Field Research:
A Sourcebook and
Field Manual

Edited by

ROBERT G. BURGESS

Professor of Sociology, University of Warwick

London and New York

First published 1982 by Unwin Hyman Ltd
Fifth impression 1989

Reprinted 1991, 1994
by Routledge
11 New Fetter Lane, London EC4P 4EE

Simultaneously published in the USA and Canada
by Routledge
29 West 35th Street, New York, NY 10001

Printed and bound in Great Britain by University Press, Cambridge.

British Library Cataloguing in Publication Data

A catalogue record for this book is available from the British Library.

Library of Congress Cataloging in Publication Data

A catalog record for this book is available from the Library of Congress.

ISBN 0–415–07893–8

Contents

page

Series Editor's Preface

The structure of the social sciences combines two separate elements, theory and empirical evidence. Both are necessary for successful social understanding; one without the other is barren. The *Contemporary Social Research* series is concerned with the means by which this structure is maintained and kept standing solid and upright, a job performed by the methodology of social research.

The series is intended to provide concise introductions to significant methodological topics. Broadly conceived, research methodology deals with the general grounds for the validity of social scientific propositions. How do we know what we do know about the social world? More narrowly, it deals with the questions: how do we actually acquire new knowledge about the world in which we live? What are the strategies and techniques by means of which social science data are collected and analysed? The series will seek to answer such questions through the examination of specific areas of methodology.

Why is such a series necessary? There exist many solid, indeed massive, methodology textbooks, which most undergraduates in sociology, psychology and the social sciences acquire familiarity with in the course of their studies. The aim of this series is different. It focuses upon specific topics, procedures, methods of analysis and methodological problems to provide a readable introduction to its subject. Each book contains annotated suggestions for further reading. The intended audience includes the advanced undergraduate, the graduate student, the working social researcher seeking to familiarise himself with new areas, and the non-specialist who wishes to enlarge his knowledge of social research. Research methodology need not be remote and inaccessible. Some prior knowledge of statistics will be useful, but only certain titles in the series will make strong statistical demands upon the reader. The series is concerned above all to demonstrate the general importance and centrality of research methodology to social science.

Robert Burgess's anthology on *Field Research* breaks new ground in the way in which he treats a style of research originally closely identified with social anthropology, but now widely used by sociologists, criminologists and social psychologists, and by social researchers in social administration, industrial relations and education. His collection of material illuminates the main phases of field research, with a particularly welcome emphasis upon the practicalities of such research. Participant observation is much more than having a sharp eye, a good memory and an ability 'to get on with people'. Robert Burgess brings out the need to consider carefully different aspects of the process of inquiry in conducting such research, from broad issues of how theory and data interrelate down to severely practical questions of how to take notes successfully when doing observational studies. Another welcome emphasis is the extent to which he draws upon the work of social anthropologists and historians to throw light upon the conduct of field research. With the attention he shows to the origins of this style of work, *Field Research* is a worthwhile contribution to a British tradition of social science work.

MARTIN BULMER
London School of Economics and Political Science

Preface

There are now numerous textbooks, sets of readings and reflections on doing social research. Much of this textbook material is American and deals with the way in which social research and in particular social surveys should be done. These 'cookbook' approaches to social research omit discussions of the interplay between research methods and research experience. Accordingly, research biographies have been produced in which editors have invited researchers to 'come clean' about the way in which research is actually done. While such accounts are high on description of the research process, they are often low on analytic discussions of methods of social research in general and field research in particular.

This book, therefore, attempts to fill a gap in the literature by introducing students to the craft of field research using a range of British and American material. The text takes the form of a book of readings which brings together styles of field research used principally by experienced researchers in sociology and social anthropology. The extracts do not provide 'solutions' to the problems that confront researchers, but they do illustrate the rich variety of strategies and techniques available, and the problems and social processes involved in doing field research.

The specific aims of this book are to indicate the diverse approaches involved in doing field research, to examine a range of research techniques that have been used in field research (participant observation, informal/unstructured interviewing and documentary materials), to examine the problems that arise in the course of doing field research and the ways in which these problems have been handled by experienced field researchers. Each section deals with a major element of field research. The first chapter in each section is intended to locate the essays in a broader context, and to raise issues and questions that can be used when reading the materials and when reading empirical studies, and when conducting field research. At the end of each of these initial chapters is an annotated reading list that allows the reader to explore in more detail some of the issues raised by the materials.

This book of readings has been designed for two purposes. First, as a sourcebook for undergraduate and postgraduate students in sociology and social anthropology who take courses on social research and field research. Secondly, as a field manual for students and research workers who engage in field research and who want some guidance on dealing with the problems, processes and practicalities of doing field research. This book can be read from cover to cover, but has also been designed for 'dipping into'. Many of the chapters can be read and reread for the questions that they raise and the experiences they communicate to the reader.

I am indebted to many colleagues and students for the help that I have received in preparing this book. During the writing period, I have received many helpful comments on my material from: Alison

Andrew, Gi Baldamus, Martin Bulmer, Christine Buswell, Celia Davies, Wyn Lewis, Valdo Pons, Julius Roth, Marten Shipman, Peter Sidey, Meg Stacey and Elizabeth Tonkin. They have all read sections of the book and many of them have commented on the complete manuscript. I hope that they can see that their labours were not in vain, although I have not met all their remarks. Obviously, any omissions are my responsibility. In typing the final manuscript I have been very fortunate to have the expert secretarial services of Hilary Pearce, who has been meticulous in every detail. Finally, I have had the continued help, encouragement and support of my wife, Hilary, who has helped me with all the tasks associated with the preparation of this book.

ROBERT BURGESS
University of Warwick

1

Approaches to Field Research

ROBERT G. BURGESS

One of the main styles of social research used by empirically oriented social scientists is field research; a style of investigation that is also referred to as 'field-work', 'qualitative method', 'interpretative research', 'case study method' and 'ethnography'. This approach to social investigation has traditionally been associated with social anthropologists, whose 'field' consisted of a small-scale society where it was possible to do 'research' by living and working among the people. Gulick indicates that:

> When the anthropologist is in the field, field work is his total life. He copes with it by using his whole body and personality in the same way that he copes with life when he is not in the field ... Life in the field involves the same emotions as life at home: elation, boredom, embarrassment, contentment, anger, joy, anxiety and so on. To these are added, however, the necessity of being continually on the alert (of *not* taking one's surroundings and relationships for granted), and the necessity of learning new routines and cues. These necessities are likely to force a heightened awareness of facets of one's personality of which one had not been aware before. This can be an emotionally devastating experience, but it is by no means inevitably so. (Gulick, 1977, p. 90; emphasis in original)

In this respect, field research is a learning situation in which researchers have to understand their own actions and activities as well as those of the people they are studying. The main instrument of social investigation is the researcher, who has to learn the local language, live among the people and participate in their activities over relatively long periods of time in order to acquire a detailed understanding of the situation under study. Such a strategy has been adopted and adapted by sociologists; especially in studies of education, medicine, deviance, institutions (schools, factories, prisons and hospitals) and rural and urban localities. Yet sociologists have argued that we still lack basic ethnographic data on the social processes involved in many areas of everyday life (cf. Delamont, 1978). Indeed, in the field of deviance, Becker (1963) has remarked that we do not have enough studies where the researcher has been in close contact with those individuals who are studied. Accordingly, he suggests that if the researcher

> is to get an accurate and complete account of what deviants do, what their patterns of association are, and so on, he must spend at least some time observing them *in their natural habitat* as they go about their ordinary activities. But this means that the student must, for the time being, keep what are for him unusual hours and penetrate what are for him unknown and possibly dangerous areas of the society. He may find himself staying up nights and sleeping days, because that is what the people he studies do, and this may be difficult because of his commitments to family and work. Furthermore, the process of gaining the confidence of those one studies may be very time consuming so that months may have to be spent in relatively fruitless attempts to gain access. (Becker, 1963, p. 170; emphasis in original)

These accounts by Gulick and by Becker begin to address the question 'what is field research?' It would appear that field research involves observing and analysing real-life situations, of studying actions and activities as they occur. The field researcher, therefore, relies upon learning firsthand about a people, and a culture. However, if the researcher is to obtain an insider's view of situations, it is vital to maintain an outsider's perspective (cf. Powdermaker, 1966a). Field researchers therefore have to develop self-criticism and self-awareness, if involvement and detachment are to be achieved in social situations. In this respect, researchers maintain membership in the culture in which they were reared while establishing membership in the groups which they are studying; they are social-ised into another culture. This has been commented upon by Evans-Pritchard, who remarks:

> Perhaps it would be better to say that one lives in two different worlds of thought at the same time, in categories and concepts and values which often cannot easily be reconciled. One becomes a sort of double marginal man, alienated from both worlds. (Evans-Pritchard, 1973, pp. 2–3)

This is the situation for anthropologists studying other cultures and for sociologists studying their own society. The social and cultural diversity that exists within any society means that the researcher has to learn a language and establish a role. The field researcher is, therefore, an outsider; a stranger who lives among the people for the purposes of study (Srinivas, 1979).

The method of social investigation that is most often referred to in field research is participant observation which allows the researcher to work with individuals in their natural settings. However, this emphasis upon observational techniques is somewhat narrow as field researchers may complement their observations by conversations, informal/unstructured interviews, formal interviews, by surveys and by collecting personal documents (written, oral and photographic evidence). These methods can be used in different combinations depending on the focus of the social investigation and the strategies that need to be adopted. Indeed, Schatzman and Strauss (1973) consider that the strategies used in field research depend upon the questions posed with the result that the field researcher becomes a methodological strategist who engages in problem oriented methodology. For them:

> Field method is not an exclusive method in the same sense, say that experimentation is. Field method is more like an umbrella of activity beneath which any technique may be used for gaining the desired information, and for processes of thinking about this information. (Schatzman and Strauss, 1973, p. 14)

Field research involves the activities of the researcher, the influence of the researcher on the researched, the practices and procedures of doing research and the methods of data collection and data analysis. However, various writers have emphasised different aspects of field research; a situation that may be attributed to the trends and developments that have taken place in this area of study.

Some Major Approaches to Field Research

The origins of field research have been identified by Wax (1971) and by Douglas (1976) in the fifth century BC, when 'on the spot' reports were provided of foreign peoples and of the Peloponnesian wars. Wax traces developments in descriptive reporting among the Romans and the traders and ambassadors of the Islamic empires. She considers that the first Europeans to report ethnographic data were missionaries of the Catholic Church and travellers and merchants. However, she maintains that it is essential to look at developments that took place in the late nineteenth and early twentieth centuries, when field reports began to be used in academic study.

THE ANTHROPOLOGICAL APPROACH: THE INFLUENCE OF MALINOWSKI

It is usual for nineteenth-century analysis to be seen to have rested on material that was collected by missionaries, travellers and government officials all of whom were unqualified in anthropology. As a consequence, the use of field methods is often regarded as a twentieth-century innovation which can be attributed to Malinowski. Such a position, as Urry (1972) has shown, oversimplifies the situation. In particular, he examines the period 1870–1920, when four editions of the volume *Notes and Queries on Anthropology* were prepared. It is, he argues, the content of these volumes that reveal changing attitudes, fields of interest, materials that were considered to be ethnographic 'facts' and the development of field methods.

The first edition of *Notes and Queries,* prepared in 1874, pointed to the deficiencies of earlier questionnaires that had been prepared for travellers. These questionnaires, it was argued, lacked attention to the detail required by anthropologists. Accordingly, this new volume was prepared so that non-anthropologists could make more precise observations and supply the anthropologist with information. However, in this volume, and in the second and third editions, there was only information on those aspects of social life that had to be observed, but no advice on methods of observation and the collection of data.

The accounts that were provided by travellers, missionaries and administrators raised certain methodological problems. First, they often focused on what, in their terms, was exotic and romantic. Secondly, their accounts were often acquired through interpreters. Finally, as their work was concerned with change, missionaries and administrators tended to produce accounts that reflected the perspectives from which they observed the people. Numerous reports, therefore, concerned savagery and barbarity among the people. Furthermore, the reports were often based on anonymous informants. In these circumstances, Haddon, Seligman and Rivers suggested that anthropologists should bypass these accounts and collect their own data. Accordingly, in 1898 a British expedition was led by Haddon to the islands of the Torres Strait, where experts were to collect ethnographic material from the people. Meanwhile, in North America, Boas made similar trips to the North-West Coast. As few attempts were made to learn the local language, much time was spent in obtaining and keeping good informants. On these trips anthropologists confronted a series of methodological problems as they had to deal with real people and question them about their lives, avoid bias in their reporting and deal with the problems surrounding the transference of meaning from one culture to another. Indeed, Rivers argued that such expeditions containing groups of experts could interfere with the people's way of life. However, such trips which were poorly funded and short in duration did have the advantage of collecting data firsthand.

In a report to the Carnegie Institute on 'Anthropological work outside America', Rivers argued the case for intensive fieldwork. He considered this involved living with the people and studying their culture, getting to know them and using the vernacular language. In these terms, he argued it was possible to overcome the bias and inaccuracy of survey work and the superficial knowledge provided by missionaries and administrators. In short, he laid emphasis on understanding native terms and native language, obtaining and paying good informants, collecting texts, genealogies and life histories and keeping systematic notes. Some of this advice was incorporated into the fourth edition of *Notes and Queries*, which Urry considers was 'not so much a guide for travellers as a manual of advice for more highly trained observers; a handbook for a new era of anthropological research to be based on more exact methods' (Urry, 1972, pp. 51–2). Malinowski used *Notes and Queries* on his early field trips (Malinowski, 1967, p. 30). Furthermore, Malinowski's position, as outlined in *Argonauts of the Western Pacific* (Malinowski, 1922), is very similar to that of Rivers. However, it is Malinowski who is usually credited with being the originator of intensive anthropological field research as *Argonauts* contains a detailed discussion of method (Malinowski, 1922, pp. 4–25), but as we shall see it was more an ideal that Malinowski had, rather than what he actually did.

Malinowski was critical of earlier writers who had not provided sufficient detail about their methods. He considered that ethnographic material was only of value when it was possible to distinguish between direct observation, native statements and interpretations, and the inferences of the author. It was vital that some assessment could be made concerning an author's acquaintance with facts and the conditions under which observations were made. It was Malinowski who raised the question about how an ethnographer should work. He considered that ethnographers needed to know the aims of their studies, to live among the natives without other Europeans and to collect data by means of specific methods. In particular, he argued that ethnographers should cut themselves off from other Europeans and live among the natives as this was the only way to gain some appreciation of the social processes involved in everyday life, and to get to know individuals, their customs and their beliefs. Malinowski also considered that studying natives in their natural setting was preferable to using paid informants. This was basic to all field research.

In *Argonauts,* Malinowski also showed that he was aware of some of the problems associated with field research. In particular, the questions surrounding the impact of the observer on the observed and the influence of the observer upon village life were examined. However, these issues were considered unproblematic as Malinowski claimed that the constant presence of the anthropologist ceased to be a disturbing influence upon tribal life. Indeed, Malinowski advocated participation on the part of the researcher, as he remarked:

> in this type of work, it is good for the Ethnographer sometimes to put aside camera, note book and pencil, and to join in himself in what is going on. He can take part in the natives' games, he can follow them on their visits and walks, sit down and listen and share in their conversations. (Malinowski, 1922, p. 21)

Such participation, it was argued, allowed the researcher to obtain an understanding of the lives of the people studied.

However, questions can be raised about Malinowski's own research and the extent to which he achieved these ideals. Certainly, his ideas concerning the collection of statistical data, detailed observations and ethnographic statements revolutionised field research, whose ultimate goal he thought should be 'to grasp the native's point of view, his relation to life, to realise *his* vision of *his* world' (Malinowski, 1922, p. 25; emphasis in original). However, when Malinowski's private diaries were published by his widow in the late 1960s, a different view of the great anthropologist was revealed. Here, we find that Malinowski had much in common with other researchers as his diary records periods of loneliness and boredom, periods when he hated the natives and periods of deep depression. In short, rather than the idealised picture of field research that he presented in the opening pages of *Argonauts,* we are given a clear view of the difficulties involved in doing ethnographic work. Malinowski reveals that there were several problems surrounding data collection as one entry, in common with several others, records:

> The rest of day ethnographic work, but it didn't go well. I began '*Kabitam*' – copied a few *lagims* and *tabuyors*, and began to ask names: they did not know the names. I asked about *megwa* – they had no *megwa*, no personal *kabitam*, nor any *megwa* used during making of *waga* or gardens. This irritated me, I went away and began to work with Tom and Topola; it didn't go well either. I felt like stopping and reading a novel. (Malinowski, 1967, p. 240; emphasis in original)

Here, it is not only the difficulties of data collection, but his relationships with the natives that can be questioned (cf. Wax, 1972). This and other diary entries reveal hatred and dislike of the people. He writes about his work one morning in the following terms:

> On this occasion I made one or two coarse jokes, and one *bloody nigger* made a disapproving remark,

whereupon I cursed them and was highly irritated. I managed to control myself *on the spot*, but I was terribly vexed by the fact that this *nigger* had dared to speak to me in such a manner. (Malinowski, 1967, p. 272; emphasis in original)

On other occasions the native women are reduced to objects of Malinowski's sexual fantasy, as he remarks:

I met women at the spring, watched how they drew water. One of them very attractive, aroused me sensually. I thought how easily I could have a *connection* with her. (Malinowski, 1967, p. 273; emphasis in original)

Such accounts raise problems about the relationship between the observer and the observed, levels of participation and the influence this has upon data collection and analysis.

While it can be argued that these entries in Malinowski's diary do not provide the kind of detail on field methodology that is given in his research monographs, they do nevertheless provide a detailed, candid account of the researcher in the field during the colonial period. (For critical commentaries on work in this period see Asad, 1973.) Although living among the people, he was aware that he could not join in everything they did. In turn, he could not remain completely separate from Europeans and European culture, as his meetings with missionaries, travellers and traders, and long periods spent reading novels, hint at attempts to get 'outside' the society that he studied. In short, the diary provides episodes from his personal life that can complement his more idealised picture of anthropological field research. Nevertheless, even if Malinowski did not live up to the high standards that he set himself, it is evident that he did 'revolutionise' the work of the anthropologist, for as Urry remarks:

Malinowski's contribution was not only to make clearer the type of information to be collected, but more importantly, he had differentiated between the type of material on the one hand and the methods for their collection on the other. It is this clear differentiation of the modes of collection and the various forms of 'fact' that made Malinowski's contribution to field methods so original. (Urry, 1972, p. 53)

The period of intensive anthropological field research had begun, for Malinowski's style of work was to influence many anthropologists in the twentieth century (Powdermaker, 1966a, pp. 33–45).

EARLY ENGLISH SOCIAL RESEARCH

Alongside these research developments by early British anthropologists, were developments in social research by those associated with social reform. Crude over-simplification of the work of investigators such as Charles Booth and Sidney and Beatrice Webb see them engaged in survey work and the collection of statistical data. Booth's work goes beyond the narrow definition of a survey. His study *Life and Labour of the People of London* (Booth, 1889–1902) was designed to apply the method of observation, reasoning and verification to the problem of poverty. Indeed, Booth's work was not just survey-based, but involved detailed observation of individual families, for he was aware that many of the descriptions of individuals in books were unrealistic and lacking in colour. Accordingly, Booth decided to gain personal experience of family life in the East End of London by taking up the position of a lodger. He reports:

Of personal knowledge I have not much. I have no doubt that many other men possess twenty or a hundred times as much experience of East End people and their lives. Yet such as it is, what I have witnessed has been enough to throw a strong light on the materials I have used, and, for me, has made the dry bones live. For three separate periods I have taken up quarters, each time for several weeks, where I was not known, and as a lodger have shared the lives of people who would figure in my schedules as belonging to classes C, D and E. Being more or less boarded as well as lodged, I became intimately acquainted with some of those I met, and the lives and habits of many others came naturally under observation. My object, which I trust was a fair one, was never suspected, my position never questioned. The people with whom I lived became, and are still, my friends. (Booth in Keating, 1976, pp. 124–5)

Such an account of exploration in England bears marked resemblance to Malinowski's experiences in the Trobriand Islands. Booth took the role of an observer, who participated with the people he studied; although it is doubtful whether the people with whom he lodged knew of his research intentions. In addition to his own experience of life in the East End of London, Booth also gathered further data from informants. In particular, he reports that thirty-four school attendance officers were questioned for twenty hours about the families with whom they worked. Furthermore, material was also obtained from school teachers, rent collectors and sanitary inspectors, who were able to report on social conditions. Finally, visits were carried out to the East End of London and documentary evidence was used in the course of his study.

Such an account modifies the traditional picture of Booth as a social investigator, who was firmly located in the survey tradition. Indeed, it is evident that some elements of field research were used to complement survey work. Wax (1971) argues that Booth's researchers were the first to combine statistical data with interviewing and participant observation. Quantitative data could, therefore, be supported by qualitative material that Booth and his associates obtained by first-hand observation. Furthermore, it was possible to use different methods of investigation to verify the data obtained. Booth's work did not, therefore, rest upon a single method or a single problem.

However, such work also raises a series of problems concerning the methods that were employed and the data that were obtained. Booth had used a number of investigators in conducting his study which poses the problem of how the data they gathered could be compared. While he provided detailed descriptions of particular individuals and groups, questions can be raised about the extent to which the people selected were representative. Thirdly, the data that were provided by his informants and the data derived from his own observations raise questions concerning the relationship between fact and opinion. Finally, his investigations reflect his class position and his values, which influenced the perspective from which he worked. Nevertheless, Booth's work is of interest to us as an early attempt by a social investigator to apply intensive methods to his own society.

One of Booth's social investigators was Beatrice Webb, who claims that her work with Booth was part of her apprenticeship as a social investigator before she began her better-known work in partnership with Sidney Webb. Despite the fact that their social investigations spanned the turn of the century, it is not until the early 1930s that the Webbs produced a discussion of their methods of social investigation. Their book *Methods of Social Study* (Webb and Webb, 1932) and Beatrice Webb's autobiographical account *My Apprenticeship* (Webb, 1926a) draw on research experience that indicates their use of various research methods rather than mere surveys. They maintain that the routine of social investigation is:

> the art of note taking, the methods of personal observation and the interview, the use of documents and literary sources, and the collection and manipulation of statistics – the predominant requirements are patience and persistence in work; precision in the use of words and figures; promptitude of decision in picking out new facts and ignoring what is only 'common form'; a genuine satisfaction in continuing to progress along a previously determined course; above all, that particular form of intellectual curiosity that delights in unravelling complicated details irrespective of their immediate relevance to the main lines of the enquiry. (Webb and Webb, 1932, p. 50)

Such an account indicates that the Webbs wanted the researcher to be acquainted with much more than a series of research techniques. Indeed, they indicate that the researcher needs to pose questions, avoid loaded questions, and overcome bias. In turn, they consider

that the researcher should study an institution in whole or in part and not a social problem. This puts them in line with the style of investigation that had been advocated by Malinowski ten years earlier. However, unlike anthropologists, they do not advocate the study of common occurrences which are an essential part of any field study. As far as they are concerned, note taking and data recording are vital as it is through systematic note taking that discovery and data analysis takes place. Finally, they discuss a range of research methods which includes the written word (documents), the spoken word (interviewing) and watching the institution at work (observation and experiment).

The Webbs considered observation an essential element in social research, as they remark: 'An indispensable part of the study of any social institution, wherever this can be obtained, is deliberate and sustained personal observation of its actual operation' (Webb and Webb, 1932, p. 158). Certainly, Beatrice Webb had extensive experience of observational methods not only in her work with Booth, but in her own investigations. In *My Apprenticeship* she reveals how she collected rents in order that she might observe the conditions of tenants in lower-class property, publicise their conditions and provide some remedies. Beatrice Webb discusses this work in the following terms:

> About the harmlessness of this intrusion of the relatively well-to-do into the homes of the very poor I had no misgivings; rents had to be collected, and it seemed to me, on balance, advantageous to the tenants of low-class property to have to pay their money to persons of intelligence and goodwill who were able to bring hardships and grievances to the notice of those who had power to mitigate or remedy them. And this occupation was certainly well fitted to form part of my apprenticeship as a social investigator. Unlike philanthropic visiting under the parochial clergy, or detective visiting under a C.O.S. committee, one was not watching instances of failure in the way of adaptation to this world or the next. What was under observation was the whole of a given section of the population: a group of families spontaneously associated in accordance with the social and economic circumstances of the particular district. From the outset the tenants regarded us, not as visitors of superior social status, still less as investigators, but as part of the normal machinery of their lives, like the school attendance officer or the pawnbroker. (Webb, 1926a, pp. 223–4)

Here, Beatrice Webb used the particular role of rent collector to gain direct access to particular families for the purposes of social investigation. However, her value position and the perspective from which she observed individuals not of her class is apparent.

Nevertheless, observation was crucial to Beatrice

Webb's work. In her study of the 'sweating system', she visited tailoring shops, obtained work as a 'plain trouser hand' for the purposes of observation, and interviewed workers, owners and factory inspectors in the wholesale clothing trade. Similarly, in her industrial and trade union studies, it was her observations of trade union branches and trades councils that helped her to formulate her ideas. Observational work provided material for her diary and was vital for providing and clarifying ideas and developing hypotheses (Webb, 1926a, pp. 265–80).

More importantly, the Webbs were aware that observational methods had to be combined with other methods in the course of social investigation. Here again, the similarity with the anthropological approach to field research advocated by Malinowski is evident in the use of systematic note taking and data recording, participation in everyday activities in order to gather data, and combining different methods of social investigation. In short, the work of Charles Booth and Sidney and Beatrice Webb bears some of the hallmarks of field methods that were, in that period of time, being devised by anthropologists working in other societies. Indeed, it has been claimed that social investigations by the early English social reformers have contributed, to some extent, to the development of field methods that have been used by sociologists (cf. Stacey, 1960, p. v).

THE CHICAGO SCHOOL

Turning to America, at the beginning of the twentieth century, it is the Chicago School of sociologists that developed an interest in field research and field methods. Here, field methods did not merely include observation and interviewing, as many of the Chicago researchers used documentary evidence, and collected life histories. The emphasis was upon qualitative methods, although the particular mix depended on the problems posed. The formative period of the Chicago School was 1920–30, although its influence upon American sociology has been wide-ranging down to the present day. The Chicago School brought together a number of researchers who were interested in the 'real world', and included Park, Burgess, Cressey, Anderson, Thrasher and Shaw. Probably the most influential member of this group was Robert Park, who as early as 1916 drew up a programme of research for the group (Easthope, 1974).

It was Park's idea that the city could become the social laboratory of the social investigator, who could examine human beings and their social behaviour in the city of Chicago. The style of research that Park expected is revealed in the following statement recorded by Howard Becker, while being taught by Park at Chicago in the 1920s:

You have been told to go grubbing in the library thereby accumulating a mass of notes and a liberal coating of grime. You have been told to choose problems wherever you can find musty stacks of routine records based on trivial schedules prepared by tired bureaucrats and filled out by reluctant applicants for aid or fussy do-gooders or indifferent clerks. This is called 'getting your hands dirty in real research'. Those who thus counsel you are wise and honourable; the reasons they offer are of great value. But one thing more is needful; first-hand observation. Go and sit in the lounge of the luxury hotels and on the doorsteps of the flophouses; sit on the Gold Coast settees and on the slum shakedowns; sit in Orchestra Hall and in the Star and Garter Burlesk. In short, gentlemen, go get the seat of your pants dirty in *real* research. (McKinney, 1966, p. 71; emphasis in original)

Real research was in Park's view based on observation; on walking around the city of Chicago, on watching crowds and listening to individuals. In short, sociology was an activity that could as easily be conducted in the street as in the university; both were at the hub of social research. Many of the studies, therefore, focused upon individuals (*The Hobo* (Anderson, 1923), *The Jack Roller* (Shaw, 1930)); institutions (*The Gang* (Thrasher, 1927), *The Taxi Dance Hall* (Cressey, 1932)); and natural areas (*The Ghetto* (Wirth, 1928), *The Gold Coast and the Slum* (Zorbaugh, 1929)).

As far as methods of investigation were concerned, Park considered that an anthropological approach could be used in Chicago, as he remarked:

The same patient methods of observation which anthropologists like Boas and Lowie have expended on the life and study of the life and manners of the North American Indian might be even more fruitfully employed in the investigation of the customs, beliefs, social practices and general conceptions of life prevalent in Little Italy on the Lower North Side in Chicago, or in recording the more sophisticated folkways of the inhabitants of Greenwich Village and the neighbourhood of Washington Square, New York. (Park, 1952, p. 15; originally published in *American Journal of Sociology*, 1916)

He also believed that methods of study could be based on the journalistic tradition of observation and unstructured interviewing and the literary naturalism of Zola, Dreiser and Upton Sinclair. However, Chicago sociologists also used surveys, documentary evidence and statistical data alongside more unstructured material.

Many Chicago School studies utilise a range of methods, although the investigators are unexplicit about their methodology. Indeed, we have only to look at *The Hobo* (Anderson, 1923), the first major study published by a member of the Chicago School; here, Anderson tells us:

I found myself engaged in research without the preparation a researcher is supposed to have. I couldn't answer if asked about my 'methods'. In my research efforts, however, I did have two resources that could be put to good use – a capacity for interviewing and a capacity for reporting what I had seen and heard. (Anderson, 1923, pp. xi–xii)

This account provides us with a wider notion of field research, field method and the research process. Furthermore, Anderson explains that his own experience of the hobo way of life derived from his own family background and was used to orientate his studies. He did not consider his work to be based upon participant observation, but rather on watching, listening and talking. In addition, his intensive data collection was complemented by sixty life histories that allowed him to distinguish five types of homeless men.

Thrasher's study of *The Gang* (Thrasher, 1927) is based on a wide range of data that had been collected over a seven-year period from 1,313 gangs. Here, the researcher interviewed the boys, and obtained reports from social workers, policemen and politicians. Twenty-one boys were asked to write life histories of themselves, and in addition newspaper evidence and other unpublished material was gathered. The research report could, therefore, draw on all this material.

Among many of the investigations conducted by members of the Chicago School, traditional field methods in the form of observation and unstructured interviews are complemented by life history documents. The study by Shaw entitled *The Jack Roller* (Shaw, 1930) consists of the life history of one boy, Stanley, whom Shaw knew over a period of six years. The life history consists of the boy's own story written as an autobiography and as a diary, but recorded in the first person in his own words, although it is the researcher who has decided what to select for inclusion in the research report. However, this material, Shaw argues, needs to be supplemented by additional records such as family history, medical and psychiatric records, and court records of arrests, offences and convictions. These help to authenticate the story and provide a reliable interpretation of experience. Such a story, Shaw maintains, highlights the delinquent's view of his world, his interpretation of his role, his culture and his personal situation.

It is evident from these examples that the studies conducted by the Chicago School were not restricted in terms of their methods. Indeed, one of the hallmarks of the Chicago School was the wide use of various methods, which combined observational materials with different types of documentary evidence. The result was urban ethnography based on highly detailed descriptive studies of natural areas, institutions and individuals in the city of Chicago (Hannerz, 1980). In short, it is as Fairbrother (1977) indicates, a sociology of the street rather than a sociology of the academic; a

sociology that is built upon the experiences of research workers as well as from surveys and documents. This approach was partly based on journalistic methods using an unstructured interview with informants, and partly on an anthropological approach to field research in which observational methods were central.

The work of the Chicago sociologists has been examined by Douglas (1976), who argues that this approach to field research does not reveal the processes among groups in urban society as it is based upon assumptions of a 'little community', where conflict and complexity are missing. In turn, Douglas criticises the low level of analysis of the Chicago School studies which he maintains reported little more than raw data. In short, he considers that the Chicago sociologists were merely natives disguised as scientists whose reports were only of value to natives. However, it could be argued that these reports are also of value to social scientists. Nevertheless, Park did encourage Chicago researchers to go on to the streets to gather rich, detailed data; an approach that was taken up by sociologists studying urban and rural localities.

FIELD RESEARCH IN URBAN AND RURAL LOCALITIES

Sociologists who have engaged in studying urban and rural localities have drawn upon field methods that have been developed in sociology and social anthropology. Indeed, a 'community studies' tradition has developed in complex societies. Some writers have claimed that 'communities' are not just objects of study, but are samples of cultures. In this respect, the study of a 'community' becomes a method of social investigation (cf. Bell and Newby, 1972, pp. 54–81).

However, does a community study method mean any more than the mechanics of doing research? Is method equated with the techniques that are used to study the 'community'? Vidich, Bensman and Stein (1964) suggest that we should look at the methodology of 'community studies' rather than community study method. This allows us to critically examine the problems surrounding the concept of 'community' (Stacey, 1969b), the methods used in the studies and the data gathered by the researcher.

The methodology that is used to study localities is of interest here as it has direct links to earlier developments in field research. There are links back to Robert Park and the Chicago School of sociologists, and in particular to Park's idea that the researcher should tramp the streets, observe people and listen to what is said. Certainly, this advice has been taken by some investigators in Britain, such as Rex and Moore (1967), who in studying Sparkbrook based their approach very much on the Chicago tradition, and by Bell (1977), who comments that while working in Banbury he saw himself as a latter-day Robert Park. A further link goes beyond Park to the anthropological tradition, where field researchers took as their unit of study small-scale territorial communities.

It is usual for the researcher engaged in the study of a locality to go and live among the people. Certainly, this was the situation in the first and second studies of Banbury (Stacey, 1960; Stacey *et al.*, 1975), where the researchers lived in different sectors of the town; a situation that facilitated a study of neighbouring. When researchers live in a locality, they share some of the experiences of the inhabitants, as for example in Pons's study of *Stanleyville* (Pons, 1969), where he became a member of a mock-formal association that met to brew and drink beer. Such situations bring the research into close contact with those who are studied and may give colour, depth and richness to the research report. However, Miller has argued that such close involvement with individuals raises the danger of over-involvement with informants (Miller, 1952). When studying localities, it is usual for the researcher to fit in with the ongoing patterns of interaction by establishing a series of roles that have to be communicated to the people. This occurred in Pons's study, when he took the roles of photographer and local letter-writer to avoid being allocated to the standard European roles of 'missionary', 'trader', or 'administrator'.

Although participant observation is the principal method of investigation that is used to study urban and rural localities, several other research techniques have been used. In the classic research reports on *Middletown* (Lynd and Lynd, 1929) and *Middletown in Transition* (Lynd and Lynd, 1937) five different techniques of data collection are identified. Much of the data was collected using observational methods while the researchers lived in Middletown. Secondly, documentary evidence was gathered in the form of census data, records and yearbooks. Thirdly, statistical sources in the form of work records were used. Fourthly, interviews both formal and informal were conducted and finally, questionnaires were sent out to local experts, and members of clubs and associations whom the Lynds had contacted. Similarly, if we turn to other studies, we find that a variety of methods are used. In Pons's study of Stanleyville (now Kisangani) (Pons, 1969) participant observation was the main method of study, but this was complemented by interviews, letters and diaries. In Gans's study of Levittown (Gans, 1967) participant observation was used together with a questionnaire. Furthermore, in the first and second studies of Banbury (Stacey, 1960; Stacey *et al.*, 1975) the observational work conducted by the teams of researchers was complemented by a sample survey and the collection of documentary materials. In these studies field research involved a variety of research strategies. However, central to the research process were the researchers themselves, who played a variety of roles to gain wide experience of the social setting.

Such a situation allows us to assess some of the problems that are involved in conducting field research

in urban and rural localities. First, there is the question of access. How does the researcher gain access to individuals and groups? In some cases, with small groups, access has been gained through informants. Whyte (1955) gained access to the inhabitants of his slum district through 'Doc'; while Pons (1969) gained access to the inhabitants of Avenue 21 through a number of key informants. On a larger scale, when the Nuffield Foundation awarded a grant for the second Banbury study, they insisted that the researchers should obtain permission for the research to be done. The result was that the presence of a research team in the town was communicated to the people of Banbury at a public meeting and through announcements in the local press. However, access still remained problematic, for it is debatable whether access can be negotiated with 25,000 people. A second problem associated with field research in a locality concerns the role of the researcher. Certainly, according to Bell's account of the Banbury study (Bell, 1977), there was the problem of what role to take and what to do, as he considers that there was a danger of being too involved with particular members of the town. Frankenberg (1957) reports that in his study of Pentrediwaith, he participated in meetings and took the role of assistant secretary to the local football club. Gans (1967) also reports that he was a participant in his Levittown research and that his level of participation in the neighbourhood assisted data collection. Such participation can open up some areas for investigation, while simultaneously closing off others (cf. Harrell-Bond, 1976). Further problems arise when data are collected in an unsystematic way. Questions can be raised about the validity of the data and the completeness of the research report.

Various attempts have been made to overcome some of these problems. First, research teams can gather data from different perspectives as is shown by the first and second studies of Banbury. In the second Banbury study each team member 'joined' a different political party to study local politics in the town. Secondly, the use of male and female researchers means that the activities of men and women can be systematically investigated by members of those categories. Finally, the use of a team of researchers means that some check can be made on individual investigators and the quality of their observations. A further attempt at overcoming some of the problems associated with data collection in localities has been made through the restudy. This approach was used by the Lynds to study Middletown a second time (Lynd and Lynd, 1937); and by Gallaher (1961), who conducted a second study of Plainville, a town that had originally been studied by West (1945), and by Lewis (1951), who conducted a second study of Tepoztlán which Redfield (1930) had studied. In Britain, Stacey conducted a second study of Banbury, a town where she had initially done research in the period 1948–51 (Stacey, 1960). However, as Stacey reports (Stacey *et al.*, 1975), researchers engaged in restudies confront problems associated with data comparability, changes in the research team, in the discipline of sociology and in the area studied. Nevertheless, despite the problems that researchers have encountered in using field methods in studying localities, they have still used this approach when working in other substantive areas. Indeed, as Goffman remarks:

> any group of persons – prisoners, primitives, pilots or patients – develop a life of their own that becomes meaningful, reasonable, and normal once you get close to it, and that a good way to learn about any of these worlds is to submit oneself in the company of the members to the daily round of petty contingencies to which they are subject. (Goffman, 1968, p. 7)

Doing Field Research

Field research has undergone a number of developments in the twentieth century. However, the question that still confronts researchers is 'how do you do field research?' The difficulty of this question even for acknowledged experts was revealed by Evans-Pritchard when he remarked:

> When I was a serious young student in London I thought I would try to get a few tips from experienced field workers before setting out for central Africa. I first sought advice from Westermarck. All I got from him was 'don't converse with an informant for more than twenty minutes because if you aren't bored by that time he will be.' Very good advice, even if somewhat inadequate. I sought instruction from Haddon, a man foremost in field-research. He told me that it was really all quite simple; one should always behave as a gentleman. Also very good advice. My teacher Seligman told me to take ten grains of quinine every night and to keep off women. The famous Egyptologist, Sir Flinders Petrie, just told me not to bother about drinking dirty water as one soon became immune to it. Finally, I asked Malinowski and was told not to be a bloody fool. (Evans-Pritchard, 1973, p. 1)

Perhaps this supports Paul Radin's point that nobody really knows how to go about field research. Indeed, field research depends upon the researcher, the researched, the problems posed, the methods of investigation that are used and the data that are gathered. Even when this has been said, it is still difficult to provide a specific guide to those about to do field research because as Freilich remarks:

> No specific techniques exist to help the young ethnographer transform a group of hostile natives into friendly informants; no specific and operationally useful rules exist for translating raw data into information that is meaningful for anthropological analysis; and no specific techniques exist for drawing productive generalizations from such information. (Freilich, 1977b, p. 15)

Sociologists have also indicated that field research is fraught with difficulties for the researcher. As Hughes has commented:

> the observer, in greater or less degree, is caught up in the very web of social interaction which he observes, analyzes and reports. Even if he observes through a peephole, he plays a role: that of spy. And when he reports his observations made thus he becomes a kind of informer. If he observes in the role of a member of the group, he may be considered a traitor the moment he reports. Even the historian, who works upon documents, gets caught in a role problem when he reports, unless there is no person alive who might identify himself with the people or social group concerned. The hatred occasionally visited upon the debunking historian is visited almost daily upon the person who reports on the behavior of people he has lived among; and it is not so much the writing of the report, as the very act of thinking in such objective terms that disturbs the people observed. It is a violation of apparently shared secrets and sentiments. (Hughes, 1960, p. xii)

These writers indicate that field research raises difficult questions concerning validity, reliability and the ethics and politics of doing research. However, no recipe can be provided on how to do field research, for it is more than a series of methods that can be applied to a range of problems. Field research involves the researcher in a relationship with those who are studied; it is a social process in which the researcher plays a major part. Material has been selected for this book not because it provides a definitive account of how to do field research, but because experienced field researchers demonstrate how they have handled various dimensions of the research process. Some of the researchers provide discussions of methodology, while others discuss research procedures and research experiences. The accounts are, therefore, resource guides that indicate ways in which field problems have been handled and, in turn, provoke questions about the conduct of field research today.

Suggestions for Further Reading

This chapter has taken up a number of themes and has assumed some knowledge of social research. The following references are intended to provide the reader with an opportunity to fill gaps in knowledge and gain familiarity with the material. The list has been restricted as more detailed suggestions for reading, together with commentary on individual books, is provided after the first chapter in all the other sections of this book.

ON SOCIAL RESEARCH

A range of basic British and American texts and readers that discuss social research are:

Bulmer, M. (1977) (ed.), *Sociological Research Methods* (London: Macmillan).
Denzin, N. K. (1970), *The Research Act* (Chicago: Aldine).
Moser, C. and Kalton, G. (1971), *Survey Methods in Social Investigation* (2nd edn) (London: Heinemann).
Selltiz, C., Wrightsman, L. S. and Cook, S. W. (1976), *Research Methods in Social Relations* (3rd edn) (New York: Holt, Rinehart & Winston).
Shipman, M. (1981), *The Limitations of Social Research* (2nd edn) (London: Longman).
Stacey, M. (1969), *Methods of Social Research* (Oxford: Pergamon).

For a tape-recorded discussion of the processes involved in social research:

Stacey, M. and Burgess, R. (1979), *'The research process'* (Oxford: Sussex Publications), taped discussion.

For further detailed references on aspects of social research methods, see the course bibliographies that have been collected in:

Burgess, R. (1979) (ed.), *Teaching Research Methodology to Postgraduates: a Survey of Courses in the U.K.* (Coventry: University of Warwick).
Wakeford, J. (1979) (ed.), *Research Methods Syllabuses in Sociology Departments in the U.K.* (Lancaster: University of Lancaster).

REFLECTIONS ON DOING RESEARCH

A series of texts in which the editors have invited researchers to 'come clean' about studies they have conducted; many of the accounts can be read alongside the empirical work to which they relate:

Bell, C. and Encel, S. (1978) (eds), *Inside the Whale* (Oxford: Pergamon).
Bell, C. and Newby, H. (1977) (eds), *Doing Sociological Research* (London: Allen & Unwin).
Golde, P. (1970) (ed.), *Women in the Field: Anthropological Experiences* (Chicago: Aldine).
Habenstein, R. W. (1970) (ed.), *Pathways to Data* (Chicago: Aldine).
Hammond, P. (1964) (ed.), *Sociologists at Work* (New York: Basic Books).
Rynkiewich, M. and Spradley, J. (1976) (eds), *Ethics and Anthropology: Dilemmas in Fieldwork* (New York: Wiley).
Shipman, M. (1976) (ed.), *The Organization and Impact of Social Research* (London: Routledge & Kegan Paul).

Spindler, G. D. (1970) (ed.), *Being an Anthropologist: Fieldwork in Eleven Cultures* (New York: Holt, Rinehart & Winston).
Srinivas, M. N., Shah, A. M. and Ramaswamy, E. A. (1979) (eds), *The Fieldworker and the Field: Problems and Challenges in Sociological Investigation* (Delhi: OUP).
Vidich, A. J., Bensman, J. and Stein, M. R. (1964) (eds), *Reflections On Community Studies* (New York: Harper & Row).

ON FIELD RESEARCH

The basic texts and sets of readings reflect American writing in sociology and anthropology.

Texts

Douglas, J. D. (1976), *Investigative Social Research* (Beverly Hills, Calif.: Sage).
Johnson, J. M. (1975), *Doing Field Research* (New York: The Free Press).
Lofland, J. (1971), *Analyzing Social Settings* (New York: Wadsworth).
Schatzman, L. and Strauss, A. L. (1973), *Field Research: Strategies for a Natural Sociology* (Englewood Cliffs, NJ: Prentice-Hall).
Wax, R. (1971), *Doing Fieldwork: Warnings and Advice* (Chicago: University of Chicago Press).
Williams, T. R. (1967), *Field Methods in the Study of Culture* (New York: Holt, Rinehart & Winston).

Readers

Becker, H. S. (1970) (ed.), *Sociological Work* (New York: Transaction Books).
Filstead, W. J. (1970) (ed.), *Qualitative Methodology: First-hand Involvement with the Social World* (Chicago: Markham).
McCall, G. J. and Simmons, J. L. (1969) (eds), *Issues in Participant Observation: a Text and Reader* (Reading, Mass.: Addison-Wesley).
Sjoberg, G. (1967) (ed.), *Ethics, Politics and Social Research* (London: Routledge & Kegan Paul).

THE ANTHROPOLOGICAL APPROACH: THE INFLUENCE OF MALINOWSKI

For a discussion of the research tradition developed by Malinowski, there is no substitute for his monographs and diary.

Malinowski, B. (1922), *Argonauts of the Western Pacific* (London: Routledge & Kegan Paul).
Malinowski, B. (1929), *The Sexual Life of Savages* (London: Routledge & Kegan Paul).
Malinowski, B. (1935), *Coral Gardens and their Magic* (London: Allen & Unwin).
Malinowski, B. (1948), *Magic, Science and Religion* (Glencoe, Ill.: The Free Press).
Malinowski, B. (1967), *A Diary in the Strict Sense of the Term* (London: Routledge & Kegan Paul).

For commentary, see:

Firth, R. (1957) (ed.), *Man and Culture* (London: Routledge & Kegan Paul).
Kuper, A. (1973), *Anthropology and Anthropologists: the British School, 1922–1972* (London: Allen Lane).
Urry, J. (1972), 'Notes and queries on anthropology and the development of field notes in British anthropology, 1870–1920', *Proceedings of the Royal Anthropological Institute of Great Britain and Ireland,* 1972, pp. 45–57.
Wax, M. (1972), 'Tenting with Malinowski', *American Sociological Review,* vol. 37, no. 1, pp. 1–13.

EARLY ENGLISH SOCIAL RESEARCH

The material produced by the Webbs is most relevant here:

Webb, B. (1926), *My Apprenticeship* (London: Longmans, Green).
Webb, B. (1948), *Our Partnership* (London: Longmans, Green).
Webb, S. and Webb, B. (1894), *History of Trade Unionism* (London: Longman).
Webb, S. and Webb, B. (1897), *Industrial Democracy* (London: Longman).
Webb, S. and Webb, B. (1898), *Problems of Modern Industry* (London: Longman).
Webb, S. and Webb, B. (1932), *Methods of Social Study* (London: Longmans, Green).

THE CHICAGO SCHOOL

The research tradition developed by the Chicago sociologists can be examined by carefully reading the monographs produced by members of the Chicago School:

Anderson, N. (1923), *The Hobo: the Sociology of the Homeless Man* (Chicago: University of Chicago Press).
Cressey, P. G. (1932), *The Taxi-Dance Hall: a Sociological Study in Commercial Recreation and City Life* (Chicago: University of Chicago Press).
Shaw, C. (1930), *The Jack Roller: a Delinquent Boy's Own Story* (Chicago: University of Chicago Press); reprinted with an introduction by Becker (1966).
Thrasher, F. (1927), *The Gang* (Chicago: University of Chicago Press).
Zorbaugh, H. W. (1929), *The Gold Coast and the Slum* (Chicago: University of Chicago Press).

FIELD RESEARCH IN URBAN AND RURAL LOCALITIES

There are a number of articles that discuss methodology and provide a useful background to the studies.

Methodology

Arensberg, C. M. and Kimball, S. T. (1965), *Culture and Community* (New York: Harcourt Brace Jovanovitch).
Banton, M. (1966) (ed.), *The Social Anthropology of Complex Societies* (London: Tavistock) (see the essays by Mitchell, 1966, and by Frankenberg, 1966).
Bell, C. and Newby, H. (1972), *Community Studies* (London: Allen & Unwin).
Kluckhohn, F. R. (1940), 'The participant observer technique in small communities', *American Journal of Sociology,* vol. 46, no. 3, pp. 331–43.
Stacey, M. (1969), 'The myth of community studies', *British Journal of Sociology,* vol. 20, no. 2, pp. 134–47.

Empirical studies

In Britain

Dennis, N., Henriques, F. and Slaughter, C. (1956), *Coal is Our Life* (London: Methuen).
Frankenberg, R. (1957), *Village on the Border* (London: Cohen & West).
Littlejohn, J. (1963), *Westrigg* (London: Routledge & Kegan Paul).
Stacey, M. (1960), *Tradition and Change: a Study of Banbury* (Oxford: OUP).
Stacey, M., Batstone, E., Bell, C. and Murcott, A. (1975), *Power, Persistence and Change: a Second Study of Banbury* (London: Routledge & Kegan Paul).
Williams, W. M. (1956), *The Sociology of an English Village: Gosforth* (London: Routledge & Kegan Paul).

In America

Gans, H. J. (1962), *The Urban Villagers* (New York: The Free Press).
Gans, H. J. (1967), *The Levittowners* (London: Allen Lane).
Liebow, E. (1967), *Tally's Corner: a Study of Negro Street Corner Men* (Boston, Mass.: Little, Brown).
Lynd, R. S. and Lynd, H. M. (1929), *Middletown: a Study in Contemporary American Culture* (New York: Harcourt Brace Jovanovitch).
Lynd, R. S. and Lynd, H. M. (1937), *Middletown in Transition* (New York: Harcourt Brace Jovanovitch).
Whyte, W. F. (1955), *Street Corner Society* (2nd edn) (Chicago: University of Chicago Press).

Section One

Starting Field Research

2

Early Field Experiences

ROBERT G. BURGESS

Field research involves the study of real-life situations. Field researchers, therefore, observe people in the settings in which they live, and participate in their day to day activities. The methods that can be used in these studies are unstructured, flexible and open-ended. Wax reports that

> strict and rigid adherence to any method, technique or doctrinaire position may, for the fieldworker, become like confinement in a cage. If he is lucky or very cautious, a fieldworker may formulate a research problem so that he will find all the answers he needs within his cage. But if he finds himself in a field situation where he is limited by a particular method, theory, or technique, he will do well to slip through the bars and try to find out what is really going on. (Wax, 1971, p. 10)

Indeed, it has been argued that field research involves flexibility as a variety of approaches can be used (McCall, 1978; Shaffir, Stebbins and Turowetz, 1980). However, such a position poses problems for those individuals about to embark on a field study. How do you prepare for field research? Where do you begin? When do you begin? How do you begin? Although much has been written about field research, relatively little material is available on how to prepare and when to start and the problem of access and how to obtain it. The start of field research is quickly passed over in many texts or remains relatively unexplored. Indeed, McCall and Simmons have discussed this aspect of the research process in the following terms:

> Once our organization or situation has been selected as the subject of a participant observation study and initial steps have been taken toward gaining entrée to it, the researcher will find himself developing a suitable and comfortable blend of the research techniques at his disposal. (McCall and Simmons, 1969, p. 61)

This account raises questions about how a research topic is selected, how access is obtained and how the researcher establishes a series of field roles. Such questions are not easy to answer as the preparation that

can be done and the access that can be obtained will depend on the researcher, the field situation and the problem to be investigated (Evans-Pritchard, 1973). Yet standard methodology texts (Bailey, 1978; Moser and Kalton, 1971; Selltiz, Wrightsman and Cook, 1976) see the selection of a research problem and the design of the investigation as the first stage in all research. However, experienced researchers (Becker *et al.*, 1961; Goffman, 1963; Dalton, 1964; Strauss *et al.*, 1964) indicate that in field studies, research design and the collection and interpretation of data take place simultaneously. Furthermore, Becker *et al.* (1961) point out that their study did not start with a research design, as they remark:

> In one sense, our study had no design. That is, we had no well-worked-out set of hypotheses to be tested, no data gathering instruments purposely designed to secure information relevant to these hypotheses, no set of analytic procedures specified in advance. Insofar as the term 'design' implies these features of elaborate prior planning, our study had none. (Becker *et al.*, 1961, p. 17)

In a similar way Morris Freilich sums up the situation for anthropologists in the field, when he writes that the researcher

> is not just a dogged follower of an artistic research design; he is not a puppet programmed to follow automatically a plan of research operations; he is not just the bearer of research tools, he is not just a 'reader' of questions found on questionnaires and he is not just a dispenser of printed schedules. He is the *project*: his actions will make the field trip either a success or a failure. What he does in the field will tend either to attract or to repel information. He is the information absorber, the information analyzer, the information synthesizer and the information interpreter. (Freilich, 1977b, p. 32)

As a consequence, the data that is gathered during field research depends on the actions and activities of the researcher and the theoretical framework that is adopted. Nevertheless, the way in which researchers establish themselves and their projects will influence the pattern of events that occur in the field, the degree of access that they are given, and the relationships that they establish with their informants. In short, it is important for researchers to define their projects and their roles as this will influence the whole of the research process. However, these projects and field roles will often be redefined by those who are researched. Freilich (1977b) indicates that the problems that exist at the start of a project do not neatly disappear, but appear and reappear in different guises throughout the research. As Geer (1964) indicates, direct links can be made between the start of a research project, data collection, analysis and publication.

This raises the question of the researcher's initial orientation to the field of study, In short, 'how does one begin doing field research?' Kassebaum (1970) maintains that the initial orientation of the researcher will depend upon whether the research is established to deal with a set of theoretical or practical problems. However, Habenstein (1970b) argues that no matter what perspective is adopted by the researcher, it is vital to develop a conceptual framework that can be modified and used throughout the research process. A similar view is expressed by Glaser and Strauss, who argue that the researcher should not approach reality as a *tabula rasa*: 'He must have a perspective that will help him see relevant data and abstract significant categories from his scrutiny of the data' (Glaser and Strauss, 1967, p. 3). Here, the theoretical framework is of paramount importance, as this will influence the questions that are posed and the data that are collected. For the data that is gathered by the field researcher is shaped by the themes that emerge during the investigation. It would appear, therefore, that effective field research depends upon the theoretical framework, the research problem, the researcher and the conditions in which field research takes place. This situation raises several questions. First, how does a field researcher demarcate a field of study? Secondly, how do field researchers gain access to the situations that they decide to study? Thirdly, how do field researchers establish their roles? Finally, how do field researchers operate in their early days in the field?

The idea of defining a field of study brings us back to a discussion of the field researcher's theoretical perspective and initial training in sociology or anthropology. Strauss *et al.* (1964) indicate that the events on which they focused in their hospital study were related to the general problems that they had in hand and their basic theoretical framework. In this context, researchers might consider the extent to which the Marxist perspective employed by Beynon (1973), Nichols and Beynon (1977), and Willis (1977), has influenced the problem of study, the methods of investigation and the collection of data. However, the limits that are placed on a field of study will depend on several issues. Devons and Gluckman (Chapter 3)

indicate ways in which field researchers can limit their studies, and ways in which the studies relate to previous work in other social science disciplines. In short, they are concerned with the ways in which field researchers can set boundaries to their studies. On the basis of their reflections on sociological and anthropological studies (Gluckman, 1964), they are able to distinguish five procedures by which field researchers can demarcate their field of study. They stress that there are no rules that can be applied to the field setting, as ultimately the decisions concerning the limits of a study depend on the field researcher's professional judgement in relation to the problems which are posed. However, this presupposes that researchers can impose themselves on people who do not limit their fields of study. In these circumstances Devons and Gluckman's position might be considered somewhat naïve, especially in the light of the experiences of Cohen and Taylor (1972; 1977) doing prison research, and Wallis (1976; 1977) working with Scientologists. In both studies the researchers' fields of investigation were limited by those who controlled the research settings.

Once researchers have some conception of the problems that are to be studied, they can begin to limit their studies to particular locations. However, before research projects begin, researchers have to gain access to a research site. In some instances, researchers are already members of the institution to be studied. Roth (1963; 1974) was already a hospital patient, and Dalton (1959) was already a manager, in the organisations they studied. However, as Burgess (1980) has shown in the case of teachers doing research in their own schools, access still needs to be negotiated otherwise covert research will be done. In considering questions of access to a research site Schatzman and Strauss (1973) indicate that the researcher should 'case the joint' in terms of three criteria. First, to determine whether the selected site meets the researcher's substantive requirements. Secondly, to consider whether the size of the site, its population, complexity and special layout is appropriate given the resources of time. Finally, to prepare suitable tactics for more formal negotiation and further access. Spencer (Chapter 4) highlights the particular problems involved in gaining access to the Military Academy at West Point. This case study allows him to analyse why groups, and in particular elite groups, shun the researcher. He also outlines the mechanisms that can be employed by a group for limiting and controlling access, and indicates the strategies that can be employed by the researcher to gain data and overcome some of these problems. He demonstrates that the researcher has not merely to gain access to a research site, but also to documents and to individuals.

In any investigation, the researcher has to decide whom to contact. Should researchers contact the person whom they see as most powerful in a particular setting? Should the leader of a group or an institution be the first person to be contacted? Group leaders and the institutionally powerful are seen by some researchers as the gatekeepers who can grant access. Doc assisted Whyte's study of a street corner gang (Whyte, 1955), as in similar circumstances did Tally in Liebow's study (Liebow, 1967) and Tim in Patrick's study of a Glasgow gang (Patrick, 1973). However, gatekeepers can also restrict access to researchers, as Cohen and Taylor found when they approached the Home Office for access to long-term prisoners (Cohen and Taylor, 1972; 1977). Walker (1980) has argued that research contact always has to be sponsored. However, he maintains that it is sponsored by individuals who have authority over those whom the researcher wishes to study. Several questions can be raised in this connection: what right has any individual to grant or withhold access to a researcher who wants to conduct research with other informants? Will the researcher become identified with the gatekeeper? Does the researcher have any obligations to the gatekeeper (cf. Burgess, 1980)? Furthermore, do gatekeepers or sponsors limit or extend access in a research setting? Harrell-Bond (1976) and Burgess (1979a) have indicated how these questions raise practical, political and ethical implications for a researcher.

Access does raise ethical questions in a direct way. Some sociologists have conducted all or part of their studies without gaining formal access from any group or individual. Humphreys (1970) in studying homosexuals did not indicate his research role, nor did Wallis (1977) in his preliminary investigations on Scientology. In such cases, covert research where no formal access is negotiated raises questions concerning the rights of the citizen and obligations of the researcher to society in general, and to the academic community in particular (Barnes, 1979; Bulmer, 1982). However, even when research intentions are declared, the question still remains about whether the researched fully understand what is being done.

What do researchers do once they have gained access? How do they begin to observe situations, select and record data? How do they learn about the setting and the people? How do they establish themselves? The anthropological literature emphasises the importance of learning terminology and language. However, sociologists working within their own culture have discussed the importance of understanding how to use a native language. Becker *et al.* (1961) explain how they discovered that the term 'crock' was used by student doctors to refer to non-preferred patients and, in turn, was significant in terms of student expectations of medical education. Similarly, McCall (1980) found that once she understood the terminology used among artists, she needed to revise the concepts and categories that she was using in her study. In this respect, an understanding of the native language is essential if the researcher is to comprehend the way of life in a social setting.

In addition to learning the language, researchers have to focus their studies and establish roles for themselves. Lupton (1963) worked within the factories that he studied. Similarly, Hargreaves (1967) and Lacey (1970) took roles within the schools that they studied, as they were researchers who taught classes. However, in these circumstances only a limited number of classes were taught, so that observation, interviewing and the writing of field notes could be done (Lacey, 1976). In the final chapter in this section (Chapter 5) Valdo Pons illustrates what field researchers do when they begin their research. In his study of a small area of an African community (Avenue 21 in Kisangani – formerly Stanleyville) he illustrates how his initial experiences allowed him to pose problems and queries about social relationships as they first occurred to him. This approach links us directly back to Devons and Gluckman and the notion of establishing a specific field of study. It also links up with Geer (1964) and her idea that researchers should devise a series of questions that she refers to as 'working hypotheses'. Pons also discusses how he gained access to the people in Avenue 21 and established a field role.

The extract from Pons's study of Kisangani is of wide-ranging significance as it highlights the processes involved in starting field research, namely, defining areas of investigation, getting to know people, developing and establishing roles in relation to the local inhabitants, making systematic observations that can be cross-checked against other data and engaging in the preliminary analysis of data. Here, we have come full circle, as Pons's early field experiences point us towards a number of themes which appear and reappear throughout the field research process. Many of these themes will reappear in later sections of this book, as they are central to the process of doing field research.

Suggestions for Further Reading

METHODOLOGY

Bell, C. and Newby H. (1977) (eds), *Doing Sociological Research* (London: Allen & Unwin). Accounts from British field projects. The reports by Bell (1977) on the Banbury restudy, Cohen and Taylor (1977) on prison research and Wallis (1977) on Scientology are all useful discussions on early experiences. Each of these papers also raise ethical questions in different ways.

Brown, C., Guillet De Monthoux, P. and McCullough, A. (1976), *The Access Casebook* (Stockholm: THS). Especially useful for the general discussion in chapters 1–3. The access cases that are reported predominantly concern organisational and industrial settings and should be used selectively.

Burgess, R. G. (1980), 'Some fieldwork problems in teacher-based research', *British Educational Research Journal*, vol. 6, no. 2, pp. 165–73; examines the problems for researchers who are already members of the institutions in which they conduct research. A section of the paper deals with questions of access.

Freilich, M. (1977) (ed.), *Marginal Natives at Work: Anthropologists in the Field* (New York: Wiley). Contains first person accounts by anthropologists together with a good introduction by Freilich (1977b) that raises key issues concerning the start of the field research process.

Geer, B. (1964), 'First days in the field', in P. Hammond (ed.), *Sociologists at Work* (New York: Basic Books), pp. 322–44. A discussion that makes links between initial observations, field notes and analysis.

Gluckman, M. (1964) (ed.), *Closed Systems and Open Minds: the Limits of Naïvety in Social Anthropology* (Edinburgh: Oliver & Boyd); contains papers written during the years 1957–8 by members of the Department of Social Anthropology and Sociology, University of Manchester. The papers cover the study of African tribes, Indian villages and factory workshops and examine links between methods and analyses.

Habenstein, R. W. (1970) (ed.), *Pathways to Data* (Chicago: Aldine). A collection of accounts that were specially commissioned from American researchers. The editor asked authors to answer specific questions in their papers – one of these questions concerned access. The papers by Beck (1970), Becker (1970b), Geer (1970) and Roy (1970) are especially good.

Schatzman, L. and Strauss, A. L. (1973), *Field Research: Strategies for a Natural Sociology* (Englewood Cliffs, NJ: Prentice-Hall); reviews the basic issues on getting started in the field and contains a useful bibliography.

Shaffir, W. B., Stebbins, R. A. and Turowetz, A. (1980) (eds), *Fieldwork Experience: Qualitative Approaches to Social Research* (New York: St Martin's Press); contains a useful collection of essays that address the topic of access – see especially West (1980), Hoffman (1980) and Karp (1980).

Spindler, G. D. (1970) (ed.), *Being an Anthropologist: Fieldwork in Eleven Cultures* (New York: Holt, Rinehart & Winston). A further collection of autobiographical accounts that include discussions of access in other cultures.

Vidich, A. J., Bensman, J. and Stein, M. R. (1964) (eds), *Reflections on Community Studies* (New York: Harper & Row); contains essays on field research in villages, towns, cities, street gangs and hospitals. The essay by Diamond (1964) is especially good on access problems.

EMPIRICAL STUDIES

There are numerous studies that make reference to the early days in the field. Among those studies that discuss early field experiences are:

Beattie, J. (1965), *Understanding an African Kingdom: Bunyoro* (New York: Holt, Rinehart & Winston).

Douglas, J. D., Rasmussen, P. K. and Flanagan, C. A. (1977), *The Nude Beach* (Beverley Hills, Calif.: Sage).

Gans, H. J. (1967), *The Levittowners* (London: Allen Lane).

Humphreys, L. (1970), *Tearoom Trade* (London: Duckworth).

Parker, H. (1974), *View From the Boys*, (Newton Abbot: David & Charles).

Patrick, J. (1973), *A Glasgow Gang Observed* (London: Eyre-Methuen).

Plant, M. (1975), *Drugtakers in an English Town* (London: Tavistock).

Pons, V. (1969), *Stanleyville: an African Urban Community under Belgian Administration* (London: OUP for the International African Institute).

Whyte, W. F. (1955), *Street Corner Society* (2nd edn) (Chicago: University of Chicago Press).

3

Procedures for Demarcating a Field of Study

ELY DEVONS AND MAX GLUCKMAN

Initially, as stated in the Introduction,[1] we thought that we were dealing with two sets of issues. First, since 'the passage of events' is 'infinite', we asked, 'how does an anthropologist decide where to demarcate a field of data, or a set of purposive activities, out of the total flow?' Secondly, there was the problem of how an anthropologist decides whether or not to take notice of the work of investigators in other social sciences who are studying the same events by other techniques and modes of analysis. And finally, what limitations did these decisions impose on his ability to explain the nature of reality?

In working through the essays in this book,[2] and through other researches in which these issues have arisen, we have come to realise that there are more than two sets of issues, and we now distinguish five procedures by which fields of study are demarcated. These procedures can be usefully distinguished from one another, even though an anthropologist may employ all simultaneously and though it is sometimes difficult to decide which he is using, because they shade into one another:

(1) There is delimitation of a field in space and in time. Every anthropologist uses this procedure to isolate a manageable amount of interconnected data, as when he studies social relations in a tribe or in a factory over a certain period. This delimitation may also be of what Fortes calls a 'domain' of activities, such as domestic relations, or political relations, or the interpersonal linkages between kinsfolk, or the relation between legal or religious activities and social relationships. This procedure of closing off a field will be called *circumscribing* a field of research. When an anthropologist circumscribes his field, he cuts off a manageable field of reality from the total flow of events, by putting boundaries round it both in terms of what is relevant to his problems, and in terms of how and where he can apply his techniques of observation and analysis. Establishing the boundaries is a major separate procedure, which may involve some of the following procedures, though they have their own logic of application.

(2) The anthropologist may take for granted, as 'given' facts, some events which exert marked influence in his field. He does not bother about their internal complexity and can completely neglect the disciplines which study them. Thus, every anthropological study of a tribal society begins from the fact that rain falls in certain quantities at certain times, and this affects the growth of crops and grazing and therefore social life, but no inquiry is made into what determines the rainfall and the growth of crops. Anthropological studies of factories take for granted that there is machinery, but they do not worry about how it works, though they are concerned with how the technological process affects social relations. We propose to call this procedure by which certain events are taken for granted, as given basic facts, *incorporation*,[3] on the mixed analogy that the anthropologist merely *incorporates* them into his field.

(3a) The next procedure has to be applied with greater care. Frequently, an anthropologist has to base his analysis on more complex combinations of relations between facts, where these relations are appropriately studied by another discipline. Thus, the question of whether a particular tribe has an abundance of land, or is running short of land, is relevant to many anthropological studies,[4] and an anthropologist may even discuss in detail the relative availability of different types of land.[5] Accurate judgement on this point requires considerable ecological and agricultural knowledge and research.[6] Similarly, when an anthropologist states that a particular dance, or form of leechcraft, involves 'dissociation' or 'hysteria', he is making a statement the validity of which can only be tested by skills which are not normally part of the anthropological battery.[7] This kind of statement about a complex of facts falling outside the anthropologist's competence cannot be taken for granted in the same way as facts which we have said can be *incorporated*. Conclusions by other scientists have to be summarised, and often simplified, and we propose therefore to call this procedure by the distinctive term, *abridgement*. If an anthropologist *abridges* research carried out by appropriate specialists on any complex of relations of this type, it is *validated abridgement*. But where, in the absence of research by such a specialist, he nevertheless has to make a judgement on some complex in order to proceed with his analysis, it is *postulated abridgement*, and he should be careful, after trying to 'validate' his summary statement as well as he can, that he does not build more of his analysis on it than it can warrantably carry. Thus, it is possible for an anthropologist to assess to some extent, though not accurately, the availability of types of land by using the opinions of Africans themselves, and particularly by judging the efficacy of fallowing; but this inexpert judgement sets limits on the extent to which he can judge, for example, immediate developments which depend on this factor.[8]

(3b)   Abridgement moves a step further when the anthropologist takes over not only complex combinations of fact appropriate to the investigations of other disciplines, but even their postulates and hypotheses. For example, Turner concludes that

> the ritual symbol, we may perhaps say, effects an interchange of qualities between its [ideological and sensory] poles of meaning. Norms and values, on the one hand, become saturated with emotion, while the gross and basic emotions become ennobled through contact with social values.[9]

This might appear to abridge the psycho-analytic thesis of sublimation: we discuss later[10] whether we believe that it does. It exemplifies a possibility which we classify with abridging the conclusions of another discipline, for though we think it important to distinguish hypotheses from conclusions, for our purposes we do not need another term to cover this distinction. Clearly, arguments based on the abridgement of hypotheses must be more carefully scrutinised, since they depend on the validity of the findings in the other discipline. Later it will be necessary to refer simultaneously to both the procedures of incorporating and abridging, and this will be called *compression*.[11]

(4)   As against abridging the findings of other disciplines, whether by validated or postulated abridging of conclusions or by abridging of hypotheses, the anthropologist may make *naïve assumptions* about the complexes of events which lie at the boundaries of his circumscribed field, or about the aspects of events which are studied by other disciplines. In doing this, he considers that he is entitled to disregard the researches and conclusions of those other disciplines as irrelevant to his problems. We wish to restrict *naïvety* – artlessness – to this procedure. We believe that most social anthropologists are in this sense naïve about researches into human personality, and that their naïvety is a *justified naïvety*. Political scientists are usually still more naïve about the personalities of individuals in their fields of study, for, unlike anthropologists, they rarely concern themselves even with the possibility of unconscious motivations influencing these persons. When economists assume that individuals are consistently and consciously rational and are motivated by enlightened self-interest, they are plunging still deeper into naïvety. Correspondingly psychologists studying the human personality may be naïve about social, political, and economic aspects of life. We again believe that this naïvety may be justified, if the investigator concerned is to proceed with his own research and analysis.

It is in defining the procedure of starting from naïve assumptions that we go beyond the views of most writers on methodology in the social sciences, though many practitioners use this procedure. Clearly, in many instances the making of naïve assumptions is quite distinct from compression, which is a process dealt with by some of these writers on methodology. But since naïvety and compression shade into one another, they have not been distinguished. 'Naïvety' is not a question of parsimony in research (Parsons, 1952),[12] or of economy in phrasing under which an investigator takes over the findings of other disciplines and states them in 'shorthand,' without spelling them out in detail (Nadel, 1951).[13] We consider that if a social scientist is to set himself a manageable aspect or field for study, about which he can say significant things, he may often have to make assumptions which will appear to be distorting or even false to the practitioners of other disciplines. We go so far as to say that he has a duty to be naïve in this way about his 'outside' assumptions, and a duty to avoid attempting to deal with aspects of reality which can only be adequately handled by some discipline other than his own. Provided that it is appropriately used, the naïvety will not mar his work. On the contrary, getting entangled in considering, let alone studying, other aspects of reality, tempting though this may often be, might be an impediment to his understanding of those aspects of reality which are properly the concern of his own discipline. If so, these basic assumptions themselves set limits to what a particular analysis can explain, and the investigator must not draw conclusions beyond those which the assumptions can bear. Leading scientists have sometimes failed in this respect to recognise what we call 'the limits of their naïvety', and have in practice gone on to claim that their analysis of some aspect of reality explains a quite different aspect.

(5)   A social scientist follows a quite different kind of procedure *within* his circumscribed field. There he has to simplify the facts and variables; and we propose to specialise the word 'simplification' for this procedure. In any complex field under study there is bound to be some simplification of this kind, but the degree of simplification depends both on the nature of the discipline and on the particular problem set. In social science the raw material to be analysed is almost always far too complex to be presented *in toto*, and it has to be simplified to some extent.[14] We consider that on the whole social anthropology does this *relatively* little, since it is concerned with complexity within narrowly circumscribed fields, while economics and political science simplify to a relatively high degree, since they deal with fewer, and more aggregated, variables in wider fields. This process of simplification raises difficult problems with which we are not on the whole concerned in this book,[15] but we draw attention to its importance in relation to the procedures we are discussing, because the rules for the application of incorporation, abridgement, and naïvety, apply also to simplification.[16]

Since everyone must restrict his field of analysis, these five procedures are of necessity applied by all social and behavioural scientists. As many do not recognise this necessity adequately when considering the work of their colleagues, we again state emphatically that there is a *duty of abstention*, which requires that if we are to solve certain problems we have to abstain from studying other, though apparently related, problems, and leave these to our colleagues, whether in the same or in some other discipline. In research, as in other activities, gluttony can choke one. Properly applied, the duty of abstention involves a *rule of disciplined refusal to trespass* on the fields of others.

In carrying out this duty of abstaining, a social scientist is entitled to perform *warranted* limitation, by using *justified* circumscription, compression (incorporation and abridgement), naïve assumptions and simplification. For example, naïvety, the procedure which has been most queried, is warranted and justified, if the naïve assumptions are not essentially involved in the analysis of the field. A fair test is to ask whether the analysis would stand, if different naïve assumptions were adopted. In these circumstances the investigator must *accept the consequences of his own naïvety* (or circumscription or compression) by recognising *the limits of his accepted naïvety*, and he should not draw conclusions about the relations between events involved in that naïvety. If he does, he commits *the error of ignoring the limits of his own naïvety*. Correspondingly, there is an error in criticism which we call *the error of unjustified allegation of naïvety*. This error is made when an investigator is rebuked because he has accepted naïvety on some point about which the critic believes he should be more sophisticated, when that sophistication is irrelevant to his mode of analysis, though not irrelevant to understanding of the total reality one of whose aspects he is investigating.[17] We emphasise at the outset that the limits of warranted naïvety, and of warranted circumspection, compression and simplification, cannot be set theoretically. They shift with the problem which is being considered.

Notes: Chapter 3

Reprinted from Max Gluckman (ed.), *Closed Systems and Open Minds: the Limits of Naïvety in Social Anthropology* (Edinburgh: Oliver & Boyd, 1964), pp. 162–9, by kind permission of Mary Gluckman.

1   See Devons and Gluckman (1964a), pp. 13–19.
2   See Gluckman (1964).
3   We feel that it is not altogether a satisfactory word, but have failed to find a better.
4   See, for example, Richards (1939), an outstanding anthropological report on a people's use of their land.
5   See, for example, Wilson (1938), an excellent study.
6   For an exposition of how difficult it is to make a judgement on these points, see Allan (1949) and Allan (1965).
7   These examples are given by Nadel (1951), p. 213. We state immediately that we do not accept Nadel's view that there is a hierarchy of sciences (see Devons and Gluckman, 1964b, pp. 172–4).
8   As an example of these difficulties, we cite Gluckman (1943), in a study of an area later investigated by an agriculturalist: Peters (1960).
9   See Turner (1964), p. 32.
10   See Devons and Gluckman (1964b), pp. 216–17.
11   Nadel speaks of both these processes in terms of a science which is higher in the hierarchy of sciences using 'shorthand', for reasons of economy, to cover the findings of sciences lower in the hierarchy (Nadel, 1951, pp. 290 ff.). We have already stated that we do not consider that the sciences are related hierarchically: we also consider, and hope to show, that Nadel's way of formulating this problem obscures the procedures used.
12   Parsons, (1952), pp. 9 f. 'Parsimony' in scientific method is also used to cover other procedures (see Hall and Lindzey, 1957, p. 14).
13   See n. 11, above.
14   We are specialising the word 'simplification' in this context: the same root in the form of 'simplicity', has been used to describe the procedure of choosing between

alternative theories (Hall and Lindzey, 1957, p. 14). These authors also use 'parsimony' to define this process, though Parsons uses it quite differently. We have searched diligently throughout for words which have not been used in other contexts of discussion of scientific method, as we wished to avoid confusion, but could find no new term to cover what we call 'simplification', as we have succeeded in doing for the other procedures.

15   See Gluckman (1964).

16   There is an excellent analysis of this procedure – and of others – in chapters 1 and 2 of Homans (1950). The tendency to construct 'models' in social anthropology, as in the other works of Lévi-Strauss, Leach and Needham, falls under this category and, hence, is outside our scope.

17   For a detailed pointing out of this kind of error in criticism, see the introduction to Gluckman (1963). Gluckman considers critiques of his analysis of political relations of ritual based on (a) the mistaken view that he was making a psychological instead of a sociological analysis; and (b) the view that he should make a more sophisticated psychological analysis, in addition to his sociological analysis.

4

Methodological Issues in the Study of Bureaucratic Elites: A Case Study of West Point

GARY SPENCER

Sociology, a generalising science, seeks not only to understand the nature of social relationships caught in a specific time and place, but also to identify more general principles of human interaction that have applicability across a wide range of social reality. The goals of this chapter are, therefore, twofold. The first is to share with the reader some of my own experiences in attempting to study a specific societal elite, the military, and a specific elite institution, the US Military Academy at West Point. My second purpose is to work towards a more general model for viewing the problems faced by sociologists in their attempts to study large-scale bureaucracies and the elites who control them.

The study of bureaucratic elites is perhaps one of the least researched areas in sociology. Yet we are a society that is highly bureaucratised, highly centralised and highly manipulated. The challenge of C. Wright Mills (1956, 1959) for sociologists to turn their sociological imaginations to the study of bureaucratic elites has gone largely unheeded. Most of our research efforts have been in the service of these elites. But now, in the 1970s, there is a growing unrest that our major societal institutions are not serving the public interest and that these institutions must somehow be made more visible and accountable to the public-at-large.

Large-scale bureaucracies entrusted with the public interest are 'commonweal' organisations. Blau and Scott (1962), in their typology of formal organisations based upon a concept of 'prime beneficiary', view a commonweal organisation as one where the 'prime beneficiary is the public-at-large'. They succinctly point out that the major 'issue posed by commonweal organizations is that of *external* democratic control – the *public* must possess the means of controlling the ends served by these organizations'.[1] In this context it is a major problem for a democratic society to maintain control of its military, police, public utilities, governmental agencies, and so on, rather than have a situation where the authority and resources entrusted to these groups are utilised to serve their own interests or the interests of a specific segment of the society. The credibility, accountability and public interest decisions of major societal institutions are today under attack.

Institutional response to public demands for facts and explanations are too often met with secrecy, harassment and public relations news releases. The problem is that when sociologists, journalists, or other professional researchers attempt to gain access to these institutions, they find that their presence is unwelcome and that they are likely to incur personal harassment and to fail in obtaining usable data.

Using the study of military elites as an example, or more specifically the US Military Academy as a case study, I shall attempt to demonstrate the sociological and societal significance of studying bureaucratic elites in commonweal organisations. A descriptive model is presented for understanding why bureaucratic elites shun outside researchers. A discussion of mechanisms adopted for limiting and controlling access to data and research populations is then presented, followed by a discussion of strategies and problems involved in obtaining data.

The Study of Military Elites

My own research interests have been in the study of military elites. Substantively I have concentrated on the selection, socialisation and career development of cadets and officers from the US Military Academy at West Point. This research is predicated on the assumption that West Point is the initial starting-point in the formation of the army elite. In 1970, for example, 100 per cent of all generals reporting directly to the Army Chief of Staff were West Point graduates, over 90 per cent of the generals with two or more stars were West Point graduates and 75 per cent of all brigadier generals were Academy graduates.[2] While West Point officers represent a small minority of all officers in the army, they represent a large majority of the careerists who find their way into the elite nucleus of military decision-making.

The influence of the Military Academy graduate extends beyond the internal military bureaucracy. In the past twenty years, 33 per cent of all West Point officer retirees who embarked upon second careers entered the civilian defence industry, and 32 per cent entered the teaching profession (Spencer, 1971). Former West Point officers hold high appointive positions both in industry and government.

At West Point this potential elite is selected, sifted and socialised. One guiding hypothesis for my research is that military elites are formed through a 'tunnelling' process of initial selection, and then selective attrition, into an elite corps which is becoming both highly inbred and highly conservative. For example, 21 per cent of a recent West Point class reported having fathers who are or were career military. By graduation the percentage was 23 per cent. After the initial required five-year tour of military duty, men from career military families comprised 31 per cent of the active West Point officers, with 18 per cent reporting that their spouse was also from a career military family. In the post-five-year period to retirement, 37 per cent of the West Point careerists were from military families. In short, through a process of initial selection and selective attrition the military elite emerges as highly inbred.

As a second case in support of the hypothesis, 25 per cent of the entrants to a recent West Point class reported having 'liberal' political views, 43 per cent reported 'middle-of-the-road' and 32 per cent reported that their political views were 'conservative'. Yet during the first year at West Point when resignations are typically high, 42 per cent of the resignees were from the liberal group, 33 per cent from the middle group and 25 per cent from the conservative group. Of those graduates who remained in the active military service beyond their initial five-year tour, only 11 per cent were liberal, 22 per cent middle, while the remaining 67 per cent reported that they held conservative political views. Thus, twice as many liberals resign as remain, the middle group is evenly split and the majority of conservatives remain on active duty.

One pattern of selective attrition within the military elite is not simply of sociological interest. It has wide-ranging implications for the relationship of the military to the larger society which it serves. As Blau and Scott (1962) point out, 'The existence of such a (military) force creates the danger that it can be used to dominate the society that produced it, thus destroying democratic control or other forms of civilian government'. They go on to point out that 'the problem of maintaining democratic control over the military is accentuated by the background and the political orientation of its senior officers'.[3] The makeup and functioning of bureaucratic elites is as important to the larger society as the makeup and functioning of non-elite lower participants are to the bureaucratic elites who control them. The latter receives extensive attention both in organisational in-house research as well as contract research. Access to bureaucratic structures in order to study higher elites has met with much less interest or success.

Why Bureaucratic Elites Shun Research by Outsiders

At an analytic level, there are essentially five basic reasons why commonweal organisations attempt to control and delimit access for the purpose of conducting social research: (1) bureaucratic rigidity and threat to personal careers; (2) the potential threat to the power of that institution; (3) the threat to the subjective reality constructs of that institution; (4) the problem of the legitimacy of the researcher; and (5) the problem of exchange. Examples from the military will be illustrative.

Most commonweal organisations are highly bureaucratised. Characteristically they function within a highly elaborate system of formal rules in a hierarchical structure of authority and communication. Informal networks, which are often as complex as the formal system, also emerge and function with their own norms and communication systems. Incumbents in bureaucratic positions typically enter the system upon completion of some formal training and embark upon an elaborate career where upward mobility is highly dependent upon the incumbent's success in both the formal and informal systems.

An outside researcher presents a problem for the bureaucracy in that the researcher does not 'fit' into the system. He does not fit into the formal chain of command, but moves back and forth at all levels of the organisation. He is not subject to the same rules or constraints as organisational participants. As such, the researcher is a relatively uncontrollable element in an otherwise highly controlled system.

The threat that the outside researcher holds for the career of the bureaucrat is also highly significant and more readily apparent. The researcher is in a position to observe activities that are not visible to all parts of the organisation. By making these activities visible through his reporting, the researcher provides data for evaluation both within and outside the system. If information is provided that is perceived as unfavourable to the institution, the career of the informant is in jeopardy. In my own research of military elites, the lack of clearcut formal rules for dealing with me plus the threat perceived to personal careers have been major impediments to obtaining data. As one colonel put it, 'I am not anxious to read one of your reports that may criticise the military, quoting me!'

Commonweal organisations hold the potential for wielding great power, because they are entrusted with a society's instruments of force or with the management of its scarce resources. In the Weberian sense, commonweal organisations have authority to use these instruments so long as they use them properly and in the interests of the society which they serve. To do otherwise is to employ power, not authority. To the extent that social research demonstrates that the utilisation of these resources is not in the public interest, it exposes their illegitimate use and, therefore, represents a threat to the organisation's power.

Commonweal organisations are often threatened by the presence of outside researchers, because the latter may not believe in the organisation to which the personnel are so dedicated and from which they derive their self-images as well as their livelihood. The uninvited researcher is viewed not so much as a threat to the existing power of the institution, as a threat to the individual's own identity and the identity of the organisation. In my own extensive interaction with military elites, for example, I rarely had the feeling that I was talking with a power-hungry person who was trying to convince me of something in which he did not believe himself. The clear impression was rather that of a person honestly and totally committed to military life and its 'mission'.

The subjective reality construct which sustains West Point is complex, highly steeped in tradition, and deeply ingrained, both formally and informally, into cadets and cadres. West Point views itself as a kind of last bastion of America's virtues, while it views the larger society as permissive towards youth and discipline. Military careerists suffer from feelings of rejection by a larger society which they seek to protect. There is a pervasive attitude that only the military can understand things military, while civilian meddling only reduces effectiveness. West Pointers are ingrained with the need to protect their traditions and public image from those who would seek to destroy it. The formal image which is West Point extolls the virtues of 'duty, honour, country', and seeks to protect its honour code which states that 'a cadet will not lie, cheat, or steal, or tolerate those who do'. But cadets, like other military personnel, are subject to an extensive informal lore that tells them to 'co-operate and graduate', 'play the game', 'maintain the image', 'get your tickets punched', and 'cover your ass'. The strength of these powerful informal norms go far in explaining military behaviour contrary to the public interest. The dilemma faced by organisational participants is the need to protect the formal public image of West Point while, at the same time, to prevent backstage access to the more powerful informal norms.

The military believes strongly that it is acting in the national interest and views many outside researchers as a potential threat. The researcher may view the military as potentially acting in ways adverse and threatening to the public interest. An in-house researcher at West Point expressed his confusion in attempting to define my role by asking, 'It is clear to me that you are not for the military. But at least are you for the United States?'

Simply put, the bureaucrat concerned with the problem of legitimacy asks, 'Just who is this fellow anyway who calls himself a sociologist, and what right does he have to come barging into my organisation?' While many sociologists view their professionalism as provid-

ing legitimacy for the dispassionate 'debunking' of social myths, they have no legal sanction, normative appeal, or legal immunity to enter public bureaucracies for the purpose of conducting a 'social audit'.

Most research arrangements involve some conception of fair exchange among researcher and the researched. The normative pattern is direct and utilitarian. That is, the organisation, in return for giving the researcher rights to publication, remuneration, or both, receives information and professional advice useful to its purposes. A variation of this exchange is often more indirect and symbolic. The organisation, while receiving no direct benefit from the research, at least is not hurt by it and may believe that somehow the cause of science and education is being served. In the type of research discussed in this chapter the researcher is providing information to the public-at-large at the potential 'expense' of the organisation actually being studied; and thus from the viewpoint of the organisation, the exchange is inequitable.[4]

Institutional Mechanism for Controlling Access to Data

Given the efforts by the bureaucracy to protect its public image and by the bureaucrat to protect his individual career chances, it is easy to see why it is difficult to carry out independent research on questions which are controversial to the military. Therefore, officials at the Military Academy are extremely apprehensive and defensive whenever a journalist or researcher attempts to gain entrée that departs from the standard public relations tours, briefings, or press releases.

The Military Academy attempts to prevent controversial reports by denying or controlling access to data. The following represent the major tactics:

(1) Refusal to allow access on the basis that it is an infringement upon the individual liberty and right to privacy of personnel.
(2) Assignment of sensitive security classification to controversial documents.
(3) Liberal use of the quasi-classification, 'For Official Use Only'.
(4) Specification of data for administrative purposes internal to the functioning of the organisation and, therefore, not applicable under the 'freedom of information' laws.
(5) Concealment of information that is potentially available.
(6) Limited access to data, making it incomplete or misleading.
(7) Controlled access to data, making it distorted and 'managed'.
(8) Lengthy bureaucratic delays to dissuade the impatient.

(9) Harassment and sanctioning of the researcher, if he is within the military.
(10) Stipulation of prior written approval before publication of independent research utilising military data.
(11) Personal discrediting of a researcher who has published data viewed as unfavourable to the military.

Blanket refusal under the guise that it constitutes an infringement upon the privacy of personnel is a popular means of preventing access to military populations. Use of the archives in the West Point Library is thus refused by this tactic. There is no question that individual rights must be protected, but too often this guise is used illegitimately for protecting the institution. The data presented earlier in this chapter in no way infringe upon the rights of the researched. In point of fact, the data themselves come from questions asked by West Point researchers for institutional use in selection and recruitment; the data are denied to those who might use them in another way. This is evidence, I would suggest, that the protection of the military as an institution is what is at stake, not the protection of its personnel.

The next three methods for preventing access to data are similar in that each involves some form of classificatory system. Classifying documents as sensitive and, therefore, unavailable to people without government security clearance and a 'need to know', is the surest way to prevent access, but it is also the most difficult to justify. Technically, a document is given a sensitive security classification if divulging of the document could seriously damage the national security. In practice, the assignment of a sensitive security classification is used, with little if any reference to national security, to avoid damage to the image and power of the organisation. The use of this system of classification allows the military to prevent other segments of the civilian population from obtaining information that could be embarrassing to the command. The Pentagon Papers are perhaps the most recent example of improper utilisation of secrecy labels. At West Point the secrecy label is not often used, but is used to keep some controversial studies in locked cabinets.

The following example demonstrates what I think is an illegitimate use of secrecy labels: A small group of cadets, along with cadets from the other service academies, filed a case in Federal court that the practice of compulsory attendance at chapel was an infringement upon their constitutional rights and should be abolished. A group of young lawyers in the Judge Advocate Corps wrote an opinion that the military did not have a proper defence and should not fight the case. The report met with such consternation that it was given a 'secret' classification and locked away while the higher-ranking Army lawyers wrote their own opinion arguing that compulsory chapel was a training exercise

that would help the young officers in counselling troops. The general feeling among many of the officers with whom I have spoken was that compulsory chapel was probably unconstitutional, but that if the military went down fighting, they could then blame the American Civil Liberties Union for the demise of religion at West Point, rather than be responsible themselves by voluntarily changing the regulation. A survey of cadets indicated that only a small minority would attend services weekly, if they were not ordered to do so.[5]

The 'For Official Use Only' label (FOUO) is attached to documents that can only be viewed by official personnel who have a need to know the contents of the document. This label is supposed to refer to unclassified documents that may contain sensitive portions such as personnel records of criminal investigations. In practice, however, many documents receive this label and are not available to the outside researcher. These documents include the actual regression weights which are used to determine entrance qualifications of cadets, several reports concerning black cadets, and other potentially controversial information. Reports are made official simply to control their circulation.

The refusal to release documents because they pertain to the internal functioning of the organisation is another technique for limiting access. The various regulations dealing with the release of public information stipulate that documents which pertain only to the internal administrative functioning of the organisation do not have to be treated as public documents. In practice, this definition is muddled; for all intents and purposes, just about anything at the Military Academy can be classified under this label.

If the researcher is able to gain access to research data, or to the West Point population, the next three methods of concealment will often reduce the ability to obtain full, reliable and accurate data. These include concealment of the data actually available, limited access to data making them incomplete or misleading, and controlled access which results in essentially the same distortion.

To the extent that the outside researcher is an unwelcome and threatening force, his presence is treated guardedly and with suspicion. Often he is given little assistance in learning just what data are available for his particular purposes. If specific questions are answered, little is volunteered beyond a succinct answer. At the same time failure to provide requested data often derives from ignorance of what is actually available. Most of the research at West Point is done by a single agency, and its reports have very limited circulation.

In point of fact, there is probably more research carried out at West Point with regard to its 'student' population than at any other educational institution in the USA. Most of the research is done by the Office of Institutional Research, an agency reporting directly to the Superintendent through the Chief of Staff. This office co-ordinates all research conducted at the

Military Academy. In 1971 alone, there were 114 research projects carried out on some phase of the Academy's operation. Most of the studies dealt with such topics as why cadets came to West Point, the commitment of cadets to military careers, prediction of academic success or attrition, and the characteristics of graduates. Each year the Office administers a questionnaire to the entire corps of cadets to obtain data for various ongoing projects, and it conducts a survey of graduating seniors. The point is that many of the kinds of questions in which the outside researcher would be interested could be examined through secondary analysis of the existing data tapes. A great deal of information could be obtained from the reports of these research projects, if one knew they existed, and if one could gain access.

Limitation of access to data is also accomplished by selecting out the data that will and will not be available. The subjective criteria for access revolve around whether or not data are controversial, or whether or not they reflect the desired image of West Point. In one visit to West Point, only four of the twenty-six reports I requested were obtained.

Controlled access to potential data is perhaps the most interesting technique for limiting and distorting information. Controlled access is accomplished by escorting the researcher around the Academy, so that the only people to whom he talks are those who are considered safe. The only data he sees are those which the Academy wants him to see. Thus, within a relatively short period of time independent articles about West Point appeared in the *New York Times*, the *Washington Post* and *Atlantic Monthly.* They all quoted essentially the same reflections of the same small group of officers who spoke rather eloquently of the changing and liberalising Academy and Army. In reality, these officers had little power to introduce change but served as an important public relations link to the liberal press.

The other methods used to limit access to research include extensive bureaucratic delays as letters are exchanged asking for more specific information about what is wanted, as numerous staff meetings are held to decide whether or not access should be allowed, and as opinions are sought from higher levels outside the Academy to assure that the release of data is appropriate. The damper which is placed upon nearly all attempts to enlist the co-operation of the Academy is the proviso that the finished report must have the approval of the Superintendent prior to its publication. All research reports emanating from the Academy itself carry the proviso that

> This document is prepared for official purposes only. Its contents may not be reproduced or distributed (in whole or in part) without specific permission of the Superintendent, US Military Academy, in each instance.

This last point deals with the control of research carried out by in-house researchers. Great care is taken to assure that control of research findings is maintained by the Academy, not by the individual researcher. Academy regulations specify that the release of data must be approved by officials before such data can be presented at professional meetings or published in journals. These delays discourage the professional research staff from formally presenting data to their professional colleagues outside the Military Academy. Research release that is not sanctioned is likely to bring about harassment or removal of the researcher.

The following excerpt is taken from a book by Heise (1969) entitled *The Brass Factories.* Heise's observations concerning the access he was given to data and the way in which he was controlled illustrate many of my own observations and serve as a form of external validation for the analysis just presented:

> Upon arriving at the Point, the present writer (Heise) was immediately informed that he would be under restrictions, and that he would be accompanied at all times – 'to assure that you get the full story', as a nervous colonel in the information office phrased it. Initially this meant that an information officer peered over my shoulder while I checked entries in the library's catalog or paced up and down in front of my carrel where I examined documents. My constant companion – always pleasant – would appear at breakfast in the academy's hotel and stay with me until he dropped me off at its front door, no matter how late the hour.
> On a subsequent visit, presumably because I had behaved properly during the first stay, the escort service was dropped at times. The cooperation, however, ceased when some sensitive nerves were touched. (Heise, 1969, pp. 3–4)

When Heise asked to visit the barracks when the cadets were present, he was denied because, 'You'd be invading the cadets' privacy'. When he asked if he could see copies of the manual pertaining to the training programme for first-year cadets, he was told that 'the manuals are a publication of the Corps of Cadets . . . implying that, therefore, they need not be made available'. The then Superintendent of the Academy told him that, 'such documents are considered exempted from release to the public', because they are 'documents which provide only internal guidance to Department of Defense personnel'. He was told that if he so desired he could appeal to the Judge Advocate General in Washington.

Heise also observes that he was informed by the information office at West Point that he was 'something of a hostile witness', because of a previously published article which was viewed as contrary to the Academy's interests.

In a visit to West Point I asked the head of the

information office, not the same one with whom Heise dealt, the reasons for Heise's treatment. The reply was quick in coming: Heise was known to be a dishonest person, and if he were not kept under constant surveillance, he would steal documents.

Seymour Hersh, the journalist, who uncovered and made public the My Lai massacre which implicated the then Superintendent of West Point, is another case in point. He is viewed as dishonest and lacking in journalistic integrity in order to get a sensational headline. The paradox is that while the military is quick to condemn as inaccurate any unfavourable report about itself, it is reluctant, if not outright in its refusal, to provide the accurate data when they are requested.

Finally, when adverse information regarding the Military Academy is published, the reaction usually takes one of the following three forms. First, the writer or researcher is discredited internally as being either a dishonest anti-military leftist, or a former Army officer who somehow has been thwarted by his own inadequacies and is now attempting to get back at the Army. Secondly, the view presented is discredited as being inaccurate or misleading. Thirdly, when all else fails, a rationale is adopted that after every war the military is in for hard knocks, and the storm will be weathered as in the past.

In the final analysis, the major variable in determining whether or not an outside researcher will gain access to research data is the determination of whether or not the individual is a 'friend' of the military. If one has published items favourable to the military or stated an intent to do so, then he is a friend, If one has published items viewed as unfavourable, he is not a friend. Furthermore, he will be discredited as being dishonest, disloyal, or misguided.

Research Strategies for Obtaining Data

This section deals with some possible research strategies for obtaining data from institutions under conditions of hostility and mutual suspicion. They are conditions where consensus methodologies are not appropriate. The usual reciprocal alliances between researcher and the researched do not exist. It is significant to point out, however, that the techniques are not really new to sociology. We have, for example, used deception, unobtrusive measures, and power relationships to obtain data for many years. The difference is that we have used these measures, with the knowledge and approval of higher elites, against the less powerful participants in organisations. With the complicity of higher elites, we have become participant observers in mental hospitals or work groups, stood behind one-way mirrors, misrepresented a survey instrument, and then used managerial fiat to assure worker co-operation. I am suggesting not so much new techniques, but the application of existing ones at the elite level of bureaucratic structures.

The several techniques, although not mutually exclusive, fall essentially into four categories: (1) participant techniques; (2) non-participant techniques; (3) entrée techniques; and (4) maximal utilisation of available documents. In each case I will try to give examples of the type of data that can be obtained.

Unquestionably the best way to carry out research at West Point is from the inside as a member of the institution. While the insider role gives one the greatest access to data, it also creates the greatest difficulty for publishing the data. The initial access, which served as the starting-point for my own work at West Point, came when I approached the time for entry into active duty as an ROTC officer. An interview was arranged for me at West Point, and while I was being shown around the Academy, my orders were being changed from a Signal Corps assignment to West Point.

While working at the Military Academy as a member of the Office of Institutional Research, there were, because of three factors, plentiful opportunities for pursuing relevant reseach questions. First, no one really knew what a sociologist should be doing, so one could define his own activities so long as he could convince his superiors that the research was relevant to the Academy's 'mission'. Secondly, many officers were both impressed and intimidated by the educational credentials of the young ROTC officers, thus making it easier for them to gain some autonomy. Thirdly, one had relatively free access to observe, discuss, or ask questions.

For a period of nearly two years I was able to administer questionnaires to the entire Corps of Cadets, visit classrooms, meet with cadets and attend various briefings and staff meetings. Informal activities provided excellent opportunity for participant observation. For example, the 'happy hours' in the officer's club bar were times when those assembled shed their official role and took one 'backstage'. Entertaining cadets at dinner in one's quarters or having dinner with them in the cadet mess allowed for conversations that would occasionally break through the extreme deference behaviours shown towards officers.

As I have already suggested, however, it is extremely difficult to publish research findings while on active duty in the military, or while working for the military as a civilian professional. The data collected are usually employed for in-house purposes and have very limited circulation. There are several ways that the strictures can be circumvented, but none are satisfactory when compared with the ideal of an open institution which freely makes data available to the broader society. Since this ideal has not been realised, the simplest way to obtain the data is for a person to take copies of materials with him when he leaves active duty. Nearly all of the research reports are unclassified and technically are public documents. Under these circumstances access is legal but nevertheless denied. Although the ethical implications of this duplicity are serious and cannot be taken lightly, it is important to recognise that most of our knowledge about bureaucratic elites comes from persons who previously functioned inside the organisation.

Two other methods for disseminating information to the academic community are to present the material on a panel at a professional meeting or to feed the data to someone on the outside so that he can put it into published form. It is extremely difficult to get a formal paper cleared for presentation at a professional meeting; it is somewhat easier to obtain permission to appear on a panel without a prepared paper. For example, after appearing on a professional panel where I discussed the characteristics of entering cadets to West Point, a military historian asked how he could get the information. I showed him how he could write to West Point and ask for the specific reports, two written by me, that I used in compiling the cross-sectional patterns just reported. Since he stated in his letter that he was a civilian adviser to the Secretary of the Army, the reports were sent to him without question; and he was able to present the data in an article, since reprinted in two anthologies of military sociology. I was unable to publish the data myself. In sum, the most effective way to obtain data on military populations is through actual participant observation in the military setting. This is one of the few ways to really observe what is going on backstage or to gain access to large survey populations.

The second set of methods for obtaining data is comprised of non-participant techniques. These include formal and informal contacts with in-house researchers, the use of formal institutional participants as informants, and the use of third-party sources for obtaining data. Most of the research which I have been doing utilises data already obtained during my military tour of duty, but I have visited West Point twice since my tour of duty to obtain data on new classes of cadets and to interview various personnel on current happenings and changes taking place. These visits have been viewed with hostility by the Military Academy. Primarily as a result of my previous writing, the Academy does not view me as a 'friend'. It is also likely that any professional researcher who has worked on the inside and now has continued his research in civilian life will be viewed as someone who has taken unethical advantage of his previous position.

The in-house researchers are the most important contacts to have within the Military Academy. For the most part, they are extremely competent and well-trained researchers. Together they probably know more about the Military Academy and its cadets than any other group of people. If they believe that a person is a serious professional in carrying out his research, they will try to assist him whenever possible. In a sense they 'run interference' by setting up interviews and introducing the researcher to key officials. They escort him around the Academy and, even more helpfully, they make him aware of the research in progress and

key personnel who may provide him with needed materials. The in-house researchers maintain professional reference groups and welcome an opportunity to talk about their work with fellow social scientists rather than with military personnel who often are unfamiliar with research issues. These exchanges ought to be encouraged, not expunged. The in-house researchers provide outsiders with far-different information than is provided by the Office of Public Information.

Former participants in an organisation can also be an excellent source for obtaining both qualitative and quantitative information about a system. Former instructors, cadets, or officers from West Point, now out of the military, are generally co-operative and anxious to talk of their past experience. For example, several former instructors at West Point have shared extensive information with me on the conduct of the classroom, the unique Thayer system of education which the Academy uses, the effects of the ability-grouped sections for organising classes, and other experiences.

The final way in which I have found non-participant research possible is to obtain data from third parties. In other words, if the researcher cannot obtain direct access, someone else who has that access may be able to secure the necessary data. In the military, a retired officer or a political official, but best of all a 'friend' of the military who has contacts inside, may be able to secure the information.

With respect to gaining access into the military in order to carry out research, several strategies are possible. One is at a distinct advantage, if one can be defined as a 'friend'. Although my position may be at odds with the Code of Ethics of, say, the American Sociological Association, I believe it is legitimate, under certain conditions, when dealing with powerful bureaucracies, to mask one's true purpose of seeking facts rather than the perpetuation of myths, in order to obtain the information essential to sustain a free society. The researcher should be ready, however, to accept the political and social consequences of his action; and he should recognise that he may be able to study many organisations only once; and he may block access for other researchers (at least for a time).

To be vouched for by a 'friend' of the military is extremely useful in gaining entrée. In one visit to West Point, when I encountered difficulty in obtaining new data, at least three different people suggested that I ask Morris Janowitz, who was defined as a good friend of the military, to pave the way for me. Or a sociologist might also become a journalist affiliated with a major newspaper. Such a role provides greater legitimacy in attaining entrée into the Military Academy than being an academic researcher. Although once there, a researcher with a journalistic base may encounter the usual evasions by the bureaucrats, he is apt to be able to secure many strategic interviews.

The most effective way of gaining entrée under

current conditions is to possess political clout. The military is extremely careful to maintain good relations with Congress, upon whom it relies for financial support and for obtaining nominations of candidates for cadetship. A visit to West Point as a member of a Congressman's staff, or with a letter indicating one has a Congressman's support, will open many closed doors.

A fourth suggested technique for obtaining data under conditions of hostility and mutual suspicion, one which I have found to be extremely rich as a source of information, involves maximal utilisation of published information. The military is very much like a fraternity, labour union, professional association and alumni organisation rolled into one. Like these analogous organisations the military publishes a wide variety of bulletins, magazines and yearbooks. All of these provide excellent data, if the researcher has the patience to content analyse and/or piece together information. For example, my paper on 'Second careers of West Point officer retirees' develops the patterned relationship between army career and second career. It also identifies the interpenetration of the military with the civilian defence industries (Spencer, 1971). It would be impossible to find such data released by the military. Yet by spending seven dollars for the West Point alumni association's annual *Register of Graduates*, it was possible, by utilising the extensive career biographies presented, to secure reliable and valid data regarding the questions with which I was concerned. The Army also publishes an annual register of its career officers, and by comparing the names of the various officers assigned to the various central commands and agencies with the West Point register, one can examine the extent to which West Point maintains its elite position in the larger military structure.

In addition to the two registers, there are several other publications which offer great insight into the activities at West Point. The alumni magazine publishes a letter from the superintendent in each issue; there are numerous speeches reprinted; articles appear that have been written by West Point researchers and instructors many of which contain extensive quantitative data. It must be noted, however, that these articles are not always available upon request. Publications by the cadets also offer great insight into the culture of cadet life.

Conclusion

Although it is possible to secure some information on such an organisation as West Point, the research strategies, outlined above, are *not* satisfactory as a means of providing a democratic society with sufficient information concerning its commonweal organisations. Even less satisfactory are the organisations' manipulation, harassment and managed news releases designed to undermine the citizen's right to know. Clearly, what is needed are institutionalised mechanisms that recognise this right and give it primacy. More exchange, not less, is needed between commonweal organisations and academic researchers. Social scientists must establish their legitimacy to conduct research at the level of bureaucratic elites, and not simply conduct research which serves these elites. If legitimacy cannot be established, then conflict methods should continue to be utilised. The social control of society by bureaucratic elites is an inversion (and perversion) of the democratic process and represents a major threat to us all. C. Wright Mills (1959) writes in *The Sociological Imagination*:

> I do not know the answer to the question of political irresponsibility in our time or to the cultural and political question of the Cheerful Robot. But is it not clear that no answers will be found unless these problems are at least confronted? Is it not obvious, that the ones to confront them, above all others, are the social scientists of the rich societies? That many of them do not do so is surely the greatest human default being committed by privileged men in our times. (Mills, 1959, p. 176)

Notes: Chapter 4

Reprinted from *Social Problems,* vol. 21, no. 1, 1973, pp. 90–103, by kind permission of the Society for the Study of Social Problems and the author. This is a revised version of a paper read at the Annual Meeting of the American Sociological Association, New Orleans, Louisiana, USA, 28–31 August 1972. Grateful acknowledgement is made to the Social Science Research Council of the University of Florida for their support, to Timothy Lehmann of Colorado State and Felix Berardo of the University of Florida for their comments on drafts of this paper.

1 See Blau and Scott (1962), p. 55.
2 Unless otherwise noted, West Point data are from unpublished research in progress by the author.
3 See Blau and Scott (1962), p. 55.
4 It is interesting to point out, however, that this is exactly what happens when sociologists study lower participants in organisations under an exchange arrangement with the higher elites. The lower participant supplies the data, providing information for the sociologist that may be used by management to further exploit or control the lower participant.
5 In December 1972 the US Supreme Court upheld the ruling of a lower court in declaring compulsory chapel at service academies unconstitutional.

5

Launching a Neighbourhood Study in an African Town

VALDO PONS

The Social Landscape of Avenue 21

Avenue 21 is the name I have previously give to twenty-three dwelling compounds situated in one of the peripheral areas of Kisangani.[1] The avenue led on to the Irumu Road which constituted the southern boundary of that quarter of the town. The twenty-three compounds faced each other across one end of a long avenue which contained a total of seventy dwelling compounds. The avenue lay about four kilometres away from the central market, from the administrative offices of the African townships, and from the centre of the 'European town'. A subsidiary market on the inlying border of the quarter was just over a kilometre away. Across the Irumu Road, and within two minutes' walk from the avenue, were a few European dwellings, a sawmill and a general workshop. These establishments employed several men living in the avenue, though the majority worked in or near to the town centre.

Avenue 21 had been first settled in 1930, and had thus been in existence over twenty years. It formed part of one of the quietest areas of the town, and few people from the busier areas ever had cause to visit it unless they had friends or kinsmen there. There was one brick house in the avenue occupied by the mistress of a European who had paid for its construction and who called there from time to time. A brick house was a rank exception in Avenue 21 and its environs, and the occupant's lover was the only non-African I ever saw in the area. In addition to the brick house there were on the same compound two native-type houses of good quality, the unusual feature of a well with cement walls and a latrine enclosed by a permanent structure instead of a rough barrier of sticks and leaves as on most other compounds. The total value of the property on this compound was over 15,000 francs. At the other end of the scale, there was a compound in the avenue with only one rough native-type house of two rooms worth no more than 300–400 francs. Most compounds had at least two dwellings (see Figure 5.1) and were worth from 1,500 to 4,000 francs. Ten of the twenty-three dwelling compounds had their own wells, which cost 200–300 francs to dig by hired labour. Most compounds had a few palm and other fruit trees, and several had small gardens of pineapples and sugarcane, and of cassava and other vegetables. There were three small shops in the avenue, and one of them was run in conjunction with a tearoom. Up and down the avenue there were several irregular and illicit beer vendors but, somewhat exceptionally for the area, there was no regular bar selling native wines.

Conditions of daily life in Avenue 21 were such that most residents, even if of only a few weeks' standing, were able to identify numbers of persons in the immediate locality. The compounds were open and a large part of the daily domestic routine of preparing food, cooking, eating and washing was conducted out of doors. People could see what their neighbours were doing, they could watch comings and goings, and they could talk to each other from compound to compound. The inhabitants of compounds without wells normally drew their water from the wells of neighbours. Neighbours and near-neighbours were also often in contact with each other as customers and clients for various goods and services. People were thus continually thrown together, and privacy and anonymity were virtually impossible.

The seemingly ready mixing of people was a feature which attracted my attention very early during the course of my fieldwork. On one of my first visits to the avenue, for example, I made a note of the following incident. Two men, a woman and her small child returned late one afternoon from a trip to a rural village. The lorry in which they had travelled drew up in front of compound no. 15, where one of the men lived. As the four jumped out of the lorry, a few fellow-passengers began to pass down bunches of bananas and other produce brought back from the countryside. Several avenue people immediately gathered round the lorry and helped to carry the goods to the main house on the compound, but at this point the owner discovered that he had lost the key to the padlock on his front door. The lorry drove away but a group of about ten people was left standing in front of the house. A woman strolled across from compound no. 18 and, on seeing what the problem was, shouted to a woman from compound no. 22, asking her to bring her bunch of keys to try on the padlock. The woman from compound no. 22 joined the assembly and, as she did so, untied a bunch of keys hanging from her headscarf. She then herself tested her keys on the padlock. The child who

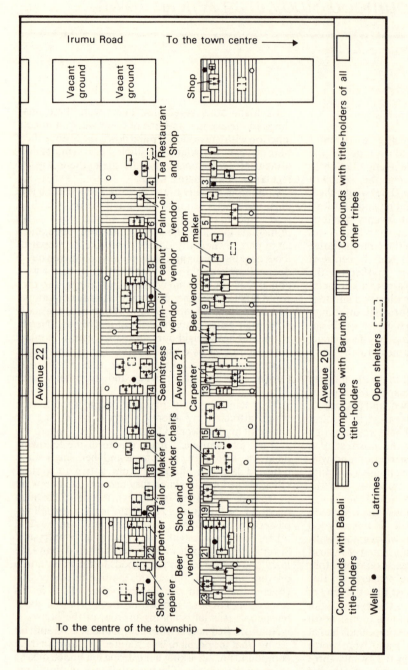

Figure 5.1 *Sketch map of Avenue 21.*

had returned on the lorry began to cry and was picked up by his mother. Another woman who had been looking on from compound no. 17 ran across and took the child from his mother's arms. Two men strolled down the avenue and paused to ask questions of the group. I recognised one of these men as a resident from compound no. 13. As the struggle to open the door continued, yet another man walked across from compound no. 22 accompanied by his small daughter. The owner of the house had by this time withdrawn to the periphery of the assembled group and was discussing his trip with yet another woman who had joined the group. After a few minutes, the door was opened and nearly all the people who had gathered entered the house. The whole incident lasted only five to ten minutes but had involved some fifteen to twenty people. Not knowing most of the participants at the time, I gained the impression that they knew each other intimately. In the light of later fieldwork, however, I now very much doubt that they all knew each other well. I was later to come to see that fleeting incidents of the kind reported above were often the means whereby people new to the area identified older-established residents for the first time, and *vice versa*. As Clément (1956) has noted in a general description of social life in the town, every newcomer was very 'quickly spotted, observed, catalogued, located with reference to his tribe, the village he came from, the relations who were putting him up, etc'.[2] This was particularly true in the outlying areas of the three townships where, in contrast to the inlying areas, there was a lower population density and little traffic. Apart from specific incidents like the one reported above, people frequently lingered in the roadway to chat to passers-by or to converse with neighbours as they worked or relaxed outside their houses. Yet many were newcomers, who knew few of the other residents at all well.

A second impression from my early period of fieldwork was that the neighbourhood was relatively self-contained and self-sufficient for a certain range of social activities. Most men went to work daily, most women went to market once or twice a week, and most children went to school; for all these purposes and for a wide range of others the inhabitants had to leave the immediate neighbourhood. Yet daily life still struck me as markedly localised and this impression was over time largely confirmed both by my regular observations, and by certain more systematic analyses. For example, I scrutinised the addresses of all persons from the immediate environs of Avenue 21 who appeared before the urban courts in 1952 as parties to cases other than matrimonial suits (that is, mainly cases of thefts, fights and insults). Defining 'the immediate environs' of Avenue 21 as extending to two avenues on either side of it I found that about 50 per cent of the court cases involving one party from within this area also had their second party from the same area. In 30 per cent of the cases the second party was resident beyond 'the

immediate environs' but in the same township, and only 20 per cent involved a party residing beyond the boundaries of the township. Moreover, over a half of all cases involving two parties from 'the immediate environs' were between persons resident in the same avenue. These figures suggest that my early impression of a relatively intense local life was substantially correct. The avenue and its immediate environs were obviously not a discrete area, but they were an area of concentrated interpersonal contacts.

The People

We have previously seen that the neighbourhood in which Avenue 21 was situated had a tribally heterogeneous population. No single tribe outnumbered all others, but the Bakumu and the Babali between them made up nearly 50 per cent of all household heads in the area. There was also a smaller concentration of Barumbi making up about 10 per cent of the total. Each of these three tribes had marked clusters of residents in the neighbourhood, and two clusters – one of Babali and one of Barumbi – cut across Avenue 21 (see Figure 5.1). We also have to recall that the mean monthly wage in this area was low, that is, about 704 francs as against 959 francs in the town as a whole and well over 1,000 francs in some inlying areas of the African townships. There were few white-collar workers in the area and none who was considered to be *évolué*. The male wage-earning population was approximately evenly divided between ordinary labourers and specialised manual workers.

Table 5.1 *Avenue 21: Population Movement Over an Eight-Month Period in 1952–3*

	Number	Percentage
Residents throughout the period 29 July 1952–1 April 1952	82	50·0
Residents on 29 July 1952 who had left by 1 April 1953	32	19·5
Persons who came to the area after 29 July 1952 and were still there on 1 April 1953	29	17·7
Persons who came to reside in the area after 29 July 1952 and had left again before 1 April 1953	21	12·8
Total	164	100·0

A complete enumeration of the inhabitants of the twenty-three dwelling compounds in Avenue 21 at one point in time yielded a *de facto* population of 128 men, women and children, but there was a high rate of movement in and out of the avenue. An impression of the volume of movement is conveyed by Table 5.1. Over one eight-month period during which I attempted to

Table 5.2   The Turnover of Population on Dwelling Compound No. 17, Avenue 21, between August 1952 and March 1953

Person	Approximate age	Sex	Tribe	Marital status	Relation to title-holder or to household head	Arrival	Departure
(1) Christine	45	F	Mongandu	S	Title-holder	Resident since 1947	—
(2) Limela	34	M	Mongandu	M	'Fictitious' kinsman, not paying rent but helping No. 1 in various ways	Resident since 1950; came here from another part of the same township	Left in November 1952 to become a tenant in a nearby avenue
(3) Rosina	30	F	Mangbetu	M	Wife of No. 2	Resident since 1951; came here from a small outpost in the hinterland to rejoin her husband from whom she had been separated for a number of years	Left in September 1952 to stay with a friend next door following on a quarrel with No. 1
(4) Etienne	2	M	Mongandu	S	Child of Nos. 2 and 3	Resident since 1951; came with his mother	Left with mother in September 1952
(5) Cornet	Under 1	M	Mongandu	S	Child of Nos. 2 and 3	Resident since 1951; came with his mother	Left with mother in September 1952
(6)	30	M	Mongandu	M	Tenant	Resident since 1951	Left in September 1952 to stay with 'fictitious' kinsman nearby
(7)	25	F	Mongandu	M	Wife of No. 6	Resident since 1951; came with her husband	Left in September 1952 to stay with 'fictitious' kinsman nearby
(8) Patrice	22	M	Murega	M	Tenant	Resident since April 1952; came here a few days after arrival in town	Left in February 1953 for compound of a 'fictitious' kinsman in newly established part of the same township, where he had started to build his own house
(9) Sangumasi	16	M	Murega	S	Brother of No. 8	Resident since April 1952; came with No. 8 a few days after arrival in town	Left February 1953 with No. 8
(10)	30	M	Mumbole	S	Tenant	Resident since April 1952	Left in September 1952, when sent to gaol for theft of 500 francs from No. 1
(11) Prosper	30	M	Murega	M	Tenant	Arrived in August 1952; came from a nearby avenue, where he had been a tenant since his first arrival in town a few months earlier	Left in October 1952 to stay with 'fictitious' kinsman in newly established part of the same township
(12) Aluwa	30	F	Murega	M	Wife of No. 11	Arrived in August 1952; came with her husband	Left in October 1952, to stay with 'fictitious' kinsman in newly established part of the same township
(13)	3	M	Murega	S	Child of Nos. 11 and 12	Arrived in August 1952; came with his parents	Left in October 1952 to stay with 'fictitious' kinsman in newly established part of the same township

No.	Age	Sex	Ethnic group	Relationship	Arrival	Departure
(14) Mangaza	20	F	Murega	Wife of No. 8	Arrived in September 1952; came here from her village to rejoin her husband	Left in February 1953 with No. 8
(15) Kalanga	3	M	Murega	Child of Nos. 8 and 14	Arrived in September 1952; came with his mother	Left in February 1953 with No. 8
(16) Marguerite	Under 1	F	Murega	Child of Nos. 8 and 14	Arrived in September 1952; came with her mother	Left in February 1953 with No. 8
(17)	35	M	Lokele	Tenant	Arrived in September 1952	Left in December 1952 but returned in February 1953 and was still there at the end of March 1953
(18)	30	F	Lokele	Wife of No. 17	Arrived in September 1952; came with her husband	Left in December 1952 but returned in February 1953 and was still there at the end of March 1953
(19)	15	F	Lokèle	Child of Nos. 17 and 18	Arrived in September 1952; came with her parents	Left in December 1952 but returned in February 1953 and was still there at the end of March 1953
(20)	30	M	Mongandu	Tenant and later lover of No. 1	Arrived in November 1952	Left in March 1953 (destination unknown)
(21) Abeli	25	M	Murega	'Fictitious' kinsman of No. 8	Arrived in November 1952	Still there at the end of March 1953
(22) Mumbuli	20	M	Murega	Classificatory brother of No. 21	Arrived in November 1952	Left in January 1953 following a quarrel with No. 1 (destination unknown)
(23)	25	F	Musoko	Friend of No. 1	Arrived in January 1953	Still there at the end of March 1953

Note: In Column 1 named persons are those referred to individually in other parts of the text.

keep a register, the names of 164 persons were recorded as residents, excluding persons who were obviously visitors. Of these 164, 50 per cent were recorded as being resident in the avenue over the whole period, but this figure is almost certainly too high as an estimate of the proportion of people who did *not* move during the eight months under review. Keeping the register up to date was a difficult task, and it is highly probable that a few people with short periods of residence were missed. An attempt to record and classify the places of origin and the destinations of persons coming to and leaving the avenue proved more difficult. However, despite the difficulties, the attempt served to show that the bulk of the movement was between Avenue 21 and other parts of the town, and not between town and country. Compound no. 17 had the highest turnover of population (see Table 5.2). The title-holder, Christine, was a woman who had for several years largely depended on her tenants and lodgers for her livelihood. Most other title-holders who took in tenants or lodgers had fewer and chose them more discriminately. Christine's compound was exceptional for this neighbourhood; as we saw previously, rent-paying tenants were for the most part new to the area and Christine must, for several years prior to 1952–3, have been one of very few landlords or landladies in the neighbourhood.

At one point in time the twenty-three compounds in Avenue 21 accommodated forty-three households, which was a slightly higher proportion than for the neighbourhood as a whole. Nine of the compounds still had only one household each and the remainder had two or more, one having four. The growth in the number of people in the area and the rising ratio of households per compound were accompanied by an increase in tribal heterogeneity. Out of twenty-three title-holders, fifteen were either Babali or Barumbi, and we know that both were old-established tribes in the town, as were also the Bakumu and Bakusu who together contributed three further title-holders to the avenue. Moreover, most heads of non-rent-paying subsidiary households were also of these tribes. In contrast, most of the new residents coming in as tenants were members of tribes not previously represented in the avenue. The newcomers, whether tenants or not, were also younger than the old-established members, and few had been in town more than a few years. There was, too, an appreciable difference in the occupations of title-holders and all others. Only four out of sixteen male title-holders were ordinary labourers, the remainder consisting of five masons, two shopkeepers, two carpenters, one tailor, one labourer's foreman and one domestic servant; but of eighteen male heads of subsidiary households, ten were labourers and only eight were specialised manual workers. Taking all this evidence into account, it is evident that the newcomers constituted a relatively distinct category of persons whose recent intrusion was affecting the composition of the avenue's population to a marked extent.

The Beginnings of Fieldwork in Avenue 21

There is a sense in which the detailed field observations reported in this chapter started in Avenue 21 by accident. During my first few weeks in Kisangani I frequently strolled through various parts of the town to gain general impressions of the social scene. On one such occasion I passed through Avenue 21 and paused for a few moments at the entrance to compound no. 24, where Libobi was repairing shoes. He greeted me and we exchanged a few words about shoes, about his customers, and about jobs and problems of accommodation. Libobi was a Mundande, whose tribal home was in the mountain areas on the eastern borders of the country. I was subsequently to discover that he had left his home village five years earlier and that he had been in Kisangani for two years. After working in several smaller labour centres, he had come to Kisangani with his employer for whom he had continued to work as a *boy de cuisine* for a few months after his arrival. He had then been unemployed for three months but had managed to stay in the town until he found employment as an ordinary labourer. He was now an *aide mécanicien* in a garage and a self-taught shoe repairer after working hours. He had fellow-tribesmen in town to whom he referred as 'brothers', but no 'real' kinsmen with known genealogical connections. He had lived on several compounds since his arrival, sometimes free of charge and sometimes as a tenant. He was now paying rent on compound no. 24 and had been there a few months only. It was here that he had begun to repair shoes in an attempt to augment his income, but his work as a shoe repairer was as irregular as it was unskilled, and he had few customers.

Some days later I again stopped to talk to Libobi. While I was there, Lusaka, the title-holder of compound no. 22, came out of his house to work at his carpentry bench. He greeted Libobi, and came across to compound no. 24. Lusaka spoke to me in French, and I later discovered that he was the only person in Avenue 21 who had been to a secondary school. He said he had previously seen me in the area, and asked me who I was and what I was doing there. He also said that other people had commented on my visits and had come to him to inquire whether he knew who I was. This was the first indication I had that Lusaka was a person to whom others in the avenue often turned for information and guidance. I was later to see that Lusaka was much respected in Avenue 21. He was regarded as reliable and trustworthy and as knowing the ways of the town. Lusaka was a Mubali, who had lived in Kisangani all his life and in Avenue 21 since childhood. He was, thus, a true local in two senses: he had himself been in the avenue for a long time and he was a member of one of the best-established tribal colonies in the neighbourhood. He had been trained as a carpenter at school and was skilled at his job. He was now employed in the sawmill across the Irumu Road and a couple of minutes' walk from his home. He also spent long hours at the workbench in his compound, making doors, windowframes and small articles of furniture for private customers. He was never short of orders and, in fact, had an ever-increasing backlog of work which his customers were continually pressing him to complete. He had started working for private customers several years earlier, but the volume of his trade had only recently grown to its present proportions.

I returned to visit Libobi and Lusaka on several occasions during my first few months in Kisangani. The contrast between their two situations was striking. Lusaka was a townsman by birth, he was well-established on his compound, skilled in his trade and well-known in the neighbourhood. He had several 'real' kinsmen in town, and he was, in Avenue 21 and its immediate environs, surrounded by fellow Babali and *basaiba* (friends and acquaintances of long standing). In contrast, Libobi was a recent immigrant, he was unskilled, he was a tenant, and he knew, and was known by, few people in the neighbourhood. I was later to see Lusaka very frequently,[3] whereas Libobi was soon to leave Avenue 21, and I lost contact with him. But there were other men in the avenue in situations similar to Libobi's and my fieldwork inevitably became in part a study of the contrasts between old-established inhabitants of the avenue and the newcomers who were often transient residents.

An Afternoon on Lusaka's Compound

As I came to know Lusaka, I began to see that his compound was one of a series of nodal points of social contact in the avenue. I found that lingering on his compound as he worked at his bench was a sure way of getting to know people, of gathering news and gossip, and of assessing various norms of behaviour in the community. And many of the local inhabitants clearly found the same. This is well illustrated by the following record of the events and conversations which took place on his compound between 4 p.m. and 6 p.m. one Sunday afternoon. At the time of recording these observations I had been working in the avenue nearly nine months. I had already spent many hours on Lusaka's compound, and my presence in the avenue had largely ceased to attract the kind of attention which my initial visits had drawn. I had myself become part of the social landscape.

Lusaka was filing his saws, after working at his bench most of the day. His mother, Samenyao, was sitting on the compound listening to his conversations with callers and passers-by. In between these conversations, Lusaka passed comments to his mother on people who happened to walk down the avenue. Sometimes he addressed her in Swahili, sometimes in Kibali. His tenants of two months' standing were not on the compound. His 'wife', Bernadette, was visiting her kin in another township.[4] She was a Mubua, and was also of

Kisangani birth. His daughter, Safi, was spending the day elsewhere in the township with her mother, Antoinette, Lusaka's former wife.

Limela, a Mongandu who had previously been a near-neighbour and was a workmate and a good friend of Lusaka, passed the compound. He had until recently been a resident of compound no. 17 and was a 'fictitious' kinsman of the title-holder, Christine. He was now on his way to visit his 'sister' but, seeing Lusaka, he stopped to greet him, came on to the compound, and began to chat. He first told Lusaka of the progress made with the new house which he was building in a newly established quarter of the same township, and for which he had already placed orders for doors and windowframes with Lusaka. Limela spoke broken French, and the conversation was partly in French, partly in Swahili. They tended to start comments in French and to lapse into Swahili as they came closer to making a point. From time to time one or the other interrupted the conversation to exchange a few words with passers-by.

Limela explained to Lusaka that he was planning his new house in such a way that it would be necessary for the children to pass through his own bedroom to go outside. Lusaka expressed approval saying that it was particularly wise for growing girls who needed to be kept under strict supervision. The conversation went on until Asumani, the title-holder of compound no. 16, came on to the compound. He, too, was strolling down the avenue when he saw Lusaka chatting to Limela and decided to stop. Asumani was, like Lusaka, a Mubali. He had been in town seven or eight years, but had only recently acquired a compound in Avenue 21. He knew Lusaka fairly well as a fellow-Mubali and near-neighbour, but he and Limela knew each other by sight only. He was less 'civilised' than either Lusaka or Limela. (Lusaka once described him to me as a man who did not 'hold "civilisation" well'.)

Asumani spoke no French, and after his arrival the conversation was almost entirely in Swahili, though at first he himself took little part in it. Lusaka and Limela continued to talk of house-building, and Lusaka explained that in the new house he was building there would be a room for visitors, but that when his elder half-brother, Kisubi, came out of gaol any visitors would have to go into an outhouse. At this point in the conversation, Elizabeth, a Mubali woman from another avenue, walked past and greeted Lusaka who responded by chiding her with the fact that she had recently taken her lover to live on the compound of her kinsmen.

Neither Limela nor Asumani knew Elizabeth, and Limela inquired from Lusaka who she was. Lusaka explained that she was the *habara* (mistress) of Henri, who used to live on compound no. 9 with his (Henri's) 'fictitious' kinsman, Bernard. Henri, Elizabeth and Bernard were all three Babali whom Lusaka knew fairly well. Bernard was a title-holder of some years' standing in the avenue. He and Lusaka were very cordial to each other if they met in the street or passed each other's compounds, but they were not intimate and did not visit each other. (Lusaka once described Bernard as 'a man of good influence'. But he was not 'civilised'. He was, as Lusaka put it, 'a man whose heart is still in the village'.)

In the course of conversation Lusaka explained to Limela and Asumani that Henri, whom neither of the two listeners knew, was not like Bernard whom they did know. Bernard was a stable man, but Henri was 'a vagabond, a man who never stayed still, and who was always wandering about the town'. Lusaka then went on to explain how Henri had recently left Bernard's compound to live on the compound of a kinsman of Elizabeth. Limela expressed surprise and disapproval that a man should leave his 'brother's' compound to live with a brother of his mistress. This led to a long discussion of the similar case of Milambo, who had recently come to the avenue to live with his mistress, Zahabu, who was the title-holder of compound no. 23, almost opposite Lusaka's house.

The case of Milambo and Zahabu was known to Limela but not to Asumani who now questioned Lusaka about Milambo. He asked what his tribe was, where he worked, what he did, how long he had been with Zahabu, and what kind of man he was. Lusaka gave the details while Limela, who did not know Milambo as well as Lusaka did, made one or two contributions to the effect that Milambo was 'a Topoke, a *musendji* straight from his village'. (Milambo was in fact a Mumbole, not a Topoke. I later discuss the significance of this mistake.)

Lusaka and Limela agreed that it was always reprehensible for a man to live on the compound of his mistress, and particularly so in this case because Zahabu was much older than Milambo, and also because, Lusaka said, 'everyone had advised Milambo over and over to leave the compound'. In the previous few days, Milambo had repeatedly quarrelled with Zahabu's mother who was also living on the compound. Lusaka conceded that the quarrels were largely the fault of Zahabu's mother, but from one point of view this only made Milambo's failure to leave the compound more difficult to understand. Milambo was, Lusaka said, like 'a man who had lost his memory'. In the end, however, he simply laughed saying that it must be a matter of *plaisir* (meaning sexual pleasure).

Limela now left to visit Christine, and shortly afterwards Maua, a young Mubali woman, walked across from compound no. 21. Maua was the classificatory sister of a man whom Lusaka knew well as a fellow tribesman and near-neighbour from another avenue. Maua herself was not a regular resident of the neighbourhood. She was an ordinary prostitute as distinct from a semi-prostitute.[5] She was not registered as a *femme libre* and was not officially entitled to reside in the town. She spent most of her time in a fashionable residential area of the town, but would occasionally come to Avenue 21 for a few days or weeks on end to stay with 'fictitious' kin. On walking across to compound no. 22, Maua greeted Lusaka and then sat down next to Samenyao to whom she talked for a while. When a lapse occurred in the conversation between Lusaka and Asumani, Maua inquired whether she might borrow Lusaka's bicycle to go on an errand to the other end of the township. Lusaka lent her his bicycle and she left.

At this point Alphonse and Amundala, residents of compound no. 18, passed down the avenue in a lorry belonging to Alphonse's employer. Alphonse and Amundala were both Babali whom Lusaka and Asumani knew very well. Amundala was the title-holder of compound no. 18 and had lived there for four years. He and Lusaka were close personal friends and 'fictitious' kinsmen in town (Amundala came from the same village as Lusaka's mother's kin, and Lusaka normally addressed Amundala as *muyomba* in Swahili or *oncle* in French). Lusaka often visited Amundala on his return from work and *vice versa*.

Lusaka greeted Alphonse and Amundala as they passed, but then immediately began to discuss with Asumani the illicit use of an employer's vehicle. He expressed strong disapproval of this, saying that it was foolish and that he was surprised that Amundala should be a party to this with Alphonse. (The implication here being that while Alphonse could not be expected to know better, Amundala should have known that it was a foolish thing to do.) If they had an accident, how would they explain themselves?

Lusaka and Asumani discussed at length instances of men who had used their employers' vehicles without permission. The conversation then developed into a general discussion about Europeans as employers. Lusaka drew contrasts between employers who were strict and those who were lenient and, later, between officials in the administration who had foresight, ability and understanding, and those who, according to him, lacked all these abilities and simply relied on seniority for promotion.

The conversation will still in progress when Maua returned bringing Lusaka's bicycle back. She again sat down next to Samenyao, and gathered from her that Lusaka and Asumani had been discussing Alphonse and Amundala. Asumani soon left and Maua now began to discuss Alphonse with Lusaka and particularly the recent visit to the avenue of Alphonse's sister, Veronique. Veronique was a *femme libre* and a semi-prostitute. She was a striking woman who dressed fashionably. She was known in the avenue as a woman who had been to Leopoldville (now Kinshasa), and who was said to associate either with European men, or with African *évolués* in one of the more fashionable African residential areas. Her brief visit to Avenue 21 had aroused considerable attention and comment. After two days, she had quarrelled with Alphonse and had left on bad terms with him. Maua questioned Lusaka about Veronique's relation to her brother, and wanted to know whether it was true that on leaving Veronique had thrown a piece of burning wood on the compound thus indicating that she was not prepared to be reconciled with Alphonse. Lusaka gave a brief account of the quarrel, and Maua then continued to discuss the incident in Kibali with Samenyao. At this point I myself left the compound.

I have given this detailed account of the events and conversations around Lusaka's workbench on one afternoon partly to illustrate the general atmosphere on one compound in the avenue, and partly because the account contains several incidents which I use in my analysis. Lusaka's compound was, of course, not the only one on which there was a continuous exchange of news and gossip – I refer to several others in this chapter – but it is one of particular interest on account of Lusaka's influential position in the avenue. Moreover, the early part of my fieldwork was to an appreciable extent conducted from this base.

Getting to Know People

At this stage when, knowing only Liboli and Lusaka, I began to concentrate on the study of Avenue 21 and its neighbourhood, my first immediate concern was to identify and classify people. I soon found this relatively easy to do because many of the people I met were themselves constantly doing the same thing. The questions which Asumani asked Lusaka concerning Milambo, for example, were of much the same kind as I myself had repeatedly put to Lusaka when I first began to frequent his compound. In a situation where most persons were in the course of a day in contact with many others, and where there was a high turnover of population over the weeks and months, people were of necessity constantly engaged in finding and checking their social bearings. In so doing, they naturally used any pre-existing social connections which they may have had with kinsmen, fellow-tribesmen, workmates, and others.

My own position in attempting to get to know people in the avenue was different from that of the inhabitants. As a European, I was conspicuous and out of place in the area, and I had no pre-existing links there. Nor did I enjoy many of the advantages that actual residence in the avenue carried for establishing social contact. Yet my position turned out to be less disadvantageous and, in a few respects, more similar to that of *some* inhabitants that I had anticipated. I was an outsider but so were many of the inhabitants, and the common feature in their situation and my own helped me to see some of the important implications of the high rate of population turnover and of the marked and increasing degree of social heterogeneity in the neighbourhood. A number of social networks were open and dispersed, and I was frequently able to enter *certain* social

relationships as easily as many of the inhabitants did.[6] I was a customer at the local shops, and I bought beer, fruits and nuts from women vendors; I had occasion to use the services of Lusaka as a carpenter and of one of his neighbours as a tailor; and I was myself a 'photographer', taking (and sometimes selling) photographs in the area. Also, more importantly, I had time on my hands which made it possible for me to linger endlessly on the more 'public' compounds (such as Lusaka's) and to perform a series of practical services for members of the population. I sometimes wrote letters of introduction to European doctors in the town to whom direct access was often difficult for the inhabitants; I advised people on the procedures they were expected to follow in registering at the labour exchange and at the offices of the township; I sometimes read and wrote letters for illiterates, and I occasionally helped schoolboys with their homework. In addition, as illustrated by my first encounters with Libobi and Lusaka, I had as a European *some* advantages for making social contacts which African inhabitants of the avenue did not have. I was a rank and conspicuous outsider, but in the situation my status as a European and my very conspicuousness carried marked advantages as well as disadvantages. I found that I came to know and identify people more rapidly than many a newcomer to the avenue, and the information which I accumulated over the course of a few months enabled me in some cases to follow conversations about local people better than *some* of the residents themselves. In the particular instance of the conversation about Milambo, for example, I already knew the answers to the questions which Asumani asked of Lusaka. Moreover, as my knowledge of people and situations in the avenue built up, I came to see that even a man like Lusaka was in conversations on his compound not solely a giver of news and information, but also often an inquirer. Though he had a large fund of knowledge built up since childhood about people who had lived in the neighbourhood a long time – and especially about Babali residents – he was himself partly dependent on persons outside his better-established networks for keeping up to date with information on the more recent arrivals, and even in some cases, on non-Babali who had been in the neighbourhood for many years. There were in the avenue many people who knew each other very well, yet no one could live there without also interacting with newcomers and strangers.

I also came to see both from personal experience and from my observation of others that the process of adjusting to the avenue was much affected by the sheer multiplicity of tribal elements represented there. Though ethnic heterogeneity was less marked than in some other areas of the town, it was sufficient for even an urban-born resident like Lusaka to occasionally find himself interacting with members of tribes whose customs were unfamiliar to him. This had an important bearing on the actions and behaviour of all the inhabitants. The process of living in the avenue involved not only becoming acquainted with individual personalities, but also *learning* to differentiate between various tribal elements in the urban population. A first step towards determining one's relationship with a stranger was to ascertain his tribe, but this in itself could be a process conducted over time and sometimes requiring considerable knowledge. To appreciate this, we have to consider the wide variety of ways in which members of different tribes could be distinguished from one another. Some tribes or groups of tribes could be distinguished with varying degrees of precision on the basis of facial marks or other physical peculiarities (for instance, the elongated skulls of the Mangbetu and related tribes whose custom it was to strap heads in babyhood). Often, too, ethnic identification could be established with a relatively high degree of accuracy on the basis of certain features of dress and ornamentation, or on the possession of distinctive articles of native manufacture such as stools, kitchen utensils and musical instruments, which commonly varied in type and style from one tribe to another or, perhaps, from one region or culture cluster of the hinterland to another. Again, identification was usually possible for persons with the requisite knowledge on the basis of speech which might be in a vernacular tongue or which, even if in Swahili or Lingala, was liable to include a phrase in a vernacular tongue or particular expressions which betrayed one or other ethnic background. The very fact of whether a person tended to speak more spontaneously in Swahili or Lingala was an indicator of some reliability as to whether he or she came from the east or west, and so on. Yet again, there were some gross behavioural indicators, such as style of native dancing, and there were more subtle ones in certain minor physical mannerisms. There were equally broad indirect indicators related to urban occupations and practices. Thus, for example, anyone who had lived in the town for some time would know that a white-collar worker was more likely, other things being equal, to be a Lokele than, say, a Topoke, though on the basis of a number of other possible criteria the cultural affinity between these two tribes might well have led to a man from the north or the east to fail to distinguish between them. Similarly, an experienced Kisangani dweller would always, other things being equal, be more likely to assume that a fashionable *femme libre* was a Mubua, and that a woman trading on the market was a Lokele, rather than the other way round.

With so many possible indicators, and with their varying degrees of reliability, it sometimes happened that people made errors in their assessments of each other's tribal affiliations. In this connection, it is revealing to consider the particular reference in my account of an afternoon on Lusaka's compound to Milambo's tribal identity. We saw that Limela referred to Milambo as a Topoke, whereas he was in fact a Mumbole. It would have been a gross error for Limela

to mistake Milambo for, say, an Azande or a Mangbetu, but the Topoke and Bambole were peoples from the same region who were in many urban situations likely to be considered, and to consider themselves, as 'brothers'. Thus, in many situations, his slip might have been of little consequence even if he had been face to face with Milambo at the time; but the fact that the Topoke were generally considered to be less 'civilised' than the Bambole could in other situations have led to Limela's slip to be construed as a deliberate insult. It is, however, of interest to note that had Limela been face to face with Milambo, he would in all probability not have made the mistake in the first place; Limela was a Mongandu, and the Mongandu were themselves a tribe with some cultural affinity to the Topoke and the Bambole. That Limela did make the mistake thus illustrates a further implication of ethnic heterogeneity for interpersonal relations. To Lusaka –or to me after some months of fieldwork in the town –Limela's error inevitably conveyed a good deal about his (Limela's) relationship with Milambo: it clearly indicated that he did not know Milambo at all well and that he had very probably never spoken to him. Had he known him better, it is highly probable that he would not have made the mistake and, indeed, that in the particular conversation on Lusaka's compound, he would have referred to an aspect of Milambo's personal situation and character – as Lusaka had done – rather than to a general classificatory characteristic such as his tribal affiliation.

Assessing Situations and Norms of Behaviour

As my account of an afternoon on Lusaka's compound shows, the conversations around his workbench were not confined to the identification of people and the straight exchange of news. During the course of two hours in the afternoon I have described, the character and behaviour of several people had been discussed and evaluated in terms of moral worth, wisdom, 'civilisation', and the like. For example, although Asumani was, in the discussion about Milambo, primarily concerned to get factual information, Limela and Lusaka were, with different degrees of knowledge and insight, more interested in trying to find an explanation for Milambo's behaviour. In the event, their conclusions –Limela's that Milambo was a 'Topoke, a *musendji* from the village', and Lusaka's that Milambo's conduct could only be understood by taking into account the question of *plaisir*, and was therefore amusing –pointed to important factors affecting variation in the local norms of conduct between men and women.

Similarly, Lusaka's exchanges with Limela over the rearing of children in town, his comments to Asumani about Alphonse's use of his employer's vehicle, and

Maua's questioning about the behaviour of Veronique, were in effect part of a process of consultation and discussion about one or other aspect of problems of personal behaviour. As such, they inevitably led Lusaka on to discuss the setting of these problems and to volunteer his views on more general subjects. On the afternoon in question, for example, he was led to discuss relations between European employers and their African employees and the promotions of different types of European administrators.

On many other occasions, Lusaka's comments on particular items of news and gossip drew him into general comparisons of the ways of life in town and in native villages. As a townsman born and bred, he had marked anti-village and pro-urban sentiments. He often maintained, for example, that 'village people are "jealous" of us in town', that 'a man is never free from difficulties in the village', whereas in town 'he is only troubled if he is a trouble-maker'. 'In town', he said, 'a man has liberty, and his eyes are opened to the world and to "civilization"'.

In listening to the wide variety of discussions that took place on Lusaka's compound I found that these were quite as much a part of an ongoing process of evaluating behaviour, of seeking solutions to problems and of weighing up different norms (or sets of norms) as they were part of a process of incorporating newcomers to the avenue into a developing set of social relations. On his compound, as on many others, social norms were in effect constantly being examined, learnt and taught at the same time as they were in the process of change, development and elaboration.

This had important implications for fieldwork, as it obviously has for any analysis of the data gathered. In the field, it often facilitated my participation in social life. In situations where people are in effect engaged in exploring modes of behaviour and discussing the relative advantages of different cultural solutions to common problems, relative lack of consensus can serve to lessen the embarassment which an outsider may cause. Thus, on *some* occasions at least, my presence was undoubtedly seen by *some* people, Lusaka amongst them, as an advantage and a positive value. For example, discussions bearing on differences in the relations between men and women in *Kizungu* and *Kisendji* frequently caused participants to ask me to talk about relations between the sexes in European society. And this was also the case, in varying degrees, in discussions on a wide range of other subjects such as kinship obligations in town, the rearing of children and relations between fellow-workers. In the process of analysing social relations, on the other hand, the fact of relative fluidity and variety in the norms governing people's actions is, of course, a complicating factor which calls for detailed observational studies, for constant comparison between different groups and, wherever possible, for the assessment of change over time in one and the same group.

The Notions of 'Civilised' and 'Uncivilised'

Lusaka's conversations with other people frequently produced references to 'civilisation', to 'civilised' behaviour, and to 'civilised' people. He himself was by common agreement in Avenue 21 'the most "civilised" man here'. Yet his concern with 'civilisation' was no personal idiosyncrasy. Throughout the avenue some people were commonly considered, and referred to, as more 'civilised' than others, while some were thought of as rankly 'uncivilised'. At first I was inclined to think of 'civilised' and 'uncivilised' primarily as assessments of moral worth for people would at times use the term 'uncivilised' to refer very loosely to behaviour that was considered harsh, ill-mannered and objectionable. Thus, if a man beat his wife or got boisterously drunk or was inhospitable to his friends and kinsmen, people might in effect say: 'What can you expect of him? He is not "civilised".' But individuals and their behaviour were also frequently assessed as 'civilised' and 'uncivilised' independently of moral worth. We have seen, for example, that Lusaka considered Bernard as a good and trustworthy man though he described him as 'not well civilised', explaining that 'his heart still lay in the village'.

The following selected examples help to convey the more general meaning and usage of 'civilised' and 'uncivilised':

(1) Mayala was a man of about 50 years of age who had travelled throughout the country as a domestic servant and who had been away from his native village for thirty or forty years. He was the title-holder of compound no. 4, where he ran a small tearoom and shop. He was not liked in the avenue, and was often referred to as miserly and self-seeking. He lived alone and people said he was too miserly to keep a wife. The well on his compound had a wooden lid which was always padlocked to prevent others from drawing water there, and this too was often cited as an example of his selfishness. People also said that he never greeted those who passed his house, and he was sometimes referred to as '*Muzungu wa ine*' – 'the European of No. 4' – an appellation which underlined his aloofness and unwillingness to share. He was, however, described to me as 'a well "civilised" man'. He was unpleasant and disliked, but he knew the ways of the town.

(2) Antoine, the title-holder of compound no. 9, was another elderly man who had spent the greater part of his life working for Europeans after having left his village as a child. He was highly respected in the avenue and was often called out to settle quarrels, especially between husbands and wives, and it was said that in days gone by the chief of the African townships had 'appointed' him as 'counsellor' to the avenue. Of him, Lusaka said: 'He is a very "civilised" man; he has always been in *Kizungu* and has learnt "civilised" ways even though he never went to school. He sometimes says that he is a Mohammedan, but he does not

know the ways of the *Arabisés*.' Another man assessed him somewhat similarly, saying: 'He is a good man; people listen to him and he understands their affairs. He is "civilised".'

(3) Dominique, a tenant on Antoine's compound, was a much younger man who had been in Kisangani a few months only after working in several smaller labour centres. On the compound where he lived he was called *Bwana Muzuri* (Mr Nice) on account of his gentle manner, and he was described to me as a man who behaved in a quite exemplary way towards his family and neighbours. But, one man said, 'as far as "civilisation" goes, he is only half-way. He does not understand, he is not yet awake'.

These cases show that social approval and disapproval bore no constant relation to 'civilised' and 'uncivilised'. More generally, 'civilisation' denoted familiarity with 'urban' norms, an attitude of mind responsive to non-traditional associations, and a way of life that could be, and was, practised by both good and bad men. The notions were closely related to those of *Kizungu*, the way of life with and of Europeans, and of *Kisendji*, a term which was occasionally used to refer very particularly to the African way of life in pre-European days but more commonly to the current tribal way of life in villages. To test whether 'civilised' status was associated with educational and occupational achievements, I asked three men – Lusaka, Limela and Likuta who, like Limela, was a former resident of Avenue 21 – to classify as 'civilised', 'less civilised', or 'more civilised' all adult men in the avenue whom each knew personally. All three were men who considered themselves, and were considered by others, as being more, rather than less, 'civilised'. I gave the exercise separately to each man and discussed his classification at length with him. The assessments of all three men showed definite though limited degrees of correlation with the educational-occupational grades of the subjects. Just as revealing as this degree of correlation, however, were two points which emerged from the way in which the three assessors carried out the exercise. First, there was the facility and confidence with which each did his grading once he had grasped what was required of him. To be asked to grade people according to degree of 'civilisation' was a meaningful task and this in itself tended to confirm my impressions based on participation in the avenue of the importance

of 'civilisation'. Secondly, the assessments were clearly made on a relative basis. In the course of the exercise, each man came to his final assessment through a process of measuring various individuals against each other. Moreover, I found that Limela was less disposed to think of people as little 'civilised' than were either Lusaka or Likuta, and the discussion I had with him about his classification strongly suggested that his results differed from those of the other two, because he was himself the least 'civilised' of the three. The notion of 'civilisation' was important and certainly relevant in day to day life, but it was, in the exercises as in daily life, a relative and largely subjective concept.

Notes: Chapter 5

Adapted from Valdo Pons, *Stanleyville: An African Urban Community Under Belgian Administration* (London: OUP for the International African Institute, 1969), pp. 128–34, 136 and 139–50, by kind permission of the International African Institute and the author.

1   See Pons (1961). (Kisangani was officially known as Stanleyville during the colonial period, but was always referred to as Kisangani by Africans in the region even before its name was officially changed after Independence.)
2   See Clément (1956), p. 375.
3   I later engaged Lusaka to help me with my work. He drew detailed diagrams of the dwelling compounds in Avenue 21, he helped me to keep my population register up to date and he did some census-type interviewing for me. He was also one of half a dozen men who later kept diaries and detailed records of income and expenditure for me.
4   Lusaka and Bernadette were not married, but were partners to a 'trial marriage'.
5   I use the term 'semi-prostitute' to refer to women who had one or more 'lovers' from whom they habitually received presents in return for sexual favours. Maua was an 'ordinary prostitute', in the sense that she normally received cash payments for her sexual services and her clients were not her regular 'lovers'.
6   If my knowledge of Swahili was often less than adequate, so, quite commonly, was that of some of the participants. And when conversation was wholly or partly in French, it was I who had the advantage. On the other hand, of course, I was always at a complete disadvantage when conversations were in any one of the many tribal vernaculars or in Lingala. But as most residents in Avenue 21 and its environs were from the north, east and south-east, Lingala was seldom used there.

Section Two

Field Roles and Field Problems

6

Some Role Problems in Field Research

ROBERT G. BURGESS

The principal method that has been used by anthropologists and sociologists to conduct field research is participant observation. As Powdermaker remarks, this method:

> was forged in the study of small homogenous societies, in which the anthropologists lived for an extended period of time, participated in them, learned the language, interviewed and constantly observed. (Powdermaker, 1966a, p. 285)

Meanwhile, sociologists have also utilised the method of participant observation as they have gone about studying small-scale situations in their own societies. Participant observation is not merely a method of conducting field research, but also a role that is used by the researcher. The task of the participant observer is well summarised by Becker, who states:

> The participant observer gathers data by participating in the daily life of the group or organization he studies. He watches the people he is studying to see what situations they ordinarily meet and how they behave in them. He enters into conversation with some or all of the participants in these situations and discovers their interpretations of the events he has observed. (Becker, 1958, p. 652)

This supports the view that the main instrument of data collection is the researcher. Such a situation means that researchers who become participant observers have to develop certain qualities, if they are to learn about the people with whom they are involved.

The qualities that are demanded of participant observers flow naturally from Becker's definition. They need to share in the lives and activities of those whom they study and take roles which are effective in the setting under study. They need to learn the language that is used in the setting, to remember actions and speech and to gather data from a range of individuals in a range of social situations. In this respect, participant observers need to understand the skills that they require and the roles that they take in research settings. Chapters 7 and 8 in this section, by Frankenberg and by Gans, focus on the participant observer. Here, the authors draw on British and American material respectively to explore the personal qualities of the participant observer, the diverse roles that the participant observer is expected to play, the relationship between the researcher and the researched and the sources of anxiety involved in being a participant observer.

The literature on participant observation is vast and much of the material examines how participant observers should present themselves. An early contribution to this discussion by Schwartz and Schwartz (1955) indicates that the roles of the participant observer could be formal or informal, concealed or revealed. They argue that participant observation can be placed on a continuum, with 'passive' participant observation at one end of the continuum and 'active' participant observation at the other. The 'passive' participant observer role is an ideal type, in which the observer interacts as little as possible with the observed. Meanwhile, the 'active' participant observer role is another ideal type, where the participant observer maximises participation to gather data, while integrating with other individuals in the social setting. These ideal types have been extended into four 'master roles' in a discussion by Gold (1958), in which he distinguishes at either end of the continuum the complete participant role and the complete observer role. Meanwhile, between these extreme positions he is able to identify the participant-as-observer role and the observer-as-participant role.

The role of complete participant, Gold suggests, is used in situations where the researcher does not reveal the fact that research is being conducted. Here, the researcher may become a member of the group that is being studied. A classic example where this role was employed is in Festinger, Riecken and Schachter (1956), in which the researchers became members of a religious group. More recent studies of sectarian groups by Wallis (1976) and by Homan (1978) have used this approach, as has Humphreys (1970) in his study of homosexuals. It can be argued that this style of research overcomes the problem of gaining access to a group. Furthermore, it is maintained that groups whose behaviour might be influenced by the presence of a researcher can be studied in their natural setting.

However, such arguments have to be placed against the objections that can be raised. First, if the people involved in a social situation are not aware that they are being researched, it makes it virtually impossible for the participant observer to pose questions to them. Secondly, the role that is taken puts the researcher in the position of being a spy (cf. Hughes, 1960). Thirdly, the role may mean that it is impossible for researchers to distinguish their everyday roles from their research roles with the result that they 'go native' and fail to pursue their research activities. Finally, it can be argued that even if participant observers can overcome role problems that confront them in the field, there are still unanswered questions about the ethics of reporting and publishing data that were gathered covertly.

Another 'master role' identified by Gold is that of the participant-as-observer. Here, the researcher and the researched are aware that their relationship stems from the research. Certainly, this role is advocated by Roy (1970) in his study of labour unions and is used in countless studies where the researcher participates with the informants and takes a particular role (for example, Hargreaves, 1967; Lacey, 1970). Here, both researcher and researched need to consider their relationships and the extent to which the researcher and the researched can overidentify with each other. In this respect, it is essential for the researcher to remain a 'stranger' while being involved in the situation under study (cf. Jarvie in Chapter 10).

The remaining 'master roles' are not so frequently used in field research. Gold discusses the role of observer-as-participant. Here, the observer role is made public from the start of the research. However, although there is less risk of 'going native' attached to this role, it is probably the least satisfactory in that the relationship established with informants is very brief, so that little detailed data can be obtained. Finally, Gold identifies the complete observer role which entirely removes the researcher from interaction with informants. A similar approach to research has been used by King (1978) in his study of infants' classrooms, where he engaged in non-participant observation. He argues that he was able to 'effectively disappear' in the classroom by avoiding conversations or being engaged in activities with teachers and pupils. Such an approach comes very close to the situation that might exist when observations are made in a laboratory. It is a role that is rarely used in field research.

While the four 'master roles' are clearly distinguished by Gold, it is important to remember that they are ideal types, and that in the course of any piece of field research, all these social roles may be used. The result is that participant observers have to learn to take and play roles in essentially the same way as they play roles throughout life (cf. Cicourel, 1964). However, in the case of taking roles in field situations, participant observers have to be able not only to take and play roles, but also to evaluate them, to evaluate their

relationships with their informants and the influence that their role performance may have on the data that they collect.

Participant observers have to consider how far they may influence the settings in which they work, how far their perceptions and analyses of the settings are influenced by the personal relationships that they form with their informants, how far their work should be secret, and how far their personal attributes (for instance, age, sex, dress, social class, speech and ethnicity) influence the research. In short, participant observers have to assess their involvement and detachment in social situations. These issues have been perceptively summarised in a question by Schwartz and Jacobs, who ask: 'how does a social scientist mesh himself into the world so that he finds out the things he is interested in while simultaneously avoiding the danger that his "enmeshment" will become a source of distorted information?' (Schwartz and Jacobs, 1979, p. 52). The remainder of this chapter addresses some of these issues by focusing on the way in which participant observers engage in covert and overt research, the influence of their personal attributes and other aspects of their position on the research and the operationalisation of their roles in the society or aspect of society that is studied.

One of the basic issues which any participant observer has to confront is the choice between engaging in covert or overt research. In a recent discussion on covert methods of participant observation, Homan (1980) considers that this approach to doing field research is justified with particular groups such as the old-time Pentecostal group that he studied. Homan indicates that without the use of covert methods, this group would not have been accessible to study. Here, we might consider the question posed by Bulmer (1980) in a rejoinder: 'is secret observation justifiable or desirable?' Certainly, Homan maintains that secrecy is justifiable as it merely poses problems concerning personal and professional behaviour. Yet he argues that his clandestine activities were less disruptive than if he had gone openly into this field of study. In his rejoinder, Bulmer (1980) raises several objections to Homan's position. First, he argues that the principle of informed consent has been ignored. Secondly, he considers that Homan's position constitutes betrayal of trust and involves an invasion of personal privacy. However, Bulmer does not consider that covert methods should never be used, but that a decision to utilise such methods should be taken carefully.

Here, the participant observer might consider if a distinction can be made between covert and overt methods. Roth (1962b) maintains that a distinction between secret and non-secret research cannot be sustained, as he claims it is never possible to tell the researched 'everything'. Furthermore, he argues that there are public settings (for example, schools, hospitals, pubs and crowd situations) in which it is impossible for the researcher to indicate to all the participants that research is being conducted. In this respect, Roth considers that secrecy is something that has to be continually confronted in social research.

Meanwhile, some researchers (Whyte, 1955; Liebow, 1967; Olesen and Whittaker, 1967) indicate that research should be open and researchers and research activities should be made public. In these circumstances, it is argued that participant observers can move about, ask questions and structure their research. Polsky indicates that in some investigations, such as the study of criminal behaviour, it is vital for participant observers to let criminals know who they are, as he warns somewhat sharply:

> in doing field research on criminals you damned well better *not* pretend to be 'one of them' because they will test this claim out and one of two things will happen: either you will . . . get sucked into 'partici- pant' observation of the sort you would rather not undertake, or you will be exposed with still greater negative consequences. (Polsky, 1969, p. 122)

If participant observers have any doubts about the roles they take, their relationship with their informants and the way this can influence their research, they might carefully consider Polsky's warning which has applica- bility beyond the study of deviance.

A further area of concern for the participant observer is the extent to which personal characteristics will influence roles, relationships and data. One area that has been considered in some detail is the influence of sex and gender on field research (Golde, 1970; Warren and Rasmussen, 1977; Wax, 1979; Roberts, 1981a). Much of this literature considers the position of women in field research. Easterday *et al.* (Chapter 9) look at the extent to which ascribed gender status and sexuality is a feature of participant observation and how it can influence the validity and reliability of field data.

In an analysis of anthropological research Golde indicates how it is important to systematically scrutin- ise 'how the chief instrument of research the anthropologist herself may alter that which is being studied and may be changed in turn' (Golde, 1970, p. 5). In particular, Golde indicates that specific behaviour is triggered off by women. She indicates that the stereotyped view of women, as vulnerable in terms of their relative weakness and openness to sexual attack, means that it is assumed by many informants that they require protection and greater assistance than men. The result, she maintains, is that women are given roles such as 'child', 'sister', or 'grandmother', that minimise their range of contacts to predominantly children and women (cf. Dua, 1979; Gupta, 1979). Furthermore, she argues that age and marital status can also influence the role to which a woman is assigned. In particular, she maintains that young, unmarried

women are considered by their informants to be in need of protection. These aspects of ascribed role and status have been commented upon by Wax (1979). She illus- trates from her field experience at Pine Ridge how separate studies had to be conducted with men and women, given the way in which particular activities were related to specific sexes. On the basis of this experience, Wax concludes that the most effective research on a 'whole' culture can only be done by research teams that are mixed in terms of age and sex. Furthermore, she argues that given the problems that arise from the female stereotype for young women, it would appear that mature women have the greatest scope for doing field research as they are usually not provided with a protected role.

The problems that confront the young female field- worker are discussed in more detail by Easterday *et al.* (Chapter 9). Further evidence on how masculinity and femininity influences field relations has been explored by Warren and Rasmussen (1977). They have also extended the discussion to examine the extent to which sex, defined by them as youthfulness and attractiveness, influences research relationships. Using Rasmussen's research on the nude beach (Douglas, Rasmussen and Flanagan, 1977) they indicate that Rasmussen (the male researcher) encountered difficulties in working with men, while Flanagan (the female researcher) encountered difficulties in working with women, with the result that joint work was considered more appropriate in this setting. In a further example from sex research, Warren indicates how she used her femaleness in working among gay males and suggests that being male or female is crucial in gaining access to data in such settings (cf. Humphreys, 1970). A further dimension to sex and gender in field research occurs when women are treated as sex objects which may result in different roles, situations and activities being presented to men and women, as some activities may be regarded as unsuitable for female observation (cf. Gupta's difficulties in studying a political situation, Gupta, 1979). Furthermore, as Golde (1970) suggests, women may be regarded with less suspicion than men due to the attributes associated with the female stereo- type. In these circumstances, field researchers might consider the extent to which ascribed roles through age, sex and gender can provide or restrict access to field data when they take the role of participant observers.

Finally, a theme which recurs in the literature on participant observation is the relationship between the participant observer's outside role in society and inside role in the research setting. This has been summed up by Powdermaker, when she remarks:

> To understand a strange society, the anthropologist has traditionally immersed himself in it, learning, as far as possible, to think, see, feel, and sometimes act as a member of its culture and at the same time as a trained anthropologist from another culture. This is

the heart of the participant observation method – involvement and detachment. (Powdermaker, 1966a, p. 9)

This dual role of outsider and insider gives the participant observer greater opportunity of being able to 'step in and out' of the setting under study; to participate and to reflect on the data that is gathered during participation. Indeed, Trice (1956) has argued that this dual role is exceedingly valuable for data collection, as the outsider role may help prevent the individual from being overidentified with the group that is being studied. It may help in preventing problems of over-rapport (Miller, 1952) and assist in data collection. However, this question of the relationship between taking the role of outsider and insider, the role of stranger and of friend, is considered by Jarvie when he argues that participant observation involves a clash of roles. Jarvie considers that the participant observer is caught in an ethical dilemma which, he maintains, can only be resolved by taking the stranger role. Such a dilemma confronts every participant observer, and indicates the complexity of the task that is involved in taking field roles in order to gather data.

Suggestions for Further Reading

METHODOLOGY

There is a vast literature on participant observation. The material suggested here has been selected for its relevance to the issues discussed:

Bulmer, M. (1982) (ed.), *Social Research Ethics* (London: Macmillan); contains papers that review some of the main ethical issues in doing participant observation.

Filstead, W. J. (1970) (ed.), *Qualitative Methodology: First-hand Involvement with the Social World* (Chicago: Markham); this is a collection of predominantly American papers on issues relating to participant observation. See especially parts 2 and 3 that include discussions of field roles, and part 6 on ethics.

Golde, P. (1970) (ed.), *Women in the Field: Anthropological Experiences* (Chicago: Aldine); consists of anthropological accounts that demonstrate the influence of sex and gender on field research.

Homan, R. (1980), 'The ethics of covert methods', *British Journal of Sociology*, vol. 31, no. 1, pp. 46–59; attempts to justify the use of covert methods. See the critical rejoinder by Bulmer (1980) in the same issue.

McCall, G. J. and Simmons, J. L. (1969) (eds), *Issues in Participant Observation: a Text and Reader* (Reading, Mass.: Addison-Wesley); this is another collection of American papers on participant observation. There is considerable overlap with the papers in Filstead (1970).

Olesen, V. L. and Whittaker, E. W. (1967), 'Role-making in participant observation: processes in the research-actor relationship', *Human Organization*, vol. 26, no. 4, pp. 273–81; discusses the relationship between researcher and researched and role development.

Polsky, N. (1969), *Hustlers, Beats and Others* (Harmondsworth: Penguin); contains a useful chapter entitled 'Research method, morality and criminology' that raises important principles involved in doing participant observation together with useful warnings and some advice.

Powdermaker, H. (1966), *Stranger and Friend: the Way of An Anthropologist* (New York: Norton); has an introduction and epilogue that provide a good commentary on questions of involvement and detachment in participant observation; the book is based on the author's experiences of doing research.

Roberts, H. (1981) (ed.), *Doing Feminist Research* (London: Routledge & Kegan Paul); discusses the influence of feminism and feminist methodology on research (see especially the papers by Roberts, 1981b; Oakley, 1981; Pettigrew, 1981; and Morgan, 1981).

Warren, C. A. B. and Rasmussen, P. K. (1977), 'Sex and gender in field research', *Urban Life*, vol. 6, no. 3, pp. 349–69; this is a useful discussion of sex and gender by sociologists who have engaged in participant observation.

EMPIRICAL STUDIES

There are a vast number of studies that utilise participant observation for data collection. I have selected some of the studies that I consider are most useful, interesting and entertaining. The list is divided into British and American studies:

British studies

Bell, C. (1968), *Middle Class Families* (London: Routledge & Kegan Paul).

Cohen, S. and Taylor, L. (1972), *Psychological Survival: the Experience of Long Term Imprisonment* Harmondsworth: Penguin).

Cunnison, S. (1966), *Wages and Work Allocation* (London: Tavistock).

Davis, A. and Horobin, G. (1977) (eds), *Medical Encounters: the experience of Illness and Treatment* (London: Croom-Helm); see especially the essays by Atkinson (1977) and by MacIntyre and Oldman (1977).

Ditton, J. (1977), *Part-Time Crime: an Ethnography of Fiddling and Pilferage* (London: Macmillan).

Frankenberg, R. (1957), *Village on the Border* (London: Cohen & West).

Hargreaves, D. H. (1967), *Social Relations in a Secondary School* (London: Routledge & Kegan Paul).

King, R. (1978), *All Things Bright and Beautiful? A Sociological Study of Infants' Classrooms* (Chichester: Wiley).

Lacey, C. (1970), *Hightown Grammar: the School as a Social System* (Manchester: University of Manchester Press).

Littlejohn, J. (1963), *Westrigg* (London: Routledge & Kegan Paul).

Lupton, T. (1963), *On The Shop Floor* (Oxford: Pergamon).

Nash, R. (1973), *Classrooms Observed* (London: Routledge & Kegan Paul).

Parker, H. (1974), *View from the Boys* Newton Abbot: David & Charles).

Patrick, J. (1973), *A Glasgow Gang Observed* (London: Eyre-Methuen).

Stacey, M., Batstone, E., Bell, C. and Murcott, A. (1975), *Power, Persistence and Change: a Second Study of Banbury* (London: Routledge & Kegan Paul).

Wallis, R. (1976), *The Road to Total Freedom: a Sociological Analysis of Scientology* (London: Heinemann).

Williams, W. M. (1956), *The Sociology of an English Village: Gosforth* (London: Routledge & Kegan Paul).

Woods, P. (1979), *The Divided School* (London: Routledge & Kegan Paul).

American Studies

Becker, H. S., Geer, B., Hughes, E. C. and Strauss, A. L. (1961), *Boys in White: Student Culture in Medical School* (Chicago: University of Chicago Press).

Becker, H. S., Geer, B. and Hughes, E. C. (1968), *Making the Grade* (New York: Wiley).

Festinger, L., Riecken, H. W. and Schachter, S. (1956), *When Prophecy Fails* (New York: Harper & Row).

Gans, H. J. (1962), *The Urban Villagers* (New York: The Free Press).

Gans, H. J. (1967), *The Levittowners* (London: Allen Lane).

Humphreys, L. (1970), *Tearoom Trade* (London: Duckworth).

Jacobs, J. (1974), *Fun City: an Ethnographic Study of a Retirement Community* (New York: Holt, Rinehart & Winston).

Liebow, E. (1967), *Tally's Corner: a Study of Negro Street Corner Men* (Boston, Mass.: Little, Brown).

Roth, J. A. (1963), *Timetables* (New York: Bobbs-Merrill).

Spradley, J. P. and Mann, B. J. (1975), *The Cocktail Waitress* (New York: Wiley).

Strauss, A. L., Schatzman, L., Bucher, R., Ehrlich, D. and Sabshin, M. (1964), *Psychiatric Ideologies and Institutions* (New York: The Free Press).

Whyte, W. F. (1955), *Street Corner Society* (2nd edn) (Chicago: University of Chicago Press).

7

Participant Observers

RONALD FRANKENBERG

If one lives at the boundaries of two subjects like sociology and social anthropology, weeks arise in which one spends the first half with sociologists and the second with social anthropologists. One becomes acutely aware of definitions and methods. Sociologists seem to lack a unity of purpose, a group consciousness, which social anthropologists have. This is perhaps the more surprising, in that anthropologists' experience nowadays is not confined to the South Seas or to Africa. Members of the professional association may have done their fieldwork in villages in Europe, or in a London borough, or even in Manchester factories.

What they all have in common is the experience of having submerged themselves for anything from a year to three or four years in a cultural environment different from their own. What few recognise is that they can never look on society in quite the same way again. Indeed, the constant reference back of all new situations to their original fieldwork can be one of the irritating attributes of social anthropologisits. Barbara Pym in her novel *Excellent Women* describes what it looks like from the sidelines:

Now that the ball was rolling, other speakers followed in quick succession. In fact they were jumping up and down like Jacks-in-the-boxes, hardly waiting for each other to finish. It seemed that they all had 'done' some particular tribe or area and could furnish parallels or contradictions from their own experience. (Pym, 1952, p. 93)

Each member of any society learns the custom of that society, the little secular ceremonies which place people in their social groups, gradually as he grows up. This knowledge is acquired relatively painlessly and etiquette is carried out unconsciously by most people. The learning of new customs and new values by the hard road of trial and error is an experience which many people must go through. The immigrant, the army recruit, the chronic hospital patient, are all examples which have a considerable literature. The participant observer deliberately submits himself to this not usually in a group, but alone. Furthermore, since his action is deliberate and intended to add to knowledge, the experience is analysed and assimilated

ready to pass on. I think it is not too fanciful to see in this an analogy with the situation of the patient in psychoanalysis. Here again, through the transference situation, processes once lived through are relived, with the analyst taking the place of former love-objects.

For this way the participant observer is resocialised with another society substituted for his own. As in analysis the next stage is progressive dissolution of the transference, so the participant observer, in order to make his experiences intelligible to his colleagues, must also break off his attachment to the society he has studied. That he is not usually completely successful is the reason that Barbara Pym could make the comment quoted.

Faced with some inexplicable custom of the Swazi, Sir James Frazer seemed to ask himself the question 'if I were a Swazi why would I think this?' The modern participant observer thinks back to the first society he studied and says 'if one of my people thought like this, why would it be?' This is a step towards objectivity. It is as necessary to the participant observer as transference to the patient under analysis. I do not think this particular parallel with psychoanalysis is the only possible one. A central paradox of the participant observation method is to seek information by not asking questions.

Professor Gluckman in an article in the *New Statesman*[1] reminded us that the great observer Malinowski was collecting myths from an inhabitant of the Trobriand Islands and kept telling him to stop boasting about his clan right to tell the myth and get on with the story. Later he realised what the islander was telling him was more important than the answers to the questions he was asking. Similarly, an early patient reproved the young Freud for interrupting her flow of reminiscences to ask questions, thereby helping him towards the method of free association.

It often happens to the field worker that the questions he is asked are more important than the questions he asks. This is because in social science, while one knows the problem one is interested in, one does not necessarily know at first the precise questions to ask, or whom to ask, and when to ask them. Sometimes one cannot be sure of a truthful, accurate, or full reply. It is sometimes quicker and more economical to wait for questions and answers to come to you. Thus, W. M. Williams in his study of Gosforth[2] learnt a great deal about social status by the questions people asked him. 'What University did you go to – Oxford or Cambridge? – *is* there a *University* at Aberystwyth?' asked the gentry. 'Have you got a car? What sort is it?' asked the up-and-coming. 'How do you manage to get paid for just messing around?' asked the wage-earner.

People in the village I studied which was called Glynceiriog[3] revealed the importance of kinship to me by asking 'who are you belonging to?' before they asked 'where are you from?' or 'what do you do for a living?' The participant observer is not only asked questions, but things happen to him. In Glynceiriog I was baffled by the contradiction between the dislike of strangers and the important part they play in social life. Thus, in the course of my work I attended village meetings, including the annual general meeting of the Football Club. To my surprise (and indeed against my protests at first) I was elected to the committee and, because I had a typewriter, made assistant secretary. Villagers had strong feelings of equality and were reluctant to take the chair at meetings. I, therefore, often found myself in the chair. When villagers disagreed among themselves, I felt forced by the logic of the situation to make suggestions. When there was a dispute about which village organisation should have the cash proceeds of a football competition, I took sides. So did a Lancashire businessman and a cockney miner living in the village. We were all three subjected to informal pressures during the days that followed. Villagers pointed and whispered. I heard rumours ascribing ignoble motives to our behaviour. When the committee met again, we changed sides. At the time I thought this was in response to a changed knowledge of the rights and wrongs. Later I came to recognise a consistent pattern of behaviour in the relations of outsiders to villagers. I now understood the meaning of informal social pressures and was able to generalise the experience into a theory about the part played by strangers in rural society.

In each activity there was a 'stranger'. He might be an outsider like the examples I have given. He might be odd in that situation only. The Wesleyan chairman of a predominantly Baptist parish council, or the man chairman of women's football supporters' club are examples. It was always the stranger who took the initiative which brought hidden conflicts into the open. This was because they were not as immediately sensitive to informal opinion as the others. Their unpopularity was also to some extent insulated. It was not so likely to spread to other social activities in the village. A quarrel sparked off by a Baptist parish chairman would have carried over into his chapel's organisation. A woman chairman of the supporters' club who suggested a line of action unpopular with even a minority of other committee women would have had to face their hostility not merely at meetings, but in the sewing group, at whist drives and in the shops. The

male chairman only met his fellow committee members as a group in the one context. A study which started out to look at the effects on family life of a journey to work was profitably (I think) diverted to the effects on village unity and politics. This, I think, was the interesting problem posed by the village which could only have been discovered by living there and taking part in its activities. In a South Wales village I studied I attended the funeral of a man who had befriended and helped me and through ignorance of custom found myself among his relatives in the chapel. Many villagers after this ascribed me to his kindred. Once again my own experience gave me an insight into community I could not have got in any other way.

Participant observation is all right in villages, it may be said, but is not always practicable or desirable elsewhere. This is true enough of course, although when I first went to Glynceiriog and saw its housing estate with each family shut up in their little box, I thought despairingly and enviously of my teachers' African villages, where everything happened (or so they told me) in the sunny open air. I did, in fact, in both villages I have studied, supplement participation with asking questions in a house-to-house survey. This gave me added depth. Similarly, I think that a resident's eye view would greatly modify the rather depressing picture of Woodford, Essex, given by a questionnaire survey in Willmott and Young's *Family and Class in a London Suburb* (1960).

Another objection that is made to participant observation is that one can only participate in a small group and that this may not be typical of the society as a whole. This again is partly true, but two comments are worth making on it. First, people in general participate in societies (however large) through small groups. Sharing their experience is the most direct way of seeing how the characteristics of the larger society affect them. Secondly, it is always possible to check hypotheses formulated in participant observation studies by a large-scale survey. A further objection may be levelled that the observer by his participation may change the situation he is studying. This I think is a question of sensitising the observer to the changes he may make. I do not think a single observer in, say, a village or a tribe is going to change custom and practice built up over years or even centuries. If he does, this is something that needs analysis. What is more likely to happen is that he may prove a catalyst for changes that are already taking place. On the occasions when I was thrust into positions of leadership in Glynceiriog when I was called upon to influence decisions, I do not believe I really did so. Villagers had their differences of opinion. In a village society a difference cannot be isolated to the activity in which it arises. A quarrel about football may have repercussions in the chapel. The chapel repercussions may affect may affect relationships in a group of kin, and so on. Those societies which have the greatest overlap of personnel in different activities, the greatest multiplicity of ties linking individual to individual, also have the greatest possibility of conflict. Their conflicts are also potentially the most disruptive of the social order. They are also the easiest to study by participant observation methods. If these differences are brought into the open not by the action of villagers, but by some outsider, the possibility of open dispute is minimised. A participant observer fits very well into this role. It may be uncomfortable while it lasts but it is productive of contented villagers who have an outsider to blame for their internal difficulties. It is also incidentally productive of good field material.

I suspect that many industrial psychologists, sociologists, economists and other applied social scientists may really function in this way. If, in a family business, the managing director and father wishes to pass over his son-in-law in favour of an abler man, he may avoid trouble at home and in the factory by putting the blame on the industrial consultant. It has been suggested that work study men are used in this way by both sides in industry and that statisticians fulfilled this role in wartime ministries.

Possibly even the awesome figures of Lindeman and Tizard in Snow's parable of wartime scientific overlordship were pawns in the hands of warring factions at Admiralty and Air Ministry. Alas, none of the participant observers seem to have been anthropologists or sociologists.

Even apart from these latent functions, I think that there is no doubt that a spell of participant observation is useful from the point of view of training fieldworkers and even theoretical sociologists. It gives you an idea of interaction and the interrelationships of social relations in a group, and a sense of process which you cannot get in any other way. I often find myself thinking, somewhat arrogantly, about the work of some theoretician or demographer, 'if only they lived in a society'. No doubt they do but, since it is their own, they take it for granted and have never stopped to consider its informal mechanisms.

I am, of course, aware that it is possible that theoreticians and demographers may justifiably bemoan my lack, as participant observer, of a sense of history, theoretical design, and the meaning of quantitative data.

Another set of institutions which lend themselves to participant observer study are organisations, hospitals, factories, prisons, schools and other areas of social interaction bounded by 'four barriers to communication'. The study of these reveals the same advantages and disadvantages for participant observation. Here, however, the ethical and moral problem which arises even in villages, arises even more sharply. Should the observer reveal his purpose in the institution, or should he maintain secrecy until the time arrives to publish a report?

To me there can be no doubt about this at all. If the observer cannot participate with the knowledge and approval of the people to be studied, he should not be there at all. The observer has a positive duty to be open that his intentions are to observe, to report and to publish an account of what he sees in print. The difficulty which arises over this is not the obvious one. People do not dry up or behave self-consciously or unnaturally because you tell them you are writing a book about them. One does, however, have difficulty in persuading people that one really is writing about what one says one is and not history, local legends, or whatever they consider to be a suitable subject to write on. The temptation is, in the desire to please, to let people think that they are right about your interests.

Again in factories, management may suspect you of being hostile, and workers of being a management spy. Conformity with local norms and a refusal to be trapped into revealing the secrets of either side are what the fieldworker needs to deal with this problem. The keeping of personal confidences until they no longer matter is not only moral, but expedient. For if sociology is to advance, participant observation studies must become more frequent. It is a cardinal principle of scholarship that no researcher has the right to make impossible the studies of those who will follow him.

Notes: Chapter 7

Reprinted from *New Society*, 7 March 1963, pp. 22–3, by kind permission of the publishers and the author.
1   See Gluckman (1960).
2   See Williams (1956).
3   See Frankenberg (1957).

8

The Participant Observer as a Human Being: Observations on the Personal Aspects of Fieldwork

HERBERT J. GANS

I

Sociology is currently undergoing change at a faster rate than almost any other scholarly discipline. Once taught only at the more cosmopolitan universities and confused by many laymen with socialism or social work, sociology is now firmly ensconced in the public area. Its annual meetings are covered by newspapers and magazines; its more literate practitioners are writing regularly for sophisticated and even for popular magazines; sociologists are being hired by governmental agencies and private firms, and journalists with undergraduate sociology credits are straining towards sociological analyses in the features they write for the Sunday supplements.

Inside sociology itself, two seemingly contradictory changes are taking place. On the one hand, the new affluence, both of enrolment and research funds, is leading to rapid growth. Sociological studies are becoming bigger and more bureaucratised; the big questions these days are not tackled by lone scholars, but by computer-equipped research teams. At the same time, however, there is a revival of participant observation research and a sudden interest in the sociologist as an individual researcher and a person, exemplified by anthologies in which sociologists report on how they conducted their studies, and how they felt while doing so.[1]

Perhaps it is incorrect to talk of a revival of participant observation; what may be happening is that the post-Second World War students of Everett Hughes and other advocates of participant observation are now mature enough to publish their own studies and to send *their* graduate students into the field. Perhaps the autobiographical articles are only a result of the fact that sociology, like show business, has its stars, and that the fans want to read about them as people. Nevertheless, ever since William F. Whyte added a long methodological and personal appendix to the second edition of *Street Corner Society* in 1955, and the Schwartzes wrote about 'anxiety as a source of distortion in participant observation' that same year, sociologists, and particularly participant observers, have begun to pay more attention to the personal dimensions of their work.[2]

When I was a graduate student at the University of Chicago just after the Second World War, no one talked much about participant observation; we just did it. Like many of my fellow sociology students, I enrolled in Everett Hughes's course 'Introduction to fieldwork', and like them, I found it a traumatic introduction; we were sent to a census tract in nearby Hyde Park and asked to do a small participant observation study. Everett Hughes gave us some words of introduction and of instruction, but good father that he was, he quickly pushed us out of the nest and told us to fly on our own.

Only later did Everett Hughes himself talk about the personal aspects of participant observation. In his introduction to Buford Junker's *Field Work* he writes:

> It is doubtful whether one can become a good social reporter unless he has been able to look, in a reporting mood, at the social world in which he was reared. On the other hand, a person cannot make a career out of the reporting of reminiscences unless he is so far alienated from his own background as to be able to expose and exploit it before some new world with which he now identifies himself. (Hughes, 1960, pp. v–xv; quote at pp. xi–xii)

He also suggested one of the personal problems: 'I have usually been hesitant in entering the field myself and have perhaps walked around the block getting up my courage to knock at doors more often than almost any of my students. (I have been doing it longer.)'[3]

Yet other problems confront the participant observer as a human being, and since the methodological issues of fieldwork are now being discussed widely by practitioners and theorists, this chapter will be limited to some of the personal elements of participant observation which I have experienced in my own fieldwork: in Park Forest, a new suburb near Chicago; among a working-class Italian-American population in Boston's West End; in Levittown, New Jersey, another new suburb near Philadelphia; and in my current research in the agencies that create America's mass media fare.

II

Participant observation is not a sociologist's monopoly; the anthropologist does little else; the newspaper reporter uses the method to get material for an exposé or an inside story; and novelists of empirical bent, Philip Roth, for example, often report on the participant observation they have carried on in their own social circles. Moreover, even in sociology, the term participant observation refers to a multitude of activities and roles: the term is only a loose and inaccurate label that covers the many varieties of participation and observation, and distinguishes them from formal interviewing or library research. Thus, Everett Hughes writes: 'The unending dialectic between the role of member (participant) and stranger (observer and reporter) is essential to the very concept of field work, and this all participant-observers have in common: they must develop a dialectic relationship between being researchers and being participants.'[4] Among the diversity of roles this dialectic imposes, he distinguishes between being a part-time participant and part-time reporter; privately participant and publicly reporter or publicly participant and secretly reporter.[5]

The activities and roles of participant observation can also be classified in terms of the fieldworker's emotional relationships to the people he is studying. In my own work, I have distinguished three types of roles. One is the *total participant*, the fieldworker who is completely involved emotionally in a social situation and who only after it is over becomes a researcher again and writes down what has happened. For example, I was often a total participant when I joined my neighbours in Levittown on Saturday morning bull sessions while we were all ostensibly mowing our lawns. A second is the *researcher participant*, who participates in a social situation but is personally only partially involved, so that he can function as a researcher, as, for example, when I went to parties given by the people I was studying, and sometimes steered party conversations to topics I was researching. The third is the *total researcher*, who observes without any personal involvement in the situation under study, as, for example, when I attended a public meeting, or carried out informal interviews.[6]

Actually, even these categories may not be quite accurate, for emotionally, the participant observer is a researcher twenty-four hours a day. Even when he momentarily forgets his research role and becomes really involved in a social situation, he soon remembers who he is and what he is doing and quickly returns to his research. Being a total participant is probably the most fruitful kind of participant observation, for only by being completely immersed in an event as an involved person can one really confront and grasp the social and emotional incentives and pressures that act on people in groups. Total participation is psychologically very difficult for the researcher, however; it is almost impossible for him to be both a total participant and an observer of himself and other people. Sometimes, one can be a total participant for a short time, and thus obtain empathy into the situations and for the people under study in a personal and direct fashion. (In

fact, the fieldworker ought to aim for at least some total participation if at all possible, so that he learns to see the world as it is seen by the people he studies.) In most instances, however, whatever the participant observer's formal role and degree of behavioural participation, he is emotionally first an observer and only secondarily a participant.

In my own fieldwork, at least, I was almost always the researcher-participant, involved in the research but not the participation. I played the required participant role, but psychologically I was outside the situation, deliberately uninvolved in order to be able to study what was happening. Uninvolvement was easiest at public meetings, for there I had only to be a passive observer and, besides, as a researcher I was not a total or real resident of the community, and thus could remain detached from the political issues under discussion. At parties or during conversations with friends and neighbours, however, the temptation to become involved was ever-present. I had to fight the urge to shed the emotional handcuffs that bind the researcher, and to react spontaneously to the situation, to relate to people as a person and to derive pleasure rather than data from the situation. Often, I carried on an internal tug of war, to decide how much spontaneous participation was possible without missing something as a researcher, or without endangering the neutrality which the researcher must maintain when he is studying more than one group, so that he does not risk being rejected by opposing groups. It was not so difficult to be spontaneous when the conversations dealt with subjects which I was not studying or had already studied sufficiently (for example, the ritual discussions about cars, sports and sex that men always resort to); but when the discussion turned to topics I was studying, like relations with neighbours, I had to be careful to remain aloof and to keep my opinions about specific neighbours to myself, to be free to observe (and memorise what was being said) and to retain my neutrality.

Generalising from one's own experience is dangerous, but I suspect that most participant observers are psychologically on the margins of the social situations and relationships they study. Participant observation, then, is the taking of a formal participatory role in a social situation without the emotional involvement that normally accompanies participation; it requires the surrender of any personal interest one might have in the situation in order to be free to observe it, and the people who are creating it. As the Schwartzes put it, 'participant-observation becomes . . . a process of registering, interpreting and recording'.[7]

This marginality distinguishes the sociologist from the newspaperman and the novelist, both of whom are as interested in their own feelings in a situation as in what other people are doing. But the sociologist is a kinsman of the anthropologist who, being in a strange culture, is almost by definition a marginal man.

The anthropologist can never participate totally, because he cannot ever internalise the norms and values of another culture, and woe befalls the researcher who tries to go native. The sociologist is, more often than not, in a similar position; as Everett Hughes points out, modern participant observation began when middle-class sociologists studied working- and lower-class communities and, although they shared a common nationality, large cultural differences remained.[8] Such differences exist even when the middle-class sociologist studies middle-class people, as I had occasion to do in Levittown. Although I shared many values with upper-middle-class Levittowners, and was similar to them in age, occupation, income and education – some of them were also academics – we differed in that they were total residents of the community, and I was not. As a result, they had concerns and perspectives which I, as a research-resident, could not share even though I came to understand them. Indeed, I would go so far as to say that the participant observer cannot study his own people; he probably cannot work in a setting so close to his own life situation that he does share concerns and perspectives; for example, he could not study the department of sociology of which he is himself a member. Even if he were able to persuade his colleagues to treat him as a researcher rather than as a colleague, which is unlikely, it is doubtful that he could give up the temptation to participate, or to shed the feelings he had about his colleagues before he started to study them. Unless he is totally uninterested in his own department, he might want to act when he should observe; to like or dislike when he should research, and to argue when he should be listening.

Needless to say, the participant observer becomes involved unconsciously and, despite all I have said, he becomes involved somewhat as well on a conscious level. Because he is a participant, even if he announces to people that he is there to study them (as I did most of the time in all my fieldwork), people soon forget why he is there, and react to him as a participant. They treat him as a person even if he treats them as subjects of study, and if he wants to remain in the group, he is obligated to participate behaviourally and to express feelings of interest. Strangeness of culture is no barrier here; the required act may be no more than a friendly hello which even the anthropologist studying an African tribe can respond to when he sees people on the street.

Consequently, the fieldworker is under pressure from those he studies to involve himself, although rarely do they demand intense involvement. For example, in Levittown, when I observed governmental meetings which were poorly attended, I was sometimes viewed as a citizen rather than as a researcher and, indeed, I was once publicly praised for my regular attendance by the city fathers, all of whom 'knew' I was there as a sociologist. However, the behavioural participation required no emotional involvement. During election campaigns, politicians sometimes asked me how I would vote, but I could not reveal my party preferences without losing my neutrality or, for that matter, without becoming involved personally in the issues being debated. I always voted, of course, but I tried not to dwell on how the issues and candidates would affect me personally – although they rarely did – for then I might have wanted to do more than vote. In the West End of Boston, however, I could not maintain my personal detachment when the city threatened to tear down the neighbourhood as a slum, and I had to restrain myself from dropping the study and joining the West Enders who were trying to fight the renewal project. Indeed, had I not known that it was too late to stop the bulldozer by the time the West Enders organised, I might have got into the battle. As it was, I continued my research but, immediately after it was over, wrote and published a critical analysis of how slum clearance was handled in the West End.[9]

As this example suggests, the external pressure to participate is much weaker than the internal pressure – and desire – to become involved. Even when the situation under study is less dramatic than it was in the West End, the mere act of participant observation means becoming part of a group and making friends, and the group pressures become internal pressures as well. Aside from not wanting to alienate the people one is studying, the participant observer also wants to be liked and, in his own marginal way, to feel part of the group. He wants to belong a little, and this helps to create one of the problems of participant observation, identification with the people being studied (to be discussed subsequently). The extent to which the need to belong affects the fieldworker is described in moving detail by Laura Bohannan in her fictional report on her fieldwork with an African tribe.[10]

The participant observer is also driven towards involvement by participating in situations in which his values are being questioned or attacked. As Mrs Bohannan explains, one cannot really shed one's own values even in an African tribe and an action based on opposing values evokes, at the minimum, an internal reaction in the fieldworker. When one studies people in one's own country, this happens more often. I had no trouble remaining uninvolved in local zoning disputes in Levittown, but when people talked disparagingly about racial integration or when they resorted to anti-intellectualism, I became involved, and the urge to argue became strong. Sometimes, this urge can lead to open involvement. When I first came to Levittown, its government was still run by old residents who were all conservative Republicans (the township in which Levittown was built had never elected a Democrat in its almost 200 years of existence) and, although I was not aware of it, listening to their attacks on liberal and radical ideas had evidently upset me considerably. After three months of fieldwork among them, I ran into four men who were about to form a Democratic club

.nd, as an independent who often votes for Democrats, I was so pleased that I impulsively said so, and even offered to do what I could to help. Ten minutes later, the possible consequences of my remarks suddenly dawned on me; if people found out I was a Democrat, my future chance of obtaining data from Republicans was nil. I rushed back to the club founders, withdrew my offer and made them promise never to mention what I had said to them. (As far as I could tell, they never did, and my own political position remained a secret in Levittown.) Most often, one can keep one's cool enough not to offer foolishly to participate, but the urge to argue remains, and must be suppressed constantly, except when it is used as an interviewing method.

In addition, participant observation means frequent contact with specific people, and the fieldworker, no different from anyone else, forms likes and dislikes. He likes some of the people he is studying better than others, because they share his values, are easier to talk with, are more open in interview situations, or are just friendlier. There are dangers aplenty here. If one gravitates more towards people one likes and is at ease with, the pleasures of participant observation increase significantly, but the sampling of people and situations – always in danger of being skewed anyway because there is only so much a single participant observer can do – may become badly distorted. This is particularly dangerous in a general community study, when one is trying to get a sense of how a whole community of many people acts and thinks and feels; it is less dangerous when one is studying a specific topic or institution, for then one's choice of people to talk with is determined much more by the topic. If one becomes too enthusiastic about someone who is being interviewed regularly, and wants to make friends with him, another danger develops. Being friends with people means being open with them and acting as a person rather than as a fieldworker. If the person one befriends is marginal in the community and sympathetic towards sociological perspectives, this is no problem, but if he is active in the community, friendship may threaten the participant observer's neutrality. Not only is he tempted to give his friend confidential information to help him, but even if he can resist that urge, other people will begin to suspect that he is no longer neutral and has developed political alliances. For example, in Levittown I became friendly with the town's few liberals, who were also leaders in the struggle for racial integration and, when it came time to sell my house, my neighbours were sure I would sell it to a black. (They were right about my feelings but wrong about my intentions; I wanted to do so, but because I feared it would endanger the fieldwork I still planned to conduct after leaving, I did not do so.)

Being marginal and neutral is a constant strain, and the participant observer is always tempted to find someone to whom he can talk freely about his problems as a participant observer and about his opinions on community issues. More generally, he wants to be able to act as a real person, because, most of the time, he is playing a role which does not entirely satisfy his personal needs. For this reason, a spouse, friends and colleagues outside the community are very important; the participant observer – or at least this one – must have someone with whom he can talk personally about his work.

My observations about the emotional marginality of the participant observer may appear to conflict with those of the Schwartzes, who have written that:

> if the observer works continuously in a situation ... he will inevitably become involved in and with the observed's emotional life. Much of this involvement may go on outside of awareness; between observer and observed there will be a continuous process of moving away from and moving toward sympathy and disgust, anger and affection, fear and trust based on conscious and unconscious motives ... These affective relations ... link observer and observed in mutually important integrations despite their individual wishes. (Schwartz and Schwartz, 1955, p. 350)

I suspect that we are both right. Community studies and research dealing primarily with sociological topics may create less involvement that is beyond awareness than studies which draw the participant observer into intensive relationship with a small number of people, or those which deal with institutions like a mental hospital, where the relationships among the people studied are more conflicted and traumatic, and may evoke some of the reseacher's personal difficulties. But whatever the study, it is likely that the participant observer will become involved in ways of which he is not aware. For all his detachment and marginality, he is still a person, and one who does research by getting into situations as a person. His style of relating to people and the very questions he seeks to answer are influenced in part by his own personality. As a result, the unconscious elements of his personality enter into his study and into the relationships he forms during fieldwork. In fact, the development of identification with the people studied, which most participant observers experience, is in large part a process that takes place outside of awareness, and represents the very involvement the Schwartzes describe. Moreover, such involvement, particularly with situations and kinds of people the participant observer has trouble dealing with in his personal life, undoubtedly add to the emotional strain of playing the participant observer role. Since what the Schwartzes call 'affective participation' can create not only personal, but methodological problems for the participant observer and can bias the data gathering process in a variety of ways, it may be wise for every participant observer to spend some time on the analytic couch: before his fieldwork to help him see what unconscious emotional factors are guiding his plans for participant observation, during the fieldwork when he has problems and afterwards to help him understand the possible distortions that may exist in his data, and in his methods of analysing them.

III

Transforming oneself into a participant observer is, as I have suggested, not an easy task, and carrying out the role may be accompanied by personal problems which deserve discussion. Among these problems, at least among those I have found most vexing, are: gaining entry into the situation to be studied, the strain and anxiety which go with the role once entry is achieved, the overidentification to which I have already referred and the guilt that develops in the participant observer because of the roles he must play.

Before discussing these problems, it is worth stressing that participant observation is hardly a continuous bout with anxiety. Sometimes, it becomes just another job, with a routine which must be followed if the study is to be at all systematic. More often than other research methods and other jobs, however, participant observation provides great satisfactions: discovering new facts, coming up with new ideas, watching people act by, and put life into, the concepts of sociological theory, and knowing always that, in contrast to any other method of social research, participant observation puts one about as close to real data and the sources of real data as is humanly possible. In addition, there is the enjoyment of being in the middle of things, meeting new kinds of people – and those one would never meet as a teacher –participating in new (and non-academic) institutions and situations; and in a community, being on the inside politically, sharing secret information. In Levittown I often felt that I was a vicarious participant in a large number of dramatic serials, some involving heroes fighting villains, others with cliff-hanger endings, and as soon as one serial came to a dramatic – or un-dramatic – conclusion, others were sure to have begun.

The participant observer's first problem is that of entry. He gets his data on the basis of his ability to be admitted to the situations he wants to study and, once there, to persuade people to let him stay. Whether entry becomes a problem depends partly on what the researcher has chosen to study and what research role he has decided to take. The criminal underworld is more difficult to enter than a suburban community, and a working- or lower-class group more difficult than a middle-class one, at least for a middle-class researcher. The researcher who hides his research role can enter more easily than the researcher who describes himself as such, and begs admittance on the basis of persuading people that scientific research is useful and desirable.

If one is studying entire communities, one cannot hide one's research identity – and be, in Junker's terms, a complete participant – for that participant can enter only a few of the many groups that make up the community, and he will probably be unable to enter competing or opposed groups. Consequently, I have always told people right from the start that I was a researcher, and hoped that they would accept me as such. In Levittown, this created no problem; I explained I was studying how a group of strangers makes a community, and this was a nicely impersonal subject in which the Levittowners, then still strangers to one another, were also intensely interested. In the West End, entry was more difficult, for working-class people are less familiar with research and more suspicious of middle-class intruders of any kind. They will not talk easily with an outsider or let him into their groups, which, being based largely on kinship, have little room for the visiting strangers. Eventually, however, they do permit entry to the researcher, provided they see him often enough to establish trust in him, and have no reason to doubt the purpose of his research. Indeed, my experience suggests that in time almost everyone will admit the researcher, for people enjoy being studied. It provides variety in their lives, and the attention which the researcher gives them is flattering. I have often been told by friends and colleagues that such and such a study could not be done; I would not be allowed in. Such warnings are as dangerous as they are wrong; if he convinces himself that people will not let themselves be studied, the uncertain researcher can set a self-fulfilling prophecy in motion. The only solution is to ask for entry, to hope for the best and, above all, to play it straight.

Asking for entry requires the researcher to sell himself to the people whose groups he wishes to enter. I am not sure how one does this; I have had few refusals and so have not had to think about it consciously. My forte, if that is what it is, seems to be an honest face, a visible earnestness about wanting to do research, and a quiet demeanour that perhaps tells people I will not be a threat to them. The last is the most important, for, if the researcher appears threatening, he is not likely to be admitted. He must play it straight; to announce himself as a researcher from the start in those situations in which it is possible without doors slamming in his face immediately and to make it clear to people that neither he nor his research will be threatening. He must attempt to figure out quickly how he could be threatening, and to respond appropriately as soon as people start to ask – or to make jokes – about why he is there. Soon after I began my current research in the mass media, some of the people I was observing began to joke about my being a spy from a competitor. I joked back, but also made it clear that I was not a spy, by postponing questions that might arouse their suspicion and by showing them, wherever possible in the same joking manner they had used, that the sociological issues which I was studying would hardly interest their competitors.

Despite my success in gaining entry, the process is for me one of great anxiety, and I often expect to be refused when the people I am studying have already accepted me. People for whom it is easy to make friends with strangers and to sell themselves may find entry less trying. Paradoxically, my anxieties about the entry process make me prefer participant observation to interviewing, for however anxiety-arousing the former may be, it is for me less so than door-to-door interviewing where one must sell oneself to more people more often than in participant observation. Until I feel that I have been accepted, the research process is nerve-wracking; I lack the personal security to banish rejection anxieties, to feel free to observe fully and to take in as much data as possible. Telling people one is a researcher from the start is helpful here, for being honest about one's mission makes it easier to face strangers, and the announcement itself facilitates moving into the marginal position needed for the research. In the West End, where I had only one year's time to do my fieldwork and gaining entry was an extremely slow process, I was initially beset with severe doubts about my ability as a fieldworker. I constantly looked for excuses not to do fieldwork and to stay in my apartment, but since there was no other alternative and time was short, I finally drove myself out on the street and eventually I made enough contacts to get into some family circles and peer groups. (Before that, I visited William F. Whyte to find out how I could meet a 'Doc' who could take me into these groups, but there is no method for finding such people, and although I did find a co-operative gatekeeper he lacked Doc's wide contacts in the community.) As I began to develop friendly relations with some West Enders, I saw that the difficulties were less the result of my drawbacks as a fieldworker than their suspicion of middle-class outsiders, and that I had to be in the West End and be seen for a while before anyone would talk with me. In Levittown, where everyone was a stranger, there were no entry problems, and in the mass media, too, they have been minor. Indeed, the main problem was to discount my fears of possible rejection, based partly on doubts expressed by colleagues, which stemmed from the belief of intellectuals that the people who work in the mass media are engaged in a conspiracy they want to hide from others. Needless to say, this is not the case; if anything, the people who create mass media fare are not sure of what they are doing, and welcome the researcher who is coming to find out. When I was observing the creation of a programme at one television network, I was approached by producers of a couple of others, who asked when I would come to study *them* and help them figure out what they were doing. Their requests made me certain that the entry problem had been licked.

After entry is achieved and the participant observer feels sure enough to develop a working routine, new problems develop. For one thing, achieving entry does not necessarily put an end to anxiety over possible rejection; nor does it guarantee that the fieldworker's rapport will always be smooth. In addition to continuing fears that he may be refused entry in a specific situation, which are sometimes justified sometimes not, the participant observer must expect occasional anxiety about his presence from the people he is studying. Even if he has been accepted, there may be days when he is not wanted, or there may be tensions among the people he is studying which make them use the fieldworker as a scapegoat. A hectic community meeting may cause someone to wonder whether the fieldworker is a spy; a need to change the programme just before airtime may cause a television producer to direct his anxiety at the fieldworker rather than at his colleagues – and sometimes the fieldworker may just get in the way of the people he is observing. When such reactions occur, and they have occurred more often in my mass media study than in my community researches, the fieldworker must try not to take the attack personally, and should get out of the way temporarily. This is not the time to take notes or ask questions, but to sympathise with the problems of the people who are under strain and to make oneself as unobtrusive as possible until the tension is relieved. It is a good time to go the bathroom.

Other anxieties develop from the management of the research, and since these are generic to all research, vary with the kind of study, and are not central to the management of relationships with the people studied and with the self, which are my central topics, I shall describe them only briefly. One source of anxiety during research is the constant worry about the flow of research activities: is one doing the right thing at the right time, attending the right meeting, or talking to the right people? This may be a particular problem of community research; the community is, after all, a complex of many ongoing institutions, and to study it properly, one must be in many places at the same time. This being impossible, one must make the right choice of what to study every day, and even so there is always the danger of having missed something and of never being able to retrieve an event that has already become history. But much the same problem has developed in my media research, for the production of a single television programme is the effort of several teams working independently, and one cannot be with all of them at the same time. The fieldworker who has missed something important can always go back to interview the participants in the event, but he will always wonder what he lost by not being there.[11] These worries are ever-present, but they do not last long; the next day's work brings new problems, and later, when the data are analysed and the report is written, the researcher often finds that the event he thought so important at the time of fieldwork was actually quite insignificant. Other study topics and settings generate different problems and anxieties, of course, and many more autobiographical accounts are needed before it is possible to determine which problems and anxieties are generic to the management of research in participant observation.[12]

A second source of anxiety generic to the management of my research at least, is how to make sense of what one is studying, how not to be upset by the initial inability to understand and how to order the constant influx of data – and of the inability to understand – sufficiently to make plans for the next day's and week's research. I have found that the best solution for the inability to understand is not to worry too much about it and to take copious notes, for what seems confusing at one point in time may be explained later. One can never escape the uncertainty, but it also adds to the joy of fieldwork, for there is great satisfaction when a mystery is suddenly cleared up.

A third source of anxiety during fieldwork pertains more to the participant observer's relationship with the people he is studying, and stems from his peculiar role. He is, as I have already suggested, pretending to be other than what he is, for, even while he acts as a participant, he is emotionally principally a researcher – but always also an individual with personal needs. Participant observation requires the suppression or postponement of satisfying these personal needs, and it also means pretending to feelings about the participation itself that may not be real. The fieldworker is, thus, in some ways like a politician; he participates with a hidden agenda and cannot talk freely about himself. The participant observer also functions like an actor, for he lives a role rather than his own life, and his participation is always, at least to some extent, a performance. Unlike an actor, however, the participant observer cannot be trained to memorise his role, and he does not get a chance to rehearse. Of course, his audience is smaller and less attentive than the actor's, and the participant observer is permitted more fluffs than the actor. He is also allowed to be more of a person than the politician, who must always be polite, interested and yet noncommittal, and can never stop playing his role when he is with his constituents.

Emotionally speaking, participant observation is thus strenuous and tense work. Studying a small group is perhaps most difficult, for then the participant observer must participate actively, even while he is trying to take mental notes of what is happening and develop questions about the event that he will insert into the conversation later. Being an observer of a larger group, such as a social gathering, requires less active participation, but it is more strenuous in other ways, for the temptation is to try to observe everything, to participate in one conversation and to listen to others at the same time. Going to meetings is probably the easiest kind of participant observation, for one can sit and even take notes, without having to participate directly, and often many of the events to be observed are predictable, having been published beforehand in an agenda. While studying Levittown, I went to meetings almost every week night for the first year, but going to meetings was relaxing; I did not have to work half as hard as in more intimate situations.

A final source of anxiety is the deception inherent in participant observation. Once the fieldworker has gained entry, people tend to forget he is there and let down their guard, but he does not; however much he seems to participate, he is really there to observe and even to watch what happens when people let down their guard. He is involved in personal situations in which he is, emotionally speaking, always taking and never giving, for he is there to learn and, thus, to take from the people he studies, whereas they are always giving information, and are rarely being given anything. Of course, they derive some satisfaction from being studied, but when they ask the participant observer to give – for example, help or advice – he must usually refuse in order to maintain his neutrality. Moreover, even though he seems to give of himself when he participates, he is not really doing so and, thus, deceives the people he studies. He pretends to participate emotionally when he does not; he observes even when he does not appear to be doing so, and like the formal interviewer, he asks questions with covert purposes of which his respondents are likely to be unaware. In short, psychologically, the participant observer is acting dishonestly; he is deceiving people about his feelings, and in observing when they do not know it, he *is* spying on them. Even if his espionage is not intended to transmit information to enemies or possible exploiters, and even if it does not injure those whom he studies, his activity is still, psychologically, a form of espionage. This has two personal consequences: a pervasive feeling of guilt and, partly in compensation, a tendency to overidentify with the people being studied. The participant observer often feels guilty about deceiving people. He can, and must, tell himself that he has no other choice, for often the only way to get honest data is to be dishonest in getting it. He can be open at the start and explain that he has come as a researcher, but if he were honest and open about all his research aims while he is observing, people would suppress facts and feelings of which they are ashamed and, thus, hide some of the data which are significant to understanding any social situation.

The researcher can perhaps persuade himself that his deception is in the interest of science, but I have never found this argument persuasive. I am not convinced by the assumption that science is disinterested, or that being a scientist allows the researcher to assume a *noblesse oblige* relationship to those he studies, for then he is both judge and jury in determining that his activities are for their own good. The social scientist does his work for the same personal motives as anyone else, including the hope of a higher income and career advancement, and even if his choice of a research topic is not based on overt ideological concerns, the research itself, once published, may have political consequences which cannot be explained away by the appeal to scientific objectivity. The participant observer can do his job to the best of his ability, and can try to minimise the social, political and psychological costs of his research for the people he studies, but when all is said and done, participant observation, like all other kinds of fieldwork, requires some deception, and the resulting guilt accompanies the fieldworker throughout his research.[13]

At the same time, the fieldworker identifies with the people he studies, partly because so much of his life is tied up with them and in them that he cannot help but identify, and partly also, I believe, because of the deception inherent in his method. Deceiving people and catching them unawares makes the fieldworker feel both guilty and sorry for the people he is studying, and, in partial recompense, he identifies with them, taking their troubles to heart, and sometimes even accepting the validity of their causes. The extent to which one identifies or overidentifies varies with the situations and people one is studying. I have found it strongest in myself when I studied people who were also being deceived or exploited by society, and when I lived with the West Enders who were about to lose their neighbourhood to slum clearance, I became, emotionally at least, their advocate. They were underdogs, and I wanted to help them. They were misunderstood by the rest of society, which described them as slum-dwellers and undeserving poor, and I felt impassioned to correct this impression. I suspect that this happens whenever one studies people who are falsely stereotyped; when, whatever one's method of research, one obtains data which show up the inaccuracy of the stereotype. Much of my research has been among people who have been stereotyped inaccurately, and, when I studied the Levittowners, who were not underdogs, I became antagonistic to the journalists and critics who had drawn false pictures of suburban life. In studying the mass media, I have become equally antagonistic to those who feel popular culture is manufactured by greedy hypocrites and unfeeling hacks.

Overidentification is not only a response to guilt or social injustice, however; it is also a way by which the participant observer compensates for his marginal position. If he cannot be truly a part of the group, he can at least adopt some of their values and beliefs so as to satisfy his feelings for belonging. In studying one television programme I soon shared the staff's disdain for its competitor on another station and, when I later studied the competing programme, turned emotionally on the people with whom I had identified before. There are pitfalls galore in overidentification and in the other problems of participant observation, both methodological and personal. For example, if one becomes too identified with the people being studied, one is likely to ignore behaviour they consider undesirable or unethical, and this can lead to partial or distorted

findings. Similarly, the fieldworker can become so involved with the people he is studying that he stops wanting to be a researcher and becomes a true participant. He must, therefore, discover early in his fieldwork which emotional consequences he is prey to and deal with them. This is easier said than done, but one means is to become aware of one's problems and anxieties, and then to find out whether they are generated by the participant observation role, by the situation and people under study, or by personal difficulties which surface because of the research. If the researcher is unable to do this himself, a sympathetic colleague or a knowledgeable psychotherapist may be helpful. Sometimes, the fieldworker need only realise that his problems are not unique, and that his anxieties are not the result of his failings, but that they are inevitable as well as universal consequences of participant observation. Merely knowing, for example, that all participant observers identify somewhat with their subjects helps one to deal with the personal and methodological impact of overidentification. Of course, problems and anxieties cannot always be eliminated, but awareness can prevent their seriously interfering with the research, or depressing the researcher's morale.[14] Moreover, they vanish once the fieldwork is done, and whatever bias they have created in the data can be dealt with, at least in part, during the analysis and writing phases. And, once the book or article about the study is completed, one usually remembers mainly the many pleasures and joys of participant observation.

IV

I should emphasise once more that what I have written about participant observation is based on my own experiences, and more important, on the needs and patterns of my own personality. Other fieldworkers may have other ways of gaining entry and achieving rapport: they may create other kinds of relationships with respondents, face other kinds of problems and develop other feelings about their work. For example, my temperament is such that I find it difficult to gather interview data by arguing with my respondents, but a more extroverted researcher may be able to do so, and come up with richer material as a result.[15]

Participant observation is the most personal of all sociological research methods, and little can or should be done to eliminate the personal element. Instead, the method and its practitioners must themselves be researched to discover how these personal elements affect the data gathering process and the gathered data. Soon, someone must do a study of participant observers, to find out what kinds of people take to this research method and why, and particularly to learn what personality types are drawn to the marginal social relationships which are the essence of participant observation. I have often asked this question of myself, and have wondered about my fellow participant observers. My hunch is that fieldwork attracts a person who, in Everett Hughes's words, 'is alienated from his own background', who is not entirely comfortable in his new roles, or who is otherwise detached from his own society; the individual who is more comfortable as an observer than as a participant. This is the stuff of which intellectuals and novelists are also made, but while literary observers may celebrate their marginality, sociologists must understand it, and see how it affects their work if they are to be social scientists. If we can discover the psychodynamics that create fieldworkers, then participant observation can truly become both a personal and a scientific method.

Notes: Chapter 8

Originally published in Howard S. Becker, Blanche Geer, David Riesman and Robert S. Weiss (eds), *Institutions and the Person: Papers Presented to Everett C. Hughes* (Chicago: Aldine, 1968), pp. 300–17, and reprinted by kind permission of the author.

1 See, for example, Hammond (1964), and Vidich, Bensman and Stein (1964).
2 See Schwartz and Schwartz (1955).
3 See Hughes (1960), p. vi.
4 See Hughes (1960), p. xi.
5 For more detailed analyses of the various roles of participant observation, see Gold (1958), and Junker (1960), chapter 3.
6 See also Gans (1967), pp. 440 ff., and Gans (1962), pp. 338–9.
7 Schwartz and Schwartz (1955), p. 344.
8 Hughes (1960), p. xi.
9 For a more detailed description of my feelings about the slum clearance during the fieldwork, see Gans (1962), pp. 305–7.
10 See Bowen (1964).
11 As Robert Weiss suggests, this is a minor problem in most studies, for the sociologist is interested in recurring behaviour, and the event he has missed will take place again. It was a special problem for me in Levittown, because my study dealt with historical as well as with recurring events.
12 For a detailed and extremely honest account of the personal facets and problems of participant observation, see Schwartz (1964).
13 For an insightful discussion of the ethical aspects of deception, see Erikson (1967).
14 For a more detailed discussion, see Schwartz and Schwartz (1955), and Schwartz (1964).
15 On the virtues of argument as a device for gathering data, see Riesman (1964).

9

The Making of a Female Researcher: Role Problems in Fieldwork

LOIS EASTERDAY, DIANA PAPADEMAS, LAURA SCHORR AND CATHERINE VALENTINE

Social scientists do research in hopes of discovering how society works. Years are spent in graduate training, learning how to gather, record and analyse data. Courses are not segregated by sex, and we are told that research is research, regardless of one's gender. Our experiences have led us to believe differently. Being single females doing fieldwork, we discovered there were research problems related to that status. The methodological literature[1] and the women studies literature[2] do not mention the effects of sex on research relationships, or how these can be dealt with in fieldwork. A few sociologists comment on female observers (Douglas, 1976; Riesman, 1964; Stein, 1954; Wax, 1960), and others consider more general problems, such as the participant observer as a human being (Gans, 1968), or friendships and personal feelings (Johnson, 1975). Also, some anthropologists have described their status as women in other cultures (Bowen, 1964; Golde, 1970; Powdermaker, 1966b) that are suggestive of some of the issues of this chapter.

We focus on specific problems of being a female field researcher in relation to general methodological issues, such as the establishment and maintenance of rapport and research relationships. We do this by extracting observations from our twelve research studies. These include an art museum, an embalming school, a funeral parlour, a medical team in a nursing home, a military photography programme, a morgue, a newspaper, two social service agencies, a stock brokerage office, a television station and a university film-making programme. We additionally present a typology of sex roles and power. We then discuss varieties of sex role relationships in those settings, showing disadvantages and advantages. Our conclusions offer suggestions on how young women researchers can minimise the liabilities of their sex status in fieldwork.

Typology of Settings and Sex Roles

While being young and being female represent two ascribed criteria influencing social interaction in any setting, the configuration of social relationships in a particular organisational setting further defines our opportunities and limitations as researchers. As Kanter (1975)[3] indicates, 'In addition to sexual and cultural issues, there are also status and power issues when men and women interact, a function of the structural positions and organisational class membership of the sexes'.

A simple typology characterises the research settings in terms of sex roles and power: primarily male (those dominated both in number and power by men), traditional male–female (those dominated in power but not in number by men), non-traditional male–female (those in which women occupy some positions of power). Primarily male settings include a morgue, a military photography programme and a university film-making programme. Traditional male–female settings include an embalming school, two social service agencies, a medical team and a stock brokerage office. Non-traditional male–female settings include an art museum, a funeral parlour, a newspaper, and a television station.

The morgue is primarily a male setting of doctor and attendants, so sex role differentiation is not customarily part of their definition of work. The perspective of the morgue director towards women is expressed in the absence of female attendants; as he says, 'there are no sleeping facilities to accommodate them', and bodies are 'too heavy' for women to carry when they are retrieved at great distances. The attendants have no objections to hiring female attendants, but the authoritative dominance of the director prevents their presence. Also, women who come to the morgue to identify bodies of relatives are defined as more emotional than men and are in need of protective handling. The female researcher is subject to similar paternalistic treatment.

The military photographer training programme is exclusively male. Like the morgue, establishing rapport was easier with subordinates in the setting than with directors, who upheld traditional attitudes towards women. Their authority defined the work situations for all participants, to the exclusion of females as employees and researchers. Dissimilarly, the university film-making programme, while predominantly male, encouraged female students (and the researcher) to participate. The director's encouragement was not a perspective shared by male students, who saw females in the setting as 'coeds' playing at a male occupation. In traditional male–female settings, our general status liability was compounded by specific role expectations attached to women in the organisation. For lack of female authority models, we often found ourselves lumped together with other female subordinates in the sexual stratification system of the setting. And we were treated accordingly:

A short two-day study was designed to observe medical teams of doctors, social workers and nurses while they conducted an evaluation study of health care facilities. As a group of observers studying several teams, we found common situations in the relationships among the team members. Among the team members it was expected that the doctor would 'take charge' over the team as the male member of an all-female team. As a young female observer, I found the passive role to be an accepted role among the other team members during the formal part of the health care study. At lunch I seemed to be one of the 'women' on the team, referred to by first name while the doctor was deferred to and called by title.

In the brokerage office, largely male-dominated (one female broker among ten, and a customer population of retired men), young single females were not present. The researcher in this setting was defined as 'cute' and 'the girl' or 'the young lady here'.

Our sex status often caused us to be 'channelled' into particular activities, thus potentially curtailing the range of our data collection:

Although not rigid, the division of labour in television newswork follows male–female roles. As a female observer, I was expected to be more interested in the features and human interest stories than the political or crime news. One woman reporter looked deflated the day I decided to go with a reporter covering a presidential candidate rather than with her to do a feature on a magician.

Traditional male–female settings are sometimes sexually segregated, creating difficulties for the researcher establishing rapport with all persons:

A sharp characteristic of the gatherings at the brokerage office was sex role separation among customers. Women talked with women and men with men. Female customers identified the female broker as 'theirs' although her customers were male as well. Early in the fieldwork, I found it easier to approach the women informally rather than the men. Later in the field after developing an informant relationship

with one of the customers, a male university professor who was amused by my being there, I was introduced to other customers as 'the girl from the university' or simply 'this young lady' who wants to learn more about the stock market and why people are here.

In certain organisational settings, the professional power of male administrators is intertwined with and enhanced by their personal, sexual dominance as men. The male director of a predominantly female-staffed social service agency allegedly employed his personal attractiveness as a means of increasing allegiance to his administration by acting seductively towards some of the women –including the researcher. The charisma attached to his position as effective leader of the organisation, as well as his legitimate authority over the professional activity and conduct of the staff, enhanced his status. Although the agency publicly encouraged autonomy and administrative participation on the part of female group leaders, it was clear that the chief administrator had the final word on important decisions and policies. In addition, the administrator was regarded by many as being skilful at political interaction with regional superordinates and staff members alike. The nature of one of our encounters as a young female researcher with him reflected this institutionalised pattern of relationships in which women are professionally, personally and politically subject to male authority.

Non-traditional male–female settings included the art museum, the funeral parlour, the television station and the newspaper. While women occupy positions as directors, assistant directors, museum curators, reporters and photographers, they do not dominate the work situation. In these settings relationships can become a problem of 'over-rapport', where coupling-off and male–female pairing are the practice among members, or where the researcher finds herself more attracted to 'feminist' men and women. Tensions among non-feminists and feminists in such settings are problematic; the researcher may find herself typed as a 'female libber' and tested for 'where she stands' – as either friend or enemy, but clearly as female. As can be seen, our typology is fluid enough to include a variety of sex role relationships. We will further discuss some of these.

Varieties of Sex Role Relationships

THE FRATERNITY

On entering male-dominated settings, female researchers often have difficulty gaining access to the setting itself. One of us established rapport with the photographers of a special military photography programme by being a photographer and knowing their language. The relationship was sustained by insisting that the researcher not be photographed as a model, but rather that she be 'one of the boys' on the other side of the lens. In an attempt to gain approval for the study from the programme's director, the researcher was denied full access with the statement, 'It won't work. The men in the programme are a close bunch, and the talk is rough. They wouldn't be themselves if you are there'.

Once a female researcher gains entrée to a setting, she may find it necessary to break into female groups similar to the male fraternity. Among the client population of a social service agency were parent groups composed primarily of poor, divorced women in their twenties and thirties. Since the contact was infrequent over two years, rapport among them in some cases took that long to establish. Stereotyped observations of the researcher went something like, 'How can you [single, childless] understand what it's like for us?' We felt the best way to counter this was to show genuine interest in things of importance to them like children, the absence of stable marriages and partners, and having a good time. Over time, while we recognised our different situations, close relationships emerged on the basis of 'we women' having similar problems of loneliness, being 'stuck here', not finding work that pays enough or is interesting, and other common plights.

HUSTLING

One of the problems a young single female researcher has to deal with is 'hustling'. Particularly in male-dominated settings where the observer is talking to one male at a time, the male–female games come early to the fore. Two researchers observing the same setting (the morgue) at different times (one year apart) experienced very similar problems in this regard:

I was in the midst of industriously questioning the attendant about his job at the morgue and he came back with, 'Are you married?'
Observer: No. How long have you worked here?
Attendant: Three years. Do you have a steady boyfriend?
Observer: No. Do you find this work difficult?
Attendant: No. Do you date?
Observer: Yes, Why isn't this work difficult for you?
Attendant: You get used to it. What do you do in your spare time?
And so our interview went on for over an hour, each of us working at our separate purposes. I doubt whether either of us got any 'usable data'.

In instances such as these, the researchers either had to avoid the informant or avoid letting him talk about other subjects he was interested in. In the one instance, in the morgue, the researcher avoided visiting the setting when one particular male was there. She was unable to discuss anything without the conversation being overshadowed by discussions of dating, marriage, or 'getting together'. However, it is not always possible to avoid such problems. At the funeral home run by a black husband–wife team, the wife became increasingly hostile towards the researcher:

I increasingly became aware of his wife's coolness towards me, although I tried in my dress and in my demeanour to be as professional as possible. When I raised this problem to the husband, asking if it would be advisable for me to leave the site, he brushed off the wife's hostility towards me, with 'Oh, you know women, they get jealous. But we know there's nothing between us, right?' About a month after my entrée at the site, the husband called me at home on three occasions, apparently on the pretext of assuring me that I would not be thrown off the site by his wife. At the conclusion of two of these calls, he reminded me not to mention to his wife he had telephoned me.

The source(s) of the wife's hostility can only be hypothesised. Perhaps it was a combination of sexual jealousy, racial hostility, or professional protectiveness. In any case, the hostility became so intense that the researcher terminated observations at the funeral home:

She told me in a friendly tone of voice that she thought I had accumulated enough observations, and that if I needed more data, I should interview her instead of her husband. She claimed my presence at the funeral services, as the sole white presence was conspicuous and disturbing to the mourners (an observation which I wholeheartedly agreed with). I told her I thought it would be better if I left the site.

At the social service agency, the story was different. Staffed by fifty women and three men, one of whom was the top administrator, multiple female–female relationships were problematic, since these were defined in relationship to the male director. Frequently 'on the make', the man used his position in the authority structure of the agency to assert himself as boss, commanding deference.

It often appears that the researcher has only two options. She can totally reject the advances of the hustler and risk his feeling that he has been rejected, or she can welcome his advances and allow the female–male relationship to develop. However, either can have detrimental effects on the research. An informant who feels rejected as a person is not likely to be a wealth of information and co-operation. In some instances he can disrupt her relationship with other informants, and possibly even have her ejected from the setting. This would be especially true, if the male happened to be in a supervisory position:

To establish rapport with the females in the situation, I adamantly refused the approaches of the director. The other consequence of that 'no' response on my part was a reciprocal denial in the way of avoiding me personally, and delaying and denying, covertly, important information about the project.

Similar pressures occurred at another social service agency:

> During my first week at the agency, the male administrator and a group of outside consultants held an 'in-service' meeting to improve staff rapport. The day after this session, the administrator approached me while I was helping a child, took my hand in his, and said to me, 'Any time you want, we can have our own private little in-service'. The same week, I saw him in the parking lot, and he asked me, 'When are you inviting me over to your place for dinner?' On another occasion, when I went into his office to request some information, he said kiddingly, 'Bribe me'. . . . Every encounter became a balancing act between cordiality and distance.

The young single female researcher must be careful that her behaviour, when designed to discourage hustling, does not backfire. This might result in stimulating the desire of the 'hustler' to conquer the woman, whose behaviour is (mis)interpreted as elusive; thus, she becomes a real trophy to possess.

On the other hand, 'getting involved' with an informant could also result in termination of the fieldwork. It could result in bad feelings among the other informants, jealousy, or exclusivity. A relationship such as this could also colour the data and make it unusable or very 'skewed' and inaccurate. For some researchers, there are great ethical dilemmas over these sorts of involvements, both professionally and personally. Few want to 'use' persons and relationships to get data. Therefore, the researcher often finds herself walking a tightrope between rejection and involvement. It seems that each situation of this nature must be evaluated and dealt with carefully. There are some men who, as hustlers, never give up. It is probably best to avoid extended interaction with them. Other situations can be handled honestly, by emphasising one's research role. One of us simply told a man she was interviewing that her role could not permit her to respond to his insistent overtures. Other men are not serious about or committed to 'scoring' and can be discouraged with no hard feelings.

THE GO-FER

In some settings the female researcher may be cast in the role of 'go-fer', a typical role for the young woman, to which men can easily relate:

In a social service agency, the male staff member I was assigned to observe continuously devised clerical errands for me to do – partly, it seemed, to keep me from observing him, but also to provide secretarial assistance. On more than one occasion I politely protested that I was employed to observe him rather than be his assistant, but he curtly informed me that I could not observe him unless I provided this kind of aid.

THE MASCOT

Unlike the 'go-fer', who is expected to do things, the mascot is accepted simply for her 'being':

> In a peer setting [university students in a film-making programme] efforts were made to characterise my participation at times as 'mascot' with statements like: 'We like your company', and 'It looks good to have a pretty girl along'.

> I asked to observe some visiting professionals at work in the morgue. One of the attendants introduced me and conveyed my request. The response was, 'Of course. Who wouldn't want a pretty girl watching them work?' There were no questions about the purpose of my observations. In a similar instance, I requested access to a particular procedure, but this request was turned down, due to legal restrictions. In reporting the refusal, one man stated, 'He said you can't watch this time, but some other time. But don't worry, he still loves you'.

FATHER–DAUGHTER

Older males in a setting may interact with a young female researcher in a manner we describe as paternalistic. Given the legitimacy of traditional sex role relationships, the father–daughter relationship offers older males – threatened by young women or unable to interact with young women as peers – a safe, predefined interactional context. At a morgue, one of us experienced such a relationship with an older and powerful male in that setting:

> The Medical Examiner (M.E.) treated me very paternalistically. When I was to observe an autopsy, he took me in hand, protectively.
> *M.E.:* Have you ever seen a dead person?
> *Observer:* Yes, once before while I was here.
> *M.E.:* Well, you know, all nurses have to attend autopsies. For some, it takes two or three, others are not bothered at all . . . Now, if you feel you need to leave, do so.
> He also protected me by discouraging attendants from showing me 'bad cases'.

Experiences with males in a social service agency and at the funeral home were also, at times, paternalistic, despite our efforts to emphasise the research role.

Advantages

Although the thrust of our essay concerns the liabilities connected with being a female field researcher, we and others have found definite advantages. The previously mentioned problem of not being taken seriously can work to one's benefit. If a researcher is not taken seriously because she is a young female, this can facilitate entrée into an otherwise difficult or inaccessible setting. In one instance, one of us was granted access to a school of mortuary science to which an older, well-known female researcher had been denied access. The young researcher was taken in on a 'mascot' basis by one of the male faculty members. The researcher's position and work were fully described to the 'gatekeeper', the dean of the school. In a rather offhand way – 'oh sure, come on in' – he granted the access. His only concern was that the researcher always dress appropriately for the setting.

Also, if the researcher is not taken seriously, people in a setting may confide in the researcher or let her hear things because they perceive her as powerless and non-threatening. Lofland (1971)[4] writes of the observer as acceptable incompetent, 'Or the observer may be a women of any age, and "everybody knows" that women don't know anything about much of anything that is important'. Elsewhere, Douglas (1976)[5] has written similarly that the 'boob ploy' benefits women researchers, sometimes unintentionally. Women in research teams sometimes were thought by people in settings (for example, a drug rehabilitation centre), to be ineffective enough to be harmless.

Personal interest in the researcher can also work to the researcher's advantage after she is in the setting. An informant who is attempting to 'hustle' an observer may, at times, reveal more than he otherwise would in an attempt to show how friendly, co-operative and accommodating he is. Stein (1954),[6] in Gouldner's work on industrial bureaucracy, talks about how a young woman was taken into the field, and how, despite the concern of other male team members, she was well-received by men in the gypsum plant: 'Actually she got along wonderfully with the men, who in an effort to impress her, would often give her more revealing data than they might to a male interviewer.'

One may, if skilful and if willing to take the risks involved, use one's femininity and desirability to manipulate males in a setting for information. As Wax (1960)[7] notes, 'a coquette is in a much better situation to learn about men than a nun'. Complications can arise, however, leading to over-rapport problems. And one is not advised to adopt views or practices one does not accept. One's values may undergo changes as a result of field experiences, which may be beneficial if one sees them as broadening experiences. There is also a component to being a marginal person, an outsider, 'the other' throughout one's life, which can contribute to the perceptiveness a woman brings to field research. In a personal correspondence to one of us, Blanche Geer writes:

> The most handicapped observer is the one doing people and situations he/she is closest to. Hence, women are in luck in a male-run world. They can see how few clothes the emperor has on, question the accepted, what is taken for granted.

Suggestions for Field Tactics

People experience their relations with one another problematically: it is not necessary to conduct field research to learn that. While there are no set procedures that would anticipate all potential problems, there are certain tactics we suggest to minimise the liabilities and enhance the benefits of being a female field researcher. Improved research reliability suggests appropriate behavioural guidelines for those doing fieldwork.

A general rule we have followed has been to avoid personal involvement with subjects as intimate friends. Ethical and practical problems such as over-rapport (Miller, 1952) suggest reasons for this rule. Generally, problems include researcher bias, data distortion and limitation, reactivity and observer effects. As we encountered these potential problems in our researches, we developed tactics in our relationships and guided our orientations towards the research enterprise. For example, we tried to manage potential over-rapport problems by equalising time with all people in the field situation, by not discussing details of the research with the informant/friend, and by checking comments and behaviour of others in the field as a way to verify observer perceptions. Other suggestions are to emphasise the research role in gaining entrée and to develop a 'spiel', choosing and accepting roles (as participant and observer) that facilitate observations, avoiding participants who monopolise research time and activity, fabricating information about oneself (for example the boyfriend back home), and recording and evaluating with honesty and rigour all observations, including feelings about participants during the research process. Our discussion of sex role problems in a variety of field settings reflects both the disadvantages and advantages of being a young woman, as we have experienced them. Research courses and methodological texts only teach students how research ought to go, rather than how it does go in the real world. As social scientists, we have an obligation to share experiences with other researchers in order to develop our research skills and enterprise.

We do not feel that admitting the effects of an observer's ascribed statuses sacrifices objectivity.

Rather, we feel that 'No observation can become objective unless the observer is also observed objectively' (Mitroff, 1974).[8] Sharing our analysis with others is a step in that direction. Thus, the statuses of young, single females acting as fieldworkers emphasises a set of problems. It would be beneficial to all field researchers to take a look at the problems and benefits their status characteristics present.

What is it like to be a young, single male or an older, married male field researcher in a female-dominated setting? What about being a black researcher in a white setting? Or what happens if one is an older, married female in a male-dominated setting? When teams of researchers enter a setting, are there differences between the experiences of men and women, young and old, single and married, and so forth? Most important, how do these differences affect reality perspectives in any setting? Further study may suggest the extent to which ascribed status affects the research process. Continued discussion of these and related problems will further our understandings not only of field methods, but also of theoretical areas such as sex role theory, minority group study, and the sociology of knowledge.

By looking at sociologists, at ourselves as participants in a society in which we are both defining and being defined by others, we can recognise our part in the social drama and perhaps achieve our hopes for discovering how society works.

Notes: Chapter 9

Reprinted from *Urban Life*, vol. 6, no. 3, October, 1977, pp. 333–48, by kind permission of the publisher, Sage Publications, Inc. and the authors.

1 See, for example, Adams and Preiss (1960), Bogdan and Taylor (1975), Bruyn (1966), Junker (1960) and McCall and Simmons (1969).
2 See, for example, Bernard (1966), Epstein and Goode (1971), Huber (1973) and Rossi (1965).
3 See Kanter (1975), p. 55.
4 See Lofland (1971), pp. 100–1.
5 See Douglas (1976), p. 185.
6 See Stein (1954), pp. 265–6.
7 See Wax (1960), p. 97.
8 See Mitroff (1974), p. 238.

10

The Problem of Ethical Integrity in Participant Observation

I. C. JARVIE

Introduction

A curious problem arises in connection with the notion of the participant observer, a problem partly ethical and partly methodological. It seems not to have been clearly seen and stated, although solutions to it exist –in practice, as it were. The problem arises like this. Standard accounts of the method of participant observation require, I would argue, an anthropological observer to be both a stranger and a friend among the people he is studying. Yet one person cannot be a stranger and a friend at the same time: the roles are mutually exclusive. This being so, it is *a fortiori* impossible to play either role in integrity while trying to combine them, with the result that an uneasy compromise is liable to be forged.

The unresolved identity crisis precipitates an integrity crisis, and only by allowing one role to override the other can the two crises be resolved.[1] The anthropologist must choose the role of the stranger, because only that role allows him to act in what he and the society he comes from would consider to be his integrity as a member of that society in general and as a scientist in particular. However, I would go further and press this to the point of arguing that to some extent the success of the method of participant observation *derives from* exploiting the situations created by the role clashes insider/outsider, stranger/friend, pupil/teacher. If I am right, the standard discussions of participant observation need drastic revision.[2]

The Ideal of Participant Observation

Modern anthropology is often distinguished from old anthropology by citing the innovation of participant observer fieldwork. As Forge (1967) has written, there is an official story that this was invented in May 1915 when Bronislaw Malinowski pitched his tent at Omarakana in the Trobriand Islands and set about learning the local language.[3] Both factors – tent and language – were claimed to be vital: a tent down among the native houses so that the observer is physically close to the native life; and learning the language, not using pidgin or interpreters, so that the observer can participate in the life he wishes to observe just as it is lived. The hardships of thus cutting oneself off from one's own tribe and plunging into another tribe have never been concealed. Recently, some autobiographies have appeared which go into some welcome detail about the experience and which reveal interesting problems of identity and integrity hitherto not much discussed (Forge 1967; Malinowski 1967; Powdermaker 1966a).[4]

The very notion of 'participant observer' needs a lot of unpacking. Junker (1960) sees a spectrum of postions within it: complete participation; the participant doubling as observer; the observer doubling as participant; and the complete observer. He notes that, if one begins as a member of the group and then secretly trains as a social scientist, the problems of being a traitor may arise; and that if the social scientist seeks to penetrate from outside, he may face the problems of a spy. The complete participant must conceal his character as observer/reporter if he does not want drastically to affect the processes he is observing. At the other extreme, the pure observer, seeing but not interacting, is more imaginary than real. Gold (1958) confines the observer-as-participant to the one-visit interview.

This leaves the participant as observer and the problem, as Junker sees it, of striking a balance between being a 'good friend' and a 'snooping stranger'. On the one hand, is the aim of participating fully, of identifying entirely with the alien way of life; on the other, is the danger of betraying trust. To observe a way of life best, it seems, involves living that way of life. This assumption invites two criticisms, each of which has both a theoretical and a practical aspect. First, is 'the inside' a privileged observation point? There is nothing especially privileged about the observations of a parade made by those in it. Spectators may be in a better position, television viewers in a still better one. Which vantage-point you choose must surely be a matter of what you want to observe and why. Secondly, can one join 'the inside', or must one have been born there? For some anthropologists, the question is purely practical:

they prefer building or buying a local-type hut to living in a tent. Evans-Pritchard (1937)[5] tells us the amusing fact that he used the local oracles for regulating his affairs when he was with the Azande. Participation may mean purchasing and looking after cattle, if these are the principal means of assessing status in that society. Some anthropologists are alleged to have taken native 'wives' – although Forge believes that in general this is not the practice. In short, participation approaches what is deprecatingly or half-jokingly called 'going native'.

Such a practical attitude may help, but it makes no impact on the theoretical difficulty of becoming an insider. There are limits inherent in the situation. First, an anthropologist is required not to go native altogether, not even as much as the local white beach-comber, since he is an observer. According to Paul (1953)[6] Goldenweiser has endorsed going native, but Radin says nothing is to be gained by it, and Herskovits says it is neither possible, nor desirable, for an anthropologist. Vidich argues:

If the participant observer seeks genuine experiences, unqualifiedly immersing and committing himself in the group he is studying, it may become impossible for him to objectify his own experiences for research purposes; in committing his loyalties he develops vested interests which will inevitably enter into his observations. Anthropologists who have 'gone native' are cases in point; some of them stop publishing entirely. (Vidich, 1955, p. 357).

Miller (1952) presents some examples illustrating this point.

Further, among the duties the fieldworker accepts – whether rightly or wrongly – is the duty to explain to the native population as clearly as possible the reason for his presence among them. Unlike someone who has dissipated his substance and 'honestly' (we say) 'gone native', the honest anthropologist carefully avoids giving the impression that he is joining his hosts for-ever; he even makes it clear that sooner or later he will leave. Williams (1967) says that 'the ethic of science is ill-served by fraudulent methods of study' and argues that if falsehoods would be necessary to fieldwork in a particular place, it would be better to go elsewhere 'to avoid compromise of the value that science is a public process, honestly discussed and conducted'.[7] Thus from the beginning of his study, the fieldworker is torn between pure participant and pure observer roles (for example, should he or should he not take a local wife?).

Failure to participate to the full, then, is unavoidable; and in any case, there are few cultures in which an outsider can ever completely overcome his role as stranger. Even when he is highly integrated, he may still occupy some such role as 'newcomer'. (Williams, 1967, ignores this when he writes, 'Most societies can find ways of incorporating the anthropologist . . . given an opportunity to search out positions to fit his roles'.[8]) Sometimes his attempts at integration call forth institutional means of putting him apart (even in the American and Canadian melting-pots we use the markers 'first-generation', 'second-generation' and 'new Canadians'). Paul (1953) argues that at most the anthropologist achieves partial penetration of the society: he comes as a stranger, and always keeps his outsider status. He cites Nadel (1939): 'The anthropologist can only be a freak member of the group, not only because of the conspicuous differences in physical characteristics which often exist but also because of inevitable social incompatibilities.' Lohman goes a little deeper:

The history of a relationship between an individual and the people in the community is a record of growth. One does not settle down and commence to traffic in the life of the community. A person is accepted to the extent that he displays like interests and purposes and to the extent that he fits into the economy of the community. He must carve a place for himself. That place not only involves acceptable and traditional practices within the group, but the relationship of the individual with external society is to be defined as essentially the same which members of the community generally hope with reference to the larger social world. The individual's struggle for a livelihood and certain essential satisfactions is to be regarded as the same one which every member of the group has for himself. (Lohman, 1937, p. 893)

Clearly, then, however well the anthropologist may be liked and trusted, however long he has been known and been got used to, he is unlikely ever to become an ordinary insider, a full member of the society he studies.

Ethical Conflict in Participant Observation

Not only is the anthropologist trying to play two roles, participant and stranger, but he is also liable to confront situations in which these roles violently clash. This brings me to my central point. My concern is with neither the theoretical nor the practical difficulties in the path of the participant observer; whether observing inside is better, whether one can be inside – these are discussed elsewhere in the literature (Kluckhohn, 1940; Paul, 1953; Schwartz and Schwartz, 1955; Vidich, 1955; Junker, 1960; Bruyn, 1966; Williams, 1967). Here I wish to air my uneasiness about the fieldworker's uneasiness: his struggle to be honest, fair and truthful. I believe that there is a conflict between his methodological theory and his practice, and that it is a good thing his practice deviates from his theory. The conflict is easily stated: the fieldworker as a scientist is seeking the truth; that very quest involves eliminating prejudice and bias when studying other societies; and that seems to demand relativism. Anthropologists sometimes call it the principle of cultural relativity and deny that it involves ethical nihilism. Of course in practice it never does, since anthropologists, so far from being nihilists, are usually deeply humane and 'committed' men. They see cultural relativity – or contextualism – as a counter to prejudice and ethnocentrism.[9] In Piddington's words (1957): 'The moral behaviour of individuals or groups of human beings must be considered in the light of what they have learned to regard as right or wrong, as forbidden or permissible'.[10] This is very bold. It exculpates juvenile delinquents as well as cannibals and head-hunters. Prejudice against these groups is bad, but so is what Gellner (1963) has called the Principle of Universal Charity. This principle is as follows: when faced with a practice that is unintelligible (or objectionable), assume that if enough of its context were known it would become unintelligible (or innocuous).[11] Yet the whole point of the practices may well lie in their unintelligible (or objectionable) character. The path between the Scylla of unreasonable ethnocentric prejudice and the Charybdis of Universal Charity is very difficult to steer, and the woolly notion of cultural relativity does not map the currents and submerged rocks.

How, then, do anthropologists in practice avoid falling into relativism while sustaining their aim of seeking the truth? Sometimes, the fieldworker, trying to make it clear that he belongs to another society to which he will one day return, will regale the host people with stories and descriptions of life among his own people. Of course, he may simplify his description and make his 'tribe' sound similar to theirs. Suppose he strives to be honest? Easier thought than acted: what shall the honest anthropologist say, if he is asked how many cattle his lineage has? Shall he interpret it as a question about his wealth and answer it literally? This, in the societies anthropologists specialise in, will probably make him appear an incredibly wealthy man, even if he lives strictly on a professor's salary. Or shall he be even more literal and indicate that he has no lineage or cattle? He may then try to explain that cattle do not signify overmuch in his society. The poor fellow more than likely will fail to get this message over, in which case he will paint himself to his hosts as a rather pathetic case. Whichever way he takes the question, his answer will not help him integrate. What if he is asked how many wives his paramount chief has? Shall he try to indicate that all his fellows have only one wife at a time, and so on? Will he be their informant as they are his? Is such a reciprocity possible? Or should he become as ethnocentrically 'bad' an anthropologist as they evidently are?

Let us press the decent anthropologist striving to be honest even harder. What sort of attitude should he adopt when faced with unhygienic food preparation, mutilation of children, human sacrifice?[12] Where is his integrity to be found? Anthropologists sometimes mention dysentery as an essential initiation into the profession: and they are only half-joking. They forget the anthropology of half-jokes; let us bring it home to them. What should the fieldworker confronted with dysentery do? He has a supply of drugs, and he guesses that the water supply is polluted. Does his integrity demand that he get dysentery, like the rest of the population? Obviously not. Should he be unlucky enough to get it, must he abjure all but local remedies in order to observe and participate? This principle might put future research at hazard. So let us allow him to avoid dysentery and to take medicine, if he gets it. What now of the people he is stranger/friend to? Does his devotion to observing rather than interfering prevent him from handing out drugs, which might preclude observation of local curative rituals, potion-preparing, and so on? Should he refrain from handing out his magic, because it will enhance his status and prestige in the society in a way he wishes to avoid? And what of his knowledge of the polluted water? We allow that he does not have to drink it; should he enlighten the natives, or will that too be both an interference and an acquisition of prestige which might jeopardize further observation?

Should, in brief, our honest anthropologist participate to the point where the boundaries of his freedom to comment on what is going on will be set by the primitive society which he is so anxious to join? It is all too easy to imagine probable situations where the honest anthropologist would be failing in his moral duty as our society conceives it, if he did not comment or even protest about some practices. Vidich (1955) thinks this keeps the anthropologist socially marginal and that marginality is an advantage.[13] Other anthropologists, like Herskovits (1948a), embrace relativism: to participate in a society, to treat it as worthy of living in, one must respect it. If it has values that clash with yours, who are you to judge? Can you claim to know their values are not right for their situation? This moral relativism is being accepted in the name of science; Schwartz and Schwartz have said:

> It is essential [to] recognize the importance of participating with the observed on a 'simply human' level . . . he must share . . . sentiments and feelings with the observed on a sympathetic and empathic level. Thus the observer and observed are bound together through sharing the common role of human being. When the observed become convinced that the observer's attitude towards them is one of respect and interest in them as human beings as well as research subjects, they will feel less need for concealing, withholding, or distorting data. (Schwartz and Schwartz, 1955, p. 347)

These authors are generalising from work among mental patients, which perhaps accounts for the stress on countering wilful interference with the facts rather than inadvertent interference. What is more serious is that they underplay the role in normal relations between human beings of argument, dispute, criticism and censure. Part of respect for strange peoples must include not lying to them and not patronising them. Let us look at what happens in practice.

The Ideal Versus the Practice

What in fact do fieldworkers do? Powdermaker (1966a) faced the dilemma when she was working in the southern USA.[14] She ran into a lynch mob and had a sleepless night wondering what she could do. In the end she did nothing, made no attempt to seek out the victim and aid his escape, expressed no strong opinions to those participating and condoning. Instead she observed and recorded it all. This story, fortunately, has a happy ending: Powdermaker breathed a sigh of relief when the man (who, it transpired, was innocent) got over the state line. But one may argue, as she does, that in any case she was helpless; if she had gone to the police, nothing would have been accomplished; if she had made censorious remarks, her position as a participant observer would have been seriously jeopardized.

Another example is Hunter S. Thompson's sojourn with the Hell's Angels, the motorcycle thugs of California. While he was witness to far less moral and legal crime than might have been expected, he nevertheless observed fights, thefts, assaults, and a semi-public gang-rape. For all his pains in disclosing none of this to the police (that would have jeopardized his status, although he also acted as an intermediary with the police, thus keeping one foot outside any total identification with the Angels), he was himself brutally beaten because he did not accede to the demands of some Angels that he pay them money for the privilege of observing their activities and later making money writing about them (Thompson, 1967).[15] His argument was that journalistic observers make a practice of not paying; their argument was that he was getting something out of hanging around them, so why shouldn't they get something out of having him hang around? The problem is a very sticky one.

It is one thing to agonise over a lynch mob, another to conceal crime for the purposes of science. But where does integrity start? The scientist is saying that above all he must be true to the search for the unbiased truth. In the name of this value of his society, he jettisons ancillary values of his society – or at least he talks as though he thinks he should. Faced with a clash of values in his own society, he would not hesitate vigorously to prosecute an argument over the issue. Why does he hesitate to do so as an anthropologist? The anthropologist, it seems to me, is in danger of forgetting that as well as being a scientist he is a member of the society he came from and will return to and should avoid giving a misleading impression to his hosts either by words or deeds.[16] Truth cuts both ways – he wants not to alienate them, but do they want him to mislead them? Again, what happens in practice?

Fieldworkers watching leaves being put on sores, or incantations being said over tracoma, will often intervene with penicillin. They, thus, break out of the 'humble participant' role and enter the 'powerful-new-medicine' stranger role.[17] Williams (1967) justifies such intervention in the name of truth: 'We could have refused to [give] medical assistance. In doing so, we would have cut off a valuable source of . . . data.'[18] La Farge (1947) utilised suspicion that he was a shaman to force retraction of a curse he felt would endanger the lives of those who had worked for him. Holmberg (1955) chose straightforward intervention to see how it would develop. It seems to me that intervention is probably for the best, since it is more honest both to the natives and to the fieldworker himself. The fieldworker usually comes from a rich and powerful society, possessed of much 'strong medicine', and has education in a cognitive system that is more powerful than the one he is confronting: it does not serve the truth to conceal these facts, however tacitly.

Once again, what happens in practice seems a better guide than the amateurish philosophy of relativism. The fieldworker as a humble supplicant is obviously not often the case. Many people would not tolerate the white stranger snooping around were it not that he belongs, as far as they are concerned, to the powerful white society which they hesitate to brush with. Churlishness and xenophobia may for this reason be curbed and thereby research forwarded. One could argue that this has been the case with research among the Indians on their reservations in the USA and among the Bantu and other people in areas of South Africa, and even with Western research in China. Moreover, fragments of evidence exist which suggest that in the field situation conscious use may have to be made of the 'stranger' position of the stranger in order to elicit information. Bribery in one disguise or another, and even a certain amount of direct bullying, seem to be not uncommon. Malinowski is very frank about this in his diary, where he describes shouting at his informants, and even punching one in the face; and although in other respects the diary is a salutary work, he fails to say that he was obviously exploiting a position of privilege in being rude. A true participant in the society would hardly get away with that!

It can be plausibly argued, it seems to me, that the observer does himself no harm if he acts in integrity towards *his* society and *its* values as far as possible. There is no reason to think the host people will not respect him more for this than for attempting to curry favour by pretending to go along with things that in truth offend, horrify, or disgust him. Deception and hypocrisy are difficult enough to defend in the name of science; and integrity *as a scientist* cannot be overridden in the name of science. If we think science is served by entering into a full and equal relationship with the subjects of study, then both human and scientific integrity require that we do not artificially exclude from those relationships the tensions and clashes which enrich normal relationships. By and large anthropologists act on this, but they do not give it due credit in their methodological discussions.

Notes: Chapter 10

Reprinted from *Current Anthropology*, vol. 10, no. 5, December, 1969, pp. 505–8, by kind permission of the publisher, University of Chicago Press and the author. © 1969 Wenner-Gren Foundation for Anthropological Research. The present chapter was read as a paper to the biennial meeting of the Philosophy of Science Association, Pittsburgh, Pennsylvania, USA, 11 October 1968, and was submitted for publication in *Current Anthropology* on 22 April 1968. Together with a paper by Kloos (1969), which was submitted coincidentally at the same time, it was sent to fifty scholars. The following responded with comments: Joseph P. Aceves, Raymond Apthorpe, H. Russell Bernard, John J. Bodine, Ernest Brandewie, R. S. Freed, Peter C. W. Gutkind, Donn V. Hart, Paul Hinderling, Dorothy L. Keur, Ralph Piddington, Peter Skalnik, Jack O'Waddell and Thomas R. Williams. Their comments are printed in *Current Anthropology*, vol. 10, no. 5, pp. 512–21, and are followed by replies by Jarvie, pp. 521–2, and Kloos, pp. 522–3.

1 For the notions of identity crisis and integrity crisis, see Erikson (1958), pp. 248–57.
2 For an acute dissection of the ambiguities of participant observation which I have labelled 'role-clashes', see Martin (1969). Jarvie (1967) is also relevant. These two papers and the present one, written quite independently, complement each other in interesting ways. Thanks to Michael Martin and Joseph Agassi, both of Boston University, for helpful comments on earlier versions.
3 Doubtless the story involves British claim-staking. The claims of Cushing (fieldwork, 1879–84), Boas (fieldwork, 1883–4) and even Radcliffe-Brown (fieldwork, 1906–8) have been pushed aside by the Malinowski public relations effort.
4 Paul (1953), who reviews the literature, and Barnes (1963) confine themselves to the problems of privacy, publication, stratification and relations with the local authorities.

5 See Evans-Pritchard (1937), p. 270.
6 See Paul (1953), p. 438.
7 See Williams (1967), p. 45; cf. also Forge's (1967) touching description of how he had to list all the relatives he would never see again in order to find a strong enough argument to justify his departure from the field to return to his own society.
8 See Williams (1967), p. 45.
9 Williams (1967), p. 61, sees it as a practice: 'Cultural relativism is an attitude of mind, an awareness of self that can be imparted only to a very limited extent in the classroom, or gained from a text. It must be gained finally in the experiences of living and working for a long period in another culture . . . the attitude . . . is one of being liberated from the parochial truths of one culture.'; cf. Jarvie (1967), pp. 230–1.
10 See Piddington (1957), p. 601.
11 Benedict (1934) and Herskovits (1948a) seem to push this far into relativism; the latter is devastated by Bidney (1953); see also Howard (1968).
12 For maximum *frisson* I recommend the paper on sub-incision by Singer and Desole (1967). At one point the authors comment that their film of 'this initiation rite . . . has made medical psychoanalysts and analyzed psychiatrists blanch and look away'.
13 He suggests that remaining marginal permits freer social movement, but that in addition, the socially marginal anthropologist may find his best sources among socially marginal informants.
14 See Powdermaker (1966a), pp. 188–90.
15 See Thompson (1967), pp. 277–8.
16 There are subtleties here. 'Truth above all' is a value of the subsociety of science located within the wider society. Because the wider society values science, it does not follow that it endorses all the values of its subsocieties. This is a special case of the general problem that every participant observer is not simply 'an example of an often quite alien culture system' (Williams 1967, p. 45) but a possibly atypical product of a society that is to him more of an ideal type than anything else; cf. Lohman (1937), p. 890.
17 Compare the incident described by Heyerdahl (1963), pp. 220–1.
18 See Williams (1967), p. 46.

Section Three

Sampling Strategies in Field Research

11

Elements of Sampling in Field Research

ROBERT G. BURGESS

Sampling is traditionally associated with survey research, yet it is an essential element of all social investigation. It is a means by which a selection is made from the basic unit of study. Clearly, in any population or in any social setting it is impossible to observe or interview everyone and everything. In these circumstances, a sample is used for detailed study. The methodological literature makes a distinction between various types of sampling and it is to these that we now turn. In terms of statistical sampling the basic distinction that is made is between probability and non-probability sampling. Chein has distinguished these forms of sampling in the following terms: 'The essential characteristic of probability sampling is that one can specify for each element of the population the probability that it will be included in the sample' (Chein, 1976, p. 516). While: 'In non-probability sampling, there is no way of estimating the probability that each element has of being included in the sample and no assurance that every element has *some* chance of being included' (Chein, 1976, p. 516; emphasis in original).

In these terms probability sampling includes: simple random sampling, stratified random sampling, cluster sampling, multi-stage sampling and stratified cluster sampling, all of which are discussed in some detail by Moser and Kalton (1971). Non-probability sampling includes: accidental samples, quota samples, judgement samples and snowball samples, all of which are discussed in less detail in the basic methodology texts. A common error has been to equate sampling with survey research and to assume that field research does not involve any form of sampling. Such a position oversimplifies the situation. First, field research, especially in urban and rural localities, has involved surveys of the population which have utilised some form of probability sampling (Stacey, 1960; Stacey *et al.*, 1975; Pons, 1969). Secondly, field researchers employ non-probability sampling in their studies when they select research sites and informants, although it is rare for researchers to provide accounts of the criteria that were employed in such non-probability sampling. However, Honigmann (Chapter 12) does outline the main forms of probability and non-probability sampling that have been used by anthropologists and evaluates the use of these sampling strategies in his own research.

Such work focuses upon statistical sampling. Meanwhile, theoretical sampling has been identified by Glaser and Strauss in the following terms: 'Theoretical sampling is the process of data collection for generating theory whereby the analyst jointly collects, codes and analyses his data and decides what data to collect next and where to find them, in order to develop his theory as it emerges' (Glaser and Strauss, 1967, p. 45). Researchers can, therefore, engage in selection in terms of theoretical sampling which will allow particular categories to emerge out of the data that is gathered. In this way, field researchers can develop, extend, modify and test hypotheses and concepts. As Glaser and Strauss (1967) demonstrate, theoretical sampling confronts the researcher with basic questions: what groups and subgroups are used in data collection? For what theoretical purpose are the groups and subgroups used? Theoretical sampling, therefore, forces researchers to consider what groups to observe, when to observe them, when to stop observing them and what data to gather. Such a position involves researchers in a different sampling strategy as they are directed towards collecting, coding and analysing data during the sampling process.

Denzin (1970) has identified two approaches to sampling that he defines as non-interactive and interactive sampling. The former involves statistically rigorous samples using variables, while the latter involves the analysis of 'natural' behaviour. Denzin considers that theoretical sampling is a variant of interactive sampling and, in turn, suggests differences between theoretical and statistical sampling. First, theoretical sampling does not end until new concepts and categories no longer appear, while statistical sampling ends when a predetermined sample has been observed. Secondly, theoretical sampling is judged by the quality of theory, while statistical sampling is judged by the extent to which it conforms to the 'rules' of sampling theory. Nevertheless, Denzin has identified a series of principles involved in all forms of sampling. First, all sampling must be theoretically directed. Secondly, the researcher must locate and enumerate elements of the sampling frame. Thirdly, the sample must be representative of the population. Fourthly, sampling must continue until a grounded theory is developed. Fifthly, sampling of natural settings must occur, so that observations relevant to theory can be collected. Sixthly, sampling must involve the use of comparisons; and finally, all sampling procedures must be made public. Such principles it is argued, apply to all sampling procedures, and so it is relevant for the researcher to consider the extent to which these principles are used in sampling methods involved in field research. While these principles are useful for the researcher to keep in mind, they are somewhat perfectionist, as actual examples will use different strategies depending on the researcher, the research setting and the theoretical framework of the study. Field researchers need to consider where to observe, when to observe, whom to observe and what to observe. In short, sampling in field research involves the selection of a research site, time, people and events.

The Selection of a Research Site

It is important for researchers to decide where to locate themselves and their studies as this will influence the kind of data that can be gathered. The kinds of questions that all field researchers need to consider are outlined by Strauss *et al.* (1964). Although their questions are directed towards the study of hospitals, they can be utilised by field researchers studying a variety of social settings. Strauss *et al.* (1964) had to consider which hospitals were to be studied. Which wards in the hospitals? Where in the wards should the researchers locate themselves? Should researchers make studies of other locations? Should they attend meetings in the hospitals, and if so, which ones? They argue that, if researchers select one location, it provides them with a particular perspective of the institution, gives them a sense of its rhythm, helps them to piece together recurrent events and builds up their ideas concerning this location. However, this approach may provide researchers with a limited perspective. They suggest that researchers should, therefore, select research sites where they can move around and make comparisons between different groups. In this way, the different perspectives that are employed by participants can become the subject of study. However, if different perspectives are to be examined in an institution, it is vital for the researcher to negotiate entry to different areas of the research site (cf. Mauksch, 1970).

Spradley (1980) has indicated that when selecting a research site a series of factors need to be considered, among which is research mobility. He considers that the researcher needs to select a research site such as a village or a school that will, in turn, provide other situations and subsites for investigation. Secondly, he considers that settings need to be selected for the degree of access they provide, together with the entry that they allow the researcher. Finally, he considers that settings need to be selected that allow researchers to participate in the activities that they plan to study. Sampling,

therefore, begins in field research when the researcher selects one research site rather than another in relation to the research problem that has been formulated.

Time

Within a social organisation, activities may vary with time. Researchers, therefore, have to consider the time dimension in all field situations. They have to sample the activities and events that occur over a period of time (cf. Foster *et al.*, 1979, on long-term field research), as well as the activities that occur at particular hours in the course of a day. In a school there are regular routines associated with breaktimes and lunchtimes and with the division of the day into teaching periods. Here, researchers might utilise the divisions that the participants use to subdivide time, or they might investigate particular aspects of the timetabled day by analysing the activities that take place in a forty-minute lesson (cf. Flanders's interaction analysis, Flanders, 1970, which allows researchers to code and record categories of classroom talk every three seconds). Another structured approach to time sampling has been used to study children in hospitals. Stacey (1969a) indicates that in her study of hospital wards, the researcher devised a system to observe children on the wards during the period 7 a.m. to 7 p.m., this being regarded as their waking hours. The time period was divided into twenty-minute intervals and during five minutes of each of these intervals the child's interaction was recorded in detail, each five-second period being recorded separately. Further details of this method are provided in Stacey *et al.* (1970), where this data is used together with data derived from diaries. A further discussion of this approach to time sampling is provided by Cleary (1979), whose study includes detailed extracts from diaries that observers used to record activities on a children's ward at particular times of the day. It is this type of approach that is discussed by Brookover Bourque and Back (Chapter 13), who indicate ways in which time sampling can be conducted using a 'diary' method and using observations made by the researcher.

In addition to time sampling being conducted over a twelve-hour period or a twenty-four-hour period, some attention has to be given to other aspects of this approach. In a hospital setting it may be important to distinguish between activities that take place by day or by night, during weekdays and weekends and on quiet nights and disturbed nights. Only in this way is it possible for the researcher to arrive at an understanding of the rhythm of the research setting. Another dimension to time sampling occurs in organisations such as hospitals and factories, where shift systems operate. Here, it is important to identify the routines associated with the 'day shift' or the 'night shift'. Further observations may be made by linking these times with observations on different weekdays, or on weekdays as opposed to weekends. In addition, observations can be made at periods that overlap both 'day' and 'night' shifts, so that further comparisons can be made. Time sampling is, therefore, a means by which the field researcher can gather detailed systematic data in a social setting that can be compared with observational material and with data gathered by other methods.

People

Once a researcher has decided where to do research and when to do research, decisions have to be made about the people who are to be researched. In some studies, groups such as patients on a particular hospital ward or children within a particular class, can be clearly defined by the researcher. However, as Ardener (1975) has shown, some groups are subjectively defined by the individuals themselves. Meanwhile, as Becker (1970b) has indicated, some groups such as deviants cannot be clearly defined. In these circumstances, researchers find difficulty concerning whom they should study. This situation has been resolved by some researchers by means of snowball sampling, whereby researchers use informants to introduce them to other members of their group. Such an approach has been utilised by Plant (1975) in studying drugtakers, and by West (1980) in studying deviants. This approach has also been used by other investigators studying groups that they found difficult to contact (for example, McCall, 1980, studying artists, and Hoffman, 1980, studying the directors of a hospital board).

Another major facet of field research is the way in which data is collected from particular informants in some depth. Key informants not only provide detailed data on a particular research setting, but also provide the researcher with introductions to other informants and to other situations. In short, key informants can act as gatekeepers in any study and facilitate access for the researcher. However, as Harrell-Bond (1976) has warned, informants may also close off situations. Furthermore, the 'best' informants may be marginal to the setting under study. Nevertheless, some informants become as well known as the studies in which they appear as, for example, 'Doc' in Whyte's study of *Street Corner Society* (Whyte, 1955). Certainly, anthropologists have also written about the importance of their informants for their field studies (Casagrande, 1960). However, in these circumstances, we might consider the basis upon which individuals are selected. Honigmann indicates that the selection of key informants can be based upon the judgement of the field researcher, or on opportunism when the selection and use of key informants does not follow a strict logical plan, but when the informants are utilised for the special knowledge which they possess. Meanwhile, Tremblay (Chapter 14) indicates a specific set of criteria according to which key informants were chosen

for the Stirling County study.

Key informants can be selected to cover different status levels within an organisation as in Strauss's hospital study (Strauss *et al.*, 1964) where informants were selected to cover different roles and different perspectives. This approach has been advocated by Mauksch (1970) to overcome the problem of management bias in hospital studies that was identified by Roth (1962a). However, the approach can be applied to other settings in which researchers work.

Finally, Spradley (1979) has indicated how informants can be selected by adopting a specific set of criteria. First, he considers that any individuals who are selected to be key informants should have been part of the social setting for at least a year. However, it may be useful to use new members of an organisation as they have other insights. Secondly, he argues that researchers should consider the kind of involvement that their informants have as it is vital for the researcher to use experts. However, novices can provide another useful perspective of the research setting. Thirdly, he maintains that informants need to be chosen for the extent to which they may represent a cultural scene and for their non-analytic abilities. However, this depends on the purpose of the study. Finally, he claims that informants need to be chosen for the detail that they can provide. However, in this context Miller (1952) has warned field researchers to beware of focusing too much on the articulate as they may become ill-tuned to the inarticulate.

Events

Field researchers may need to follow up particular situations and events depending on the hypotheses which they develop, or the theories which they wish to generate. Schatzman and Strauss (1973) have indicated that it is important for the field researcher to distinguish between three discrete sets of events: the routine, the special and the untoward. By routine events, they have in mind situations that regularly occur. Special events are defined as situations that are fortuitous, but nevertheless anticipated; while untoward events are defined as emergency situations (a theme which will be taken up in more detail in Section Nine, especially in the work of Turner (Chapter 33) and Morgan (Chapter 34)). These different kinds of events may need to be selectively sampled over a specific week in which the research occurs, or over a longer period of time. In some cases, events such as a wedding (Leonard, 1980) or a funeral (Loudon, 1961), may only be observed on one occasion during the course of field research. However, a single event may be compared with similar events which researchers might have reported to them by their key informants. Finally, as Honigmann indicates, events and situations may be systematically observed using a field guide as was done by Whiting and his associates in the study of socialisation (Whiting *et al.*, 1966).

In sampling events, the field researcher also utilises the sampling strategies that have been employed elsewhere, as the events that are observed may depend on the research site that has been selected, the key informants that have been used and the times when observations have been made. Sampling is a research strategy that needs to be carefully considered by the field researcher as it can help in the systematic collection of data. However, it is not always possible to use statistical sampling procedures. Researchers need to adopt sampling strategies that will focus on the sociological characteristics of the groups and individuals that are studied. In this respect, field researchers need to understand the principles involved in sampling strategies and the way in which they can be combined. For, in practice, the researcher has to apply sampling strategies to particular research problems as it is rarely possible to follow the ideal strategies outlined in textbooks.

Suggestions for Further Reading

METHODOLOGY

Adams, R. N. and Preiss, J. J. (1960) (eds) *Human Organization Research: Field Relations and Techniques* (Homewood, Ill.: Dorsey Press); provides a range of sociological and anthropological papers on field research. See the chapters on the selection of informants.

Arrington, R. E. (1943), 'Time sampling in studies of social behaviour: a critical review of techniques and results with research suggestions', *Psychological Bulletin*, vol. 40, no. 2, pp. 81–124; provides a detailed appraisal of time sampling and contains an extensive bibliography.

Boehm, A. and Weinberg, R. A. (1977), *The Classroom Observer: a Guide for Developing Observational Skills* (New York: Teachers College Press). See unit five that provides a discussion of time and event sampling in classrooms.

Casagrande, J. (1960) (ed.), *In the Company of Man* (New York: Harper & Row). A collection of essays by anthropologists on their key informants.

Glaser, B. G. and Strauss, A. L. (1967), *The Discovery of Grounded Theory: Strategies for Qualitative Research* (Chicago: Aldine); the third chapter provides a useful discussion of theoretical sampling.

Kish, L. (1965), *Survey Sampling* (New York: Wiley); gives a highly technical discussion of sampling that is worth examining.

Moser, C. A. and Kalton, G. (1971), *Survey Methods in Social Investigation* (2nd edn) (London: Heinemann); contains a series of chapters on sampling. Although the discussion focuses on surveys, it is not inappropriate to field research.

Naroll, R. and Cohen, R. (1973) (eds), *A Handbook of Method in Cultural Anthropology* (New York: Columbia University Press); a collection of papers that emphasises some quantitative aspects of field research. See the papers in part 3.

Pelto, P. J. and Pelto, G. H. (1978), *Anthropological Research: The Structure of Inquiry* (Cambridge: CUP). A basic text on the use of positivist methods in anthropology. See chapter 7.

Schatzman, L. and Strauss, A. (1973), *Field Research: Strategies for a Natural Sociology* (Englewood Cliffs, NJ: Prentice-Hall); contains a useful chapter on sampling strategies (chapter 3).

Selltiz, C., Wrightsman, L. S. and Cook, S. W. (1976), *Research Methods in Social Relations* (3rd edn) (New York: Holt Rinehart & Winston); contains a good appendix on probability and non-probability sampling (Chein, 1976).

EMPIRICAL STUDIES

There are numerous empirical studies that utilise sampling techniques in the course of doing field research. However, very few studies explicitly discuss sampling strategies in this context. Studies that utilise probability and non-probability sampling:

Pons, V. (1969), *Stanleyville: an African Urban Community under Belgian Administration* (London: OUP for the International African Institute).

Stacey, M. (1960), *Tradition and Change: a Study of Banbury* (Oxford: OUP).

Stacey, M., Batstone, E., Bell, C. and Murcott, A. (1975), *Power Persistence and Change: a Second Study of Banbury* (London: Routledge & Kegan Paul).

Studies that utilise key informants:

Liebow, E. (1967), *Tally's Corner: a Study of Negro Street Corner Men* (Boston, Mass.: Little, Brown).

Parker, H. (1974), *View from the Boys*, (Newton Abbot: David & Charles).

Patrick, J. (1973), *a Glasgow Gang Observed* (London: Eyre-Methuen).

Whyte, W. F. (1955), *Street Corner Society* (2nd edn) (Chicago: University of Chicago Press).

For studies using snowball sampling:

Plant, M. (1975), *Drugtakers in an English Town* (London: Tavistock).

Shaffir, W. B., Stebbins, R. A. and Turowetz, A. (1980) (eds), *Fieldwork Experience: Qualitative Approaches to Social Research* (New York: St Martin's Press) (see especially the essays by Hoffman, 1980; McCall, 1980; and West, 1980).

For studies using time sampling:

Foster, G. M., Scudder, T., Colson, E. and Kemper, R. V. (1979) (eds), *Long-Term Field Research in Social Anthropology* (London: Academic Press).

Hall, D. and Stacey, M. (1979) (eds), *Beyond Separation: Further Studies of Children in Hospital*, (London: Routledge & Kegan Paul) (see the essay by Cleary, 1979).

Stacey, M., Dearden, R., Pill, R. and Robinson, D. (1970), *Hospitals, Children and their Families*, (London: Routledge & Kegan Paul).

12

Sampling in Ethnographic Fieldwork

JOHN J. HONIGMANN

Two Kinds of Sampling

An ethnographer cannot avoid selecting some people, objects, or events for study, thereby renouncing, for a time at least, the possibility of studying others. From a vast range of possibilities, he takes up work in a particular tribe, village, or town; questions certain respondents; employs a few informants; observes some artefacts, situations, or behavioural events, and makes observations at restricted times. If the word 'sampling' is used so broadly, then fieldworkers are constantly sampling the universe of people, situations, objects and behavioural events with which they are occupied. Seldom, however, do they keep track of how they drew a sample or report its composition. Even statements as general as my pseudonymous list of principal Kaska Indian informants and subjects,[1] and Margaret Mead's 'neighbourhood maps',[2] identifying the adolescent and pre-adolescent girls she observed, are rare. An anthropologist characteristically extends his remarks beyond his sample and talks about 'the' Kaska Indians and Samoan girls or about child rearing, quarrels and pottery techniques in general – as though he had studied the community, category, or topic exhaustively. The usual spoken implication is that for his problem, the sample adequately represented a larger universe of actors, topics, culture patterns, techniques, or other units under study and, therefore, could provide reliable information about that universe as it existed at a particular time. A statistically conscious observer might object and point out that for a sample to be considered in a strict sense representative of the universe whence it came, it must have been selected in a suitable manner. Anthropologists are likely to respond by protesting that it is not they who decide what persons or events to use as sources of data; such decisions are practically made for them when certain individuals volunteer their help, some groups extend welcome, and some techniques happen to be accessible to observation.[3] That units force themselves on a researcher's attention, is merely a figure of speech. It overlooks the fieldworker's readiness to respond positively or negatively to certain cues in the field situation and ignores his active involvement in deciding how to respond to environmental opportunities or when to surrender to unbreachable limitations.

However strongly some stimuli 'compel' the ethnographer's attention, it will repay him to be aware of the character of his sample, beginning with the basic distinction between non-probability and probability methods of drawing it. The first term refers to sampling in the general sense in which I have so far used the word. Probability sampling designates a method that specifically intends every unit in the universe under study to have the same known probability of being studied. If the universe totals 100 people, houses, hours, or garden plots, and we want to study ten, then the probability of any unit being included in the sample is one in ten. Actual selection of a probability sample follows definite rules, the most important one requiring the units of the sample to be drawn at random; hence the familiar name for such sampling, random sampling. The unparalleled advantages of probability sampling, which recommend it for certain kinds of social science research, will be pointed out in due course. My object in this chapter is to review both types of sampling as they have been or can be applied in ethnography. I shall develop, first, how anthropologists use and defend use of non-probability sampling methods in studies of culture and then review random sampling. Since certain procedures connected with defining the universe to be sampled before actual sampling begins are common to both probability and non-probability sampling, they will be mentioned in both places.

Non-Probability Sampling

SELECTING A PLACE TO WORK

If cultural anthropology is ultimately concerned with achieving generalisations applicable to man in general, then sampling begins when an ethnographer chooses to explore the lifeways of one social aggregate rather than another and, having made that choice, narrows down his objective to look for a locality to settle in. John Beattie (1965)[4] chose Bunyoro on the advice of an Africanist after discovering that another anthropologist had already begun to work with the group of his first choice. Out of the many local communities constituting Bunyoro, he sought one that, as far as he could judge at the time, was 'reasonably representative . . . as typical as possible of rural Bunyoro'. Judgement sampling of this sort, which seeks to meet specific criteria, is most likely to be successful when it is informed by expert knowledge. Beattie, being a novice, gained such knowledge from others, a relatively rich literature undoubtedly assisting him in making his choice. He also wanted a community off the main roads and away from bureaucratic centres, yet reasonably accessible. Criteria for selecting a site may follow logically from the research problem and accompanying theory. Southall and Gutkind (1956)[5] in their survey of Kampala sought two areas for their sample survey, one to represent the densest type of uncontrolled and primarily African urban settlement in the Kampala area, and the other an intermediate situation representing a transition towards maximal density from a previously rural community. In 1952 I went to Pakistan to study the impact of US informational films on rural audiences, the country itself having been designated for me by an agency in the State Department.[6] Available time would permit me to pay reasonably close attention to only three villages and I determined to concentrate them in West Pakistan. Here, I sought to sample as much of heterogeneous territory as possible by studying one village in three of the most populous provinces out of the ten or so political units then constituting the country's west wing. This allowed me to include three major languages in my sample, for, I asked myself, if the country possessed several languages, how did films containing only Urdu narration communicate their content? When it came to selecting villages, logistics and a sufficient degree of isolation from urban influence became critical guides in judging suitability. In Karachi, Lahore, Peshawar and an upcountry town, I sought to make contacts with knowledgeable people who could recommend a village that would be accessible to a mobile unit carrying projection equipment. Guarantees of welcome and a place to live also influenced my decision where to settle. Specifications for an eligible unit to study may be even more explicit, like those Whiting and his associates (1966) demand for a primary social unit (PSU).[7] Defined as a stable social group located within a larger social group, consisting of about thirty mutually interacting families set off from the larger society by some social factor in such a way that they conceive of themselves as a kind of social unit, a PSU must provide the investigators with variables both antecedent and consequent to child rearing. It represents a culture 'cut down to manageable size'. Factors of temporal stability and spatial homogeneity listed in decreasing order of importance are: territorial unity; membership in a common kinship group, like a clan; membership in a common school district; common religion; membership in a common economic association; membership in the same social class; and membership in the same recreational group.

Once he settles down in a locality and begins to work,

an ethnographer has no way of knowing how the behaviour patterns and artefacts he observes represent the social system's larger culture, except as reading or informants extend his knowledge. Yet he may title his monograph to refer to the culture or social system as a whole, only in the prefatory pages incidentally designating the precise universe he investigated.

SELECTING PEOPLE TO STUDY: JUDGEMENT AND OPPORTUNISTIC SAMPLING

Further sampling occurs when the fieldworker chooses steady informants, perhaps following criteria like those Tremblay (1957) specifies for key informants or else working with whoever turns up and shows a readiness and ability to provide information. Note that I am not so much drawing a distinction between the degrees of intensiveness with which an anthropologist works with people – the informants who are steadily employed and may become practically surrogates of the fieldworker compared to those only casually observed or engaged in conversation. I am stressing the deliberateness with which any subjects are chosen. Informants selected by virtue of their status (age, sex, occupation) or previous experience, qualities which endow them with special knowledge that the ethnographer values, are chosen by a type of non-probability sampling best called judgement sampling. The ethnographer uses his prior knowledge of the universe to draw representatives from it who possess distinctive qualifications. He may, for example, select informants or subjects according to class strata, occupational status, sex, age, or length of residence in the community. Spindler (1955)[8] to a large extent employed judgement sampling in obtaining sixty-eight adult Menomini males, all recorded as being at least one-half Menomini Indian. He selected subjects 'to represent all degrees of observable socioeconomic status from the richest to the poorest; and all degrees of cultural participation', or acculturational status. While he would have preferred to draw his sample by some random method, he knew it to be even more important to have subjects of different economic and cultural status with whom he could establish rapport sufficient to obtain the intimate social and psychological data his research problem demanded. He later allowed his subjects a hand in choosing additional respondents:

> At each sociocultural level, a few known individuals, friendly to me, were treated with first, then a minimum of three names of other persons was obtained from them and at least one of these persons was obtained as a case, using his acquaintance with the first subject as a means of introduction. These cases in turn designated other possibilities. A number of other cases were 'picked up' as contacts were made in many casual conversations.

Spindler recognised the possibility of bias serious

enough to affect the outcome of his research arising from the possible selection of persons corresponding to certain personality types. Unconscious selection of persons to whom he could relate, he acknowledges, would have tended to reduce the variability of personality types in his sample. However, inspection of his data gave no evidence that such selection actually operated, except for the fact that only four people he chose declined to co-operate with him. Another example of judgement sampling comes from my own experience. In Frobisher Bay, Baffin Island, I had available abundant payroll records of the town's largest employer of Eskimo labour, the government. My wife and I sampled them for only four months, July and December (1962) and March and May (1963). We sought to cover the year without over-representing the summer season when employment is very high and winter when jobs are scarce.[9] Definite limits restrict the extent to which judgement sampling can be applied before the fieldworker knows something about the composition of the universe being investigated. The population may have to be carefully stratified to allow sufficient representation for important constituent categories, as well as explicity defined, for example to determine who is a Menomini Indian or what summer and winter are at the latitude of Frobisher Bay. Anthony F. C. Wallace (1952)[10] is exceptionally clear concerning the way he went about choosing a sample that represented the age and sex distribution of Tuscarora Indians, to whom he proposed to administer Rorschach tests. His census revealed a total of 353 persons aged 16 and older who were sociologically Tuscarora. (He specifies the conscious rule by which he decided who in that sense was a Tuscarora.) Then he calculated the number of records necessary to preserve in the sample the same proportions that existed in the population at large, calculating these figures on the expectation that he could deal with a total of about 100 persons (or Rorschach records). He first allowed an informant to select individuals of requisite age and sex. Later, as Wallace got to know more people, he himself suggested subjects for testing. He justifies logically his belief that these methods of selection introduced very little bias, though once his guide shocked him by commenting on twenty persons who had already been tested, saying they represented the 'better element' of Tuscarora society. Apparently the assistant used the word 'better' to describe people whom he personally knew and liked and, therefore, had chosen. This revelation distressed Wallace less than the thought that 'better element' might have referred to socioeconomic levels, to which he had given no consideration in preparing his sampling design.

Non-probability judgement sampling demands a clearcut definition of the universe about which the sample is intended to provide information. Such a decision is often difficult to make. What is the community and where are its boundaries?[11] How are people in a PSU connected? How shall a Tuscarora Indian be defined? What situations are likely to be most rewarding with certain kinds of information? I will have more to say about the critical judgement required in designing sampling frames in the section devoted to random sampling.

If the concept of sampling is strictly limited to some such *deliberate* selection of typical or representative units, then an anthropologist's partly self-selected informants or subjects for observation are not obtained by sampling at all. However, I have already indicated that I propose to ignore such strict usage. The term 'opportunistic sampling' is available for the familiar process by which fieldworkers find many of the people who provide them with ethnographic information. Such sampling follows no strict, logical plan.[12] The perimeters of the sampled universe are poorly drawn and the procedure itself is so situationally variable, as well as being idiosyncratically influenced by the personal qualities of the particular ethnographer, that it becomes well-nigh impossible for another person to replicate. I recall one use of opportunistic sampling during my first ethnographic trip to West Pakistan. The abundant visitors who voluntarily came to my home served as respondents for innumerable questions; I sought to plumb their motivations and other personality characteristics, and in some cases begged them to take the Rorschach test. Occasionally I solicited my guests with my interview schedule (that had been prepared for a random sample) to learn if they had attended the motion-picture showings, and if so, what they had seen and heard. Responses from such opportunistically selected subjects were kept separate from those of randomly selected subjects. Subsequently I compared both samples, as I will report later in this chapter. My wife and children also utilised invitations to the homes of relatively well-to-do or high-ranking families as opportunities to observe certain aspects of domestic life and to obtain other information, though success in such matters depended on the extent to which hosts were bilingual or could be conveniently interviewed through a bilingual relative. Such opportunistic sampling can also be called 'chunk sampling', meaning that the researcher resourcefully seizes any handy chunk of the universe that promises to reward him with relevant information: he observes whatever children or mothers are available, visits receptive households, tests willing adults, records remarks he overhears or has volunteered to him, and attends almost any public meetings, church services and entertainments that he happens to hear about. But since this method calls for acting opportunistically in all such situations, we might as well call it opportunistic sampling.

Judgement and opportunistic, non-probability sampling represent degrees of deliberateness exercised in choosing informants, subjects, situations, or behavioural events. One type does not exclude the other. Opportune social contacts may be exploited for the special knowledge they possess, as my wife and I did with the lawyers, farmers, teachers, Islamic scholars, women and political leaders we met in Pakistan. The information provided by such casually selected respondents is interpreted or evaluated according to the status he or she represents, and it possesses limited value until significant dimensions of the person's status have been identified. I shall have more to say about identifying opportunistically selected people or situations and about interpreting the information they provide. Such procedures, which in effect convert opportunistic into judgement samples, have been called distinctive of ethnographic fieldwork.

SELECTING BEHAVIOUR AND SITUATIONS TO OBSERVE

I have spoken about sampling places and people in non-probability fashion but only incidentally have I mentioned sampling behavioural episodes themselves (which, to be sure, always include people). An ethnographer from time to time deliberately assigns himself to observe particular situations and events. Undoubtedly, he initially learns much about an as yet unfamiliar culture by seizing convenient opportunities to study behaviour and artefacts that catch his eye and ear. Casual observations of cattle returning to the village, men, ploughing, carpenters repairing a cart-wheel and mothers interacting with children eventually serve him to construct ethnographic statements about agriculture, industries and child rearing. Informants may themselves be asked to sample by reporting cases of certain kinds of behaviour they have observed, thereby extending the ethnographer's observational range. The photographs and drawings of objects in published monographs report 'typical' samples chosen by non-probability methods. 'Typical' in this sense means that an object has been selected for illustration, because the author judges it characteristic of the class of objects to which it belongs. In the same way, a typical wedding, game, or other behavioural event may be written up at length. (On the other hand, an episode occurring only once during the researcher's presence in the community is better reported as a single case without any assumption about its typicalness unless informants provide comparative information.)

Sampling for behaviour can be quite systematically organised when the ethnographer goes into the field equipped with a carefully planned research design. Whiting and his associates (1966)[13] in a fieldguide they prepared for studies of socialisation in five cultures list a number of observations to be made of children, the object of which is to learn about prescribed situations that arise in various settings in which children spend their day and about how they respond in such situations. 'Settings' means general cultural activities limited by time and place (for example, sleeping, break-fast, playing in the schoolyard after school, and so on), and 'situations' designates specific social conditions that instigate responses. Twelve situations likely to promote responses are specified, including assaults, insults, hurts, encounters with difficulties, requests for help and reprimands. The manual contains procedural rules for identifying such situations and responses in culturally specific terms as well as instructions for classifying the data. An observer is told to construct a schedule of a child's typical day in the PSU where he is working, and where he is able to identify specific children. The schedule will indicate settings to be sampled for the situations they contain. He is instructed to make twelve five-minute observations on each child spaced as widely as possible over time and setting to yield a one-hour sample of each child's behaviour. The fieldworker has a problem of distributing his time among the various settings in a way that will maximise observation in settings yielding the richest data and still cover a representative sample of the child's activities. In general, he is told to divide his time in proportion to the time children spend in each setting, to undersample settings (like sleeping) where the twelve situations occur rarely, or where response varies little, and to oversample settings where situations occur abundantly and response varies greatly. He is also advised to photograph and even to take movies of the most frequent settings a child encounters in a community. The twelve five-minute observations are expected to indicate frequency with which the twelve prescribed situations arise and the probability with which each type occurs. The data will later permit cross-cultural analysis of differences in the probabilities of occurrence as well as differences between subgroups and individuals belonging to the PSU. The fact that instructions had to be altered after the ethnographers had reached the field and begun to report on problems facing them in their various locations indicates the difficulty anthropologists face in preplanning their sampling and general research designs before learning something about the culture.

EVALUATING NON-PROBABILITY SAMPLING IN ANTHROPOLOGY

Non-probability sampling in ethnography along with associated practices like reliance on non-quantitative procedures and on unimodal patterns of behaviour undoubtedly consitute the most debated technique in the fieldworker's armamentarium. Not only do persons in adjacent disciplines voice scepticism, but also, particularly when certain kinds of research like national character studies are involved, anthropologists themselves.[14] Critics point out that judgement and opportunistic sampling allow no way of knowing precisely the degree to which a sample corresponds to the universe it represents and therefore casts doubt on the reliability, perhaps even the general validity, of the information it provides. To argue that a sample of 600 Vassar College girls mostly of middle-class background adequately reflects the predominantly middle-class culture of the USA does not compensate for the lack of any empirical information about, say, lower-class girls.[15] Wallace (1952)[16] sampled to ensure a representative age and sex distribution in his adult Tuscarora protocols, but did he not invite serious bias to enter his sample by allowing his assistant to select 43 per cent of the tested subjects? Bias so introduced may indeed be minor, but the degree to which those subjects represented the Tuscarora adult universe in other than age or sex characteristics must remain clouded by some doubt. Many anthropologists have been troubled by such criticism. Yet most of us continue to use judgement and opportunistic samples, and I would not dream of suggesting we cease. We use such samples not primarily because our field problem is usually so enormous and our time so limited that we cannot afford to use the several probability samples that our multifaceted research would require in order to be clearly representative. Our adherence to traditional anthropological fieldwork methods of sampling rests on the assumption that the questions put in research can frequently be satisfactorily answered through samples selected by non-probability methods.

Why should we expect that non-probability sampling will work in the study of technology, social structure and idea systems as anthropologists commonly pursue such topics? What logical reason do we have for believing that judgemental and more casually chosen samples will provide an ethnographer with satisfactory factual information about particular cultural systems? As a minimum definition of satisfactoriness, I would demand that the empirical propositions in an ethnography be objectively replicated in a high proportion of cases. While some notable differences of fact have indeed arisen between anthropologists who have reported on the 'same' culture, when the few restudies we have are considered, the extent of agreement between professional investigators who have reported on the 'same' culture (given a loose, unstandardised criteria of agreement) seem to outweigh disagreements.[17] This indicates that anthropological sampling works and is to a tolerable degree reliable, given the current standards of ethnographic reliability and my qualitative method of appraising reliability. The question I ask is: why does it work as well as it does? A general answer holds that a common culture is reflected in practically every person, event and artefact belonging to a common system. In a community, nearly every source of data an ethnographer consults – each informant, subject, event and artefact – in some degree or in some way reveals consistencies with many other sources (corresponding to the same or a different type) that he consults. Accounts of child rearing by several informants partially fit together with one another and agree with observed instances of child rearing. The fit may not be as perfect as the interlocking of pieces in a jigsaw puzzle, but such an analogy is nevertheless useful. A Sindhi landlord's actions, though vastly different from his tenant farmer's, meshes with certain aspects of the latter's, and the landlord's luxurious rural dwelling is in some respects comparable to the tenant's hovel or referable to the tenant's labour, passivity, powerlessness and so on. It is with such consistencies and comparable aspects abstracted from the sample that we build up an integrated picture of a culture. No two reporters use the same facts in the same way, but some of the same facts recognisably appear in different anthropologists' treatments of the same culture or social system. Use of judgement and opportunistic samples in fieldwork is predicated on the researcher's primary interest in the *system* of behaviour rather than in the way behavioural traits or individuals with specific characteristics are distributed in a known universe whose systematic nature is either taken for granted or ignored.[18] If the system is composed of subgroups, then such subgroups are sampled for whatever information they can contribute concerning the whole system.

The person who has most tried to explain how traditional anthropological sampling works is Margaret Mead.[19] Confining her discussion mainly to the selection of people by non-probability methods, she points out the vital importance of identifying informants by salient characteristics they possess which are capable of affecting the validity of information they produce. (The same rule, as I will bring out later, applies to certain kinds of cultural products.) Hence, accomplished ethnography calls for 'skill of evaluating an individual informant's place in a social and cultural whole and then recognizing the formal patterns, explicit and implicit, of his culture expressed in his spontaneous verbal statements and his behaviour'.[20] When the sample is a human being, his identification is made in terms of more than his representative status or social characteristics:

the validity of the sample depends not so much upon the number of cases as upon the proper specification of the informant, so that he or she can be accurately placed, in terms of a very large number of variables – age, sex, order of birth, family background, lifeexperience, temperamental tendencies (such as optimism, habit of exaggeration, etc.), political and religious position, exact situational relationship to the investigator, configurational relationship to every other informant, and so forth. Within this extensive degree of specification, each informant is studied as a perfect example, an organic representation of his complete cultural experience. This specification of the informant grew up historically as a way of dealing with the few survivors of broken and vanished cultures and is comparable to the elaboration with which the trained historian specifies the place of a crucial document among the few and valuable documents available for a particular period. (Mead, 1953)[21]

Again like a historian working with documents, an anthropologist drawing information from expressive cultural products like novels or films notes salient characteristics of their authors 'so as, in the end, to be able to discount . . . individual differences'.[22] A single life history is representative of a community's culture to the degree that the individual it portrays has been involved in experiences common to other (not necessarily all) individuals. To that degree, the subject's life history becomes a model of his culture which the anthropologist can use in building *his* model.[23] Even a relative stranger, like the Hudson's Bay Company manager serving an Indian community in northern Canada, or the visiting missionary, becomes representative in the sense that he is capable of providing information about the Indians' culture, but his special cultural and social position must be known and carefully considered in appraising what he says or does.[24]

Such diverse sources of data open ethnography to the charge that it relies on unstandardised modes of procedure and is haphazard or impressionistic in its approach, charges that Mead (1955) takes pains to rebut when she emphasises that an anthropologist in his work follows rules different from those employed in other social sciences but does not operate totally without discipline. The ethnologist who combines information from novels, from living informants and even utilises his own personal experience in another culture to construct his final model of the culture or social personality may have sampled informants and behavioural settings opportunistically, but he did not do so haphazardly if he kept in mind what his sources represented. Safeguards in anthropological sampling include cross-checking information one receives from different sources, using every datum to test the soundness of the model as it is built and comparing each to data employed before, examining it for inconsistencies, contradictions, and incongruities. 'Anthropological sampling is not a poor and inadequate version of sociological or sociopsychological sampling, a version where *n* equals too few cases', Mead (1953) claims, '*it is simply a different kind of sampling*'.[25]

With so much importance put on identifying salient characteristics of human samples in fieldwork, it becomes imperative for the ethnographer to keep records of the people he studies – not merely their names but generous amounts of biographical and other data relevant for understanding information they provide. Indexing of fieldnotes not merely by categories like those given in the *Outline of Cultural Materials*, but by names, is essential so that the full set of notes referring to any individual can be used to augment

formal biographical data available about him and, thus, round out knowledge of him that will help to place any particular behaviour or statement referring to him in the fullest possible, meaningful context. What *X* tells me on one occasion is apt to assume special significance, once I know certain of his previous behaviour, and have retrieved it from my records. In this way, long-term research in single communities will someday benefit through comprehensive data banks established for persons and for entire families.[26] When the ideal of full, individual identification becomes unrealisable, as in studying a large community like a nation or a city involving many subjects who, therefore, must remain for the most part anonymous, other methods can be employed to achieve a similar result. Mead (1953)[27] suggests random sampling, or 'positional studies in which small complex parts of the total structure are carefully localised and intensively studied', like organisations or several shops in a factory. Or else 'the intensive analysis of segments of the culture which are unsystematically related to each other and overlap in a variety of ways' are consulted (in Russian national cultural studies such segments have included novels, proceedings of the Communist Party congress, and controls on Soviet industry). Rhoda Métraux (1943)[28] also speaks of positional sampling used to interview specific groups for information about food habits, including grocers and persons waiting in line to register for ration cards. In a heterogeneous social system, therefore, work in any sampled subgroup is done knowing, or while learning, salient characteristics of that subgroup with respect to the whole, just as in sampling persons or cultural products. Special attention might have to be given to a subgroup, if its members are playing a particularly decisive political role in a nation.

Anthropological methods of sampling, Mead (1952; 1953)[29] maintains, are logical as long as the fieldworker expects mainly to use his data not to answer questions like 'how much' and 'how often' but to solve *qualitative* problems, such as discovering what occurs, the implications of what occurs, and the relationships linking occurrences. Anthropological sampling serves the ethnologist, who is primarily engaged in searching for patterns that occur and recur in diverse sets of social relations, 'between employer and employee, writer and reader, and so on', including between parents and children.[30] Such patterns can be constructed from information provided by identified living informants augmented by bits of data obtained from cultural productions, like paintings, plays, or movies. The latter data are 'cross-integrated' with observed behaviour and statements provided by informants.[31] She illustrates from linguistics:

If one wants to know the grammatical structure of a language, it is sufficient to use very few informants about whom the necessary specified information has been collected; if one wants to know how many people use a certain locution or a particular work in preference to another, then sampling of the wider type is necessary.

Mead's account of judgement sampling stops short of demonstrating how the information so obtained is utilised in ethnographies in ways that avoid undue overgeneralisation. It hardly suffices to be told that 'any cultural statement must be made in such a way that the addition of another class of informants previously unrepresented will not change the nature of the statement in a way which has not been allowed for in the original statement',[32] or to be warned that the representativeness of the informants must be included in statements as, for example, 'These statements are made about the culture prevailing in the rural south among people living in communities of less than twenty-five hundred people'. Can all new information by hitherto unrepresented samples be anticipated? How precisely can samples be identified in ethnographic statements? I doubt if such rules can regularly be followed when large amounts of information must be reported. Such criticism, however, may be unfair, for one of the crucial problems in traditional anthropological method, and one we understand very poorly due no doubt to the extent to which a personal element is involved, is precisely the matter of what happens to data after they have been collected in the field and prior to the point where they turn up in the stylised prose of a monograph.

It is well to guard against using the term 'anthropological sampling' without bearing in mind that no probability methods of sampling apply in anthropology only to the extent that ethnographers, in fact, pursue research interests like those stated, or interests consistent with ends such sampling can serve. I think it noteworthy that Mead does not defend non-probability sampling by referring to the predominant homogeneity of small-scale communities which renders random sampling unnecessary.[33] Neither homogeneity nor heterogeneity by itself constitutes a sufficient basis for choosing between probability or non-probability sampling methods. We may safely assume that in any community, regardless of whether it is large or small in scale, individuals embody or enact culture differently, and so do families. To that extent, a degree of heterogeneity is universal. A research problem that seeks to capitalise on internal ('intracultural') variations of behaviour between a fairly large number of individuals or families in communities of any scale would undoubtedly find probability sampling advantageous.

Probability Sampling

SELECTING A SAMPLE[34]

A probability sample is called for whenever it is useful to know within precise margins of error how often units (people, artefacts, activities, attitudes, or opinions) with particular features occur in a universe of such phenomena that is too large or for some other reason difficult to investigate *in toto*. The word 'features' covers any question that can be incorporated in an interview schedule and any variable to which an observer can give attention. The carefully planned process of selection used to obtain a probability sample comes close to creating a miniature, unbiased replica or cross-section of the sampled phenomena. Due to the underlying mathematical theory of probability sampling,[35] such samples can be employed with considerable, known confidence for the light they throw on the universe from which the sample was drawn. Laws of chance or probability, rather than expert knowledge or self-selection, govern the way representatives of that universe are chosen. The very role that chance plays in drawing the sample can be known. Put another way, the probability sampling tells us what percentage of the time we can expect our sample to be representative of the universe from which it is drawn. Such practical and mathematical advantages are important reasons for the widespread use of sampling in science. In what follows I will be mainly concerned with random sampling, the best-known method of probability sampling. In this method, each unit in the sampled universe enjoys an equal chance of being drawn.

In preparing to choose a probability sample by random selection, the first step is to construct a sampling frame. A sampling frame is the sampled universe drawn together in some convenient fashion for sampling. It often differs from the target universe, that is, from the total population which the anthropologist may be studying. In a moment I will bring up some of the problems connected with generalising from the sampled universe to the target universe. Here, it suffices to say that all the safety we enjoy in making statistical inferences from the random sample to the sampled universe disappears once we extend knowledge gained from the sample beyond the sampling frame to the target universe. The sampling frame may consist of a stack of newspapers, a herd of cows (if the object is, say, to discover milk yield), a street map of a city, or a list of people. A satisfactory census or other enumeration of people may already be available in the community or at some capital to serve as a sampling frame. If not, or if the census is suspected to be incomplete, the fieldworker will have to make his own enumeration. He can often save time in doing so by utilising available knowledge, as Fortes and his co-workers[36] did when the Ashanti survey began its enumeration using lists of household heads taken from the taxrolls. Often it proves too difficult or impossible to construct a sampling frame that coincides with the target universe which the ethnographer is studying. Baeck (1961)[37] was interested in the consumption patterns of well-to-do

Congolese in Leopoldville, but restricted himself to drawing a sample of government clerks earning incomes above a certain figure who were also household heads. He used a payroll list as his frame. His sample, of course, included no other occupations that may have been represented among well-to-do Congolese. Peter Marris (1961)[38] would have preferred to sample households in Lagos, but because he found no adequate list of such units, he had to settle for individuals drawn from a census. In Pakistan I wanted to know about both men's and women's presence at, and reaction to, the motion pictures shown in the three villages I had selected, but purdah did not permit me to construct sampling frames including women's names. In Frobisher Bay we wanted to know about Eskimo drinking, but could best find out the Eskimo men who had received permits to deal with the Territorial liquor store. We used a 100 per cent sample of such people.[39]

There is a danger of error whenever the researcher generalises beyond the sampling frame. To avoid or reduce such error, the ethnographer may specify the relationship between the sampling frame and the target universe, for example, the degree to which well-to-do Congolese are represented by government clerks earning above a certain figure. He may decide to restrict his conclusions to the sampled universe, at that point shedding all interest in the target universe. We did this to a large extent when, under the heading of 'Eskimo drinking', I confined most of our discussion to purchases made by permit-holders in Frobisher Bay, merely indicating that there were some teetotalers and that a small, unknown amount of illegal home-brewing occurred. The ethnographer may also, if time permits, increase the number of sampling frames in order to cover as large a portion of the target universe as possible. In Leopoldville, for example, he might have added to the payroll list a tax list of household heads and drawn from it a random sample of householders who pay amounts above a certain figure. If one employs the sampling frame to make wider generalisations, it can be done by basing what is said on well-founded knowledge of the target universe and of the subject matter being studied. Thus, because many Pashto-speaking male respondents in Pakistan failed to understand the filmtrack's Urdu narration, it was even less likely that Pashto-speaking mature women would; their seclusion, I reason, has allowed them little opportunity to learn Urdu. Often the sampling frame represents a more or less satisfactory compromise between studying the target universe directly and utilising available sources of information or working within time limits available to the ethnographer. Compromise cannot go to all lengths. Frames must possess some relevance to the problem being investigated, if they are to be useful. For a researcher interested in the inheritors of land, a list of *all* taxpayers or households will not do; he needs a sampling frame of persons who have inherited land or a list of estates whose owners he can track down to solicit the required information.[40] One is justified in wondering what Geoffrey Gorer (1955) accomplished by way of getting to know about 'English character' with a sampling frame consisting of 10,524 questionnaires returned by persons who in response to an appeal published in a popular newspaper, consented to complete such an instrument.

Sampling frames are sometimes hard to construct, because the universe itself (for instance, well-to-do Congolese in Leopoldville) is conceptually ambiguous. Much thought has to be given to formulating rules concerning what is to constitute the frame, and why. Are men working away from the village to be included in the household? Should I include members of satellite villages in the universe to be sampled? What time limits are sufficient or required for my problem? Solutions to such questions depend on the research objectives and on knowledge of relevant factors in the community's culture and history. For example, in Frobisher Bay it was very desirable to have data on liquor purchases that went back before the date when new regulations entered into force; such data would enable me to tell what difference, if any, the regulation made. Obviously, previous knowledge of an area and its history will provide valuable guidance both for constructing sampling frames, and for generalising beyond them.[41] If the essence of art lies in applying skill to overcome limits imposed by one's tools, materials, and personal resources, then designing a sampling frame calls for considerable art.

The sampling frame contains all the units or observations that will be sampled; the sample contains the number of units actually studied (including those that cannot be found or refuse to collaborate). The second step in collecting a sample consists in determining how many such units are needed (assuming that circumstances do not permit a 100 per cent sample) and then randomly drawing that number from the frame. Sample size depends on the amount of variability in the sample and the degree of confidence that the researcher wishes to establish for his results. In general, the larger the sample, the smaller the probable error and the greater the confidence attached to the results. However, beyond a certain size, gains to be expected rapidly decline, making large samples relatively inefficient to use. Listing units in the frame and assigning each a serial number or numbering houses and blocks permits convenient sampling by use of a table of random numbers,[42] for to draw a large number of cases by lot would be a clumsy, time-consuming procedure. A list or series of items, like pages or newspapers, can be random-sampled by numbering them or numbering areas of the page and lines of type. This is an appropriate place to point out that sampling pages, newspapers, or printed lines by selecting units at regular intervals is not true random sampling, because the selection of each unit fails to be independent of the others. Regular-interval sampling is random only if the arrangement of the series is free from bias, for example, if the pile of newspapers has been mixed so that choosing every seventh does not result in only Sunday papers being drawn. Similar precautions must be taken in stopping to question people or vehicles at regular intervals, when the interviewer must also be cautious that he does not depart from the sample design and unconsciously show partiality in making his selection. In sampling a list of names at regular intervals danger lies in oversampling the initial letter and omitting the least common letters. Returning to random sampling procedures, a numbered grid placed over a large-scale map allows random selection of places to be visited for investigation. In two-stage or multi-stage sampling, once such places are randomly chosen their constituent units are again random-sampled. Peter Marris (1961)[43] contemplated drawing a grid over a plan of Lagos and sampling the squares. However, the density of population made this unthinkable; each square would have included too many people to sample further and an adequate sampling frame would have been hard to construct.[44]

No matter how carefully drawing occurs, bias resulting in a misleading sample, one that under- or overrepresents certain kinds of units, cannot be completely eliminated. Failure of people to respond or to be located, inaccessibility which deters an interviewer from going to certain places, and the readiness of some respondents to co-operate all contribute to bias. I respect the fortitude of my Pathan assistant in a large North-West Frontier village as he patiently accompanied me on long treks across hot fields in search of respondents, whose wells and fields we had located through inquiring in the market place. Even then we could not locate an unallowably large proportion (26 per cent) of the sample which had been chosen from a voter's list, the validity of which I came to doubt.[45]

STRATIFIED RANDOM SAMPLING

The simplicity characteristic of simple random sampling disappears when the basic method which I have described is applied in more complex circumstances, for example, in national samples of public opinion. It would be merely academic for me here to go into such variations of random sampling as area or cluster sampling.[46] However, I will briefly describe one well-known variation, stratified random sampling, because it is likely to be helpful in ethnographic research. This type of probability sampling occurs when the universe under study is heterogeneous; that is, the units vary in characteristics which are apt to be significant for the problem being studied. For example, a population contains persons of different ages or members of different ethnic groups. These features, the investigator suspects, might influence other features

that he is studying. He takes care to draw a sample that will proportionately represent the likely significant features in the universe. He divides the sampling frame into strata or categories (cells), each homogeneous with respect to a certain characteristic. Then he draws a random sample of proportionate size from each cell. In a small Sindhi village of about 500 persons my initial census of males 18 years old or more revealed a population stratified in six tiers; non-cultivating landlords; cultivating landholders; tenant cultivators; craftsmen and tradesmen, including domestic servants; Marwari, a Hindu enclave; and Brahui-speaking transients living on the settlement's outskirts. My sample of forty subjects represented each of these categories in proportion to its weight in the total population. Circumstances, however, made it impossible to complete interviews with each designated respondent, the suspicious Brahui putting themselves beyond reach.[47] Constructing a frame for stratified random sampling obviously requires prior knowledge about the composition of the universe, so that its probably significant characteristics can be defined. To a very large extent, I relied on my Sindhi-speaking assistant for such knowledge.

ADVANTAGES AND DISADVANTAGES OF PROBABILITY SAMPLING

Major justification for using probability samples in any discipline lies in the precision with which they allow inferences drawn from the sample to the sampled universe to be statistically grounded. Speaking less exactly: when sampling is used to control for bias, one is relatively safer in generalising from the few to the many. As I pointed out, such safety vanishes upon leaving the sampled universe (or sampling frame) in order to extend results to a larger aggregate of which the frame itself is but a part, unless one knows precisely how the frame fits the target universe. Probability sampling can conveniently and confidently answer questions concerning the frequency with which features are distributed in a large population: the number of people who possess certain amenities in their homes, are gainfully employed, possess certain cognitive and emotional traits as measured by the Rorschach test, or immigrated to the community in various years. The technique need not involve people directly. It can, for example, be effectively used to discover the number of times a certain value or sentiment is expressed in newspaper editorials and reports of political speeches during an election campaign (Garrett and Honigmann, 1965). Beyond such descriptive use, probability methods are even more important for the way they lend themselves to discovering predictive relationships in a given universe. Do mental health ratings vary with income or with other indicators of socioeconomic status?[48] Hypotheses following from such questions can often be confidently tested with the aid of samples drawn by some method of random selection.

Probability sampling may be to some extent inappropriate when the aim of research is to understand a social or cultural *system* to whose operation or dynamics individual actors or artefacts offer only clues. When interest then lies in discovering the logical relationship that exists between norms, statuses, organisations, or patterns of overt behaviour, both deviant and non-deviant, the incidence of those phenomena is not a crucial question. Such a problem is little concerned with generalising data from a few to the many units comprising a universe. Research problems, however, rarely correspond solely to quantitative or qualitative matters. It is rare that results obtained through one procedure cannot be enlightened by results obtained in another way. Consequently, it will more often than not be advantageous to apply probability methods along with other fieldwork techniques. At least, one will be wise always to weigh carefully the possibilities in using or not using probability sampling and in estimating its relative advantages and disadvantages.

A latent function of probability sampling deserves attention. The careful planning it requires forces an investigator to give much thought to what he wants to learn about, and why. Therefore it is especially appropriate to problem-oriented research, where it helps in defining the crucial variables which, in turn, are often few enough to allow an adequate sampling frame to be efficiently constructed.

Turning now to disadvantages, the care and time required to construct sampling frames which in the end probably do not fully cover the target universe must certainly be taken into account.[49] Perhaps it would be more efficient to sample opportunistically, carefully identifying the pertinent characteristics of the informants, particularly if precise estimates of frequency are unimportant. Furthermore, in culturally unfamiliar social systems, an adequate sampling frame cannot be constructed until much preliminary study has been done. By that time the knowledge to be gained by probability sampling may be very small pickings indeed, especially if research is not problem-oriented. The relatively few variables involved in problem-oriented research constitute an advantage that allows an adequate sampling frame to be efficiently constructed. In comparison, it is very difficult if not impossible to sample by probability techniques for all the information that is pertinent when studying a total culture. In our study of town-dwelling Eskimo in Frobisher Bay we would have needed a staff of several people and much more time than we had to cover by probability sampling all the sources we actually explored; that is, to sample the local radio station's output, school-attendance records, aims and goals of the town's various organisations, activities and learning opportunities in the various shops, earnings and expenditures, amount of fresh food that full- and part-time hunters brought in, attitudes of Euro-canadians toward Eskimo, child rearing, and so on.[50]

Although several large-scale random sample surveys have been successfully conducted under conditions of extreme suspicion and fear,[51] in some parts of the world people randomly selected for interviewing would very likely so often refuse to answer questions that the proportion of uncompleted interviews would destroy the sample's representativeness. There will always be some people in a random sample who refuse to provide information for which they are solicited, or who will be unavailable for interviews. They, in fact, did not have a chance equal to that of the more willing of the sample to be interviewed. Confidence in the results of a random sample is seriously impaired, if the proportion of non-collaborators becomes too high, say 10 per cent of the total sample or more (Cochran, Mosteller and Tukey, 1954). The implication, then, is that those who responded constitute a select and unrepresentative selection. In a study of sexual behaviour they are, perhaps, the high performers, exhibitionists, or extroverts who distort what actually occurs in the universe.[52] Resistance to being interviewed, I suspect, is likely to be frequently encountered in relatively small-scale communities. When it occurs, it springs not only from hostility or suspicion, but also from inexperience with, and little taste for, the kind of introspection, reporting and forethought that people in a different type of society so effectively manage when they are asked to respond to a host of apparently unrelated questions.[53] We failed largely to overcome such unwillingness in Frobisher Bay Eskimo and as a result could barely complete even a simple household census.

PROBABILITY AND NON-PROBABILITY SAMPLES COMPARED

It is interesting to look at two experiments in fieldwork which employed both probability and non-probability samples under controlled conditions. A hypothesis I tested with data obtained in three Pakistan villages predicted that random and opportunistic samples would be significantly different in composition (Honigmann and Honigmann, 1955). Results show that male subjects appearing in the combined opportunistic samples for the three villages differed in socio-economic status from those in the combined random sample. The combined random sample shows 9, 60 and 31 per cent of the respondents coming from the upper, middle and lower socioeconomic groups, respectively. In comparison, the opportunistic samples drew 17, 46 and 37 per cent of the respondents from those strata. Apparently, by querying men who came to our attention, spoke English and proved to be willing informants, we had especially shown a bias for the uppermost stratum. Why lower-status men were also oversampled, is not clear. I can only suggest that my intention to avoid unduly representing high-status people made me zealous in contacting men from the opposite end of the continuum. I also compared the Sindhi and Punjabi to see if the random and opportunistic samples would be different not only in composition, but in two types of response: attendance at the film performances, and number of people showing correct awareness of the government presenting the films. (For this purpose I did not use data from the North-West Frontier province village, where sampling had proven to be very difficult.) Differences at the 0·05 level of probability or lower occurred with respect to both types of response. This suggests, by the logic of probability sampling, that I would have been mistaken had I relied solely on the opportunistic sample to inform me about the behaviour of village population from which those helpful and informative men came.

Among Cree Indians in Attawapiskat in 1955 I used card II of the Behn Rorschach test to discover whether information obtained from a random adult sample ($N = 20$) in response to a controlled stimulus would differ significantly from adults opportunisitically selected ($N = 23$) (Honigmann and Carrera, 1957).[54] I predicted that the samples would differ in respect to eight scored response categories (for example, animal content, human content, total responses, incidence of colour, incidence of rejection). Differences between the means of the random and opportunistic samples turned out to be statistically non-significant. However, a second test hints that the stimulus itself was non-discriminatory; for when the two Cree Indian samples were compared to ninety-six undergraduate college students, no significant differences showed up between means of those two groups.

From these experiments it is possible to conclude that the more homogeneous the universe, the more likely it is that probability and non-probability samples will manifest similar characteristics and results. The reason is clear: the small variability in the universe means that all respondents are likely to respond in similar ways to the same situation.[55] The more stratified the universe, the more likely that probability and non-probability samples drawn from the same strata will respond similarly. Again the reason is clear: the relative homogeneity within each stratum means that all respondents coming from it are likely to respond in similar ways to the same situation. Presumably anthropologists in small-scale homogeneous communities take advantage of the community's slight variability when they sample opportunistically and generalise from the sample to the population at large. When Margaret Mead, speaking of large-scale heterogeneous social systems, advises carefully identifying pertinent characteristics of opportunistically chosen informants, she is in effect saying that the anthropologist who confronts consider-able variability must create and sample more categories in which variability is reduced. Sampling opportunistically from homogeneous strata reduces the possibility that different results would be obtained between probability and non-probability samples.

Notes: Chapter 12

Reprinted from Raoul Naroll and Ronald Cohen (eds.), *A Handbook of Method in Cultural Anthropology* (New York, Columbia University Press, 1973), pp. 266–81, by kind permission of Doubleday & Company, Inc.

1 See Honigmann (1949), p. 27.
2 See Mead (1928), pp. 250–52.
3 See Festinger and Katz (1953), p. 173.
4 See Beattie (1965), pp. 3–13.
5 See Southall and Gutkind (1956), pp. ix–x.
6 See Honigmann (1953), p. 2.
7 See Whiting, *et al.* (1966), chapter 6, cf. Firth (1951), p. 49.
8 See Spindler (1955), pp. 10–11.
9 See Honigmann and Honigmann (1965), p. 70.
10 See Wallace (1952), pp. 40–1.
11 See Leighton *et al.* (1963), p. 40.
12 See Parten (1950), pp. 242–5.
13 See Whiting, *et al.* (1966), chapter 5.
14 See Mandelbaum (1953), p. 182.
15 See Codere (1955), pp. 65–7.
16 See Wallace (1952), p. 42.
17 I believe Kroeber originally made this point.
18 Compare Kroeber (1957), p. 193.
19 Her views mainly appear in Mead (1951b; 1953; 1954; 1955; 1961), and Mead and Métraux (1953), pp. 1–53; see also Zelditch (1962), reprinted in this book as Chapter 23.
20 See Mead (1953), p. 646.
21 See Mead (1953), pp. 645–55.
22 See Mead (1961), p. 19.
23 See Mead (1953), p. 653.
24 See Mead (1951b), p. 77.
25 See Mead (1953), p. 654.
26 For example, see the use Goldfrank (1948) makes of such information in analysing versions of myths.
27 See Mead (1953), p. 652.
28 See Métraux (1943), p. 88.
29 See Mead (1952), pp. 402–3, and Mead (1953), p. 655.
30 See Mead (1953), p. 655.
31 See Mead (1951a), pp. 109, 116.
32 See Mead (1953), p. 648.
33 See, however, Mead (1932), pp. 10–12.
34 In describing how probability samples are selected I follow mainly Parten (1950), pp. 116–22, and Riley (1963), pp. 284–7.
35 For the theory of sampling, see any of the following: Deming (1960); Hansen, Hurwitz and Madow (1953); Kerlinger (1965), chapter 4; Kish (1953); Wallis and Roberts (1956), chapters 4, 10 and 15; also Naroll (1973), pp. 889–926.
36 See Fortes *et al.* (1947), p. 177.
37 See Baeck (1961), p. 162.
38 See Marris (1961), pp. xii–xiv.
39 See Honigmann and Honigmann (1965), pp. 204 ff.

40   Compare Leach (1958).
41   Compare Smith (1963).
42   See Wallis and Roberts (1956), pp. 631 ff.
43   See Marris (1961), p. xiv.
44   For more on the mechanics of drawing samples, see Parten (1950), pp. 265–72, 277–80.
45   See Honigmann (1953), p. 57.
46   For information on these and other methods, see Hansen, Hurwitz and Madow (1953) or Parten (1950).
47   See Honigmann (1953), pp. 10–11.
48   See Srole *et al.* (1962), pp. 32 ff., 210 ff.
49   See Hill (1963), p. 8, and Parten (1950), pp. 111–12, 225–6.
50   I forbear going into the arguments concerning the validity of responses obtained by use of questionnaires. For discussions of this question, see Vidich and Bensman (1954) and Zelditch (1962) (reprinted in this book as Chapter 23).
51   Compare Southall and Gutkind (1956), p. 235.
52   Compare Himelhoch and Fara (1955), chapters 7–11.
53   See Lerner (1958), p. 147.
54   The Wenner-Gren Foundation for Anthropological Research supported the fieldwork in Attawapiskat.
55   I am indebted to Donald R. Ploch for the following conclusion and for a very critical and helpful reading of the section dealing with probability sampling.

13

Time Sampling as a Field Technique

LINDA BROOKOVER BOURQUE AND KURT W. BACK

Three methods of data collection have traditionally been used to investigate human behaviour in a social situation: interviewing, participant observation and the small-group experiment. Each of these methods has been subjected to criticism and has fairly serious disadvantages. The information collected from interviews may be clouded by the problem of recall. Participant observation is costly, because it demands a high ratio of observers to observed. Further, this method presents the problem of the selection of relevant behaviour. The small-group experiment removes the behaviour from its usual context and, hence, leads to a lack of clarity about the importance of effects observed to general behaviour.

Sociologists and anthropologists need a new method of data collection which combines the rigour of the small-group experiment with the representativeness of field sampling. Brunswik,[1] in studying perception, dealt with a similar problem. He was concerned with obtaining measurements of perception which were representative of the individual's pattern of perception in his daily life. Brunswik devised what he called 'representative design' as a solution to this problem:

> Combining active command of the situation with representativeness rather than with artificial systematic design leads to the establishment of what may be called *representative experimental design.* Certain residuals of systematic procedure may hereby be retained to great advantage . . . Aside from representative variation and co-variation, representative experimental design also implies that the choice of the variables themselves should be sensitized to their biological relevance. (Brunswik, 1944, p. 152)

Representative design is a method of sampling the perceptions of an individual as the person moves within his typical environment. The experimenter follows the subject during the experimental period. At certain times, predetermined by the experimenter, the subject is asked to describe his perception of some aspect(s) of his surrounding environment according to certain pre-established criteria. Brunswik considered the data collected with such a method more accurate and, thus, more valuable than data collected through other methods of measuring perception.

With certain modifications, the method developed by Brunswik should be applicable to other areas of behavioural inquiry. A complicating factor in Brunswik's research design is the one-to-one ratio between subject and experimenter. A diary-type questionnaire which could be filled out by the subject himself at the predetermined time might alleviate this problem, and might yield information similar to that obtained by a participant observer. Diary questionnaires have often been questioned, because they place too much responsibility on the respondent. However, Foote and Meyersohn[2] found that if a diary questionnaire was sufficiently simplified it could be made to work.

If we combine the findings of Foote and Meyersohn, and Brunswik, we might be able to develop a representative, economical method for measuring communication. Ackoff and Halbert[3] attempted to do this in investigating the dissemination of information among scientists. A specific set of questions can be asked at random time intervals over an experimental period. To fulfil Brunswik's ideal of representativeness, the emphasis can be placed on actual communication in which the respondent is engaged.

If such a valid concise method to ascertain the structure of communication as it occurs can be constructed, it might be very useful in solving the problems of both group research and field research. Among other things, a simple checklist questionnaire designed to determine what a person was doing at a particular predetermined time, if accurate, could allow an experimenter to: (1) study the actual behaviour of a given population; (2) study processes of social change over time; and (3) indicate whether an individual's stated behaviour coincided with his actual behaviour as obtained by such a measure. The purpose of this study is an attempt to develop such a method of measuring existent situations, particularly as they are manifested in patterns of communication.

Method

THE SETTING

In order to develop and apply a workable method, it is necessary to have a well-defined population in which processes might be observed and change might occur. The population chosen was the students in the Duke University School of Nursing. There are approximately 275 girls in the school at any given time. Ninety students are generally admitted to the freshman class, and between fifty and sixty girls graduate each year. Since something is occurring to the student as a result of her association with the nursing professionalisation process, this seems a good situation in which to develop a method for systematically observing behaviour.

Duke offers a four-year programme in nursing which leads to a BS degree. The first year is devoted entirely to a general liberal arts curriculum, with the exception of one introductory course in nursing fundamentals. In September of their sophomore year the girls are given their uniforms and caps, and receive their first clinical ward experience. They continue to take some liberal arts courses, but the emphasis is on the academic sciences, that is, chemistry, anatomy and physiology. Both the junior and senior years are devoted almost exclusively to clinical nursing courses. One entire summer and part of at least one additional summer are spent on campus in addition to the four academic years. The nursing students live in isolation from the rest of the undergraduate population. They are approximately two blocks from the hospital, and closer to both male undergraduates and graduate students than to other undergraduate women. Their principle contact with undergraduate women occurs through their liberal arts courses. Sophomore student nurses at Duke University were used as the subject population in this study. Our objective was to measure the interaction between attitude change, normal behaviour and patterns of communication. The sophomore year represents the students' first direct exposure to the role of professional nurse. This exposure combines their first experience in uniform on the hospital wards with the nursing fundamentals course, which they take during the fall semester of the sophomore year. It is during this year that the dropout rate due to un-happiness with, or inability to perform, nursing duties is the highest. The two crisis situations to be used in this research design are drawn from experiences related to this sophomore fundamentals course. They are: (1) the mid-term examination (the first formal evaluation by the instructor); and (2) the student's first distribution of patient medication. The two crises are likely to affect the students' pattern of communication, interaction and attitude change over the experimental period.

EXPERIMENTAL PROCEDURE

The class was divided into high- and low-attitude groups, according to a standard attitude measure given in the spring of 1963. The schedule used measured the students' attitude towards the nursing profession and the Duke University School of Nursing. It was part of a larger questionnaire administered by the Duke University Department of Sociology and Anthropology, in their extensive panel study of the nursing professionalisation process. These two groups were then divided into three comparable groups: each containing an equal number of girls with attitudes defined as 'high' and 'low'. One of these groups was placed on a longitudinal plan, another on a time–place situational experimental plan and the third was used as a control group. The purpose of including both a time–place situational experimental group, and a longitudinal experimental group, was to ascertain which methodological situation provided the best observation and measurement of the interaction of all situational variables on the subject at the given time and place. Once the three experimental groups were defined, the sophomore class was approached as a group, and their co-operation was obtained. One of the authors then met with each of the two experimental groups immediately prior to the pretest, and explained the procedure that they were to follow.

DIARY GROUP

The first group on the longitudinal plan was designated 'diary'. This group was given questionnaires designed to ascertain what the individual was doing at a given time of the day, that is, specifically we were interested in determining: (1) whether she was being exposed to any type of communication; (2) who was present at the time; (3) whether she initiated the activity or communication; and (4) how she judged those around her as reacting to it. These questions were put in the form of a one-sheet checklist. The categories were: (1) number of people and identity; (2) type of activity; (3) purpose of activity; (4) type of exposure to activity; (5) who initiated discussion or activity; (6) who dissented in the discussion or activity; and (7) whether the respondent agreed or disagreed with the major viewpoint expressed. At the bottom of the sheet was placed a more open-ended question. This asked for the major viewpoint or purpose expressed and for any secondary activity, conversation, or thought in which the girl might be engaged.

Eight times between 7 a.m. and 11 p.m. were chosen at random and assigned to subjects for each of the experimental days. At each time, the subject was asked to complete one questionnaire. She was asked to do this during four sets of two- to three-day sequences: 7 and 8 November, 18, 19 and 20 November, 5, 6 and 7 December and 15, 16 and 17 December; 7 and 8 November was the period immediately after the mid-term examination; 18, 19 and 20 November came between the beginning of the medications crisis and after the return of the mid-term examinations; 5, 6 and 7 December and 15, 16 and 17 December came during the medications experience, and also during a period when the girls were taking a number of examinations in their academic science courses. The questionnaires were distributed to the girls on the evening preceding the first day of each experimental period.

TIME–PLACE GROUP

The second group was designated 'time–place'. In this group essentially the same information was being sought, that is, what was the student doing at a pre-assigned time. However, instead of having the student relay this information by way of a self-administered questionnaire, an investigator placed herself in situations in which it was predetermined nursing students might be. These places were determined by asking the girls to note where they were at particular times of the day on the week preceding the pretest. These observation places included the wards, the dormitory, libraries, classrooms and the cafeteria. The same data were then collected by observation on whichever student or students(s) first appeared, or were nearest to the researcher. These observations were made during the same eleven days as those of the diary group.

THE CONTROL GROUP

The third group was designated as a control group. No contact was initiated with this group until the end of the experimental period. At that time, all three groups were given the same attitude and self-evaluation measures that they had been given the previous spring, in order to determine whether any change had occurred.

Problems in Method

The objective of this study is to develop a structured but flexible method to measure behaviour. A method, to be useful, must be concise, accurate and feasible from the point of view of both the subject, and the experimenter. It should not make unrealistic demands on the subject population's time or energy, and it should present a comprehensive picture of the activities engaged in by the specified population. This includes the interactive characteristics and the environmental conditions in which the activity occurs. Thus, the next step is to investigate the methods' ability to: (1) obtain data; and (2) give a comprehensive and representative picture of what sophomore nursing sudents are doing.

METHOD FEASIBILITY

Our first concern is to decide whether the format of the study was feasible. Three types of feasibility are relevant in this study. The first might be called general feasibility: will subjects provide the information we want? The second and third types might be called method feasibility: do the time–place and diary groups provide us with economical and representative data. The loss of three subjects at the beginning of the

experiment demonstrates the problem of general feasibility. One low-attitude girl dropped out of school at the beginning of the experiment, and two other low-attitude girls refused to participate. Since only one other low-attitude subject was available, two of these girls were not replaced. Thus, the total number of low-attitude subjects in the total sample was reduced from eighteen to sixteen, and the number of low-attitude subjects in the control group was reduced from six to four. Since these losses occurred before the girls knew what the experiment demanded of them, we assume that the method itself had nothing to do with their refusal to participate.

It was quickly learned that one person could not adequately collect participant observation data on the fifteen subjects in the time–place group. The maximum amount of data that it would be possible to collect would not be comparable to the data collected on the diary group. In addition, during about 20 per cent of the time periods no student appeared in the places to which the researcher assigned herself. The maximum number of observations that were attempted by one person was about 100. However, only seventy-eight yielded actual data. Thus, although data were collected for the entire experimental period, it was decided that no definite analysis could be made on this data, and that it would be used only as a reliability check on the diary group.

The diary method proved more feasible as a sufficient number of usable forms were returned. Each girl received eighty-eight questionnaires. The six low-attitude girls had a mean return of 57·3, and the nine high-attitude girls had a mean return of 65·2. Thus, we can conclude that the diary method was feasible, and the time–place method was not. In the following sections the diary method will be investigated more fully, using the time–place method, when applicable, and additional control.

VALIDITY OF THE METHOD

It would have been possible for girls to distort their responses. It can be assumed that such distortions would show up as inconsistencies. These inconsistencies could occur either between the students' reported behaviour and what was known to be possible according to their formal schedule of classes and activities, or between areas of analysis within the questionnaires. The time–place observations were used as a validity check. Cross-sorts were made on the various areas in order to get an impression of how the variables measured on both the diary questionnaires and the time–place observations were related to various independent variables. The independent variables used were: (1) time of day; (2) day of the week; (3) attitude groups; and (4) experimental periods. Since the subject's accuracy in answering a diary-type questionnaire in the absence of the experimenter could reasonably be disputed, the frequency distribution of diary questionnaires was then compared to the frequency distribution of the time–place observations. In addition, validity checks were made simply on the basis of common sense and knowledge of the students' schedules.

Interaction with men was indicated as being highest on Saturdays and after 6 p.m., which is reasonable considering that dates normally fall on weekends and during the evening. In addition, attendance at movies was twice as high for Saturday nights as for any other one night. No association with either nursing, or non-nursing instructors, was reported as occurring after 6 p.m. or on Sunday. Nor was any time indicated as being spent on the hospital wards, or in the men's graduate centre cafeteria on Sunday. Sophomores, unlike juniors and seniors, would have no reason to be on the hospital wards on Sundays, and like juniors and seniors, would eat in the hospital cafeteria on Sundays, since the men's graduate centre, where they normally eat, is closed. Presence in physiology is listed only for Friday and sociology only for Thursday, which are not the *only* days during which sophomore nurses could be in these classes, but are reasonable days in view of their schedules. Attendance on the wards is by far the highest in the morning, which is logical since *all* ward classes occur in the morning.

All of the above data were supported by the amount of participant observation, time–place data available. In addition, it was found that girls in the diary group indicated that 57 per cent of their conversational and lecture activity occurred in the afternoon. When the purpose of the activity is broken into 'to instruct' and 'to entertain', the girls see 81 per cent of instructional activity as falling during the morning and afternoon. Both of these measures are substantiated by the time–place data: 63 per cent of conversational and lecture activity was observed in the afternoon, and 82 per cent of the purpose being 'to instruct' was considered as occurring in the morning and afternoon. The consistency found in the relatively straightforward information above indicates that the girls were generally accurate and consistent in filling out questionnaires, and that the items on the questionnaire were generally interpreted in the way the researcher meant them to be.

Each of the three groups in this study had a different amount and type of contact with the experimenter. The control group had the least contact, and the time–place group had the most contact. This difference in contact might have influenced attitude change within groups. It is also possible that the type of contact might be a factor in the change process. For example, girls completing questionnaires in the diary group might, due to the nature of the questionnaire, become more aware of their own communciations, and consequently have a pattern of attitude change that differs from that of the other two groups and the total population.

This analysis had two objectives: (1) to determine whether the three experimental groups differed as groups in their pattern of attitude change; and (2) to determine whether individuals within groups differed in their pattern of attitude change. We find in doing simple comparisons of the means and standard deviations that the attitude level, regardless of experimental group, falls slightly and that the range of attitude within experimental groups is extended slightly. Thus, we can say that there was a slight, but not significant, lowering of the attitude level in all groups.

In order to find out whether the structure within groups changed, we used Pearson-Product Moment correlations between the pre- and post-experimental attitude measures for each group. The correlations obtained indicate that the control group differs from the two experimental groups. We find that the control group shows a consistently lower correlation. This suggests some structural changes within the control group, that is, possibly a reversal of position between those with high and low attitudes within the groups. The time–place and diary groups show much more consistency in their attitudes. It is possible that this greater consistency is the result of some aspect of the experimental procedure.

Since it was available as part of the data collected by the Department of Sociology in a more inclusive study, we made use of the questionnaires six months later in order to check on the permanence of the intragroup distribution of attitudes. Analysis of these data did not provide any clarification primarily because almost one-third of the girls in the study did not answer this third questionnaire. The solution to the problem would be to use the method again with a much larger sample size.

Method Used as an Overview of Behaviour

One immediate use of this method might be to show how student nurses spend their time. It can be assumed that most of the students' time is devoted to classroom demands. The questionnaires, when they were coded, were classified by the type of activity in which girls were engaged. Most of these categories were determined by the formal structure of the nursing programme and the sophomore students' position in the nursing programme. A large proportion of the students' formal classtime during the sophomore year is spent in nursing courses or on the hospital wards. Each of these activity areas was designated as a category of behaviour. Ward experience was separated from the nursing classroom experience, because it represents the practical application of the classroom theory and because students do not work on the hospital wards prior to their sophomore year. Since the hospital ward is a new environment for the student, and since it is her first direct contact with routine nursing techniques, an additional category, 'professionalisation adjustment', was made. The fact that girls drop out of school more often during the sophomore year may be connected with the ward experience. Therefore, the designation of a 'professionalisation adjustment' classification was made as an attempt to determine how much actual time the student devoted to discussing and thinking about her potential success as both a student, and professional nurse.

Other categories of activity were also used. The category, 'study and classroom in subjects other than nursing', accounted for time spent studying, in class, discussing and thinking about courses taken outside the school of nursing, such as physiology, anatomy and sociology. 'Self-maintenance' accounted for time spent eating, sleeping, dressing, ironing, bathing and so on. 'Social activities' included both on- and offcampus events, and dating and non-dating behaviour. Two 'other' categories were constructed: one for activities in which the girl was alone, and one for activities in which the girl was probably with others.

With the exception of the last two, each of the categories constructed included times when: (1) a girl was both alone and with others; (2) a girl was both formally and informally involved in an activity; and (3) the activity indicated was either the only activity indicated, or when it was one of two or three simultaneous activities. One of these other methods of classification could have been used, but classifying by type of activity seemed to be the best way of obtaining a comprehensive picture of how the student nurse spends her time.

Table 13.1 *Frequency and Percentage Distribution of How Sophomore Student Nurses Spend Their Time*

	High Attitude		Low Attitude		Total Group	
	N	% age	N	% age	N	% age
Professionalisation Adjustment	18	3·1	7	2·0	25	2·9
Coursework within the School of Nursing	91	15·7	51	14·8	142	15·4
Ward experience	24	4·1	15	4·3	39	4·2
Self-maintenance	111	19·1	78	22·6	189	20·4
Coursework outside the School of Nursing	146	25·2	87	25·2	233	25·2
Social activities	70	12·1	19	5·5	89	9·6
Other						
Alone	45	7·8	23	6·7	68	7·4
Not alone	75	12·9	65	18·8	140	15·1
Totals	580		345		925	100·0

Sophomore student nurses spend most of their time involved in self-maintenance, and in studying for and in class in courses outside the School of Nursing. Surprisingly enough, they spend more time with their non-nursing courses than they spend in all their nursing courses. They devote about 15 per cent of their time to nursing classwork, 4 per cent of their time to the hospital ward, and 3 per cent of their time to concern about their 'professional adjustment'. Dividing the population into groups according to high and low attitude towards the profession does not cause any appreciable change in distribution. Low-attitude girls spend less time in social activities and more time in various 'other' activities than do high-attitude girls.

Table 13.2 *Frequency and Percentage Distribution of Formal and Informal Ways in which Sophomore Nursing Students Spend Their Time*

	Low Attitude		High Attitude		Total	
	N	% age	N	% age	N	% age
Professionalisation Adjustment						
Formal	7	1·2	2	·6	9	1·0
Informal	13	2·2	6	1·7	19	2·1
Nursing classes						
Formal	33	5·7	16	4·6	49	5·3
Semi-formal	6	1·0	2	·6	8	·9
Informal	57	9·8	15	4·3	72	7·8
Ward experience						
Formal	15	2·6	7	2·0	22	2·4
Informal	9	1·6	8	2·3	17	1·8
Self-maintenance						
Eating	15	2·6	9	2·6	24	2·6
Sleeping	60	10·3	36	10·4	96	10·4
Other	23	4·0	20	5·8	43	4·6
Study in other courses						
Formal	67	11·6	31	9·0	98	10·6
Semi-formal	18	3·1	8	2·3	26	2·8
Informal	65	11·2	50	14·5	115	12·4
Social activities						
Formal	15	2·6	1	·3	16	1·7
Informal	12	2·1	7	2·0	19	2·1
Total	580*		345*		925	

* Totals are for all questionnaires, while formal and informal breakdown does not include all questionnaires.

FORMAL AND INFORMAL DISTRIBUTION OF TIME

Numerous other observations can be made by making more complex frequency counts of the types of activities in which the subject is engaged. The environmental and interactive conditions of the behaviour can be investigated. For example, it is possible to divide the above activity categories into formal and informal exposure. Formal activities are those activities which are more or less predetermined in the students' lives, such as class attendance. Informal activities are those activities which occur during periods of time, such as dating and studying.

Categorisation by formal and informal exposure to activity shows that sophomores spend less formal time in nursing classes and on the wards than they spend in other classes. Students also spend more informal time in activities related to non-nursing courses. When they are grouped according to high and low attitudes towards the profession, it is found that students with a high attitude towards nursing spend more informal time in activities related to nursing and less time in activities related to other courses than do students in the low-attitude group. Interestingly enough, all sophomores spend more than 10 per cent of the time between 7 p.m. and 11 p.m. sleeping.

Table 13.3   *Frequency and Percentage Distribution of Places Where Sophomore Nursing Students Spend Their Time*

	Low Attitude		High Attitude		Total	
	N	% age	N	% age	N	% age
Campus classrooms	33	9·8	70	12·3	103	11·4
Nursing classrooms	25	7·4	53	9·3	78	8·6
Dormitory rooms	105	31·3	204	35·9	309	34·2
Libraries	46	13·7	67	11·8	113	12·5
Cafeteria and coffee lounge	21	6·3	54	9·5	75	8·3
Hospital, not ward	9	2·7	16	2·8	25	2·8
Hospital wards	6	1·8	13	2·3	19	2·1
Means of transportation	35	10·4	19	3·3	54	6·0
On campus	7	2·1	20	3·5	27	3·0
Off campus	18	5·4	40	7·0	58	6·4
Totals	336*		568*		904*	

* Since not all questionnaires were used in analysing distribution by place, the totals are greater than the frequencies would indicate.

DISTRIBUTION OF TIME BY PLACE

Information can also be subdivided according to the places where the student was during the day. In this study, thirty-four different locations were given by the students on the various questionnaires. All students spend the greatest part of their time in their dormitory rooms. They spend one-eighth of their time in various libraries, one-tenth in classrooms on campus, one-tenth in nursing classrooms and on the ward, and slightly less than one-tenth of their time in the cafeteria or coffee lounge. When places are analysed by high- and low-attitude groups, it is found that high-attitude students spend more time in their rooms, in nursing classrooms and on the wards, in the cafeteria and coffee lounge and in campus classrooms. Low-attitude students spend more time in libraries and on modes of transportation.

Table 13.4   *Amount of Time Spent with Other People*

Number of people	High Attitude		Low Attitude		Total Group	
	N	% age	N	% age	N	% age
No one	137	23·5	65	19·1	202	22·0
One person	107	18·3	88	25·8	195	21·1
Two to five persons	168	28·8	96	28·2	264	28·7
More than five persons	172	29·5	92	27·0	259	28·7
Total	584		341		920	

Interaction with other people and time of day is related to *allocation of time*. 'Time of day' and 'the number of people interacted with' are the last categories that were investigated in trying to obtain an overview of sophomore student nurses' interaction pattern and environment. The majority of their time is spent with more than two people: close to one-third of their time is spent with two to five people, and another one-third of their time is spent with more than five people. Equal amounts of time are spent alone, and with one other person. High-attitude girls spend more time alone and less time with one other person; low-attitude girls spend less time alone and more time with one other person.

If interaction over time is observed, it can be seen that interaction with more than five people is very high during the late morning and the middle of the afternoon. These are periods when all the sophomores have large lecture courses scheduled. Interaction with only one person is relatively high in the early morning. It then drops, and begins to rise at 3 p.m. Neither interaction with two to five people or no interaction with people established any very definite pattern over the day (see Figure 13.1).

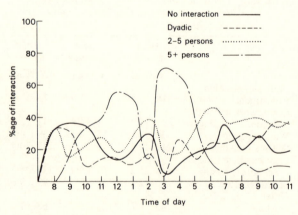

Figure 13.1   *Patterns of interaction*

Conclusion

Granted methodological reservations, this method appears useful. Although it was impossible with the data available to investigate the potential usefulness of what we call the time–place method, we did find that diary questionnaires were particularly effective in measuring who the student was with at a particular time, the size formation of the group, and the student's concept of the pattern of interaction being engaged in at the time.

Notes: Chapter 13

Reprinted from *Human Organization,* vol. 25, no. 1 pp.

64–70, 1966, by kind permission of the Society for Applied Anthropology and the authors. This article is based on the first author's MA thesis under the direction of the second author and was supported by a grant from the Office of Naval Research, Group Psychology Branch (Contract No. 1181 11, Project NR 177470), and the National Institute of Health (Contract No. GM 06912 04). The authors would like to thank Dr H. H. Winsborough and Mr Richard Warnecke for their assistance.

1   See Brunswik (1944).
2   See Foote and Meyersohn (1961).
3   See Halbert and Ackoff (1958), and Ackoff and Halbert (1958).

14

The Key Informant Technique: A Non-Ethnographic Application

MARC-ADÉLARD TREMBLAY

There has been extensive use of the key informant technique[1] in anthropological fieldwork but relatively few attempts have been made to spell it out, especially from the viewpoint of its planning and its place in a structured, yet flexible, research design for data gathering. This chapter, which draws its material from the Stirling County study,[2] will explain why and how key informants were selected for a particular phase of the research (that of identifying the poorest and wealthiest communities of the county) with the hope that from detailed presentation of a specific case, some general principles of use can be drawn.

In this chapter we shall define what we mean by the technique, and then analyse its use in gathering data. This will be followed by a section on the kinds of data we hoped to discover through the use of the technique. Our research design will then be outlined and the reasons for deviating from the original design will be explored. Finally, the manner in which the operation was carried out will be described. The procedures for the analysis of the data as well as the results are not pertinent to this essay and are, therefore, omitted from it, but they can be found elsewhere (Tremblay, 1955).

The Key Informant Technique

(1) *Definition of terms*

As used here, the term 'key informant' has a more delimited definition than is usual. In traditional anthropological field research, key informants are used primarily as a source of information on a variety of topics, such as kinship and family organisation, economic system, political structure and religious beliefs and practices. In brief, they are interviewed intensively over an extensive period of time for the purpose of providing a relatively complete ethnographical description of the social and cultural patterns of their group. In that particular fashion, a few informants are interviewed[3] with the aim of securing the total patterning of a culture. The technique is preeminently suited to the gathering of the kinds of qualitative and descriptive data that are difficult or time-consuming to unearth through structured data gathering techniques such as questionnaire surveys.

Although the emphasis is on qualitative aspects, it is also possible to get a great deal of valuable concrete quantitative data. For instance, by interviewing a sawmill operator, one is likely to get a large amount of specific data such as the number of thousand feet of lumber sawn in a day, the number of workers required to maintain a certain rate of woodcutting, the predicted production of a piece of woodland, and so forth. This, of course, does not mean that qualitative data of great importance cannot be obtained in a survey. Many surveys, for instance, have open-ended questions which allow respondents to give a good deal of qualitative data, as in the Morale Survey, USSBS (Leighton, 1949). This kind of interviewing, labelled 'key informant technique', is often named 'the anthropological technique' or referred to as 'unstructured interviewing'. In our opinion, there is some objection to using either term. As for the first, despite the fact that anthropologists have made a major contribution to the development of this approach and laid down many of its principles, it cannot be considered as belonging solely to that discipline. It has been used in economics and in the political sciences, and it is also a common procedure in journalism.

On the other hand, the term 'unstructured interviewing' creates the impression that the technique is of limitless plasticity and has a lack of system. As we shall demonstrate later, the technique can have structure, although it is a different kind from that used in the design and administration of questionnaire surveys. In using key informants, one chooses them strategically, considering the structure of the society and the content of the inquiry. Furthermore, in the interview itself, although the informant is given latitude to choose his own order and manner of presentation, there is a systematic attempt on the part of the researcher to cover completely the topic under analysis. When we use key informants, we are not randomly sampling from the universe of characteristics under study. Rather, we are selectively sampling specialised knowledge of the characteristics. It should be noted that there is usually considerable difference between an anthropologically selected key informant and a statistically drawn respondent. The former is able to make comparisons between communities of the county and differentiate the poorest from the richest, mainly because this had been the criterion for selecting him. Most respondents of a questionnaire survey, being more limited in scope and knowledge, could hardly make these comparisons.

There is also emphasis on progressive restructuring of both the choice of additional informants, and the content of the interviews, as a result of the information gathered; that is to say, 'feedback'[4] is an important element in the conception and operation of the method.

The term 'key informant' seems to avoid the connotations of these other terms. It does not suggest any single scientific discipline, and at the same time it does imply, at least indirectly, some structuring in the selection of informants.[5] The type of interviewing may increase or lessen structure depending upon the problem.

(2) A focused use of key informants

We have used key informants, in the traditional anthropological sense, during preliminary phases of the Stirling County study and during intensive community studies. In this operation, however, our use of informants has been in the study of specific aspects of a cultural setting rather than the cultural whole usually detailed in ethnographies. The technique was in this sense very limited: the narrowness of our interest meant that we searched not for informants who might add to our total understanding of the culture, but for informants who might be expected to have specialised information on particular topics. Yet it compares with ethnographic usage in that schedules are not used in the interview situation, nor are informants randomly selected as in a sample survey interview. However, it differs from the traditional anthropological technique in that a large number of key informants are selected and interviewed within a restricted framework of questions with highly focused objectives. If we were to take as our research setting a relatively unexplored culture, our interviewing procedure might be as follows: the use of ethnographic key informant technique as the first stage of investigation; the use of the focused key informant technique at the second stage of the inquiry, to be followed, at the third stage, by sample surveys. A focused use of key informants is, thus, intermediate in nature. It assumes broad general knowledge of the area, but precedes the ability to choose the relevant alternatives incorporated in a well-designed sample survey.

This chapter will be concerned primarily with the relatively unexplored focused use of key informants mentioned above. It is structured in the sense that the interviewer, familiar with the type of material sought from the informant, has a framework of questions in mind. This framework, which gives an idea of the type of material sought and which limits the universe to be studied, is told to the key informant at the beginning of the interview in order to give him some orientation. If the informant's conversation is irrelevant to the topic or if he veers repeatedly from the main focus of the interview, the research worker interjects comments or questions intended to bring him back, but without forcing him to adopt a predetermined pattern of conversation. The technique is flexible in that the informant is allowed considerable leeway in regard to the content of his answers and the manner of presentation. He is encouraged to follow, by associative processes, from one thought to the other with relative freedom. A salient feature of the informant researcher interaction is that the former is encouraged to bring out all the facts pertinent to the researcher's interest. Clues are followed and clarifications requested, so that the informant's interest is continuously revived and sustained. The technique is self-developing, since the researcher can refine his interviewing method during the course of a session, or through repeated contacts, as the amount of knowledge about the problem increases and as the ability of the informant is fully revealed. The interview process develops the informant's skills to recall facts and situations, stimulates his memory and facilitates the expression of these recollections.

Objectives of the Key Informant Technique in this Research Operation

The self-developing quality of the technique and the nature of the interview data made the technique pre-eminently suitable for some phases of research in the Stirling County study. A further reason for choosing it was that the size of the county, the large number of communities, and the overall research design ruled out more extensive and expensive methods of data gathering. Study planning called for comparisons of all true communities in the county on seven conditions. The key informant technique was applied to one of these, poverty–affluence, with the idea that if it proved sufficiently accurate for research purposes, it could then be applied with relative ease to the remaining variables.

There were three types of data that we wanted from key informants: definitional, objective and judgemental. These types of data were to be brought to bear on the following research objectives:

(1) To develop a definition of the dimensions involved

One purpose was to evolve a conception of the nature of poverty, and its opposite, as specific phenomena in Stirling County. This is in accord with the feedback mechanism and the process of self-development alluded to earlier. We wanted to use the informants' own terms for 'poverty' or 'wealth' instead of more abstract or more measurable terms. We feared that such terms might, by their unfamiliarity, lead the informants to unnecessarily imprecise or erroneous judgements. As a matter of procedure, the researcher gave a preliminary general assessment of what he was looking for. In response, key informants would either identify the poorest communities, in which case they would be asked to define what they meant; or they would translate our cues into their own terms for describing poverty, after which they would be asked to identify the extremes. If we had an absolute scale, this would imply a comparison of Stirling communities against communities in general in that part of the world. But in a relative scale of the type developed here, there have to be richer communities to compare against the middle range, as well as poorer communities.

As a result of this practice, we came to define poverty as existing in communities (or subcommunities) in which the residents had no capital, few goods or possessions, low credit, no skills of economic value and both low and irregular incomes. As the informants suggested, these conditions manifested themselves in dilapidated and unpainted houses, roofs in disrepair, untidy yards, broken windows, loose lapboards, broken steps and shacks or big houses that had deteriorated. In the course of identifying and characterising poorest communities, a number of key informants made comments which indicated their awareness of some of the most noted characteristics associated with poverty, for example, lack of normal social controls, aspirations and values comparable to those prevailing elsewhere in the county.

(2) To discover boundaries of communities

Another objective of the key informant technique was to delineate the boundaries of those communities which were identified as being either the poorest, or richest. Since it was suspected that formal boundaries, such as school, postal, electoral and church districts did not necessarily coincide with natural communities, it was important to let informants define the communities they named. The idea behind this procedure was to find groups of people, even though they might belong to two different administrative units, who regarded themselves as belonging together and as being different from those surrounding them, and who were regarded by their neighbours as being different. As it turned out, key informants mentioned a number of communities which were not administrative entities and were not recorded on our maps of the county. This was especially true of the poorer sections, which were often submerged in larger and richer areas. For instance, north-west Jonesville and The Bog were mentioned again and again as 'natural' areas (an assertion which was later verified by intensive anthropological participation in these areas). They are not administrative or political units and, hence, do not appear on county maps as separate entities.

(3) To identify extremes

Another general research objective was to identify the most extreme communities in terms of poverty and affluence, that is, the poorest and richest communities in the county. This required a relatively straightforward evaluation by the informants, although it was based on their own impressions and other subjective data, as well as whatever objective information they might possess. The details of having informants rank communities between the extremes will be described later in this chapter.

(4) To increase knowledge of the problem

The final goal, which is more indirect than the others but more in line with traditional fieldwork, was to maximise the chances of collecting relevant information not explicitly stated in the research design and, by this means, to gain further insight into some of the phenomena pertaining to the variable under investigation.[6]

Preliminary Research Design

(1) Criteria for selection of informants

To get the data required, it was necessary to have the best possible informants. The following criteria of the 'ideal' informant were delineated:

Role in community. His formal role should expose him continuously to the kind of information being sought.

Knowledge. In addition to having direct access to the information desired, the informant should have absorbed the information meaningfully.

Willingness. The informant should be willing to communicate his knowledge to the interviewer, and to co-operate with him as fully as possible.

Communicability. He should be able to communicate his knowedge in a manner that is intelligible to the social scientist.

Impartiality. As an ideal, personal bias should be at a minimum, and such biases as do exist should be known to the research worker. For instance, if the informant has a bias conditioned by his class position, this should be known to the interviewer so that its effects can be properly appraised.

Of these five criteria of eligibility, only role in community can be determined in advance. The other qualifications are apt to be largely matters of personality, rather than positions in the social structure. Once individuals performing key roles in the economic structure are detected, the other four criteria serve as a screening device for separating the 'good' from the 'poorer' informants. This means that, after having prepared an ideal list of informants on the basis of their roles in the community, we could expect to make some changes as a result of personal contact and appraisal. It was also anticipated that repeated contacts with informants might lead to the best ones being singled our for more attention. For judging the information provided by the informants, and in fact the informants themselves, the following criteria were considered important: internal consistency, productivity and reliability. These criteria are preliminary to checks against outside standards, for example, census materials, surveys and intensive fieldwork in the locations. Let us spell out these preliminary checks:

Internal consistency. This is a necessary, although not sufficient, condition for accurate information. Such consistency can be checked in the course of data collection and analysis of each informant. Furthermore, there should be a cogent explanation for any specialised knowledge which key informants exhibit in the interview situation. This is especially true when the richness of detail goes beyond what one would expect. For example, one individual was particularly detailed in his accounts of the economic and social relations of families in one section of the county. Upon being asked why he knew all these facts, he cited his participation in numerous fund-raising campaigns, his career as a newspaper reporter, and his work in local government committees concerned with taxes, education and police administration.

Productivity. Productivity implies the ability to tell a lot about the problem. In our case it meant that the informant knew a large number of communities and a great deal about their economic structure.

Reliability. In a technique of this kind, cross-comparison is feasible and should be utilised as much as possible during data collection. This will give some indication of reliability and reveal areas of discrepancy where more intensive interviewing may be needed.

It is worth noting that in every sizeable community there are one or two individuals with particular skills as informants. We have come to designate them 'natural observers'. This term was suggested by Alexander H. Leighton, from whose experiences as a fieldworker many of our observations are derived. These people have been lifelong students of the human scene. They are interested in the behaviour of their fellow men, observe the development of institutions and often speculate and make inferences about both. Usually, there is no one in the community where they live with whom they can exchange these interests, and the appearance of the social scientist seems to afford them considerable satisfaction. The qualities of the 'natural observer' appear in a variety of roles. Such people sometimes have very limited horizons, as in isolated farms and small villages. More often, however, they occupy positions from which they can derive a broad knowledge of human affairs, for example, police magistrate, municipal clerk, teacher, or doctor in rural districts.

(2) *Preliminary selection of informants*

On the basis of formal role participation, a preliminary list of informants was developed. Our choice of roles was determined both by the nature of the information sought, and by the political structure of the county. The first, the distribution of poverty and wealth, meant choosing informants whose roles might provide them with wide and accurate knowledge of financial conditions in the county. Among these were the more obvious roles of bankers, large-scale employers and local government and welfare personnel, as well as such roles as those of newspaper reporters and doctors, whose work might be expected to lead to wide general knowledge of the county. The second determinant was the fact that the county is divided into two dissimilar municipalities. To keep our data symmetrical, we imposed the requirement of aiming for an equal number of informants, as well as comparable role-representation, in each sector. The number of people in the county who filled these two qualifications of role-eligibility and symmetry are indicated in Table 14.1.

Table 14.1 *Frequency of Formal Roles in Stirling County*

Roles	Number
Municipal Councillors	21
Municipality Wardens	2
Municipal Clerks	2
Sawmill Owners (large), and Co-operative Managers	8
Medical Doctors and Welfare Officers	12
Local Bankers	5
Newspaper Reporters	2
Total	52

Research Operations

(1) *Deviation from the preliminary design*

Deviations were introduced into the design as it was applied in the field. There were a number of causes for deviation: the overlapping of roles; the application of the last four criteria for informants to those selected on only the first criterion (role-participation); the discovery of individuals who fulfilled these four criteria but who did not occupy formal positions that suggested their special knowledge; and limitations inherent in the field situation (see Table 14.2).

The overlapping of roles. Some individuals occupied more than one of the roles selected as a point of departure. Some of the sawmill operators and co-operative managers, for instance, were also municipal councillors. Thus, where the symmetrical design called for two separate interviews, the field operation yielded only one.

Lack of knowledge. This factor was the basis for eliminating many individuals from the original list. A short contact with people occupying some of the formal roles made it evident that a prolonged interview would yield little valuable information.

Table 14.2   *Deviation from the Design in Key Informant Interviewing*

Roles	No. in Design	No. Interviewed
Municipal Councillors	21	6
Municipal Wardens	2	2
Municipal Clerks	2	2
Newspaper Reporters	2	1
Sawmill Owners and Co-operative Managers	8	6
Doctors and Welfare Officers	12	7
Bankers	5	2
Farmers	0	3
Member Legislative Assembly	0	2
Electric Power Superintendent	0	1
Tax Collector	0	1
Store Owner	0	1
Fisherman	0	1
Priest	0	1
Fish Plant Owner	0	1
Salesman	0	1
School Inspector	0	1
Agronomist	0	1
Garage Owner	0	1
Total 19 roles	52	41*

*Altogether there were twenty-eight key informants who occupied a total of forty-one major economic roles. The difference between the two numbers results from duplicate roles.

Discovery of new informants. In the course of contacting and interviewing people occupying the listed roles, some individuals suggested others whom they considered particularly well qualified as informants. In a number of cases, contact was made and relevant data were collected.

Intensive versus extensive interviewing. A few informants were highly productive and exceptionally well qualified by all the criteria mentioned earlier. In order to get the full detail of their knowledge, it was essential to interview them more often than was anticipated. Particularly in the urban centre of Bristol, numerous interviews of three and four hours each had to be secured, and one key informant was interviewed at regular intervals during three months. Since time was limited, this made it impossible for us to contact some potential informants listed, although we aimed at interviewing a maximum number.

Personality factors. As with lack of knowledge, a few individuals had to be left out mainly because of personality factors that interfered with, or made impossible, communication between fieldworker and informant.

Operational inconveniences. This refers to practical factors in the field. One example was the impossibility of interviewing two of the bankers in the largest town in the study area, because it was thought necessary to get permission from the companies' head offices in Montreal. By the time this could have been accomplished, the research as a whole would have passed beyond the deadline for this particular operation.

In brief, the selection of informants was not based on representativeness of age, sex and locality of residence. The latter would have been important, if these individuals had been randomly selected respondents rather than judgementally selected key informants. The selection was based almost exclusively on intensive knowledge of many communities in the county and ability to impart that knowledge to the interviewer. The symmetrical design was of great utility in maximising the chances of locating individuals who combined a high degree of knowledge with the ability to communicate it accurately. In short, it was a device for finding 'good' informants by first looking into the formal roles which they were likely to occupy.

(2) *Management of the interview*
As noted earlier, many of the informants had been previously interviewed by members of the project and, therefore, had a fairly sophisticated knowledge of the general nature of our work. The few who did not know the study's goals and activities were given a general introductory explanation and a printed brochure as means of orientation. However, all key informants needed explanations on the nature of the immediate task. A standard, yet flexible, procedure was developed by the two main interviewers in order to maximise consistency and to get comparable qualitative data.

As the first step, the study's interest in grading and comparing communities of the county from the standpoint of material wealth was discussed. The key informant was then given a map and asked to consider the communities he knew best, and to rate them on a continuum of material wealth. It was decided to use a map rather than a checklist of the place names as a memory aid, because of the quality of the data we hoped to procure. A checklist would probably have resulted in maximally standardised procedures (that is, entire coverage, same order of presentation of communities, and so on). However, it would probably have minimised the informant's sense of freedom to concentrate his discussion on the communities he knew best, regardless of instructions. He might have felt obliged to discuss all names, whether he was well informed on them or not.

The use of the map would avoid this disadvantage. Used only as a visual aid to stimulate the informant to organise his material himself, it would encourage his thinking on those very communities he did know best. The disadvantage to this system was that the informant was likely to overlook some communities. This could be overcome to some extent by having the interviewer ask directly about any areas of the county which the informant had not discussed, after the informant had given detailed information on the communities he knew best.

After the informant had a chance to examine the map, he was asked to pinpoint: (1) the poorest and (2) the richest communities. The order was to sharpen the informants' sense of contrasts between the extremes of poverty and affluence. After the informant had enumerated all the communities which he tagged either poorest, or richest (and the reasons therefor), he was then asked to single out: (1) all the poorer than average communities which were not so poor as the poorest; and (2) all the better than average communities which were not so affluent as the richest. After additional queries had been made, communities which had not been rated were therefore either unknown to the informant, or considered as average. In such cases, communities which the informant considered average or did not know, were often undifferentiated by this procedure.

After all the ratings had been completed for these four categories, the informant was asked to rank-order the communities he had mentioned within each class of wealth. For instance, if a respondent had mentioned Loomervale, The Bog and Monkeytown as belonging to the poorest class, he was then asked to rank-order these three from poorest to least poor. In numerous instances, however, informants felt that they could not make such refined distinctions; they were not pressed further. Because rank-orderings within wealth categories were incomplete, it was impossible to develop a method which could refine further the within-class-rating of informants.

In accord with our aim of defining poverty and wealth in the local idiom, we encouraged informants to explain their reasons for rating the communities as they did. We also encouraged them to delimit and describe the places they rated, since we were interested in isolating all true communities in the area. We tried to record the interviews as fully as possible. Coloured pencils were supplied and informants were encouraged to use them to spot the communities they discussed. Such maps were kept as part of the interview record. Informants were interviewed to the fullest extent compatible with their knowledge. Some required only one interview to exhaust the relevant information, while others needed more interviews. Extensive notes were taken during the interviews, and on some occasions total recordings were made.

Conclusion

Although this chapter deals with the illustrative case of poverty, this procedure was repeated for other socio-cultural factors similarly relevant to our main problem. On the basis of these focused key informant operations, we were able to gather the information necessary for the design of a sample survey to be used in the study area as a whole, and for the preliminary selection of focus communities for intensive analysis with both 'structured' and 'non-structured' techniques of interviewing and observation. Thus, the technique not only provided us with the information essential for the refinement of the overall research design, but it also dictated the steps whereby its validity could be checked through comparison with the findings of subsequent research operations.[7]

Notes: Chapter 14

Reprinted from *American Anthropologist,* vol. 59, no. 4, pp. 688–701, 1957, by kind permission of the American Anthropological Association and the author.

1 This term has been employed in professional writing at least as early as 1939 by Nadel (1939), pp. 317–27. It has received wide recognition, since it avoids the terminological difficulties of either the 'anthropological method', or 'unstructured interviewing'.
2 The Stirling County study was conducted by Cornell University in collaboration with the Department of Public Health of the Province of Nova Scotia and with the co-operation of Acadia and Dalhousie Universities. Invaluable help was also provided by the Faculté des Sciences Sociales, Université Laval. Within Cornell, the Stirling County study was attached administratively to the Social Science Research Center and was sponsored by the Department of Sociology and Anthropology and the Department of Psychiatry of the New York Hospital and Cornell Medical College. Financial support was provided by the Carnegie Corporation of New York, the Department of National Health and Welfare of Canada, the Department of Public Health of the province of Nova Scotia and the Milbank Memorial Fund. In the preliminary phases of the work, help was given by the American Philosophical Society, Cornell University, and the Wenner-Gren Foundation for Anthropological Research. The staff of the project consisted of the following, who are listed according to their functions in the study: Alexander H. Leighton, Director; Allister M. MacMillan, Deputy Director; Bruce Dohrenwend, Social Analyst; Christopher Haffner, Chief of the Psychiatric Clinic; Bernard Hébert, Clinical Psychologist; Charles C. Hughes, Social Scientist; Ruth Kent, Administrative Assistant; and Dorothea C. Leighton, Assistant to the Director. In addition to help given by the staff mentioned above, the author wishes to acknowledge his gratitude to Professors Alexander H. Leighton and Emile Gosselin, who

carried out the major part of the field operation and contributed many of the ideas expressed in this chapter, and to express his indebtedness to Morris E. Opler and Toshio Yatsushiro, who read the chapter and made useful comments; to Norman A. Chance, who made a review of the literature; and to Alice Longaker for editorial assistance.

3 There are a number of studies in anthropology based on a single key informant (for example, Osgood, 1940, and Yang, 1945, the latter being the author's retrospective reconstruction of his own native village). An account of the division of labour in a northern Indian village is reported by Opler and Singh, the latter being the informant (Opler and Singh, 1948).

4 Feedback can be described very briefly as a 'self-corrective process'; see Wiener (1954), pp. 24–6, 49–50, 58–61, 63, 96, 151–3, 156–8, 164 ff. Here is a passage which appears on p. 61: 'Feed-back is a method of controlling a system by inserting into it the results of its past performance. If these results are merely used as numerical data for the criticism of the system and its regulations, we have the simple feed-back of the control engineers. If, however, the information which proceeds backward from the performance is able to change the general method and pattern of performance, we have a process which may well be called learning.' See also the excellent statement on this process by Spicer (1952), pp. 125–6.

5 John Madge (1953), pp. 144–253, discusses the subject of key informants. In his chapter on 'Interview' he identifies three types of respondents: (a) potentate, or individuals occupying authority positions; (b) expert, or individuals with specialised knowledge; and (c) people, or the lay public. In this scheme, most of the Stirling key informants for the identification of extremely poor and extremely rich communities would be considered as occupying authority positions and as having special knowledge.

6 This is what Merton called 'serendipity'; see his notes on the term (1949), pp. 12, 98–102, 376–7.

7 For further references and discussions, see Bartlett (1937), Becker (1954), Bennett (1948), Boas (1920; 1932; 1940a; 1940b), Cannell and Kahn (1953), Chapple (1949a; 1949b; 1950), Dean (1954), Dotson (1954), DuBois (1937), Festinger and Katz (1953), Garrett (1942), Hallowell (1956), Herskovits (1948b; 1954), Jahoda, Deutsch and Cook (1951), Kluckhohn (1945a; 1945b), Maccoby and Maccoby (1954); Madge (1953), Malinowski (1922; 1935b; 1944), Mead (1933; 1939; 1940), Merton (1947), Merton and Kendall (1946), Nadel (1939; 1951), Osgood (1955), Paul (1953), Radin (1933), Redfield (1948), Rogers (1945), Royal Anthropological Institute (1951b), Sewell (1949), Stavrianis (1950), Steward (1950), Warner and Lunt (1941), Whiting *et al.* (1954), Whyte (1953; 1955) and Wormser and Selltiz (1951).

Section Four

Conversations in Field Research

15

The Unstructured Interview as a Conversation

ROBERT G. BURGESS

Conversation is a crucial element of field research. Certainly, the classic field researchers indicated the centrality of conversation in their empirical work. Malinowski (1922) writing in *Argonauts of the Western Pacific* indicated the importance of talking to natives, so that ethnographic statements could be collected that would 'grasp the native's point of view'. Such a position was echoed in the field manual prepared by Vivien Palmer (a member of the Chicago School of sociology). Palmer indicated that: 'The ability of the objects of social research to converse with each other and with the scientific investigator is so vital a characteristic of the subject matter of the social sciences that it cannot be disregarded in any well rounded study' (Palmer, 1928, pp. 168–9). Indeed, Palmer continues: 'The conversations of human beings are an important part of the data of social research, as well as an important part of social research technique' (Palmer, 1928, p. 169).

The notion was also reflected in the writings of Sidney and Beatrice Webb. In *Methods of Social Study* (Webb and Webb, 1932) they conclude that:

> For the greater part of his information the investigator must find his own witnesses, induce them to talk, and embody the gist of this oral testimony on his sheets of notes. This is the Method of the Interview, or 'conversation with a purpose', a unique instrument of the social investigator. (Webb and Webb, 1932, p. 130)

Here, conversation is presented as crucial data for the social scientist, as well as being a method of social investigation.

Contemporary textbooks on social research tend to focus on interviews and interviewing. The interview is shown to take many forms and can be placed on a continuum with structured interviews at one end and unstructured interviews at the other. In these texts, the emphasis is placed upon the structured interview with its specified schedule, fixed order and form of questions, together with specified alternatives. As Bechhofer (1974) suggests, structured interviews define situations in advance and do not allow the researcher to follow up any interesting ideas. The result in that talk, conversation and elements of everyday life often go unrecorded within formal interviews; yet these provide basic data for the field researcher. It is the intention of this section to examine unstructured interviewing as a form of conversation that incorporates elements of everyday life into the conduct of field research.

The aims of the unstructured interview have been well summarised by Palmer (1928), who considers that they provide the opportunity for the researcher to probe deeply, to uncover new clues, to open up new dimensions of a problem and to secure vivid, accurate, inclusive accounts from informants that are based on personal experience. In these terms, it is argued that a standard set of questions would be far too narrow and would restrict the researcher's perspective. The unstructured interview therefore:

> assumes the appearance of a natural interesting conversation. But to the proficient interviewer it is always a controlled conversation which he guides and bends to the service of his research interest. (Palmer, 1928, p. 171)

The unstructured interview may, therefore, appear to be without a structure, but nevertheless the researcher has to establish a framework within which the interview can be conducted; the unstructured interview is flexible, but it is also controlled. Palmer suggests that the researcher must keep the informant relating experiences and attitudes that are relevant to the research problem and encourage the informant to discuss these experiences naturally and freely. It is suggested that:

> A few comments and remarks, together with an occasional question designed to keep the subject on his main theme, to secure more details at a given point of a narrative, or to stimulate the conversation if it tends to lag, are the usual means by which the interviewer accomplishes the first part of his task. Gestures, the nod of the head, smiles, facial expressions which reflect the emotions narrated are a very important factor in obtaining the second objective. (Palmer, 1928, p. 171)

In this respect, researchers need to have understanding and sympathy for the informant's point of view. They need to follow their informants' responses and to listen to them carefully in order that a decision can be made concerning the direction in which to take the interview. In short, researchers have to be able to share the culture of their informants. Certainly, Becker and Geer (1957) have warned sociologists that this is just as important when they conduct investigations in their own culture as it is when anthropologists conduct studies in other cultures. Indeed, the Webbs point to the importance of detailed preparation of an unstructured interview, so that researchers are acquainted with the various shades of meaning that informants attach to situations, since they remark:

> For instance to cross examine a factory inspector without understanding the distinction between a factory and a workshop, or the meaning of the 'particulars clause'; or a town clerk without knowing the difference between getting a provisional order, promoting a local Act or working under a general Act, is an impertinence. Especially important is a familiarity with technical terms and a correct use of them. To start interviewing any specialist without this equipment will not only be waste of time, but may lead to a more or less courteous dismissal after a few general remarks and some trite opinions; at best the conversation will be turned away from the subject into the trivialities of social intercourse. (Webb and Webb, 1932, p. 136)

Researchers, therefore, require a knowledge of technical terms and an ability to ascertain cultural meanings, if they are to obtain detail, verify statements, elucidate contradictory data and obtain information that will allow them to evaluate their informants' statements. In short, researchers need to ascertain meaning and get access to unspoken elements of social life. Researchers need to be able to decide what questions to ask and how to ask them, if they are to get at gossip and move beyond generalisations in the course of conversations with their informants.

Strauss *et al.* (1964) maintain that researchers need to become members of the social settings they study, if they are to understand the positions that informants adopt in situations. However, they acknowledge that as time proceeds, the researcher can no longer take the role of a new member, with the result that the researcher has to use specific questions if data is to be obtained. They suggest that four different types of questions can be used to encourage an informant to talk about a situation. First, the devil's advocate question, in which the informant is presented with an opposing point of view. In this respect, they argue that it is possible to discover the informant's position through the responses that are given. Secondly, they consider that the researcher can pose hypothetical questions to

find out what the informant might do in particular circumstances. Thirdly, they argue that, if the researcher asserts an ideal position, it is possible to discover how the informant perceives ideal persons, situations and conditions. Finally, they consider that researchers can begin to offer their interpretations of situations towards the end of a research programme. This may stimulate informants to confirm the researchers' findings or to respond with counter-information which may set them on another line of inquiry. However, no matter what questions are posed, it is vital for researchers to allow informants to talk in their own terms, providing some guidance and support when these are required. This has been summarised by Dean, Eichorn and Dean in the following terms: 'the researcher should be a thoughtful and analytic listener, or observer, who appraises the meaning of emerging data for his problem and uses the resulting insights to phrase questions that will further develop the implications of these data' (Dean *et al.*, 1967, p. 302). However, they are aware that these principles will vary with the situation and will depend upon the informants, the purpose of the interview and how the interview is to be used. Nevertheless, interviewers need to be good listeners as well as questioners. Some projects (Rainwater, 1970; Platt, 1976; Cottle, 1978) have utilised untructured interviews alone, while others have utilised unstructured interviews in relation to observational material (cf. Nash, 1973; Woods, 1979, in the study of schools and classrooms). Unstructured interviews have also been used in relation to personal documents; the collection of life history material (Shaw, 1930; Bogdan, 1974), oral testimony (Ewart Evans, 1970; Vansina, 1973; Thompson, 1978) and the elucidation of data recorded in diaries (Zimmerman and Wieder, 1977). In these circumstances, unstructured interviews take different forms. Among the main forms of unstructured interview that have been identified are: the non-directive interview, the group interview and the conversation. However, no matter what form of interview is used by the researcher, there are significant problems that have to be confronted.

Non-directive interviews allow informants to take the subject of discussion in whatever direction they prefer. Certainly, Gouldner (1954) in his study *Patterns of Industrial Bureaucracy* reports that the interviews were partially non-directive as the informants were allowed to take the interviews in any direction they wanted them to go. Indeed, he indicates that the researchers started with a crude list of questions that were modified on the basis of their interviews. A similar experience has been reported by Platt (1976) in her study of sociological research projects. Here, she indicates that interviews with members of research teams were modified on the basis of her interview experiences with chief investigators and other team members. While such an approach has the advantage of taking up issues that are considered crucial by the informant, it also raises problems concerning the way in which the responses can be utilised and compared.

A form of unstructured interviewing that was strongly advocated by the Webbs was the group interview. Group interviews have been discussed in some detail by Banks (1957) and by Chandler (1954), and have been used in a number of educational studies where groups of children have been interviewed by researchers (Nash, 1973; Corrigan, 1979; Woods, 1979). Such a situation provides informants with an opportunity to discuss their world and to argue over the situations in which they are involved. These interviews may afford glimpses of competing views and how consensus or difference is arrived at. However, the members of the group interview will normally only produce views that can be stated publicly. While this provides further data on the dynamics of social relationships between informants, it also raises a problem, as less detailed material can be gathered from individuals. In turn, group interviews also raise the problem of comparability in terms of the questions that are covered; a situation that can only be partly resolved, if the researcher sets out with a similar list of topics rather than questions that will be covered in all interviews.

Finally, at the far end of the spectrum of interview technique is the situation where the interview is based on a conversation with the researcher. The principal exponent of this method of working has been Cottle (1972a; 1973b; 1974), who argues (Cottle, 1977) that it is important for the researcher to become involved in the lives of those individuals who are studied. He considers that the researcher has to actively participate in conversation, and that the participation should be recorded in the published account. He states that:

> To make the monologue a dialogue, as all interview situations are, is to make more complex the social reality and accounting of the dialogue by both participants, and to set the conversation more securely within the province of the sociological enterprise. (Cottle, 1977, p. 21)

While this approach provides moving stories, illuminates social situations and provides detailed portraits of individuals, it raises a series of ethical, political and methodological issues. How can the researcher claim to know about people? How can the researcher provide detailed accounts of individuals yet preserve their personal privacy? Should the presence of the researcher be recorded in the final research report? Certainly, there are no definitive answers to these questions that confront all researchers who engage in interviews that demand vivid, detailed personal stories, feelings, attitudes and opinions from informants. Indeed, this approach raises further questions: how do we know the informant is telling the truth? Do informants tell us what they think we want to hear? How do researchers develop relationships with informants? Can men interview women, whites interview blacks, old people interview young people? These kinds of questions need to be considered in relation to unstructured interviewing, and in relation to the data that are gathered using this approach. Ultimately, we might ask why researchers working with similar groups using unstructured interviews obtain very different data. As Shipman (1981) indicates in his discussion of the work of Scharff (1976) and Willis (1977), both authors used unstructured interviews to examine the transition from school to work among young people in inner-city schools in the 1970s. However, as Shipman indicates, although there is some similarity between the two studies, there is much conflicting evidence. Scharff's pupils were satisfied with their schooling, while Willis's pupils hated school. Shipman considers whether both explanations are possible. However, he also indicates that, if we are to evaluate the data gathered from similar groups using similar methods of study, we should consider the values of the investigators and the theoretical framework within which they work. It is, therefore, important to consider the links between the theoretical framework, the data collected and the methods used in particular studies.

The materials that are included in this section by Whyte and by Cottle have been included not because they provide answers to the questions that have been raised, but because they discuss various ways in which unstructured interviews can be conducted and confront some of the issues that emerge in this kind of work. In short, they demonstrate that interviewing is much more than the staccato conversation conducted on the doorstep by some market researchers. Unstructured interviews involve the sort of conversation that is developed through a sustained relationship between the informant and the researcher. Such interviews can yield a variety of rich material. However, researchers need to listen to their informants for, as Cottle remarks: 'Without allowing people to speak freely we will never know what their real intentions are, and what the true meaning of their words might be' (Cottle, 1978, p. 12).

Suggestions for Further Reading

METHODOLOGY

American Journal of Sociology vol. 62, no. 2, 1956, pp. 137–217; special issue devoted to interviewing. Contains methodological papers and examples of the problems involved when interviews are conducted in particular social settings.

Banks, J. A. (1957), 'The group discussion as an interview technique', *Sociological Review,* vol. 5, no. 1, pp. 75–84. One of the few available discussions of the group interview.

Chandler, M. (1954), 'An evaluation of the group interview', *Human Organization,* vol. 13, no. 2, 26–8. A comparison of group interviews and individual interviewers.

Cohen, S. and Taylor, L. (1977), 'Talking about prison blues', in C. Bell and H. Newby (eds), *Doing Sociological Research* (London: Allen & Unwin), pp. 67–86; examines the use of conversation in a research project.

Cottle, T. J. (1977), *Private Lives and Public Accounts* (New York: New Viewpoints). One of the few detailed expositions that Cottle provides of his conversational approach to doing research (see especially part 1).

Dean, J. P., Eichorn, R. L. and Dean, L. R. (1967), 'Observation and interviewing', in J. T. Dolby (ed.), *An Introduction to Social Research* (2nd edn) (Des Moines, Iowa: Meredith Corporation), pp. 274–304. A useful account of interviewing.

Gorden, R. L. (1980), *Interviewing: Strategy, Techniques and Tactics* (3rd edn) (Homewood, Ill.: Dorsey Press); discusses the main communication problems involved in interviewing.

McCall, G. J. and Simmons J. L. (1969) (eds), *Issues in Participant Observation: a Text and Reader* (Reading, Mass.: Addison Wesley). See the series of papers by Becker and Geer (1957; 1958), and by Trow (1957), that detail a debate concerning participant observation and interviewing that originally took place through the pages of *Human Organization.*

Palmer, V. M. (1928), *Field Studies in Sociology: a Student's Manual* (Chicago: University of Chicago Press). A text prepared by a member of the Chicago School of Sociology –the chapter on interviewing looks at the interview as a form of conversation, see pp. 168–79.

Richardson, S. A., Dohrenwend, B. S. and Klein, D. (1965), *Interviewing: its Forms and Functions* (New York: Basic Books). A useful textbook discussion of strategies involved in interviewing.

Spradley, J. P. (1979), *The Ethnographic Interview* (New York: Holt, Rinehart & Winston); presents a developmental research sequence for interviewing.

EMPIRICAL STUDIES

There are numerous field studies that utilise various forms of interviewing as a major research tool. The following studies have been selected to demonstrate the diversity involved in interviewing:

Bott, E. (1971), *Family and Social Network* (2nd edn) (London: Tavistock).

Cottle, T. J. (1978), *Black Testimony: Voices of Britain's West Indians* (London: Wildwood House).

Corrigan, P. (1979), *Schooling the Smash Street Kids* (London: Macmillan).

Gouldner, A. W. (1954), *Patterns of Industrial Bureaucracy* (Glencoe, Ill.: The Free Press).

Nash, R. (1973), *Classrooms Observed* (London: Routledge & Kegan Paul).

Pahl, J. M. and Pahl, R. E. (1971), *Managers and their Wives* (London: Allen Lane) (see the appendix by Corbin, 1971).

Platt, J. (1976), *The Realities of Social Research: an Empirical Study of British Sociologists* (London: Chatto & Windus for University of Sussex Press).

Rainwater, L. (1970), *Behind Ghetto Walls* (Chicago: Aldine) (issued by Penguin, 1973).

Scharff, D. E. (1976), 'Aspects of the transition from school to work', in J. M. M. Hill and D. E. Scharff, *Between Two Worlds: Aspects of the Transition From School to Work* (Richmond: Careers Consultants), pp. 66–332.

Stimpson, G. and Webb, B. (1975), *Going to See the Doctor: the Consultation Process in General Practice* (London: Routledge & Kegan Paul).

Willis, P. (1977), *Learning to Labour* (Farnborough: Saxon House).

Woods, P. (1979), *The Divided School* (London: Routledge & Kegan Paul).

16

Interviewing in Field Research

WILLIAM FOOTE WHYTE ·

The anthropologist or sociologist gathers a large part of his research data through field interviews. Interviews may be of various types, ranging from the questionnaire administered in writing and the orally administered interview schedule of predetermined questions to the more freely structured interview common to studies in social anthropology. In the present chapter I shall give only incidental attention to questionnaires and interview schedules, since they are systematically discussed in a number of already available books. I shall concentrate upon the method in which the interviewer does *not* follow a standard order and wording of questions.

Nature of the Interview

The interview we use is often called 'non-directive'. This is a grave misnomer. The 'non-directive' interview was a therapeutic development based on the theory that a patient would make progress best, if he were left free to express himself on his problems as he wished, stimulated by an interested and sympathetic listener. While the good research interview may have a therapeutic side-effect, it is structured in terms of the research problem. The interview structure is not fixed by predetermined questions, as it is in the questionnaire, but is designed to provide the informant with freedom to introduce materials that were not anticipated by the interviewer.

Whatever its merits for therapy, a genuinely non-directive interviewing approach simply is not appropriate for research. Far from putting informants at their ease, it actually seems to stir anxieties. Once, while studying human relations in restaurants, I decided that I would be just as non-directive as I could. I began each interview simply by asking the informant to tell me whatever he cared to that was important to him about the job situation. The usual answer was :'what do you want to know?' Some informants were willing to respond to questions, but no one poured out his feelings in response to my general invitation. Rather, the approach seemed to make the informants quite uneasy, and I quickly shifted to providing a good deal more structure in the interview.

Sometimes, when an informant does need to get something off his chest, the researcher can quite appropriately play a non-directive role – at least for the first part of the interview. Even here, however, the informant will usually leave out aspects of the problem that are significant for the interviewer. These can be brought out only through questioning or otherwise encouraging talk along certain lines. The rules we follow in interviewing are, indeed, based on those for the non-directive interview. But there are important differences. Like the therapist, the research interviewer listens more than he talks, and listens with a sympathetic and lively interest. He finds it helpful occasionally to rephrase and reflect back to the informant what he seems to be expressing and to summarise the remarks as a check on understanding. The interviewer avoids giving advice and passing moral judgements on responses. He accepts statements that violate his own ethical, political, or other standards without showing his disapproval in any way. Generally he does not argue with the informant, although there may be justification for stimulating an argument as a prod to determine how the informant will react. This, however, should be a part of a conscious plan and not be done simply because the interviewer disagrees with the informant and cannot contain himself on the point.

The therapist is told not to interrupt. For the researcher the advice should be: don't interrupt *accidentally*. In normal social intercourse a person interrupts because he is impatient and needs to express himself. This is no justification for interruption in a research interview. However, some people will talk forever, if they are not checked. Since they seldom pause for breath, anything that anyone else says to them is necessarily an interruption. Such people circle the same topic with an infinite capacity for repeating themselves. The interviewer who waits patiently for new material will hear only variations on the same theme. I have described an extreme type of informant, rarely encountered in this pure form. However, experienced fieldmen recognise that for informants of this tendency one must learn to interrupt *gracefully*. This is not as difficult as it sounds; such people are quite accustomed to being interrupted in ordinary social intercourse, as this is the major way others communicate with them. The interviewer need not feel that an occasional interruption will antagonise his informant. In non-directive therapy the interviewer designs his questions to help the patient express himself more fully on matters on concern to him. In research we want the informant to talk about things of vital interest to him, but we also need his co-operation in covering matters of importance to the researcher, though possibly of little interest to the informant. Although I have thus far compared the non-directive with the research interview as if they were two different and distinct types, it should be possible to measure the degree of directiveness that the interviewer uses. If so, the interviewer can vary the degree of directiveness not simply in terms of his own personality, but in response to the interviewing situation and the problem he is studying. Research by Dohrenwend and Richardson[1] has shown the way here, and I shall present a modified and simplified version of their work.

In analysing interviewers' behaviour, there are, of course, other categories besides directiveness in which we will want to make discriminations. We will consider here also what Dohrenwend and Richardson call 'restrictiveness' as to type of answer and suggestion of the content of the answer. The following scale should enable us to evaluate the degree of directiveness in any question or statement by the interviewer by examining it in the context of what immediately preceded it during the interview. The scale goes from low to high directiveness as we go from 1 to 6:

(1)   'Uh-huh', a nod of the head, or 'That's interesting'. Such responses simply encourage the informant to continue and do not exert any overt influence on the direction of his conversation.
(2)   Reflection. Let us say the informant concludes his statement with these words: 'So I didn't feel too good about the job.' The interviewer then says: 'You didn't feel too good about the job?' – repeating the last phrase or sentence with a rising inflection. This adds a bit more direction than response 1, since it simplies that the informant should continue discussing the thought that has just been reflected.
(3)   Probe on the last remark by the informant. Here, as in response 2, attention is directed to the last idea expressed, but the informant's statement is not simply reflected back to him. The interviewer raises some question about this last remark or makes a statement about it.
(4)   Probe of an idea preceding the last remark by the informant but still within the scope of a single informant statement. In one uninterrupted statement an informant may go over half a dozen ideas. If the interviewer probes on the last idea expressed, he follows the informant's lead. In turning to an earlier remark, the interviewer is assuming a higher degree of control over the interview.
(5)   Probe on an idea expressed by informant or interviewer in an earlier part of the interview (that is, not in the block of talking that immediately preceded the interviewer's probe). By going further back in the interview to pick up a topic, the interviewer has a much broader choice, and consequently exercises more control than is the case if he simply limits his choice to immediately preceding remarks. It seems logical to distinguish between probes on ideas earlier expressed by the informant and those by the interviewer. However, I find in practice that this is a difficult discrimination to make because most probes of this type can be related back to remarks made both by the informant, and by the interviewer.
(6)   Introduction of a new topic. Here, the interviewer raises a question on a topic that has not been referred to before.

In using this scheme, I follow the convention of categorising a remark with the lower number when it might be categorised by two or more different numbers. For example – a probe related to the last informant remark – 3 – may also refer to a remark made earlier in the interview – 5. Following our convention, we would show it as response 3.

My brief practice with this adaptation of the coding scheme indicates that coders too often disagree on the number to be assigned to a given comment. If the coding scheme is to be used for research on research methods, then its reliability must be further tested. However, if we are interested in field–research training, then we need only require that the effort to make appropriate discriminations in analysing his own interviews should provide the apprentice researcher with a useful learning experience.

Following further on the Dohrenwend–Richardson approach, we find that the interviewer may influence the length of informant responses through asking closed or open questions. A closed question can be either a yes–no, an explicit alternative, or an identification question. For example: 'Did you go to town?' 'Did you go to town yesterday or the day before?' 'Who went to town with you?' The informant can answer with short responses, such as 'Yes', 'Yesterday' and 'John Smith'. Open questions are a residual category. Any question that cannot be answered politely with a short answer is an open question. The word 'politely' refers to the ordinary expectations of social intercourse. The question 'Would you like to tell me what happened last night?' could be answered, literally, by 'Yes' or 'No'. This is not expected in ordinary intercourse, however. In effect, the question calls for a much more extended set of remarks.

The interviewer's questions can point to an appropriate content for the response. A question may call for an objective response ('Who did that?') or a subjective response ('How did you feel about it?'), or it may be non-specific in this respect. 'What kind of evening did you have?' can be answered by the word 'Lousy', an evaluative statement, or by 'We played cards', a descriptive statement. Either satisfies the question, since the interviewer does not ask specifically for a report of feelings or of events. These coding schemes do not in themselves tell us whether the interviewer is performing well or badly, but they do provide a reasonably objective basis whereby an interviewer can evaluate himself. For this purpose, he needs to tape-record several of his interviews so that he will have an exact record of what he has done. One's own memory is likely to be very faulty in these matters.

The fact that an interviewer's statements average quite high on the directiveness scale does not necessarily mean that the interview was a poor one. However, a high-directiveness average, combined with the feeling that the interview was choppy and that the informant did not talk very freely, suggests that a less directive approach might be more effective with this particular informant. On the other hand, a very low average on the directiveness scale, combined with an apparent lack of progress from one idea to the next and a lack of materials relevant to his research, suggests the desirability of introducing more direction.

On the restrictiveness dimension, beginning interviewers commonly find themselves asking a number of closed questions. They start with questions demanding a yes-or-no, a choice of one alternative, or an identification of an individual or a place. Of course, many informants will talk at length on a question that can be answered with a single word, but there are many informants who will give short answers whenever possible. The beginning interviewer, therefore, gets questions answered faster than he can think up new ones, and he finds this a most disturbing experience. Only as he learns to put open-end questions into the early stages of the interview does he find that he can relax, listen and develop worthwhile questions out of the informant's responses.

Regarding the mix among descriptive, evaluative, and non-specific questions, there is no single correct proportion. If the interviewer asks a high proportion of evaluative questions, he needs to ask himself whether he is really learning what has been going on. With descriptive questions the disadvantage is not quite so clear, because few people can report events without at the same time referring to their feelings about them. However, the interviewer who asks few evaluative questions should ask himself whether the informant is also providing evaluative material – provided that he wishes both types of data.

Specifying Process and People

The interviewer will often find that an open-end question is poorly answered the first time he puts it. The problem is that most informants are vague in identifying people and in dealing with social process. For example, the informant may say, 'We faced a problem with them'. He then goes on to state the nature of the problem and, in the next breath, the solution. No mention is made of who 'we' or 'they' are. Even when the identification of the individuals is obvious in the context of the interview, the interviewer would do well to check his understanding. I find that I have often gone wrong guessing on such identification. Furthermore, the informant has mentioned the nature of the problem and its solution but has said nothing about the social process of recognition, decision, choice of actions, and so on, all of which may be of more interest to the social researcher than is the problem itself.

In one interview with a union leader, for example, my opening question about a problem situation elicited a response of about 500 words. No doubt the informant considered this a full response, as indeed it was, by ordinary conversational standards. However, I was dealing with a problem of some technical complexity as well as one of specifying people and process. It took me eighteen questions or statements before I felt that I had the problem adequately covered. Even then, upon reviewing the transcription later, I found important elements I had overlooked.[2]

Stages in Interviewing

The researcher does not generally hope to cover all relevant areas in the first interview. Often he is initially greeted with suspicion. Even though he promises that what people say will remain confidential, there is no reason for believing this assurance from a complete stranger. Therefore, if the interviewer ventures into the touchiest emotional areas at the outset, he finds people responding in a guarded and superficial manner and observes unmistakable signs that they would be happier if he went away and left them alone.

The first concern of the interviewer is to build rapport, to establish a relationship in which people will feel comfortable and confident in talking with him. The interviewer deliberately keeps the conversation away from evaluative topics and tries to get the informant to talk most about descriptive matters. The interviewer may begin by asking the informant just what his job consists of, what he does at what time and how his job fits into the whole production process. From this topic, the interviewer may ask the informant how he got this particular job, and in this way learn something of his work history. On such topics the informant need not feel pushed to reveal his inner feelings about the company, the foreman, the union, or other possibly touchy topics. On the other hand, since these topics involve human relations, the informant can easily refer to other people if he feels so inclined. In the first interview the researcher should follow up such references with caution. When they are not volunteered, he must patiently wait for another occasion when increased familiarity may give the informant more confidence and enable him to talk more easily.

Occasionally, in the first interview an informant will unburden himself of a great deal of emotionally loaded material. Although the beginning interviewer may be delighted by such a reaction, this entails certain hazards. Realising that the interviewer will be talking to many other people, the informant may become anxious and wonder if he has said too much. The interviewer may then find in the second interview that this particular informant is quite hesitant and reserved.[3] Clearly, the interviewer in such a first interview cannot refuse to listen to the informant, but he should recognise the hazards and should not probe for further information. Also he should not terminate the interview just at the point at which the informant has had his say on the most emotionally loaded materials, but should bring him up out of the depths and conclude the interview with some casual smalltalk. Furthermore, to guard against the sudden cooling off of such an informant, he should be contacted further for a casual discussion, if not another interview, soon after the first interview.

Every experienced fieldworker recognises that informants are not of equal value to the research. There are some individuals who, no matter how skilled the interviewer, do not notice what is going on around them or perhaps have difficulty in expressing themselves. The best informants are those who are in a position to have observed significant events and who are quite perceptive and reflective about them. Some such key individuals may be identified early in the study, since they hold a formal position of importance to the study. Others, who hold key informal positions, are not so evident initially. To locate such people, the interviewer can make a practice of asking each informant to name several people who would be especially helpful to his study. The chances are that the several lists will converge on a few names.

As the study proceeds, the researcher should be thinking of getting some key individuals to become collaborators. It can be of inestimable value to have one or two individuals who know what the researcher is looking for and can give him the expert guidance that can be based only upon such full information. It is a mistake to think of informants as passive instruments. In a long interview with a union steward, I was trying to learn what had led to the downfall of a once very popular foreman. None of my specific questions brought much light on this. It was only when I told the steward frankly what puzzled me that he provided a full and systematic story.

Verification

The first step in the analysis of research data involves a weighing of the validity of statements made by the informant. What are we to make of it when he tells us how he feels? Or when he tells us what happened? All interviewing methods necessarily deal with this problem. The researcher dealing with a questionnaire or interview schedule can only seek to put into the same instrument several questions bearing upon the same topic, thus bringing to light possible inconsistencies in response which may indicate ambivalence of feelings – or confusion as to the meaning of the questions.

The interviewer proceeding along the lines discussed here sacrifices the questionnaire advantages of ready quantifiability in attitude or sentiment responses, but he gains in exchange freedom to use a variety of techniques to test the meaning of the responses he gets in the interview. In asking informants 'what happened?' the interviewer enters into an area of data not amenable at all to the questionnaire approach. Here, too, informant reports are not simply accepted, but are tested in various ways. I am not suggesting that skilful interviewing can ever tell us, in any absolute sense, how the informant feels or even what happened. I am only claiming that the techniques to be discussed will enable us to assess, with more justified confidence, what the informant is telling us. The meaning of his remarks must be tested in some of the following ways.[4]

THE INFORMANT'S REPORT OF EVALUATIVE DATA

The problem here is how to assess the informant's feelings about some subject under investigation. At the outset we must recognise that there are different kinds of evaluative data: (1) the informant's *current emotional state*, such as anger, fear, anxiety, or depression; (2) the *values* of the informant, that is, the feelings that may be presumed to underlie opinions, attitudes and behaviour; (3) the informant's *attitudes* or *sentiments*, his emotional reactions to the subjects under discussion; and (4) the informant's *opinions* or cognitive formulation of ideas on a subject There is no reason to expect that the data gathered in these four categories will fit together consistently. Nor, in case of a conflict, do we try to determine which data represent the informant's 'real' feelings. Discovery of the conflict may, indeed, be the most important subjective information we obtain.

This approach puts a different light on the problem of using behaviour as a way of validating attitudes. For example, a young housewife expressed herself so much in favour of careful budgeting that she and her husband carefully made out envelopes in which they put the money allocated for various purposes. When shopping with a close friend with whom she felt a good deal of social competition, however, she bought a dress which was out of line with the budget. It is not very meaningful to say that her behaviour in buying the dress 'invalidates' her opinions in favour of budgeting or to ask what her 'real' attitudes are. Even if this young housewife had been asked what she would do if she ran across an unusually attractive dress which was not within her budgetary planning, she might have said that she should refuse to buy it and would work out some way to purchase such a dress in the future. The sophisticated interviewer expects neither consistent well-thought-out attitudes and values on the subjects he is inquiring about, nor rational and consistent pictures of informants' sentiments and behaviour. The difficulties in interpreting subjective data are increased when the informant is recollecting past feelings or attitudes. Recollections of past feelings are generally selected to fit more comfortably into one's current point of view. But perhaps the major consideration that complicates the assessment of evaluative reports is that they are so *highly situational.* If, for example, a Democrat is among Republican friends whose opinions he values highly, he will hesitate to express sentiments that might antagonise or disconcert these friends. With other friends, who think pretty much as he does, however, he will not hesitate to express a Democratic point of view, and if he is at a Democratic party meeting, he may be swept up in this enthusiasm and express such sentiments even more strongly. The interview situation must be seen as just *one* of many situations in which an informant may reveal subjective data in different ways.

The key question is this: what factors may influence an informant's reporting in the interview situation? The following factors are likely to be important:

(1) *Ulterior motives* may affect the informant's reporting. On one occasion a foreman of a South American company expressed great interest in being interviewed. He went on to express enthusiasm about every aspect of the company. When the interview closed, he said, 'I hope you will give me a good recommendation to the management'.

(2) The informant may *desire to please* the interviewer, so that his opinions will be well received. An interviewer identified with better race relations might well find informants expressing opinions more favourable to minority groups than they would express among their own friends.

(3) *Idiosyncratic factors* may cause the informant to express only one facet of his reactions to a subject. For example, in a follow-up interview an informant was told that she had changed her attitude towards Jews. She then recalled that, just before the initial interview, she had felt that a Jewish dealer had tried to cheat her. She recalled that she was still angry about this incident and had reacted in terms of it to the questions about Jews in the interview. A few days earlier or a few days later, she would probably have expressed herself quite differently. Mood, wording of the question, individual peculiarites in the connotations of specific words and extraneous factors, such as the baby crying, the telephone ringing, and so on all may influence an informant.

When present, such factors may cause serious misinterpretation of the informant's statements. To minimise the problems of interpretation, the interview situation should be carefully structured and the interview itself should be carefully handled. Some distractions can be avoided by prearranging an appropriate time and place for interviewing. Ulterior motives can sometimes be counteracted by pointing out that the researcher has no position of influence. Bars to spontaneity can be reduced by assurances to the informant that his remarks will be kept confidential. The confidence that develops in a relationship over a period of time is perhaps the best guarantee of sincerity, and important informants should be cultivated with care and understanding. Idiosyncratic factors of connotation and meaning are difficult to account for, but a good precaution is to ask questions in many different ways, so that the complex configuration of sentiments can be better understood. While we never assume a one-to-one relationship between sentiments and overt behaviour, the researcher is constantly relating sentiments expressed to the behaviour he observes – or would expect to observe – in the situation under discussion.

In one field situation the informant was a restaurant supervisor. The restaurant owner was a graduate dietician, who placed a great deal of stress upon maintaining high professional standards. In the course of the interview the supervisor casually remarked that she herself was the only supervisor in the restaurant who was not a college graduate. She did not elaborate, nor did the interviewer probe the point at this time. A few minutes later the interviewer returned to the topic: 'I was interested in something you said earlier: that you are the only supervisor here who is not a college graduate.' Before another word was uttered, the supervisor burst into tears. Clearly, the affect attached to the earlier statement was repressed and became evident only in subsequent behaviour, when she cried.

In some cases the informant may be trying to convince himself, as well as the interviewer, that he does not have a certain sentiment. In the case of Joe Sloan,[5] a highly ambitious gasoline-plant operator, the interview took place shortly after Sloan had been demoted. He reported calmly that in a subsequent talk with the plant manager and the personnel manager they had not been able to encourage him about his future with the company. Since Sloan had earlier expressed strong sentiments against management – with apparent relish – one might have expected him to be even more explosive with this new provocation. The researcher was puzzled when he said, 'I'm nonchalant now. Those things don't bother me any more'. Neither his gestures, nor his facial expression revealed any emotion. A week later, Sloan suddenly walked off the job in response to a minor condition that had recurred often in the past. Reflecting on the incident later, we could see that Sloan's 'nonchalant' statement was a danger-signal. Recent events had intensified his negative sentiments towards management, being unable or unwilling to 'blow his top' as before, he no longer had a safety-valve and might have been expected to take some rash and erratic action. These cases suggest the importance of seeing discrepancies between sentiments and observed (or expected) behaviour as an open invitation to focus interviewing and observation in this problem area.

THE INFORMANT'S REPORTING OF
DESCRIPTIVE DATA

Frequently the interviewer wants to determine what actually happened on some occasion. Can we take what the informant reports at face value? The answer, of course, is 'No'. An informant who reports that people are plotting against him may reveal merely his own paranoid tendencies. But even though plots of this kind are rare, it may just happen that people actually *are* trying to undermine the informant. The researcher must know in what respects an informant's statement reflects his personality and perception and in what respects it is a reasonably accurate record of actual events. The objectivity of an informant's report depends on how much distortion has been introduced and how this can be corrected. The major sources of distortion in first-hand reports of informants are:

(1) The respondent did not observe what happened, or cannot recollect what he did observe, and reports instead what he supposes happened.
(2) The respondent reports as accurately as he can, but because his mental set has selectively perceived the situation, the data reported give a distorted impression of what occurred. Awareness of the 'true' facts might be so uncomfortable that the informant wants to protect himself against this awareness.
(3) The informant quite consciously modifies the facts as he perceives them in order to convey a distorted impression of what occurred.

Naturally, trained research workers are alert to detect distortion wherever it occurs. How can they do this? First of all, there is an important negative check – *implausibility*. If an account just does not seem at all plausible, we are justified in suspecting distortion. For example, an informant living near the campus of a co-educational college reported that a college girl had been raped in a classroom during hours of instruction by some of the male students. She was quite vague as to the precise circumstances, for example, as to what the professor was doing at the time. (Did he, perhaps, rap the blackboard and say, 'May I have your attention, please?') While this account lacked plausibility, it did throw light on the informant's personal world. Through other reports we learned that a college girl had indeed been raped, but the offence had taken place at night, the girl was not on the college campus, and the men were not college students. The woman who told the original story was a devout member of a fundamentalist sect that was highly suspicious of the

'Godless university'. In this context, the story makes sense as a distortion unconsciously introduced to make the story conform to her perception of the university. The test of implausibility must be used with caution, of course, because sometimes the implausible *does* happen.

A second aid in detecting distortion is any knowledge of the *unreliability of the informant* as an accurate reporter. In the courtroom the story of a witness is seriously undermined by any evidence that he has been inaccurate in reporting some important point. First interviews provide little evidence on an informant's reliability, unless he is reporting on a situation about which we have prior knowledge. After what the informant has told us has been checked or corroborated by other reports, we can form some idea of how much we can rely on his account. Even though we learn to distinguish reliable from unreliable informants, we must never assume that an informant who has proved reliable in the past will never require further checking. A third aid is *knowledge of an informant's mental set*, and how it may influence his perception and interpretation of events. Thus, we would be on guard for distortion in a labour-union leader's report of how management welched upon a promise it made in a closed meeting.

Perhaps the major way to detect and correct distortion is by *comparing an informant's account with accounts given by other informants*. And here the situation resembles the courtroom setting, since we must weigh and balance testimony of different witnesses, evaluate the validity of eye-witness data, compare the reliability of witnesses, take circumstantial evidence into account, appraise the motives of key persons and consider the admissibility of hearsay information. We may have little opportunity in field research for anything that resembles cross-examination but we can *cross-check* accounts of different informants for discrepancies and try to clear these up by asking for further clarification.

Since we generally assure informants that what they say is confidential, we are not free to tell one informant what another has told us. Even if the informant says he does not care, it is wise to treat the interview as confidential, since repeating what informants say stirs up anxiety and suspicion. Of course the researcher may be able to tell what he has heard without revealing the source; this may be appropriate where a story has wide currency, so that an informant cannot infer the source of the information. But if an event is not widely known, the mere mention of it may reveal what a specific informant has said about the situation. How can data be cross-checked in these circumstances?

In a field study in a glassworks, Jack Carter, a gaffer (top man of the glass-making team), described a serious argument that had arisen between gaffer Al Lucido and his servitor (no. 2 man) on another workteam. Lucido and his servitor had been known as close friends. Since the effect of intra-team relations on morale and productivity were central to the study, it was important (1) to check this situation for distortion; and (2) to develop the details.

Carter's account of the situation seemed plausible, and our experience indicated that he was a reliable informant. We had no reason to believe that he was so emotionally involved or biased towards this other workteam as to give him an especially jaundiced view of the situation. Furthermore, some of the events he described he had actually witnessed, and others he had heard about directly from the men on the particular workteam. Nevertheless, wishing an account from one of the men directly involved, I scheduled an appointment with Lucido one day after work. To avoid disturbing Lucido and the others by asking directly about the argument, I sought to reach this point without revealing my purpose. Lucido was encouraged to talk about the nature of his work and about the problems that arose on his job, with the focus gradually moving towards problems of co-operation within the workteam. After Lucido had discussed at length the importance of maintaining harmonious relationships within the workteam, I said: 'Yes, that certainly is important. You know I've been impressed with the harmonious relationships you have on your team. Since you and the servitor have to work closely together, I guess it's important that you and Sammy are such close friends. Still, I suppose that even the closest of friends can have disagreements. Has there ever been a time when there was any friction between you and Sammy?' Lucido remarked that, indeed, this had happened just recently. When I expressed interest, he went on to give a detailed account of how the friction arose and how the problem between the two men had finally worked out. It was then possible to use Lucido's account to amplify the data on a number of points that Carter had not covered. The informant in this case probably never realised that I had any prior knowledge of the argument. This suggests how the use of information already in hand can guide the researcher towards data that will reveal distortions in the initial account and give a more complete understanding of what actually happened.

Secondhand reports compound the problems of distortion, since they combine the original distortion by the witness with subsequent distortions by the informant. Of course, a shrewd informant may be able to take into account distortions or bias in the reports he receives, and it may even be that his lines of communication are more direct and intimate than any the research worker can establish. If so, the picture the informant gives may have greater objectivity than the reports of eye-witnesses.

This is illustrated by the case of 'Doc' in *Street Corner Society*.[6] Doc was an extraordinarily valuable informant. Whenever checked, his accounts seemed highly reliable. He was also well informed about what was happening in his own and other groups and organisations in his district. This was due to the position he occupied in the community social structure. As the leader of his own group, other leaders discussed with him what they were doing and what they should do. Hence, he knew developments in the 'foreign relations' of the group before his followers, and usually in more direct and accurate form.

Because of the wide variation in quality of informants, the researcher is always on the lookout for informants such as Doc, who can give a reasonably accurate and perceptive account of events that the research is interested in. These special informants are frequently found at key positions in the communication structure, often as formal or informal leaders in the organisation. They can weigh and balance the evidence themselves and correct for the distortions incorporated by their sources of information. Of course, they may withhold or distort information too, so wherever the researcher has to rely on secondhand reports he must be particularly cautious in his interpretation.

On Evaluating Interview Data

Interviewing can never pin down with absolute certainty 'what actually happened'. However, the research man who follows the procedures outlined above should be able to achieve a fairly close approximation of reality. Furthermore, even when he is unable to resolve conflicting evidence, his interviews should clarify the nature of the conflict and help to explain the bases of the different accounts. In dealing with subjective material, the interviewer is, of course, not trying to discover the *true attitude or sentiment* of the informant. He should recognise that ambivalence is a fairly common condition of man – that men can and do hold conflicting sentiments at any given time. Furthermore, men hold varying sentiments according to the situations in which they find themselves. The research task is, then, not simply to discover a particular sentiment, but also to relate that sentiment to the events and interpersonal relations out of which it arises.

Recording the Interview

Interviews yield voluminous data. How are the data to be recorded? The answer to this question depends upon the nature of the study undertaken, the stage of learning of the researcher and the stage of development of the study. Whatever the purpose of an interview, a student should learn early in his training to record as close to verbatim as possible. Among other things, this helps the student stretch his powers of observation and his memory. It is easy enough later to cut down on the volume of recording; it is very difficult to build up an adequate record later on the basis of brief skeletonic reports. Regardless of the stage of a researcher's training, when he first undertakes a study he should strive for a fuller recording than he thinks he will need later on. A special value of this type of interview is that it reveals new angles to explore. If the research man records only items whose significance is apparent to him at the time, he will lose data that could open up for him promising new avenues of exploration.

For the actual mechanics of recording the interview, the research man has three choices: (1) tape recording the actual interview; (2) taking notes on the interview as it progresses and writing a fuller report later; and (3) making notes on the interview after it has terminated and then writing it up.

While a tape recorder on the spot provides the fullest recording, it is expensive and formal. The expense of the machine is the smallest part of the problem. Transcription of an interview is an exceedingly time-consuming task, even for an experienced stenographer. If expense is no problem, the interviewer still has to cope with the additional formality in the situation provided by the recording equipment. Informants are likely to talk more 'for the record' with the machine than without, even when they have been told that the interviewer is going to write up the interview later. Where the interviewer has strong rapport, informants may accept the machine with little hesitation, but in the early stages of the study the introduction of the machine may place a serious obstacle in the way of his efforts to get himself established.

The use of concealed recording machines raises both ethical and practical questions. The ethical question is so obvious that it needs no discussion. The practical question involves the chances of detection. For any given interview, the researcher may be confident that he can arrange things so as to escape detection. However, after a number of months in the same community or organisation, the chances are that he will give away his secret through carelessness or that an informant will somehow stumble upon it. The secret, once out, will spread through the organisation or community in no time at all. At this point the researcher will find no explanation that is satisfactory to the people he is studying. Their faith in him will have been destroyed. Even on strictly practical grounds, the risk seems hardly worth taking.

Should the interviewer take notes in the course of the interview? While having the undoubted advantage of providing a fuller and more accurate record than can possibly be recaptured by memory, this advantage must be balanced against two possible disadvantages. Note-taking adds to the formality of the occasion and may inhibit the informant – especially in the early stages of the study. This is not always and uniformly the case. There are some informants who express anxiety when the interviewer is not taking notes, or who feel that this means that what they are saying is not worth remembering. Even if the assets and liabilities of note-taking balance each other out from the standpoint of

their effect upon the informant, they affect the interviewer himself. An interviewer who takes notes cannot give full attention to the informant. Physical movements, gestures, and facial expressions give clues not to be found in the words themselves, and some of these fleeting non-verbal cues will be missed while the interviewer is writing.

Furthermore, a good interviewer cannot be passive. At all times he must reflect upon what is being said, ask himself what each statement means and how he can best encourage the informant to clarify a certain point or give detail on an item only hinted at. He must be ready at the conclusion of each informant statement to raise a question or make a statement to develop the account further on the items most pertinent and appropriate for the interview at this stage. The interviewer who is busy taking notes cannot be as alert at picking up productive leads as the interviewer who is paying full attention to the informant. Note-taking is likely to interfere with the flow of the interview in another way. The interviewer is always a little behind the informant in his note-taking. Let us say that the informant has just concluded a statement, rich in data, that should be followed up at once. Instead, the interviewer needs a few more seconds at least to finish writing up what the informant has said. Then, after he has rushed the note-taking to a conclusion, he needs a few seconds more to formulate a good comment to stimulate further discussion. Such delays will embarrass the interviewer and make him want to hurry his own statements, with a consequent deterioration of their quality.

The beginning student, who makes notes later and tries to reconstruct the interview completely from memory will be oppressed by how little he can bring back. Even a small amount of practice increases enormously the ability of most interviewers to reconstruct what has been said. However, even the most skilful interviewer will not come very close to a verbatim recording in this method. At best, he will present an interview that is accurate in its main outlines but that condenses and organises the data. This is probably an inevitable feature of the recording process. Our memory needs pegs to hang things on, and we tend naturally to think in terms of topics. The informant may have talked on a certain topic on three or four occasions during the interview, but we tend to group comments on the same topic together and record them together.

Condensation and reorganisation in themselves rarely lead to serious errors, but distortion may occur in the process. In everyday life, we often find ourselves quoting a person so inaccurately as to change the sense of what he said. On other occasions, we attribute to someone else a sentiment we ourselves expressed, simply because the other person did not flatly disagree with us and we unconsciously credited him not simply with agreement, but with actual authorship. There are no sure ways of detecting distortions, but one method for the student to use on himself is to arrange for practice interviews with a tape recorder. Following the interview the student writes it up as fully as he can from memory, and then checks it against the tape recorder for omissions and, particularly, for distortions.

Often the interviewer is unable to write up his interview immediately after it has been concluded. He may have no dictating machine or typewriter handy and no time for a full pencil-and-paper report. Often we have an opportunity to make a second interview immediately after the first, and as a general rule, it is not wise to forgo potentially productive interviews simply to take care of our recording problems. When pressed in this way, the interviewer should try to jot down brief notes, referring to points in the interview and a few key phrases or sentences that suggest particularly telling points that he knows he will want to write in detail later. Such brief notes are of inestimable value when the interviewer is not going to be able to handle the full recording until some hours later.

Projective Aids to Interviewing

There is no need for the interviewer to limit himself to verbal and gestural stimuli. In fact, there are situations in which verbal stimuli are entirely inadequate to bring out the data the researcher is trying to elicit. In such cases the interviewer may wish to develop his own projective devices. Projective techniques are commonly used in clinical psychology to probe the individual's personality. In this chapter, however, we are not concerned with personality. Our concern is with the individual's sentiments and the social world in which he participates, and we therefore use devices much closer to the social environment that we are studying than the Rorschach ink blot or even the thematic apperception test pictures. Three examples will indicate the possibilities.

In the Stirling County study of mental health and social stress, John Collier[7] photographed all the houses in a community and a number of workareas in a local factory. The project staff found the pictures a distinct aid in eliciting statements that seemed to go into full and rich detail. Talking about the pictures also added enjoyment to the interview for the informants. The pictures of factory interiors were particularly helpful in interviews made in the home. A number of researchers have noted that the home is psychologically quite distant from the workplace for most informants. The factory pictures helped the worker place himself in that scene and helped the interviewer place the informant in the technology and workspace.

Leonard Sayles used photographs to advantage when studying worker–management relations. In one situation he found many workers hesitant about expressing their feelings towards the grievance procedure, whereby an individual or group of workers is represented by a union official in arguing the worker's complaint before management. The union contract explicitly recognised that the grievance procedure was the appropriate way of handling differences between workers and management regarding interpretation of contract provisions. Furthermore, the union literature presented the grievance procedure as an essential aspect of democracy in the workplace and implied that a worker should take pride in it. Nevertheless, Sayles picked up indications that workers were anxious about using the grievance procedure.

To elicit such sentiments more readily and to probe more deeply, Sayles developed a set of seven photographs depicting significant social scenes at various stages in the process of grievance-handling. He describes the selection of the scenes in these words:

> In general, people in the plant who thought about using the grievance procedure, envisioned themselves as participating in these group interactions or successive steps of the settlement process: (1) informal discussion with one's fellow workers on what to do about a complaint, (2) informal discussion with a union official, (3) informal meeting with the foreman and union official and worker involved, (4) formal meeting in personnel director's office with the union official and worker present, (5) a formal hearing for the union member before the union executive board, (6) formal discussion of the grievance with the union member present at the plant labor–management committee meeting, (7) an informal discussion in the work group concerning the outcome of the case. (Sayles, 1954, p. 169)

Sayles found it advantageous to present the pictures in sequence to each informant in a rather structured manner. While he tried a number of variations of this procedure, he generally presented each picture with a statement as to the situation it represented and as to who the characters were. The informant was then asked to give his own impression as to what was happening in the picture.

Sayles does not argue that this method gave him material distinctively different from that gained through interviewing but shows that the same types of material are elicited. For example, consider the following responses of the same individual to a photograph and to an interview on another occasion.

Informal discussion with one's fellow workers on what to do about a complaint.
Response to the photograph:
You can tell by their faces just what they're saying. They're telling him, 'You can go ahead if you want to – *but*,' and you can be sure it's a big *but* they're adding. The question is whether or not he has a legitimate grievance. You can see by how he looks that he's sure that he has a legitimate grievance, of

course; that's always the way. He's probably still going through with it, in fact. But by the looks of them, it seems like he is making trouble for the group all the time. If those other fellows are a cross section of the plant, they'll probably be thinking the same as the grievance committee though, and he is going to lose his case. In fact, I'm sure he'll lose it. But at the end he will have made some trouble for them.

Interview response:

Very few fellows in a department like to be in a position of having a grievance – it usually stops a lot of other people from getting something. Most of the grievances fellows have are against each other. You can tell though who it is who's going to have the grievances. It's just like in the Army – you know who's going to squawk. (Sayles, 1954, pp. 171–2)

What, then, is the advantage of the projective approach? Sayles puts it in this way:

the average depth interview was two hours, and this did not include the researcher's previous efforts over a six-week period to develop rapport with his informants. On the other hand, the projective photographs were administered in approximately ten minutes to volunteer subjects that the researcher had not met prior to the picture interview. To be successful, the depth interviews had to be undertaken at the informant's home; the picture interviews were done in the plant. (Sayles, 1954, p. 173)

I have found a projective method very helpful in a glass-work study.[8] These workers, particularly the gaffer and the servitor, were highly skilled. The workteams made a complete product, from beginning to end, and the products are well known as art objects. We wondered whether the workers derived some aesthetic satisfaction from making these products, but we had great difficulty in getting meaningful worker reactions to the mental and physical processes involved in the work itself. We could not tackle the question directly without embarrassing ourselves and the workers. Frustrated in our direct approach, we devised an indirect approach through asking the gaffer or the servitor to arrange a set of cards, each one representing a job his team performed, in order of preference. We then asked each individual to explain why he ranked the cards the way he did. While we got no data of particular value out of the ranking itself, the explanations of the rankings revealed feelings about the work process itself that were not expressed in the ordinary interview. It should be noted that some men found it difficult to make any rankings. Thus the method, as used, was not standardised, but served as a useful supplement to other methods.

Some of the gaffers at least were able to verbalise their

pride in the creative process. One commented as follows: 'When you get done, you've got a nice piece of work there . . . It really looks like something . . . When I can say I made that piece, I really swell with pride.' Another gaffer, after commenting on other aspects of a piece he disliked, said, 'That little mug don't look like nothing when you're done'. A third gaffer commented on his favourite piece, 'When you're finished, you've got something'. We also found them verbalising feelings which could be categorised under their reactions to achievement, pressure and timing, amount of work, variety and sense of contribution. These are described in detail elsewhere.[9] Finally, we found the card-ranking method exceedingly useful in some cases in bringing out data on personality, status and human relations. For example, one ambitious young gaffer evaluated his pieces primarily in terms of the degree of difficulty each design offered. The more complex the production problem, the more prestige to him if he succeeded.

Indexing

The researcher who uses questionnaires has little difficulty with problems of indexing. A well-designed questionnaire provides its own organisation of data. The type of interview we describe does not automatically order the data. Furthermore, it provides a voluminous body of data. At first the researcher may remember where to find any particular point, but as the numbers of interviews pile up, he finds himself swamped. He may spend endless hours of reading and rereading his notes unless he has devised some effective manner of indexing them.

In the Appendix for *Street Corner Society* I describe how I approached the indexing problem:

As I gathered my early research data, I had to decide how I was to organize the written notes. In the very early stage of exploration, I simply put all the notes, in chronological order, in a single folder. As I was to go on to study a number of different groups and problems, it was obvious that this was no solution at all.

I had to subdivide the notes. There seemed to be two main possibilities. I could organize the notes topically, with folders for politics, rackets, the church, the family, and so on. Or I could organize the notes in terms of the groups on which they were based, which would mean having folders on the Nortons, the Italian Community Club, and so on. Without really thinking the problem through, I began filing material on the group basis, reasoning that I could redivide it on a topical basis when I had a better knowledge of what the relevant topics should be.

As the material in the folders piled up, I came to realise that the organization of notes by social groups fitted in with the way in which my study was developing. For example, we have a college-boy member of the Italian Community Club saying: 'These racketeers give our district a bad name. They should really be cleaned out of here.' And we have a member of the Nortons saying: 'These racketeers are really all right. When you need help, they'll give it to you. The legitimate businessman – he won't give you the time of day.' Should those quotes be filed under 'Racketeers, attitudes toward'? If so, they would only show that there are conflicting attitudes toward racketeers in Cornerville. Only a questionnaire (which is hardly feasible for such a topic) would show the distribution of attitudes in the district. Furthermore, how important would it be to know how many people felt one way or another on this topic? It seemed to me of much greater scientific interest to be able to relate the attitude to the *group* in which the individual participated. This shows why two individuals could be expected to have quite different attitudes on a given topic.

As time went on, even the notes in one folder grew beyond the point where my memory would allow me to locate any given item rapidly. Then I devised a rudimentary indexing system: a page in three columns containing, for each interview or observation report, the date, the person or people interviewed or observed, and a brief summary of the interview or observation record. Such an index would cover from three to eight pages. When I came to review the notes or to write them, a five-to-ten minute perusal of the index was enough to give me a reasonably full picture of what I had and of where any given item could be located. (Whyte, 1955, pp. 307–8)

As I moved on into industrial studies, I made the index somewhat more elaborate. In one column, together with names of people interviewed, I added, in parentheses, the names of people referred to in the interview. Thus, I was able to note at a glance not only with whom the interview was, but what people were referred to or discussed in the interview. In another column I recorded not only topics, but also relationships. For example, a discussion of a problem of incentives might be indexed with the following headings: piecerates, foremen – time-study man, foreman –worker, worker – steward, steward – foreman. This would indicate to me that a certain section of the interview, in which the informant is describing a piecerate problem, contains statements referring to events or sentiments between people in the categories separated by the dashes. I have not found it profitable to separate sentiments from interactions in my index, because informants almost invariably run them together in their own statements.

I do not consider it advisable for the researcher to determine his indexing categories before he starts the field study. While most significant relationships can be set forth on the basis of the formal structure of the organisation, exactly what topics will be of most significance to the study cannot be completely predetermined. After eight or ten interviews, the researcher should have the feel of the situation sufficiently, so that he can develop a reasonably adequate indexing system. At this point he might reread his first interviews and pencil the appropriate indexing categories on the margins of each page. If he then continues this practice as he goes along, he will find that it will take him perhaps just a few minutes of typing to transfer his marginal notes from the interviews themselves to index pages.

The researcher ready to write a report can work directly from the index to the outline of the paper he is writing. A few minutes spent in rereading the whole index gives him a fairly systematic idea of the material he can draw on. Then, for each topic covered in the report, he can write into his outline the numbers of the interviews and the pages in those interviews where he will find relevant material. For example, if in a restaurant study, he is writing a section on relations between hostesses and waitresses, he writes in his outline some general heading referring to the supervision of waitresses. Then he notes in the outline all interviews where he finds in the index 'waitress – hostess' – plus the page numbers of those particular interview sections. This may refer him to a dozen or more interviews. Perusal of the index will refresh his memory on these interviews, and he will recall that some of the interviews merely duplicate each other. He pulls out of the file perhaps half a dozen interviews, turns to the sections where 'waitress – hostess' is marked on the margin, rereads these sections, and finally uses material from three or four of these interviews. While indexing is an essential part of the mechanics of fieldwork and report-writing, it is far more than a mechanical operation. The indexing system should evolve in line with the type of analysis the researcher eventually intends to make. In this way, the process of indexing the materials is in effect a preliminary analysis of the data. When the fieldwork is completed, therefore, the index not only helps find materials, but serves as a start of the analysis.[10]

Notes: Chapter 16

Reprinted from R. N. Adams and J. J. Preiss (eds), *Human Organization Research: Field Relations and Techniques* (Homewood, Ill.: Dorsey Press, 1960), pp. 352–74.

1   See Dohrenwend and Richardson (1956).
2   This case is taken from Whyte (1953).

3   I am indebted to Stephen A. Richardson for this point.
4   The following section is adapted from Dean and Whyte (1958).
5   See Whyte (1956).
6   See Whyte (1955).
7   See Collier (1957).
8   See Whyte (1957). This study was carried on in collabora-

tion with Frank Miller. We are indebted to Al Callender, the plant superintendent, for suggesting the card-ranking method.
9   See Whyte (1957).
10 For further discussions on interviewing, see Dean (1954), Fenlason (1952), Garrett (1942), Kahn and Cannell (1957) and Merton and Kendall (1946).

17

The Life Study: On Mutual Recognition and the Subjective Inquiry

THOMAS J. COTTLE

I

For several years, my research has been based on visiting with families in poor neighbourhoods of Boston.[1] I have met most of the families by chance, often through encounters with their children in the street, at schools, or after school in local restaurants, pharmacies, tailor shops and flower stores, where in the winter it is particularly warm, and in pool halls too. From the start, the families learn that I might write about them, and describe their histories for others, as well as the way their lives presently are led, and how it is they are able to endure what they themselves call 'life's most difficult hardships'. In some cases, naturally, there is no friendship to be established; I am turned away by a family, and told not to speak with the children.

Briefly, the work is built on long-term friendships and conversations which may take place at any time and in any setting. No questionnaire is used, the conversations simply taking their own course. I do not use a tape recorder, but instead take notes either during the conversation or more likely after it has been completed. Conversations typically last one to two hours, and if our schedules permit, meetings take place about once a week, although sometimes considerably more often. In most instances I find that the actual writing does not begin until I have visited with a particular family for about two years. In the beginning, especially, the work generates serious problems for these families: why have I chosen them? What really do I want of them? What kinds of things are they supposed to talk about with me? And, how do we overcome the differences that showed in the instant of our first encounter, and the advantages I possess by nature of my position in the society and my role in conducting the research?

Unlike many social scientists, I often have no adequate answers for these families. I use words like description and observation, and tell them I believe in having their words heard by those who live in other parts of America. The young children with whom I speak are not overly concerned with my stated purpose; they have already made their decision of whether or not I look like a good bet for a friend. Older children and parents, for good reason, are more suspicious and scrutinising, if not perplexed. In one regard, I am still another person coming to their home uninvited, ready to *take* something from them. In another sense, they may feel that my presence, like that of any researcher, means a chance to talk and be heard, to be recognised, and maybe, too, honoured by this new friendship, however contrived it may seem at first. And so, I do my best to convince them of my interest in them, and express my hope that they might be willing to share some hours with me. Sometimes, for as I say I am turned away, they will reply, in their way, I am not sure what this is all about, but I will take a chance, let you come in, and tell you what you want to know, or what you ought to want to know, and learn something of you as well.

I cannot say why, exactly, of all the families in these neighbourhoods, I specifically selected certain ones for more intensive study. As the research is predicated on the establishment of care, as well as mutual acknowledgement and recognition, very human sorts of attractions play a role in the choices of friends and 'subjects' for observation. Most of the families could well be chosen for this work, although some, clearly, appear a bit more relaxed with me, a bit freer, perhaps, to share experiences. Perhaps, too, I feel freer in their presence, and better able to confront my own reactions to them, as well as the thoughts their words evoke in me.

I make no pretence at objective assessments of these people's lives, the inquiry being subjective and dependent on my relationship with these families, and on paying attention to what is transpiring. One encounters people, listens to them speak about what matters to them, hears the attitudes and opinions they only naturally cultivate and then records what they say. A danger, therefore, some might argue, is that these families are not representative of the urban poor. Moreover, as they are special, if only because they meet with me, their words cannot be made the basis of any generalisations. Actually, the families are careful to speak only for themselves. Even when I encourage them to characterise the attitudes of their friends, they pull back slightly. They speak of their own lives and histories, and about what makes it possible for them to sustain themselves, their pride and dignity in the face of all sorts of injustices. Thus, it is I who prefer to think that these families speak for a larger group of people than any of us could ever know making this type of inquiry.

Still, the question of the representativeness of these families can be addressed, for their perceptions and attitudes have been well studied. Indeed, the social and political features of urban poverty, and especially of poor black families, and the cognitive, political and social psychological development of these families have been the subject of literally hundreds of studies and accounts.[2] Thus, the research, lying closer perhaps to a tradition established by cultural anthropologists, participant observers, and journalists, among others, is always complemented and enlightened by the more traditional research of the social sciences.

Before elaborating certain features of this type of research, two points should be made. First, names of families are always changed so that confidentiality is preserved. Furthermore, families read the manuscripts and grant permission for their publication. Their reading provides a check on the accuracy of reporting, as well as a chance to learn whether the work has honoured them and affirmed our friendships. Secondly, the families who participate in this inquiry have not been selected because of some psychological problem they were experiencing. In no way are they seen as patients.

II

Each of us knows the many roles situations demand that we play. We sense too, the qualitative shifts in personality that these situations generate. We come away from one home and say, I was uncomfortable there, I was not myself. We come away from another home and report feeling free to be the person we believe we genuinely are. In many of the homes I visit, I do not feel free to say things I may let myself say elsewhere. If for no other reason, the asymmetry in my friendships with these families makes us all feel the weightiness of observation and constant self-regard. In our giving to one another, we also hold back; although in our holding back we give each other still another part of ourselves, a part with which we may or may not be satisfied.

Both sides, the families and the investigator, observe new selves emerging, the selves that 'belong' to this special situation. On the one hand, a mother remarks on her son's 'good manners' and articulate ways when he is with me. On the other hand, I see myself at times bumbling, groping for words, for a good question or generous response in a manner I feel to be discrepant from my manner at other times. I find myself too, coming upon new words just as some of the children find whole new families of words and images which they feel to be inappropriate for school but somehow right for me. So we are all on our guard, watching each

other, and most especially, watching ourselves watching each other. And in our changing ways, we seek to be respectful and caring of one another, and try not to be inhibited by the different circumstances of our lives or by the different appearances of our bodies. One result of this brand of work, then, is to consecrate a series of settings and relationships that transcends the settings and forms of relationships normally experienced by the participants. Thus, a boy softens the lighting in his bedroom when we speak, and a girl prepares a kitchen table in some special way. And all of us think of one another as 'that special friend', and work to attain the feelings of mutual recognition, mutual acknowledgement.[3]

There is an important point to be made about this transcendent setting and 'special friend' kind of friendship. When I began the work in these neighbourhoods eight years ago, I looked at the families strictly as illustrations of some 'problem', 'phenomenon' or 'condition'. In addition, I found myself 'ghettoising' everything until the families became little more than neighbourhood informants, representatives of poverty, poignant objects that I could hold up to make a case for their intelligence, political sophistication and need for legal rights. As long as I used fragments of speech and worried about what their words meant, the families remained newspaper photographs, postcards, some-*thing* to regard as illustration, but not people to be taken seriously in and of themselves.

Even more, I believed that to gain the confidence of these families, and to be certain that what we experienced was 'valid', the settings and relationships had to put us all at ease. Any cue that reminded us of my own participating observation would render all responses stilted, self-conscious, invalid. Patronising actions, undue cordiality or ingratiation necessarily implied failure in friendship, failure in investigation, failure in science. Personal accounts, I felt, had to be put aside through my sociological expertise or so-called clinical insightfulness. Or, even if I listened in the 'right' and 'open' manner, I distanced myself from these 'subjects' by taking myself out of the writing altogether, so that no one would be reminded that I had been with them and been touched by them. In the name of objective social science and proper psychological and political demeanour, no one should know how I felt about them. Later, I made an equally imprudent mistake when I came to believe that little in sociology or psychology seemed pertinent to my discussions with the families. In fact it was the people themselves who encouraged me to call upon sociological and clinical perspectives just as they were doing.

After eight years I have turned these beliefs around. My periodic stumbling ways and ungainly silences, along with the children's occasional formalities and so-called 'best behaviourisms', symbolise our collective desire to create that transcendent situation of mutual recognition. For within it lies the care that each of us has for the other, a care that derives in part from the awareness that our relationship is to some extent unnatural, even contrived. Still, the act of contriving a role or presence can be a creative act, one of giving and of increased consciousness of self. It can be an offering. Surely Mrs Rosalie Counter Williams, with whom my friendship remains brittle and unsettled, even after five years, realises that I have more knowledge on certain topics than I may share with her at a given time. But I know that she has knowledge and feelings that she keeps out of my sight as well. Sadly, our culture continually assesses the differences between us and the materials we share and keep from one another in terms of equalities and inequalities.

This matter too, enters our friendship and causes us to be self-conscious and on guard. Both of us are aware of those who are suspicious of the fact that at times I can find nothing to say to her or to her children, or that I might be overcome by feelings, even childlike feelings. We are aware, too, of those who chastise her for restraining herself with me, or perhaps for merely allowing me to enter her home. As best we can, therefore, we play out political roles, the politics, that is, of our experiences together, hoping to combat the asymmetries produced by the culture, the society, our age, sex, race and social standing, and by the rights and privileges that put me at an advantage in doing this type of work.

There is little, then, about this form of research that allows for so-called objective inquiry. Even if I chose to assume the role of indifferent observer, as if that role yielded objectivity, I know that the families would never let it pass; not after all these years. Invariably they remark on those days when I appear more dishevelled than usual, just as they remark on those instances when I fail to tell them of feelings my face and body are already emitting. Upon hearing their remarks, I am reminded of the subjective nature of the inquiry, and that what I observe and record is not only material experienced by me, it is, in part, generated by me. I often think that the aspects of the families' lives that I might record with some modicum of objectivity are the very aspects wherein I never confront them. Yet even these aspects would receive subjective responses, responses that are in no way inferior to the knowledge gained through so-called objective assessments.

Again, the research builds upon encounters with human beings, who by nature act egoistically. The encounters are themselves processes of mutual inquiry, observation and expression; explication and under-standing lie in the encounters. The emphasis, therefore, rests on the single case, and the growing series of single involvements. A genuine encounter, moreover, precludes comparison and assessment. To assess these families, in effect, is to transcend them, and thereby to negate the mutuality of recognition and the politics of equality. The self-consciousness, finally, born in these encounters, connotes both wariness and self-awareness, clearly precursors of human conscience and tolerance.

In writing about these families, I constantly feel the predisposition to over-romanticise them. At very least I feel a need for something with which to counteract the reality of their circumstances. But merely to reveal an awareness of this problem in no way resolves the dangers of over-romanticising their lives. I am certain that I have invested feelings in them as well as indulged in my own thoughts when it might have been 'better' to 'stand back' and assume an air of objectivity, or the traditional role of 'outside' observer. Indeed, one might think, given the disparities between my life and the lives of these families, that an outsider's role would be easily assumed.

The withholding of feelings, both in conversation, and in writing, is something with which I continually struggle. If there is a rule about this form of research, it might be reduced to something as simple as pay attention. Pay attention to what the person says and does and feels; pay attention to the scene, the streets, rooms, textures, colours and lighting; pay attention to what is evoked by these conversations and perceptions, particularly when one's mind wanders so very far away; and finally, pay attention to the response of those who might, through one's work, hear these people. Paying attention implies an openness, not any special or metaphysical kind of openness, but merely a watch on oneself, a self-consciousness, a belief that everything one takes in from the outside and experiences within one's own interior is worthy of consideration and essential for understanding and honouring those whom one encounters. More importantly, the expression of the investigator's feelings contributes to the reality of the situation, as the situation itself is comprised in part by the investigator. It is through the investigator that one hears these families. Like the families, readers, too, want to know whether the investigator can be trusted.

Feelings, naturally, cannot shape the intellectual and legislative processes required in the determination of human rights. Yet, when anger never appears, when day to day heartache and anguish and personal responses to them are deemed inappropriate for intellectuals, researchers and legislators, then that transcendant situation of mutual recognition, as sub-jective as it must be, is never approached, and the traditional distances and inequalities between people are reiterated and affirmed. Then too, institutions and government need never change, and the words of these families remain poignant, and sensitive, but not legitimate influences of personal consciousness or social change, nor testimonies of the need for political and economic enfranchisement.

Here may be the crucial point of separation between myself and these families. I have no doubt that they 'open up' with me, as we say, and share personal and tender experiences as well as some hurtful ones. We also hold back things, and recognise that certain issues, and the emotions connected to them, are better left unsaid. One such issue is that I can leave them, there, in their inadquately heated homes, with a meagre amount of food ready to be placed on the table, and return to my own home, my own race, my own social position and cultural securities. Many hold back anger from me, partly because I am for them, along with others, a symbol of the very culture that constrains them. Pressure is put on some of the black families to stop talking with white people, and I understand this, just as pressure is put on me to terminate my relationships with them. But more than just what they say or I say, it is the encounter, the two cultures coming together to yield words, ideas and passions that predominates. Our behaviour together, coupled with the respective evolution of our peoples, keeps their anger out of sight; not out of hearing distance, but out of sight. And so our friendships for the moment are safeguarded.

Nothing, then, is more troublesome than to leave these families each day, realising how much empty space remains between them and me, and that all of us are aware of this space. It is a space of politics, receiving my blind spots and patronising gestures, as well as their feelings of attachment, 'identification', ambivalence, or just plain caring. It is where the politics begin and end, where disenfranchisement, oppression and colonisation breed, and where research of the sort I have reported takes place. Words, intellects and emotions, live in this space, as do laws, customs, history and scholarship. Each word we speak constitutes a molecular tension, relative quiescence followed by frenzied action of human relationships. This, in essence, is the space of my encounters with these families; it is the site of the distillates of America's political system in this one moment, and in this one context.

III

In undertaking the research, I confess to wondering whether the relatively small number of families would be 'enough', and whether the absence of abstract interpretation and analysis of attitudes would cause some to feel that something vital was missing. As much as the practice of psychotherapy at times demands interpretations of language and behaviour, in this different sort of enterprise, I believe that people's words stand on their own, and that often an overriding analysis is uncalled for, if not an outright impertinence.

Clearly, analysis of social, political and psychological phenomena, an inevitable operation in a society dominated by technological rationality, is useful and enlightening. But analysis can also mean the distancing of people, the gratuitous 'upgrading' of human groups, or the fact that in order to speak for oneself and one's people, one has to learn the appropriate 'mother tongue', or the language of vocal and powerful leaders. Analysis implies that the words of someone, a resident of some community, a patient in psychoanalysis, are by themselves incomplete bits of data waiting maturation.

What makes them 'complete' is the analysis; rational explanation; their systematic placement not just in a particular context or series of categories – for these operations we all undertake in listening to speech – but in some higher order and abstracted level of comprehension. For the present work, analysis would mean not only making something of the words spoken by these families, but using their words to develop an overarching statement, a theory of the self in contemporary society.

Without doubt, the task of rendering everyday reality into conceptualisations and explanatory theories is a formidable one, and essential for understanding our single lives and our cultures, as well as for the development of intellectual discourse. Yet the generation of social science theory and the act of abstracting human expression to achieve levels of more comprehensive awareness is not the goal of this research. It is not the reason I came to know these families. Interpretation and analysis none the less remain a part of this enterprise. They are, however, performed implicitly. In the selection of the material, in the inevitable editing of dialogues and personal reflections and reactions rest interpretation, theory, conceptualisation and, just as important, the moments of polemics and moralising.

As is true with most types of theory-building and interpretation in the social sciences, this implicit almost playwright form of interpretation carries its own brand of prejudgements and unabiding perspectives. They are unavoidable. In making interpretations and analyses in the form of experiencing, selecting and ordering, one hopes that the truth is accurately described, and that the ethic of enhancing life is never lost, but one can never be certain. Pure, abstract analysis, like the structured interview, often masks the uncertainties and vagaries of the reality from which the analyst can never be extricated unless, of course, the analyst never encounters the reality chosen for analysis. But when one does play a part, when one is implicated in the lives of those one observes or 'studies', then abstract analysis becomes a more difficult psychological and intellectual chore. Distancing oneself becomes an impossible strategy, an implausible experience, and using these people's words as grist for one's intellectual machinery, an ugly if not incongruous undertaking. When, finally, I go back and analyse, in the typical sense, I negate the encounters and deny the truths of the subjective inquiry.

In this context, I understand, but am saddened nevertheless, by two expressions I often hear made in connection with this kind of work. The first goes something like, 'It's good that you're going out there to those homes, talking with those families and having their dirt rub off on you'. Strangely, it is rarely suggested that one might be cleansed in his contact with the poor, the obscure, the disenfranchised. Still, apart from whether one is dirtied or cleansed, does this expression mean that one is in some way made less a person because of his association with families living in poverty? Is one now half a man because so many of his hours are spent associating with children in ways we normally characterise as being feminine? Does the fact that women engage in the care of children more than men influence our perceptions of children generally, and of those men who enter into friendships with children and their families, and become in small measure, a part of their lives? If, because of a subjective posture, one becomes half a man, then indeed he is a child, expressive rather than analytic, filled with sentiment, and catering to unrealisable dreams and ambitions, all of which suggests he is not yet ready to be taken seriously. He often bumbles, sits in silence, has outbreaks of temper, generally 'overidentifies' with those he visits, and in no way resembles the image we maintain of a scholar or scientist.

The second expression goes, 'I don't know what to do with the words of these families, what to make of them or think about them'. The expression reminds me of my own reactions to concerts, where I feel an uneasy urge to wait for the following morning's review before deciding whether I liked what I heard. Undoubtedly, analysis enhances one's appreciation of music, or language in the present context. It must never detract, however, from one's ability to hear and pay attention, or minimise one's belief in one's capacity to hear, appreciate and respond. While analysis, be it explicit or implicit, aids in understanding and offers the possibility of enlarging the sensuous experience, it can also be a self-imposed inhibitor of the feelings evoked by the experience, a constraint, in other words, on reaction.

Similarly, the structured interview, while yielding valuable information, purposely acts as a constraint on personal reaction. In a sense, the structured interview becomes a barrier between people, albeit a porous one, as well as a means of keeping responses of all kinds under control. Whereas the content yielded through the structured interview is unpredictable, the interaction describing the interview is more or less prearranged. This is not to say that so-called 'free form' interviews, what we have called encounters, are free of restraints on behaviour and feeling. They are not. Indeed, these restraints may be the basis of the tension one experienced in becoming implicated, if only by reading, in the lives of other persons, particularly those with whom one rarely associates.

The tension, then, is between structuring and analysing material, and remaining vulnerable to whatever has been evoked by this material, without utilising techniques to control and shape the material. It is not merely a tension caused by a competition between intellectual and emotional resources. Rather, the tension is caused partly by the political, economic and educational disparities in our culture, and partly, too, by our social roles and positions, our stations in life and our learned beliefs about what is appropriate and inappropriate behaviour for ourselves, for those richer and more powerful than us and for those poorer and less powerful than us.

It is a tension caused, moreover, by those we feel to be transgressing in some ways, those who seem capricious in their manner, and somehow less respectful of style, custom and protocol. Analysis may be a means of combating these transgressors, these persons who travel where they are not meant to travel, work where they are not meant to work, commune with those with whom they are not meant to commune, and subjectively experience what they ought to be objectively describing and assessing. It may also be a means of counteracting the feeling that we have been intruded on; that our feelings, in other words, have been accidentally ignited. Abstract, depersonalised analysis, then, is an essential intellectual and creative act that expands learning. It is also an encumbrance; a blockade to feeling and human contact; a filibuster to quintessential human expression and exchange.

IV

A common accusation levelled at those of us doing this kind of research, is that we 'work out' our identities through the lives of those we interview, teach, or simply observe. While the accusation is cryptic, and the use of the word identity not sufficiently comprehensive, the import of the accusation contains a truth. Decisions to work with certain families in a somewhat open manner may well affect one's identity. But any decision may influence the continuity of the self over time and the sense of inner sameness that are, theoretically, foundations of identity. Confronting these families, or anyone for that matter, necessarily affects our sense of personal evolution and commitment, and touches the chords of our identity. Encounters, implying as they do mutual acknowledgement of persons, must affect our sense of identity, for they cause us to become reacquainted with ourselves.

The accusation of working out one's identity with families in poverty is extremely serious, if truths are distorted and identity formation found to be the reason for engaging children in the first place. But these potential dangers hold true in any human contact, be it with an employer or colleague, parent, or friend. For any encounter may cause someone to feel that his or her identity has been affirmed, or put somehow into jeopardy. And that this happens is not necessarily a sign that one is 'insecure', but rather that the capacity to become reacquainted with one's history and imagined destiny endures.

Still, when the work involves children, the question of 'identity seeking' is more frequently heard, probably because we believe that those who study, teach, or treat children have never completely resolved the childlike components of their own identity. While this remains a matter for psychiatrists and psychohistorians to decide, unless of course children begin to publish their investigations of us, one takes from this 'identity seeking' accusation the contention that possessing childlike components in one's adult identity is pathological, and this fact has serious implications for our fundamental perceptions of ourselves and our children.

V

One final point. I began the research with the idea of sampling families from various economic levels of society – what we ordinarily conceive of as the lower, middle and upper classes – so that a genuine comparison of families' attitudes and experiences might be achieved. I gradually changed my mind, however, believing that at certain times one must speak about the few families one knows and no one else, and refrain from comparing them with their age counterparts someplace, or even with other families in their own neighbourhood. For in the comparison process one can too easily lose an appreciation for the single human being who stands before us, the knowledge and feelings of the person, and the glory that must be that person's history and future. While clearly a useful and valid method of research, the comparison process can also further, albeit unintentionally, the very standards and criteria that lead to such imputations as 'disadvantagedness', and 'inferior performance and intelligence'. The goal, therefore is not to study poor families for the purpose of constructing behavioural criteria to be used later with rich families. The goal is to establish and preserve human rights, rights sanctified by law, culture and psychology, that honour human beings and safeguard the time during which they walk upon the earth.

Under any political system that evolves in a truly equitable society, individuals will continue to need help of one sort or another. They will be in pain or feel despair, they will seek advice on how to read faster, or perhaps how to raise their children, or grow their produce. Their requests, however, in this equitable society will be interpreted as acts of strength, not as ineptitude. At present, the overriding message of those who periodically dip into poor communities as if testing icy water with their toes, is that the people of America's inner cities are weak, ignorant, primitive, filled with 'raw' capacities and unwilling to 'help their own cause'. These reports then make their way into the minds of American's citizens, their abiding legislation, newspapers and textbooks. The result is captured in my own surprise several years ago, when I simply had to acknowledge how splendid are the minds of the young people I was meeting in communities like Roxbury, Dorchester, Somerville and Roslindale. The result is captured, too, in my own blind spots, my patronising gestures and my inability at times to transcend a proper role or agreed upon expectation, and in the encounter listen to what was being said to me, about me and within me.

Notes: Chapter 17

Reprinted from *Urban Life and Culture,* vol. 2, no. 3, October, 1973, pp. 344–60, by kind permission of the publisher, Sage Publications, Inc. and the author.

1   See Cottle (1971; 1972a; 1972b; 1972c; 1972d; 1973a; 1973b and 1974).
2   See, for example, Aberbach and Walker (1970), Billingsley (1968), Clark (1965), Coles (1967; 1969; 1971a; 1971b), Coles and Piers (1969), Deutsch (1967), Greenberg (1970), Hannerz (1969), Kardiner and Ovesey (1951), Liebow (1967), Marx (1967), Parsons and Clark (1966), Pettigrew (1964), Rainwater (1970), Riessman (1962) and Riis (1970).
3   This discussion has been influenced by the work of William Earle: see Earle (1972).

Section Five

Historical Sources and Field Research

18

Personal Documents, Oral Sources and Life Histories

ROBERT G. BURGESS

The emphasis in field research conducted by sociologists and social anthropologists is upon the observed present. Certainly, if we turn to basic texts in field research (Lofland, 1971; Wax, 1971; Schatzman and Strauss, 1973), we find no space devoted to a discussion of historical materials. Similarly, if we turn to ethnographic studies, we find that historical data is neglected. Warner's studies of Newburyport in the Yankee City series (for example, Warner and Lunt, 1941; Warner and Low, 1947) have ignored the history of the community as available in documentary sources, with the result that he misrepresents a number of patterns of social life (Thernstrom, 1965). A similar point has been made about Whyte's classic study of *Street Corner Society* (Whyte, 1955). Thernstrom (1968) questions the extent to which Whyte's evidence reflects the historical period in which the data was collected. As Pitt (1972) has argued, the field researcher is in danger of misinterpreting the present if historical sources are ignored.

Here, we might ask what constitutes an historical source? A classic statement is provided by Langlois and Seignobos, who maintain that 'The historian works with documents ... For there is no substitute for documents: no documents, no history' (Langlois and Seignobos, 1898, p. 17). Indeed, they go on to remark: 'The search for and the collection of documents is thus a part, logically the first and most important part, of the historian's craft' (Langlois and Seignobos, 1898, p. 18). While the latter statement has much to commend it, in terms of indicating the style of research, the former statement concerning documents is problematic, as they restrict their meaning of the term 'document' to written sources alone. Such a definition can only add strength to the field researcher's argument for omitting historical material, as it can be maintained that many groups with whom field researchers work often do not produce a sufficient range of written documentary materials. But this puts an unduly narrow construction on both field research and documentary evidence.

There are two major questions here. First, what constitutes documentary evidence? Secondly, what constitutes a written document? As far as the writers in this section are concerned, documentary evidence is taken to include both written and oral sources. Mean-while, the term 'written document' can be taken to include personal documents such as biographies, autobiographies, letters, diaries, sermons, poems, plays and novels. However, field researchers should be aware that historians use a wider range of data sources (census materials, parish registers, wills and inventories) and methodologies. Hobsbawm (1974) has indicated how social history has been influenced, shaped and stimulated by the methods, techniques and questions of other social sciences with the result that quantitative approaches are now used in historical studies (Wrigley, 1972), especially by the Cambridge Group for the History of Population and Social Structure. In a discussion on the use of quantitative methods for the study of social data, Schofield (1972) has explained how a sample of historical documents should be drawn and how the results should be evaluated, while Anderson (1972) has discussed how quantitative and non-quantitative descriptive data can be used in historical studies. While a wide range of historical materials, techniques and approaches are available, the emphasis in this section is upon the collection of historical evidence construed in its broadest sense to include personal accounts of situations that are provided through oral and written sources.

The written sources of documentary evidence are varied. As Samuel shows (Chapter 19), there is a standard range of written documents that it is usual to gather in the study of local history. However, the documents that are available influence the perspective that is taken, as Samuel has commented elsewhere:

> It is remarkable how much history has been written from the vantage point of those who have had the charge of running – or attempting to run – other people's lives, and how little from the real life experience of people themselves. (Samuel, 1975, p. xiii)

The result, according to Samuel is that we only obtain one perspective on the past, namely, that which is embodied in official documents. However, as Carpenter (1980) has shown, another perspective can be obtained from elite documents by interrogating them from another perspective. Nevertheless, Samuel

(1975) maintains that we need to find out about factory life from informants other than factory inspectors, prison life from informants other than prison reformers and to concentrate more attention on how people lived their lives. He argues that documentary evidence needs to embrace personal experience and oral testimony, if we are to successfully interpret the past.

A similar line of argument, in respect of written documents, has been advanced by Burnett, who claims that accounts of personal experiences need to be gathered from autobiographies and diaries, as

> they are direct records of the person involved in the situation from which he or she writes at first hand. There is no intermediate reporter or observer to change the situation. The writer himself and alone selects the facts, incidents and events which are to him most important and in doing so he also unconsciously reveals something about his own attitudes, values and beliefs. (Burnett, 1977, p. 10)

Such accounts, together with those obtained from letters, biographies, speeches, sermons and other personal documents do indicate the way in which the individual perceived situations. However, as Okely (1978) has argued, this range of material often leads to gaps in the literature on women as they have rarely produced such materials.

It can be argued that the field researcher who collects personal documents is obtaining firsthand accounts from informants in the past. Certainly, Pons's discussion of contemporary interpretations of Manchester in the 1830s and 1840s (Pons, 1978) relies on participants' accounts (by Engels, Kay, Cooke Taylor, Parkinson, and others) to examine the salient features of Manchester society during the period. In this context, the informants provide observational material on nineteenth-century Manchester through documentary evidence. Several questions can be raised concerning the reliability, accuracy, representativeness and validity of these first-person accounts. The field researcher needs to consider: is the material trustworthy? Is the material atypical? Has the material been edited and refined? Does the autobiographical material only contain highlights of life that are considered interesting? Furthermore, it could be argued that the material is automatically biased as only certain people produce autobiographies and keep diaries; there is self-selectivity involved in the sample of material available; they do not provide a complete historical record. Nevertheless, such material does provide a subjective account of the situation it records; it is a reconstruction of part of life. Furthermore, it provides an account that is based on the author's experience. Angell (1945) has argued that personal documents can be used in a variety of ways: to secure conceptual hunches, to suggest new hypotheses, to provide a series of facts and the formulation of rough hypotheses from the facts. He maintains

that personal documents can also be used to verify hypotheses, to obtain an historical understanding of a person, group, or institution, and to provide an exposition.

However, for some groups with whom the field researcher works there is no written documentation and, in these cases, it is important for the researcher to consider using oral sources. Writing from an anthropological perspective Vansina defines the oral tradition as 'hearsay accounts, that is, testimonies that narrate an event which has not been witnessed and remembered by the informant himself, but which he has learnt about through hearsay' (Vansina, 1973, p. 20). Among African oral traditions, Vansina includes: rituals, lists of place names and personal names, official and private poetry, stories, and legal and other commentaries. He indicates that as these oral traditions were socially important in pre-literate societies, there were specific systems for handing down the testimony from one generation to another. Here, there is a danger of seeing oral testimony as something which is exclusive to pre-literate African societies that are discussed by Vansina. However, every society has topics that are not documented in written records, so that oral sources need to be used to make these topics visible. If we examine the folk tradition in England, we find that oral sources are important. This is clearly evident in the following remarks from Cecil Sharp, concerning the English folk song:

> One of the most amazing and puzzling things about the English folk song is the way in which it has hitherto escaped the notice of the educated people resident in the country districts. When I have the good fortune to collect some especially fine songs in a village, I have often called upon the Vicar to tell him of my success. My story has usually been received, at first, with polite incredulity, and, afterwards, when I have displayed the contents of my notebook, with amazement. Naturally, the Vicar finds it difficult to realize that the old men and women of his parish, whom he has known and seen day by day for many a long year, but whom he has never suspected of any musical leanings, should all the while have possessed, secretly and treasured in their old heads, songs of such remarkable interest and loveliness. (Sharp, 1972, p. 131)

This point has been recognised not merely by those interested in rural culture, but also by those researchers who are interested in industrial contexts and the recent past. Indeed, Samuel (Chapter 19) highlights the importance of oral evidence.

Given this diversity of sources, to what use can they be put in field research? Paul Thompson (1978) has claimed that oral sources can provide a new dimension to research. Oral history, it is argued, provides material on individuals from whom or for whom very little written documentary evidence is available. Secondly, it is argued that through oral history it is possible to obtain an account of everyday life and work. Finally, oral history gives people an opportunity to provide interpretations of their own lives. In these terms, it is considered that oral history can counteract the bias that exists in written historical sources. Above all, Gittins (1979) maintains that oral history provides an opportunity to 'get close' to the data in order that one can see how people interpreted their social relationships in the past. Such claims suggest great strengths for oral history, but against these claims a series of questions can be posed. How reliable is the evidence of oral history? How does it compare with other historical materials? How does it complement other data? Is it inferior to a document? How do you check the reliability of oral evidence? Here, we are confronted with questions concerning the validity, reliability and representativeness of oral sources. One way in which these data can be checked out is by comparing them with other sources. Meanwhile, they can also be checked for their own internal consistency.

Certainly, oral history has been used to bring forward a different perspective of the past. In particular, the work of George Ewart Evans (1970) has provided a unique chronicle of accounts of agricultural life in eastern England, as provided by a variety of country craftsmen: the saddler, the ploughman, and the gardener among many other country people. Similarly, Mary Chamberlain (1975) has provided a portrait of women in Gislea, an isolated village in the Fens. Such studies complement each other, as they provide accounts of another class or gender and give fresh insights into rural life. They complement written accounts about work in rural England. Similarly, accounts by researchers working in industrial and urban situations have filled gaps in our knowledge (for example, Ewart Evans, 1976). Bundy and Healy (1978) have used oral evidence to provide firsthand accounts of what poverty 'felt like' in Manchester, while Thorn (1978) uses oral history to provide insights into the significance of women's work at the Woolwich Arsenal during the First World War. Further accounts have been provided of dockyardmen (Waters, 1977), mining families (Harkell, 1978), and the trawling industry (Edwards and Marshall, 1977), that complement written accounts on work experience. In these circumstances, oral history provides a collection of 'stories' concerning people's lives. However, questions can still be raised concerning the representativeness of the individuals interviewed, their reliability as witnesses and the problem of the accuracy of their memories.

When E. P. Thompson (1976) reviewed Robert Moore's study of the Methodists in the Deerness Valley (Moore, 1974), he took the opportunity to raise several critical comments concerning oral testimony. Moore had used oral history interviews to gather data about Wesleyans and Primitive Methodists, who had merged in the 1930s. Thompson, however, considered that the informants had provided evidence of a 'golden past' and date about their own self-image rather than any evidence from the past. Furthermore, he questioned the extent to which these elderly informants could know about the elements of life that were important to their parents and grandparents. In this respect, it is important for cross-checks to be made between oral evidence and documentary sources.

One form of historical data that combines both written and oral evidence is the life history. Life history materials have been widely used by social anthropologists as shown by Langness (1965). In sociology the classic life history was provided by Thomas and Znaniecki (1918–20), in their study of the peasant Wladek. Further life histories were collected by members of the Chicago School, among which Shaw's account of Stanley (a jack roller) is probably best known (Shaw, 1930). Despite such studies being based on autobiographies, letters, diaries, court records, newspaper accounts, interviews with the key informant and with others, they are still regarded with some suspicion. Questions are raised concerning reliability, typicality and representativeness. Furthermore, as Faraday and Plummer (1979) indicate, questions can be raised concerning the extent to which life history materials assist sociological understanding. Evidence in favour of the use of life history material has been well documented by Denzin (1970) and by Becker (1966), who argue that life histories can help evaluate theories and provide a subjective assessment of institutional processes. They can also provide participants' accounts and help us to examine social processes and generate new questions. However, further work is required in this area, if we are to assess the utility of life histories. As there are few accounts of how to collect and analyse life history data, the chapter by Mandelbaum (Chapter 20) has been included in this section. He indicates how the field researcher can get beyond a collection of chronological materials when gathering life history data.

The use of documentary sources raises several questions concerning historiographical method. Central to written and oral materials are problems concerning the authenticity of documents, their availability, their selection, the inferences that can be drawn from them, the interpretation of data and the presentation of results. In addition, oral materials also raise ethical questions concerning the rights of the individual, the relationships between the researcher and the researched and the conflicts and obligations involved in data collection (Klockars, 1977; Faraday and Plummer, 1979). As a result of these questions, it would seem that any researcher using documentary evidence would need to know about the document, the informant and the context in which observation and data recording took place.

However, the problems do not end there. As E. P. Thompson demonstrates (Chapter 21), there are further questions to consider concerning the use of historical context, the application of sociological or anthropological concepts and the extent to which it is possible to generalise on the basis of the data that has been gathered. Here, Thompson has identified some of the classic pitfalls involved in using historical materials. However, if these can be avoided, it is evident that historical sources can provide the field researcher with a rich vein of material to complement the ethnographic present and provide deeper sociological insights into the way in which people lived their lives.

Suggestions for Further Reading

METHODOLOGY

Becker, H. (1966), 'Introduction' (to the Jack Roller), in C. Shaw, *The Jack Roller: a Delinquent Boy's Own Story* (Chicago: University of Chicago Press, Phoenix edition). A classic statement by a sociologist on life history materials.

Bloch, M. (1976), *The Historian's Craft* (Manchester: Manchester University Press). A personal account of historical method in which the author indicates how history should be practised.

Carr, E. H. (1964), *What Is History?* (Harmondsworth: Penguin); raises fundamental questions about the relationship between history and the social sciences.

Faraday, A. and Plummer, K. (1979), 'Doing life histories', *Sociological Review*, vol. 27, no. 4, pp. 773–98; examines the problems involved in doing life histories: social science problems, technical problems, ethical and political problems, and personal problems.

Foster, J. and Sheppard, J. (1980), 'Archives and the history of nursing', in C. Davies (ed.), *Rewriting Nursing History* (London: Croom Helm), pp. 200–14; provides a useful discussion of archives together with appendices on references books, background reading and addresses of archives.

Gittins, D. (1979), 'Oral history, reliability and recollection', in L. Moss and H. Goldstein (eds), *The Recall Method in Social Surveys* (London: University of London Institute of Education), pp. 82–97; discusses the problems of oral history, the way in which problems may be avoided and an overview of the strengths of the approach.

Gottschalk, L., Kluckhohn, C. and Angell, R. (1945), *The Use of Personal Documents in History, Anthropology and Sociology* (New York: Social Science Research Council). Three essays on the way in which anthropologists, sociologists and historians utilise personal documents.

Klockars, C. B. (1977), 'Field ethics for the life history', in R. S. Weppner (ed.), *Street Ethnography* (Beverly Hills, Calif.: Sage), pp. 201–26. An interesting account on the ethics of doing life history based on the author's experiences of working on *The Professional Fence* (Klockars, 1974).

Langlois, C. V. and Seignobos, C. (1898), *Introduction to the Study of History* (London: Duckworth). A classic statement on historiography.

Langness, L. L. (1965), *The Life History in Anthropological Science* (New York: Holt, Rinehart & Winston). An overview of life history material from an anthropological perspective.

Lipset, S. M. and Hofstadter, R. (1968) (eds), *Sociology and History: Methods* (New York: Basic Books). A series of essays on history and sociology in America – contains several useful essays on concepts and methods.

Platt, J. (1981), 'Evidence and proof in documentary research: some specific problems of documentary research', *Sociological Review*, vol. 29, no. 1, pp. 31–52.

Platt, J. (1981), 'Evidence and proof in documentary research: some shared problems of documentary research', *Sociological Review*, vol. 29, no. 1, pp. 53–66. Two related articles that provide a useful discussion of documentary materials. These articles synthesise a range of sources and provide critical commentary and a personal account.

Samuel, R. (1981) (ed.), *People's History and Socialist Theory* (London: Routledge & Kegan Paul); brings different types of historical work (for instance, local history, oral history, labour history and feminist history) into dialogue with one another.

Thompson, E. P. (1976), 'On history, sociology and historical relevance', *British Journal of Sociology*, vol. 27, no. 3, pp. 387–402. A review article concerning *Pit-Men, Preachers and Politics* (Moore, 1974). Thompson provides a critical discussion on the use of historical sources and a critique of oral history.

Thompson, P. (1978), *The Voice of the Past: Oral History* (London: OUP). A basic text on oral history that provides a very detailed bibliography and suggestions for further reading.

Vansina, J. (1973), *Oral Tradition* (Harmondsworth: Penguin). A detailed discussion of oral tradition as a means of reconstructing the past.

Wrigley, E. A. (1972) (ed.), *Nineteenth Century Society* (Cambridge: CUP). A series of papers on the use of quantitative methods for the study of social data.

EMPIRICAL STUDIES

There are many studies that now utilise historical sources; the following have been selected as they highlight the use of particular approaches.

Written documents

A collection of personal accounts or studies based on personal accounts:

Bulmer, M. (1978 (ed.), *Mining and Social Change* (London: Croom Helm) (especially part 2, containing personal accounts by Benney, 1978; Chaplin, 1978; and Williamson, 1978).

Burnett, J. (1977), *Useful Toil* (Harmondsworth: Penguin).

Pons, V. (1978), 'Contemporary interpretations of Manchester in the 1830s and 1840s', *Stanford Journal of International Studies*, vol. 13, pp. 51–76.

Samuel, R. (1975) (ed.), *Village Life and Labour* (London: Routledge & Kegan Paul).

Samuel, R. (1977) (ed.), *Miners, Quarrymen and Saltworkers* (London: Routledge & Kegan Paul).

Oral history

On rural situations. A series of accounts that all relate to rural life in eastern England. Some are based entirely on oral sources, some use oral material alongside other historical sources:

Blythe, R. (1969), *Akenfield* (Harmondsworth: Penguin).
Chamberlain, M. (1975), *Fenwomen* (London: Virago).
Ewart Evans, G. (1970), *Where Beards Wag All: the Relevance of the Oral Tradition* (London: Faber).
Newby, H. (1977), *The Deferential Worker* (London: Allen Lane) (see chapter 1).

On industrial situations. A series of accounts that have been published in the journal, *Oral History:*

Edwards, P. J. and Marshall, J. (1977), 'Sources of conflict and community in the trawling industries of Hull and Grimsby between the wars', *Oral History*, vol. 5, no. 1, pp. 97–121.
Frank, P. (1976), 'Women's work in the Yorkshire inshore fishing industry', *Oral History*, vol. 4, no. 1, pp. 57–72.
Harkell, G. (1978), 'The migration of mining families to the Kent coalfield between the wars', *Oral History*, vol. 6, no. 1, pp. 98–113.
Hay, R. and McLauchlan, J. (1974), 'The oral history of Upper Clyde shipbuilders', *Oral History*, vol. 2, no. 1, pp. 45–58.
Thorn, D. (1978), 'Women at the Woolwich Arsenal, 1915–1919', *Oral History*, vol. 6, no. 2, pp. 58–73.
Waters, M. (1977), 'Craft consciousness in a government enterprise: Medway dockyardmen, 1860–1906', *Oral History*, vol. 5, no. 1, pp. 51–62.

Life histories

A series of studies that utilise life history materials:

Bogdan, R. (1974), *Being Different: the Autobiography of Jane Fry* (New York: Wiley).
Jacobs, J. (1974) (ed.), *Deviance: Field Studies and Self-Disclosures* (Palo Alto, Calif.: National Press Books) (see part 2).
Klockars, C. (1974), *The Professional Fence* (London: Tavistock).
Plotnicov, L. (1967), *Strangers to the City* (Pittsburgh, Pa.: University of Pittsburgh Press).
Shaw, C. (1930), *The Jack Roller: a Delinquent Boy's Own Story* (Chicago: University of Chicago Press).
Thomas, W. I. and Znaniecki, F. (1918–20), *The Polish Peasant in Europe and America* (2nd edn) (New York: Dover), pp. 1831–2244.

19

Local History and Oral History

RAPHAEL SAMUEL

Local history, despite attempts to bring it into line with other forms of historical practice, is still very much the province of enthusiasts. The merest squiggle on a parish register may set the historian's imagination alight – a reference to the death of a 'nurse child' or the marginal note of some ancient local cure. Or he may be horrified by the casual brutality revealed in workhouse records or the 'removals' itemised in parochial accounts, such as those reproduced by Reginald Hine, the historian of Hitchin, in his *Relics of an Un-Common Attorney* (these examples are from 1710):

> For a woman's lodging and victuals and to be rid of her, 1s 3d. Paid to a woman big with child and two children to go out of town, 4d. Paid Mary Gregory to go away, her children having the Small Pox, 7s. (Hine, 1946)

An old smithy or brewhouse may set him on the track of local trades, or a rusty old adze, hanging on its hook, or the chance discovery of a Day Book. He may be excited by a story in an old newspaper (or by the advertisements, or by the inquests, or by police court reports); fascinated by Roman remains; or puzzled by the legend of some half-remembered incident which demands an explanatory setting (the Grimsby riot is a good example). Or again, his sympathies may have been aroused by the struggle of his forebears, as they were for Methodist writers of the nineteenth century, tracing the humble origins of the chapel, and as they are for the trade unionist, writing of Tolpuddle times – or the General Strike – today. The sources, once a project has been taken up, are infinitely various, encompassing archaeological finds as well as literary remains, material culture as well as manuscripts and archives, dialect and speech as well as the printed word. Yet they are never so unlimited that the researcher is likely to get lost in them, and much of his time (or hers) will be spent in chasing fugitive facts, dating a wall or a building, mapping a driftway, completing a family tree. Harvesting, at least for the historian of early modern times, is not so much a matter of separating the wheat from the chaff as of reaping (or gleaning) the solitary ear of grain.

Local history demands a different kind of knowledge than one which is focused on high-level national developments, and gives the researcher a much more immediate sense of the past. He meets it round the corner and down the street. He can listen to its echoes in the marketplace, read its graffiti on the walls, follow its footprints in the fields. The abstract categories of social class, instead of being assumed, have to be translated into occupational differences and individual life careers, the impact of change measured by its consequences for particular households. The basic materials of historical process have to be constituted with whatever materials are locally available, or the structure will not stand.

The newcomer will find the path well signposted by aids.[1] Tate[2] – or the local vicar – will elucidate the mysteries of the parish chest; Emmison[3] – or the County Record Office staff – will act as guide to the Militia Lists, Hearth Tax returns or Quarter Sessions. At the town hall the chief committee clerk will use his keys to open up the basement muniments, though this may need patience and tact (at Barrow-in-Furness the historian of the town has only recently been given access to the corporation records, after a diplomatic contest lasting twenty years), while in the local library the researcher will often find a well-stocked and elaborately indexed collection of printed matter and ephemera, including perhaps the notebooks deposited by antiquarian predecessors and, for more recent times, the newspaper cuttings filed by the library staff. (In an old-established central library, such as Birmingham's or Manchester's, there will be obituaries of local worthies stretching back a hundred years). Secondhand bookshops can be a great help too: many of them specialise in local books and, if a wanted item does not come the way of the stockrooms, they can advertise for it in the trade.[4]

Local history also has the strength of being popular, both as an activity and as a literary form. Nineteenth-century provincial newspapers would devote as much as half a page a week to antiquarian jottings (the serialised form in which many local histories of that time appeared); today newspaper publication is rarer, but local diarists – such as the ever-helpful 'Anthony Wood' of the *Oxford Mail* – are often hungry for the items which the researcher can provide (the same is also true of local radio) and a local history pamphlet, whatever its quality, is assured of being a local best-seller.[5] People are continually asking themselves questions about where they live, and how their elders fared. They have a keen sense of heritage, treasuring iconography – old apprenticeship indentures or Valentines, bronze attendance medals, Sunday-school prize books, holiday postcards – and once their curiosity has been aroused, they may be only too anxious to help, rummaging around in old papers to see what they can dig up, submitting to detailed questions and volunteering information of their own. Often the local historian will be drawing on the accumulated reflection of his or her own life experience, and it is no accident that so many town and parish histories have been compiled by men and women actively engaged in local affairs, from clergymen and solicitors in the past to community-based agitators, such as the authors of *Fly a Flag for Poplar*,[6] or the editors of the 'People's Autobiography of Hackney' today. Veteran trade unionists, after a lifetime's activity, will take on the history of the trades council, retired teachers will chronicle the local school, JPs and aldermen the record of municipal affairs. The old socialist makes himself a library and archive (Alf Mattison's, now divided between Leeds Central Library and the Brotherton, is a major source of local history); the inveterate rambler, with a stout pair of boots, reconstructs the vanished landscape; the Women's Institute (they were responsible for some of the best local histories of the inter-war years) make an inventory of the home.

Why, then, is so much local history, though undertaken as a labour of love, repetitive and inert? Why, under the historian's microscope, do trades councils, board schools, or family businesses look so alike? Why do the localities themselves, when reconstituted over time, look so interchangeable? In the older parish histories there was a well-worn set of topics, the squire and his relations, the church and its incumbents, the manor and its court. There might be extensive notes on folklore and etymology, and if the author was a keen botanist 'flora and fauna' would be given a chapter (or an appendix) to themselves. Catholics and Noncomformists, though duly noticed, would often get less attention than the fabric of the parish church or the memorials on family gravestones, while industry and trade would often be relegated to the chapter of miscellanies at the end. The bourgeois revolution in local history – a twentieth- rather than a seventeenth-century affair – has changed all that, and today more attention is likely to be given to municipal worthies than to vicars, to philanthropically minded manufacturers than to medieval knights and squires. Transport and communication occupy the chapter once allotted to plants, population changes excite more attention than genealogy, ratebooks take the place of manorial entries and fines. The new conventions however, though different, can be just as imprisoning as the old.

One difficulty lies in the nature of the documents, which vary remarkably little from place to place, and are heavily biased towards local government. One set of churchwardens' accounts – a staple fare for the historian of the eighteenth- and early nineteenth-century parish – is very much like another and the same may be said of school logbooks: at least from the coming of the School Boards in the 1870s both the form and the matter of the entries were rigorously prescribed. Parish censuses, or the enumerators' returns, tell you little more about family life than household size and, as the Cambridge demographers have been at pains to argue, this shows a broad similarity over time, and comparatively slight local variation. They are an equally unsatisfactory source for the discussion of occupational structure, which often resolves itself into a head count of trades. Charities and poor relief are given an altogether disproportionate space for no better reason than the comparative abundance of their documentation, and the same may be said, in nineteenth-century town histories, of drainage.[7] As a result one local history tends to read very much like another, and though the historian is likely to pounce on any oddity which comes his or her way (churchwardens' payments for hedgehogs, for instance, or mercantilist-inspired instructions for burial in wool), the oddities themselves are apt to be repetitive, reflecting conventional vestry functions or standardised administrative forms. In urban history the administrative bias of the documents is reinforced by the preoccupation with 'improvement', which provides the writer with a ready-made documentation and theme. Victorian Wantage and Victorian Exeter can look very much alike when treated under such headings as the increase of population, public health measures, or the spread of schools.

The bias of 'family' papers – at least of those encountered in the town or county archives – can be quite as limiting as that of borough records, workhouse minutebooks or the parish chest. The great bulk of those deposited in a record office are estate papers and solicitors' accumulations and that mass of conveyances, wills and deeds which take up page after page in the catalogues. They are for the most part landlord–tenant agreements, preserved for accounting reasons, or legal documents resulting from disputes. As a result landownership and property transactions occupy a disproportionate amount of space in many local histories, and there is a one-sided emphasis on great estates. The history of a suburb, for instance, is likely to be dominated by the roadmakers, the housebuilders and the property developers simply because they have left more enduring and more systematic evidence of their activity than anbody else. It is easier, for instance, to reconstruct the building history of Belsize Park, as F. M. L. Thompson has done in his much admired *Hampstead; Building a Borough*,[8] than to satisfactorily account for such more fugitive

appurtenances of local life as the Adelaide Branch of
the Communist Party, the chessmen at Prompt Corner,
or the busmen's ranks on South End Green; the
creation of Swiss Cottage gets an interesting chapter to
itself, but there is not a word about nursery life in the
1890s (despite the splendidly detailed memoir of
Eleanor Farjeon which might have served as a starting-
point), nor a hint of what went on in those gigantic
drawing rooms in the days before German refugees and
Indian students – the penniless intelligentsia of the
1930s and 1940s – took them over from the
bourgeoisie. Wills and deeds – the local historian's
stock-in-trade – can be made to yield a great deal of
economic information, and imaginatively used, as
Hoskins has shown for the probate inventories of the
sixteenth century, they provide a sensitive indicator to
stock-holding and household possessions. But there are
limits to their reach. Estate papers can be full of
information about tenancy agreements, yet have little
or nothing to say about husbandry; conveyances, for all
the elaboration of their detail, may tell us little about
occupancy – the way in which buildings or farms were
used. Business records can be even more unyielding.
They tell us more about the marketing of goods than
about the people who made them (or who sold them),
more about wages than about work (even wagebooks
are comparative rarities); ledgers and daybooks make it
comparatively easy to write about growth and
consolidation, while giving no indication at all of the
fissiparous tendencies working in the opposite
direction, family rivalries, for instance, scheming
managers, or partners who took to the bottle.
As a result economic activity is often seen through the
eyes of the valuer and surveyor – or for more recent
times the accountant – rather than that of worker and
employer.

In recent years local historians have called on visual
evidence in an attempt to get more sense of the
particular, and convey a more immediate sense of
place. One dominant preoccupation has been with the
making of the landscape and the locational analysis of
industries, housing and trade. The difficulty with this
kind of work is that it is almost too rewarding, so that
the historian's attention is diverted from the people to
the place. In the city every stone can tell a story, while
in the country there is the abundant testimony of the
hedges and fields. Old sites can be identified, field
systems mapped and street lines drawn out on a grid.
Moreover almost any kind of local document is likely
to yield topographical information of some kind, even
if it is useless for anything else. The material, in short, is
abundant, and the compulsive note-taker (as the
present writer can testify) will soon find his files bulging
and his headings well filled. The material also provides
the writer with a unifying theme. Community life can
be intimately related to (and often explained by) the
physical peculiarities of the environment; its history
can be set out in well-ordered phases of growth, from
the geographical factors affecting the original conditions of settlement to the centrifugal forces at work
today; structural continuities can be emphasised, while
at the same time due allowance is made for development and change. Despite the accumulation of detail,
however, it is possible for the people to remain at one
remove. The shapes on the ground, as in an aerial
photograph, appear with brilliant clarity – Celtic
survivals, Roman earthworks, or the sprawling lines of
modern villadom; ridge and furrow (the plough lines of
the Middle Ages) stand out in sharp relief, houses can
be picked out by the rooftops; the inhabitants, on the
other hand, from the panoramic nature of the vantage-
point – or the absence of comparable material – may
remain comparatively indistinct. The same is even
more true of such related enthusiasms as industrial
archaeology, which have made such a fruitful contribution to local history in recent years. The workplace is
lovingly reconstructed but the workers themselves
can remain mere shadows, dwarfed by the physical
setting.

The pilot studies of the demographers – another
major recent influence on local history – offer an even
more aerial view. They have opened up new areas of
inquiry, and parachuted into what was previously
unexplored terrain, but the sample surveys so far
published suggest a bleak landscape, inhabited by
statistical variables, and sociological rocks. As with the
topographers and the industrial archaeologists, theirs is
an attempt to make up for the silence of the records and
to recover the texture of life in the past. But household
shape and size, the categories they deal in, part
company with the social reality they are intended to
expose: the ebb and flow of personal relationships, the
to and fro of daily life. The documentation on which
they rely, whether by necessity or choice (parish
registers and census enumerators' returns) precludes
the encounter that they seek. Instead of family life, we
are given elaborate charts of births, marriages and
deaths. The statistical material pre-empts the
historian's attention, and provides him or her
simultaneously with a subject matter and a
problematic, not only a scaffolding but the bricks and
mortar, too. As in the case of local government records,
the sheer weight of the material (and the preponderance
of a single source) is apt to impose itself. When 'social
structure' (the demographers' term for class divisions)
is derived from these documents, the construct is liable
to be both static and unreal. Instead of the world of real
economic relationships – patrons and clients, landlords
and tenants, buyers and sellers, exploiters and
exploited, employers and employed – we are offered
statistical aggregates.

So far as the historical demographers are concerned –
the pioneers in this field – such misgivings are beside
the point. Their effort is avowedly comparative. They
are interested in structure, not events, in stratification
rather than relationships, in quantifiable variables

which can be assimilated to cross-cultural analysis. Their 'case studies' are cast in local form, but even though the ostensible subject is a village or a town, the sense of place is deliberately eschewed. Alan Armstrong's study of York,[9] for instance, devotes some thirty pages to 'economic characteristics' and about the same to 'social characteristics', and then gets on to the real meat of the study: 'growth of population'; 'mortality'; 'marriage and fertility'; 'household and family structure'. It is no accident that the censuses which provide him with his chief material, appear in the very title of his book, or that 'mortality' should be the subject of one of the longer chapters. His aims are frankly stated at the outset:

> This study . . . may be regarded as an example, albeit imperfect, of both the new social history and urban history . . . I have eschewed descriptions of the provincial 'season', sporting and cultural activities, colourful and quaint illustrations of customs, manners and social events, etc. The spheres of local politics and ideology, important though they are, have been left to others . . . instead there is a heavy emphasis on social structure and demographic trends.

Michael Anderson's study of early Victorian Preston[10] is equally severe. In all its elaborate discussion of the household, and subdivision according to numbers and makeup, there is little mention of individual Preston families by name, or of single instances to illustrate the life cycles and correlations so confidently set out. What he says may be true, but we have no autonomous validation: the world is one utterly enclosed by his constructs. Servant-owning households are singled out for attention, as a class,, but there is scarcely a reference to the millowners, the great cotton magnate, nor the Masters' Association of 1853–4 are so much as mentioned). Reference is made to the Irish, as a component of the working population, but not to their streets, to their ferocious attacks on the police (the Quarter Sessions records at Preston have a particularly affecting instance), nor to such interesting and important characters as Micky Gallaher, one of the strike leaders in 1853–4 and, in later years, a local Orange firebrand. Very few streets are mentioned by name either: there is no 'Orchard' for strike meetings to be held, no 'Fishergate' for high street promenades. There is no reference either to Temperance (a national movement founded by the Seven Men of Preston in the 1830s); to Chartism, to trade unionism (despite the existence of an excellent contemporary account of the spinners by their secretary, Thomas Banks); or to Orator Hunt, who was for a time the town's MP. Strangest of all, in a study whose focus is on mid-century, there is not so much as a word about the great Preston strike of 1853–4, the subject of Dickens's lurid but memorable fiction, *Hard Times*[11] (Dickens went up to witness the strike before writing the novel), and arguably the single most important industrial event in nineteenth-century Lancashire, a terminal point for three decades of near-insurrectionary struggle; nor is any use made – even for the considerable light it casts obliquely on domestic life – of the fine collection of strike material housed in the Harris library or the County Record Office, both of them conveniently sited in the very centre of the town. The omissions are all the more striking, because on its chosen topics the book is so thoroughly researched; they are the result not of oversight, but as in Alan Armstrong's fastidious exclusions at York, of programmatic intent.

A final difficulty concerns the very notion of local history: the idea of place as a distinct and separate entity which can be studied as a cultural whole. In the older antiquarian histories almost anything which happened locally was liable to be treated as significant, irrespective of its intrinsic importance, or place in an evolutionary scheme. Strikes and riots rubbed shoulders indiscriminately with 'remarkable occurrences' such as floods, the village stocks might be sandwiched in a paragraph between monumental brasses and an account of local inns. Documents would be faithfully transcribed and affectionately reproduced simply because they were old – 'the actual words written at the time' – and much of the historian's ingenuity would be focused on whimsical sidelights. Miscellaneous chronicles of this kind have always given a great deal of pleasure, and they are unlikely to disappear, however many strictures are directed against them.[12] But the local historian today, following the direction pioneered by Hoskins,[13] Finberg[14] and the Leicester School, is characteristically more selective. In place of the picturesque, they are more likely to be on the look-out for regularities. The preoccupation with place is just as intense as it was in the past, but for those who follow the Leicester School the focus of attention is more likely to be on patterns of development than on individual documents and events. Locality is seen as a distinct phenomenon, with its own peculiar time-scale and laws of growth, a living organism with its own distinctive life cycle which can be studied continuously over long periods of time both in terms of occupational structure, and topographical peculiarities. 'The business of the local historian', as Finberg wrote in 1953, in a much-quoted passage 'is to re-enact in his own mind, and to portray for his readers the Origin, Growth, Decline, and Fall of a local community'. The notion of community, as in the above passage, is often invoked – 'a group of people bound together by certain common interests', 'a true society of men, women and children, gathered together in one place' – and the whole thrust of local history in recent years has been towards identifying community types.

No one who cares about English history can fail to have been excited by one or other aspect of this work, or to acknowledge the major advances in scholarship and understanding which have resulted from it. But it is possible to be uneasy about some of its suppositions even while welcoming, and being thankful for, the results. In particular the notion of 'community', though freely invoked, is, or ought to be, problematical. In urban history it is little more than a convenient fiction, which can only be maintained by concentrating on civic and municipal affairs. In the countryside it often carries an unwarranted assumption of equilibrium, which it might be the task of the historian to question rather than to affirm. It is possible to live in the same place while inhabiting different worlds, whether as man and wife, parent and child, employer and employed. The lady's maid and the carpenter, even if they eventually marry, will have been shaped by fundamentally different work experiences and give their allegiance to strongly contrasted ideologies: one will have known only the protective patronage of the great house, while the other, however skilled, will have led an itinerant, jobbing life, surrounded by insecurities (in a country town, for instance, victimisation when his trade unionism became known); one would rely on a character reference when it came to a change of job, the other on the unofficial building workers' grapevine. Even in marriage their outlook, shaped by such different experience, would by no means be the same.

Instead of assuming the existence of equilibrium, it might be better if historians were to fathom some of its undercurrents, and to distinguish between interests which were conflictual and those which in some sense were shared. The recent work of the Leicester School has shown that religious divisions can be treated in this way, and in Margaret Spufford's *Contrasting Communities*[15] – a magnificently detailed and thoughtful reconstruction of life in three Cambridgeshire villages of the sixteenth and seventeeth centuries – one can see the precious insight they give into class and economy, as well as bringing us closer to the mentality and consciousness of the time – to the ways which people thought and felt and grouped themselves. Or again, instead of taking locality itself as the subject, the historian might choose instead as the starting-point some element of life within it, limited in both time and place, but used as a window on the world. This is what, on a modest scale, Ruth Hapgood[16] did with her study of women's work at Abingdon between the wars, and Graham Rawlings[17] in his account of the three working classes in Bath in the 1930s: studies like this can give one more sense of the individuality of a town than much weightier tomes laden with borough records. It would be good to see this attempted for nineteenth-century London. A study of Sunday trading in Bethnal Green, including the war waged upon it by the open-air preachers (at the time of the 1851 religious census, only a tiny proportion of the local population were churchgoers); of cabinetmaking in South Hackney, or of Hoxton burglars (according to one of Booth's investigators in the 1890s, some of them were skilled

artisans, neither rough nor poor, but, as he chose to call them 'criminal', who went out safecracking as an evening recreation) would take one closer to the heartbeat of East End life than yet another précis of Hector Gavin's *Sanitary Ramblings*,[18] G. R. Sims's *Horrible London*,[19] or James Greenwood's *Low Life Deeps*.[20] Courting and marriage in Shepherd's Bush, domestic life in Acton, or Roman Catholicism among the laundrywomen and gasworkers of Kensal Green, might tell one more about the growth of suburbs than logging the increase of streets, and the same might be said, on the further fringes of London, of market gardening in Barking, boatmen at Brentford, gypsies at Wandsworth, harvest or haymaking at Tottenham Hale. The study of social structure, too, might be made more intimate and realistic if the approach were more oblique, and focused on activity and relationships. A study of childhood in Chelsea (of whom you could or couldn't play with, or where you were allowed to go), masculinity in Mitcham, the journey to work in Putney, or of local politics in Finsbury, would tell one a great deal about the way class differences were manipulated and perceived, and social allegiances expressed in practice, even if not a word were said explicitly of social structure. Gwyn Williams's little study of Merthyr politics in the 1830s,[21] in which he shows how a cadre of radically minded Unitarian tradesmen transformed the political complexion of the town, brings us much closer to the ambiguities of class feeling than a more flat-footed approach, taking the Registrar General's five-fold divisions as markers.

By using a different class of record – such as the depositions discussed by David Vaisey[22] – or with the aid of living memory (or both) the historian can draw up fresh maps, in which people are as prominent as places, and the two are more closely intertwined. He or she can then explore the moral topography of a village or town with the same precision which predecessors have give to the Ordnance Survey, following the ridge and furrow of the social environment as well as the parish boundaries, travelling the dark corridors and half-hidden passageways as well as the byelaw street. Reconstructing a child's itinerary seventy years ago the historian will stumble on the invisible boundaries which separated the rough end of a street from the respectable, the front houses from the back, the boys' space from the girls'. Following the grid of the pavement you will come upon one stretch that was used for 'tramcars', another for hopscotch, a third for Jump Jimmy Knacker or wall games. 'Monkey racks' (such as the one described by Derek Thompson in interwar Preston)[23] appear on the High Street, where young people went courting on their Sunday promenades, while the cul de sac becomes a place where woodchoppers had their sheds and costers dressed their barrows. The physical environment will come alive too, if seen as an arena of activity rather than as an impersonal ecological force or a repository of archaeological remains. Particular fields or woods or commons are remembered by their use, by the work done in them, or the provisions foraged: here mushrooms and firewood could be found or rabbits trapped; there potatoes were dug or horse illegally grazed or long summer days were spent at haymaking or harvest.

Oral evidence makes it possible to escape from some of the deficiencies of the documentary record, at least so far as recent times are concerned (namely, those which fall within living memory), and the testimony which it brings is at least as important as that of the hedges and fields, though one should not exclude the other. There are matters of fact which are recorded in the memories of older people and nowhere else, events of the past which they alone can elucidate for us, vanished sights which they alone can recall. Documents cannot answer back, nor, beyond a point, can they be asked to explain in greater detail what they mean, to give more examples, to account for negative instances, or to explain apparent discrepancies in the record which survives. Oral evidence, on the other hand, is open-ended, and limited only by the number of survivors, and by the ingenuity of the historian's questions, and by his or her patience and tact. It is surprising how unwilling local historians have been to admit it, except in a subordinate role. W. G. Hoskins, the doyen of English local history, writing in 1972, warned that while it was 'not to be dismissed altogether', it had to be subject to rigorous checks, and he plainly regards it as inferior, as well as different in kind, to manuscript and material remains.[24] Yet there are certain kinds of inquiry which can only be undertaken with the aid of living testimony, and whole areas of life in which its credentials are beyond question. A man or woman talking about their work know more about it than the most diligent researcher is likely to discover, and the same is often true of childhood, where people's memories are apt to be peculiarly precise if the historian can find the right key to unlock them. Oral evidence can also be crucial for a background understanding. It can give us living contexts which the documents themselves, however closely pressed, fail to yield. The spare entries of a diary, for instance, can take on new meaning if we are able, from other sources, to reconstitute the character of the writer or of the circumstances to which the entries refer. The obscure hieroglyphics of a wages book become comprehensible in the light of the sub-divisions and classification of the work, as it can be described by those who were themselves involved, the measuring book in the light of piecework, the price list in the memory of those who haggled over its terms. Sources like this may only come to life when there are people to explain, to comment and to elaborate on them, when there are other kinds of information to set against them, and a context of custom and practice in which they can be set. Oral evidence can also help to bring the residues of material culture into play. The copper stick or the dolly mop cease to be inanimate objects if one listens to

the men or women who used them, the cooper's cresset fills again with fire, the stained black knives are cleaned with Bath Brick or house sand, the dirty old pinny is worn again for Sunday-school, starched white.

As well as making a more extended use of the existing records, an oral history project can also add to them, and build up a whole new documentation of its own. There are in the first place the recordings and their transcripts whose greatest value may still lie unperceived; they will (if safely preserved) be archives for the future as well as answering to the particular purpose of the work in hand. Then there are the autobiographies which an oral history project can encourage, such as Alice Foley's *Bolton Childhood* (a fine, harsh account of a Lancashire childhood in the early 1900s),[25] or those which have been published as the 'People's Autobiography of Hackney'[26] one of the Hackney authors, after writing his own life, has now gone on to produce a 120,000-word reconstruction of his family). Others may be brought to light in the course of research, preserved as family heirlooms – the little history which a Methodist may write of his chapel or the shopkeeper of his shop, the 'brief account' which a grandfather in the closing years of his life will draw up for his descendants, tracing family origins or relating the times he has seen (so far I've found no grandmother's). Then there are the family papers, handed down from older generations, which occasionally make their way into the record offices, but for the most part are treasured, or neglected, in the privacy of the home and which, below the level of the gentry and the high bourgeoisie, escape the investigations of the Historical Manuscripts Commission or the National Register of Archives. Family letters are particularly precious, though much more difficult to find than such more decorative ephemera as Valentines or apprenticeship indentures. The Welsh Coalfield project has been collecting them along with lodge minutebooks, miners' libraries and individual tape recordings. Some of them are from newcomers to the coalfield in the 1900s, writing home, and they give us precious insights into the process of migration which could hardly have been arrived at in any other way. Documents like these will only come the historian's way, if he or she asks for them. The same is true of diaries. In any locality there are likely to be numbers of them waiting to be collected which the historian will only come upon inadvertently, in the course of visits to local homes. The rescue of old photographs is another possible byproduct of an oral history project, and if it is deliberately pursued great numbers of them are likely to turn up.[27] They will be useful anyway as illustrations, evoking the past for those who never saw it, and stirring new memories in those who were there. Sometimes too they will provide new information, or independent corroboration. At their best they will provide the historian with a benchmark, exposing a reality which it is then his or her task to explain. Finally, though more occasionally, there are the private hoards – cuttings, handbills, posters, diaries – of those who have made themselves unofficial archivists of local activities and events. The best local documents, in short, will be found not in the library or the record office, but in the home.

Oral evidence makes it possible not only to fill in gaps, but also to redefine what local history can be about. Instead of allowing the documents to structure the work – or having it filtered through the categories of law, accountancy, or local government – the historian can make his touchstone the real-life experience of people themselves, both domestically and at work. He can deal with the ordinary unreported troubles of everyday life as well as with such better-documented catastrophes as floods, with family feuds as well as with suicides and murders, courtship and marriage as well as bastardy, working practices as well as strikes. He can take the pulse of daily life as well as registering the more occasional tremor of great events, follow the seasonal cycle, plot the weekly round.

Interview and reminiscence will also enable the historian to give an identity and character to people who would otherwise remain mere names on a street directory or parish register, and to restore to some of their original importance those who left no written record of their lives. Some of them will emerge in the course of family reconstitution, if the historian will pause for a profile at each name in the network of kin, starting from the grandparents and their siblings and working downwards. Some will crop up in the course of personal reminiscence, or stories of incidents and events. Names culled from newspapers of the time can be used as a source of questioning and prompts. Or again, more systematically, it is possible with the aid of a directory or an electoral register to attempt a living reconstruction, house by house and shop by shop, of long-since-vanished streets. In some cases a chain of living testimonies can be brought to bear upon a single character – the woman round the corner who was called in when people were sick, or when there was a baby to deliver, or body to be laid out or a funeral to prepare; the backstreet moneylender who was relied upon for weekly or seasonal loans; the man with the horse and cart, or barrow, who helped out on moonlight flits. This is what Hackney WEA have done in *The Threepenny Doctor*[28], their composite portrait of Dr Jelley, an unfrocked doctor and abortionist who practised locally between 1910 and 1930: in the space of thirty-odd pages it tells us more about popular medicine, and the ways in which illness was coped with in the home, than volumes of Medical Officer of Health reports. Biographies like these will not only make the historian's account more readable, they will also provide a bank of information which could hardly have been arrived at in any other way, and in the course of compiling them the historian will discover all kinds of unofficial networks, hidden from history so far as the documents are concerned, which nevertheless once

played a crucial part in backstreet and neighbourhood life. The historian can take down the portraits of worthies and still find his gallery well filled.

Oral evidence makes for a much more realisitc appreciation of capitalist enterprise than one which relies on business records alone. The shopkeeper steps out of the columns of his ledgerbook to become a busy, pushy man, renowned for his penny-pinching ways; the rent collector comes round on a Monday morning, wing-collared and straw-hatted, only to be told that mother is out; the master printer turns out also to dabble in slum property, to have an interest in a public house, and to share his warehouse with a furnisher. Close questioning about custom and practice makes it possible to learn what went on in the counting houses as well as what was reproduced in the books, to take up place beside the small master at his bench and travel with the trader on his rounds; in the case of small farms, as David Jenkins has shown in his fine study of Cardiganshire in the 1900s,[29] it is possible to redress the imbalance in the records, with their bias in favour of the large farms and the great estates, and recover some of the missing elements of peasant life in the past. Class relations can be explored at the point of production rather than by their distant echo, perfunctorily recorded, if at all, in trades council minutebooks, or the surviving records of the local trade union branch: the workplace, instead of being merely listed as plant, can be explored as a social arena.

The notion of work, too, can be complicated and refined. Instead of merely listing occupations – or ranking them according to sociological notions of prestige – the historian can discover what they actually entailed. The labourer, that catch-all title favoured by the Census enumerators, turns out in many cases not to have been a labourer at all, but a man with a definite calling – a holder-up in the shipyards, a winchman at the docks, a welldigger or drainer in the countryside, a carrier or a freelance navvy; conversely the artisan, when one inquires into the succession of his jobs, seems forever to be crossing occupational boundaries, notwithstanding his apprenticeship to one trade; the stonemason, when out of work, turns to furniture-making or carving mantels, the bricklayer to welldigging, the cabinetmaker to hawking tea. The labour process itself is something which with the aid of oral evidence can be reconstituted with great precision – as George Ewart Evans has shown for the ploughmen, the haymakers and the harvesters of East Anglia.[30] People's memory of their work, like that of childhood, is often peculiarly vivid, and extends to incidents and events and stories which give precious insights into the workplace, as a total context and cultural setting – the ambiguities of foremanship and the difficulties encountered by authority, the nature of the learning process, the subdivision of the different classes of work, the shifting balance of power between employer and employed. *Working Lives*, Hackney WEA's collection of work autobiographies, is an example of the illumination this can bring.[31] Here, for instance, is an extract from the account of Mr Welch, a demolition man of the 1920s, when the work was 'all done by hand', which throws a flood of light on what was then, even more than it is today, a very murderous trade. It tells us something not only of the dangerous quality of the work itself, but also the way people steeled themselves against dangers, and the psychic mechanisms which came into play to cope with accidents, both when they happened and also retrospectively, in stories where, London-style, the tragedy is played for the laughs:

It was dangerous work. You were always hearing of casualties from the other men on the jobs. If you had been in the game long you would have met most of the demolition men in the London area, including characters with names like 'Bootnose' and 'Gutsache'.

Bootnose himself was killed at Cannon Street, when a cast iron girder fell on him. At Peter Robinson's one bloke fell off the front wall. Arthur Lovell, his name was. As he fell off the wall, he hit the fan. He hit the guard and bounced . . . into the road. For any ordinary man that should be death. They put him into a wheelchair for about 2½ years and he got £250 compensation. It ruined his life and that is all he got. He spent it to buy a greengrocer's business. He did not do all that well with it; with him being like that, his wife had to do all the work. He had to sell it out in the end. It was not a happy life and I heard that he died a couple of years later. My father fell several times. Once he fell when he had been down Covent Garden Market, where the pubs open early. Being a good drinking man, he had been in the pub and had his usual morning drink. He always did this to steady him up to go to work. But this day he was so drunk that when he got to the top (the foreman had told him to pull down a chimney breast).

'I didn't know which was which,' he told us afterwards. 'There should be six flue holes, but there were eighteen of them.'

He hit down the bottom where there was already a pile of rubbish (we were knocking down a slum) otherwise it would have been his lot. He rolled out into the open and the foreman came out to see if he was still breathing just as he was scrambling to his feet.

'You all right, Jim.'

'Aw, me back!'

So the foreman said to one of the other chaps: 'Take him up the Middlesex 'Ospital. See what's 'appened. If 'e's not fit, take 'im 'ome.'

Of course, they had a couple on the way, and then they got to the hospital Dad had an argument with the doctor: 'I didn't want to come to the bleedin' barber's,' he said. (He thought because he had a white coat on he was a barber!)

The doctor gave him an examination. He was a mass of bruises, nothing else.

'Right, take him back to the job.'

He should have gone home, but they came out, sampling the pubs on the way.

'I'll get back to work now. I'm all right,' said Dad. The beer made him like that – he wanted to get back to work. (People's Autobiography of Hackney, 1976, pp. 36–7)

Oral history can also provide a different perspective on the family (and give much more space to it) by bringing qualititative evidence to bear. The approach of local historians in the past was largely genealogical – the identification of family origins, the tracing of family trees. More recently, under the influence of the Cambridge Historical demographers, the focus of attention has shifted to household size, but the accounts – despite the importance attached to 'family reconstitution' – remain obstinately external. Names are abstracted from the parish registers, Census returns quantified, but little or nothing may be said about household economy, or the emotional realities of family life. Oral evidence makes possible a much more phenomenological account. Close questioning about specific situations – such as those used in the Essex Oral History project – will reveal a great deal about the inner texture of household life, and enables the historian to explore the different and changing meanings which attached to the notions of a home. Instead of treating the family as a monolithic unity, it is possible to explore specific relationships – mother–daughter, father–son, brother–sister as well as those of the marriage partners themselves. Children are often left out of the demographers' accounts entirely, except as statistics: the frequency or otherwise of their births are recorded and the median age of their marriages, but little else. In an oral history account of the family, by contrast – it is both a weakness and a strength – children are likely to occupy a disproportionately prominent place, if only because informants will be calling on memory drawn from their childhood years. For the same reason the mother is also in the forefront, in many cases overworked and underfed (in a struggling Edwardian home the father would often be given the lion's share of the available food, while the women and children had his leavings), but also chancellor of the family exchequer, strategist and manager, and gaining in authority as her children grew up, while her husband's earning powers waned. Living standards can be explored in the light of the family life cycle, and the peculiarities of the household economy. Instead of looking at earnings only, the historian can inquire into the management of a debt, which in a poor family (or an improvident one) could be as important as wages in the day to day struggle for survival. Earnings themselves will often appear as a family affair, rather than the concern only of the senior male breadwinner. Double banking, secondary employments, totting and foraging, backstreet dealing and trade will often be revealed in people's memory and nowhere else. The same is true of women's home earnings – so often unrecorded in the Censuses – and of child labour, which in the 1890s and 1900s could still make a big contribution to a family's well-being even if, below a certain age, it was prohibited by law.

Oral evidence is important not just as a source of information, but also for what it does to the historian who goes out into the field, as an invisible corrective and check. It can help to expose the silences and deficiency of the written record and reveal to the historian – in Tawney's fine phrase – the 'shrivelled tissue', which is often all that he has in his hands. It serves as a measure of authenticity, a forcible reminder that the historian's categories must in the end correspond to the grain of human experience, and be constituted from it, if they are to have explanatory force. To say this is not to exalt one kind of evidence over another, but to propose a continuous interplay between them, and a more extended use of both. Oral evidence should make the historian hungrier for documents, not less, and when he finds them, he can use them in a more ample and more varied way than his sedentary colleagues, who confine themselves to the library carrel, or the Record Office search room. He will need them for indications of phenomena which lie beyond the reach of memory, for dates where it may be mistaken, for precisions which it cannot, or will not, supply. He will need them to enrich and inform his questioning, to allow the dead to speak to the living and the living to the dead. Above all he will need them to establish the dimensions and peculiarities of change, if he is not to be chronologically limited by the lifespan of his older informants.

Local history does not write itself but, like any other kind of historical project, depends upon the nature of the evidence and the way that it is read. Everything about it is contingent, from the choice of theme to the subject matter of the individual paragraphs. The whole shape of a work can be pre-empted by the adoption of a particular method – family reconstitution, for example, or the derivation of 'social structure' from the Census enumerators' returns. The questions the historian starts with will, to a large extent, determine the answers. Women and children will only appear if he looks for them, domestic labour if he asks about it, family quarrels if he is alert to their tell-tale signs. Documents are decisive too as an unacknowledged source of bias, especially when the historian is heavily reliant on a single main source: you get a different picture of life from local newspapers than from borough records, from petty sessions than from constabulary reports. Often the crucial evidence for what the historian wants to write about is missing, and it might be better to acknowledge the fact, and signal it to readers, rather than to present a partial picture as though it were the whole. Whatever the limits of the material the historian

still has a wide range of optics. The landscape, for instance, will take on quite different hues, depending on whether it is seen through the lens of activity, or the evidence of material remains; the class system will look transparent or opaque according to the materials with which it is reconstituted, and the angle of vision from which it is seen. Precisions can often only be achieved by narrowing the field of vision, perspective by widening it, and the historian should make the reader aware – and recognise himself – the loss which inevitably accompanies either gain.

Documents, I have tried to argue in this chapter, are the most contingent factor of all. Their survival is hazardous and uneven and it is the more bureaucratic and financial class of records which are the most likely to have been preserved: doctors' case notes are a great rarity (there is a good set in the Stockport public library) while board of guardian minutebooks abound. A local history project, however, can generate its own archives and sources as well as drawing on those which have already been deposited or amassed in the record offices, and the historian, even if he does not set out with that intention, will soon find himself the custodian of all kinds of miscellanea. Documents will turn up in the unlikeliest places once you begin to look for them, and the historian who ventures outside the library can bring all kinds of other evidence into play. He will have privileged access to information networks which depend on friendship and word of mouth, to unclassified source materials which are stored as personal hoards, and to men and women who are walking documents, living testimonies to the past. He can supplement the written word with the spoken and call on the visual evidence of the environment, on household iconography and remains. The lottery element in local history can never be eliminated, but for recent times at least it can be substantially reduced.

It would be a great pity if oral history were fetishised, like historical demography, as a project on its own. There are certain kinds of inquiry which can only be undertaken with the aid of oral evidence, others in which its contribution is more marginal. The oral historian is just as likely as anybody else to be stuck in the groove of methodological circularities, and a local history based on oral evidence alone runs as much risk of being routinised – and radically incomplete – as one which depends on the parish chest, even though the repetitions would be different. It would also carry its own characteristic biases. Recalling their past, people will often have much more to say about home life than politics, about habit and custom than about individual occurrences and events (memories of the General Strike are often disappointingly perfunctory, while children's games can cover pages of a transcript). Memory has its own selectivity and silences just as the written record has its bureaucratic biases and irrecoverable gaps. It may be strong on general outline, but fickle when it comes to facts, reticent on some areas of experience while on others it is unexpectedly vociferous. It cannot tell us how reality was perceived at the time, even when it can be recalled in the uttermost detail; and it is only too easy for difficulties to be softened in the warm afterglow of nostalgia. The threads of consciousness are particularly difficult to unravel, because past and present attitudes are so liable to be tangled up. As in everything the historian must be alert to the nature of the evidence presented, whether it is being retailed at first- or at second- and thirdhand, hearsay and gossip, or the testimony of direct personal experience, 'folklore' polished by frequent repetition, and elaborated by the storyteller's arts, or the surprised revelation of incidents and events long since buried in the unconscious. The value of the testimonies depend on what the historian brings to them as well as on what he or she takes, on the precision of the questions, and the wider context of knowledge and understanding from which they are drawn. The living record of the past should be treated as respectfully, but also as critically, as the dead.

Notes: Chapter 19

Reprinted from *History Workshop Journal*, no. 1, 1976, pp. 191-208, by kind permission of the editors.

1 See, for example, Stephens (1973), Tate (1946), Royal Commission on Historical Manuscripts (1973), Harley (1972), HMSO (1964), Wrigley (1972), Mills (1965), Steer (1962), Brunskill (1970), Parker (1970), Hoskins (1969), Emmison and Gray (1961), Emmison (1966), Gough (1968), Travis (1896), Herbert (1948), Mackenzie (1865–6), Peel (1888; 1893), Cox (1879), Pugh (1954), Wake (1925), Boase (1956), Hine (1946), Finberg (1953), Hoskins (1968; 1972), Dyos (1972), Rogers (1972), Everitt (1970) and Spufford (1974).
2 See Tate (1946).
3 See Emmison (1966).
4 *The Director of Dealers in Secondhand and Antiquarian Books* (published annually) is a worthwhile buy for those who want to do their own chasing.
5 *Otmoor and its Seven Towns* (Hobson and Price, 1967) has sold some thousands of copies since it was first published in 1961, while the People's Autobiography of Hackney reaches sales of over 1,000 for its pamphlets within a matter of months.
6 See Richman (1975).
7 *Trowbridge's Fight for Pure Water, 1864–1874* (Lansdown, 1968) is the expressive title of a West Wiltshire Historical Association pamphlet, and it could be matched by comparable chapters in many other works.
8 See Thompson (1974).
9 See *Stability and Change in an English County Town, a social study of York, 1801–1851* (Armstrong, 1974).
10 See Anderson (1971).
11 See Dickens (1854).
12 *'Tis a Mad World at Hogsdon* (Coombs, 1974), which has sold some 2,000 copies in and around Shoreditch, East London, since it was first published in 1974, is a representative recent example.
13 See Hoskins (1968; 1969; 1972).
14 See Finberg (1953).
15 See Spufford (1974).
16 See Hapgood (1975).
17 See Rawlings (1975).
18 See Gavin (1971).
19 See Sims (1883).
20 See Greenwood (1876).
21 See Williams (1966).
22 See Vaisey (1976).
23 See Thompson (1975).
24 See Hoskins (1972).
25 See Foley (1973).
26 See People's Autobiography of Hackney (1976; 1977).
27 The second *Hackney Camera* (People's Autobiography of Hackney, 1974a) is a selection from 280 glass negatives discovered in a cellar.
28 People's Autobiography of Hackney (1974b).
29 See Jenkins (1971).
30 See Ewart Evans (1970).
31 See People's Autobiography of Hackney (1976; 1977).

20

The Study of Life History

DAVID G. MANDELBAUM

Life Passage and Life History Studies

In their observation of the development of a person, anthropologists have used two main approaches: life passage studies, and life history studies.[1] Life passage (or life cycle) studies emphasise the requirements of society, showing how the people of a group socialise and enculturate their young in order to make them into viable members of society. Life history studies, in contrast, emphasise the experiences and requirements of the individual – how the person copes with society, rather than how society copes with the stream of individuals. This difference in emphasis in anthropological studies is also found in sociological and psychological studies.[2]

Comparisons of life passage events in different cultures have brought out certain general similarities;[3] even more, they have highlighted the vast differences among peoples in their methods and standards of socialisation.[4] The life passage studies, in general, have made us aware of some constants in the life experience of man as a member of his species and of the enormous cultural variations that are possible in his experience as a member of his particular society.[5] But these studies have not usually been concerned with the dynamic and adaptive aspects of the life experience, with the relations between one stage of life and the next, with the cumulative patterns of personal conduct, with the relevance of personal experience to social institutions, and with the impact of personal choice on social change. Such questions are more likely to be raised by life history studies, those which follow the individual through the course of his career.

A life history is the account of a life, completed or ongoing. Such an account obviously involves some kind of selection, since only a very small part of all that the person has experienced can possibly be recorded. Certain salient facts about a person are likely to be recorded by any narrator, but much of any life history has to be chosen for inclusion according to some principles for selection. Often enough, such principles as are used are unstated or unwitting or inchoate. Most social scientists who have pointed out the great potential of the life history approach for their respective disciplines have seen as its chief difficulty the lack of accepted principles of selection, of suitable analytic concepts to make up a coherent frame of reference.

Three procedural suggestions are given here as a possible start for such a frame. The ideas of the dimensions, turnings and adaptations in a life history may be useful as guidelines for the collection and analysis of life history data. These ideas are not intended to be inviolable classifications; nor are they substantive concepts, though using them may help us develop such concepts.

Life History Studies in the Social Sciences

The art of biography has long been cultivated by historians, and there is a considerable literature on the writing of biography for historians' purposes.[6] But the study of lives for purposes of social science has been more advocated than practised. At one time the Social Science Research Council gave special attention to the use of life histories and of related personal documents.[7] Other psychologists and sociologists have also given directives for the study of life history and have outlined programmes for research.[8] But not many have as yet done much recording and analysis of life histories as wholes. Longitudinal studies, notably those conducted in the Institute of Human Development at the University of California, Berkeley, USA have yielded many significant observations of growth and social development, but these have yet to be placed in their social and cultural contexts.

Anthropologists have recorded life histories since the beginnings of the discipline. Many of these have been published.[9] Many have not, perhaps because the recorders have not been very clear about what to do with a life history in the way of anthropological analysis.

The stimulus to record them has been, I believe, not so much the outcome of a deliberate research plan as the result of a characteristic phase of the anthropologist's own life experience. When an anthropologist goes to live among the people he studies, he is likely to make some good friends among them. As he writes his account of their way of life, he may feel uncomfortably aware that his description and analysis have omitted something of great importance: His dear friends have been dissolved into faceless norms; their vivid adventures have somehow been turned into pattern profiles or statistical types.

This dilemma is not peculiar to anthropologists; in a way it is part of the human condition. Sapir (1949)[10] once wrote that our natural interest in human behaviour vacillates between what is imputed to the culture of the group as a whole and what is imputed to the psychic organisation of the individual himself. In familiar circumstances and with familiar people, our interest usually centres on the individual. In unfamiliar circumstances and with unfamiliar roles, our perceptions are likely to be cultural rather than personal. 'If I see my little son playing marbles', he wrote, 'I do not, as a rule, wish to have light thrown on how the game is played. Nearly everything that I observe tends to be interpreted as a contribution to the understanding of the child's personality'.

To redress the balance between these two perspectives, a good many anthropologists have taken down the story of an informant's life. Radin (1913; 1920; 1926) was one of the first to give a rationale for doing so; his purpose was 'to have some representative middle-aged individual of moderate ability describe his life in relation to the social group in which he had grown up'.[11] Radin noted how difficult it was to get 'an inside view of their culture' from informants,[12] and showed that a life history narrative could add much to an ethnological account. Radin's footnotes tell a good deal about the culture and about the narrator, but there is almost no analysis. Although a main theme of Crashing Thunder's story is his quest for a good way of life, Radin's notes are more on the culture than on the society or personality, more on cultural patterns than on social or personal adaptation, more on descriptive presentation than on conceptual development.[13]

Dollard's (1935) *Criteria for the Life History* was a major attempt to provide some theoretical underpinning for the use of life history data. Dollard formulated seven criteria for the study of life histories, of which the first six stipulate in various ways that the subject must be understood in his social and cultural context. The seventh is that 'the life history material itself must be organised and conceptualised'. Dollard recognises that this is the crucial criterion. As he says, life history material does not speak for itself. But Dollard could then offer very little in the way of concepts or clues to organisation.

Dollard's book reflected and also stimulated increased interest in life histories, or at least in the kind of perspectives on human behaviour that life histories might yield. When Kluckhohn (1945a) surveyed the use of personal documents in anthropology, a number of life histories had recently been published or were in preparation. Boas, among others, had been dubious about their scientific value, and in one of his last papers, published posthumously in 1943, concluded that 'they are valuable rather as useful material for a study of the perversion of truth brought about by the play of memory with the past'.[14] But Kluckhohn's thorough and thoughtful survey reached very different conclusions. Kluckhohn recognised the many problems of reliability, validity and interpretation that are involved in the use of life histories, but saw their potential advantages for studies of social change, as clues to implicit themes, as documentation on roles, as demonstration of socialisation and enculturation as an entry into understanding personality, as a view of the 'emotional structure' of a way of life, as a means towards understanding variations within a society, and also of seeing the 'common humanity' among peoples. Yet the use of life histories, as he appraised it in 1945, was more promise than actuality: 'Perhaps the most salient conclusion which emerged from our survey of published life history documents was the deficiency of analysis and interpretation.'[15] He added that personal documents had served as little more than interesting curiosities and that pitifully few new theoretical questions had been asked of them.[16]

The other surveys in the series sponsored by the Social Science Research Council came to similar conclusions. Allport's (1942) appraisal of the use of personal documents in psychology ended with a recommendation that more conceptual, analytical work with such materials should be encouraged. Angell's (1945) review of sociological studies found that Thomas and Znaniecki's *The Polish Peasant in Europe and America* (1918–20) remained a monumental example of the method and that, while Blumer's (1939) appraisal of that work was relevant and stimulating, there had been very little theoretical development of this field.

More than twenty years later, several updated reviews of the use of life history materials appeared. Becker (1966), considering the state of such studies in sociology, emphasises the great importance of presenting the actor's subjective evaluations of his experiences and of giving the context in which he undergoes his social experience. He discusses the great potential of life history data as a wellspring for theory and as a means of testing concepts. He notes that such materials offer basic evidence about social interaction and process, that they can provide a vivid feeling for what it means to be a certain kind of person. 'Given the variety of scientific uses to which the life history may be put', he observes, 'one must wonder at the relative neglect into which it has fallen'.[17]

Becker attributes this, in part, to sociologists' greater concern with their own abstract categories than with those held by the people studied. Life history materials do not lend themselves well to sociological emphases on structural variables, on synchronic analysis and on group attributes. A further reason, Becker notes, is that life history studies do not yield the kind of findings that sociologists have expected research to produce. The emphasis has been on the self-sufficient and self-contained single study, in which the researcher's hypothesis is tested against what is discovered in that one piece of research. A life history, like the life itself, is not so self-sufficient or self-contained, nor can it readily be deployed to prove or disprove any one hypothesis. Becker concludes with the hope that 'a fuller understanding of the complexity of the scientific enterprise will restore sociologists' sense of the versatility and worth of the life history'.[18]

Edinger (1964), in his survey of the use of political biography in political science, notes that while such study is generally accepted as vital, it has been much neglected. The reasons for this neglect are mainly in the discipline's preference for group rather than individual manifestations and for the 'scientific' models of the behavioural approach. For behaviourally oriented American political scientists, Edinger observes, 'the most notable lack in modern political biography is that it has no explicit, conceptual framework for the selection, organization, and presentation of data'.[19] He offers a possible framework, but it has not been quickly seized upon by other political scientists. Davies (1967) calls attention to the research leads for political science in Dollard's work. Greenstein (1969) gives a fine overview, including a chapter on the biographical, 'single-actor' study; he, too, mentions the lack of conceptual tools and recommends increased development of this approach in political science research.

The trends of research in anthropology have not raised the kinds of barriers to the use of life histories that have been noted for political science and for sociology. Anthropologists have generally been more aware of the people's categories and perhaps less attached to their own favourite abstractions. Nor have they commonly sought for self-sufficient single studies in the same way that some sociologists have done, or for mass behavioural analysis in the manner of some political scientists. Yet, a resurvey of the anthropological use of life histories by Langness (1965) reveals little more development than has occurred in these other disciplines. Langness observes, 'Indeed, unfortunate as it seems, we can use virtually unchanged the summary statements made by Kluckhohn in 1945'.[20]

Many life histories were collected during the intervening two decades, and a number of excellent narrative accounts were published. But though they give the reader some insight into the central figure and a feel for his society and culture, they add little to a body of general concepts. Few have much to offer in the way of analysis, but those few show the life history to be a rich, though still largely untapped, vein for anthropological investigation. Thus, Alberle's (1951) analysis of *Sun Chief* (Simmons, 1942), the autobiography of a Hopi Indian, sheds new light on such aspects of Hopi culture as witchcraft, and illumines certain general problems such as the diversity of interpretation of the same culture by different observers. Mintz's (1960) fine life history of a Puerto Rican makes vividly clear, as few

other anthropological studies have done, the social factors and personal motivation that are involved in religious conversion.

The most extensive life history materials published in this period are those recorded on tape by Lewis and presented by him in a widely read series of books. In the introduction to his *La Vida* (1965), Lewis discusses the important concept of the culture of poverty, evidence for which he gained in considerable part from the autobiographies he collected in his studies of Mexican and Puerto Rican families. Langness (1965) says that these are masterful accounts, but that Lewis's work 'is almost exclusively descriptive and involves very little in the way of analysis or "problem- orientation" '.[21]

The need for intellectual form in the study of life history was well expressed by Redfield (1955).[22] This approach, he noted, could show the social life of a community not only as a structure of interrelated parts, but more as a 'succession of added comprehensions'. It would raise new questions and problems, such as the changing states of mind in the span of a life, the prospective quality of a person's life, the influence of ideals on behaviour, and the differences among what a man thinks ought to happen, what he expects to happen and what he actually does. Such queries would bring the anthropologist to 'the real and ultimate raw material' of his study; they would provide him with a direct means of examining social change. But they also involve the special difficulties of giving strong consideration to the people's modes of thought, rather than assuming the more comfortable categories of the observer. All these discussions of the use of life histories convincingly tell of the great potential benefits of the method and properly warn workers in this field of the precautions to be observed, but provide few guiding ideas for actually doing this research.

Procedural Suggestions

The jumbled, often profuse flow of data in a life history that an anthropologist collects has to be channelled in some preliminary way before much analytic headway can be made with it. Three ways of doing so are suggested here beyond sheer chronological succession. They are in noting: (1) the dimensions or aspects of a person's life; (2) the principal turnings and the life conditions between turnings; and (3) the person's characteristic means of adaptation. The dimensions provide categories for understanding the main forces that affect a life. The turnings mark major changes that a person makes and, thus, demarcate periods of his life. A focus on adaptation directs our notice both to changes he makes, and to continuities he maintains through his life course.

DIMENSIONS

A dimension of a life history is made up of experiences that stem from a similar base and are linked in their effects on the person's subsequent actions. One such dimension is the biological, based on the individual's organic makeup and somatic development. Other distinguishable dimensions I have labelled the cultural, the social and the psychosocial. To these must be added the unique, individual aspect of each life that is a basic consideration in life history study.

The *biological* dimension is the best documented for the human species as a whole. Each person's biological development has been broadly preprogrammed for him in the course of human evolution. Each one's programming is affected by his genetic constitution, and this differs among groups as well as among individuals, though the behavioural significance of the group differences is far from clear. And in discussing biological development, the inclusive pronoun 'he' must be put aside in some respects, since the biological development of males and females differs both in timing and in kind.

The biological factors set the basic conditions for a life course; cultural factors mould the shape and content of a person's career. The *cultural* dimension lies in the mutual expectations, understandings and behaviour patterns held by the people among whom a person grows up and in whose society he becomes a participant. Each culture provides a general scenario for the life course that indicates the main divisions, tells when transitions should be made, and imputes a social meaning to biological events from birth through death. Each scenario interprets and affects the biological dimension in its own way; each provides its own chart for the progress of a life.

This cultural life plan is more a schematic outline than a detailed code. Within this outline, more detailed prescriptions of roles and behaviour patterns are stipulated for particular sections of the society. These specifications commonly provide options among which the individual can make some choice. Such narrower specifications and broader choices provide the individual with his principal guides to actual social interrelations.

The *social* dimension of a life history includes the effective interplay and real relations in the course of which the actors may alter the roles, change the nature of the choices and shift the cultural definitions. So the cultural expectations for a life course may be revised in mid-course of actual lives. In focusing on the social dimension the observer studies those acts of personal choice that are characteristic of the person's group and the common ways of working out the recurrent conflicts of life. Some of these regularities are recognised by the participants, others are not.

The cultural and the social dimensions, as devices for analysis, often overlap, but the difference in emphasis is clear and the distinction seems to be analytically useful. The cultural dimension has to do with expectations and known forms shared by the people of a group with the cognitive and normative thought they have in common. The social dimension, in contrast, has to do with their social acts, conflicts, solutions and choices. It includes the emotional experiencing of reward and penalty and the outcome of action in maintaining or changing behaviour patterns.

Within the study of the *psychosocial* dimension, the observer focuses on the individual's subjective world, his general feelings and attitudes. These are individually experienced, but each individual's subjective experience is likely to be similar, in some considerable part, to that of others in his culture and society. Psychosocial development in the course of a life has been more extensively discussed than have characteristic developments in the cultural and social aspects.[23] Freud's formulations provided a foundation for Erikson's (1964; 1968a; 1968b) influential scheme of the individual's development. Erikson outlines eight stages through which all persons pass, each characterised by a particular psychological encounter in which a person must somehow cope with opposing trends in himself. (In the earliest stage of infancy, for example, the encounter is between basic trust and mistrust.)[24] The sequence, Erikson says, varies 'in tempo and intensity' according to cultural and personal differences. This outline resembles a profile of biological development, in that it is postulated as universal to the human species and the development is taken to be epigenetic. That is, the organism is seen as unfolding gradually in time and becoming more differentiated by cumulative stages. The psychological dispositions listed in this sequence have to do with a person's general attitudes towards others, and with his feelings towards an image of himself. The observer's emphasis in this view is on subjective response more than on biological capacity, on introspective feeling more than on prospective pattern, on generalised attitudes more than on social interaction.

Other postulated sequences emphasise different psychological variables and deal mainly with the earlier years of life. Piaget (1968) has contributed a long and important series of studies, in which he and his colleagues have formulated stages of cognitive development and of adaptive behaviour. Kohlberg (1968) has worked out a series of stages in the development of moral judgements. Leovinger (1966) has sketched an overview of stages of ego development. Leighton and his colleagues have done extensive research in social psychiatry, taking a psychobiological approach and using life history materials.[25] One contribution of this research is an extensive life history, with considerable analysis, of a Navaho Indian (Leighton and Leighton, 1949). Important psychological studies on life history materials have been done by Bühler (1933), and Frenkel (1936). More recently, Bühler (1962)[26] has formulated a chart of basic psychological tendencies in the development of the self, which shows the stage at which each tendency is particularly important.[27]

These studies of psychosocial aspects have dealt mainly with persons from European or North American societies; the research methods used have been more those of clinic and questionnaire than of long-term observation and direct recording in the context of reality. Their results should, therefore, be tested and amplified in the light of broader studies of life history.

Underlying all formulations about life development is that aspect of a life history that is special and unique. Out of the study of individual lives, all life history generalisations are distilled. General concepts must be tested against individual experience. Yet, a person's life cannot be neatly summarised and totally wrapped up in our generalisations. Simmons (1942)[28] notes that each person is a creature and carrier of his culture, a manipulator in his society and also, even if only in a minute way, a creator of culture. While illuminating studies can be made about the conditions and limitations of creativeness in a society, each person's creativity cannot be fully accounted for by such studies.

This limitation to generalisation is no more than the limit on all social research that abstracts common features from particular instances. But it becomes more poignantly apparent to those who try to study the whole life of a real person. And in the study of a life, the student tends to become especially aware of the person as an active doer and seeker, and not only as a passive recipient or a subject for scientific generalisations. Despite this ungeneralisable aspect of life history, cogent generalisations about a single account and comparative generalisations about many life histories, across cultural lines, can usefully be made. The guideline of dimensions is one sorting device for doing so; the ideas of turnings and adaptations complement it.

TURNINGS

The principal periods of a life are marked by the main turnings, the major transitions, that the person has made. Such a turning is accomplished when the person takes on a new set of roles, enters into fresh relations with a new set of people, and acquires a new self-conception. The turning, thus, combines elements of three dimensions, the new roles being mainly cultural, the new interactions being social, and the new self-conception being psychosocial. A turning may occur through a single event or experience, a 'turning-point', or it may be a gradual shift. A marriage ceremony can be a turning-point, while the shift from active adult to less active elder is often a gradual process. Some turnings are ascribed, others are more self-chosen. Certain turnings are quite absolutely ascribed, for example, entrance of every child into school in American society or early marriage for girls in the com-

munity in which Gandhi grew up. Other turnings are left to family or individual choice. The manner of carrying out some turnings may be prescribed in detail; other turnings are more improvised. Some improvisation takes place even in a closely prescribed ritual, such as a funeral or a wedding. Conversely, a person who improvises a turning in his life commonly follows some established patterns. A person's own view of the watersheds in his life may not exactly coincide with the significant turnings that an observer may notice, but that view may none the less be important in the way in which he directs his life. Any one turning, then, may be relatively more ascribed or self-chosen, prescribed or improvised, quick or protracted, but each provides an index to the person's conduct after the turning. Once we understand the major transitions, we also know something about the main parts of his life, that is, about his salient roles, social relations and self-conception from one transition to the next.

ADAPTATIONS

A life history develops over time, and so the parts entail periods of time. These periods are commonly drawn as segments along a curve, yet the depiction of a life as a trajectory, rising out of nothing, ascending to a zenith of something, and falling back to nothing, is not a very useful analogy. A life does not proceed in a projectable, unilinear curve like a cannon shot. Rather it involves ongoing development in various spheres of behaviour; it includes continuous adjustment and periodic adaptation. Personal adaptations are both the source of social adaptation, and also responses to it.

Adaptation is a built-in process, because every person must, in the course of his life, alter some of his established patterns of behaviour to cope with new conditions. Each person *changes* his ways in order to maintain *continuity*, whether of group participation or social expectation or self-image or simply survival. Some of these new conditions are imposed by his own physical development. Others arise from changing external conditions, whether of custom or climate, family or society. Changes in behaviour that remove particular stimuli to action have been labelled adjustments. Personal adaptations, by contrast, are changes that have major effect on a person's life and on his basic relations with others. Kluckhohn (1962) applied the term 'adaptive' to behaviour that contributed to the survival of the individual or the group. Questions about adaptation in the study of a life history can be especially useful, when an outline of the turnings and dimensions is available. We can then look to the main opportunities and limitations that the person faced at each juncture and ask how and why the person adapted his behaviour (or failed to do so) at this point, what he tried to change and what he tried to maintain.

Notes: Chapter 20

Reprinted from *Current Anthropology*, vol. 14, no. 3, June, 1973, pp. 177–82 and 195–6, by kind permission of the publisher, University of Chicago Press, and the author. © 1973 Wenner-Gren Foundation for Anthropological Research. The present paper was submitted for publication in *Current Anthropology* in final form on 9 July 1971. It was sent for comment to fifity scholars of whom the following responded: Akinsola A. Akiwowo, Michael M. Ames, Nirmal Kumar Bose, Charlotte Bühler, Fred I. Greenstein, George G. Haydu, L. L. Langness, Sidney W. Mintz, Herbert P. Phillips, Susanne Hoeber Rudolph and Lloyd I. Rudolph, M. Brewster Smith, André Varagnac and Jack Waddell. Their comments are printed in *Current Anthropology*, vol. 14, no. 3, pp. 197–204, and are followed by a reply from Mandelbaum, pp. 204–6.

1 This study was begun in the spring of 1969, when I was associated with the Institute of Human Development, University of California, Berkeley, USA. The help of the Institute and its staff is gratefully acknowledged. Bibliographic assistance was most ably given by Kathryn Hansen.
2 Thus, Smith (1968), p. 276, has noted that the psychological study of social competence should 'keep in simultaneous view the two perspectives that are differently emphasised by Inkeles and by Foot and Cottrell; that of society and its 'manpower' needs, and that of the person himself, as the locus of humanistic values.'
3 See, for example, Van Gennep (1960).
4 See, for example, Mead (1928; 1935; 1970a).
5 Compare Richards (1970), and Clausen (1968), pp. 47–8.
6 Compare Garraty (1957).
7 See Blumer (1939), Allport (1942), Gottschalk (1945), Kluckhohn (1945a) and Angell (1945).
8 Compare Park and Burgess (1924), Bühler (1933; 1968a; 1968b), K. Young (1952), P. Young (1966), Becker (1966) and Denzin (1970).
9 Compare Langness (1965), pp. 54–82.
10 See Sapir (1949), p. 590.
11 See Radin (1920), p. 382.
12 See Radin (1920), p. 383.
13 Compare Lurie (1966), pp. 96–106.
14 See Boas (1943), p. 335.
15 See Kluckhohn (1945a), p. 133.
16 See Kluckhohn (1945a), p. 147.
17 See Becker (1966), p. xvi.
18 See Becker (1966), p. xviii.
19 See Edinger (1964), p. 426.
20 See Langness (1965), p. 18.
21 See Langness (1965), p. 14.
22 See Redfield (1955), pp. 56–65.
23 Compare Bühler (1967), pp. 83–5.
24 See Erikson (1968b), pp. 286–7.
25 Compare Leighton (1959).
26 See Bühler (1962), pp. 108–9.
27 See also Bühler and Massarik (1968).
28 See Simmons (1942), p. 388.

Anthropology and the Discipline of Historical Context

E. P. THOMPSON

(EDITOR'S NOTE: This material was originally published as a review article in which E. P. Thompson reviewed *Religion and the Decline of Magic* by Keith Thomas (London: Weidenfeld & Nicolson, 1971) and *The Family Life of Ralph Josselin, A Seventeenth-Century Clergyman*, by Alan Macfarlane (Cambridge: Cambridge University Press, 1970.)

An interesting – if sometimes tedious and provoking – book from Dr Macfarlane, and an immensely important and stimulating book from Mr Thomas! Both raise questions of historiographical method. Macfarlane's study is subtitled 'an essay in historical anthropology'. Thomas published an important article in *Past and Present* in 1963, on 'History and anthropology',[1] followed (in 1964) by a study of 'Work and leisure in pre-industrial society',[2] which located further problems in this area. In 1966 he published a *credo* in *The Times Literary Supplement*, in which he called for 'a more systematic indoctrination' of historians 'in the social sciences', which sciences were defined as including not only anthropology and demography, but also social psychology and sociology:

> If the analysis of the past is to be rigorous, then the construction of an historical typology, a means of classifying and comparing, is an urgent *desideratum*. It cannot come from sociology alone, but an education in the concepts of sociology seems the quickest way of attaining it. (Thomas, 1966, pp. 275–6)[3]

How far do these books signal the arrival of a new history, with distinctively new methods? Macfarlane (in this sense) offers most, but his accomplishment is modest. He submits Ralph Josselin's diaries to patient and intensive scrutiny, supplementing their evidence where possible from other sources, and the questions which he puts to this source material are prompted by his anthropological training. The originality of this method – and, in particular, the systematic examination of a single source – has perhaps led some readers to overestimate its productivity, and to underestimate several of the difficulties inherent in the method. Macfarlane rightly warns the reader that 'the very fact that he kept a diary suggests that [Josselin] was slightly exceptional'.[4] He does not, however, in any serious sense seek to validate and identify the nature of his own source, except where objective events (births, deaths, law suits, and so on) can be checked against alternative sources. Since Josselin – a dull, acquisitive, unadventurous man – was not given to romancing, or to inventing diary entries, this does not invalidate the greater part of the material studied: property transactions, weather notes, the comings and goings of kin and of friends. But where the entries indicate attitudes and beliefs,[5] one must clearly be more cautious.

A diary is addressed to an audience, even when its motive is confessional and the audience is confined to the author and to God. In the case of Josselin, the motives are clearly mingled: confessional, self-disciplinary examination, useful memoranda and annual accounting. Where attitudes are expressed, we must always be aware when we have evidence not of a spontaneous, unmediated attitude, but of this transcribed into an approved self-image (perhaps with approved doctrinal afterthoughts), like someone arranging his face in a looking-glass. On 26 August 1644 Josselin entered in his diary: 'leaping over the pales I scratched my face, but God be praised I had no further hurt though I might if providence had not preserved mee, & also in our fall when my wife and I pulling downe a tree with a rope with our pulling all fell together, but no hurt God bee praised'.[6] Macfarlane cites this as illustrative of Josselin's 'awareness of the precarious world he lived in', and of his 'everlasting anxiety, mixed with relief and gratitude to God'; and, in a wider context, as illustrative of the anxieties of men living in an age of low life expectations, demographic hazards, poor medicine, no insurance companies, and the rest. One nods contentedly over the argument, reassured by anthropological footnotes, until one recalls that Ben Jonson – if he had seen the passage – would have unhesitatingly cited it as exemplifying

Puritan self-deception and humbug: Tribulation Wholesome in his person, with his lack of humour and of self-criticism, his timidity, his self-importance, and his crafty eye for the main chance. And one might be led from that to reflect that other men in the sixteenth and seventeenth centuries (also without the protection of insurance companies, and so on) were able to face inconceivable hazards with equanimity.

One is concerned not with this disputable point, but with the method: how can one, in using a diary, distinguish between the man's actuality and his approved self-image? How can one detect the gap (if one exists) between a man's motives and his rationalisation of these motives, and further, the ideological or doctrinal gloss which he places upon these rationalisations? Macfarlane has read his diary with enormous patience and critical awareness, but he has not confronted this problem, nor has he any critical method to bring to bear upon it. As a result, his study contributes little to the understanding of the Puritan sensibility.

What of the stricter examination of Josselin's family life and economy? He is hindered here by the deficiencies of his source. In some pages central to his study one notices that the diary provides no evidence as to the cause of the miscarriages of Josselin's wife; no evidence as to birth control, or as to sexual relations between husband and wife;[7] no discussion of the problems of puberty;[8] scarcely any evidence as to the rearing of children;[9] no reference to the 'natural functions'; or to the chastisement of children;[10] and so on. Where the source is more communicative, one is not always sure that Macfarlane is asking the right questions: just as the historian who is innocent of anthropological discipline may impose twentieth-century categories upon seventeenth century material, so the anthropologically trained may be in danger of imposing categories from a wholly different social culture.

This is critical to the problem of method, so we must take examples. It is by no means self-evident that studies of *Nupe Religion*[11] and of *The Sherpas of Nepal*[12] can serve as 'models' for understanding funeral rites in seventeenth century Essex.[13] J. K. Campbell's fine study, *Honour, Family and Patronage*[14] is drawn upon repeatedly, usually for purposes of contrast, sometimes with the suggestion that Campbell's findings refer to 'Greece' as a whole.[15] The unprompted reader is not informed that Campbell's study is of an unusual and isolated society of mountain shepherds. At one point (discussing kinship ties) Macfarlane writes:

> The children of Josselin's uncles, his first cousins, might be expected to form another important kinship category, as they do in another bilateral kinship society where 'Cousins are the most significant of a person's kinsmen both for purposes of practical co-operation and for simple companionship'. (Macfarlane, 1970, p. 136)

(The reference is to Campbell.) The anthropological category imposed here ('another bilateral kinship society') prepares the mind to envisage that a significant comparison is being made, whereas in fact the functions of both practical co-operation and of companionship are rather different in a partially nomadic society of herdsmen and in a seventeenth century Essex village (from which the subject's cousins are separated by distance, differences of occupation and status). The comparison is not significant: it is either muddled or pretentious. Campbell's work succeeds not because he has isolated this or that facet of his shepherd community, but in so far as he shows how all the parts relate to each other in a coherent and internally consistent cultural and social system. This is what much of the best anthropology is about, and British anthropologists are generally cautious (some would say excessively so) as to carrying generalisations across from one society to another, even when these are at comparable levels of development. The increasing tendency to abstract some anthropological or sociological finding from its context, and to flourish it around as if it was possessed of some intrinsic value as a typological fact about all human societies is actively injurious to history.

Macfarlane's anthropological training prompts him to ask many interesting questions, and often (although not, perhaps, as often as he implies) these are questions which historians have neglected to ask. It does not, however, equip him to answer these questions, except in so far as he submits them to more orthodox tests of historical evidence. And occasionally it actively obscures his view. An example may be taken from one of the most successful and important findings of the book, the examination of the age at which the Josselin children left home, for education, service, or apprenticeship: in the case of the girls, between the ages of 10 and 14, in the case of two boys at 15. These interesting findings[16] are supplemented by the very useful appendix B,[17] which brings additional evidence from conventional historical and demographic sources to argue that this pattern was widespread, and most marked in middling economic groups, excluding the wealthy and the very poor. But Macfarlane is inhibited from a full exploration of this problem by the supposition that the relevant fact, in the sending out of children, must be the onset of puberty: 'it is surely more than a coincidence that it was exactly at this age that they all left home to be subjected to outside discipline and freed from the incestuous dangers of crowded living'.[18] (By a similar logic of 'coincidence' one might argue that the progressive raising of the legal minimum age for factory children in the nineteenth century was occasioned by a rising age at puberty.) 'Incestuous temptations'[19] is not, as an explanation, a satisfactory substitute for an examination of the traditions of education and of 'house-keeping', the institution of apprenticeship and the manifold other factors contributing to the upbringing of adolescent children at that time.

Macfarlane's preoccupation with the incestuous dangers to which the Reverend Ralph Josselin's household was exposed were perhaps prompted by reminiscences of Melanesian islanders; but he is able to call also upon the findings of sociologists in the 1950s and 1960s in Britain and the USA. Thus he brings to bear upon the relationship of Ralph Josselin to his wife the category of 'joint-role relationship', which (in the terms of 1957) was defined as entertaining together, sharing friends and the care of the children, taking 'joint decisions over matters previously discussed together' ('shall we go to Majorca again this year, darling?') and participating 'generally in one another's activities'. On the basis of the most slender evidence – Josselin and his wife fell over together while pulling down a tree (and from this it is inferred that they 'helped one another in the farm work') they discussed together the suitability of their daughters' suitors (from which it is inferred that 'all important decisions were jointly taken') – Macfarlane comes up triumphantly with the portentous judgement that 'this marriage could be classified sociologically as a "joint-role relationship" and described as an emotional success'.[20]

If this is indeed so, one can only add: 'so much the worse for sociology.' An instrument designed for unpicking the inwardness of mid-twentieth century marital adjustments cannot be applied without modification to seventeenth century Essex. There is no evidence that Josselin consulted his wife on any of his important property transactions, or that he gave way to her judgement on any of his political or religious decisions, or that they did indeed in any sense share the 'farm work', or that Mrs Josselin took any comparable part in disciplining the refractory adolescent or adult children, or that he consulted her about his sermons, or that they ever took a holiday together in Majorca. (We do know that he bequeathed to her some land and personal effects, together with 'three or foure Roomes of the Mancon house wherein I now dwell together with free ingresse, egress, and regress out of the same'.) Macfarlane has in fact got into a bad muddle here, by bringing to the problem too lumpish and unsubtle a category.

Perhaps these muddles, which are inevitable when two disciplines impinge upon one another, can be fruitful. Certainly, the related – and even more profound – muddle about 'patriarchalism' cries out for some resolution. In this case the anthropological inclination towards a strongly characterised typology leads Macfarlane, in an extraordinary passage of verbo-synthesis,[21] to assimilate Laurence Stone's comments of patriarchal father–son relationships to reports from Turkey, Melanesia, the Gold Coast and the Ruanda ('among the Ruanda the father even had access to a son's wife') – all presumably, comparable 'patriarchal' societies – then to demonstrate that, in contrast to these, Josselin showed affection and concern for his sons (and failed to discipline his younger son), and

eventually to emerge with the suppositious disproof of the views (held by 'some historians') that Puritan fathers were 'austere' and showed 'patriarchal aloofness'.

The questions here are too large and too complex to pursue at this point. But they cry out for research, and for research more subtle than is offered in this book. Patriarchal values need, by no means, imply aloofness or lack of affection; but the degrees by which patriarchalism shades into paternalism require scrupulous definition. Macfarlane does not propose that matriarchal values dominated the Josselin household and, presumably, there may be a weak, equivocal, un-self-confident patriarchal authority? (Patriarchalism need not *necessarily* imply that the father has access to the son's wife.) The point is that, if anthropologists are right to propose this kind of question, they carry with them no bag of conjuring tricks which enables them to provide answers by shortcuts and out of tidbits of abstracted information. Only when the evidence is studied within its whole historical context – the rules and expectations of inheritance, the role of influence and interest, the norms and expectations not of 'society', but of different social groups – can it bring fruitful results.

The great merit of Macfarlane's book is that it poses questions; it teaches historians to look much more closely, and in new ways, at familiar evidence; it brings familial relationships into the centre of scrutiny; and it offers, in a significant way, the unit of one man's life, and of one man's economic fortunes, as a focus of study. In attending to certain demerits my comments are ungenerous: the author does not propose infallibility, and is at times disarmingly tentative, and invites criticism or confirmation. The demerits have been singled out, because they are characteristic not of Macfarlane alone, but of many current attempts to apply anthropological or sociological or, indeed, criminological or demographic concepts *to* history.

The difficulties are of several kinds. (1) It is generally true that anthropology, sociology and criminology have evolved either as unhistorical disciplines, or with an inadequate historical component, or with an actively anti-historical bias. Hence, they cannot offer – what Mr Thomas asked for in *The Times Literary Supplement* – 'an historical typology'.[22] The discipline of history is, above all, the discipline of context; each fact can be given meaning only within an ensemble of other meanings; while sociology, let us say, may put many questions to historical material which historians had not thought of asking, it is most unlikely that any 'sociological concept' can be taken, raw, from twentieth century suburbia (or from Melanesia) to seventeenth century England, since the concept itself must be modified and refined before it will be appropriate to the ensemble of seventeenth century meanings. This should not require saying: but there are fashions around which require it. In some eyes, the 'systematic indoctrination' of historians 'in the social sciences' conjures up a scene of insemination, in which Clio lies inert and passionless (perhaps with rolling eyes), while anthropology or sociology thrust their seed into her womb. But the encounter between partners is going to be a good deal more active than that; and it is difficult to believe that the complacency of some anthropological and (in particular) sociological typologies will not be as much shattered by historical examination as the reverse. (2) There is not, in any case (*pace* Mr Thomas) any such thing as 'the concepts of sociology', but a mass of conflicting and disputed concepts. Sociology more than most 'social sciences' has been deeply marked by the ideological pressures of the microscopic quantum of historical time in which we now live. Hence, even the bringing of such concepts to bear, in asking questions of historical material, requires great selectivity. (3) Where the influence of the social sciences is undoubtedly most fruitful it is, at exactly the same point, most treacherous: in the comparative method. For it is precisely at the point where these seventeenth century families become the Nuclear Family: where these thirteenth century Russian peasants and those nineteenth century Irish cottiers become the Peasantry: where these Chartist plug rioters and those communards become Violence in Industrial Society: where, indeed, eighteenth century Birmingham and a bazaar in twentieth century Persia and a village in twentieth century Ecuador become assimilated as Pre-Industrial Society – it is at this point that the integument of the historical discipline comes under extreme strain, and is in danger of being punctured to let in a gush of abstract typological air. The danger is worth taking; but each new concept so gained must be thrust back into the ensemble of meanings of a specific historical context once again, and many of the concepts – perhaps the majority – will crumble to mere dust of irrelevancy in the immersion. Perhaps the continual making and breaking of the integument is the best that we can do.

Macfarlane, in this work at least, does not signal a new history. What of Thomas? There can be no doubt that his work is of the greatest importance; the extent to which it signals new methods requires more careful examination. In his *Times Literary Supplement* credo of 1966[23] his enthusiasm for the new history touched at times a millennial note:

> In America the new econometric history, less than ten years old, is already sweeping all before it. Resting upon an alliance between mathematically sophisticated tools of measurement and the construction of elaborate theoretical models, it promises a definitive solution to such problems as the economic efficiency of slavery, etc.

By contrast to this, his book impresses first of all by its massive command of more or less traditional means of scholarship. He uses, in fact, no econometrics; nor

could he, in his chosen area. The insights which he has derived from anthropology are subdued to the historical discipline. He needs none of my sermons.

The book is, in fact, a superb example of sustained historical argument. It is in itself an ensemble of meanings: the church in its doctrines and in its sociological presence, the various dimensions of the several magics of popular religion, prophecy, wisemen and witches, astrologers and their customers – all are related to one another, and seen within the perspective of decomposing magical notations of the accidents of nature and of human occasions. The method of which one is most aware is that of acute, and patient, logical inference; an even intelligence, rarely rising and even more rarely falling in intensity, patiently teasing out interconnections and recovering forgotten modes of perception; a subtle rationalism always ready to explore the irrational with sympathy.

In a more limited technical sense, one admires at every stage the aptness of the sources deployed to the particular inquiry in hand. For the doctrines of the church and of the Puritans, he has the pamphlets and sermons of the Bodleian; for conjurors and wisemen, the depositions of church courts; for astrologers, he has their own casebooks of consultations; for witchcraft, he has legal proceedings; for all areas, he has a formidable command of the published and secondary sources, including an enviable freedom of movement among the often-neglected provincial antiquarian and folklore publications of the nineteenth century.

This is to say that, although some of the subject matter of *Religion and the Decline of Magic* is new, one is impressed less with a sense of a new methodology than with the evidence of the extension of a traditional historical discipline into new areas of research. And yet there is clearly a substantial anthropological impulse in Thomas's thought, most evident in the analysis of wisemen and of witchcraft, but operating also in the wider framework of the book (in its definition of the character and function of magic) and in the manner in which he discloses the rationality of the irrational. There are times when anthropological data of dubious relevance appear to obtrude – most commonly in footnotes, but on at least one occasion in the text,[24] where Melanesian cargo cults are deployed to illuminate the Fifth Monarchy Men, only to be snubbed politely and sent away on the next page. Far more often the concepts are not cut, raw and bleeding, from the side of context and applied to seventeenth century England: they are first assimilated, tested against the material, modified. The principles which can be taken across from one society to the other are few, although large in significance; for example, the notion that if a community believes that magic works, it will, within limits, work (the man who is cursed will become ill, the thief who knows that the wizard is searching him out will, for fear of discovery, return the stolen goods, and so on); above all, the understanding gained from the study of African witchcraft that a crucial point of purchase for its examination may be to isolate the social and personal relations between the accuser and the accused.

It is questionable how far the accession of such insights as these can be said to constitute a new method: one would hesitate to describe it as 'historical anthropology'. Thomas, as it happens, leans heavily upon African example, where the best studies by British anthropologists have been made. If his borrowings had been less cautious, if he had not subjected each inference to the test of its historical relevance, he would have come up with ludicrous results; it is immediately evident from a glance at his footnotes on certain pages that the societies under comparison are grossly dissimilar, and that if comparable material had been available from, say, nineteenth century India, where popular superstition and an oral tradition coexisted with sophisticated religious institutions and literacy, its use would have been preferable. Indeed, for a study of this scope and significance, Thomas's comparative range is limited, precisely because he is wary of generalisations which escape from the discipline of context: even when considering witchcraft, his glances at Europe and New England are brief and tentative and, more seriously, he avoids even a Scottish comparison.

We cannot, then, say that this is a comparative method, nor is it an anthropological method except in the sense that the mind of the historian has been informed, his perspectives extended, his awareness of significances aroused, by a reading of anthropology. This is probably the proper way in which such influences, as between disciplines, should be taken through. One hopes that some anthropologists will return the compliment.

What, then, are we to make of the millennial Mr Thomas of *The Times Literary Supplement* (1966)? Is it just that he does not practise what he has preached? This is partly so; or, rather, he is too good a historian to have submitted himself to the 'systematic indoctrination' of the social sciences for which he called, and has accepted from them a far more selective influence. But there is perhaps one area in which Thomas (1966) can be felt as an inhibition upon Thomas (1971): his uncritical deference, at the level of theory, to quantities. In his preface he apologises for his failure to provide 'exact statistical data'; in the absence of such materials he has had to 'fall back upon historian's traditional method of presentation by example and counter-example', although the computer has made this technique 'the intellectual equivalent of the bow and arrow in a nuclear age' (the inadequacy of the thought betrays itself here in a most uncharacteristic cliché). He laments that there is 'no genuinely scientific method of measuring changes in the thinking of past generations'.[25] This chimes in well with the millennial note of 1966, and with the assertion:

A great proportion of the statements made in a

history book are ultimately statistical in their implications. All historical propositions relating to the behaviour of large groups, for example, about illiteracy or religious activity, are susceptible of treatment in this way, and *indeed permit of no other.* (My italics)

This is of course the mumbo-jumbo of those latter-day astrologers, who stem from Conjuror Bentham, whose spells are woven each quarter in the *Economic History Review*, and who for 200 years have been trying to persuade us that nothing is real that cannot be counted. It is difficult to refute it without immediately calling down on oneself accusations of being a black (as opposed to white) witch; one who does not believe in counting, who rejects the computer, who is unaware that increasingly sophisticated techniques are enabling it to count in areas (such as 'social distance', the history of crime, of family relations) where counting had not before been possible; one who rejects science in favour of old spells and potions out of Trevelyan's Herbal.

But may we put this behind us? Let all that may usefully be counted, be counted, amen! Nevertheless, if men's actions can be counted in increasingly subtle ways, it is improbable that counting will always (or even often, on its own) reveal their significances. The behaviour of even 'large groups' is made up of individual behaviour, and religious activity supposes belief and experience, literacy supposes education and literature (of some kind), and attempts to count the quality and meaning of these will always be cumbersome and insensitive. In the end men consume their lives in the form of experience; for their experience, their illusions, and their self-understanding, we must rely upon 'literary' sources; and if historians cease to be interested in understanding how past generations experienced their own existence, that will be a large oversight. Perhaps at that stage historians will invent the bow and arrow once again.

This is one area in which one is disposed to be critical of Thomas's method, both in detail and in implication. In points of detail he is curiously chary of employing 'literary' sources. One notices that Thomas (1966) while calling upon the social sciences makes no reference to literary criticism, a discipline which has made its own advances in past decades. While making no pretensions to being a 'science', textual criticism, with its sensitivity to tone, its awareness of the inner consistency of text and of the significance of imagery, is a discipline – or habit of reading – of which historians stand in as much need, when dealing with literary texts, as they need numeracy when dealing with quantities. But it is not in fashion to mention this.

In points of detail, then, this is one place where Thomas's reading appears to be sketchy or even (as with a reference of Marlowe)[26] dated. Elizabethan drama provides so many fully realised expressions of exactly the tensions in consciousness which Thomas explores (at a score of points the text shouts out for *Lear*) that it seems impossible that this material should not be deployed, not as 'illustrations' to a point, but as major evidences. Moreover, critics and literary historians have been exploring these tensions for decades, on parallel lines to Thomas (although often needing for correction his command of actualities). Thomas does not even mention that T. S. Eliot's diagnosis of dissociation of sensibility', unsatisfactory as it may be, curves closely alongside his own descriptions of the intellectual decline of magic.

The material, if drawn upon, would have confirmed, perhaps enriched, but not substantially revised Thomas's account. When shopping so extensively among the Azande, he might have placed one or two orders nearer home. But at other points his work is actively weakened by his reluctance to draw upon 'literary' sources: religion, magic, astrology, prophecy – all operate in a language of symbolism which, when translated into rational argument, loses a portion of its meaning and all of its psychic compulsion. And the symbolic or 'poetic' meanings will always have been most powerful at the popular level, where the superstitious believer had least need to erect rationalist defences around his beliefs. The failure to treat his materials in their sense as poetry weakens, in particular, his chapters on 'Prayer and prophecy' and on 'Ancient prophecies'.

One other consequence of Thomas's attitude towards counting is methodologically evident. He proceeds, again and again, by the accumulation of instances, presented in rapid sequence, with often no more than one sentence allowed to each. At times – for example, in documenting the activities of wisemen, or the customers of astrologers – the method is immensely impressive, wholly convincing. At other times it is like flicking through a card-index, when every now and then one glimpses an unusual card and wishes to cry: 'stop'! Thomas, one feels, is convinced that he can only look the computer in the face, if he can provide twenty instances at each point of substance; if he had offered two or three only, he would be defenceless before the charge of untypicality or (worst accusation of all) 'impressionism'. But in following this method he denies himself the space for micro-study, and for exploring the inwardness – and the irregularities as well as regularities – of the evidence. To boil down twenty instances to a line or two apiece must, after all, entail much selectivity and the suppression of much attendant evidence. The reader must still place his confidence in the historian, who has decided that this feature only (and not all those others) of the evidence shall be singled out for remark; although he is not as much a victim as he is before the gross reiterative impressionism of a computer, which repeats one conformity *ad nauseam* while obliterating all evidence for which it has not been programmed.

In the end, however 'scientific' our pretensions, we must make an act of faith (based upon the evidence of the text and of our own knowledge of the materials) in the judgement of the historian or the subtlety of his programme. One places confidence in Thomas's judgement with little hesitation, except where symbolism and 'poetic' meanings are involved. On occasion, of course, he must nod. Thus, he boils down to one line an incident at Calne, Wiltshire, in 1618, and assimilates it to a list of instances of 'mob action' against arsonists, witches and scolds.[27] The action was taken, in fact, against 'a skimmington', and so far from being a 'mob action' was carefully prepared and highly-ritualised; and the Quarter Sessions deposition recording it is (to my knowledge) one of the richest early evidences of the character of a skimmington-riding which we have. Close study of the document (with its objective extrusion from human community of 'a' skimmington, as of 'a' witch) would have fed back a dimension to the understanding of witchcraft accusations.

In this case Thomas may have strayed by taking his information from an inadequate secondary source. But the problem of method remains, and it is a difficult one. In my own current work on such problems as 'rough music' and the sale of wives I face it repeatedly, and I find that I can only solve it by presenting occasional detailed case studies, rather fuller than any offered by Thomas. Thus, to understand why some sexual offenders (and not others) were victims of rough music, it is important not to have 100 instances which are imperfectly understood, but to have ten, or even five, in which one can disclose something of the personal history of the victims, the flagrancy of the offence, the kinship relations in the neighbourhood, the insights afforded by some revealing phrase in a deposition. Such inscape is hard to come by, and one still faces the problem of 'typicality'. Thomas, by the accumulation of examples, goes some way towards answering this objection and, hence, vindicates his method. What one wishes is that he had supplemented it with a few case studies, of wisemen, of conjurors, of witches, at critical points in his argument – stopping the movie and holding on to a long, clearly focused still of this victim within this or that social context.

These two limitations: (1) the failure to give to literary evidence its full weight, and to handle poetic meanings with an appropriate critical discipline; and (2) the absence of microstudy, are sufficiently grave to make *Religion and the Decline of Magic* fall short of greatness. The limitation is felt, here and there, along the way; but, most of all, in a failure to synthesise his own findings, to present an integrated view of popular religious beliefs, or to draw together the book into a satisfying conclusion.

In his early chapters, where he discusses the 'Magic of the medieval church', and religion and the people, there are passages which have a quaintly bookish, rationalist air. A dozen of the superstitions recorded with surprise in fact survive in this country to this day (one need only ask old people in the West Riding to find the belief that unchristened children 'don't get on'). Thomas is curiously apologetic as to the complicity of the church in this 'magic', and is at pains to show that reputable theologians were not responsible for popular belief. But reputable priests understood and, in Catholic rural societies, understand it perfectly well: to the degree that the ritual calendar year chimes in with the agrarian calendar, the authority of the church is strengthened. Moreover, despite his sympathetic handling of the irrational in popular belief, he tends to have two yard-sticks for the irrational, according to its intellectual reputability. 'Even after the Reformation', he writes, 'organized religion continued to help men cope with the practical problems of daily life by providing an explanation for misfortune and a source of guidance in times of uncertainty'.[28] But in fact he has shown that most of the explanations were false, and the guidance misguidance. In what sense, then, could it help men 'cope with practical problems'? Anthropology (Radcliffe-Brown and Malinowski) comes to his aid: religion provided 'appropriate rites of passage', it was a 'ritual method of living'.[29] Popular magic, by contrast, offered not a system, but fragmentary remedies: 'it never offered a comprehensive view of the world, an explanation of human existence, or the promise of a future life. It was a collection of miscellaneous recipes, not a comprehensive body of doctrine'.[30]

It is a helpful distinction; but one is not finally convinced, at a popular level, that it was so. Thomas scarcely takes into his categories other social functions of religion; for example, the imposition upon the people by the established church of a rigmarole best calculated to inculcate the values of deference and of order. Religion need not only provide a socially neutral 'ritual method of living'; it may seek to enforce that particular ritual method of living which makes the people most serviceable and least disobedient to their masters. But once a class dimension is introduced, the problem of intellectual reputability assumes a different form. For in so far as the common people sensed that they were being 'got at' by the church, to that degree the elements of an anti-culture will have formed, assimilating these doctrines, rejecting those, knitting together Christian ritual with surviving pagan beliefs, translating doctrine into a symbolism more appropriate to their own life experience.

Keith Thomas cites with apparent surprise the case of the old man, a lifelong attender at sermons, who thought God 'was a good old man', Christ 'was a towardly young youth', that his soul 'was a great bone in his body', and that, after death, 'if he had done well he should be put into a pleasant green meadow'.[31] Thomas comments that this case illustrates the 'inadequacies of popular education' and 'popular religious ignorance'. Possibly so: but is it also a glimpse into that process of translating doctrine into a more meaningful, an altogether more relevant symbolism –of

accepting from the church only so much doctrine as can be assimilated to the life experience of the poor. Thomas also cites the fourteenth century shepherd who, asked if knew who the Father, Son and Holy Ghost were, replied: 'The father and the son I know well for I tend their sheep but I know not that third fellow; there is none of that name in our village.' This, again, he attributes to 'popular ignorance'. But would it really have helped this shepherd to have coped 'with the practical problems of daily life' if he had memorised some theological catechism about the Holy Ghost? It is curious that a historian of so rational a cast of mind should imply, in so many ways, that the sophisticated magic of theology was reputable, but that the symbolic magic of the poor was not.

The image of the soul as a 'great bone' laid after death in 'a pleasant green meadow' implies, at a poetic level, so much: the assimilation of both death and paradise in the single image of rest from daily labour, the modest, taciturn expectations of eternity. According to Chafin's *Anecdotes of Cranbourn Chase*,[32] an eighteenth-century gamekeeper had more luxurious fantasies. He had heard the parson talk about a place that he called Paradise: 'it seemed to be a desperate pleasant place . . . but if there was but a good trout-stream running down Chicken Grove Bottom, Fernditch Lodge would beat it out and out.' One could multiply such examples, and one might well collect others today. But one cannot usefully analyse them in terms of intellectual reputability. 'Ignorance' is far too blunt an analytic tool, for ignorance may indicate evasion, or translation, irony in the face of the church's homilies, or very often, active intellectual resistance to its doctrines. Folklore gives us repeated instances where the people, clinging to their own rituals of passage, knew better what was 'real Christianity' than did the parson. Of a wife sale in the late nineteenth century a West-countryman said: 'You may ask any one if that ain't marriage, good, sound, and Christian, and everyone will tell you it is.'

Can we reconstruct this mixture of popular religion and folklore, and discover how systematised it was – how far its parts were related to the occupations and life-experience of its adherents – how far it also offered (no less than Christian doctrine may have done to the literate) a 'comprehensive view of the world' and a 'ritual method of living' for West Country villagers, Cornish tinners, or Aberdeen fishermen? This problem some anthropology might help us to answer: we might even be aided by observation in contemporary Calabria or Southern Ireland. It cannot be answered, however, from the pamphlet collections of the Bodleian, since one is dealing above all, in folklore and in folk ritual (even the ritual of a bread riot or of a rough music) with an orally transmitted culture. And hence (one must repeat) the importance to the historian of popular culture of all the techniques of literacy. Just as an earlier benighted generation of historians supposed that they were numerate because they had performed their maths Schools Certificate, so the present generation suppose that they are literate because they have an O level in English. But the literate historians of the future will perhaps require some training in linguistics; they will be familiar with the use of dialect dictionaries; and they must certainly read their texts with a sensitivity to poetic as well as rational or numerate meanings. Both dialect and old Welsh and Gaelic are studded with words which point not only towards forgotten tools, measures and things, but also towards forgotten modes of thought and habits of work. The Welsh *buchedd* (I am told) is untranslatable, in a literal sense, because it entails not only the notion of a man's life, but also of the quality of his life, his life as it was lived, his 'way'. The translator's difficulty signals a large change in customary consciousness. It will be at this difficult and expert level that, in the end, an analysis of the symbolism of popular magic and of witchcraft must be made.

One substantial comment remains, which I had intended as the theme of this chapter. One cannot read *Religion and the Decline of Magic,* nor Hill's *Society and Puritanism in Pre-Revolutionary England,*[33] without noting that both studies point, insistently, towards that great vacancy which is where eighteenth century social history should be. Both here, and in some of Laslett's work, there is a sense of hiatus: seventeenth century custom is contrasted with the practices of industrial (that is, nineteenth century) society. But what happened in between? And if magic (and 101 other things) were in decline, why was the decline so long?

Thomas is cautious at this point. He is at pains to qualify his description of the decline of this or that superstition with indications of eighteenth- or nineteenth century survivals. But in general he leaves the reader with the impression that in the mid-seventeenth century reputable intellectual opinion discarded more and more areas of 'magic', parting company with a popular culture in which magic survived, but as fragmentary survivals, which must, inevitably, decompose over the decades, even if decomposition was sometimes a surprisingly lengthy process. His final chapter discusses some of the possible processes of disseminating enlightenment: literacy, communications, new technology, new aspirations, a capitalist agrarian stance attaining to the control of natural forces. But, as he warns us when discussing witchcraft (in the words of John Selden): 'The reason of a thing is not to be enquired after, till you are sure the thing itself be so. We commonly are at *what's the reason for it?* before we are sure of the thing.' And the thing, in this case, is the reality of the 'decline' in the popular culture of the eighteenth century. I am myself chiefly impressed by the extraordinary vitality, the robustness, of popular culture (and of rituals of a kind which hitherto have been largely the preserve of folklorists) in that century. Moreover, one appears to confront a system of beliefs with its own coherence, even if this is most clearly seen in relation to particular occupational groups.

One may suggest, very tentatively, that the presupposition of a unilinear, progressive process of 'decline' may be unhelpful. The fascism of this century reminds us that progressive enlightenment does not always move in one way. And while no analogy is intended from this, it may set us on our guard against the impression that eighteenth century intellectual development was necessarily unilinear (did magic 'decline' or did it change its form?), or that changes in reputable literate belief necessarily communicated themselves to the poor and the illiterate by a process of seeping down.[34] If the polite culture abandoned magic, this marked a dissociation not only of sensibility, but between the polite and the vulgar cultures. Finding little relevant in the symbolism of the polite doctrinal sermons of the Enlightenment, people may have reacted by withdrawing the more determinedly into a vivid symbolism of their own. ('No other preaching will do for Yorkshire', John Nelson told Wesley, 'but the old sort that comes like a thunderclap upon the conscience. Fine preaching does more harm than good here'.) From the standpoint of the common people, the magic and charisma of the established church had been immeasurably weakened by the commencement of the eighteenth century, although it maintained its sociological presence in the village. Hence, the feasts, the sports, the songs and the rituals of the people developed independently of the calendar of the church. One encounters a culture which at times appears as almost pagan; it is not so much scepticism or indifference (absence from church) as an alternative system of beliefs and sanctions. (The rituals around the gallows may provide one example.) I can see no inherent reason why this system of belief may not have been more vigorous in 1750 than in 1650.

Moreover, this might help us to understand the true character of Wesleyanism as explicitly a movement of counterenlightenment. In returning to his pastoral duties to the poor, Wesley perforce must leap a gap of sensibility between two cultures, even though leaping that gap meant reaffirming scores of superstitions which Thomas confidently describes as being in 'decline'. Among these were bibliomancy, old wives' medical remedies, the casting of lots, the belief in diabolical possession and in exorcism by prayer, in the hand of providence, in the punishment (by lightning stroke or epilepsy or cholera) of ill-livers and reprobates. Rule (1971) in an unpublished study of the Cornish tinners has shown exactly this process at work: Wesleyan superstition matched the indigenous superstitions of tinners and fisherman who, for occupational reasons which are examined, were dependent upon chance and luck in their daily lives. The match was so perfect that it consolidated one of the strongest of Methodist congregations.

When one describes this popular culture as a system

of belief, one is not so much employing rational tests as the notion developed by such critics as Hoggart and Williams of a consistent structure of feeling, a whole way of apprehending the world. Nor was this mode of apprehension limited to the very poor or to the rural outback. It was, repeatedly, Thomas Hardy's achievement to chart these tensions in consciousness, between the old modes and the new. *The Mayor of Caster-bridge*[35] might be added as a superb appendix to Thomas's book – and as a refutation of some points in its last chapter. For Hardy here consciously puts together into a convincing whole in the character of Henchard, who carries with him throughout life the sensibility of his plebeian origin, this way of apprehending the accidents of life. His tragedy commences with the folk ritual of a wife sale; retribution comes in the folk ritual of a skimmety. He visits, half-sceptically, half-superstitiously, a wise man to foretell the harvest; in misfortune he believes that someone may be roasting his waxen image. At no critical point in his life does Christian doctrine enter. But this sensibility is seen (in ways which Thomas fails to do, since he never integrates all his bits of magical belief into one given social context or personality) as integrally related to Henchard's mode of work and economic relations: 'He used to reckon his sacks by chalk strokes all in a row like garden-palings, measure his ricks by stretching with his arms, weigh his trusses by a lift, judge his hay by a chaw, and settle the price with a curse.' Farfrae, his rival in business, introduces also a different mode of rational apprehension; 'he does it all by ciphering and mensuration', and when Farfrae triumphs in Henchard's former granaries, 'the scales and steelyards began to be busy where guess-work had formerly been the rule'.

Beyond this we cannot go. Thomas is aware of the vigorous recrudescence of millennial movements in the 1790s and thereafter, with sufficient force (for example) to impel thousands of poor Englishmen on the route to Salt Lake City. All this, and much more, of nineteenth-century irrationalism, is already under examination. (One did not – if one waspish note be admissable –require Thomas's footnote[36] to be reminded that 'the prophetic literature of the 1790s would repay analysis'.) Historians of this century will learn much from *Religion and the Decline of Magic*, but the historian of eighteenth century popular culture will learn most of all. It will be in testing his thesis of 'decline' that one's intellectual debt may be most helpfully repaid, even if the repayment entails a rewriting by Thomas of his final chapter. I do not think that Thomas will mind; despite the rational patina of his prose, one suspects that his heart is with the conjurors and wisemen after all. Why else should he have worshipped, in 1966, before the magic totempole of the computer?

Notes: Chapter 21

Reprinted from *Midland History*, vol. 1, no. 3, 1972, pp. 41–55, by kind permission of the editor.

1   See Thomas (1963).
2   See Thomas (1964).
3   Quotation on p. 276.
4   See Macfarlane (1970), p. 11.
5   One chapter is entitled 'Attitudes to pain, sin and God'.
6   See Macfarlane (1970), p. 171.
7   See Macfarlane (1970), p. 83.
8   See Macfarlane (1970), p. 88.
9   See Macfarlane (1970), p. 89.
10 See Macfarlane (1970), p. 90.
11 See Nadel (1954).
12 See Führer-Haimendorf (1964).
13 Implied on p. 99.
14 See Campbell (1964).
15 See Macfarlane (1970), for example, pp. 117, 178.
16 See Macfarlane (1970), pp. 92–8.
17 See Macfarlane (1970), pp. 205–10.
18 See Macfarlane (1970), p. 92.
19 See Macfarlane (1970), p. 205.
20 See Macfarlane (1970), pp. 108–10.
21 See Macfarlane (1970), p. 117.
22 See Thomas (1966), pp. 275–6.
23 See Thomas (1966), pp. 275–6.
24 See Thomas (1971), p. 143.
25 See also Thomas (1971), p. 449.
26 See Thomas (1971), p. 167.
27 See Thomas (1971), p. 533.
28 See Thomas (1971), p. 151.
29 See Thomas (1971), p. 76.
30 See Thomas (1971), p. 636.
31 See Thomas (1971), p. 163.
32 See Chafin (1818).
33 See Hill (1967).
34 See, for example, Thomas (1971), pp. 646–7.
35 See Hardy (1886).
36 See Thomas (1971), p. 145.

Section Six

Combining Strategies in Field Research

22

Multiple Strategies in Field Research

ROBERT G. BURGESS

Does survey research give breadth, while field research gives depth? Is field research no more than doing participant observation? Is participant observation a better method of doing research than interviewing? When such questions have been posed by researchers, they have received few answers and sharp criticism. Indeed, when Becker and Geer (1957) asserted that participant observation was superior to interviewing, they received a sharp rejoinder from Trow, who commented:

> Let us be done with the arguments of 'participant observation' *versus* interviewing – as we have largely dispensed with the arguments for psychology *versus* sociology – and get on with the business of attacking our problems with the widest array of conceptual and methodological tools that we possess and they demand. This does not preclude discussion and debate regarding the relative usefulncss of different methods for the study of specific problems or types of problems. But that is very different from the assertion of the general and inherent superiority of one method over another on the basis of some intrinsic qualities it presumably possesses. (Trow, 1957, p. 35)

Certainly, the coverage given to field research within this book suggests diversity of method, strategy and tactic. In these circumstances, the researcher has to consider ways in which different methods can be used and different data collected in order to address a variety of theoretical and substantive problems. Such a position points, as Wax (1971) suggests, to the disadvantages of rigidity and the advantages of flexibility in doing field research. The field researcher, is therefore, seen as a methodological pragmatist, who 'sees any method of inquiry as a system of strategies and operations designed – at any time – for getting answers to certain questions about events which interest him' (Schatzman and Strauss, 1973, p. 7). In short, the field researcher is concerned with operations that yield profound, meaningful and valid data.

Various writers have suggested ways of assessing the validity of social research. Stacey (1969a) suggests 'combined operations', while Denzin (1970) suggests 'triangulation' and Douglas (1976) suggests 'mixed

strategies'. All these writers have different ideas for overcoming the narrowness of approach that can exist in social research. In this way, this chapter attempts to synthesise their different ideas using the notion 'multiple strategies'. Nevertheless, these writers do hold one thing in common; namely, the use of diverse methods to tackle a research problem. The articles that have been included in this section focus on the multi-method approach of doing research. Zelditch (Chapter 23) suggests that narrow definitions of field research are inadequate and that the method should encompass observation, informant interviewing and sampling. Meanwhile, Sieber (Chapter 24) goes beyond the notion of broadening particular techniques of research. He points to the benefits of using field methods and survey methods in conjunction with each other in the design, collection and analysis of data within one study. In short, he indicates the way in which particular methods can be integated in approaching a research problem. While these papers stress multiple methods, it is important to examine discussions on the use of multiple investigators in a study, as well as the debate from Denzin (1970) on data triangulation (multiple sets of data) and theoretical triangulation (multiple theories). It is, therefore, the purpose of this chapter to consider the multiple strategies that are available to field researchers who wish to overcome the problems of the single-method, single-investigator, single-data, single-theory study.

Multiple Methods of Investigation

Anthropologists and sociologists have been aware, for some time, of the limitations of single method studies. Malinowski indicated that the goal of ethnographic fieldwork had to be approached in three ways:

(1) *The organisation of the tribe, and the anatomy of its culture* must be recorded in firm, clear outline. The method of *concrete, statistical documentation* is the means through which such an outline has to be given.

(2) Within this frame, the *imponderabilia of actual life*, and the *type of behaviour* have to be filled in. They have to be collected through minute,

detailed observations, in the form of some sort of ethnographic diary, made possible by close contact with native life.

(3) A collection of ethnographic statements, characteristic narratives, typical utterances, items of folk-lore and magical formulae has to be given as a *corpus inscriptionum*, as documents of native mentality. (Malinowski, 1922, p. 24)

However, Malinowski's approach to field research raises several problems. First, a researcher cannot glibly assume that there is a tribe. Secondly, researchers need to consider the economic, social and political context in which their observations are obtained. For despite Malinowski's major contribution to field research, his work does raise several conceptual problems for the contemporary researcher (cf. Gluckman, 1960). Nevertheless, he was concerned with the ways in which field research could embrace intensive methods of observation and interviewing together with survey methods.

A similar point of view can be detected in the work of Lazarsfeld, writing from a sociological perspective. In a special foreword to the English edition of *Marienthal* (Jahoda, Lazarsfeld and Zeisel, 1972) he draws on an unpublished paper written in 1933 to outline four principles involved in doing research:

(1) For any phenomenon one should have objective observations as well as introspective reports.
(2) Case studies should be properly combined with statistical information.
(3) Contemporary information should be supplemented by information on earlier phases of whatever is being studied.
(4) 'Natural and experimental data' should be combined. By experimental I mean mainly questionnaires and solicited reports, while by natural I meant what is now called 'unobtrusive measures' – data derived from daily life without interference from the investigator. (Lazarsfeld, 1972, p. xvi)

Again the emphasis is placed on combining methods, so that data can be collected from different perspectives. However, researchers need to consider the problems associated with attempting to make objective observations.

While these early statements point to the necessity of using different methods and integrating those methods, it is evident from Sieber's article that this has rarely been achieved. Numerous studies in anthropology (Mitchell, 1956b; Fraser, 1960; Anderson and Anderson, 1964) and in sociology (Stacey, 1960; Gans, 1962; 1967; Pons, 1969; Stacey *et al.*, 1975) have utilised a variety of methods to gain access to data. However, several questions remain. To what extent have researchers successfully integrated their methods, their theories and their data? Have different methods been used to focus upon the same unit of investigation, or to examine different aspects of the same study? Gans (1962) explains that his study involved six approaches: three approaches to participant observation, formal and informal interviewing, the use of key informants and observation. Here, it was possible for the researcher to cross-check between various forms of participant observation: where the researcher acted as an observer, where the researcher participated as a researcher and where the researcher acted as a participant. Similar cross-checks can be made between data obtained from participant observation and interviews. However, it is only when observational and interview data are integrated that the full potential of multiple field methods can be realised.

Multiple Investigators

In order to address some of the problems associated with the single-investigator, 'lone-ranger' approach to doing field research, investigators have come together in a variety of different relationships.

PARTNERSHIP RESEARCH

This approach involves separate but co-ordinated activities within an investigation. A classic study in which this approach was used was *Deep South* (Davis, Gardner and Gardner, 1941). In studying the relations between blacks and whites in one old Southern city, four social anthropologists (a black husband and wife, and a white husband and wife) lived in the city for almost two years. Although they were all working on the same project, they concealed their collaboration from the people studied. More recently, this approach has been used by Fujisaka and Grayzel (1978) in their study of a maximum security prison. Here, both researchers used participant observation but in a very different way, based upon their personal background and use of different informants. This approach minimised the personal biases of the researchers and they 'were able to avoid making a clear and difficult choice between obtaining either an in-depth single-faceted perception of prison reality or a more generalised multifaceted view' (Fujisaka and Grayzel, 1978, p. 178). Indeed, this style of research allows activities to be co-ordinated and facilitates the cross-validation of data collection and analysis.

TEAM RESEARCH

A more conventional approach to solving the problem of the single-investigator study is the use of team field research; a situation that Douglas considers

> involves a number of people working together in a flexibly planned and coordinated manner to get at

the multiperspectival realities of a group, constructing the team to achieve the research goals of the project in the concrete setting, utilizing the specialized abilities and opportunities of the various team members, providing both support and cross checks on the work of each member by the other members, and all members (ideally) providing creative inputs to the research, the grasping, the understanding and the final report. (Douglas, 1976, p. 194)

Such an account provides a picture of team research in ideal terms. However, research teams will operate in different ways depending upon the research context (cf. Platt, 1976). In commenting upon her first study of Banbury, Stacey (1969a) indicates that the three researchers who comprised the research team reflected three different social classes: the titled upper, the lower-middle and the working class. The background characteristics of this team were such, she argues, that they were able to work in different segments of the town; a situation that provided a variety of data that could be pieced together at regular weekly meetings. The relative success of this team approach to field research led Stacey to gather together a further team of research workers to conduct the second study of Banbury (Stacey et al., 1975). Here, she tried, to some extent, to replicate the first team, in terms of researchers coming from different social-class backgrounds and by appointing Anne Murcott to the team, in order that data could be collected on women by a woman. Despite Stacey's good intentions, the account of this team's work that is provided by Bell (1977) indicates that real problems arose in the Banbury restudy, concerning what was to be studied and how it was to be studied. Indeed, it is evident from Bell's account that the second Banbury research team faced problems concerning their workloads, research design, division of labour in data collection, the ownership of data and the rights of team members concerning publication. Neverthless, we only have an account of Bell's research experience in Banbury; no doubt if Batstone, Murcott and Stacey provided separate accounts, we would get closer to learning about the politics of team-based research. Furthermore, we would be nearer to understanding what really happened in Banbury.

Meanwhile, other researchers have pointed to the potential strength of a research team comprised of different people. Mead remarks:

a husband-and-wife team, or a team in which there is a great discrepancy of age, whether of the same or opposite sex, works better than a team of two men or two women of the same age. Each piece of knowledge that either member of the team acquires speeds up the learning of other or others. If this is accepted enthusiastically, without rivalry, then any team of whatever composition, but especially one contrasted

in sex or age, will be able to do, not twice, but four or five times as much work as one person working alone. (Mead, 1970b, p. 326)

Certainly, this point is supported by Wax (1979), who argues that the virtues of the Sioux study in which she was involved were due predominantly to the co-operation of a diverse group of people who became a research team that reflected the old, the young, the male, the female, the American Indian and the white.

INTER-DISCIPLINARY AND MULTI-DISCIPLINARY RESEARCH

It is Stacey (1969a) who has distinguished between inter-disciplinary and multi-disciplinary research. While the former involves links being forged between members of a research team drawn from different disciplines, the latter involves team members from different disciplines being involved in separate studies within a broad area. Stacey argues that some research problems call for members of a research team to be drawn from different disciplines. The study of children in hospital (Stacey et al., 1970) called for a team of sociologists and psychologists to work together to understand individual and collective facets of the children's experiences. In these circumstances, the members of inter-disciplinary research teams need to establish common problems and common knowledge, and to develop a common theoretical link, if their disciplines are to be related. However, as Luszki (1957) argues, such teams may generate interpersonal problems that can lead to difficulties in communication among team members. Meanwhile, multi-disciplinary projects involving researchers from different disciplines working on separate studies have been conducted in areas such as health and illness, education and housing. The study of the Lower Swansea Valley (Hilton, 1967) provides an example of multidisciplinary research, whereby six university departments focused upon one geographical area to see how it could be restored. Each department conducted its own investigations but informed the other departments of its work. In this respect, the projects were conducted from a variety of perspectives and were not so closely linked as an inter-disciplinary project.

Nevertheless, no matter what form of multiple investigator strategy is involved, at its best it can involve researchers in projects where support, stimulation and help can be maximised to achieve valid data. However, ideal situations are rare and multiple investigator projects can hold much potential both for creative research, and political conflict.

Multiple sets of data

In his consideration of multiple strategies of doing research (triangulation) Denzin (1970) considers that a researcher needs to collect multiple sets of data. He argues the need to obtain different data relating to different phases of the research, different settings and different participants. Such a strategy brings us back to questions of sampling (see Section Three). Denzin (1970) advocates the use of different times, persons and situations in any study, so that researchers can obtain several different accounts of any single event.

This approach to field research is used by Becker *et al.*, (1961), in their study of medical students where research on students and hospital staff is synthesised. Nevertheless, such work is not without its difficulties, as Gans (1967) indicates in his study of the Levit-towners. Here, as in *The Urban Villagers* (Gans, 1962), he indicates that multiple methods and multiple points of access resulted in more data than he could handle. His experience is summarised as follows:

> I made no real attempt to integrate the findings reached . . . More such integration would have been desirable, but I had such vast amounts of data that it took me a long time even to organize them into a single narrative. (Gans, 1967, p. 449)

Such a revelation indicates the difficulties that multiple data can bring, as well as indicating the potential for integration and for detailed research reports.

Multiple Theories

A further strategy that is advocated by Denzin (1970) is that of multiple theories (theoretical triangulation). Here, Denzin closely follows the work of Westie (1957), who argues that theoretically guided and informed research cannot be achieved while there is theoretical incongruence. Indeed, Westie argues that it is usual for researchers either to resort to empiricism and let facts speak for themselves, or to select a particular proposition from what is already known or to create new propositions. He argues that researchers should utilise all possible theoretical propositions as they exist together with all their contradictions and inadequacies.

This, Westie argues, can be achieved, first, by noting all the empirical relationships that might turn up in a project; secondly, by listing the possible range of interpretations; and finally, by selecting all those relationships that are found to pertain. Such a procedure, Westie considers, increases the chances of using a variety of theoretical interpretations in a project. Certainly, Denzin (1970) supports this notion, as he considers that it can help a researcher to collect a variety of data using a range of research methods. However, while it might seem that this approach holds some potential for theoretical synthesis, there is also the danger of theoretical eclecticism. In these circumstances, researchers need to consider whether different theoretical perspectives are linked to one another within individual studies. Furthermore, some con-sideration needs to be given to the virtues and vices of combining theoretical perspectives in the course of social investigation.

The use of multiple methods, investigators, sets of data and theories in field research can provide flexibility, cross-validation of data and theoretical relevance. However, field researchers rarely conduct investigations in ideal circumstances, with the result that the strengths of using multiple strategies have to be considered alongside various problems and constraints concerning the collection and analysis of data. While multiple strategies are useful, they can also prove costly in terms of time and money.

Suggestions for Further Reading

METHODOLOGY

Bell, C. (1977), 'Reflections on the Banbury restudy', in C. Bell and H. Newby (eds), *Doing Sociological Research* (London: Allen & Unwin), pp. 47–62. An account of team-based research which has been the subject of much criticism from reviewers (Larner, 1977; Burgess, 1978) and from fellow team members. Nevertheless, it raises useful questions.

Bennett, J. W. and Thaiss, G. (1967), 'Survey research and socio-cultural anthropology', in C. Glock (ed.), *Survey Research in the Social Sciences* (New York: Russell Sage Foundation), pp. 271–313; reviews the fusion of survey methods and intensive field research in anthropological studies.

Caudill, W. and Roberts, B. H. (1951), 'Pitfalls in the organiza-tion of interdisciplinary research', *Human Organization*, vol. 10, no. 4, pp. 12–15; discusses the problems of inter-disciplinary research and examines the demands it makes on the researcher.

Denzin, N. K. (1970), *The Research Act* (Chicago, Aldine). A basic text, where the term 'triangulation' is used. Triangulation, it is argued, is a major principle of social research and a major theme in this book.

Douglas, J. D. (1976), *Investigative Social Research* (Beverly Hills, Calif.: Sage); contains useful discussions of 'mixed strategies' (defined as methods) for doing research. The book also contains an extended discussion of team research.

Fujisaka, S. and Grayzel, J. (1978),' Partnership research: a case of divergent ethnographic styles in prison research', *Human Organization*, vol. 37, no. 2, pp. 172–9. A detailed discussion of the author's partnership research in a prison.

Luszki, M. B. (1957), 'Team research in social science: major consequences of a growing trend', *Human Organization*, vo. 16, no. 1, pp. 21–4; examines the strengths and weak-nesses of team-based research.

Newby, H. (1977), 'Editorial note concerning "Reflections on the Banbury restudy"' (Bell, 1977, in C. Bell and H. Newby (eds), *Doing Sociological Research* (London: Allen & Unwin), pp. 63–6. A commentary on the difficulties surrounding the publication of Bell's article.

Perlman, M. L. (1973), 'The comparative method: the single investigator and the team approach', in R. Naroll and R. Cohen (eds), *A Handbook of Method in Cultural Anthro-pology* (New York: Columbia University Press), pp. 353–65. A useful discussion of team research from an anthropologist.

Platt, J. (1976), *Realities of Social Research* (London: Chatto & Windus for University of Sussex Press); provides a useful discussion of team research and the politics of doing research.

Roth, J. A. (1966), 'Hired hand research', *American Sociologist*, vol. 1, no. 4, pp. 190–96; discusses the problems involved when numerous investigators are hired to conduct research.

Stacey, M. (1969), *Methods of Social Research* (Oxford: Pergamon). A basic text with a useful chapter on 'combined operations' that involves multiple methods and investigators, together with a discussion of inter-disciplinary and multi-disciplinary research.

Webb, E. J., Campbell, D. T., Schwartz, R. D. and Sechrest, L. (1966), *Unobtrusive Measures: Nonreactive Research in the Social Sciences* (Chicago: Rand McNally); contains a useful discussion of triangulation.

Westie, F. R. (1957), 'Toward closer relations between theory and research: a procedure and an example', *American Sociological Review*, vol. 22, no. 2, pp. 149–54. A useful discussion on the use of multiple theories in empirical research.

EMPIRICAL STUDIES

There are numerous studies that employ multiple strategies (methods, investigators, data and theories). Most studies utilise multiple methods and data, while some use multiple investigators and a few use multiple theories. Some studies use one of these approaches, others use several approaches. The following list of studies have been selected as they illustrate particular aspects of multiple strategies that have been discussed in this introduction:

Anderson, R. T. and Anderson, B. G. (1964), *The Vanishing Village: a Danish Maritime Community* (Seattle: University of Washington Press).

Becker, H. S., Geer, B., Hughes, E. C. and Strauss, A. L. (1961), *Boys in White: Student Culture in Medical School* (Chicago: University of Chicago Press).

Douglas, J. D., Rasmussen, P. K. and Flanagan, C. A. (1977), *The Nude Beach* (Beverly Hills, Calif.: Sage).

Fraser, T. M. (1960), *Rusembilian: a Malay Fishing Village in Southern Thailand* (Ithaca, NY: Cornell University Press).

Gans, H. J. (1962), *The Urban Villagers* (New York: The Free Press).

Gans, H. J. (1967), *The Levittowners* (London: Allen Lane).

Hilton, K. (1967) (ed.), *The Lower Swansea Valley Project* (London: Longman).

Mitchell, J. C. (1956), *The Yao Village: a Study in the Social Structure of a Nyasaland Tribe* (Manchester: University of Manchester Press).

Stacey, M. (1960), *Tradition and Change: a Study of Banbury* (Oxford: OUP).

Stacey, M., Batstone, E., Bell, C. and Murcott A. (1975), *Power, Persistence and Change: a Second Study of Banbury* (London: Routledge & Kegan Paul).

Stacey, M., Dearden, R., Pill, R., and Robinson, D. (1970), *Hospitals, Children and their Families* (London: Routledge & Kegan Paul).

Woods, P. (1979), *The Divided School* (London: Routledge & Kegan Paul).

23

Some Methodological Problems of Field Studies

MORRIS ZELDITCH, Jr

The original occasion for this chapter was a reflection on the use of sample survey methods in the field: that is, the use of structured interview schedules, probability samples, and so on, in what is usually thought of as a participant observation study. There has been a spirited controversy between, on the one hand, those who have sharply criticised fieldworkers for slipshod sampling, for failing to document assertions quantitatively, and for apparently accepting impressionistic accounts – or accounts that the quantitatively minded could not distinguish from purely impressionistic accounts;[1] and, on the other hand, those who have, sometimes bitterly, been opposed to numbers, to samples, to questionnaires, often on the ground that they destroy the fieldworkers' conception of a social system as an organic whole.[2]

Although there is a tendency among many younger fieldworkers to accent criticisms made from the quantitative point of view,[3] there is reason to believe that the issue itself has been stated falsely. In most cases field methods are discussed as if they were 'all of a piece'.[4] There is, in fact, a tendency to be either *for* or *against* quantification, as if it were an either/or issue. To some extent the battle-lines correlate with a relative concern for 'hardness' *versus* 'depth and reality' of data. Quantitative data are often thought of as 'hard', and qualitative as 'real and deep'; thus, if you prefer 'hard' data, you are for quantification, and if you prefer 'real, deep' data, you are for qualitative participant observation. What to do, if you prefer data that are real, deep *and* hard, is not immediately apparent.

A more fruitful approach to the issue must certainly recognise that a field study is not a single method gathering a single kind of information. This approach suggests several crucial questions: *What* kinds of methods and *what* kinds of information are relevant? How can the 'goodness' of different methods for different purposes be evaluated? Even incomplete and imperfect answers – which are all that we offer here – should be useful, at least in helping to restate the issue. They also pose, order and to some extent resolve other issues of field method, so that in pursuing their implications this chapter encompasses a good deal more than its original problem.

Three Types of Information

The simplest events are customarily described in statements predicating a single property of a single object at a particular time and in a particular place. From these descriptions one may build up more complex events in at least two ways. The first is by forming a configuration of many properties of the same object at the same time in the same place. This may be called an 'incident'. A more complex configuration but of the same type would be a sequence of incidents, that is, a 'history'.

A second way to build up more complex events is by repeating observations of a property over a number of units. Units here can be defined formally, requiring only a way of identifying events as identical. They can be members of a social system or repetitions of the same type of incident at different times or in different places (for instance, descriptions of five funerals). The result is a frequency distribution of some property.

From such information, it is possible to deduce certain underlying properties of the system observed, some of which may be summarised as consequences of the 'culture' of S (S stands here for a social system under investigation). But at least some portion of this culture can be discovered not only by inference from what is observed, but also from verbal reports by members of S – for example, accounts of its principal institutionalised norms and statuses. The rules reported, of course, are to some extent independent of the events actually observed; the norms actually followed may not be correctly reported, and deviance may be concealed. Nevertheless, information difficult to infer can be readily and accurately obtained from verbal reports. For example, it may take some time to infer that a member occupies a given status, but this may readily be discovered by asking either him, or other members of S.

We, thus, combine various types of information into three broad classes:

Type 1 – *Incidents and Histories*. A log of events during a given period, a record of conversations heard, descriptions of a wedding, a funeral, an election, and so on. Not only the actions observed, but the 'meanings', the explanations, and so on, reported by the participants can be regarded as part of the 'incident' in so far as they are thought of as data, rather than actual explanations.

Type 2 – *Distributions and Frequencies.* Possessions of each member of *S*, number of members who have a given belief, number of times member *m* is observed talking to member *n*, and so on.

Type 3 – *Generally Known Rules and Statuses.* Lists of statuses, lists of persons occupying them, informants' accounts of how rules of exogamy apply, how incest or descent are defined, how political leaders are supposed to be chosen, how political decisions are supposed to be made, and so on.

This classification has nothing to do with what is *inferred* from data, despite the way the notion of reported rules and statuses was introduced. In particular, more complex configurations of norms, statuses, events which are 'explained' by inferring underlying themes or structures involve a level of inference outside the scope of this chapter: the classification covers only information *directly* obtained from reports and observations. Moreover, this classification cuts across the distinction between what is observed by the investigator, and what is reported to him. Although Type 3 consists only of reports, Types 1 and 2 include both observations by the investigator himself, *and* reports of members of *S*, in so far as they are treated as data. Later we talk of an event as seen through the eyes of an informant, where the investigator trusts the informant as an accurate observer and thinks of the report as if it were his own observation. Now, however, interest is focused not on the facts of the report, but rather on what the report reveals of the perceptions, the motivations, the world of meaning of the informant himself. The report, in this case, does not transmit observational data; it is, itself, the datum and so long as it tells what the person reporting thinks, the factual correctness of what he thinks is irrelevant. (This is sometimes phrased as making a distinction between *informants* and *respondents*, in the survey research sense.) Thus, Type 1 includes both observations (what we see going on), and the statements of members telling what they understand the observed events to mean, which is regarded as part of the event. In a somewhat different way, Type 2 also includes both reports (for example, an opinion poll), and observations (for example, systematically repeated observations with constant coding categories).

Three Types of Method

It is possible to make a pure, logically clear classification of methods of obtaining information in the field, but for the present purpose this would be less useful than one that is, though less precise, rather closer to what a fieldworker actually does. Two methods are usually thought of as characteristic of the investigator in the field. He invariably keeps a daily log of events and of relatively casual, informal continuous interviews, both of which go into his field notes. Almost invariably he also develops informants, that is, selected members of *S*, who are willing and able to give him information about practices and rules in *S* and events he does not directly observe. (They may also supply him with diaries, autobiographies and their own personal feelings; that is, they may also function as respondents.) Contrary to popular opinion, almost any well-trained fieldworker also keeps various forms of census materials, records of systematic observations, and so on, including a basic listing of members of *S*, face-sheet data on them and systematically repeated observations of certain recurrent events. Many fieldworkers also collect documents; however, we will classify field methods into only three broad classes which we conceive of as primary:

Type 1 – *Participant observation.* The fieldworker directly observes and also participates in the sense that he has durable social relations in *S*. He may or may not play an active part in events, or he may interview participants in events which may be considered part of the process of observation.

Type 2 – *Informant interviewing.* We prefer a more restricted definition of the informant than most fieldworkers use, namely, that he be called an 'informant' only where he is reporting information presumed factually correct about others rather than about himself; and his information about events is about events in their absence. Interviewing during the event itself is considered part of participant observation.

Type 3 – *Enumerations and samples.* This includes both surveys, and direct, repeated, countable observations. Observation in this sense may entail minimal participation as compared with that implied in Type 1.

This classification excludes documents on the ground that they represent resultants or combinations of primary methods. Many documents, for example, are essentially informant's accounts and are treated exactly as an informant's account is treated; they are subjected to the same kinds of internal and external comparisons, treated with the same suspicions and often, in the end, taken as evidence of what occurred at some time and place from which the investigator was absent. The fact that the account is written is hardly important. Many other documents are essentially enumerations; for example, personnel and cost-accounting records of a factory, membership rolls of a union, tax rolls of a community.

Two Criteria of 'Goodness'

Criteria according to which the 'goodness' of a procedure may be defined are:

(1) *Informational adequacy,* meaning accuracy, precision, and completeness of data.
(2) *Efficiency*, meaning cost per added input of information.

It may appear arbitrary to exclude validity and reliability. Validity is excluded because it is, in a technical sense, a relation between an indicator and a concept, and similar problems arise whether one obtains information from an informant, a sample, or from direct observation. Construed loosely, validity is often taken to mean 'response validity', accuracy of report, and this is caught up in the definition of informational adequacy. Construed more loosely yet, validity is sometimes taken as equivalent to 'real', 'deep' data, but this seems merely to beg the question. Reliability is relevant only tangentially; it is a separate problem that cuts across the issues of this chapter.

Fundamental Strategies

Certain combinations of method and type of information may be regarded as formal prototypes, in the sense that other combinations may be logically reduced to them. For example: instead of a sample survey or enumeration, an informant is employed to list dwelling units, or to estimate incomes, or to tell who associates with whom, or what each person believes with respect to some issue. The information is obtained from a single informant, but he is treated *as if he himself* had conducted a census or poll. More generally, in every case in which the information obtained is logically reducible to a distribution of the members of S with respect to the property a, the implied method of obtaining the information is also logically reducible to an enumeration. The enumeration may be either through direct observation (estimating the number of sheep each Navaho has by actually counting them; establishing the sociometric structure of the community by watching who interacts with whom), or through a questionnaire survey (determining household composition by questioning a member of each household, or administering a sociometric survey to a sample of the community). If an informant is used, it is presumed that he has himself performed the enumeration. We are not at the moment concerned with the validity of this assumption in specific instances, but rather in observing that regardless of the actual way in which the information was obtained, the logical and formal character of the procedure is that of a census or survey.

Suppose an informant is asked to describe what went on at a community meeting which the observer is unable to attend; or a sample of respondents is asked to describe a sequence of events which occurred before the observer entered S. In either case, his reports are used as substitutes for direct observation. Such evidence may, in fact, be examined critically to establish its accuracy – we begin by assuming the bias of the reports – but it is presumed that having 'passed' the statements they become an objective account of what has occurred in the same sense that the investigator's own reports are treated as objective, once his biases have been taken into account. The informant, one usually says in this case, is the observer's observer; he differs in no way from the investigator himself. It follows that the prototype is direct observation by the observer himself.

The prototype so far is not only a formal model; it is also a 'best' method, efficiently yielding the most adequate information. In learning institutionalised rules and statuses it is doubtful that there is a formal prototype, and all three methods yield adequate information. Here, we may choose the *most efficient* method as defining our standard of procedure. To illustrate: we wish to study the political structure of the USA. We are told that the principal national political figure is called a 'president', and we wish to know who he is. We do not ordinarily think of sampling the population of the USA to obtain the answer; we regard it as sufficient to ask one well-informed member. This question is typical of a large class of questions asked by a fieldworker in the course of his research.

A second example: any monograph on the Navaho reports that they are matrilineal and matrilocal. This statement may mean either of two things:

(1) All Navaho are socially identified as members of a descent group defined through the mother's line, and all Navaho males move to the camp of their wife's family at marriage.
(2) There exists a set of established rules according to which all Navaho are supposed to become socially identified as members of a descent group defined through the mother's line, and to move to the camp of their wife's family at marriage.

The truth of the first interpretation can be established only by an enumeration of the Navaho, or a sample sufficiently representative and sufficiently precise. It is readily falsified by exceptions, and in fact there *are* exceptions to both principles. But suppose among thirty Navaho informants at least one says that the Navaho are patrilineal and patrilocal. If this is intended to describe institutionalised norms as in (2) above, we are more likely to stop using the informant than we are to state that there are 'exceptions' in the sense of (1) above. We might sample a population to discover the motivation to conform to a rule, or the actual degree of conformity, but are less likely to do so to establish that the rule *exists*, if we confront institutionalised phenomena. This also constitutes a very large class of questions asked by the fieldworker.

Adequacy of Informants for Various Problems in the Field

It does not follow from the definition of a prototype method that no other form of obtaining information can suffice; all we intend is that it *does* suffice, and any other method is logically reducible to it. Further, comparison with the prototype is a criterion by which other forms can be evaluated. In considering the adequacy in some given instance of the use of an informant as the fieldworker's surrogate census, for example, we are interested primarily in whether he is likely to know enough, to recall enough, and to report sufficiently precisely to yield the census that we ourselves would make. Comments below, incidentally, are to be taken as always prefixed with the phrase, 'by and large'. It is not possible to establish, at least yet, a firm rule which will cover every case.

The informant as a surrogate census-taker. A distinction must again be made between *what* information is obtained, and how it is obtained. It is one thing to criticise a fieldworker for not obtaining a frequency distribution where it is required – for instance, for not sampling mothers who are weaning children in order to determine age at weaning – and another to criticise him for not obtaining it *directly* from the mothers. If the fieldworker reports that the average age at weaning is 2 years and the grounds for this is that he asked an informant, 'About when do they wean children around here?' it is not the fact that he asked an informant, but that he asked the wrong question that should be criticised. He should have asked, 'How many mothers do you know who are now weaning children? How old are their children?'

The critical issue, therefore, is whether or not the informant can be assumed to have the information that the fieldworker requires, granting that he asks the proper questions. In many instances he does. In some cases he is an even better source than an enumerator; he either knows better, or is less likely to falsify. Dean, for example, reports that workers who are ideologically pro-union, but also have mobility aspirations and are not well integrated into their factory of local unions, are likely to report attending union meetings which they do not in fact attend.[5] She also shows that, when *respondent-reported* attendance is used as a measure of attendance, this tends spuriously to increase correlations of attendance at union meetings with attitudes towards unions in general, and to reduce correlations of attendance at union meetings with attitudes more specifically directed at the local union. The list of those actually attending was obtained by an observer, who, however, had sufficient rapport with officers of the local union to obtain it from them.[6] Attendance, largely by 'regulars', was stable from meeting to meeting so that the officers could have reproduced it quite accurately.[7]

On the other hand, there are many instances in which an informant is *prima facie* unlikely to be adequate, although no general rule seems to identify these clearly for the investigator. The nature of the information – private *versus* public, more or less objective, more or less approved – is obviously relevant, yet is often no guide at all. Some private information, for example, is better obtained from informants, some from respondents. The social structure of S, particularly its degree of differentiation and complexity, is also obviously relevant. An informant must be in a position to know the information desired, and if S is highly differentiated and the informant confined to one part of it, he can hardly enumerate it. Probably to discover attitudes and opinions that are relatively private and heterogeneous in a structure that is relatively differentiated, direct enumeration or sampling should be used.

The informant as a 'representative respondent'. An 'average' of a distribution is sometimes obtained not by asking for an enumeration by the informant, nor even by asking a general question concerning what people typically do; sometimes it is obtained by treating the informant as if he were a 'representative respondent'. The informant's reports about himself – perhaps deeper, more detailed, 'richer', but nevertheless like those of a respondent in a survey rather than an informant in the technical sense – stand in place of a sample. Where a multivariate distribution is thought of, this person is treated as a 'quintessential' subject, 'typical' in many dimensions. Some fieldworkers speak favourably of using informants in this way, and it is likely that even more of them actually do so.

Since, as yet, we have no really hard and fast rules to follow, it is possible that in some cases this is legitimate; but, by and large, it is the most suspect of ways of using informants. It is simply a bad way of sampling. The legitimate cases are probably of three types: first, as suggestive of leads to follow up; secondly, as illustration of a point to be made in a report that is verifiable on other grounds. But in this second case the proviso ought to be thought of as rather strict; it is not sufficient to 'have a feeling' that the point is true, to assume that it is verifiable on other grounds. The third case is perhaps the most legitimate, but is really a case of using informants to provide information about generally known rules: for example, using informants to collect 'typical' genealogies or kinship terms, the assumption being that his kin terms are much like those of others (which is not always true, of course) and his genealogy sufficiently 'rich' – this being the basis on which he was chosen – to exhibit a wide range of possibilities.

The informant as the observer's observer. The third common use of the informant is to report events not directly observed by the fieldworker. Here, the investigator substitutes the observations of a member for his own observation. It is not simply interviewing that is involved here, because participant observation was defined earlier as including interviewing on the spot, in conjunction with direct observation. Thus, some of the most important uses of the informant – to provide the meaning and context of that which we are observing, to provide a running check on variability, and so on – are actually part of participant observation. It is the use of informants as if they were colleagues that we must now consider.

Such a procedure is not only legitimate, but absolutely necessary to adequate investigation of any complex structure. In studying a social structure by participant observation there are two problems of bias that override all others, even the much belaboured 'personal equation'. One results from the fact that a single observer cannot be everywhere at the same time, nor can he be 'everywhere' in time, for that matter – he has not been in *S* forever, and will not be there indefinitely – so that, inevitably, something happens that he has not seen, cannot see, or will not see. The second results from the fact that there exist parts of the social structure into which he has not penetrated and probably will not, by virtue of the way he has defined himself to its members, because of limitations on the movement of those who sponsor him, and so on. There has never been a participant observer study in which the observer acquired full knowledge of all roles and statuses through his own direct observation, and for that matter there never will be such a study by a single observer. To have a team of observers is one possible solution; to have informants who stand in the relation of team members to the investigator is another. The virtue of the informant used in this way is to increase the accessibility of *S* to the investigator.

Efficiency of Sampling for Various Problems in the Field

Sampling to obtain information about institutionalised norms and statuses. It has already been argued that a properly obtained probability sample gives adequate information about institutionalised norms and statuses but is not very efficient. Two things are implied: that such information is *general* information, so that any member of *S* has the same information as any other; and that the truth of such information does not depend solely on the opinions of the respondents – the information is in some sense objective.

The first of these implications is equivalent to assuming that *S* is homogeneous with respect to the property *a*, so that a sample of one suffices to classify *S* with respect to it. It then becomes inefficient to continue sampling. The principal defect in such an argument is a practical one: By what criterion can one decide *S* is homogeneous with respect to *a* without sampling *S*? There are two such criteria, neither of which is wholly satisfactory. The first is to use substantive knowledge. We would expect in general that certain norms are invariably institutionalised, such as incest and exogamy, descent, inheritance, marriage procedures, patterns of exchange of goods, formal structure of labour markets, and so on. We may assume *a priori*, for example, that a sample of 200 Navaho is not required

to discover that marriage in one's own clan is incestuous. But the pitfall for the unwary investigator is that he may stray beyond his substantive knowledge, or apply it at the wrong time in the wrong place.

A second is to employ a loose form of sequential sampling. Suppose, for example, that we ask an informed male in *S* whom he may marry, or whom any male may marry. He answers: 'All who are *A*, but no one who is *B*.' We ask a second informant and discover again that he may marry all who are *A*, but no one who is *B*. We ask a third, a fourth, a fifth. and each tells us the same rule. We do not need to presume that the rule is actually obeyed; that is quite a different question. But we may certainly begin to believe that we have found an institutionalised norm. Conversely, the more variability we encounter, the more we must investigate further. The pitfall here is that we may be deceived by a homogeneous 'pocket' within which all members agree but which does not necessarily represent all structural parts of *S*. For this reason, we try to choose representative informants, each from a different status group. This implies, however, that we are working outward from earlier applications of this dangerous principle; we have used some informants to tell us what statuses there are, thereafter choosing additional informants from the new statuses we have discovered.

The second implication – that in some sense the truth of the information obtained depends not on the opinions of respondents, but on something else that is 'objective' in nature – simply paraphrases Durkheim: institutions are 'external' to given individuals, even though they exist only 'in' individuals; they have a life of their own, are *sui generis*. Illustrating with an extreme case: a 'belief' of *S*'s religion can be described by an informant even where neither he nor any living member of *S* actually believes it, although if no member ever did believe it, we might regard the information as trivial. In other words, this type of information does not refer to individuals living at a given time, but rather to culture as a distinct object of abstraction. It is this type of information that we mean by 'institutionalised norms and statuses'. It bears repeating at this point that, if one Navaho informant told us the Navaho were patrilineal and patrilocal, we would be more likely to assume he was wrong than we would be to assume that the Navaho had, for the moment, changed their institutions.

Sampling to obtain information about incidents and histories. If we had the good fortune to have a report from every member of *S* about what happened in region *R* at time *T*, would it really be good fortune? Would we not distinguish between those in a position to observe the event and those not? Among those who had been in the region *R* itself, would we not also distinguish subregions which provided different vantage-points from which to view the event? Among those viewing it from the same vantage-point, would we not distinguish more and less credible witnesses? Enumeration or not, we would apply stringent internal and external comparisons to each report in order to establish what truly ocurred. Formally, of course, this describes a complex technique of stratification which, if carried out properly, would withstand any quantitative criticism. But if all the elements of a decision as to what is 'truth' in such a case are considered, it is a moot point how important enumeration or random sampling is in the process.[8]

Informants with special information. Some things happen that relatively few people know about. A random sample is not a sensible way in which to obtain information about these events, although it is technically possible to define a universe U containing only those who do know and sample from U. A parallel case is the repetitive event in inaccessible parts of a social structure. A social structure is an organised system of relationships, one property of which is that certain parts of it are not readily observed by members located in other parts. There is a considerable amount of relatively esoteric information about S. It may be satisfactory from a formal point of view to regard S as consisting in many universes U_i, each of which is to be sampled for a different piece of information, but again the usefulness of such a conception is questionable, particularly if most U_i contain very few members.

Efficiency and Adequacy of Participant Observation for Various Problems in the Field

Ex post facto quantitative documentation. Because certain things are observed repeatedly, it sometimes occurs to the fieldworker to count these repetitions in his log as quantitative documentation of an assertion. In such cases, the information obtained should be subjected to any of the canons by which other quantitative data are evaluated; the care with which the universe is defined and the sense in which the sample is representative are particularly critical. With few exceptions, frequency statements made from field logs will *not* withstand such careful examination.

This sharp stricture applies only to *ex post facto* enumeration of sampling of field logs, and it is because it is *ex post facto* that the principal dangers arise. Events and persons represented in field logs will generally be sampled according to convenience rather than rules of probability sampling. The sample is unplanned, contains unknown biases. It is not so much random as haphazard, a distinction which is critical. When, after the fact, the observer attempts to correlate two classes of events in these notes, very misleading results will be obtained. If we wish to correlate a and b, it is characteristic of such samples that 'a' will be more frequently recorded than '*not-a*' and '*a and b*' more frequently than '*not-a and b*' or '*a and not-b*'. As a general rule,

only those data which the observer actually intended to enumerate should be treated as enumerable.

There are, of course, some valid enumerations contained in field notes. For example, a verbatim account kept of all meetings of some organisation is a valid enumeration; a record kept, in some small rural community, of all members of it who come to the cross-roads hamlet during a year is a valid enumeration. These will tend, however, to be intentional enumerations and not subject to the strictures applicable to *ex post facto* quantification. A much rarer exception will occur when, looking back through one's notes, one discovers that, without particularly intending it, every member of the community studied has been enumerated with respect to the property a, or that almost all of them have. This is likely to be rare, because field notes tend not to record those who do *not* have the property a and, of all those omitted in the notes, one does not know how many are *not-a* and how many simply were not observed. If everyone, or almost everyone, can be accounted for as either a or *not-a*, then a frequency statement is validly made.[9] But, if such information were desired in the first place, participant observation would clearly be a most inefficient means of obtaining it.

Readily verbalised norms and statuses. It is not efficient to use participant observation to obtain generally known norms and statuses so long as these can be readily stated. It may take a good deal of observation to infer that which an informant can quickly tell you. Participant observation would in such cases be primarily to check what informants say, to get clues to further questions, and so on. It is, of course, true that the concurrent interviewing involved in participant observation will provide the information – it is necessary to make sense out of the observations – but it comes in bits and pieces and is less readily checked for accuracy, completeness, consistency, and so forth.

Latent phenomena. Not all norms and statuses can be verbalised. Consequently, there remains a special province to which participant observation lays well-justified claims. But certain misleading implications should be avoided in admitting them. Because such phenomena may be described as 'latent' – as known to the observer but not to the members of S – it may be concluded that *all* latent phenomena are the province of participant observation. This does not follow. The term 'latent' is ambiguous; it has several distinct usages, some of which do not even share the core meaning of 'known to the observer, unknown to members'. Lazarsfeld, for example, refers to a dimension underlying a series of manifest items as a 'latent' attribute; it cannot be observed by anyone, and is inferred by the investigator from intercorrelations of observables. But the members of S may also make these inferences. (They infer that a series of statements classify the speaker as 'liberal', for example.) The most advanced techniques for searching out such latent phenomena are found in survey research and psychometrics, not in participant observation.

These are matters of inference, not of how data are directly obtained. The same is true of the discovery of 'latent functions'. Often the observer is aware of connections between events when the members of *S* are not, even though they are aware of the events themselves. But again, relations among events are not the special province of any one method; we look for such connections in *all* our data. In fact, owing to the paucity and non-comparability of units that often plague the analysis of field notes, it might be argued that participant observation is often incapable of detecting such connections. The great value of participant observation in detecting latent phenomena, then, is in those cases in which members of *S* are unaware of actually observable events, of some of the things they do, or some of the things that happen around them, which can be directly apprehended by the observer. Any other case requires inference and such inference should be made from *all* available data.

Table 23.1   *Methods of Obtaining Information*

Information Types	Enumerations and Samples	Participant Observation	Interviewing Informants
Frequency distributions	Prototype and best form	Usually inadequate and inefficient	Often, but not always, inadequate; if adequate, it is efficient
Incidents, histories	Not adequate by itself; not efficient	Prototype and best form	Adequate with precautions, and efficient
Institutionalised norms and statuses	Adequate but inefficient	Adequate, but inefficient, except for unverbalised norms	Most efficient and, hence, best form

Summary and Conclusion

Table 23.1 offers a general summary. With respect to the problem with which this chapter originated the following conclusion may be drawn: because we often treat different methods as correctly different types of study rather than as analytically different aspects of the same study, it is possible to attack a field study on the ground that it ought to be an enumeration and fails if it is not; and to defend it on the ground that it ought to be something *else* and succeeds only if it is. But, however we classify types of information in the future – and the classification suggested here is only tentative – they are

not all of one type. True, a field report is unreliable if it gives us, after consulting a haphazard selection of informants or even a carefully planned 'representative' selection, a statement such as, 'All members of *S* believe that' or 'The average member of *S* believes that' and (1) there is variance in the characteristic reported, (2) this variance is relevant to the problem reported *and* (3) the informants cannot be seriously thought of as equivalent to a team of pollsters, *or* (4) the investigator has reported what is, essentially, the 'average' beliefs of his *informants*, as if *they* were a representative, probability sample of respondents. But to demand that every piece of information be obtained by a probability sample, is to commit the researcher to grossly inefficient procedure and to ignore fundamental differences among various kinds of information. The result is that we create false methodological issues, often suggest quite inappropriate research strategies to novices, and sometimes conceal real methodological issues which deserve more discussion in the literature – such as how to establish institutionalised norms given only questionnaire data. It should be no more satisfactorily rigorous to hear that everything is in some way a sample and, hence, must be sampled, than to hear that everything is in some sense 'whole' and, hence, cannot be sampled.

Notes: Chapter 23

Reprinted from *American Journal of Sociology*, vo. 67, no. 5, 1962, pp. 566–76, by kind permission of the publisher, University of Chicago Press and the author. © 1962 University of Chicago. This chapter reports part of a more extensive investigation of problems of field method in which Dr Renée Fox is a collaborator. The author gratefully acknowledges the partial support given this investigation by funds from Columbia University's Documentation Project for Advanced Training in Social Research.

1   See, for example, Alpert (1952); and Hanson (1958).
2   See Warner and Lunt (1941), p. 55; Arensberg (1954); Becker (1956); Becker and Geer (1957); Kimball (1955); and Vidich and Bensman (1954).
3   See particularly Lewis (1953), p. 455n; also cf. Becker (1958); Colson (1954); Eggan (1954); Driver (1953); Herskovits (1954); and Spindler and Goldschmidt (1952). And see the section 'Field methods and techniques' in *Human Organisation*, especially in its early years and early editorials. Some qualification has been characteristic of 'field' monographs for a very long time; cf. Kroeber (1917). Such classics as *Middletown* (Lynd and Lynd, 1929) and the Yankee City series (Warner and Lunt, 1941; 1942; Warner and Srole, 1945; Warner and Low, 1947; Warner, 1959) are studded with tables.
4   A significant exception is a comment by M. Trow directed at Becker and Geer. Becker and Geer, comparing interviewing to participant observation, find participant observation the superior method and seem to imply that it

is superior for all purposes. Trow insists that the issue is not correctly formulated, and that one might better ask: 'What kinds of problems are best studied through what kinds of methods; . . . how can the various methods at our disposal complement one another?' In their reply, Becker and Geer are more or less compelled to agree. See Becker and Geer (1957); Trow (1957); and Becker and Geer (1958).

5 See Dean (1958).

6 See Dean (1958), p. 37, n. 4.

7 See Dean (1958), p. 37, n. 4.

8 None of this applies to repeated events. If we are interested in comparing several repetitions of the same event, generalising as to the course that is typical, care must be taken in sampling the events.

9 We may make a less stringent requirement of our notes, using what might be called 'incomplete' indicator spaces. Briefly, if we wish to classify all members of S with respect to the underlying property A, and behaviours $a, b, c, d \ldots$, all indicate A, then it is sufficient for our purpose to have information on *at least one* of these indicators for each member of S. For some we might have only a, for some only b, and so on, but we might have one among the indicators for all members, even though not the same one for all members, and thus be able to enumerate S adequately.

24

The Integration of Fieldwork and Survey Methods

SAM D. SIEBER

Prior to the Second World War, fieldwork[1] dominated social research. Such classics as the Hawthorne studies, the Middletown volumes, the Yankee City series and the Chicago studies of deviant groups, not to mention the anthropological contributions, attest to the early pre-eminence of fieldwork. Following the war, the balance of work shifted markedly to surveys. This shift was largely a consequence of the development of public-opinion polling in the 1930s. Mosteller, Cantril, Likert, Stouffer and Lazarsfeld were perhaps the major developers of the newer techniques. In particular, Lazarsfeld's interest in the two major non-academic sources of social surveys – market studies and public-opinion polling – and his adaptation of these traditions to substantive and methodological interests in sociology gave special impetus to the advancement of survey research in the universities.

With the rapid growth of this vigorous infant, there emerged a polemic between the advocates of the older field methods and the proponents of the newer survey techniques. In fact, two methodological subcultures seemed to be in the making – one professing the superiority of 'deep, rich' observational data, and the other the virtues of 'hard generalisable' survey data. That the fieldworkers were more vocal about the informational weaknesses of surveys than were survey researchers with respect to fieldwork, suggests the felt security of the latter and the defensive stance of the former. An extreme point in the polemic was reached by the statement of Becker and Geer:

> The most complete form of the sociological datum, after all, is the form in which the participant observer gathers it; an observation of some social event, the events which precede and follow it, and explanations of its meaning by participants and spectators, before, during, and after its occurrence. Such a datum gives us more information about the event under study than data gathered by any other sociological method. Participant observation can thus provide us with a yardstick against which to measure the completeness of data gathered in other ways. (Becker and Geer, 1957, p. 28)

This position was strongly contested in a rebuttal by Trow (1957), who pointed out that no single technique could claim a monopoly on plausibility of inference; and, indeed, as he argued, many sociological observations can be made only on the basis of a large population. One technique is suitable for one type of information and another technique for another:

> It is with this assertion, that a given method of collecting data – any method – has an inherent superiority over others by virtue of its special qualities and divorced from the nature of the problem studied, that I take sharp issue . . . Different kinds of information about man and society are gathered most fully and economically in different ways . . . The problem under investigation properly dictates the methods of investigation. (Trow, 1957, p. 33)

In his brief rebuttal, Trow did not seek to propose a scheme for determining the suitability of fieldwork or survey research for the collection of given types of data. This task was undertaken a few years later by Zelditch (1962), who applied the criteria of 'efficiency' and 'informational adequacy' of surveys, participant observation and informant interviewing in gathering three kinds of data: (1) frequency distributions; (2) incidents and histories; and (3) institutionalised norms and statuses. Thus, if the objective is to ascertain a frequency distribution, then the sample survey or census is the 'prototypical and best form'; but not so with incidents and histories, which render the survey both 'inefficient and inadequate', according to Zelditch. This contribution was a long step forward in mediating between the two historically antagonistic styles of research.

But even this formulation showed the traces of an assumption that undergirded the earlier polemic, namely, that one uses either survey, or field methods. The fact of the matter is that these techniques are sometimes combined within a single study. If all three types of information noted by Zelditch are sought within the framework of a single investigation, then all three techniques are properly called into play. In such cases, the inefficiency of a survey in studying 'institutionalised norms and statuses' falls by the wayside; if one is conducting a survey anyway (because of other information needs), then why not proceed to measure norms and statuses in the questionnaire? Likewise with the investigation of incidents and histories by means of a survey. If combined with other approaches, according to Zelditch, the survey becomes 'adequate' for the collection of incidents and histories; so if one is already doing a survey, the question of efficiency once again becomes irrelevant. But there is a second implication of combining field and survey methods that is much more important to the progress of social research than the needed qualifications in Zelditch's scheme.

The integration of research techniques within a single project opens up enormous opportunities for mutual advantages in each of three major phases – design, data collection and analysis. These mutual benefits are not merely quantitative (although obviously more information can be gathered by a combination of techniques), but qualitative as well – one could almost say that a new style of research is born of the marriage of survey and fieldwork methodologies. Later on, we shall argue that the respective techniques need to be modified for their special roles in a set of interlocking methods. It is this combination of adjustments which, in our opinion, produces a distinctly new style of investigation.

It is curious that so little attention has been paid to the intellectual and organisational problems and to the prospects of the integration of research methods. A few methodologists have sought to compare the results of different approaches, but these endeavours were conceived within the traditional framework of mutually exclusive techniques, in as much as the problem was to determine the consequences of using either one or another technique.

The authors of a recent compendium of 'unobtrusive measures' have noted our doggedness in viewing social research as a single-method enterprise: 'The usual procedural question asked is, which of the several data-collection methods will be best for my research problem? We suggest the alternative question: which *set* of methods will be best?'[2] These authors were prompted to raise this question on the assumption that every technique suffers from inherent weaknesses that can be corrected only by cross-checking with other techniques: 'No research method is without bias. Interviews and questionnaires must be supplemented by methods testing the same social science variables but having different methodological weaknesses.'[3] In its own way, this assumption is as radical as that of Becker and Geer. To be sure, there are areas of informational overlap between methods, but there are also large areas of information which can be gained only by a particular technique. If each technique has an inherent weakness, it also has an inherent strength unmatched by other techniques. The opinions held by a large population can be measured only by survey techniques; the unverbalised normative pattern of a small group might

be measurable only by observation. Further, what if the results obtained from two or more different techniques do not agree? Are we to abandon our findings altogether, or should we re-examine the techniques to discern a special weakness in one of them that invalidates its results? If the latter strategy is chosen, then we are admitting the superiority of one of the techniques in gathering the desired information. An illustration from a class experiment at Columbia University will make the argument more concrete.

A Class Experiment

In a seminar on research methods, nine graduate students were provided with the field notes of an observer informant interviewer who had investigated the settings of Job Corps trainees in two city agencies.[4] On the basis of these notes, the project director had selected one of the settings as 'good' and the other as 'bad' in terms of the trainees' morale, opportunities for training and meaningful participation in the work of the agencies. (Although several agencies had been investigated, these two were selected as polar cases for the purpose of the class experiment.) The nine students were instructed to scrutinise the *field notes* very carefully and then to select those items from a *questionnaire* (later distributed to the trainees), which they believed would confirm the conclusions of the project director as to the value of the two settings (the *direction* of the predicted difference being obvious in most cases, since the items were clearly evaluative of morale, participation and so on). After the students had made their individual selections, the results of the questionnaire survey in each of the two agencies were tabulated and compared item by item. If at least half of the judges predicted that an item would discriminate, and it did in fact discriminate, it was classified in a category of 'congruence' between fieldwork and survey results. If less than half of the judges predicted a difference on the item, but the item nevertheless discriminated, it was classified in a 'non-congruent' category, and so on. Table 24.1 shows the percentage of 75 questionnaire items that fell into each of four logical classes.

Table 24.1 discloses that 45 per cent of the survey items were predictable on the basis of the field notes (cells 1 and 4). Virtually all of the items in cell 1 referred to the match between the trainee's interests and qualifications and the job he was performing. (Of all the items, 21 per cent fell into this cell.) Another 24 per cent of the items were accurately regarded by the judges as revealing no difference (cell 4). The items in this category focused mainly on the administration of the overall programme, such as selection procedures, training, general administration, and so on; in other words, experiences that the trainees in the two agencies were known to have shared. As these experiences were not specific to a particular agency, the judges assumed correctly that the items bearing on them would not discriminate between the agencies. Cells 2 and 3 clearly reveal incongruence between the field notes and the survey results. In cell 2 we find items that in fact discriminated, but that the field notes did not provide grounds for such discrimination (36 per cent of the items). This percentage may be taken as a rough measure of the unique contribution of the survey as perceived by the judges. The items falling into this cell were of three distinct kinds: (1) *statistical data*, such as number of hours per week with little or nothing to do, income expected from Urban Corps, present payrate; (2) *personal history*, such as how income compares with what was previously expected, whether another job was turned down to work for Urban Corps, attitude towards job when applied; (3) *personal interests and values*, such as kinds of summer jobs preferred, enjoyment of life in the city, occupational values, career plans, interest in hearing different types of speakers in Urban Corps seminars.

Table 24.1 *Questionnaire Items Classified According to Their Congruence with Fieldwork Observations (Percentage of 75 Items)*

Item Actually Discriminated between Agencies*	Consensus among Judges†	
	Half or More (5–9)	Less than Half (0–4)
Yes	(1) Congruence (prediction of difference confirmed) 21%	(2) Non-congruence (failure to predict difference) 36%
No..........	(3) Non-congruence (inaccurate prediction of difference) 19%	(4) Congruence (prediction of no difference confirmed) 24%

* 10% difference between the agencies was regarded as determining whether an item 'discriminated'.
† No. of judges predicting a difference between survey responses of trainees in two city agencies on basis of field notes.

Perhaps more lengthy exposure to the agencies and their trainees would have contributed more information on these points in the field notes. However, the survey was clearly a more economical means of disclosing such information. In addition, by being gathered in a standardised fashion, the information could be dealt with statistically in examining the differential impact of the two agencies on different trainees. For example, it now became possible to see if trainees with lower occupational aspirations were less satisfied with the 'bad' agency.

Finally, in cell 3 we find items that were expected to discriminate, but which in fact did not discriminate between the two agencies (19 per cent of the total items). Here it is plain that the field notes misled the judges into assuming that the trainees in the 'bad' agency (1) were disliked by their superiors and other regular staff, and (2) blamed the agency itself for their unsatisfactory assignment. In short, an assumption of mutual animus was conveyed by the field notes. Here are some examples of items that were mistakenly thought to discriminate between the two agencies (in each case the trainees in the 'bad' agency were expected to give the more negative response):

How do you think your supervisor would rate your performance?
If you have switched jobs, what were the reasons? (Agency or supervisor was dissatisfied.)
Have you complained to the Urban Corps staff about any aspect of your job?
When you first arrived in this agency, how much did the agency prepare you for what you would be doing?
Do you like your supervisor as a person?
Would you say your non-Urban Corps co-workers are friendly or unfriendly to you?
How would you characterise your agency? As: (*a*) open to new ideas, (*b*) bureaucratic, (*c*) sympathetic towards clients.

We encounter here a common pitfall of fieldwork that might properly be called the 'holistic fallacy' –that is, a tendency to perceive all aspects of a social situation as congruent. In the present instance, because of the wholly unsatisfactory job assignments of the trainees in one of the agencies, it was assumed that they would be displeased with the agency and, in turn, would feel resented by the regular agency staff. The survey corrected this assumption.

While the above experiment confirms Webb *et al.* (1966) in the advisability of using several techniques to validate inferences, it also demonstrates that certain information can be gathered only by means of a single technique (see cells 2 and 3 above). However, by drawing upon its special strengths, one technique may contribute substantially to the utilisation of the other technique. It is this principle that we wish to demonstrate in the remainder of this chapter.

To recapitulate: the original polemic between advocates of field methods and of survey research was mediated by the assertion of Trow and Zelditch that the nature of the problem dictates the method to be applied. Later on, Webb *et al.* (1966) rejected a commitment to any single method in solving a particular problem, because of an inherent bias in all techniques. Their argument in behalf of multitechniques is based on an assumption of interchangeability – otherwise it would be meaningless to plead for cross-validation. In contrast, we believe that survey and field research each possesses special qualities that render these methods non-interchangeable; nevertheless, each method can be greatly strengthened by appealing to the unique qualities of the other method. Despite the plausibility of this claim, the advantages of the interplay between surveys and field methods are seldom recognised and rarely exploited. To the contrary, it seems that most sociological research either utilises only a single method of investigation, or assigns an extremely weak role to a second. To show the value of fully integrating the respective techniques by drawing upon existing research for examples, we hope to focus serious attention on the enormous opportunities that lie at hand for improving our social research strategies.

We shall, first, deal with the contributions of fieldwork to surveys, and then reverse ourselves and consider the contributions of surveys to fieldwork. In each case we shall give illustrations that bear on the phases of design, data collection and analysis associated with each method. Then, in a final section, we shall take up the question of time-order in which the methods are applied. Considerations of time-order are of major importance to the management of a research study that seeks to benefit from both techniques. This point will become clearer when we turn to the formulation of an optimal research schedule.

Contributions of Fieldwork to Surveys

CONTRIBUTIONS TO SURVEY DESIGN

More and more, surveys are conducted among selected communities or organisations rather than among samples of isolated individuals. In these cases, a great deal of careful thought must be given to the selection of the collective. It is not unusual, therefore, to find survey researchers scouting among an array of potential collectives in order to select those that promise to maximise the advantages of comparative study. An account of one such scouting expedition is given by Wilder and Friedman, who had tentatively selected seven communities to be included in their investigation of school–community relations. (Parents, students and teachers in these communities were eventually interviewed.) We quote:

The Project Director and his assistant visited each of the communities to see whether they appeared to 'fit' their census descriptions. Since we had found it necessary at several points to compromise with our *a priori* assumptions about what constituted criteria for the various types of communities, we had certain misgivings about some parameters and cutting points and we felt it would be useful to verify qualitatively our sampling framework. In addition we were curious to *see* these communities with which we had become so familiar on the basis of census data.

In general, the tours served to confirm our expectations. Schools in settled towns were often pre-1900 vintage, while in growing communities they were either new or had new additions. Homes and people in middle-class communities 'looked' middle-class and shops displayed quality merchandise. In the working-class towns homes were smaller, lawns were tidy or non-existent, Methodist churches were predominant. Boxy developments were mushrooming in the growing working-class suburb, while more expensive split-level developments abounded in the growing middle-class suburb. The trips served to convince us that the communities we had selected on the basis of the available published data did indeed 'fit' their census descriptions. (Wilder and Friedman, 1968, appendix A)

The contribution of field observations to the study design of a survey need not be restricted to a confirmatory role, as in the above example, but can provide the sole rationale for the design. An illustration is provided by our own research on suburban schools:

While conducting exploratory interviews and observations in a single suburban school system located just beyond the crest of a migratory wave originating in a large city, our attention was drawn to the school system's vulnerability as its public composition gradually changed. In our interviews, we heard stories about a neighbouring system that had already felt the full impact of migration. The informants were fearful that the same kinds of conflict between school and community would overtake their own system in the near future. After about two months of fieldwork in the less urbanized system, we decided to include the neighbouring system in our study and to focus on the response of the schools to increasing vulnerability arising from suburbanization. Fieldwork was then pursued in both systems for several months before launching a questionnaire survey of all staff members in the two systems. Thus, the initial fieldwork sharpened the focus of the investigation on a specific educational problem by directing attention to the contrast between pre- and post-suburbanized systems, necessitating the inclusion of a second system. A survey was then conducted to gain fuller knowledge of the impact of suburbanization on the schools. Fieldwork, in sum, dictated the design of the survey investigation.

Broadly conceived, qualitative fieldwork includes any source of personal familiarity with a setting or group to be surveyed. This knowledge may be derived from non-professional sources, such as family members or previous work experience. These sources can provide insights and 'privileged' information that can make a major contribution to the development of a meaningful survey design. A striking illustration of the benefits of non-professional familiarity with a social group prior to the conception of a survey is afforded by Lipset (1964) in his 'biography' of the project that eventuated in the well-known monograph, 'Union democracy'. Lipset's interest was in explaining the high level of participatory democracy in the printers' union, a phenomenon that disconfirmed classical theories of the development of oligarchical control in socialist parties and trade unions. An innovation of the project was the sampling of collectives (union chapels), a design permitting elaborate analysis of contextual effects on individual political attitudes and behaviours. Referring to this unusual design, Lipset says: 'The methodological innovations evidenced in our sample design did not stem from any special concern with creative methodology . . . It was a sophisticated survey design precisely because years of prior investigation of the attributes of a complex system had preceded it.[5] The history of that prior investigation began in Lipset's youth:

My first contact with the International Typographical Union came when I was quite young. My father was a lifelong member of the union . . . While in elementary school and high school, I frequently overheard discussions of union matters, and occasionally my father would take me to the monthly meetings of the New York local at Stuyvesant High School – a set of experiences which was to play a role later in my conceiving of the 'occupational community' as an important part of the environment of the union. (Lipset, 1964, pp. 96–7)

Lipset's survey design was developed expressly to study the effect of varying degrees of 'occupational community' within the different chapels in promoting the members' political participation.

The contribution of field methods to survey design is by no means restricted to the study of collectives. Sometimes, for example, there are special categories of individuals whose existence is brought to light by exploratory fieldwork and which are then incorporated into the design of the survey:

In preparing for an investigation of the organization of research in schools of education, in which deans and bureau directors were to be surveyed, Lazarsfeld and I [Sieber and Lazarsfeld, 1966; 1972] interviewed expert informants. One informant noted the presence of 'faculty research coordinators,' an emerging status that had been overlooked in the study design. The informant himself filled this role in his institution. Therefore a special questionnaire was prepared for these persons. Further, since we realized that the data to be collected from these respondents would permit a comparison of organized and unorganized settings for research, the former represented by bureau directors and the latter by faculty coordinators, the existing questionnaires were modified by expanding the number of items on which comparisons would be fruitful. In effect, a new study design was adopted.

These comparisons later afforded a perspective on bureau research that was not attainable in any other way.

CONTRIBUTIONS TO SURVEY DATA COLLECTION

The exploratory interviews and observations that often precede social surveys yield valuable information about the receptivity, frames of reference and span of attention of respondents. Since a great part of the value of systematic pretesting resides in the gathering of such intelligence, it is justifiable to consider this aspect of pretesting under the rubric of qualitative fieldwork. Improvements in the questionnaire stemming from qualitative pretest information enhance rapport between interviewer and respondent, reduce non-returns of mailed questionnaires or refusals to be interviewed, and generally ease the data collection efforts of the research staff.

In addition, the instrument can be broadened or narrowed, depending upon the identification of topics that are salient to pretest respondents. That is, by identifying the respondents' level of interest and scope of concern, the instrument can be modified to avoid overtaxing each respondent, on the one hand, or underrepresenting his views, on the other. An example of expanding a questionnaire on the basis of this type of information is taken from a survey of college students on a single campus. A chronicle of the questionnaire's development contains the following observation:

The pre-test was administered to about thirty students, and the results were very heartening. Almost all of the interviewers reported that the respondents seemed to be interested in cooperating. This information caused an over-all change in the form of the questionnaire. In the pre-test, the emphasis had been on limiting the number of questions for fear of antagonizing the busy students. The interviewers' reports seemed to indicate that the fear was ungrounded and the items that had been limited could be expanded.

The general direction of the expansion was the addition of *contingent sections* to existing questions . . . The discovery of student interest *allowed* us to add more sections according to our own interests. (Langenwalter, 1967, pp. 5–6)

Pretesting is only one means of exploring issues that bear on the development of an instrument. Often a good deal of exploratory work precedes even the pretest questionnaire. As a rule, the more knowledgeable the questionnaire designer about his ultimate population, the more sophisticated the instrument and the smoother its administration.

Apart from the formulation of the questionnaire,

fieldwork often provides a means of gaining legitimation for the survey. If the population has a central leadership, contacts with leaders will often smooth the way for contacts with followers. If there are factional fights, of course, the endorsement of only a single leader may set a large number of the followers in opposition to the survey. But information about political infighting should come to the attention of the sophisticated fieldworker in the normal course of informant interviewing, thereby prompting him to gain endorsements in a way that will appeal to all sectors of the constituency.

The importance of identifying and gaining support from the appropriate authority during the exploratory phase preceding a survey, and of grasping the political context in which approval is sought, are perhaps best demonstrated by a negative instance: Voss (1966) describes the case of a school survey that was terminated by the superintendent on the grounds that it was 'unauthorised by the school'. Although in reality the superintendent was responding to pressures from a group of right-wing parents, the survey having been duly approved by lower-level administrators, he was able to claim that he had not personally endorsed the survey and could, therefore, cancel it on legalistic grounds. Voss concludes from this experience: 'Lack of familiarity with the structure of the organization may spell disaster. For some time sociologists have recognized that persons without portfolio may influence the decision of the titular head of the organization. The only means of avoiding such a problem is to obtain unequivocal support from the highest level possible.' Our investigation of two suburban districts, mentioned earlier, affords a case at the opposite end of the spectrum of co-operation: after conducting fieldwork for several months – which included the privilege of walking unannounced into the superintendents'offices at any hour and attending closed strategy meetings of the teachers' association –there was never really any question of gaining endorsements for the survey. Every administrator in the district co-operated fully in urging teachers to respond and in collecting the completed questionnaires. And the many helpful, marginal comments of the teachers, some addressing the survey designer by name, suggested that the questionnaire was completed with uncommon seriousness. (The return rate was about 90 per cent of the entire staff.) The two projects are not exactly parallel, since Voss surveyed students rather than staff members, thereby touching off community hostility; but the problems encountered by Voss are also faced in gaining access to school staff. The crucial point is that rapport which stems from fieldwork can smooth the way for the more elaborate, time-consuming and often more threatening aspects of survey data collection. Apparently, the impersonality of a survey can be counteracted by the subject's personal acquaintance with the investigator and the goals of his study.

CONTRIBUTIONS TO SURVEY ANALYSIS

Information that is gathered in the course of fieldwork can assist in the analysis and interpretation of survey data in several ways. First, the *theoretical structure* that guides the analysis can be derived wholly or largely from qualitative fieldwork. Secondly, as emphasised by Webb *et al.* (1966), certain of the survey results can be *validated*, or at least given persuasive plausibility, by recourse to observations and informant interviews. (This contribution is limited to areas of informational overlap, as noted earlier.) Thirdly, statistical relationships can be *interpreted* by reference to field observations. Fourthly, the selection of survey items for the *construction of indices* can be based on field observations. Fifthly, *external validation* of statistical constructs (indices) is afforded by comparison with observational scales. Sixthly, *case studies* that illustrate statistical and historical types are supplied by field protocols and finally; provocative but puzzling replies to the questionnaire can be *clarified* by resort to field notes. Illustrations of each of these contributions to survey analysis follow.

(1) The derivation of a theoretical structure from fieldwork is perhaps more common than appears from reports of survey work. Often, only passing acknowledgement is made of prior, personal familiarity with the situation, a familiarity that has produced rather definite ideas for research. A sociologist who conducts a survey of college faculty has made many observations of his own institutional context, which contributed, no doubt, to his theoretical guidelines, but his monograph might omit any reference to this fact. And rare indeed is the report that systematically traces the intellectual history of a study to its qualitative antecedents.

Such an effort has been made by Lipset in his chronicle of the 'Union democracy' study (Lipset, 1964). As a consequence of his personal familiarity with the International Typographers Union, Lipset says,

I had a fairly clear picture in mind of factors which had created ITU democracy and those which sustained it . . . The main task of the survey was to convert hypotheses which had been developed earlier into questions for a schedule which could be administered to a sample of union members. (Lipset, 1964, pp. 106–7)

In an investigation of high-school rebellion, Stinchcombe (1964) asserts that the four hypotheses that guided his analysis 'were developed during the course of about six months of anthropological observation and exploratory survey research in a California high school'.[6] In the preface to his monograph, Stinchcombe candidly notes his debt to informant interviewing: 'I became quite suspicious of any hypothesis that was never formulated, in one guise or another, by at least one of the teachers or administrators of the school, and many were suggested by them.' It would appear than an optimal schedule for theoretical survey research would include a lengthy period of fieldwork prior to the survey. As a result of our perusing the literature for examples, however, our impression is that this practice is rarely followed.

(2) The verification of survey findings by reference to fieldwork is especially useful when the finding is both surprising and strategic. A statistic of this kind was discovered in our study of educational research organisations (Sieber and Lazarsfeld 1966).

> Tabulation of the questionnaire showed that extremely few doctoral recipients who had worked in research bureaus as assistants remained as staff members. On the average, only .7 students per unit had stayed on after the doctorate in the past three years. It occurred to us that this fact might explain the lack of continuity in research bureaus, the difficulty of recruitment and the strong influence of each succeeding director. Here was an explanatory factor that was wholly unanticipated. But since only about two-thirds of the respondents had answered this difficult statistical question, we felt uneasy about resting our case on the survey finding alone. When we later did informant interviewing, therefore, we asked the directors how they felt about retaining research assistants as professional staff members. With only one exception, the dozen or so directors whom we talked to believed that students should be encouraged to leave the bureau after getting their degrees. The reason given was that students would not become independent of their mentors unless they took positions elsewhere. Since this viewpoint was expressed with great conviction by the informants, the field interviews lent plausibility to the survey finding.

The invalidation of survey results by qualitative methods should also be counted as a contribution to survey analysis. For example:

> In her study of working-class marriage, it was very important for Komarovsky (1962) to classify her subjects according to differing degrees of marital happiness in as reliable a manner as possible, for marital happiness was a crucial dependent variable. She therefore drew upon information gathered in a series of detailed and indirect probes. Comparing her distribution of cases with large, representative samples of the same social strata which employed more direct self-ratings, she found that her own population contained a larger proportion of unhappy marriages. In one nationwide survey only 5% of the grade school graduates were classified as 'not too happy'; while in her study, 14% were judged to be 'very unhappy.' Komarovsky accounts for this discrepancy by reference to the more subtle tech-

niques of qualitative case study, making it more difficult for the respondent to conceal the unpleasant aspects of marital relations. As she states: 'Our detailed and indirect probing may have brought to light unfavorable facts which are not readily admitted in answer to direct questions used in surveys . . . In our own interview, answers to the direct questions on dissatisfaction with communication were at variance with the admissions made elsewhere by the same people'.[7] Consequently, instead of being misled by the results of typical survey items, Komarovsky employed a more qualitative approach when classifying her subjects according to certain major variables in her study.

The testing of a survey's reliability may extend to the entire study as well as focusing on selected items or variables. Riesman visited a large number of the social science professors who had been interviewed in the study of threats to academic freedom during the McCarthy years (Lazarsfeld and Thielens 1958). He also interviewed the interviewers. As a result, he was able to arrive at the overall assessment of the survey's reliability. He states in Lazarsfeld and Thielens: 'Deficiencies in the interviewing did not seriously impair the information gathered. Or, to put it another way, the interviewing was, in general, sufficiently skillful to carry the somewhat unusual demands of this particular survey.'[8]

(3) Qualitative fieldwork is also useful for the interpretation of statistical relationships. The identification of a whole series of interpretative variables is illustrated by Kahl's study of 'common man' boys (1953).[9] Kahl found that IQ and occupation contributed independently to students' plans to attend college. He then became interested in the chain of causality linking SES to college aspirations. Through intensive interviews with the parents of a small subsample of the students (that is, those in the upper-lower and lower-middle brackets) who had completed questionnaires, he found that overt parental pressure largely accounted for the students' college plans. This variable had not been measured in the original survey. Kahl then proceeded even further in his search for interpretive variables by discerning those factors that impelled the parents to urge college upon their children. The following is my own synopsis of his findings on this point.

Parents who propelled their children towards college had adopted the upper middle-class as a normative reference group, frequently owing to the father's proximity to middle-class workers within his job setting. Because these better-trained and higher-paid employees had high visibility for the father, he had become dissatisfied with his own occupational role and, therefore, placed great emphasis on his children's getting ahead. Those who were content for their children to stay out of college seemed more oriented to peers rather than to individuals placed immediately above them in the work hierarchy. Moreover, these fathers were not socially acquainted with professionals or semi-professionals. Consequently, they tended to exhibit 'short-run hedonism', that is, a concern with present enjoyments rather than with delayed gratifications. Rather than 'getting ahead', as Kahl puts it, they were interested in 'getting by'. In summary, Kahl's interview materials permitted him to refine the original survey correlation between SES and college plans among high-IQ 'common man' boys whose chances of planning to attend college were about fifty-fifty. Direct observation of behaviour may also aid in the interpretation of statistical relationship. The following example is drawn from our own study of suburban schools.

In the questionnaire, the teachers in the two suburban systems were asked if they had easier access to administrators than most other teachers. In the smaller, less bureaucratised system, teachers with easier access held more favourable attitudes towards the administration. This was not the case in the larger district, however, where access and attitudes were unrelated. I tried to recall any difference that was observed between the two districts in the nature of personal interaction between teachers and administrators. By reflecting on my observations of actual meetings, I noted a distinction which had escaped me before. In the larger district both teacher and administrator observed formal protocol in the course of interaction. For instance, appointments were made, the participants sat with rigid postures on opposite sides of the administrator's desk and the discussion pursued a businesslike course. In the smaller district, the situation was highly informal. The teacher walked unannounced into the administrator's office, the participants sat back comfortably at a large conference table and enjoyed a smoke together, and the conversation roamed over a variety of topics. In short, a considerable amount of social distance was maintained in teacher–administrator relations in the larger district, reflecting the widely shared bureaucratic norms in that district. Consequently, personal sentiments of liking or disliking did not arise from teacher–administrator contacts. In the smaller district, the distance between formal ranks was almost obliterated by personal friendships, making it possible for mutual trust to develop more readily out of frequent interaction.

(4) The construction of indices for use in survey analysis may derive from systematic informant interviewing or from more casual observation. The value of informants is demonstrated by Carlin's study of the social factors affecting the ethical behaviour of lawyers (1966).

Before the analysis could precede, it was necessary to develop a scale to measure the ethical proclivities of the lawyers. Therefore, questionnaire items were assembled from information about the ethical conflicts that commonly arise in legal practice. Much of this information was gleaned from informal interviews with lawyers. Carlin gives the following account of his strategy: 'Detailed interviews were conducted with a dozen lawyers. They were asked certain general questions relating to professional ethics; also, they were asked to identify borderline unethical practices. Among the general questions were the following: In what ways do lawyers take advantage of other lawyers? In what ways do lawyers act unethically toward public officials? What kinds of activities do you consider unethical or improper? How do you distinguish more from less ethical lawyers? How important are such distinctions in your judgements of other lawyers?' Several hypothetical situations that presented opportunities for unethical conduct were eventually devised. Responses to these items in the questionnaire made it possible to score the lawyers according to their ethical tendencies.

A similar approach was employed in the development of an index of 'apprehension' on the part of social science professors regarding threats to academic freedom (Lazarsfeld and Thielens, 1958). The authors discuss the development of this index in great detail, but what interests us here is the preliminary phase of exploratory interviewing:

The first step was to conduct a series of detailed interviews with a number of college professors who were prevailed upon to describe in detail any situation encountered in their capacity as teachers which had somehow made them feel uneasy. We asked them to remember as much as they could of both important and trivial experiences which create problems in a teacher's professional career, experiences they had already encountered or which might arise in the future. From these preliminary interviews we selected a list of about twenty relatively specific experiences. Questions were then worded so that the respondent simply had to say whether or not these things had happened to him . . . Twenty-one items were included in the questionnaire to gauge a professor's apprehension. But further screening was necessary to select the items most suitable for the classificatory task at hand . . . As a result of this sifting, eleven items remained suitable for an index of apprehension. (Lazarsfeld and Thielens, 1958, pp. 73–4)

(5) The validation of a statistical index by reference to fieldwork is illustrated by our procedure in testing a measure of 'formal authority' among the directors of research bureaus. The index was based on replies to such questions as whether the director participated in the decision to undertake a study, whether he determined the salaries and promotions of staff members, whether he was a member of the board of directors and so on. After each director had been scored on the index, a small subsample was visited to gain firsthand

information about certain bureaus. In the course of the interviews with the directors, the interviewer sought to explore the amount of formal authority that the directors had. Finally, the directors were told that they ranked high, low, or medium on the index and asked if their score accurately reflected their position. In virtually all cases, the directors confirmed their position on the index. One director who scored very low on the index explained that he ran the bureau in a very informal manner, but nevertheless had a great deal to say about what went on. Further probing revealed that the director in question was a highly esteemed scholar, who was frequently sought out by the staff for advice and support. Thus, we were alerted to a weakness in the index that was later compensated for by using a measure of the directors' research productivity to reflect their informal status among colleagues.

(6) The use of case studies to illustrate statistical and historical types that are derived from survey analysis is so common a practice that it only seems necessary to refer to it here. Some investigators who have employed this technique are Kahl (1953), Gordon (1957), Komarovsky (1962) and Sieber and Lazarsfeld (1966). In all these cases – and the reader can undoubtedly think of his own examples – fieldwork reports were used to exemplify certain types of individuals or situations that were disclosed in the analysis of survey data.

(7) A final contribution of fieldwork to survey analysis entails the clarification of ambiguous but provocative responses to a questionnaire. In our survey of the directors of educational research bureaus, we asked the following: 'In general, how *fruitful* have interchanges been with the academic departments in the university; what *problems* have been encountered, if any; and what *directions* would you like future interchanges to take?' One director wrote the following reply: 'Professors in the liberal arts seem not to be able to make advancements within their respective departments, if they participate heavily in the activities of the Centre.' The response was curious, possibly significant, but far from clear. Later in the course of fieldwork among selected bureaus, we asked the director to clarify his answer. He explained that academic personnel who became associated with his organisation lost visibility in their departments. Their frequent absence from the department was interpreted as a lack of departmental commitment. His clarification illuminated the problem of integrating research bureaus into the universities, which became a dominant theme in our subsequent thinking.

Contributions of Surveys to Fieldwork

We now shift to the other end of the two-way street between fieldwork and survey methodologies. The contribution of surveys to fieldwork is probably less well appreciated than the reverse, but as we shall see, there are many ways in which fieldwork can take advantage of survey techniques. Indeed, on many occasions it would seem to be methodologically obligatory.

CONTRIBUTIONS TO THE DESIGN OF FIELDWORK

We noted earlier that fieldwork is useful for identifying the most suitable collectives or individuals to be surveyed. The same holds for the contribution of surveys to the design of fieldwork. When selecting collectives or individuals for qualitative case study, it is common to rely upon a statistical profile of the population containing the units to be observed. For example, in selecting schools for intensive fieldwork, we might peruse the following kinds of information about a number of districts: racial and occupational composition, density, school size, teachers' salaries and so on. These data are often used, because they are readily available. But there is frequently a need for other information which is more pertinent to the goals of a study. Thus, a field exploration of the school characteristics that promote innovative behaviour would benefit from precise data showing the range of 'innovativeness' among a number of schools. With this information in hand, it would be easy to select schools at different points on the continuum for qualitative study. Other kinds of information that are not generally available but might be collected in a preliminary survey include staff morale, educational goals of parents or school personnel, backgrounds of school board members and proportion of graduates who attend college. For example, before visiting the research units for our fieldwork (in connection with the study of graduate schools of education), we stratified the units according to certain data already collected in a national survey. The degree of emphasis on research *versus* service, whether the unit mainly facilitated faculty research or staff research, and public or private sponsorship were the stratifying variables. The first two items of information were contributed by the survey.

The purpose of selecting the research bureaus according to a sampling frame was to provide cases that represented the main types of bureaus. Another use of survey data is to select unrepresentative cases for the analysis of subtypes. As an example, Kahl (1953) used survey data to select a particular subsample of students and their parents for intensive interviewing. He examined the distribution of all cases according to IQ, fathers' occupations and the students' expectations of college attendance. Those students whose plans were least predictable on the basis of IQ and fathers' occupation – that, is high IQ and low occupation – were selected for follow-up study.

Kahl selected subjects who conformed to his theoretical expectations but who were under the cross-pressures of relatively low occupational background and high IQ. Consequently, only about half planned to attend college. The purpose of his follow-up interviews was to find out what distinguished the college- from the non-college-going students in this group. He might have chosen, however, to study those students who went counter to his expectations, for instance, the boys of high IQ and high occupational background who did not intend to enroll in college (11 per cent of his cases); or the boys of low IQ and occupational background who did intend to enroll in college (9 per cent). If he had adopted this approach in refining his theory, he would have been engaged in what has come to be known as 'deviant case analysis'. As Kendall and Wolf (1949) point out, 'Through careful analysis of the cases which do not exhibit the expected behavior, the researcher recognizes the oversimplification of his theoretical structure and becomes aware of the need for incorporating further variables into his predictive scheme'.[10] But often the researcher does not have in hand the additional information necessary for measuring the further variables. Since it is extremely rare for a survey researcher to re-enter the field for intensive interviewing after the completion of a survey, the needed information is almost never collected. This methodological embarrassment might account for the superficiality of a good many reports based on survey analysis.

Qualitative fieldworkers, of course, also search for relationships among variables. But since evidence that can be examined in tabular form is seldom collected, the identification of deviant cases is more difficult than in survey work and, therefore, more prone to escape attention. Here is where a preliminary survey can be most fruitful, for it constrains the fieldworker to notice departures from theoretical expectation and clearly identifies those cases that deviate. The fieldworker can then focus on these cases for intensive observation. In sum, a survey can improve the design of fieldwork by identifying both representative and unrepresentative cases, the former serving the goal of generalisability and the latter the function of theory refinement.

CONTRIBUTIONS TO FIELDWORK DATA COLLECTION

A common pitfall in qualitative data collection is an 'elite bias' in the selection of informants and in the evaluations of statements. There are several reasons for gravitating to the elite of a social system in the course of fieldwork. First, initial contacts are often made with the 'gatekeepers' of a group to insure access to subjects. Consequently, the fieldworker tends to feel gratitude towards the elite and is careful to keep on good terms with them, especially in the early period while establishing his credentials. These early constraints on the fieldworker's role might colour his objectivity throughout the ensuing study. Secondly, if the upper-status persons are esteemed in society at large, the fieldworker might tend to value personal association with them to the detriment of other contacts. Such

overvaluation might stem from the prestige conferred on the sociologist by familiarity with (and later specialisation in) a certain elite strata. A third reason for the elite bias is that upper-status individuals are often more articulate and give the impression of being better informed about the group than any other member. Thus, they might seem to display greater knowledge and equanimity, enhancing their qualification as informants. Finally, it is often more interesting to study elites who have remained hitherto inaccessible to sociologists than to study lower-level participants, even though a goal of the study might be to observe all strata. Consequently, the fieldworker might spend more time collecting information from the elites, ultimately giving greater weight to their viewpoints than to those of lower-level participants.

With hindsight, all of these factors probably entered into our own fieldwork in a study that set out to examine the structure of two suburban school systems, but developed into a study of school boards, superintendents, and the leaders of the high-school teachers. After conducting a survey, however, I was able to correct certain impressions that emerged from my elite bias. This can be shown quite simply. Prior to looking at the results of the survey, I predicted the proportion of teachers who would respond in particular ways to the survey questions. I then compared my predictions with the actual responses. It became obvious when observing these comparisons that I had unwittingly adopted the elites' version of reality. For example, I overestimated the extent to which teachers felt that the administration accepted criticism. Here are the relevant questions and the statistics: 'Do you think that teachers who are interested in administrative openings jeopardise their opportunities in this district by voicing criticism of present school policies and practices?' (percentage responding 'definitely' and 'possibly'):

	predicted	observed
system A	40	60
system B	40	65

Similarly, I had assumed that the teachers were more satisfied with evaluative procedures than was in fact the case: 'All in all, how well do you think the evaluation of teachers is done in your school?' (percentage responding 'as well as possible' and 'fairly well'):

	predicted	observed
system A:		
elementary	80	65
secondary	50	36
system B:		
elementary	80	74
secondary	75	56

Although to a lesser extent, I also overestimated the rank-and-file support for the leaders of the teachers association, with whom I had spent a good deal of time. In short, I had fallen prey to the elite bias, despite recent training in the dangers of giving greater weight to prestigious figures as informants.

The survey not only constrained me to see that my qualitative data collection procedures had been faulty, but also provided the opportunity to learn about an entire stratum which I was aware of having glossed over in the fieldwork, namely, the elementary teachers. Apparently the elite bias had operated also in my preference for secondary teachers, who are the more esteemed both in the profession and the community. If the survey results had been available to me in the midst of fieldwork, I would have been able to alter my data collection procedures. This sort of concurrent scheduling of field- and survey work was utilised by Vidich and Shapiro in their study of a rural community:

> The field observer, who had spent a year in the community, sought to rank a large sample of residents according to certain prestige groupings. A sociometric survey was then conducted among these individuals. In comparing the results, it was found that individuals who were not known to the observer contained a disproportionate number of those with low prestige. As the authors put it, 'Thus, even though the observer had made deliberate efforts to establish contact with lower prestige groups, his knowledge of community members was biased in favor of individuals with higher prestige . . . Without the survey data, the observer could only make reasonable guesses about his areas of ignorance in the effort to reduce bias. The survey data give him more exact information regarding the degree and kind of selectivity operating, and thereby allow him to make better compensatory allowances in planning his observational activities.' (Vidich and Shapiro, 1955, p. 31)

As in my own case, moreover, the field observers were now able to classify a large number of cases with whom they were unacquainted. In sum, here are two ways in which surveys contribute to data collection in fieldwork: (1) they correct for the elite bias in the interpretation of events; and (2) they provide information about the informants or subjects who were overlooked.

There are other contributions, too, provided that the survey is conducted prior to fieldwork. Replies to survey questions provide leads for later interviews and observations and eliminate the need to ask routine 'background' questions. They thereby afford greater realism, enhance rapport, and offer guidelines for probes. Before arriving for our appointments with the directors of research bureaus, we carefully studied the information they had given us in the questionnaires. Background data on the directors and routine organisational information gave us an imagery of the man and

his setting. And it was especially helpful to be able to forgo asking tedious questions about the activities, structure and purposes of the organisation. As a result, the interviews were relaxed, focused on subtle points of research administration, and relatively brief. In certain instances, replies to the mailed questionnaire were followed up with probes.

CONTRIBUTIONS TO THE ANALYSIS OF QUALITATIVE FIELD MATERIALS

We will discuss four contributions of surveys to the understanding of field observations: (1) correction of the holistic fallacy; (2) demonstration of the generality of a single observation; (3) verification of field interpretations; and (4) the casting of new light on field observations.

(1) *Correction of the holistic fallacy*

In our earlier discussion of a class experiment in predicting survey results from fieldwork, we referred to the 'holistic fallacy' as a tendency on the part of field observers to perceive all aspects of a social situation as congruent. This tendency is a common pitfall. The anthropological method was developed in response to the needs of studying a particular type of social setting – small, isolated, relatively homogeneous cultures. In transferring the method to industrial societies, certain intellectual assumptions underlying the technique were also transferred, that is, every social situation can be perceived in an ideal-typical fashion. When the search for congruence overrides important refinements or dictates assumptions that are unsupported by direct evidence, and especially when striking exceptions to one's theory are subtly discounted on behalf of a unified conception, one is indulging in the holistic fallacy.

It will be recalled that this tendency was demonstrated in the class experiment reported earlier: evidence that the trainees were poorly suited for their assignments was extended to their attitudes towards supervision, when in fact the survey showed that these trainees felt no more hostile towards supervisors than trainees in a more satisfactory work setting. Another example of the holistic fallacy corrected by survey results is drawn from our study of suburban schools.

It was our impression that the smaller school district approximated the *Gemeinschaft* form of society, while the larger one was much more bureaucratised, impersonal, up-to-date, that is, a *Gesellschaft* setting. In pursuing the fieldwork, I became more and more convinced that this distinction applied to almost all aspects of the two systems and would be reflected in the attitudes of the participants. The survey seemed to confirm that there was greater social cohesion in the smaller district. When asked how many of the faculty were close personal friends, 21 per cent in the smaller district stated six or more, while only 7 per cent in the other district claimed as many personal friends. But other results upset my expectations. With respect to the perception of red tape ('an excessive number of rules and regulations which hamper the abilities of the staff of my school'), there was no difference. And with respect to the perception of faculty morale and cohesion, the attitudes of the staff in the larger district were clearly more favourable. Overall, there turned out to be many more similarities than differences between the two districts. Apparently, my observation of greater informality among the staff members in the smaller district had led me to assume that morale in general was higher, and that less strain was created by bureaucratic regulations, because of the informal nature of the administration. Thus, the survey made it possible to refine the attitudinal climate so as to disconfirm those impressions that had arisen from the holistic fallacy.

(2) Demonstration of the generality of a single observation

Surveys also afford the means of demonstrating the generality of a single observation. When the observation plays an important role in the theoretical structure of fieldwork, survey data become essential for buttressing the argument. The following illustration is taken from a comparative study of school boards. The field observer was impressed by the superintendents' unwillingness to allow board trustees to discuss educational matters, including those that fell legally within the board's domain. The observation was critical for Kerr's thesis that superintendents sometimes convert the boards into 'legitimating agencies', in order to preserve professional autonomy. Since only two superintendents were observed, Kerr was uncertain as to the generalisability of their attitudes. By referring to the results of a survey conducted among the staff, he was able to show that the resistance to legally constituted lay control was generally held by school administrators:

The superintendents were not the only administrators in the districts who disapproved of the boards' intervention in professional matters which legally came under the boards' jurisdiction. For example, a questionnaire survey in the districts included a question concerning the role that the school board should play in hiring teachers: 'To what extent do you think the following persons or groups *should* influence the selection of new teachers?' (Kerr, 1964, pp. 51–2). Eight out of thirteen administrators in one district and five out of eight in the others replied that the school board should be 'not at all' involved in selecting teachers. Since legally all personnel appointments had to be approved by the board members, the survey finding confirmed the hostility of professional educators to the nominal authority of school trustees. Kerr then showed how this attitude led to manipulative measures in the interest of protecting professional autonomy.

(3) Verification of field interpretations

The verification of observations based on fieldwork is a third major contribution that surveys make to the analysis of field materials. Here, we return to the point made by Webb *et al.* (1966) that multiple techniques are often necessary for the validation of results.

In the course of fieldwork among medical students, Becker *et al.* (1961) were impressed with what they called the 'long-range perspective' of the freshmen students, a perspective characterized by a vague notion of the physician's role and an idealistic view of medicine. According to the researchers, the students conveyed this perspective mainly 'by gesture and tone of voice' and 'the innumerable other nuances of human interaction impossible to record or quantify.' In addition to the field data, however, they had materials from interviews with a random sample. When asked to express their idea of a successful physician, the freshmen rarely mentioned money, and generally responded in ways that reflected an idealistic conception. Also, it was found that the students decided on a medical career at an early age, and learned about the profession from the same sources as the public at large, that is, from movies, books, and from being patients. As the researchers sum up: 'With data from the interviews thus supporting the field work, we conclude that freshmen enter medical school full of enthusiasm, pride, and idealism about the medical profession.' (Becker *et al.*, 1961, p. 79)

(4) The casting of new light on field observations

Survey results can cast a new light on field observations, or more precisely, the serendipitous nature of some survey findings can illuminate a field observation that was hitherto inexplicable or misinterpreted. It is common to think of fieldwork as being more congenial to serendipity than survey work. Sometimes we hear that surveys should be actuated by specific problems or hypotheses, while fieldwork is uniquely qualified for exploratory investigations. But survey analysts make many observations that were unanticipated; and in another context, I argue that surveys are uniquely qualified for the measurement of unanticipated concepts (Schenkel and Sieber, 1969).

The exploratory portion of survey analysis can be exploited for the better understanding of field observations. A simple illustration will suffice. In our study of two suburban districts, it was observed that a smaller proportion of teachers turned out to vote in the bond issue election in the larger district. When this observation was shared with informants, many explanations were offered. We tentatively attributed the poor turnout to the alienation of many teachers in the more bureaucratised system. (We have already seen that this holisitic assumption was challenged by the survey data.) While perusing the distribution of responses to the survey, we noticed with surprise that 39 per cent of the teachers in the larger district resided outside of the district, compared with only 18 per cent in the smaller district. The teachers in the larger district were simply less often legally qualified to vote. The observations of poorer turnout was, therefore, reinterpreted. Moreover, we then began to explore the implications of living inside or outside the district for the teachers' involvement in the affairs of the system and in their relationships with parents.

PROBLEMS OF SCHEDULING

Many of the examples that we have given depend upon a particular time-ordering of field observations and survey work. Thus, the contribution of fieldwork to the formulation of the theoretical structure underlying a survey study requires that the fieldwork be performed prior to designing the survey study. But if the purpose of the fieldwork is to clarify or extend a survey finding, then it must be conducted after the survey. Further, several of our examples depended upon concurrent scheduling of the methods – correction of the elite bias in fieldwork, repeated pretests of a questionnaire and, perhaps, also correction of the holistic fallacy. Further, if the survey investigator is in the field during data collection, he might learn a great deal about the meaning of the survey questionnaire to respondents. To some extent, the 'obtrusiveness' of a questionnaire can be assessed and taken into account in the analyst's interpretations. This latter information is sometimes conveyed to the survey worker by professional interviewers, but firsthand experience with the instrument during its administration is probably also needed. An optimal research schedule, therefore, would entail an interweaving of field observations and survey work over the duration of the project, regardless of the primary method of data collection. (If the techniques were assigned to different staff members having special competencies, the workload on the project director would be lightened.)

The problems of integrating survey and fieldwork are reduced when studying a small number of formally organised collectives, such as schools, since the respondents are clustered within settings having definite boundaries. But even the typical large-scale survey of individuals could be rearranged so as to profit from fieldwork. In the first place, respondents could be selected who are socially related to one another. These networks could then be treated in much the same fashion that a fieldworker deals with a more formal collective. If for some reason this type of survey design

is not feasible, then every *n*th interviewer could be instructed to make certain observations, or to extend the interview into an unstructured format. Such interviewers would have to receive special training in fieldwork, or they might be recruited from among individuals who have specialised in fieldwork in the past.

In other instances, the traditional design of fieldwork might need to be modified to take advantage of a survey. Certain clusters of actors might be identified; then, a large number of such clusters could be selected in order to enhance the usefulness of statistical study. Or networks of relationships could be sought in fieldwork, in order to select individuals who will receive questionnaires. The adjustments in traditional research designs called for by the integration of field and survey methods would seem to produce a new style of research. At present there are far too few examples of this style to adduce general principles to be followed in organising future projects. The task of collecting specimens of projects that have sought to profit from the interplay of fieldwork and surveys, rather than instances bearing on a single aspect of projects, remains for the methodologist of the future – provided that the boundaries between the two traditions are dissolved and attention is turned to their intellectual integration in the interest of improving our strategies of social research.

Notes: Chapter 24

Reprinted from *American Journal of Sociology*, vol. 78, no. 6, 1973, pp. 1335–59, by kind permission of the publisher, University of Chicago Press and the author. © 1973 University of Chicago. We are especially indebted to John D. Ferguson for his stimulating ideas regarding the interplay of fieldwork and surveys.

1   That is, participant observation, informant interviewing and use of available records to supplement these techniques in a particular setting.
2   See Webb *et al.* (1966), pp. 174–5.
3   See Webb *et al.* (1966), p. 1.
4   Catherine Bodard Silver was most helpful in analysing the results of the experiment. We also appreciate the co-operation of George Nash in making available his data.
5   See Lipset (1964), p. 108.
6   See Stinchcombe (1964), pp. 9–10.
7   See Komarovsky (1962), p. 348.
8   See Lazarsfeld and Thielens (1958), p. 269.
9   The term 'interpretive variable', as used here, denotes a variable that intervenes in time between two variables whose relationship is already established.
10   See Kendall and Wolf (1949), pp. 153–4.

Section Seven

Recording Field Data

25

Keeping Field Notes

ROBERT G. BURGESS

Although the results of field experience are formally recorded in the books, monographs and articles that are published by the researcher, there are very few published records of the raw materials out of which research reports are constructed. Until relatively recently few researchers gave direct access to their field notes, diaries, journals, letters, interview transcripts and documents, yet these provide the basic data with which the field researcher works. The result has been that readers of field studies could never be sure what kind of material was initially recorded in the researcher's notebook. However, developments in data analysis, such as the extended case method or situational analysis (Gluckman, 1967; Van Velsen, 1967), have meant that actual situations recorded in field notebooks have found their way into the final analysis. Similarly, many empirical studies provide transcripts of interviews (Nash, 1973; Stimpson and Webb, 1975) and extracts from documentary evidence (Moore, 1974; Wallis, 1976). Readers of field studies can, therefore, compare the data gathered with the inferences that are made. However, the use of particular cases together with detailed illustrations from the researcher's notebook demands that records be kept in meticulous detail (Gluckman, 1961; Epstein, 1967b).

In these circumstances, researchers have to consider what data to select and record, when to record it and how to record it. Some of the basic questions involved have been set out for researchers by Lofland, when he asked a group of colleagues:

> In what manner did you keep field and/or interview notes? Typed? Carbons? Dittoed? What was the rate of data accumulation, or waves of accumulation? What work place isolation or other place and physical devices did you employ to facilitate work on getting down material and working at its analysis?
> How did you file, code or otherwise encode or sort the raw materials you accumulated? Marginal codes? Filing? Other? (Lofland, 1974b, p. 308)

Further questions concerning data recording have been posed by Beatrice and John Whiting (1973) who ask: how should observations be recorded? Should the researcher write down everything that is seen? Should field notes be written in simple language? Should cameras, tape recorders and video tapes be used? These questions are vital, if the researcher is to consider what to select, what to write down, what processes are involved in constructing notes, what types of material are to be recorded. For the recording of field data raises questions on the relationships between data collection, formal and informal theorising, data analysis and the final research report.

Note-taking is a personal activity that depends upon the research context, the objectives of the research and relationships with informants. Nevertheless, there are a series of basic principles of data recording that can be derived from the experiences of researchers who have engaged in observational work and unstructured interviewing. Firstly, a regular time and place should be set aside for writing field notes. Secondly, all field notes should contain date, time, location and details of the main informants. Thirdly, field notes should be written in duplicate or in triplicate, so that an account of a single event or material from a particular interview can be used in different phases of data analysis. Furthermore, additional copies of the field notes and interview transcripts allow different sets to be stored in different places; a precaution against damage and destruction. Fourthly, the researcher needs to consider what is to be recorded and what is to be omitted from field notes and the theoretical criteria that are used to reach these decisions. Finally, field notes can be used to begin data analysis alongside data collection.

One of the best illustrations of how these principles can be embodied in the process of note-taking comes from Beatrice Webb (Chapter 26). Here, she outlines in some detail the way in which she and Sidney Webb developed the art of note-taking as a hallmark of the Webbs' method of social investigation. She indicates that precision, detail, clarity, creativity and analysis are all part of the process of note-taking. This makes note-taking central to the research process, as it marks the beginning of preliminary analysis and theoretical discovery for the researcher.

While Beatrice Webb was concerned with basic principles of note-taking, it is important to appreciate that these principles can be applied to different types of notes. Experienced field researchers indicate that different types of notes may be kept: mental notes, jotted notes and full field notes (Lofland, 1971; Bogdan, 1972; Schatzman and Strauss, 1973; and Bogdan and Taylor, 1975). Full field notes can be established on the basis of the research problem, methodology and the process of theorising. In these circumstances, the researcher can record substantive field notes, methodological field notes and analytic field notes.

Substantive Field Notes

This set of notes will focus on the main observations, conversations and interviews which the researcher makes. Systematic note-taking can include lists of names, dates, places and events. In Pons's study of Kisangani he provides examples of the systematic notes he kept (see Section One, Chapter 5). Here, Pons gives details of the movements of individuals on one of the compounds that he studied in Avenue 21. His systematic notes that included details of the name, age, sex, marital status, tribal origin and kinship relations among those individuals on a compound in addition to their patterns of movement are summarised in Table 5.2. Another example of systematic recording is shown in Humphreys (1970, p. 35), when he reproduces one of the systematic observation sheets which he completed during the course of his field research. Further examples of field notes and interview transcripts are provided by Bittner (1968) and Werthman (1968), respectively. Meanwhile, extracts from field notes are included in the text of several monographs that utlise case materials (Turner, 1957; Kapferer, 1972), when the details of events observed are used in the analysis. In particular, Kapferer's outline of a strike situation (Kapferer,1972, pp. 311–17) highlights the detail which the researcher recorded about what happened, where it happened and when it happened. Such a detailed extract from field notes indicates that the researcher cannot merely record the details of an event, but has to include descriptions of informants, details of their conversation and the actions and reactions of groups and individuals. In short, substantive field notes include a chronological description of events, details of informants and conversations and, in the case of documentary work, details on the content of documents.

Methodological Field Notes

The substantive material often includes details about the circumstances in which the field researcher gathered the data. It is, therefore, important to keep records on personal impressions of situations and personal involvement. Here, the researcher includes details concerning field roles, the selection of informants, relationships with informants and some self-analysis that gives an account of emotional

relationships at various points throughout the research process. While I have termed these records methodological field notes, experienced researchers have recorded their experiences in various ways: as part of their field notes (Geer, 1964); as a separate journal or diary (Malinowski, 1967); and as letters from the field (Mead, 1977). The materials which the field researcher records on methodology are illustrated by Geer, when she remarks in her notes:

7/13/59: I want briefly to take a look at the kind of questions I have been asking and my general goals during this period of field work. First of all, I've been getting background data (on previewers); this is necessary if we are to understand the types of students we are dealing with. Second, I've been trying, evidently to pick up a tremendous body of facts and names, about campus organisations, slang, and customs. This is a natural thing for any field worker, trying to orient himself, to do, and I think it is particularly important in our study if we are to identify groups, as it is by these means that we are able to separate students from each other and recognise them easily and quickly. In other words, if we get all this stuff down we may be able to sort them out without going to such lengthy interviews as this (a three hour talk with a senior).

I seem to have the feeling that information of this kind is necessary in order to be able to find (the boundaries of) groups. I also seem to be developing a technique for next fall in which I talk with a student long enough to get his confidence thoroughly and make plans to meet him next fall and attend some class or activity and get to know his friends. This, I think, will be quite a reasonable way of bounding groups, at the same time learning more about the actual activity.

I think I have developed an impatience as a result of our various theoretical and methodological innovations of last year. I apparently want to go right out and put data into perspectives and tables. I am impatient with the mountain of background information that I must first learn before I can interpret any of this . . . of course, there are repeats and reiterations coming already, and these are the material of perspectives. At the same time, an outline of the place is forming in my mind, a kind of topographical map in which it becomes more and more easy to locate what the various students say to me. (Geer, 1964, pp. 326–7)

Here, the researcher uses methodological notes to reflect on her research experience, to focus on her research problem, and to consider questions relating to the selection of informants and the development of field roles.

Researchers who write separate diaries utilise them for self-expression, self-exploration and self-analysis.

The extract from Malinowski's diary (Chapter 27) gives a different view of the great researcher doing fieldwork, disliking natives, and listening to the *Fidelio Overture* while pawing native girls. The extract highlights his relationships with his informants, his physical, mental and social conditions in the field, and indicates the personal difficulties that he encountered in doing research. In particular, Malinowski's diary provides a different account of his field activities (cf. Malinowski, 1922, pp. 4–25) that allows us to review his substantive materials from another perspective.

Finally, a further firsthand account of the processes involved in doing field research comes from the letters of Margaret Mead (1977). Her letters contain reflections on field experiences that bring aspects of her personal life to view. These letters have much in common with Geer's methodological field notes and Malinowski's diary, as letter-writing provided Mead with an opportunity to analyse her own activities. In these circumstances, researchers might consider the range of formal and informal documents that they produce while recording their activities in the field.

Analytic Field Notes

Field research involves the simultaneous collection and analysis of data. In this respect, it is important that field notes provide some form of preliminary analysis. Various writers have indicated how their preliminary analysis took the form of questions and queries posed in the course of research (Geer, 1964; Pons, 1969). Geer examines the way in which working hypotheses were developed within her field notes. Field notes can, therefore, include brief indicators to the researcher about topics that can be developed, themes that can be explored and brief details of analysis, (Nash, 1973). If these notes are included within the main substantive field notes, it is essential for the researcher to indicate that these are personal analyses, so that they are clearly distinguished from the questions, queries and analyses of situations that are often provided by informants.

In addition, the researcher has to code and classify field notes as the research proceeds (Wolff, 1960). Such work can lead to the researcher using particular materials, examining particular themes and developing substantive theories from the data that have been gathered. This process can be conducted through memo-writing (Glaser and Strauss, 1967; Schatzman and Strauss, 1973), whereby the researcher codes the data and begins to develop substantive and formal theories. However, such activities may take many years.

The note-taking that is done by the field researcher covers all aspects of field research: substantive, methodological and theoretical. In short, field notes are the basis of all field research. However, in recent years field research has undergone a 'revolution' in data recording, as notebook and pencil have been comple-mented and in rare cases replaced by the tape recorder and the camera. The basic principles involved in note-taking equally apply to tape recordings and photographs. It is essential that researchers consider when to record, where to record and how to record. In addition, Mead suggests that 'at any point the technology of field work is related to the art of field work, and this in turn with the mental and physical well being of the individual field worker' (Mead, 1973, p. 250). In this respect, tape recorders and cameras cannot be super-imposed on any field setting, as the researcher has to consider the advantages and disadvantages of these instruments in relation to the field context, the informants and the process of data collection and analysis. Epstein (1967b) has argued against the use of tape recorders in particular settings, as they cannot provide the detail that is required for data analysis. Furthermore, if tape recorders are used, transcriptions have to be quickly produced, so that researchers can sift their notes, reflect on their experiences and pose questions about their data. Yet transcription work is notoriously slow and technically difficult. Tape recording is, therefore, not the new panacea for field researchers. Meanwhile, if photographic evidence is used, questions concerning the selection and significance of photographs are involved (Becker, 1980), as they do not overcome the problems of observation (Collier, 1967). More often, photographs are used to complement observations, with the result that the researcher has to consider how to co-ordinate photographs and field notes (Collier, 1957; Berger and Mohr, 1967; 1975).

Field researchers produce their own documentation in the form of notes, diaries, interview transcripts, photographs, tape and video recordings. Certainly, field notes including journals and diaries are essential, as are maps, diagrams, plans and photographs. Nevertheless, no matter what records are kept by the researcher, it is essential for them to be maintained systematically, as the record of field experiences are the detail out of which theoretical, methodological and substantive discussions are constructed in the final research report.

Suggestions for Further Reading

METHODOLOGY

Becker, H. S. (1980), 'Aesthetics and truth', *Transaction*, vol. 17, no. 5, pp. 26–8; discusses questions that can be raised on the use of photographs.

Bittner, E. (1968), 'Keeping the peace in skid row', in A. L. Strauss (ed.), *The American City: a Sourcebook of Urban Imagery* (London: Allen Lane), pp. 277–84; provides excerpts from Bittner's field diary when on patrol with policemen in Denver's skid row.

Bogdan, R. and Taylor, S. J. (1975), *Introduction to Qualitative Research Methods* (New York: Wiley); contains a useful section on field notes, together with a series of extracts from field notes in an appendix (pp. 225–36).

Collier, J. (1967), *Visual Anthropology: Photography as a Research Tool* (New York: Holt, Rinehart & Winston); provides an introduction to photographic techniques – written from an anthropological perspective.

Geer, B. (1964), 'First days in the field', in P. Hammond (ed.), *Sociologists at Work* (New York: Basic Books), pp. 322–44; contains numerous extracts from field notes that are used in an analytic way. This article deserves careful study.

Malinowski, B. (1967), *A Diary in the Strict Sense of the Term* (London: Routledge & Kegan Paul). A book that provides a different view of the great anthropologist. Useful to compare what he actually did as opposed to what he claimed he had done when his monographs were first published.

Mead, M. (1977), *Letters from the Field, 1925–1975* (New York: Harper & Row). A series of letters written to friends and relatives that reveal the researcher's field experiences.

Okely, J. (1975), 'The self and scientism', *Journal of the Anthropological Society of Oxford*, vol. VI, no. 3, pp. 171–88. Useful discussion of self-consciousness in field research and the uses of a diary.

Roth, J. A. (1974), 'Turning adversity to account', *Urban Life and Culture*, vol. 3, no. 3, pp. 347–59; discusses the processes of note-taking, analysis and report-writing with specific reference to Roth's monograph, *Timetables* (Roth, 1963).

Walker, R. and Adelman, C. (1975), *A Guide to Classroom Observation* (London: Methuen). A handbook originally designed for student teachers, although it provides useful material for field researchers. It contains a guide to the different methods that can be used to record observations: tape, videotape, slides and photographs.

Webb, B. (1926), *My Apprenticeship* (London: Longmans, Green). An autobiographical account of a field researcher.

Werthman, C. (1968), 'The police as perceived by negro boys', in A. L. Strauss (ed.), *The American City: a Sourcebook of Urban Imagery* (London: Allen Lane), pp. 285–87; consists of a series of extracts from interviews with black and Mexican boys.

EMPIRICAL STUDIES

A series of studies that use field notes and records and provide extracts from field notebooks are:

Fletcher, C. (1974), *Beneath the Surface* (London: Routledge & Kegan Paul) (see Part Two, Chapter 5).

Humphreys, L. (1970), *Tearoom Trade* (London: Duckworth) (see the verbatim accounts taken from observation sheets).

Kapferer, B. (1972), *Strategy and Transaction in an African Factory* (Manchester: University of Manchester Press).

Pons, V. (1969), *Stanleyville: an African Urban Community under Belgian Administration* (London: OUP for the International African Institute) (see part 3 and the appendices).

Turner, V. W. (1957), *Schism and Continuity in an African Society: a Study of Ndembu Village Life* (Manchester: Manchester University Press for the Institute of African Studies, University of Zambia).

For studies that use visual material in anthropological and sociological field research, see:

Bateson, G. and Mead, M. (1942), *Balinese Character: a Photographic Analysis* (New York: New York Academy of Sciences).

Berger, J. and Mohr, J. (1967), *A Fortunate Man: the Story of a Country Doctor* (London: Allen Lane).

Berger, J. and Mohr, J. (1975), *A Seventh Man: a Book of Images and Words about the Experiences of Migrant Workers in Europe* (Harmondsworth: Penguin).

Marsden, D. and Duff, E. (1975), *Workers: Some Uemployed Men and their Families* (Harmondsworth: Penguin).

Mead, M. and Macgregor, F. C. (1951), *Growth and Culture: a Photographic Study of Balinese Character* (New York: Putman).

26

The Art of Note-Taking

BEATRICE WEBB

It is difficult to persuade the accomplished graduate of Oxford or Cambridge that an indispensable instrument in the technique of sociological inquiry – seeing that without it any of the methods of acquiring facts can seldom be used effectively – is the making of notes, or what the French call 'fiches'.[1] For a highly elaborated and skilled process of 'making notes', besides its obvious use in recording observations which would otherwise be forgotten, is actually an instrument of discovery. This process serves a similar purpose in sociology to that of the blowpipe and the balance in chemistry, or the prism and the electroscope in physics. That is to say, it enables the scientific worker to break up his subject matter, so as to isolate and examine at his leisure its various component parts, and to recombine them in new and experimental groupings in order to discover which sequences of events have a causal significance. To put it paradoxically, by exercising your reason on the separate facts displayed, in an appropriate way, on hundreds, perhaps thousands, of separate pieces of paper, you may discover which of a series of hypotheses best explains the processes underlying the rise, growth, change, or decay of a given social institution, or the character of the actions and reactions of different elements of a given social environment. The truth of one of the hypotheses may be proved, by significant correspondences and differences, to be the order of thought that most closely corresponds with the order of things.

The simplest and most direct way of bringing home to the reader the truth of this dogmatic assertion of the scientific value of note-taking in sociological investigation will be first to describe the technique, and then to point out its uses. Now, it may seem a trivial matter, but the first item in the recipe for scientific note-taking is that the student must be provided not with a notebook of any sort or kind, but with an indefinite number of separate sheets of paper of identical shape and size (I have found large quarto the most convenient form), and of sufficient good quality for either pen, or typewriter. The reason why detached sheets must be employed, instead of any book, is, as I shall presently demonstrate, the absolute necessity of being able to rearrange the notes in different order; in fact, to be able to shuffle and reshuffle them indefinitely, and to change the classification of the facts recorded on them, according to the various hypotheses with which you will need to compare these facts. Another reason against the notebook is that notes recorded in a book must necessarily be entered in the order in which they are obtained; and it is vitally important to be set free from the particular category in which you have found any particular set of facts, whether of time or place, sequence or co-existence. In sociology, as in mineralogy, 'conglomerates' have always to be broken up, and the ingredients separately dealt with.

Upon the separate sheets should be clearly written, so that other persons can read them, and according to a carefully devised system, with as much precision as possible, and in sufficient detail, a statement of each of the facts, or assumed facts, whether the knowledge of them has been acquired by personal observation, by the use of documents, by the perusal of literature, by the formal taking of evidence, by the interview, or by the statistical method, or in any other way. A good deal of the ease and rapidity of the investigation, and no small part of its fruitfulness and success, will depend on the way in which the notes are – to use a printer's word – displayed; and our experience suggests the following rules.

On each sheet of paper there should appear one date, and one only; one place, and one only; one source of information, and one only. Less easy of exact application, because less definite, and more dependent on the form of the provisional breaking up and classification of the facts, is the rule that only one subject, or one category of facts, even only a single fact, should be recorded on each sheet. Of almost equal importance with this primary axiom of 'one sheet, one subject matter' – we may almost say 'one sheet, one event in time and space' – is the manner in which the fact is 'displayed' on the paper. Here, what is of importance is identity of plan among all the hundreds, or even thousands, of notes. The date (in the history of institutions usually the year suffices) should always appear in the same place on all the sheets – say, at the right-hand top corner of the paper; and the source of information, or authority for the statement, in the left-hand margin. The centre of the sheet will be occupied by the text of the note, that is, the main statement or description of the fact recorded, whether it be a personal observation of your own, an extract from a document, a quotation from some literary source, an answer given in evidence, or a statistical calculation or table of figures. Some of the sheets may record suggested hypotheses, for subsequent comparison with the facts; or even a 'general impression', or a summary of a group of facts, given in addition to a note of each of the facts themselves. On what part of the sheet to write the name of the place at which the event occurred, and the various headings and subheadings to be added by way of classification, constitutes the central puzzle-question with which the sociological investigator is confronted in devising the system for his note-taking. This cannot be definitely determined, in any elaborate or extensive investigation, except in conjunction with the principal classification or the successive classifications that may be adopted during the inquiry. Assuming that the investigation is concerned with all the social institutions of one place, and with no other places, the name of the place can, of course, be taken for granted, and not recorded on the innumerable sheets (except in so far as it may be necessary for the convenience of other persons using the same notes, when it may be given by the use of an india-rubber stamp once for all). In such an investigation the principal heading, to be placed in the centre of the top of the sheet, may be the name or title of the particular institution to which the note relates, while the subheading (which can be best put immediately under the date on the right-hand side) may denote the particular aspect of the institution dealt with, whether it be, for instance, some feature of its constitutional structure, or some incident of its activities. If, on the other hand, the investigation is concerned with social institutions in different places, the name of the place at which each event takes place becomes an essential item of the record, and it should be placed in a prominent position, either in the centre of the page at the top, or as the first subheading on the right-hand side beneath the date. The one consideration to be constantly kept in view, in this preliminary task of deciding how to record the facts that constitute the subject matter of the inquiry, is so to place the different items of the record – the what, the where, the when and the classification or relationship – that in glancing rapidly through a number of sheets the eye catches automatically each of these aspects of the facts. Thus, a carefully planned 'display' and, above all, identity of arrangement, greatly facilitates the shuffling and reshuffling of the sheets, according as it is desired to bring the facts under review in an arrangement according to place, time, or any other grouping. It is, indeed, not too much to say that this merely mechanical perfection of note-taking may become an instrument of actual discovery.

'What is the use of this pedantic method of note-taking, involving masses of paper and a lot of hard thinking, not to mention the shuffling and reshuffling,

which is apparently the final cause of this intolerable elaboration?' will be asked by the postgraduate student eager to publish an epoch-making treatise on the *History of Government*, or perchance, on the *History of Freedom*, within the two years he has allotted to the taking of his doctorate. The only answer I can give is to cite our own experience.

The 'Webb speciality' has been a study, at once historical and analytic, of the life history of particular forms of social organisation within the United Kingdom, such as the trade union and co-operative movements, and English local government from the seventeenth to the end of the nineteenth century. In these successive tasks we have been confronted, not with constitution and activities of one organisation, in one particular year, in one part of the kingdom; but with a multiplicity of organisations, belonging, it is true, to the same genus or species, but arising, flourishing and disappearing in diverse social environments, at different intervals throughout a considerable period of time, exhibiting a great variety of constitutions and functions, subject to successive waves of thought and emotion, and developing relations with other institutions or organisations within the British and, in some cases, within the world community. The task before us was to discover, for instance, in the tangled and complicated undergrowth of English local government, the recurrent uniformities in constitution and activities showing the main lines of development, together with the varieties in structure and function arising in particular places, in particular decades, or within peculiar social environments; some to survive and multiply, others to decay and disappear. The main sources of our information were, as it happens, records and persons located in the cities and villages of England and Wales, sources which, for reasons of time and expense, had each to be exhausted in one visit. But even if all this mass of manuscripts and printed records, and the hundreds of separate individuals concerned, had been continuously at our disposal, whenever we cared to consult them, it would still have been desirable to adopt a method of note-taking which would allow of a mechanical breaking up of the conglomerate of facts yielded by particular documents, interviews and observations, in order to reassemble them in a new order revealing causal sequences, and capable of literary expression. The simplest (and usually the least fertile) way of expressing the results of an investigation is to follow the strictly chronological order in which the events occur not according to their causal connections with other events, but exclusively according to the dates of their happening. But even for this narrow purpose the conglomerate notebook is an impossible instrument,[2] unless the subject matter happens to be the life history of a single organisation, the data for which are all to be found in one document, and are themselves given in that document in strictly chronological order. In our investigations, dealing as they did with the life history of hundreds of separate organisations, the data for which were to be found in innumerable separate documents, pamphlets, newspapers, or books, or were discovered in many observations and interviews, the conglomerate notebook system would have involved disentangling and rewriting, from all the separate notebooks, every note relating to a particular year. By adopting our method of one sheet for one subject, one place and one date, all the sheets could be rapidly reshuffled in chronological order; and the whole of our material might have been surveyed and summarised exclusively from the standpoint of chronology. But, as a matter of fact, we had to use the facts gathered from all these sources not for one purpose only, but for many purposes: for describing changes in the constitutional form, or the increase or variation in the activities of the organisation; or the localisation of particular constitutions or activities in particular areas, or the connection of any of these groups of facts with other groups of facts. By the method of note-taking that I have described, it was practicable to sort out all our thousands of separate pieces of paper according to any, or successively according to all, of these categories or combination of categories, so that we could see, almost at a glance, to what extent the thousands of vestries which served as local authorities in the eighteenth and early nineteenth centuries were entangled in the court leet structure; in what particular year they began to apply for Acts of Parliament closing or opening their constitutions; whether this constitutional development was equally characteristic of the statutory bodies of commissioners set up during the latter part of the eighteenth century and the early part of the nineteenth century; whether, when and why exactly the referendum and initiative were introduced and for what purpose; or at what stage of development and under what set of conditions all these authorities ceased to rely on the obligatory services of citizens and began to employ persons at wages. Or to take an example from our investigations into trade unionism. It was only by arranging and rearranging our separate sheets of paper that we could ascertain how far piecework, or the objection to piecework, was characteristic of a particular type of industry, or of a particular type of trade union, or of a particular district of the United Kingdom, or of a particular stage of development in the organisation concerned, or of the movement as a whole. Indeed, it is not too much to say that in all our work we have found this process of reshuffling the sheets, and reassembling them on our worktable according to different categories, or in different sequences – a process entirely dependent on the method of note-taking – by far the most fertile stage of our investigations. Not once, but frequently has the general impression with regard to the causal sequence of events, with which we had started our inquiry, or which had arisen spontaneously during the examination of documents, the taking of evidence or the observation of the working of an organisation, been

seriously modified, or completely reversed, when we have been simultaneously confronted by all the separate notes relating to the point at issue. On many occasions we have been compelled to break off the writing of a particular chapter, or even of a particular paragraph, in order to test, by reshuffling the whole of our notes dealing with a particular subject, a particular place, a particular organisation, or a particular date, the relative validity of hypotheses as to cause and effect. I may remark, parenthetically, that we have found this 'game with reality', this building up of one hypothesis and knocking it down in favour of others that had been revealed or verified by a new shuffle of the notes – especially when we severally 'backed' rival hypotheses – a most stimulating recreation. In that way alone have we been able 'to put our bias out of gear', and to make our order of thought correspond not with our own prepossessions, but with the order of things discovered by our investigations.

I realise how difficult it is to convince students – especially those with a 'literary' rather than a 'scientific' training – that it is by just this use of such a mechanical device as the shuffling of sheets of notes, and just at this stage, that the process of investigation often becomes fertile in actual discoveries. Most students seem to assume that it is the previous stage of making observations and taking notes which is that of discovery. I can only speak from our own experience, of which I will give two examples. When we had actually completed and published our *History of Trade Unionism* (Webb and Webb, 1894), after three or four years' collection of facts from all industries in all parts of the kingdom, which we had arranged more or less chronologically, we found to our surprise that we had no systematic and definite theory or vision of how trade unionism operated, or what it effected. It was not until we had completely resorted all our innumerable sheets of paper according to subjects, thus bringing together all the facts relating to each, whatever the trade concerned, or the place or the date – and had shuffled and reshuffled these sheets according to various tentative hypotheses – that a clear, comprehensive and verifiable theory of the working and results of trade unionism emerged in our minds; to be embodied, after further researches by way of verification, in our *Industrial Democracy* (Webb and Webb, 1897).

A further instance occurred in connection with my work on the Poor Law Commission. It had been commonly assumed on all sides that the Local Government Board and its predecessors had continued throughout to administer the 'principles of 1834'. On my insisting upon an actual examination of the policy pursued through the seventy years, I was deputed by the commission to examine and report what had actually been the policy. This involved the examination of every manifestation of policy, such as the successive statutes, general orders, special orders, circulars, and so on, numbering in all some thousands. These were all analysed by subjects, on separate sheets of paper, under my direction. To these data was added an analysis of the letters of the Local Government Board, from 1835 to 1907, addressed to a dozen of the principal Boards of Guardians (an analysis made by permission of these authorities from their letterbooks), as well as their records of the inspectors' verbal decisions and advice to guardians. When the task was completed neither the able assistants who had done the work, nor I who had directed it, had the least idea what the policy on each subject had been at each period. It was not until the sheets had been sorted out, first according to subjects, and then according to date, that the fact and the nature of a continuous but gradual evolution of policy could be detected, differing from class to class of paupers; until 1907, each class had come to be dealt with according to principles which were obviously very different from those of 1834. The report of this investigation was presented to the Poor Law Commission, with the interesting result that we heard no more of the 'principles of 1834'! It was subsequently published as *English Poor Law Policy* (Webb and Webb, 1910). I append two samples of our sheets of notes; one recording an interview, and the other an extract from an official document.

NEWCASTLE

Town Council

Interview:

Rodgers, Town Councillor and Chairman Board of Governors

1900
Audit

Got himself elected People's Auditor about 1887, in order to exclude a worthless man. For many years the Auditors had been reelected without question – in 1886 (?) a worthless man, who lived by his wits, got himself nominated at last moment, on the chance of the existing holders not taking the trouble to be formally nominated. And so got elected, for the sake of the small emolument.

Rodgers, then on the *Evening News*, got himself nominated the following year, & held it for 5 years. Found out many irregularities, which he exposed in *Evening News* – principal being the failure to collect the contributions of owners towards Private Improvements (paving streets) – there was £40,000 outstanding, on which owners were paying no interest, whilst Corpor^n was borrowing the money at interest. Corporation then turned him out of the Auditorship. He had had to fight the election every year, and lost it at last.

Recently he had been elected a Councillor. Was not satisfied with the way the business was done. Would prefer L.G.B. audit.

NEWCASTLE

Town Council

1892
Committee's
Newcastle Imp. Act 1892.

Proceedings.
Aug. 4. 1892. p. 568.

Council resolves:

'That the powers & duties of the Council under Part 9, (Sanitary Provisions), 'Part 10, (Infectious Diseases) and Part 11 (Common Lodging Houses) of the 'N'castle-upon-T. Improvement Act 1892 be delegated to the Sanitary C'tee until '9 Novr next or until the Council otherwise direct.'

Similarly, Powers relating to Streets, Buildings, and Plans are delegated to Town Imp. Ctee.

Notes: Chapter 26

Reprinted from Beatrice Webb, *My Apprenticeship* (London: Longmans, Green, 1926a), pp. 364–72, by kind permission of the London School of Economics and Political Science.©1967 London School of Economics and Political Science.

1   The art of note-taking has been recognised by German and French historians alike as necessary to the scientific historian. 'Every one agrees nowadays', observe the most noted French writers on the study of history, 'that it is advisable to collect materials on separate cards or slips of paper . . . The advantages of this artifice are obvious; the detachability of the slips enables us to group them at will in a host of different combinations; if necessary, to change their places; it is easy to bring texts of the same kind together, and to incorporate additions as they are acquired, in the interior of the groups to which they belong' (Langlois and Seignobos, 1898), p. 103. 'If what is in question', states the most learned German methodologist, 'is a many-sided subject, such as a history of a people or a great organisation, the several sheets of notes must be so arranged that for each aspect of the subject the material can be surveyed as a whole. With any considerable work the notes must be taken upon separate loose sheets, which can easily be arranged in different orders, and among which sheets with new dates can be interpolated without difficulty' (Bernheim, 1908), p. 555.

2   An instance may be given of the necessity of the 'separate-sheet' system. Among the many sources of information from which we constructed our book, *The Manor and the Borough* (Webb and Webb, 1908), were the hundreds of reports on particular boroughs made by the Municipal Corporation Commissioners in 1835. These four huge volumes are well arranged and very fully indexed; they were in our own possession; we had read them through more than once; and we had repeatedly consulted them on particular points. We had, in fact, used them as if they had been our own bound notebooks, thinking that this would suffice. But, in the end, we found ourselves quite unable to digest and utilise this material until we had written out every one of the innumerable facts on a separate sheet of paper, so as to allow of the mechanical absorption of these sheets among our other notes; of their complete assortment by subjects; and of their being shuffled and reshuffled to test hypotheses as to suggested co-existences and sequences.

27

The Diary of an Anthropologist

BRONISLAW MALINOWSKI

Wednesday, 4.11 [sic]: First half of day in Gusaweta; normal routine: got up late after bad night, had conversations with Bill about photography, etc. Examined films (after breakfast), cleaned camera, finished developing. Washed and shampooed. At 1 ready to leave; rain; wrote E. R. M.[1] All that morning I was energetic, felt well, in love with E. R. M. – In the afternoon, instead of reading novel or idling, I read my old diary. Reflections: I asked myself whether my present life achieves the maximum of intensity obtainable in view of my health and good nervous condition. *No*:[2] I interpreted the doctrine that best work is done during *leisure hours* as doctrine of following line of least resistance, as *taking it easy.* Doubts à la S. I. W. [Stanislaw I. Witkiewicz][3] – is it worth while to eliminate fruitful sources of inspiration (which every thinker and artist will find by following the line of least resistance)? But it is a fact that when you eliminate one form of inspiration you gain another, and that to eliminate line of least resistance is above all to eliminate *pure* waste of time (reading novels, sitting *extra long* in company, etc.). For instance, my present mode of life: I turn in too late, I get up at irregular hours. Too little time devoted to observation, contact with natives, too much to barren collecting of information. I rest too frequently, and indulge in 'demoralization' (e.g., in Nabwageta). I also thought about problems of keeping a diary. How immensely difficult it is to formulate the endless variety of things in the current of a life. Keeping a diary as a problem of psychological analysis: to isolate the essential elements, to classify them (from what point of view?), then, in describing them indicate more or less clearly what is their actual importance at the given moment, proportion; my subjective reaction, etc. For instance, yesterday afternoon: First version: 'I went to Sinaketa in Raf.'s *waga.*'[4] (I could give hundreds of examples of such versions.) Second version: (a) external impressions; landscape, colors, mood, artistic synthesis; (b) dominant feelings in respect to myself, to my beloved, to friends, to things; (c) forms of thought; specific thoughts, [programs], loose associations; obsessions; (d) dynamic states of the organism; degree of concentration; degree of higher awareness; [resulting] programs. – Concretely: (a) after departure from Gusaweta (I had a comfortable seat, the *waga* was heavy and *stable*), gray and dark blue clouds. Definition of the mood created by the flat *coastline* of Losuya, Kavataria: 'afternoon holiday mood and rest' (*a smiling relaxation and promise of changes*); flat and long coastline indented by shallow bays; today *jet-black under the luminous distant clouds and a clear dark blue sky with the characteristic appearance of emptiness – like a blackened-sky effect in an old master.* Then the landscape disappears; I read the diary, sailing between mangroves. Then the green lagoon of Oburaku. Oh yes, Boymapo'u *manche*: the water *dun-colored* with intense violet reflections (the dark-blue of the clouds blending with water). Oburaku lagoon: *mat, pale green, like a naked chrysoprase, on that, the intense violet; above, dark blue clouds and intense goldish green mangroves and other trees.* (b) Feelings for E. R. M. steady, am continually referring to her, but I am above all alone. I am entirely caught up in creative thoughts, seized by a wave of concentration. (c) Clearly defined ideas: the nature of psychology and to what extent introspective analysis modifies psychic states; also, is introspective analysis discredited because it modifies states? – Historical problems (?) – associations: memories of my life in Samarai; memories of Paul and Hedy[5] suddenly come to me out of nowhere. (d) Dynamically, I am in a state of concentration; I resolve not to read novels, to go to bed and get up at regular hours, to write letter to N.S., to write regularly, every day, to E. R. M.; to attain absolute mental faithfulness to her, as well as to aim at achieving 'a strong will' in the sense I gave this term previously.

After nightfall, took the boat out, punted for about 45 minutes. Then I sat watching the phosphorescent fish in the water, got two fish out of the boat. Planned trip to Vakuta[6] and work there. Arrival: Ted gone. Supper with Raf. Reading of [Musset]. My attitude was much more objective than before: I stayed *in my shell* and looked more critically at Raffael, but not without sympathy. Formula: I clearly see differences in our outlook – his ideas which I don't accept, which is *ein überwundener Standpunkt* [a point of view I have left behind] – but I check my impulse to discuss them.

Thursday, 4.12 [sic]: All day long I was in a mood of

concentration. After writing diary, I worked with Layseta.[7] After lunch, read bits of Australian poems in *Memorial for Fallen Soldiers,* and worked with another fellow here on the veranda. Both times on *kula.*[8] At 5, to see Kouta'uya;[9] spent an hour copying the list of his *karayta'u.*[10] Then at the Raffaels';[11] talked with natives; *conjuring tricks.* Moral tenets: I must never let myself become aware of the fact that other women have bodies, that they copulate. I also resolve to shun the line of least resistance in the matter of novels. I am very content that I have not fallen again into the habit of smoking. Now I must accomplish the same thing in respect to reading. I may read poems and serious things, but I must absolutely avoid trashy novels. And I *should*[12] read ethnographic works.

4.13: [*sic*]: We planned lunch together, photography, and croquet. This morning I resolve: before 10 write a few lines to E. R. M. Then 2 hours of preliminary ethnographic work. Describe *kula* for E. R. M. and make list of problems raised by *kula.* – From 10 to 12.45: I looked over notes on *kula* and copied them for E. R. M. Lunch at the Raffaels', taking pictures; I examined pearls. Came back at 3, again busied myself with *kula,* then the *boys* from Kitava came. Went again to see Kouta'uya and worked fairly well despite the sluggishness of these fellows. Then talked with a couple of fellows from Kitava on the beach. Wondered whether it would pay to go with them to Vakuta. Decided I would go. – Evening at the Raffaels'. We discussed the Germans – are they *ahead in science*? We talked about Giligili and Wright, Solomon, and other people from Samarai. Moment of heightened sympathy, when he spoke about *'looking through' a person.* He asked me whether I did this; I said, Of course I do, just like you. Then I mixed lemonade and we drank [. . .] Oh yes, also a very personal conversation about Sam's marriage and the influence of Emma. – Went back, wrote E. R. M. At night awakened by storm and nasty thunder. Terribly frightened; for a moment I thought I might never see E. R. M. again and this thought created fear. I thought about C. E. M. and how terrible death must have been for him. My precious, marvelous Elsie.

4.14: Saturday [*sic*]: In the morning sky overcast, rain. Woke up late; under the netting a tendency to let myself go, as usual, which I mastered. Planned details of excursion to Kitava, and thought about documenting *kula.* – I got ready. Wrote down conversations; *mail* to Samarai; finished letter to E. R. M. At 12:30 went to the village; conversation with Kwaywaya,[13] Toudawada, & Co. They refused to take me to Vakuta. Lunch at Raffael's; he showed me his *blisters* [blister pearls]. Came back; at 4:30 went out, made drawings of boats until 6:30. Then to Raffael's. We talked about the *natives:* their 'specific weight'; their ideas about causes of natural phenomena – he didn't know about

kariyala.[14] In the evening we talked about suicide *by means of tuva,*[15] *chagrin d'amour,* etc. Jealousy among natives (a married woman betrayed by husband takes *tuva* – is this suicide out of love?). Then we read *Phèdre.*

Sunday, 4.15 [*sic*]. Awakened by Vakuta people; the *waga* waiting for me. On the principle that it is better to visit the same place twice, I decided to go to Vakuta for a week. – I packed (unpleasant clash with Ginger *à propos* of termites; I was enraged and punched him on the jaw once or twice, but all the time I was scared, afraid this might degenerate into a brawl). Lunch at Raffael's. He showed me his pearls. I told him about my plans for a dictionary. Went back to the boat; but felt poorly. Talked a bit with the Vakuta people; but it was raining. Then, tired by talk, read *Lettres persanes,* but I found none of the ideas I was looking for, only lewd descriptions of harems . . . Night fell, behind Muwa. Arrival in Giribwa around 9. Slept in a new house. Again read *Lettres persanes* . . .

Landschaftlich [notes on landscape]: After leaving Sinaketa we sailed fairly close to the shore. In spots, tall trees on a bit of beach; elsewhere, jagged, dried *scrub* with the white arms of little boughs cutting across the green in many places – 'a disorderly mixture' is a better description. In spots, a low stretch of mangroves, and woods above. In the distance, Kayleula submerged in water; lagoons on the north shore. On the horizon, Kuyuwaywo, Yaga. From afar, we see [a drawing of the shoreline in the manuscript], as if suspended between sea and sky, Gumasila and Domdom. The overcast gray sky falls like a curtain on the flat shores and shuts them off, turning them into a specific melancholy wilderness. Between Muwa and the shore a long, narrow *karikeda.*[16] The tall trees of Muwa over the narrow stretch of land (weightless shapes, floating rather than set on any foundation) bring to mind the atmosphere of the Vistula; pushing the ship off the sandbar at Susuwa [Beach] – *generic name for a series of shallow bays and forelands.* Then night; I can't make out details but obviously the *raybwag* is close. Water plashing against stone, the shadow grows *more solid and high, instead of the choral croaking of frogs, the first chirping of crickets.* Rain more and more threatening, finally begins to fall. Marvelous points of phosphorescence emerging to the surface of the sea. Giribwa and the fairylike promontory of Vakuta. *The flat belt shown by an island or continent, like the face of a man, hiding and symbolizing his personality. First impression which can never be the real,* [to] *unveil the whole is nonetheless provoking and irritating.*

Monday, 4.16 [actually, 4.15]: In the morning, pouring rain. Curious effect: yellow (bright) sand. A group of boats from Kitava, and on this side, right beside them, on the sand, mats spread out, huddled bodies of people sleeping or cooking food underneath. All this glows in deep dull red against the bright green sea with blue reflections under the gray sky. I took a walk through the little villages – 11 huts and a couple of *bwaymas*[17] scattered pell-mell on the sand. [I went] toward the sea (my eyes and head ache); view of Kitava; two currents collide against the isthmus and form little foamy waves. Rain over Kitava. Looked at the bouquet of trees very tropically merged with the profiles of the rocks on the opposite shore. – They tell me about a *lili'u*[18] of the fish Baibai. Then to Vakuta; the clear bottom of the sea. They show me mythical stones. Headache (seasickness); I lay down and dozed. Shallow muddy waters, mangroves. We enter the *waya* [tidal creek] floating amid open watery clearings in the mangrove. The *waga* passes among the trees. *Headwater pool*; *wagas* from Kitava. Headache dominant. Walk; I arrange the house here, sleep till 6. Walk toward Kaulaka. Planning my work here. Thought of Melbourne, longed for it. Went back: the village by gentle moonlight; voices of the people; smoke surrounds the houses like a cloud and blots out the tree trunks. The tops of the palms seem suspended in the sky. Mood of return to a human environment, a peaceful village. Thought of E. R. M., of returning to Melb. [. . .] F. T. G. The mysteriousness of condensed life; artificial intensity and absurd lighting. – In the evening I sat with Kouligaga and Petai surrounded by a circle of onlookers, and we talked, the light of the lamp falling on the broad ornamented front of the *lisiga*[19] where K. with his wife sat higher up. A group of people in *buneyana*. – At night rain, insomnia; thought of *N*. [circled letter] and Tośka with sensual regret, for that which will never come back. Thought about Poland, about 'Polish woman'; for the first time deep regret that E. R. M. is not Polish. But I rejected the idea that perhaps our engagement is not definitive. I shall go back to Poland and my children will be Poles.

Tuesday, 4.17 [*sic*]: Over-all mood: strong nervous excitement and intellectual intensity on the surface, combined with inability to concentrate, *superirritability and supersensitiveness of mental epidermis and feeling of permanently being exposed in an uncomf. position to the eyes of a crowded thoroughfare: an incapacity to achieve inner privacy.* I am on a war footing with my *boys* (i.e., with Ginger), and the Vakuta people irritate me with their insolence and cheekiness, although they are fairly helpful to my work. Still making plans for subjugating Ginger, and still irritated with him. About Elsie I think constantly, and I feel *settled down*. I look at the slender, agile bodies of little girls in the village and I long – not for them, but for her.

    Events: In the morning watched the farewells of the Kitava people. After breakfast, it was too noisy here; I went to the village, talked with Samson, Kouligaga, and others. Rain. After lunch (during which I also talked) *kabitam*,[20] I went to the boats, copied the designs; rain abated. Came back, wrote a bit, then went to Kaulaka.

Formulated problems, especially those of *kabitam*. – Kaulaka is a poetic village in a long hollow amid palm trees, a kind of sacred grove. – The pleasure of new impressions – unsettled consciousness, where waves of new things, each with its well-defined individuality, flow from all sides, *break against each other, mix, and vanish*. A pleasure like that of listening to a new piece of music, or experiencing a new love: the promise of new experiences. Sat in *Lauriu*, drank *coconut* milk; they told me about *Puwari*. – Went back with Ogisa; clouds threatening; I walked fast without thinking about anything definite. Four eggs for supper; then again to the village; talked about *kula* with Petai. Sleepless night; continuous rain, nervous excitement, itch in big toe (a new form of psychopathological obsession) . . . I think about E. R. M. a great deal – how we'll make our *grande entrée* at the ball [Under the Rams] (ribbon of the Legion of Honor).

Wednesday, 4.18 [*sic*]: After bad night, awakened by cries about *kovelava*. Boats leaving to fish. Got up sluggishly. The same mood of nervous tension. They brought me a lot of [inedible things] and two decent *utakemas*. Resolved to pick one or two important Vakuta problems and develop them thoroughly. To begin with, *kabitam*. Then, local mythology. Then go over the whole range of similarities, differences, between Vakuta and Kiriwina. I carry out this decision and work well, choosing a couple of the most important questions (in the morning, traditions with Petai, in the afternoon L. T. [*lili'u tokabitam?*][21] with [. . .]. A couple of first-class informants. Rain pouring all day with one hour's interruption at 11. During lunch (*crab*) did not read. Right after lunch, M'bwasisi[22] & Co. Around 6, still raining but I feel I must go out; Beethoven melodies flit through my head (*Fidelio Overture*), longing for and thoughts about E. R. M. The *tokabitam* brings me a comb, which overjoys me. In the rain and mud I walked to Kaulaka; associations with similar walks in Zakopane [in Poland, near Cracow]. Yesterday and day before horribly sultry, like the worst days on Oburaku, everything a thick soup of fog, mist, and smoke. Mental excitement, I repress it. Planned new designs for combs. Thought of my ethnogr. work. Planned final letter to N. S. In Kaulaka, bought stones. On my way back planned article *'The New Humanism'*, in which I would show that (1) humanistic thinking *as opposed to* dead-petrified thinking is profound and important; (2) to associate this thinking with the 'classics' is a fatal error; (3) I would analyze the essence of humanism and sketch a new plan in which living man, living language, and living full-blooded facts would be the core of the situation, and *mildew, patina, and dust* would not be like a *halo on the head of a saint, making a broken, putrid, dead thing the idol of a whole thinking community, a community that monopolizes thought. A man of genius gives life to these things, but why should not he be inspired to this by life itself, why should he not take life as the first subject to analyze and understand, and then with its light to get the other things unraveled? – To begin with, the joke about the 2 Assyriologists. – As a corollary, if we want to banish this thing from our schools, we must banish it from our mature thought first.* – Went back in the evening; strong feeling of contentment with this life: solitude, possibility of concentration, work, essential ideas; true existence. – Lying on the bed, I thought about it. Supper, then wrote E. R. M. I am aiming at a 'rhythm,' work without nervous super-tension. Sleepless night again . . . Dream about St. Ig. W. and N. S. Feeling of having wronged, deceived her.

Thursday, 4.19 [*sic*]. Fine day; sunshine in spots, some rain. Got up at 8, intending to write diary and copy loose notes, but my informants came and I collected information instead of copying. Worked well, without rushing things. At 1 rested, though I was not tired. Loaded camera. At 3 worked again. *Guma'ubwa libagwo.* – At 5 went to Kaulaka. A pretty, finely built girl walked ahead of me. I watched the muscles of her back, her figure, her legs, and the beauty of the body so hidden to us, whites, fascinated me. Probably even with my own wife I'll never have the opportunity to observe the play of back muscles for as long as with this little animal. At moments I was sorry I was not a savage and could not possess this pretty girl. In Kaulaka I looked around, noting things to photograph. Then walked to the beach, admiring the body of a very handsome boy who was walking ahead of me. *Taking into account* a certain residue of homosexuality in human nature, the cult of the beauty of the human body corresponds to the definition given by Stendhal. – View of Kitava: low rocks, covered with lush vegetation blending with the stones and bending over a narrow belt of shallow water, beyond which the sea drops off to a great depth. In the distance Kitava, a dark strip against the gray horizon. The shallow water is of a dull green color, with pink stones in it. Slowly the clouds take on colors, a violet reflection on the surface kills the play of colors at the bottom, everything takes on surface colors and merges into a single dull-red harmony. Earlier I had observed the play of the fishes among the stones, and dolphins outside the reef pursued by some predatory fish. They showed me the [place] near the shore where they catch *milamala.*[23] We talked about it and went back. In the village I sat a moment on the *pilapabile*, and I pawed a pretty girl in the *lauriu*. In Kaulaka we sat and again talked about catching *milamala* and about celebrating *yoba balomas.*[24] Walked back by moonlight, composing in my mind an article on *kula*, and I questioned my companions. – In the tent (at 8.30 eggs and tea) terrible mosquitoes; went to village for a while; back at 10:30; turned in at 11.

General remarks: Work, excellent. But mental attitude toward E. R. M., bad. That lousy girl [. . .] everything fine, but I shouldn't have pawed her. Then

(morning of 4/20) I thought about Lila Peck. At the same time I thought a great deal about N.S., strong guilt feelings. Resolve: absolutely never to touch any Kiriwina whore. To be mentally incapable of possessing anyone except E. R. M. *As a matter of fact*, in spite of lapses, I did not succumb to temptations and mastered them, every one of them *in the last instance*.

Friday, 4.20 [*sic*]: Another day of intensive work, without tiredness or *surchauffage* [getting overheated], physically well and content. In the morning wrote alone and despite everything I felt a little more deserted than when the *niggers* are here. – Got up as usual. On both sides of the gray interior, green walls – on the east weeds of fresh *odila*,[25] on the west a couple of pink palms divide the upper half of the picture vertically: the road lined with [. . .] and in the distance *odila* jungle with cascades of vegetation. Interior: rotten sticks covered with pile of rubbish, and patched in a few places; in the middle Samson's mat; my bed enthroned, the table, a pile of my things, . . . etc. – *Well*, I covered a great deal systematically; around 12 the *niggers* helped me finish *kaloma*[26] and translate the texts. After lunch, Samson came back: Yaboaina, *kaloma libagwo* – I was very tired and I could not think straight. I took a walk . . . along the sandy, stony beach, then walked back. The bonfire cast flickering lights on the pastel-coloured background of palms, night fell, Kitava vanished over the distant sea. Once again upsurge of joy at this open, free existence amidst a fabulous (*sic!*) landscape, under exotic conditions (how unexotic New Guinea seems now!), a real picnic based on actual work. I also had the real joy of creative work, of overcoming obstacles, new horizons opening up; misty forms take on contours, before me I see the road going onward and upward. I had the same upsurges of joy in Omarakana – then they had been even more justified, for that was my first success and the difficulties were greater. This may have also been the cause of my joy at Nu'agasi, when suddenly *the veil was rent* and I began to collect information. – By the sea, creative ideas about '*sense of humor, manners and morals.*' I came back tired, lay down. Samson offered me his cane. I went with him and he gave me [. . .] information. Also *sawapu*. I came back late and slept well – oh yes, on my way back I went to the pool and delighted in the view of trees, water, and boats by moonlight. It's a pity that I may leave this forever. I want to write about all this to E. R. M. and to remind her that it is just half a year ago we parted.

Saturday, 4.21 [*sic*]: First day of changed clocks. Got up an hour earlier than usual, I was a bit sleepy and depressed, but my health is so good that I worked well notwithstanding, took a long walk to Okina'i, and all day long I thought creatively and intensely. Emotionally, it's rather low tide, and at night under mosquito net, disastrous relapses again: I recalled

[Nayore] and G. D., etc. In the morning I moved to the lawn in front of the house and wrote down conversations. Then I hammered away at *libagwo* with my two best informants (Tomeynava and Soapa). Then, under the *bwayma* lunch and a two hours' rest – didn't read anything, and don't remember what I thought about. Then went to the village, again got Tom. and So. and worked on [GDN], very low pressure; terrified by complications of new rites and need to change point of view. At 6 (new time) went to Okina'i. The road was not too amusing and in spots a strip on the left, fairly big *odila*, a foul stony and muddy path. The new road, the new goal interested me nonetheless. Magnificent view of the lagoon: the sun was setting; compact little clouds on the west. The mountains to the south invisible, towering cottony white cumulus clouds, probably lying on top of the mountain range. A dark mangrove belt in the direction of the *raybwag* – clearly outlined individual trees –*dark and immobile over the moving water, on which colored reflections continually come and go.* Sandy white beaches, just beyond the slimy bottom of the lagoon. I walked along the beach to Okina'i, ahead of the *niggers*; I wanted to be alone with my thoughts: initial intensity – for I feel I still have no specific theme in my mind – Okina'i and Osikweya on the sand – the smooth waters of the lagoon through the gray houses and palms bring to mind the mood in Mailu and on the South Coast. I walked alone beyond Osikweya. Formulated plans for next five months: Vakuta must be given   *No. 1 place.* Revise and formulate basic gaps: *Mwasila*[27] magic; *waga megwa;*[28] *tauva'u*[29] in Vakuta, etc., and then develop all this systematically. Eliminate Capuan[30] days in Sinaketa and Gusaweta. I must hurry in any case. Working at my present pace I should finish (?) and at all events come back as laden with materials as a camel. – On my way back by moonlight I thought about the letter I had planned to the Carnegie Institute, and my thought deviated to B. Sp. and C. G. S. –'Creative thoughts and filthy thoughts' – avoid the latter! I felt that my thoughts were becoming uncreative and I stopped them – the rest of the way I just looked, and my associations were insignificant. I drank tea in front of the house, the *boys* and *niggers* were in the kitchen. I was flooded with reminiscences of Italian songs. Thought of E. R. M., P. & H., M. H. W. as audience. 'Marie,' 'Sole,' etc. – Then Pida examined the boat I had bought, and I made two important discoveries; the models of boats are an object of *kayasa;*[31] and *Kwaykwaya* (custom of robbing houses of specific kinsmen or others under specific conditions). Walked to the village; the dogs irritated me. – Under the mosquito net, 'I burn at two ends' – thought of composing a tango with Olga Ivanova. Then disastrous thoughts – the magic of E. R. M. silenced by a wave of corruption. Fell asleep very late. Pleasant and interesting dreams. – In short, health is A-1, joy of living, existing in these conditions – I completely forget, physiologically speaking, that my conditions here are

negative. I am completely under the spell of the tropics, as well as under the spell of this life and my work. For nothing in the world would I read trashy novels, and I think with pity about people who keep taking medicine all the time! Health!!

Sunday, 4.22 [*sic*]: Got up at 6 after six hours' sleep. Sunday: I went to Tap. – *just another ethn. experience.* Dry cool breeze – *laurabada.*[32] Thought about E. R. M. – composed letter to her. Then I wrote – I wrote all day long, in the morning in a hut because of the sun, in the afternoon under the *bwayma.* At 6 I went to Kaulaka and to the shore where the *wagas* are drawn up. I was nervously exhausted and excited: I deliberately stopped my flow of thought, which was sparkling but lacked depth. Talked with the *niggers* about 'the positions' during sexual intercourse. Magnificent *cove*; sand between two rocks, crowned with a thicket of pandanus; foaming waves, misty moon. Came back very sleepy and tired. At home, irritation because of *supposed theft of* Kaluenia. – This day is a break in the intensive work. The letter to E. R. M. is a rather dead, unpolished formulation of my ideas – a duplicate of the diary, not an expression of my thoughts or feelings in relation to my beloved. – I have *a flash of insight*: physical intimacy with another human being results in such a surrender of personality that one should unite only with a woman one really loves.

Notes: Chapter 27

Reprinted from Bronislaw Malinowski, *A Diary in the Strict Sense of the Term* (London: Routledge & Kegan Paul; New York: Harcourt Brace Jovanovich, 1967, by kind permission of Routledge & Kegan Paul and Harcourt Brace Jovanovich, Inc. © 1967 by A. Valetta Malinowska.

1   Elsie R. Masson, daughter of Sir David Orme Masson, professor of chemistry at the University of Melbourne. At the time she was a nurse in Melbourne hospital. She and Malinowski were married in 1919; she died in 1935.
2   Emphasis in original.
3   Stanislaw Ignacy Witkiewicz (1885–1939), son of the renowned Polish poet and painter and an artist in his own right, who was a close friend of Malinowski's from boyhood.
4   A native term in the Trobriand Islands to refer to all kinds of sailing craft, and also a large, built-up canoe. The meaning of this term together with all native terms used in this chapter has been taken from 'An index of native terms', by Bick (1967), pp. 299–315.
5   Paul and Hedy were Mr and Mrs Paul Khuner of Vienna, lifelong friends of Malinowski, who were in Melbourne during the period 1917–18.
6   The Dobuans were expected again in Vakuta – their final destination before sailing home.
7   Layseta was a chief in Sinaketa; he had a wide knowledge of magic and had lived in the Amphletts and Dobu.
8   The famous trading cycle between Melanesian communities described in Malinowski (1922). For a brief note on *kula*, see Malinowski (1967), p. 118.

9   Kouta'uya was the second-ranking chief in Sinaketa and played a major role in the *kula* expedition between Sinaketa and Dobu detailed in Malinowski (1922). He had 116 *karayta'u* (kula partners).

10 An overseas partner in the *kula*.

11 Mr and Mrs Raffael Brudo, French pearl traders in the Trobriand area, became good friends of Malinowski's.

12 Underlined in the original.

13 Chief of Kitava Island.

14 The portent associated with each form of magic.

15 A creeper whose roots supply poison for fish.

16 Fenced path between garden sites.

17 Trobriand storehouse, sometimes with a sitting shelter or platform. See Malinowski (1935a), for a complete description.

18 The real or important myths of the Kiriwinian natives.

19 Chief's hut.

20 Skill, expertise, craft.

21 A myth about an expert carver.

22 M'bwasisi, the garden magician of Vakuta.

23 A name for the *palolo* worm, which comes up at a certain full moon and is used in fixing the date of the annual festival and return of the spirits, during the peak of prosperity; the worm's arrival is sometimes connected with the arrival of the spirits.

24 The driving away of the ancestral spirits of the dead at the close of the *milamala* festival.

25 The bush, as opposed to cultivated grass.

26 Small circular perforated discs made from spondylus shell, which are made into the necklaces used in the *kula*; the *kaloma* decorate almost all articles of value or artistic finish in the *kula* district.

27 Magic performed on arrival at destination of *kula*, designed to induce generosity in the host partners.

28 Magic, generic term; magic formula.

29 Evil anthropomorphic beings, who come from the southern islands and cause epidemics.

30 Capua: city of ancient Rome noted for luxury.

31 Contractual enterprise.

32 South-east trade wind season.

Section Eight

Theorising in Field Research

The Role of Theory in Field Research

ROBERT G. BURGESS

A key problem in sociology and social anthropology is the relationship between theory and research. Some of the discussions concerning this relationship in social science have been oversimplified. Many social science textbooks on methodology have begun by outlining an ideal scientific procedure of: theory – developing hypotheses – data collection – testing of hypotheses – conclusion. Such a procedure, it is claimed, occurs in the natural sciences and can be applied to research in the social sciences. However, such discussions do not question the relevance of this research procedure for the natural sciences. Indeed, Medawar (1964) has suggested that the way in which scientific papers are written up constitutes a fraud, as the actual process of doing research follows a different pattern from that represented in the papers. He indicates that natural science can be a creative and imaginative activity, in which hypotheses appear along uncharted paths in the research process. Among social scientists, similar remarks have been made by Wright Mills (1959), who criticises empirical researchers who surround their data with 'theory' after data collection has been completed. Such procedures, he argues, can mislead a reader into thinking that the study was specifically designed and conducted to test broader conceptions.

These remarks from the natural sciences and the social sciences bring us back to considering what is involved in the research process and, in particular, to consider the relationship between theory and research, and the process of theorising which is discussed in the chapters in this section. Turning once again to the natural sciences we find that an account of the processes involved in research on the discovery of the structure of DNA is provided in *The Double Helix* (Watson, 1968). This account is devoted to demonstrating that:

> Science seldom proceeds in the straightforward logical manner imagined by outsiders. Instead, its steps forward (and sometimes backward) are often very human events in which personalities and cultural traditions play major roles. (Watson, 1968, p. 13)

Here, we are made aware that research does not occur in 'stages' and does not follow a linear path, but instead is a social process, in which overlap occurs between all areas of the investigation. Indeed, in sociology it has been argued by Wallace (1971) that, if we are to understand the research process, it is essential to grasp how theory is interrelated with methods of research, observations, generalisations and hypotheses.

Such an argument supports Wright Mills's advice to the social researcher, when he states:

> Be a good craftsman: Avoid any rigid set of procedures. Above all, seek to develop and use the sociological imagination. Avoid the fetishism of method and technique. Urge the rehabilitation of the unpretentious intellectual craftsman, and try to become such a craftsman yourself. Let every man be his own methodologist; let every man be his own theorist; let theory and method again become part of the practice of a craft. (Wright Mills, 1959, p. 224)

This challenges social scientists to shift away from set procedures and points towards integrating theory and method. It also provides a series of questions that confront the field researcher while doing research: what is the relationship between theory and research? Do theory and research involve similar activities? Are theory and research dissimilar? If theory is separated from research, do you lose the meaning of the research? Further questions arise concerning theory and method: do theory and method relate? How are theory and method involved in field research?

Such questions turn us towards examining the role of theory in field research. Already we have seen that theory cannot be put into a separate box, but is involved in constant interplay with the selection of research problems, methods of investigation and with data collection and data analysis throughout the research process. Here, we might consider Cohen's remark that 'the word "theory" is like a blank cheque: its potential value depends on the user and his use of it' (Cohen, 1968, p. 1). Such a statement indicates that theory potentially has a wide range of uses. Indeed, Bensman and Vidich (1960) suggest a number of uses for social theory in field research. They indicate that theory can be used to provide a focus for the study; an idea for investigation. Secondly, it can provide a series of alternative perspectives for field research. Thirdly, theory can assist the researcher to formulate and reformulate the problem posed in the research. Fourthly, the limitations of a theory that is used in empirical work can be demonstrated with empirical evidence. Finally, they state that theory can be used to discover new dimensions of the research problem and to reconstruct that problem. In this respect, Bensman and Vidich (1960) argue that theory is used throughout research: in stating the problem, collecting data and analysing and publishing the results. Theory is continually refined in relation to the problem posed, the data collected and the analysis that is provided. However, theory is not merely used in terms of verification. Indeed, Merton (1968) has maintained that to see empirical research as merely testing or verifying hypotheses is to return to a model of research that fails to describe what actually occurs, as it omits several aspects of the research process. For Merton, the verification and testing of theory assigns a passive role to the research enterprise. He is more concerned with an active role between research and theory, in which research shapes, initiates, reformulates, deflects and clarifies theory. Such a position is considered by Glaser and Strauss (1967) to involve the grounded modification of theory; a position that they wish to extend.

Glaser and Strauss (1967) maintain that theory is a central part of the process of doing research. In their work, they argue a case for discovering theory from data. Theory becomes a developing entity rather than a perfected product, so that grounded theory is generated and developed from data; hypotheses, concepts and theories being derived from the process of doing research. As a variety of relationships occur between theory and research, it is important to turn to field studies and research biographies to see the way in which theory is actually involved in the research process (cf. Hammond, 1964, and the commentary on informal research procedures by Baldamus in this section). To assist in this activity Glaser and Strauss provide a series of questions that can be used to evaluate the relationship between theory and research in any study. The questions that they consider should be asked are:

(1) Is the author's main emphasis upon *verifying* or *generating* theory?

(2) Is he more interested in *substantive* or *formal* theory?

(3) What is the *scope* of theory used in the publication?

(4) To what degree is the theory *grounded*?

(5) How *dense* in conceptual detail is the theory?

(6) What *kinds of data* are used and in what capacity in relation to the theory?

(7) To what degree is the theory *integrated*?

(8) How much *clarity* does the author reveal about the type of theory that he uses? (Glaser and Strauss, 1967, p. 118)

Using these questions they maintain it is possible to decide whether investigators verify, or generate theories in their work.

On the basis of examining a range of studies, they are able to identify those that verify theories (for example, Blauner's (1964) study of alienation), those that assume verification and generate new categories and hypotheses within the original theoretical framework (for example, Redfield's (1941) study, *The Folk Culture of Yucatan*), those that organise data as against generating theory (for example, La Piere, 1938) and those that are principally involved in generating theory. Among the latter group, field research from anthropology and sociology figures large with illustrations from the work of Geertz (1963), Evans-Pritchard (1937), Goffman (1959; 1963) and Strauss *et al.* (1964). In Evans-Pritchard's study, *Witchcraft, Oracles and Magic Among the Azande*, a theory is shown to emerge from the data. Here, the field research was conducted within a general framework but alternative theories were not explicitly used to guide the research. As a result, Glaser and Strauss argue that the researcher generates grounded theory through the use of original categories and relationships that are derived from the data. As far as sociological studies are concerned, the work of Strauss *et al.* (1964) based on field research in two hospitals is used as an example of generating theory. This work was initially guided within a framework based on the 'sociology of work' and 'symbolic interaction'. In these circumstances, it is argued that categories and hypotheses were free to emerge, guide and direct further data collection that contributed towards the discovery of substantive and formal theories. In short, this study reflects the constant interplay between theory, methods and data that Glaser and Strauss argue should occur in the conduct of field research.

It is evident that a range of relationships can occur between theory and research, and these have been systematically discussed in the literature. First, the hypothetico-deductive method, where progress is made by empirically testing deductions made from a universal statement where the results are used to verify or falsify the original theory. Secondly, analytic induction, where generalisations are derived from data presented in case studies by means of refinement, abstraction and generalisation. Finally, retroduction or abduction, which focuses on the interplay of theory and data whereby the researcher reasons back to develop a theory which will account for the observations that are made.

Among sociologists who engage in field research with its flexible form of research design, data collection and data analysis there is a tendency for induction to play a more important part in the process of theorising. Analytic induction was developed by Znaniecki (1934), who intended that this approach should allow researchers to remain faithful to the data they collected, to abstract and generalise from a small number of cases and to avoid prior categorisation of data. This procedure is followed in Lindesmith's study of opiate addiction (Lindesmith, 1947). Here, a hypothetical explanation is formulated after which cases are studied to see if the hypotheses fit the data. In cases where they do not fit, the hypotheses are either reformulated, or the phenomenon is redefined. Meanwhile, in cases where the phenomenon does fit, further cases are examined until a universal relationship is established. The critics of analytic induction (Robinson, 1951; Turner, 1953) raise questions concerning the logic of explanation and whether universal relationships can be established from case studies. They argue that more often analytic induction encourages the development of typologies and assists in the definition of social phenomena.

An influential attempt at analytic induction is the grounded theory approach advocated by Glaser and Strauss (1967) and by Glaser (1978). In the most recent account Glaser maintains that: 'Grounded theory is based on the systematic generating of theory from data, that itself is systematically obtained from social research' (Glaser, 1978, p. 2). Here, it is argued that generating theory and doing research are all parts of the same process, as research activities are guided by the emerging theory. Again, the key question that emerges is on the relationship between theory and research. Glaser (1978) maintains that there are three general approaches to developing links between theory and research. First, when the sociologist reads through the data that is gathered and gives commonsense impressions in theoretical language. Secondly, when categories are developed that are described with data, and finally, when data is systematically analysed and constantly compared until a theory results. However, in this context, researchers might ask: what is data? How is data gathered and selected? What categories can be used? Overall, Glaser maintains that theory generation takes place when all the data that have been collected are conceptualised into categories and integrated into a theory that emerges during the process of doing research. Such an approach emphasises theory generation rather than theory testing, with theories being developed inductively from data as the main task of the sociologist. Yet, even with this approach, researchers still have to decide how to generate theory in the social contexts in which they work.

Bechhofer has argued that, although induction is frequently used by the sociologist, it is not a straight choice between induction and deduction, as he remarks: 'The research process . . . is not a clear-cut sequence of procedures following a neat pattern but a messy interaction between the conceptual and empirical world, deduction and induction occurring at the same time' (Bechhofer, 1974, p. 73). He illustrates this statement by making reference to participant observation, which he considers allows for continuous generation and testing of hypotheses; a point that is clearly illustrated by Geer (1964) in her appraisal of her field research.

The constant movement between theory, method and data, and the intertwining of theory and method throughout the research process, has been clearly illustrated in reflections on the research process provided by researchers in the collections edited by Hammond (1964), Vidich, Bensman and Stein (1964), Shipman (1976) and Freilich (1977a). In all these texts, autobiographical accounts by researchers highlight the relationship between theorising and empirical research. However, the word 'theorising' is defined in different ways by various researchers as they indicate the patterns of theoretical 'discovery' in their own work.

It is this theme of theoretical 'discovery', patterns of formal and informal theorising and the relationship between theory and research that is the focus of the chapters that are included in this section. In Chapter 29 Baldamus discusses the nature of 'discovery' in empirical work in social science, utilising the autobiographical accounts that are provided in Hammond (1964). Here, he raises a series of basic questions about the role of 'discovery' and of theorising in social science. Meanwhile, Chapter 30 consists of an essay by Glaser from *Theoretical Sensitivity* (Glaser, 1978), in which he raises a series of questions about generating formal theory and provides some answers about the links between data, substantive theory and formal theory on the basis of his own research experience. While neither of these chapters provides answers to the problem of the relationship between theory and research, they do indicate how theorising is a central part of the research process that influences the problem posed, the methods used, the data collected, the analysis made and the final research report.

Suggestions for Further Reading

METHODOLOGY

Baldamus, W. (1976), *The Structure of Sociological Inference* (London: Martin Robertson). A text in which Baldamus develops some of the arguments stated in the chapter reprinted here.

Bechhofer, F. (1974), 'Current approaches to empirical research: some central ideas', in J. Rex (ed.), *Approaches to Sociology: an Introduction to Major Trends in British Sociology* (London: Routledge & Kegan Paul), pp. 70–91; a good overview of the research process and a useful basic discussion of theory and research.

Bensman, J. and Vidich, A. J. (1960), 'Social theory in field research', *American Journal of Sociology*, vol. 65, no. 6, pp. 577–84; outlines ways in which social theory provides alternative perspectives on data.

Blumer, H. (1954), 'What is wrong with social theory?', *American Sociological Review*, vol. 19, no. 1, pp. 3–10. A paper in which Blumer identifies deficiencies in contemporary sociological theory.

Bruyn, S. T. (1966), *The Human Perspective in Sociology: the Methodology of Participant Observation* (Englewood Cliffs, NJ: Prentice-Hall); provides a discussion of some of the philosophical issues involved in the conduct of field research.

Bulmer, M. (1979), 'Concepts in the analysis of qualitative data', *Sociological Review*, vol. 27, no. 4, pp. 651–77; a useful discussion and critique of the use of concepts and theories in empirical research.

Dubin, R. (1968), *Theory Building* (New York: The Free Press); designed as a practical handbook for the researcher on the interaction between theory and research.

Glaser, B. G. (1978), *Theoretical Sensitivity* (Mill Valley, Cal.: Sociology Press). A text in which Glaser outlines advances in the development of grounded theory. However, there are still several unanswered problems associated with 'grounding' and 'generating' theory from data.

Glaser, B. G. and Strauss, A. L. (1967), *The Discovery of Grounded Theory: Strategies for Qualitative Research* (Chicago: Aldine). The basic critique of the theory/research relationship and a discussion of discovering theory from data.

McCall, G. J. and Simmons, J. L. (1969) (eds), *Issues in Participant Observation: a Text and Reader* (Reading, Mass.: Addison-Wesley). Reprints the papers by Robinson (1951) and Turner (1953) on analytic induction. See chapter 5 which contains a number of interesting essays on generating hypotheses.

Merton, R. (1968), *Social Theory and Social Structure* (3rd edn) (New York: The Free Press). See Merton's discussion on the relationship between theory and research and research and theory.

Mills, C. Wright, (1959), *The Sociological Imagination* (New York: OUP); this is worth reading especially for its appendix on intellectual craftsmanship.

Znaniecki, F. (1934), *The Method of Sociology* (New York: Farrar & Rinehart); provides a discussion of the procedures involved in analytic induction.

Reflections on research

Autobiographical statements on doing research provide accounts on theorising and discussions on the relationship between theory and research. The collections that take up these themes are:

Freilich, M. (1977) (ed.), *Marginal Natives at Work: Anthropologists in the Field* (New York: Wiley).

Hammond, P. (1964) (ed.), *Sociologists at Work* (New York: Basic Books).

Shipman, M. (1976) (ed.), *The Organization and Impact of Social Research* (London: Routledge & Kegan Paul) (see especially the account by Lacey, 1976).

Vidich, A. J., Bensman, J. and Stein, M. R. (1964) (eds), *Reflections on Community Studies* (New York: Harper & Row).

EMPIRICAL STUDIES

There are few studies that explicitly discuss the relationship between theory and research. However, the following studies provide useful examples of relationships between theory, methods and data:

Benyon, H. (1973), *Working for Ford* (Harmondsworth: Penguin).

Blauner, R. (1964), *Alienation and Freedom* (Chicago: University of Chicago Press).

Cressey, D. (1953), *Other People's Money* (Glencoe, Ill.: The Free Press).

Ditton, J. (1977), *Part-Time Crime: an Ethnography of Fiddling and Pilferage* (London: Macmillan).

Evans-Pritchard, E. E. (1937), *Witchcraft, Oracles and Magic among the Azande* (Oxford: OUP).

Geertz, C. (1963), *Peddlers and Princes* (Chicago: University of Chicago Press).

Glaser, B. G. and Strauss, A. L. (1965), *Awareness of Dying* (Chicago: Aldine).

Glaser, B. G. and Strauss, A. L. (1968), *Time for Dying* (Chicago: Aldine).

Goffman, E. (1959), *The Presentation of Self in Everyday Life* (London: Allen Lane).

Goffman, E. (1963), *Stigma* (Englewood Cliffs, NJ: Prentice-Hall).

Moore, R. (1974), *Pit-Men, Preachers and Politics* (Cambridge: CUP).

Nichols, T. and Beynon, H. (1977), *Living with Capitalism* (London: Routledge & Kegan Paul).

Strauss, A. L. and Glaser, B. G. (1977), *Anguish: a Case History of a Dying Trajectory* (London: Martin Robertson).

Strauss, A. L., Schatzman, L., Bucher, R., Ehrlich, D. and Sabshin, M. (1964), *Psychiatric Ideologies and Institutions* (New York: The Free Press).

Vidich, A. J. and Bensman, J. (1968), *Small Town in Mass Society* (2nd edn) (Princeton, NJ: Princeton University Press).

Willis, P. (1977), *Learning to Labour* (Farnborough: Saxon House).

29

The Role of Discoveries in Social Science

W. BALDAMUS

W. BALDAMUS

THE SERENDIPITY PROBLEM[1]

Traditionally, the advancement of scientific work is associated with the notion of 'discovery'. In so far as social sciences are based in some sense on pragmatic knowledge, it would seem probable that advancement towards new understanding is not entirely a function of scientifically formalised procedures. We should expect, in other words, that the discovery process extends into the realm of pragmatic experience. The present chapter intends to follow up these clues. Most of it involves the breaking of new ground and is therefore extremely tentative.[2]

There are various ways of exploring this question methodologically. Perhaps the most obvious prospect lies in discussion of serendipity patterns. According to Robert Merton's (1957) celebrated definition, it refers to 'the fairly common experience of observing an *unanticipated, anomalous and strategic* datum which becomes the occasion of developing a new theory or for extending an existing theory'.[3] For all its striking plausibility, this formulation has never been quite convincing as far as the social sciences are concerned: it is hardly a 'fairly common experience'! Undoubtedly, what Merton had in mind was oriented by the discovery process of the natural rather than the social sciences. He had been taking his clue from a simple descriptive account of serendipity cases by the physiologist W. B. Cannon, reported in terms of chance discoveries chiefly in physiological and medical research.[4] In view of the fact that the popular stereotype of the scientist as a discoverer is derived from the spectacular recent history of the natural sciences, it is understandable that social scientists, anxious to establish or to enhance the scientific nature of their work, like to believe that they, too, are engaged in discoveries. If we examine Merton's definition of serendipity in the light of Cannon's descriptive examples (such as the accidental discovery of penicillin), we can see why Merton places a special emphasis on 'strategic' data. 'Strategic' means that 'the unexpected fact . . . must permit of implications which bear upon generalized theory', and he adds that he refers here 'rather to what the observer brings to the datum than to the datum itself.'[5] This idea occurs in Cannon's account only casually in so far he talks about a 'prepared mind', 'sagacity', 'fresh insight', 'alert intelligence', and so on. But this is not just a difference of emphasis. What happened most likely is that Merton started off by looking at the most striking unexpected discoveries in the *physical* sciences, and then cast his mind over the range of similar incidents in sociological research. He, thus, must have noticed not only that it takes a good deal of searching around before one finds comparable incidents, but also that the few which seem to be relevant are curiously different. He realises, finally, that what is new about new observations involves a great deal of interpretation and theorising, an element, that is to say, which 'the observer brings to the datum'. It is obvious that this element weakens the whole idea of 'discovery', for what seems so impressive in the history of natural science is precisely the sheer force with which pure facts, in the sense of theoretically unadulterated events, have asserted themselves.

That the case of genuine serendipity in social science is noticeably weaker than one would hope is confirmed by the fact that Merton elaborates his definition by only one illustration from sociological research, one that is by no means particularly exciting:

> In the course of our research into the social organization of Craftown, . . . we observed that a large proportion of residents were affiliated with more civic, political and other voluntary organizations than had been the case in their previous places of residence. Quite incidentally, we noted further that this increase in group participation had occurred also among the parents of infants and young children. This finding was rather inconsistent with common-sense knowledge. (Merton, 1957, p. 105)

Obviously, to call this a 'discovery' would hardly be convincing. However, on two other occasions he does mention more startling cases; Lazarsfeld's and his associates' well-known work on voting behaviour[6] and the concept of 'relative deprivation' developed in *The American Soldier*.[7] Although the word 'serendipity' is not explicitly mentioned, a possible third example might be the 'paradoxical' (and in that sense unanticipated) findings of the Western Electric Co. experiments, which are discussed as an illustration of the 'discovery' of latent functions.[8] That is all. Though there are so few examples, they are at any rate sufficient to show up the dominance of *theoretical* interpretation over the strictly accidental 'datum itself'.

In a more recent publication, Robert Merton followed up the serendipity problem under the aspect of 'multiple discoveries'.[9] The relevant passage is this:

[the study of multiples will] help us to identify certain significant similarities and differences between the various branches of science. To the extent that the rate of multiples and the type of rediscoveries are much the same in the social and psychological sciences as in the physical and life sciences, we are led to similarities between them, just as differences in such rates and types alert us to differences between them. In short, the study of multiples can supplement the traditional notion of the *unity of all science*. (Merton, 1963, p. 243; my italics)

This suggests that the difference between the natural and the social sciences is a matter of degree only. Now the paper in which this statement occurs is dealing predominantly with multiple discoveries in astronomy, physics, chemistry, biology and medicine, an important focus being reported disputes about 'priority'. As regards specifically the 'social and psychological sciences', the following scholars involved in such disputes are discussed: Saint-Simon, Comte, Ferguson, Adam Smith, Adam Robertson, Guizot, Le Bon, Sighele, Lester Ward, Albion Small, Herbert Spencer, Marx, Mosca, Freud, Jung, Adler, Moreno, Slavson and Sorokin.[10] Now if we glance at these names, the question arises: what exactly is the nature of the discoveries which led to priority quarrels? Are they really comparable to what was at stake when Newton, Galileo, Laplace, or Darwin got involved in such disputes? Merton does not provide us with an explicit definition of the terms 'discovery' or 'multiple discoveries' or 'rediscovery'. In the context of the natural sciences he seems to allude to the 'repeated discovery of the same facts',[11] but when he discusses social scientists and psychologists, he includes '*new ideas*', and in dealing with what he calls the 'eureka syndrome' he talks about the 'socially reinforced elation that comes with having arrived at a new and true scientific idea or result'.[12] In this latter context he discusses, side by side, Kepler's third planetary law, Gay-Lussac's discoveries in the behaviour of gases, William James's 'idea of pragmatism', Joseph Henry's 'new way of constructing electromagnets', and finally Freud's early discovery of staining nervous tissue with a solution of gold chloride, as well as a later occasion when Freud reminds Karl Abraham that they had gained the 'first insights'. Evidently, any attempt to include social scientists under the category of scientific discoverers is forced to shift, once again, the emphasis from 'new facts' to 'new ideas'. Simultaneously the difficulty arises that somehow one has to be sure that the new ideas are 'true' or 'genuine' discoveries. Clearly, it

would require quite an elaborate and controversial undertaking to determine exactly to what extent and in which sense Freud's insights represent a genuine scientific discovery, notwithstanding their tremendous influence on modern social science. This difficulty will be felt even more acutely if we exclude from the social sciences economics and such approaches to psychology which remain more or less closely linked to biology, physiology, or clinical psychiatry.

No doubt one of the most impressive features of the history of the natural sciences is the occurrence of multiple discoveries. Nothing else can demonstrate so convincingly the 'objectivity' of scientific procedure than the observation that one and the same 'fact' is found independently by two or more investigators. But the suggestion that social science is equally objective and scientific because here, too, discoveries – including multiple discoveries – are a typical occurrence is likely to defeat its own purpose. I think if one sets one's mind to it, one could make quite a good case by arguing that there are no clear cases of multiple discoveries at all. Even so, the questions that emerge from this matter are important. Not only do they indicate that there seems to be something odd about the nature of the 'facts' with which the social scientist is concerned. They also prompt us to look at the ways and means by which the kind of new results are brought about that we would like to call discoveries, though we know they are not quite the real thing.

For this reason the next step is indicated by the need to to obtain a better understanding of the nature of interpreted facts within the social sciences. It is at this juncture that the role of pragmatic knowledge appears to be particularly significant. For there is sufficient evidence to assume that it is the universe of pragmatic knowledge which functions, as it were as an intervening medium between the results of systematically controlled inquiry, on the one hand, and the experience of uninterpreted reality, on the other. Obviously, this universe is of great importance to specifically sociological work. For the sociologist's observations – all that goes into codified responses, fourfold tables, and zero-order correlations – are already the products of common conceptualisations in everyday life.

Seen from this vantage-point, the social scientist's 'data' are merely derived observations, based on secondary sources. This important aspect is easily overlooked when we talk about 'commonsense data' in a casual manner. The conventional implications and meanings of the term are vague and variable, but a frequent connotation points towards unreliable, untested, non-scientific, or even non-rational beliefs. Now, if we replace this term by 'common *knowledge*' or 'practical *knowledge*', we shall move in a different direction altogether. We realise that there is more to it than simply untested beliefs. The emphasis now is on experiences which have a *cognitive* dimension, which contain observations that are in some sense valid and relevant. It should be noted that ordinarily in social research this possibility is never seriously envisaged. Whether or not the answers to a questionnaire express an element of truth is simply not taken into consideration: the aim is, rather, to obtain honest and sincere answers, no matter whether they are true or false in their own right.

As soon as we start to identify our raw material as knowledge that could be more or less accurate, valid, or true, we seem to depart so radically from the conventional scientific approach, that it takes some effort to assimilate the idea. The main difficulty is that we can hardly imagine what sort of methodological consequences we would have to face. As a first step to understand such consequences, we might point to one conspicuous advantage that arises from a recognition of the cognitive attributes of practical knowledge. This is that it explains at once the puzzle of the 'obstinate' or 'active' facts. If we realise that our raw data – our observations on elements of practical knowledge – have potentially a validity of their own, deriving from the pragmatic contexts of everyday life, we can understand how it is possible that mere observational facts have a power to assert themselves. They perpetually generate *theoretical* interpretations of the world that compete, as it were, with the researchers' own theories, hypotheses, concepts and analyses.

But although we can see now what it is that makes facts obstinate and self-assertive, on that basis it would seem even more difficult to comprehend the formal methods that we conventionally associate with social research and theory. According to thoroughly established practice, the procedural rules prescribe a unidirectional sequence of axiomatic theory, hypothesis formation, observation, testing and conclusion; there is no other way to gain verified knowledge. Obviously, if the third step – the observations themselves – tend to generate valid knowledge on their own, the sequence is broken and the procedure seems pointless.

In trying to overcome this formidable difficulty we have to look at the facts. And 'the facts' in this case are the practices and techniques actually used in the doing of scientific work. Possibly, even here, the facts exhibit an assertive power of their own. In a sense this would amount to attempting an empirical study of the available products of social science. In the course of it we would expect to come across certain bit and pieces of pragmatic knowledge: the 'knowhow' of social scientists that is acquired through constant practice and that appears to have obtained some degree of validity on account of its pragmatic usefulness in producing scientific results. In other words, we would have to presume that side by side with the official methodology that one finds in the textbooks on systematic theory, formal logic, statistical methods, survey design, or interviewing procedure, there exists a reservoir of *unofficial*, non-formalised techniques of inquiry. Evidently this kind of phenomenon is not easily got

hold of. While there is a well-established sociology of science, no systematic research has been done specifically on what would have to be called the 'sociology of social science'. It is surprisingly easy, nevertheless, to visualise the nature of unofficial techniques. What comes to mind is, for example, the exchange of personal experience, of 'gimmicks' and lucky 'hunches', of frustrations and unexpected insights, between researchers or theorists when they meet privately, at conferences, or in staff common-rooms. In addition, one could draw on the occasional autobiographical remarks in the preface to published works and, of course, on one's own accumulated experience distilled from memory and introspection.

It would, however, be premature to expect that we have now found a major difference between the nature of discovery in the physical and the social sciences. Such a conclusion might be suggested by the impression that the serendipity pattern in the physical world originates from a different sort of unanticipated events: events that occur *independently* of the theorising, interpretating, defining, conceptualising investigator (or, in the case of pragmatic knowledge, administrator). Vitamin K exists, one would think, even if it should remain undiscovered. The newly discovered fact is a physical thing that cannot generate by its own power a meaningful theoretical interpretation; it would seem to be 'obstinate' only in so far as the investigator's preconceived *theory* is obstinate and unyielding. On the face of it, the difference appears to be supported by the curious phenomenon that, while serendipity in the natural sciences has very often taken the form of simultaneous discovery – two or more observers stumbling upon the same anomalous fact independently of each other – such cases are not easily identified in the non-experimental sciences.

Unavoidably, I have to touch here briefly on certain recent developments in the philosophy of science. One of the approaches that has become prominent in recent years suggests the view, to put it very briefly, that scientific investigation (in the natural sciences) involves a continual interaction of theory with fact. There are no 'facts' as such, independent of a pre-existing theoretical framework.[13] Hence, the discovery of an 'anomalous' event is possible only if and in so far as a new theory has been created which defines it as anomalous. On this basis, therefore, the position in the natural sciences appears to be not markedly different from that in our own fields of inquiry. I shall have to revise this conclusion at a later stage, but first I want to add a few more details.

The approach of Toulmin (and others) has obtained considerable support from the work of Thomas Kuhn[14] which is centred on empirical-historical observations on the development of modern science, rather than being directly concerned with the theory of knowledge. This may explain, incidentally, why Kuhn's contributions have made a considerable impact even outside the circle of professional philosophers. What he has done is to examine closely and systematically the concrete processes by which scientific discoveries have come about. His interest was aroused by coming across, accidentally, an obscure monograph by a German physician, Ludwig Fleck's 'Entstehung und Entwicklung einer wissenschaftlichen Tatsache', published in 1935. He refers to it as 'an essay that anticipates many of my own ideas'.[15] Fleck's study is devoted to a careful and detailed examination of one outstanding case, the discovery of the famous Wassermann test as a means of diagnosing syphilis. In the centre of his analysis is the concept of *kollektiver Denkstil* by virtue of which he demonstrates that a 'scientific fact' is unthinkable without presupposing a theoretical framework and that, moreover, such theoretical orientations (in the natural sciences) are the product of collectively maintained schools or paradigms of thought. The 'discovery' of a new event, therefore, can only occur through a change in the collective style of interpretation dominant at a given time. The discovery of syphilis depended on the gradual historical emergence of a new style of thinking about the nature of venereal diseases. Discoveries are, as he puts it brilliantly, the product of *gerichtete Wahrnehmung*: directional perception. To the sociologist it may be of interest to add here that Fleck's fundamental concept of the collective thought-style is virtually identical with Karl Mannheim's collective 'thought-model' developed a few years earlier, which is remarkable because Fleck's essay shows no traces of any acquaintance with sociological sources. As far as our own problem is concerned, Kuhn's work goes much further than Fleck's pioneering effort. He accumulates powerful historical evidence that the changing collective 'paradigms' which organise the manner in which scientists define their problems and their relevant facts are systems which have a logic (as well as a vocabulary and a world-view) of their own. Different paradigms are, thus, incommensurate. To choose a telling example: Einstein's physics is in no way comparable with Newtonian physics; the basic vocabulary of such terms as 'mass', 'movement', 'space', 'time',. and so on has altogether different meanings in the two systems. To quote from a characteristic passage:

Paradigms gain their status because they are more successful than their competitors in solving a few problems that the group of practitioners has come to recognize as acute. To be more successful is not, however, to be either completely successful with a single problem or notably successful with any large number. The success of a paradigm – whether Aristotle's analysis of motion, Ptolemy's computations of planetary position, Lavoisier's application of the balance, or Maxwell's mathematization of the electromagnetic field – is at the start largely a promise of success discoverable in selected and still incomplete examples. (Kuhn, 1962, p. 24)

This idea of pragmatic 'success' is further elaborated as a form of 'correspondence' between facts and prediction: 'Normal science consists in the actualization of that promise, an actualization achieved by extending the knowledge of those facts that the paradigm displays as particularly revealing, by increasing the extent of the match between those facts and the paradigm's predictions, and by further articulation of the paradigm itself.'[16] The relevant point is here the assurance that apparently the absence of pure, uninterpreted facts is not typical of the social sciences alone; it appears to be a general affliction of scientific inquiry.

The Activity of Theorising

I propose to examine the problem of 'theory-determined facts', in the context of scientific discovery, by questioning the conventionally alleged formal connection between 'theory', 'hypothesis' and 'observation'. Accordingly I shall look at the *unofficial* techniques of work that condition or cut across the rules of formal methodology. I shall argue that the elements of the social scientist's work should be analysed behaviouristically, that is to say, as a type of prolonged and variable acitvity and, hence, as a process through time. As may be expected, however, it is as yet very difficult to maintain this approach: there is no sharp demarcation line between the formal and the informal, the published and the preparatory, the perceived and the real process of scientific discovery.

It may be recalled that for a number of reasons we were driven to the conclusion that the popular notion of a profound difference between natural and social science is misleading. As far as the discovery of facts – especially the discovery of obstinate facts – is concerned, there does not seem to be a decisive difference. Apparently the facts are, in both areas, always theory-determined. To pursue the question beyond this point would easily lead away from the main objective of the present chapter. It would force us to inquire into the logical foundations of theory-building. We would want to know, for example, whether the sort of theory which is typically used (or believed to be used) in the social sciences is essentially different from the theories of the experimental sciences. In turn this question could not be tackled without getting involved in the controversy between positivistic and anti-positivistic (phenomenological) school of thought.[17]

The whole problem may look very different on taking into account the informal processes out of which systematic theory is produced. As pointed out in an earlier discussion paper, the informal aspect of theorising refers to the inarticulated techniques, devices and practices which are customarily employed during the preparatory stages in the production of formal theories.[18] Ideally this can only be investigated by inquiring into the behavioural basis of sociological theorists at work, chiefly by means of suitably designed interviews of theoretical writers. The technical difficulties of such a method are numerous, but I do not think insuperable. However this may be, in the present context I am mentioning this possibility in order to show that the size of the gap in our knowledge of theorising is unexpectedly large. While there is an extensive and ever-growing specialisation concerned with the formal logic of theory in social science, its informal-behavioural side has virtually remained untouched. We simply do not know how in fact formal-theoretical works are brought about. It is even hard to imagine what kind of interview questions one would have to try out. It is difficult to understand why – considering the vastness of the available theoretical literature – so little has been done to identify the techniques and the skills which are normally employed in the production of theoretical writings. Partly, no doubt, the explanation is that the theorists themselves have very rarely seen the need to provide their readers with clues as to how they operate.[19]

Another reason is the peculiar manner in which statements of systematic theory are customarily presented: it takes the form of a sequence of *suggestions* which are offered without ostentive justification in terms of theoretical axioms. As A. Rapoport has pointed out, from a formalistic point of view, the initial stage of theory-building is particularly revealing in so far as it seems to involve a high degree of arbitrary selection. 'The stuff from which human relations and social structure are made is not evident intuitively. It must somehow be distilled, or abstracted from innumerable "events", and the selection of these events depends to a great extent on one's experiences, cultural background, and biases'.[20] The question whether this is inevitable because of the unique logical properties inherent in the subject matter of social science does not concern us here. From our point of view, the crucial work in the above quotation is the word '*somehow*'. The fact that the style of theoretical argumentation is cast in a distinctive mould may serve as a clue. If we take Parsons's *The Social System*[21] as the most sophisticated type of modern sociological theory, it may be significant that all its fundamental concepts are stated without formal definitions. The reader is introduced to such concepts usually by suggesting some combination of several, more or less interchangeable expressions which, in turn, merely suggest certain commonly known but technically undefined associations. Let us look, for example, at the familiar pattern variable of 'affectivity *versus* affective neutrality'. Neither of these or the associated equivalent terms 'gratification' (*versus* 'discipline') and 'expressive' (*versus* 'evaluative') interests, and so on, are specified by explicit definition. It is obvious throughout the book that the omission is intentional. Another aspect comes into view when one tries to locate the origin of the conceptual components. There are practically no footnotes in *The Social System* containing references to particular sources. It is evident, however, that the principal source is the accumulated body of abstract concepts available from current usage in social science generally. The use of specific references would be cumbersome and indeed misplaced, because it is always only a broad, and frequently merely a temporary, association with current usage that is required. The important thing is to keep within the hard core of consistent meaning of a given vocabulary. And this is all that is possible. For none of the constituent terms of a theoretical framework could be traced back to a precise formal definition at its primary source: all of them are, as we have seen, 'constructed constructs' distilled from pragmatic knowledge.[22]

So far, then, the relatively most tangible characteristic of theorising points to a process through time that can best be described as sutained '*articulation*': an initially vague and vacillating image of a complex framework is perpetually redefined, so as to produce an increasingly definite and stable structure. The most penetrating description of conceptual articulation I have come across has been presented by Michael Polanyi. Though primarily directed towards a clarification of the role of conceptualisation in the natural sciences, certain aspects of his analysis are relevant to our problem. Very briefly, his point of departure is the kind of progressively structured behaviour that is known from the dynamics of animal and child learning, commonly associated with the rudimentary trial-and-error type of problem-solving. He then proceeds from this kind of 'inarticulate learning' to the role of articulate language, the crucial basis of which devolves on the creation of 'interpretative frameworks'. Still further along this dimension Polanyi refers to the articulation process which governs certain logical operations on the level of scientific conceptualisation. Omitting here the technical details of the subsequent steps of Polanyi's exposition, of special interest to the analysis of sociological theorising is the following statement which is adapted from G. Polya's introspective account of mathematical problem-solving:

This (casting about for a solution) we do by performing two operations which must always be tried jointly. We must (1) set out the problem in suitable symbols and continuously reorganize its representation with a view to eliciting some new suggestive aspects of it, and concurrently (2) ransack our memory for any similar problem of which the solution is known. The scope of these two operations will usually be limited by the student's technical facility for transforming the given data in different ways, and by the range of germane theorems with which he is acquainted. (Polanyi, 1958, p. 128)

I am quoting this at length because of the obvious, if unexpected similarity between the highly formalised articulation in mathematical problem-solving and the apparently crude process of sociological conceptualisation.

Applied to sociological theorising, the essence of the first operation is reflected in the perpetual reorganisation, the unceasing restructuring, of symbols; whereby the 'symbols' consist in this case of the core meaning of existing conceptual elements (such as 'affective', 'gratification', 'expressive', in the example mentioned earlier on). The second operation – searching one's memory for similar problems with a known solution – reappears in the sociologist's endeavour to utilise available conceptual frameworks that have proved to be clarifying in other contexts or have become established by usage. To strengthen the comparison, I would suggest that the phrase 'known solution' of a mathematical problem might be replaced, without serious distortion, by 'other mathematical operations that have proved to be effective'. The difference, however, between the articulation process of mathematical problem-solving and sociological theorising should not be overlooked.

The decisive difference is founded upon the paramount importance of communication. Each step in the build-up of successively more sophisticated conceptual frameworks is severely limited by the prerequisite of uninterrupted communication within the community of social scientists as it exists at a given stage of development. Thus, as is well known, most of Parsons's writings move closely along the extreme limit of comprehensibility in terms of current sociological usage. This has often been attributed, erroneously, to lack of skill in his personal style of writing. But it should be clear from the foregoing that the difficulty of communication is largely inherent in the very process of progressive articulation. The available conceptual raw material can be precise only to the extent that the core meaning of the relevant symbols has already become institutionalised in the prevailing culture of the scientific community. The importance of communication to institutionalised scientific work in general has been clearly established by the study of Kuhn, mentioned earlier, and need not be elaborated here. Unsolved, however, is still the problem of the special conditions that derive from the lack of precision of sociocultural concepts. Evidently these conditions pertain to the nature of the symbols required to handle sociocultural phenomena.

Conceptual Innovations and Eclectic Discoveries

In the foregoing discussion I have suggested certain apparent similarities as well as differences between intuitive mathematical problem-solving and informal sociological theorising. It involves, by all appearances, an unceasing manipulation of both the content and the relation of particular symbols. What has to be explained next is the purpose of these operations. If this were to be done by studying the contemporary literature on the logic (or lack of logic) of social inquiry, we would be faced with a very difficult and somewhat dreary undertaking. In what follows I shall attempt a shortcut that will take us directly into the medium of unofficial practices.

This shortcut is based on the assumption that the activity of theorising is not confined to manifestly theoretical works. Some form of theorising also takes place in the execution of *empirical* studies. The advantage of using empirical work as our source rests on the fact that in such a perspective the technique of theory-building seems to be somewhat out of place: it appears to be an unofficial activity and it is, thus, more conspicuous and more tangible than in the case of overtly theoretical operations.

An invaluable source here is the collection of autobiographical reports presented in P. E. Hammond's *Sociologists at Work*,[23] in which we find a modest beginning towards a potentially systematic, comparative study of the unofficial practices of research. The contributors (among them a few outstandingly successful researchers) were asked to portray their own research activity 'as it was experienced during some *specific* investigation' and to report the actual sequence of events and ideas in the mind of the investigator, so as to 'let the reader in on the *sub rosa* phases of contemporary research'.[24] At first sight the result of this endeavour seems curiously disappointing. The reader who expects useful information about the most effective techniques that generate research discoveries finds hardly anything worth recording. Throughout these pages there is a striking contrast between the obvious success of these authors in terms of previously published works and the highly insecure, frequently trivial, and unaccountably erratic descriptions of their unofficial methods. More specifically, the following two features deserve particular attention: (1) the preoccupation with theory; and (2) the absence of discoveries.

(1) Although the chroniclers are concerned with empirical works only, all the contributors are extensively engaged in theorising or theoretical problems of one kind or another. This is remarkable because on the basis of published works, no effective interaction between theory and research seems to exist. Apparently, then, the theoretical activities take place during the preparatory (unpublished) stages only. They appear to be a private, more or less illegitimate, occupation. This curious attitude pervades the bulk of the chronicles and is, indeed, its most puzzling feature. To understand it we must first bear in mind that the author's conception of 'theory' does not easily fit into any of the established categories of conventional methodology. For example, this conception could not be described by any of the many types of social science

theory that are presented in R. Brown's *Explanation in Social Science*.[25] The way in which the word 'theory' is used here informally and loosely suggests a sort of continuous speculation without a definitive purpose. It has neither a recognisable beginning, nor an end. It certainly does not yield a theory, a specifiable end-product that can be used to design a set of hypotheses (which subsequently would be 'tested' by observation or experiment). More aptly, therefore, we should speak of 'theorising', a word that is actually employed a great deal in these reports. The ongoing nature of the process is well expressed, for example, by Stanley H. Udy: 'During this phase of the work, I "theorized" . . . during the afternoon, read my data and checked it against the afternoon's result during the evening, slept on the outcome, and tried proposing hypotheses in the morning'.[26] Another aspect, equally frequent, is the notion that informal theorising is a highly personal experience. It comes about by organising one's general ideas around a 'central theme', by steering the investigation into a certain direction. The process appears to be propelled by the desire to obtain in the end such observations as may confirm the investigator's preconceived ideas. Thus, we find an unceasing search for an 'integrating principle' (Blanche Geer), 'a new theoretical amalgam' (David Riesman and Jeanne Watson), 'a basic conceptual framework' (Robert N. Bellah), 'an organisation or synthesis which provides the essential structure into which the pieces of analysis fit' (James S. Coleman), 'a crucial insight' (Peter M. Blau), 'a major idea' (James A. Davis), 'a relevant typology' (Stanley H. Udy), and so forth.

Several of the writers describe this technique of 'theorising' alternatively as 'hypothesising'. It is, however, quite clear from the context that the word is used either to ridicule, or at least to throw doubt on the conventional concept of a rigorous hypothesis that is testable. For example:

'The research was not preceded by consciously elaborated hypotheses but grew vaguely out of my confusion and irritations . . . This was a kind of implicit hypothesizing that gave more freedom of thought and more rapid movement from hunch to hunch than initial preoccupation with formal hypothesizing about limited facts would have allowed. (Dalton, 1964, p. 63)[27]

And:

Since I had reached my 'hypotheses' by a combination of verbal reasoning and ex post facto induction (sic!), the appropriate method in most cases appeared to me to be to array frequencies in fourfold tables, with controls as appropriate. This I did, proceeding from one hypothesis to another through a verbal chain of reasoning.[28]

All this, of course, makes nonsense of hypothesis construction in the accepted sense. Yet this remarkable idea of informal theorising or hypothesising is expressed and elaborated by the various authors with such consistency that it requires some explanation. Why, for example, does it remain an unofficial, normally unreported activity?

(2) Once again it needs to be emphasised that none of the eleven contributors could be called a theoretician. The intensive preoccupation with theory takes place in the midst of empirical (including statistical) works: it appears to be an integral element throughout the process of collecting data. On that basis, however, the method of informal theorising appears to be even more perplexing. It flatly contradicts the whole idea of scientific testing. Indeed, what really goes on here amounts to a process of falsification. The investigator pursues a selected 'central theme', a pet theory that he wants to drive home; he looks around for observable facts that fit his theme; then, and only then, does he fabricate a hypothesis that fits the facts. This reversal of scientific procedure goes so much against the grain that several of the authors acutely feel the need to offer some form of apology or justification for it. It is found in what may be called the 'abundance' dilemma. 'There are so many questions which might be asked, so many correlations which can be run, so many ways in which the findings can be organized, and so few rules or precedents for making these choices that a thousand different studies could come out of the same data'[29]:

How did I know that this classification would be better than some other scheme, that is, that I could predict more about organization structure by using it than some alternative taxonomy? I did not. One never does, for in principle there exists an infinite number of ways of classifying anything. (Udy, 1964, p. 176)[30]

It is obvious, however, that the abundance dilemma, though it explains why *some* choice has to be made, cannot justify the selection of data to fit a particular preconceived theme. Moreover, it contradicts the canons of scientific objectivity in yet another point. Observations which are selected deliberately so as to make sense in the light of pre-existing knowledge are the precise opposite of empirical discoveries – of 'unanticipated, anomalous and strategic data', in Robert Merton's terms. And, indeed, as soon as one looks at the chronicles from this angle, one is struck by the total absence of genuine discoveries. As my interest in this book was initially aroused by the editor's announcement that it deals with the 'context of discovery',[31] I went through it page by page to look for them. I found none.

So once again the substance of 'discovery' seems to evaporate on closer inquiry. Perhaps these investigators just happened to be unlucky? In following up this –

admittedly somewhat unrealistic – possibility, I came to notice one element supporting it. Throughout the chronicles one finds an attitude that manifests an *expectation* of discovery: everybody is searching, casting around, exploring. In fact the word 'exploratory' stage is among the most frequently used terms to describe the informal processes. Now, supposing we take this expression literally, we would arrive at a concept of 'discovery' that is distinctively different from our previous notion. For we could say then that the kind of discoveries that the researchers are after are in the nature of 'territorial' discoveries: the exploration of uncharted areas of sociocultural entities which are relatively unknown or unfamiliar. The resultant findings would be anomalous and unanticipated but, and this is important, they would not be strategic. The word 'discovery' is, therefore, ambiguous in this context. At the most we could speak here only of 'sociographic discoveries'.

The relevance of this interpretation of the chronicles obtains further support, if they are seen in their connection with the official monographs or projects to which they refer. The subject matter of these is always the descriptive exploration of a special field, a new territory, an unusual situation: Blau's study of the behaviour of officials in a particular kind of bureaucratic agency, Dalton's equally specific description of the motives, aspirations, informal activities, 'out-of-role' adaptations of a selected group of supervisors and foremen, Lipset's inquiry into the 'deviant case' of the ITU, Wright's and Hyman's investigation into the effectiveness of training methods used by institutes of the Encampment for Citizenship, Bellah's research on the Tokugawa religion, and so on.

The predominance of sociographic specialisation explains a great deal. Not only does it account for the undaunted spirit of discovery of the explorers, it also explains the obsessive preoccupation with theorising, conceptualising, 'hypothesising', and so on. Obviously, any kind of highly situational descriptive exploration is bound to produce numerous findings that are 'new' – in the sense of observations which have not been made before in exactly the same manner. But, of course, if these can be called 'discoveries' at all, they are merely in the nature of trivial, eclectic, or peripheral data. They are in direct contrast to those which would be of central importance to the fundamental properties of society at large. Hence it becomes all the more important to theorise. In other words, it is necessary constantly to reinterpret the accumulating new findings until they finally appear in some sense to be strategically relevant to general, centrally important problems.

We have now reached a position which takes us back to the broader aspects of the serendipity problem. I think it is a safe assumption that Hammond's chronicles are fairly typical in so far as the bulk of contemporary social research produces merely eclectic

sociographic discoveries. This means our data are peculiarly deficient on account of their triviality and speciality. Hence, the need to theorise is a universal prerequisite. Earlier on I described, provisionally, the activity of theorising as a trial-and-error process by which conceptual frameworks become progressively more articulate. Although we do not know exactly how this is done, it is evident that the process involves a large element of inventiveness and creativity. The perpetual restructuring of concepts around their core meanings is essentially a matter of theoretical innovations. To see the importance of this we have only to recall a few sociological concepts that became characteristically incisive through the work of individual thinkers, for example, alienation, anomie, conspicuous consumption, bureaucracy, oligarchy, ideology, latent function, social system, pattern variables, reference group, other-directness, power elite.

These innovations manifest a sharp contrast to the observational data. Whereas the empirical findings are insignificant details of sociographic description, the conceptual frameworks are implicitly aimed at centrally important phenomena: values, ideologies, social change. Furthermore, while the data are derived from verifiabled observations, the concepts are the product of the sociologist's mind. In the last analysis, it is the inevitable triviality of social observations, the absence of genuine discoveries, which is responsible for the precarious situation of social science. There are many sociologists who, quite naturally, would not like to admit this openly. They pursue their laborious efforts in the hope that by some lucky hit they may yet stumble upon one statistical correlation that transcends the narrow triviality of sociographic data. Frequently this hope is fostered by the example of strategic statistical discoveries in economics, such as Juglar's Pareto's, or Bowley's. Now and then a fresh effort is made to prove that Durkheim's analysis of suicide rates *did* produce a discovery of general theoretical significance. It did nothing of the sort. The very essence of social observations, statistical or interpretative, precludes the possibility of yielding a 'general law'.

Double Fitting

While many of the unofficial activities remain obscure, we have come some way towards recognising their wider implications. I think we can be reasonably sure that informal theorising is a large and indispensable element of all empirical research. Furthermore, my earlier assumption, that the researcher's theoretical activities are essentially akin to the theoretician's endeavours seems fairly plausible in view of the importance of conceptual innovations. What is still puzzling is the curious repetitiveness of the process: its outstanding feature is the interminable *re*structuring, *re*defining, *re*interpreting, *re*formulating of conceptual frameworks. Linked with this is the extraordinary wastefulness of the process. Apparently a very large amount of the results of informal theorising is unusable and, therefore, unsuitable to be included in the final published work. It remains hidden away in notebooks, research files and preliminary drafts. It is this element of apparent wastefulness that more than anything else conflicts with the official notion of systematic scientific work presented in most methodological texts.

In attempting to reduce this contradiction I propose to supplement our first approximation to the trial-and-error process of 'articulation' as follows. Informal theorising (henceforth simply called 'theorising' as opposed to formal theory construction) involves a continuous restructuring of conceptual frameworks whereby a specific technique of reciprocal or *double fitting* is employed. This may be envisaged by imagining a carpenter alternately altering the shape of a door *and* the shape of the door frame to obtain a better fit, or a locksmith adjusting successively *both* the keyhole, and the key. In one sense such a technique looks like deliberate falsification: the investigator simultaneously manipulates the thing he wants to explain as well as his explanatory framework. In a strictly scientific context it would mean 'cooking the facts'.

As theorising in the shape of double fitting is evidently not defensible in terms of official procedures, its rationale is difficult to identify. It should be noted, in the first place, that the direction of the process is indeterminate. On the face of it there is merely an interminable sequence of alternating changes of a framework and its content. If so, what would be the purpose? To simplify the matter, we may argue that the final adjustment is done either to the framework, or to the content (the keyhole or the key). In the practice of scientific work this would mean that an investigator's chief interest is centred either on problems of conceptualisation or on empirical observations. Thus, although double fitting takes place all the time, the process as a whole may be conceived in two ways: it can be either dominantly theoretical, or dominantly empirical.

Theorising then reveals that kind of double fitting which is *dominantly* oriented towards inventing and articulating conceptual frameworks. Here, the process starts, arbitrarily, with some cluster of observations and it ends with a framework. At the beginning there is only a vague notion of some observed but unfamiliar or puzzling phenomenon (whereby it is of no importance at present whether the data have been arrived at by pragmatic knowledge, or quantitative methods). This first notion virtually amounts to a crude interpretative innovation. It is gradually articulated by trying to 'fit' it into a succession of combined criteria (which may be simple, dichotomous, or multidimensional). The bulk of such criteria is usually chosen from the reservoir of generally known and accepted concepts. But while one knows what they mean if taken separately, their combination may nevertheless produce new meanings

that might eventually illuminate the original unfamiliar phenomenon from which the process set out.

The importance of theorising (by means of double fitting) in empirical work is a consequence of the triviality of eclectic sociographic discoveries. The unique process which we have identified as theorising corresponds to what the autobiographical chronicles variously and uncertainly describe as the search for the central theme, the synthesis, the integrating principle, and so on. But theorising is not the only method of organising an investigation. We have seen already that the articulation process of double fitting may be directed dominantly towards empirical instead of theoretical tasks. We must now look at this other possibility. I shall call it 'hypothesising'.

As before, the substance of this technique is again an interminable sequence of alternately modifying frameworks and their contents. But this time the investigator's interest is dominantly 'empirical'. The arbitrary point of departure is now an interpretative framework, a more or less articulate theoretical statement or simply a vague generalisation that is barely more than a hunch. The focus of interest, however, is located in empirical observations. The theoretical framework is merely a means to an end, namely, to discover the existence of some regularity, some recurrent features among certain data, or some invariant relationship between factual observations. As a rule the expected findings are in the nature of causal relations, notably so in the context of sociographic discoveries. Like all causal relationships, even trivial (nonstrategic) data may suitably be treated in the light of a 'hypothesis'. But there is no need for it to be explicitly formulated. As usually employed in the practice of research, the term 'simply' means that some causal connection between certain classes of events may possibly be found to exist. The best illustration for this notion is the trial run on an IBM. Similarly, instead of actually carrying out a series of trial runs, it is often expedient simply to reflect upon the most promising possibilities. Or one may search the literature of past research for comparable cases that suggest a lead. All these informal activities may be conveniently classified as 'hypothesising'. They have in common with theorising the informal, improvising disposition of a trial-and-error process.

The suggestion that theorising and hypothesising are but two versions of one and the same process provides a partial answer to the question: what is the rationale of double fitting? It is a sort of psychological answer, not a description of the logical structure of the process. The answer points to the kind of satisfactions or the goals that are attached to sociological work. One type of satisfaction is grounded in the need for theorising, for projecting some order into the multitude of eclectic data by relating them to major problems, basic political issues, central values, and so on. To be fulfilled, this need requires value-commitments. The other type, concerned with hypothesising, stems from the striving for detachment, verification, scientific certainty. It relies on the assertive power of obstinate facts. Since both needs are deeply institutionalised in contemporary society, it is not surprising that the two corresponding activities are occurring side by side in any given piece of work. As regards individual scholars, the relative strength of the two motives will vary. Some are more theoretically minded, others more interested in empirical observations. The important thing is that either of the two specialisations has to use both operations.

Both the motivational aspect cannot fully explain the unique nature of double fitting. I shall add, therefore, one further characteristic. It is evident from the chronicles and similar sources that the interlocking of theorising and hypothesising is spread over the whole exploratory process. The interaction is continuous. Somehow it does not seem possible to specialise on the one or the other operation for any length of time. Apparently, in a concrete study one cannot engage solely in theorising for, say, one month, then change over to pure hypothesising for the next month, return to another month of theorising, and so on. In practice the two modes of double fitting are nearly simultaneous. This is clearly emphasised in the reports by the recurring phrase of 'constantly moving back and forth'. We must assume, therefore, that double fitting, no matter in which form it manifests itself, contains a directional element. It is not an activity that goes on in a random fashion for ever. Rather, I believe, it is gradually *progressing* in a uniform direction; there is some sort of progress, some advancement, some kind of product, that is gradually emerging from the innumerable trial-and-error actions. To get hold of this element, the process might properly be called '*progressive*' double fitting. To look at it from another angle, we should recall here the conspicuous wastefulness of these techniques. If there is so much wasted effort, there must also be certain positive residuals, however small their amount.

As regards that part of double fitting which I called 'theorising', the potential positive net effect is fairly obvious. It consists of a gradually rising level of abstraction. Starting from a relatively narrow cluster of observations, there is a trend which moves towards more and more comprehensive conceptual frameworks. The net effect of hypothesising is more illusive. It is particularly difficult to identify it, if one looks at any one brief period. But if we take sufficiently long periods, comparing the position at the beginning and the end, it appears that progress comes about by way of relatively increasing *complexity*: keeping the level of abstraction constant, the number of variables or phenomena that have been found to be causally (or otherwise) related to each other is larger at the end of the period than at the beginning. To be more precise about this, we would need a systematic inquiry into the actual development of concrete sociological studies during their preparatory stages. The question of how to measure the net effect of increasing complexity will certainly depend a great deal on the type of investigation. Moreover, any further elaboration of this matter would lead away from the behaviouristic approach into the problems of formal logic (set theory, and so on).

What is more important in the present stage is to realise that theorising and hypothesising are always interdependent. Hence, the overall 'progress' of the total process must involve simultaneously a relative rise in the level of abstraction as well as a relative increase in the degree of complexity. Taken together, the two effects bring about a gradual improvement in the stability of the total process. That is to say, both the emerging conceptual frameworks and the clusters of eclectic discoveries will appear in the end less arbitrary, less fluctuating, more established and more structured than they did initially. Obviously, this kind of increasing stability can only be relative. *Some* amount of subjectivity will always adhere to the theoretical frameworks, and *some* degree of arbitrariness regarding the selection of data will still be present in the finally published product. It should be noted that I am describing here only an idealised picture of the process. In a concrete case, there will be many ups and downs before a measure of stabilisation is reached that warrants the publication of the results. And, of course, it is possible that it is never reached at all (for example, the case of the project failure reported by Riesman and Watson in Hammond's chronicles). I have also neglected the further complication that even a small-scale study will always be following several lines, so that at any given moment there will be floating around side by side several unrelated frameworks and accordingly several unconnected clusters of data. But in principle we can treat each line of actual or potential inquiry as a single current of double fittings.

The particular advantage of this analysis appears to me in the possibility of treating theorising and hypothesising by a single analytical device. Since both represent a recurrent activity of double fitting, it is possible to see them as operations that are capable of interaction. At the same time it will, thus, be realised that this sort of interaction can only materialise as an ongoing process through time, a process that is at any given moment precarious and highly unstable, and does not produce a specifiable end-product. It can certainly not be seen by looking at the finalised published version of a given study. It must be remembered the problem is not *whether* there exists such interaction between theory and research. That it does exist in the practice of sociological work has hardly ever been doubted. The real question is: how can it be possible, considering that theory is concerned with interpretive innovations and empirical research with causal discoveries? The general process of progressive double fitting is also relevant to a number of other points that are well known but rarely seen in their bearing on the uniqueness of social inquiry. I would mention the notorious difficulty of the arbitrary starting-point of any piece of work (do we start with 'concepts' or 'facts'?). Then there is the familiar dilemma of value-determined theory, the vagueness of concepts and the related fact of the lack of genuine replication. Equally characteristic is the insoluble question of when to 'terminate' a given theoretical or empirical study. Questions of this sort will seem to be of minor importance when we consider that the technique of progressive double fitting is an activity *sui generis*, and that there is no other way of doing sociological work.

Conclusion

To round off this inquiry into unofficial techniques I shall try to connect it with a few aspects of formal methodology that seem to me of general interest. The topic of 'discoveries' was chosen as my main theme, because the term reflects an attitude that is very common among social scientists. It acts as a symbol of scientific objectivity and it derives from the belief that, apart from certain difficulties connected chiefly with the problems of values, social science could be just as rigorous as physical science. This attitude is often reinforced by the assumption that such imperfections are merely temporal, they are characteristic only of the 'present stage' of social science. As a consequence of this dependence on the experimental sciences, it seems to be overlooked that meanwhile an increasing amount of evidence is accumulating that suggests that the procedures actually used in the praxis of social research and theory may well turn out to be of a unique, unprecedented type. An incisive impulse in that direction came from the work of Merton, in his insistence on the need for investigating the social research behaviouristically.[32] But at that time the ideal of the logic of the physical sciences was still so deeply ingrained in our minds, as for example the preoccupation with 'discoveries' demonstrates, that it blocked the view to the *sui generis* features of our methods. Somewhat similar, in the same period, was the situation in which Lazarsfeld and his pupils started to analyse and codify the most important formal techniques of specifically sociological research. It was then already noticed that explicit hypothesis-testing was not the only legitimate method: the most typical techniques were recognised as revealing a distinctively different pattern, tentatively called 'elaboration'.[33]

I realise that my argument implies that theorising and hypothesising are epistemologically incommensurable. I have no answer to that. But in realising that the two operations have at least one basic element in common, the trial-and-error process of recurrent double fitting, we may be one step further in understanding the interdependence of theory and research. What we know about it so far suggests a type of inter-dependence that is unique to social science and, therefore, wholly out of reach to any positivistic theory of knowledge derived from the physical sciences.

Notes: Chapter 29

Reprinted from Teodor Shanin (ed.), *The Rules of the Game* (London: Tavistock), pp. 276–302, by kind permission of the author.

1 This is an abbreviated version of an essay first published as an informal discussion paper in 1965. Apart from the correction of minor inaccuracies in the presentation, my position has remained unchanged. Indeed, I have come to believe that the technique of 'progressive double fitting' is even more typical of sociological work than I thought at the time. This can now be seen by recognising the basic similarity between such apparently incommensurable works as Rosenberg (1968) and Znaniecki (1936).
2 The main topic emerged from methodological discussions with colleagues and students, I am especially indebted to Vic Allen, William M. Evan, Peter Gleichmann, Julian Nagel, Peter Rickman and Michael M. Walker. I also wish to thank Dietrich Goldschmidt, Wolfgang Lempert and Burkhard Lutz for giving me the opportunity to act as a participant observer in a large-scale survey that was carried out in Germany.
3 Merton (1957), p. 104. In taking this work as a point of departure, it should be noted that my criticism involves only minor points. As a matter of fact, it is Merton's concept of latent function that forms the basis of my analysis.
4 See Cannon (1945) pp. 68 ff.
5 See Merton (1957), p. 105.
6 See Merton (1957), p. 96, n. 18.
7 See Merton (1957), p. 229, n. 2, and p. 241, n. 13.
8 See Merton (1957), pp. 66 ff.
9 See Merton (1963).
10 See Merton (1963), p. 262.
11 See Merton (1963), p. 238.
12 See Merton (1963), p. 270.
13 See Toulmin (1961), p. 95.
14 see Kuhn (1962).
15 See Kuhn (1962). p. ix.
16 See Kuhn (1962), p. 24 and *passim*.
17 See Buckley (1957).
18 See Baldamus (1967).
19 Compare Parsons (1961).
20 See Rapoport (1959), p. 351.
21 See Parsons (1952).
22 See Baldamus (1967), pp. 10–14.
23 See Hammond (1964).
24 See Hammond (1964), introduction, p. 3.
25 See Brown (1963), pp. 165–93.
26 See Udy (1964), p. 177.
27 See, similarly, Blau (1964), p. 19 f.; Riesman and Watson (1964), p. 305; Coleman (1964), p. 202; Bellah (1964), p. 159.
28 See Udy (1964), p. 181.
29 See Davis (1964), p. 232.
30 See, similarly Bellah (1964), p. 159; Dalton (1964), p. 54; Riesman and Watson (1964), p. 307 and *passim*.
31 See Hammond (1964), introduction, p. 3.

32 See Merton (1957), pp. 100–17.
33 See Lazarsfeld and Rosenberg (1955), pp. 121–5; a further
    contribution from this school, Rosenberg (1968), reveals
    even more the specifically 'analytical' processes of
    hypothesising (including double fitting) throughout the
    methodology of survey research.

30

Generating Formal Theory

BARNEY G. GLASER

We are far more humble when it comes to generating formal theory. We remain convinced that it should be grounded, but are not sure yet, as with grounded substantive theory, of the resolutions to many specific problems of generation. For example: in choosing a core variable for a formal theory, what are the grounds for its relevancy, how does one integrate the theory, where next to theoretically sample, how dense should formal theory be? Indeed why generate formal theory at all? Once the analyst is cut loose from the grounding of a specific substantive area, answers to these questions are not readily apparent. At times it seems that formal theory can 'go' just about any way that an analyst desires.

In this chapter we shall touch on these problems, by giving answers to strategies developed through many years of experience in doing research and in writing at varying levels of conceptualisation, including two formal theory monographs.[1] We shall also give our thoughts on these problems, which have supplemented our experience and somewhat outdistanced it.[2] In the first section we consider the diverse sources of generating formal theory, with special attention to the link that substantive theory provides between data and formal theory. In the next section we discuss the differences in comparative analysis operations between substantive and formal theory, with special attention to theoretical sampling. Then we present a section on theoretical sampling for generating formal theory. Then we present a section on theoretical formulation with focus on density and integration. Lastly, we give our view of why generating formal theory is of value. Again, we reiterate that these ideas barely open up the methodology of generating grounded formal theory.

Sources of Formal Theory[3]

The several sources of formal theory can usefully be classified in three ways: grounded in systematic research, ungrounded, or a combination of both grounded and ungrounded. Speculative or ungrounded formal theory derives from any combination of several sources; whims and wisdoms of usually deceased great men, conjecture and assumptions about the 'oughts' of life, and other extant speculative theory. The usual method of developing such theory is to deduce logically from these sources. The weaving in of some grounded theory usually helps, but does not save nor even compete well with the theorist's emphasis on speculative sources.

As we have argued in *Discovery*,[4] this speculative, derived formal theory does not meet our criteria of fit, 'works', relevance, and easy modification. Indeed, because it is ungrounded, when applied to data such theory forces the data in many ways. The theory dictates, before empirical examination, presumed relevancies in problems, concepts and hypotheses, and the kinds of indicators that 'should' apply – to the neglect of emergent relevancies of processes, concepts, and their properties and indicators. Its fit and its predictions also are suspect, while modification of the theory when it does not work is regarded as requiring systematic conclusive proof, certainly not warranted by a few exceptional (often crucial) incidents. This forcing of the data by speculative formal theory has two untoward consequences: (1) some theorists, especially when young, are dissuaded from advancing and extending theories which appear useless; (2) while others settle for description made at low conceptual levels.

The principal sources of grounded formal theory consist both of the data of diverse systematic research, and the substantive theories generated from such data. In combination and separately these sources give rise to several bases of grounding: (1) one substantive area formal theory which uses 'rewriting up' techniques; (2) direct formulation from data from diverse substantive areas when no substantive theory exists; (3) expanding a single, existing substantive theory with comparative data of other areas, and comparative analysis of several existing substantive theories, which is perhaps the most powerful of these approaches. The latter is powerful because its coverage of more diverse properties of the formal theoretical area makes it apply to more diverse substantive areas with minimal qualifications. The 'rewrite' approach is, however, both the weakest and the more prevalent in sociology; Lastly, we consider (4) the Basic Social Process (BSP)[5] approach to generating formal theory; and (5) cumulative knowledge.

From Substantive to Formal Theory. Before considering these bases of grounding, let us briefly consider the essential difference and a few relationships between substantive and formal theory. By *substantive theory* we mean theory developed for a substantive or empirical area of sociological inquiry – such as patient care, race relations, professional education, geriatric lifestyles, delinquency, or financial organisations. By *formal theory* we mean theory developed for a formal or conceptual area of sociological inquiry – such as status passage, stigma, deviant behaviour, socialisation, status congruency, authority and power, reward systems, organisations, or organisational careers. Both types of theory may be considered 'middle-range'.[6] They fall between the 'minor working hypotheses' of everyday life and the 'all-inclusive' grand theories.

Substantive and formal theories exist on conceptually ordered distinguishable levels of generality, which differ only in terms of degree. In any one study each type of theory can shade at points into the other. The analyst, however, should focus clearly on one level or the other, or on a specific combination, because the strategies vary from arriving at each one. For example, in an analysis of the organisational careers of scientists, the focus was substantive (scientists' careers), not formal (organisational careers).[7] With the focus on a substantive area, the generation of theory can be achieved by doing a comparative analysis between or among groups within the same substantive area. In this instance, comparisons were made among the career stages of junior investigator, senior investigator and supervisor within two different promotional systems of the organisation. Generation of the substantive theory also can be furthered by comparisons of the organisational careers of scientists with other substantive cases within the formal area of organisational/careers, such as the careers of lawyers or military officers. Those comparisons would be used to illuminate the substantive theory about scientist's career.

However, if the focus of level of generality is on generating a formal theory, the comparative analysis is made among different kinds of substantive cases and their theories, which fall within the formal area, without relating the resulting theory back to any one particular substantive area. The focus of comparisons, to continue with our example, is now on generating a formal theory of organisational careers, not on generating a theory about a single substantive case of an organisational career. In *Organizational Careers*[8] the comparisons were between theories.

(1) *'Rewrite' techniques*

One version of rewriting techniques is simply to omit substantive words, phrases, or adjectives; instead of writing 'temporal aspects of dying as a non-scheduled status passage', one would write 'temporal aspects of non-scheduled status passage'. Substantive theory can also be rewritten up a notch: instead of writing about how doctors and nurses give medical attention to a

dying patient according to his social loss, one would talk of how professional services are distributed according to the social value of clients.

In each version of the rewriting technique, the social scientist writes a one-area formal theory on the basis of his substantive theory; he does not generate the former directly from the data. These techniques produce only an adequate *start* towards theory, *not* an adequate formal theory itself. *The researcher has raised the conceptual level of his work mechanically; he has not raised it through comparative understanding.* He has done nothing to broaden the scope of his theory on the formal level by comparative investigation of different substantive areas. He has not escaped the time and place of his substantive research. Moreover, the formal theory cannot fit or work very well when written from only one substantive area (and often only one case of the area), because it cannot be developed sufficiently to take into account many of the contingencies and qualifications that will be met in the diverse substantive areas to which it will be applied. All that happens is that it will be modified by other theories and data through the comparative method, because by itself it is too sparsely developed to use in making trustworthy predictions and explanations beyond the substantive area. Thus, in our view, the one-area formal theory still remains, in actuality, treated as a substantive theory possibly later to be generalised by comparative analysis. To be sure theory is a strategic link in advancing from substantive to formal theory, as it can be used in the comparative analysis of several substantive theories.

(2) *Data*

The linkage provided by substantive theory is not omitted when generating a formal theory directly from diverse sets of data. It is natural to the process of generating that parts of a substantive theory will emerge from the initial set of substantive data, before the theory's level of conceptualisation is raised by comparing it to data from other substantive areas. This process leads to great changes in the variable structure of the theory. For example, there is a drop out of what are only contextually significant variables – time, place and conditions of each substantive area.

(3) *Substantive theory*

The linkage between research data and formal theory, provided by substantive theory, is twofold. It occurs when a particular substantive theory is extended and raised to formal theory by the comparative analysis of it with other research data. The linkage occurs also when the substantive theory is comparatively analysed with *other* substantive theories. The theory arrived at when comparing substantive theories is more general and more qualified.

Substantive theories typically have important general relevance and become, almost automatically, springboards or stepping-stones to the development of a grounded formal theory. As stated in Glaser (1978), the core variable has general implications and can be followed through to generate a formal theory of the core.[9] For example, a substantive theory on the comparative failure of scientists leads directly to the need for a theory of comparative failure in work (or even more generally in all facets of social life).[10] Or substantive theory on deviance disavowal of people with visible handicaps leads to a formal one concerned with deviance disavowal by a much wider range of persons.[11]

Other relevant aspects provided by substantive theory for formal theory are the providing of *initial* direction in developing relevant conceptual categories, conceptual properties of categories, hypotheses relating these concepts, and in choosing possible modes of integration for the formal theory. We emphasise 'initial', because as the formal theory is generated from comparing many substantive theoretical ideas from many different cases – the relevant categories, properties and hypotheses will change in the process of generating theory. Also, in integrating formal theory, formal models of process, structure and analysis may be useful guides to integration, along with models provided by the comparatively analysed substantive theories.

(4) *BSP*[12]

A fourth approach, closely related to the above, to generating formal theory is to start with a BSP (or other core variable) and compare its phenomenon in different substantive classes. This is done both by searching the literature for where the BSP is processing on some dimension, and through memory of relevant literature, experiences and incidents. This approach requires a mature, experienced grounded theorist for several reasons. He must know a great deal of literature to draw on, he must have had experience in research for worthy anecdotes, he must have the capacity and skill to search much literature quickly and he must be experienced *in knowing when his BSP is merely a logical elaboration.* One can find specks of a BSP everywhere, but unless it was firmly grounded in at least one substantive theory, only the mature, theoretically sensitive sociologist will begin to know empirically if it is indeed relevant anywhere, *even though it sounds relevant.*

For example, it seems that BSPs such as memoing or risk-taking are relevant, but we are not that sure, never having seen them be the core variable in a substantive study. We have seen these variables in studies many times, but they never seem to emerge as core or near core. Thus, experience counsels that they would not be worthy candidates for generating a formal theory. In contrast, core BSPs such as cultivating, waiting, or faulting are very relevant BSP cores and are probably worthy of the time and effort to generate a formal theory on them. Our theory of status passage was generated on this basis – we had read, researched and experienced many forms of status passage for some years.

In searching the literature the analyst must be experienced, skilled at and sensitive to looking for the BSP in both its more general and more specific, but also different, conceptual forms. For example, to generate a formal theory of cultivating he can look at the more general processes of servicing and the more specific ones of courting, soliciting, prospecting, selling and persuading, as he varies his substantive classes of data. And the analyst can look for comparisons in BSPs that seem closely related, such as delivering, collecting, or rewarding. As this theoretical sampling proceeds, much that is preconceived and/or logically elaborated tends to be corrected by comparisons.

In writing a theory from this source of focusing on a BSP or core variable, the analyst should be careful not to mislabel the theory by referring to a unit – which both specifies it out of generality, and shifts emphasis from process to unit. Thus, a general theory of 'becoming' should be left as such and not be titled with a unit such as 'becoming a nurse', or 'becoming a professional', although it might have begun from such a source.

(5) *Cumulative knowledge*

Within these relations between social research, substantive theory and formal theory is an overall design for the cumulative nature of knowledge and theory, hence a moving force for generating higher-level formal theory. The design involves a progressive building up from facts through substantive to formal grounded theory. To generate grounded substantive theory, we need many facets for the necessary comparative analysis; ethnographic studies and direct data collection are required. Ethnographic studies, substantive theories and direct data collection are all, in turn, necessary for building up by comparative analysis to formal theory. This design, then, locates the place of each level of work within the cumulation of knowledge and theory, and thereby suggests a division of labour in sociological work.

For example, after having developed a theory of status passage, there is no reason not to link other grounded theory with this theory, provided that extant theory fits well and makes sense of our data. For example, 'awareness theory' was linked with our emergent theory of status passage.[13] Useful linkages with other grounded theories possibly will occur to other readers. In turn, our theory of status passage is subject to extension – best done through theoretical sampling and the associated comparative analysis. This extension represents a further specifying of the limits of that theory, thus an inevitable qualification of it.

The cumulative design also suggests that, besides many ethnographic studies, both multiple substantive and formal theories are needed to build up, through discovering their relationships, to more inclusive formal theories. Such a call for *multiple* theories is in contrast to the directly monopolistic implications of logico-deductive theories, whose formulators talk as if there is only one theory for a formal area or, perhaps, only one formal sociological theory for all areas. The need for multiple substantive theories to generate a formal theory may seem obvious, but it is not so obvious that multiple formal theories are also necessary. One formal theory never handles all the relevancies of an area, and by comparing many formal theories, we can begin to arrive at more inclusive, parsimonious levels of formal theory. Parsimonious grounded formal theories are hard-won by this design.

If we do not practice such modes of extending grounded theories, we relegate them, particularly if substantive, mainly to the status of respected little islands of knowledge, separated from others – each visited from time to time by inveterate footnoters, by assemblers of readings and of periodic bibliographical reviews, and by graduate students assigned to read the better literature. While the owners of these islands understandably are pleased to be visited, in due course of time they can look forward to falling out of fashion and to being bypassed. This is not how to build a cumulative body of theory.

The formal theory that we are referring to is induced by comparative analysis, and needs to be contrasted with 'grand' theory that is generated by logical deduction from assumptions and speculations about the 'oughts' of life. The logico-deductive theorist, proceeding under the licence and mandate of analytic abstraction and deduction from assumptions and conjecture, engages in premature parsimony of concepts and integrative model. He is not concerned with the theoretical-comparative analysis of data and substantive theories required to achieve a theory that fits and works in explaining and interpreting a formal area of inquiry. If sociologists continue to develop both speculative theory and general theoretical frameworks without recognising the great difference between those formulations and the theory that is genuinely grounded in data, however useful the former types may be as rhetoric or for orientation, when they are taken as theory, they simply help to forestall another generation's discovery and formulation of grounded, truly testable theory. Speculative theory and theoretical frameworks also have had the consequence of turning away many persons from theorising (because those are the only theories they recognise) in favour of syntheses[14] or publishing minimal conceptual descriptions.[15]

Generating Formal Theory by Comparative Analysis

The term comparative analysis – often used in sociology and anthropology – has grown to encompass several different meanings and thereby to carry several different burdens. Many sociologists and anthropologists, recognising the great power of comparative analysis, have employed it for achieving their various purposes. To avoid confusion we must, therefore, be clear as to our own use for comparative analysis (generating of theory) in contrast to its other uses (achieving accurate evidence, empirical generalisations, specification of a concept, and verifications of a hypothesis). Generation of theory both subsumes and assumes these other uses but only to the extent that they are in the service of generation. Otherwise they are sure to stifle it.

Comparative analysis is considered a general method, in our use of it, just as are the experimental and statistical methods – and all involve the logic of comparisons. Comparative analysis can, like those other methods, *be used for social units of any size.* Some sociologists and anthropologists customarily use the term 'comparative analysis' to refer only to comparisons among large-scale social units, particularly organisations, nations, institutions and large regions of the world. But such a reference restricts a general method to use with only the specific class of social units to which it has frequently been applied. As a general method for generating theory, comparative analysis takes on its fullest generality when one realises its power applied to social structural units of any size, large or small, ranging from men or their roles, through groups and organisations to the nations or world regions.[16]

Comparative analysis can also be used to compare conceptual units of a theory or theories, as well as data, in terms of categories and their properties and hypotheses. Such conceptual comparisons result, as we have seen, in generating, densifying and integrating the substantive theories into a formal theory by discovering a more parsimonious set of concepts with greater scope.

The basic criterion governing the theoretical sampling of comparison groups in order to compare conceptual units for generating formal as well as substantive theory is their theoretical relevance for furthering the development of emerging categories, properties, hypotheses and integration of the theory. *Any* groups may be selected that will help generate these elements of the theory. In making his selections, the researcher must always remember that he is an active sampler of theoretically relevant data, and as an active sampler of data, he must continually analyse the data to see where the next theoretical question will take him.

The criterion for selecting theoretically relevant materials is *ideational* to provide as broad and diverse a range of theoretical ideas on the formal area as possible. *This range of ideas may be contrasted to and does not necessarily mean, a broad range of data or of authors.* Ideas that fit theoretical areas or problems are the criterion of placement – not how much of an author or of a kind of data is used. The ultimate range of authors need not be great. It depends on the state of knowledge of the field.

Thus, materials are chosen to provide as many

categories, properties, hypotheses and problems on the formal theory as space permits – which, in turn, provides the range of elements for developing the formal theory. Many materials will come from exploratory qualitative research, not all of which are published yet are found in footnotes.[17] In qualitative research we usually find an abundance of general categories, hypotheses and problems, in contrast to their sparseness in quantitative research. Also, qualitative research discussions are easier and richer to read, especially for interested readers outside of sociology. The ideas of many of the materials may be applicable to several parts of the theory. But each is put where it will contribute the most ideationally to the generation of formal theory.

As said in discovering substantive theory, because groups are chosen for a single comparison only, the analyst has no definite, prescribed, preplanned number and types of groups to compare for all or even most categories, but he can cite the substantive class of groups. In research carried out for discovering formal theory, the researcher also *cannot* cite the diverse classes of substantive groups from which he collected data until the research is completed. In an extreme case, he may then find that the development of each major category may have been based on comparisons of different classes of groups. In the usual case there is considerable overlap of classes of comparison groups.

In theoretical sampling for formal theory, no one kind of data on a category, nor any single technique for data collection, is necessarily appropriate. Different kinds of data give the analyst different views or vantage-points from which to understand a category and to develop its properties; these different views we have called 'slices of data' in *Discovery*.[18] Theoretical sampling allows a multifaceted comparative investigation. There are no limits to the techniques of data collection, the way they are used, or the types of data required. The result is a variety of slices of data that would be bewildering if one wishes to evaluate them as accurate evidence for verifications. However, for generating formal theory this variety is highly beneficial, because it yields more diverse comparative information on categories than any one mode of knowing (technique of collection).

Among the slices of data that can be used in formal theory as opposed to substantive theory is the 'anecdotal comparison'. Through his own experiences, general knowledge, or reading, and the stories of others, the social scientist can gain data on other groups that offer useful comparisons. Anecdotal comparisons are especially useful in developing core categories. The researcher can ask himself where else has he learned about the category, and make quick comparisons to start to develop it and sensitise himself to its relevancies.

Rules of comparability of groups used in descriptive and verification studies do not apply in generating formal theory, because group comparisons are conceptual. Two typical, complementary rules of comparability mentioned in Glaser (1978)[19] as irrelevant are especially so when generating formal theory is the goal. One rule states that to be included within a set of comparison groups, a group must have enough features in common with them. Another rule is that to be excluded it must show a 'fundamental difference' from the others. These two rules for verificational and descriptive studies attempt to hold constant the strategic facts, or to disqualify groups where the facts either cannot actually be held constant, or would introduce more unwanted differences. In sum, one hopes that in this set of purified comparison groups spurious factors will not influence the findings and relationships and render them inaccurate.

These rules hinder the generation of formal theory. Weeding out spurious factors is not important in generating, since they are just one more theoretical idea to be included in the theory. Indeed, concern with these rules – to avoid spuriousness and inaccuracy – diverts attention away from the important sets of fundamental differences and similarities among groups which, upon analysis, become important qualifying conditions under which categories and properties vary. These conditions should be made a vital part of the theory. Furthermore, these two rules hinder the use of a wider range of classes or groups for developing categories and properties. Such a range, necessary for the fullest possible development of formal categories, is achieved by comparing incidents or ideas from *any* group, irrespective of differences or similarities, as long as the data indicates one similar category or property.

When theoretically sampling for comparison groups, several matters must be kept in mind. The analyst must be clear on the basic types of groups he wishes to compare, in order to control their effect on the generality of both *scope* of population, and *conceptual level of* his theory. As the analyst gradually shifts the degree of conceptual generality from substantive to formal theory, he must keep in mind the class of groups he selects. While the logic and process of comparative analysis remains the same, the process becomes more difficult, because of the more abstract conceptual level and wider range of groups. When the aim is to discover formal theory, the analyst will definitely select dissimilar substantive groups from the larger class, in order to increase his theory's scope while transcending substantive areas.

He will also find himself comparing groups that seem to be *non-comparable* on the substantive level but which on the formal level are conceptually comparable. Non-comparable on the substantive level here implies a stronger degree of apparent difference than does the term dissimilar. For example, while fire departments and emergency wards are substantially dissimilar, the conceptual comparability is still readily apparent; both deal with emergency systems which render immediate assistance. Since the basis of comparison between substantively non-comparable groups is not readily apparent, it must be explained on a higher conceptual level. For example, one could start developing a formal theory of social isolation by comparing four apparently unconnected monographs: *Blue Collar Marriage, The Taxi-Dance Hall, The Ghetto* and *The Hobo.*[20] All deal with facets of 'social isolation'. For another example, Goffman has compared apparently non-comparable groups, when generating his formal theory of stigma.[21]

The analyst who wishes to discover formal theory, then, should be aware of the usefulness of comparisons made on high-level conceptual categories among the seemingly non-comparable. He should actively seek this kind of comparison, do it with flexibility and be able to interchange the apparently non-comparable comparison with the apparently comparable ones. The non-comparable type of group comparison can greatly aid him in transcending substantive descriptions of time and place as he tries to generate a formal theory.

Density. Making a distinction between category and property indicates a conceptually systematic relationship between these two elements of theory. A category stands by itself as a conceptual element of theory; for example, a reversal. A property, in turn, is a conceptual aspect or element of a category; for example, the degree of clarity of a reversal. Categories and properties vary in degree of conceptual abstraction. Synthesis and integration of the theory may occur at many levels of conceptual and hypothetical generalisation, whether varying from substantive to formal theory, or within the formal level of abstraction. Levels of conceptualisation, then, is one aspect of the density of generated grounded theory. Another aspect of density is how densely a category is developed in terms of its theoretical properties. Yet another consideration of density is how well the theory is integrated within its full range of conceptualisation. We believe, of course, that a grounded substantive theory warrants much densification, so that it will fit a multitude of situations in its area. A dense theory lends itself to ready modification and formulation in order to handle yet new qualifications *required* by changing conditions in what is 'going on'. A dense theory helps relate very abstract levels to data.

A formal theory should also be dense, but in generating a formal theory *dedensification* occurs.[22] As substantive theories are compared, there is a 'fallout' of substantively specific variables, as cross-contextualisations generates the most general codes on underlying uniformities. Thus, parsimony and scope increase with comparison of different substantive classes.

The richness of substantive theory comes from the multiplication and proliferation of codes from the most abstract down in pyramiding fashion to smaller, lower-abstraction codes. In contrast, the richness of formal theory comes from dedensifying by a parsimony of underlying general ideas which 'lump' or condense some generally relevant substantive codes together as specific others 'fall-out'. Formal theory is extensive compared to the intensiveness of substantive theory.

Obviously, as the analyst extends the scope of his theory by including new substantive classes, his theoretical sampling is guided by the less dense, higher abstracting, recording process. As the abstracting process continues, formal theory densifies to the degree the scope of generality is increased by including more substantively relevant codes from different classes. In so doing, the analyst must guard against easily slipping into logical elaboration, by being sure all his comparisons are of grounded ideas.

Integration. The integration of a dense formal theory is accomplished quite differently from that of a substantive theory. The latter, as we have seen, is integrated by the emergence of a natural integration which occurs in the data of the area under consideration. Not so for formal theory; integration of small segments of a formal theory do emerge from substantive theory as it is generated. But substantive integration is likely to disappear along with fall out, condensing and depyramiding of substantive codes.

In large measure the total integration of the formal theory can become arbitrary, since core relevance is hard to be sure of. Hence, formal theory can be usefully integrated by one or more theoretical models. In *Status Passage*[23] we chose a cumulative build up of several core categories of status passage, each of which has clear relationships to the other. Thus, to recapitulate, direction and timing combine to make shape of status passage; and desirability provides the motivation to control shape and to go through a single-status passage and through multiple-status passages whether alone, in aggregate, or in concert. This mode of integrating the theory readily can be seen as arbitrary, in the light of possible alternative modes. We originally worked on fifteen core categories of status passage, which could have been reduced differently than finally chosen; and, of course, we did not work on all possible core categories. Again, logical elaboration is too easily slipped into if the analyst is not careful, and goes the way of 'neatness' and 'completeness'.

A modelled integration does not make a formal theory ungrounded, it merely makes it somewhat less grounded than if integration were achieved by the emergence of a natural integration, which includes the higher-level abstraction codes. This raises the question: can a formal theory be integrated on a grounded basis, if substantive integration does not hold? The answer, yet to be completely shown by more studies, is *perhaps.* One way is for the analyst to use the most general codes of the stages of a grounded BSP as his integration scheme.[24] The analyst then begins to theoretically sample in a variety of substantive areas for each stage of the process. For example, in diet health optimising there are three stages; pollution, purification and compromising purification with small amounts of pollution.[25] If the analyst were to develop an optimising formal theory, he could theoretical sample for each stage in various substantive areas.

Limits for theoretical sampling do not revolve around saturation, as with substantive theory, since we think it is probably impossible to saturate categories for the formal theory. There are always substantive areas to sample. Saturation, in fact, revolves only around the temporal limits, monetary resources, personal interest and knowledge of the analyst. But no matter, since new data and ideas merely modify an ever-developing formal theory by adding density, parsimony and scope while dedensifying substantive-specific codes. Another analyst, not personally saturated, can always pick up where the analyst left off.

The grounded area which yielded the BSP makes the analyst sensitive to how to begin theoretical sampling and coding by using the original substantive areas to vary the scope of his theory and generate the fall out of substantive-specific variables and condense those that uncover the cross-contextual uniformities of the formal theory. As the formal theory codes emerge, they are integrated by the general stages of the BSP, however modified. The chances that the stages will vary from the substantive integration are great, if the variation that they account for in the formal theory problem is different from that of the substantive theory; but the stages may change, they will be a grounded integration that emerged for the formal theory by cross-substantive comparative analysis of an emergent substantive integration. The above discussion also applies to the dimensions of a basic structural condition, such as shifts, or of other core variables.

The BSP integration of a formal theory has some advantages in degree over an arbitrary modelled formal theory. It tends to be more relevant, since it started from substantive relevance and the comparisons verify and modify the relevance. Its applicability is also more apparent for the same reason. It is more understandable to readers because of its emergent 'natural' integration. Arbitrary integration tends to lead to a highly dense unrelieved formal theory, since all seems relevant – logically – as more comparisons generate more codes. This was the problem of *Status Passage*.[26] The theory will also seem closer to reality, if it appears grounded in the original substantive concern; thus, it will have more grab, imagery and fewer gaps. Also the formal problems seem more relevant when they are grounded in data, not in 'sociological' interest. Parsimony and scope probably do not vary significantly between the two types of integrations. Furthermore, a formal theory based on a BSP integration can be used tentatively to open up a substantive area. This is only provided that the BSP has an emergent fit, and the analyst has not

enough resources to emerge a substantive theory from systematic research, which would clearly be more favourable. In this sense a formal theory can be a useful consultation tool. Let us examine this area.

Applied Formal Theory

Our colleagues often ask: 'Of what use is formal theory?' We assume that they accept the standard uses of formal theory: guiding substantive research; opening up substantive areas for thought, research and scholarship; verificational studies of formal theory; modifying and extending it and integrating it with other theory to increase its scope with parsimony. These are quite worthy of *grounded* formal theory as opposed to the blind alleys of logical formal theory.

An applied use for grounded formal theory exists, especially one based on a BSP. This is based on the fact that it is not generalised to other populations but *generalised to basic social processes that underlie the issues and problems of diverse substantive areas* – for which there is *yet no grounded theory*.[27] This general relevance, this transcending of substantive areas, makes grounded *formal* theory a viable, applicable tool in, for example, consultations and during negotiations. It is also useful for critiquing other sociology.

When using grounded formal theory, the social scientists need not know all there is to be known about the substantive area. A little substantive knowledge related to the emergent fit of principal indicators, allows the formal theory to be applied. For example, theory about emergency systems that is based on the standard systems of a city, can be applied to developing a new system, such as a type of 'crisis intervention'. The consultant finds that the mind-absorbing and mind-opening aspects of such formal theory make sense to the client, and soon he becomes able to supply his own indicators and substantive information. Moreover, a theorist *qua* consultant can contribute to the research enterprises of colleagues, by stimulating thought about the implications of their data (already or soon to be collected) concerning matters suggested by grounded formal theory. We have found the theory of status passages useful both for research consultation, and pragmatically addressed consultation.[28]

Often in the latter kind of consultation there is neither time nor money for the research needed to develop a relevant substantive theory; or there is yet nothing to research, or no way to research the data. Cogent suggestions are needed, and grounded formal theory is most applicable in these instances. Our theory of status passage, for instance, is fairly obviously applicable to help, guide and articulate many institutionalised status passages now in their forma-tion, expansion, or 'having problems'; such as new kinds of training programmes, illness careers and novel styles of socialisation. We have underlined the applied capability of grounded formal theory as an emerging area for sociological endeavour and theory. Applied social theory – in contrast to applied social research – only becomes realistic with the development of grounded theory that fits, works, is relevant and is readily modifiable, and it seems that formal theory is more readily applicable than substantive theory to different classes of substantive areas.

Notes: Chapter 30

Reprinted from Barney G. Glaser, *Theoretical Sensitivity* (Mill Valley, Calif.: Sociology Press, 1978), pp. 142–56, by kind permission of the author.

1   See Glaser and Strauss (1971), and Glaser (1968); see also Strauss and Glaser (1975).
2   The future of grounded formal theory requires that we do another book devoted to its methodology, *after* much more experience is gained.
3   Much of this section may also be found in slightly altered form in chapter 9 of Glaser and Strauss (1971), and the introduction of Glaser (1968).
4   See Glaser and Strauss (1967).
5   See Glaser (1978), chapter 6.
6   See Merton (1957).
7   See Glaser (1964b).
8   See Glaser (1968).
9   See Glaser (1978), chapter 6.
10   See Glaser (1964a).
11   See Davis (1961).
12   This subsection rests heavily on memos received from Odis E. Bigus, Department of Sociology, University of Tulsa, Oklahoma, USA.
13   See Glaser and Strauss (1968).
14   See Lofland (1969).
15   See Sudnow (1967).
16   See Glaser (1978), chapter 3, on the theoretical coding of structural units.
17   See Goffman (1959), and Hughes (1958), for examples of masters referring to unpublished student work.
18   See Glaser and Strauss (1967).
19   See Glaser (1978), chapter 3.
20   See respectively Komarovsky (1962); Cressey (1932); Wirth (1928); and Anderson (1923).
21   See Goffman (1963).
22   Based on material from Odis E. Bigus.
23   See Glaser and Strauss (1971).
24   Based on material from Odis E. Bigus.
25   See Hanson (1976).
26   See Glaser and Strauss (1971).
27   See Glaser (1978), chapter 6.
28   See Zetterberg (1962).

Section Nine

Analysing and Reporting Field Research

31

Styles of Data Analysis: Approaches and Implications

ROBERT G. BURGESS

Traditionally, social science research has been sub-divided into 'stages'. However, these 'stages' occur simultaneously and are complementary in field research. Indeed, Becker *et al.* writing in their study *Boys in White* indicate that:

> In this research, analysis was not a separate stage of the process which began after we had finished gathering our data. Rather . . . data-gathering and analysis went on simultaneously (Becker, *et al.* 1961, p. 31)

Here, the research process involved constant analysis as field notes were read and reread to discover relevant problems of study, hypotheses were developed in relation to the problems posed and the researchers looked for valid indications of variables contained in the hypotheses. (cf. a similar process in journalism, Bernstein and Woodward, 1974). Analysis continued throughout the study and provided an outline of many of the conclusions contained in the final research report. However, there are relatively few accounts from field researchers of the actual process of data analysis or from methodologists on how data analysis can be done in field research. (An attempt has been made to address some of these difficult issues in a series of papers on the analysis of qualitative data; (Blaxter, 1979).

Among researchers, useful accounts have been provided by Platt (1976), and by Wolff (1960). The account by Platt of her study of sociological research projects is particularly useful as she indicates what she thought she would do, as well as what she actually did. She writes:

> Originally the analysis was conceived rather vaguely. I just thought that I would identify a series of themes and write about them, and that coding, analysis and writing would be one integral process. Perhaps it could have been like that, but it was not. (Platt, 1976, pp. 197–8)

In practice, she shows that data analysis was a long process that involved reading and rereading the interviews she had conducted. To begin with, she had to establish coding categories based on themes that arose in the interviews. However, she found that when new themes arose, it was essential to go back over the interviews that had already been examined. In short, she considers that data analysis is a long and laborious process, where the researcher has to try to avoid skimping on the work.

Wolff (1960) devotes a complete paper to describing the operations involved in the collection and organisation of field materials in his study of Loma. Here, he indicates the way in which he classified his field notes into specific topics, and cross-referenced the topics while he was in the field. The result was 500 single-spaced pages of field notes divided into sixty-six topics. These notes were arranged into seven broad categories around which the main themes in the final report were organised. However, he indicates that when the process of writing up began, there were shifts between the way he intended using his material and the way in which he actually used it.

These two researchers provide an all too rare glimpse of the methodological operations involved in data analysis, which have considerable influence upon the final research report. Such accounts force the researcher to consider a number of questions about data analysis. Some of the main questions that can be posed have been summarised by Lofland:

> How did the leading ideas that organized your present analysis evolve? A suddent flash? Slowly? Other?
> What kind of models or images are you aware of employing to organize the materials? What were their sources? To what degree did you organize your analysis before writing it out in text, versus writing it and then seeing what you had?
> Did you write a little every day, around the clock in bursts, or some other way? In general, what were the most important difficulties and facilitants experienced in evolving the analysis and writing it up? How would you, or have you, modified your practices since doing the particular work described here? (Lofland, 1974b, p. 308)

It is regrettable that questions such as these have not been directly addressed by the contributors to Bell and Newby (1977), and Bell and Encel (1978), for if field researchers were to address these questions, we should begin to understand the processes involved and the technical skills required to analyse field data. Meanwhile, we can begin to examine some of the characteristics of data analysis as we attend to two questions. First, what is data analysis? Secondly, what can a researcher do with field materials that are gathered using observational methods, unstructured interviews and written and oral documents?

Numerous reseachers have indicated that data does not 'speak for itself'. Indeed, a setting may provide material from which to build the analysis but it does not dictate the analysis. Lofland (1974a) has outlined a variety of circumstances in which no sociological analysis takes place. First, there are reports based on a 'moral style', where the researcher shows empathy and sympathy for the group studied. Secondly, there are reports based on 'the "then they do this" style', which present a detailed chronological record of what occurred. Finally, he identifies a 'vacillating style', in which sociological concepts are haphazardly applied to the data collected. In an earlier account Lofland argues that the process of data analysis involves an appreciation of the way in which participants order and analyse their world. He maintains that 'the qualitative analyst seeks to provide an explicit rendering of the structure, order, and patterns found among a set of participants' (Lofland, 1971, p. 7). The field researcher, therefore, needs to describe and explain that which has been observed and to indicate further areas that require detailed study. The material obtained from a single setting may be used in a variety of analyses, as data can be selected and combined to illustrate numerous social structures and social processes. Indeed, Schatzman and Strauss (1973) have indicated that data can be used to provide a straight description that links into classes of accepted theory, an analytic description whereby an organisational scheme may be developed from the data and substantive theory which is present in any descriptive account.

Some of the basic issues involved in the analysis of field data are outlined in the paper by Becker and Geer (Chapter 32), who examine the way in which sequential analysis is done in field research and the way in which conclusions are reported. While they indicate that there are no rules for doing data analysis, there have been several suggestions about how data can be examined. In a classic paper of qualitative data analysis, Barton and Lazarsfeld (1955) indicate ways in which researchers can begin to analyse data. First, they indicate ways in which initial observations and experiences may be systematically scanned for further questions that can be posed in subsequent research. Here, we are brought back to the relationship between early field experiences and data analysis discussed by Pons (see Section One, Chapter 5), and the relationship between field notes and data analysis that has been examined by Geer (1964). Secondly, Barton and Lazarsfeld (1955)

indicate how observations can be used as indicators which they illustrate by making reference to *Deep South* (Davis, Gardner and Gardner, 1941), and to *Street Corner Society* (Whyte, 1955), where observations are used to get at complex social processes and social structures such as racial prejudice and gambling in the respective studies. Barton and Lazarsfeld also discuss what can be done with an array of observations. They suggest that field data can be used to arrive at crude lists of types and typologies. In particular, they indicate that field data can be used to classify people and situations as illustrated by the work of Chicago sociologists, such as Anderson (1923) and Wirth (1928). In each case, these writers utilise their data to provide portraits of the characters in their studies. Finally, they indicate that the most highly developed descriptive system used in data analysis is the systematic typology which is derived from basic attributes or dimensions of the data. The way in which Anderson (1923) establishes a typology of homeless men provides a classic example of this approach, while Ditton's typology of the men who deliver bread and who feature in his study (Ditton, 1977) provides a more recent example. Finally, Barton and Lazarsfeld indicate how field data can be used to suggest relationships, causes, effects and processes. In this respect, their paper highlights various levels of analytic complexity and ways in which researchers may begin to lever their data to arrive at sociological explanations.

A further detailed scheme for analysing data has been put forward by Lofland (1971). He provides a guide to the analysis of field data for the researcher. Lofland indicates that explanation and understanding can be achieved by examining six social phenomena which range along a microscopic-macroscopic continuum. He suggests acts, activities, meanings, participation, relationships and settings as the basic units of social analysis. Here, Lofland has outlined an ideal approach to data analysis that has to be applied in different ways depending on the different social settings. However, he indicates that this scheme is merely a device that can be utilised to order field data and to seek out a sociological understanding. His discussion (Lofland, 1971, chapter 2) provides numerous examples drawn from a range of sociological studies which illustrate various ways in which data analysis has been achieved by researchers working in a variety of social settings.

A further scheme for data analysis comes from the Manchester School of sociology and social anthropology. Gluckman, Mitchell, Turner and Van Velsen developed a case study method, in which social action is examined in order to arrive at a set of abstract principles. Gluckman (1961; 1967) traces the use of case study material back to Malinowski. However, he criticises Malinowski for collecting and using data merely to illustrate specific points in his argument – an approach that Gluckman refers to as the 'method of apt illustration'. Specifically, he maintains that this method is inappropriate for the analysis of the total process of social life. As an alternative he suggests taking a series of specific incidents involving the same persons or groups over a long period of time, in order to examine principles of social structure and social relations. Gluckman (1942) used a bridge-opening ceremony as a way into an analysis of the complexities of social structure in modern Zululand. Similarly, Mitchell (1956a) examined a series of incidents when he focused upon ceremonial behaviour and conducted an analysis of a team of dancers in the Copper Belt, in order to illuminate aspects of tribalism in an urban setting. A more explicit development of this approach is revealed in Turner's discussion of the concept of social drama (Chapter 33). In the social drama, crisis situations are used to examine latent conflicts in social life, in order that the researcher can 'observe the crucial principles of the social structure in their operation, and their relative dominance at different points of time' (Turner, 1957, p. 93). Here, Turner is suggesting that dramas such as ceremonies, demonstrations and disputes may be studied so that the researcher can show how the actions of informants reflect their positions in the social structure, which may generate questions that involve the collection and interpretation of further data. This approach has been elaborated by Van Velsen's discussion of situational analysis (Van Velsen, 1967), and in the network approach that has been discussed by Mitchell (1969) and utilised in several studies (Boissevain and Mitchell, 1973; Boissevain, 1974).

The article by Morgan (Chapter 34) does not merely provide an illustration of data analysis utilising Turner's notion of social drama, but also raises a series of questions concerning the ethical, social and political context in which the reporting of field research takes place. Becker (1964) has summarised some of the key questions concerning published reports, when he asks: in what form should researchers publish their findings? Under what conditions? What can be done to minimise harm to the persons studied? These are questions that all field researchers have to address concerning relationships and responsibilities with their informants.

While these questions indicate the general problems that confront the reseacher, more specific ethical issues are raised sharply by Platt, when she writes of her own research: 'People often told me things that they would not have been prepared to see published in ways that could identify them or that could have harmed them or embarrassed them or other people' (Platt, 1976, pp. 201–2). In these circumstances, the researcher has to consider whether to keep faith with the informant or to omit particular items which may render the account false and lose interesting data. Furthermore, even if attempts are made to resolve some of these problems by utilising pseudonyms for informants, it may still be possible for readers to discover the location of the research and the identity of the informants as happened

with Morgan's work. As Platt (1976) suggests, there may be circumstances in which the informants may need not only to be shielded from the academic community, but also from themselves. In an attempt to offer some protection to individuals who co-operate with researchers the British Sociological Association (1973) has drawn up a statement of ethical principles in an attempt to influence the conduct of its members. This statement provides a framework within which researchers can operate; it is not legally binding and cannot be enforced. Furthermore, such statements (cf. American Anthropological Association, 1971) really only considers one of the parties involved in the research process. The activities of informants and the recipients of research reports cannot be governed by these statements. We have only to look at Klockar's key informant who took great pains to promote and sell the book in which he appeared (Klockars, 1977), and the evidence from Morgan (Chapter 34) of the newspaper reporter who located the factory where he worked, to appreciate the complex relationships between researcher, researched and the recipients of research reports. In this respect, Roth's critical comments on statements of ethical principles and codes of ethics seem justified (Roth, 1962b). Indeed, Roth indicates that researchers are more likely to resolve some of these problems by 'Analyzing the research process of the sociologist himself than by drawing up written codes of ethics which merely perpetuate current moral biases and restrict rather than aid further ethical development' (Roth, 1962b, p. 284). For as soon as researchers begin to examine the research process, they are confronted with many questions: to whom are researchers accountable? To whom are researchers responsible? How do researchers minimise deception? Do researchers inform all informants equally? Do researchers collaborate with informants? Such questions do not have any definite answers. However, a consideration of these problems can help researchers to take informed decisions on the basis of their analysis of the social, ethical and political context of field research.

Suggestions for Further Reading

METHODOLOGY

For discussions on data analysis, see:

Barton, A. H. and Lazarsfeld, P. F. (1955), 'Some functions of qualitative analysis in social research', *Frankfurter Beiträge zur Soziologie*, 1955, pp. 321–61 (reprinted in G. J. McCall and J. L. Simmons (eds), *Issues in Participant Observation* (Reading, Mass.: Addison-Wesley), pp. 163–96, 239–44); provides a range of suggestions about how researchers can handle their data.

Blaxter, M. (1979) (ed.), 'The analysis of qualitative data: a symposium', special issue of *Sociological Review*, vol. 27, no. 4, pp. 649–827; contains a series of papers that explore problems involved in handling qualitative data.

Epstein, A. L. (1967) (ed.), *The Craft of Social Anthropology* (London: Tavistock). A collection of essays that contain discussions of the case study method of analysis. See especially the essays by Gluckman (1967); Epstein (1967b); and Van Velsen (1967).

Gluckman, M. (1961), 'Ethnographic data in British Social Anthropology', *Sociological Review*, vol. 9, no. 1, pp. 5–17; discusses case study analysis.

Lofland, J. (1971), *Analyzing Social Settings* (New York: Wadsworth); a useful text on field research that orientates its material towards data analysis (see, especially, part 1).

Lofland, J. (1974), 'Styles of reporting qualitative field reports', *American Sociologist*, vol. 9, no. 3, pp. 101–11. A short account of analysis and non-analysis.

Lofland, J. (1974), 'Analyzing qualitative data: first person accounts', *Urban Life and Culture*, vol 3, no. 3, pp. 307–9. A brief introduction to data analysis that raises a series of important questions.

Macfarlane, A. (1977), 'History, anthropology and the study of communities', *Social History*, no. 5, pp. 631–52. A useful discussion of the way in which the case study approach can be applied to historical material. See the reply by C. J. Calhoun (1978), *Social History*, vol. 3, no. 3, pp. 363–73.

Mitchell, J. C. (1969) (ed.), *Social Networks in Urban Situations* (Manchester: University of Manchester Press). A good guide to network analysis.

Turner, V. W. (1957), *Schism and Continuity in an African Society: a study of Ndembu Village Life* (Manchester: University of Manchester Press); contains the extract reprinted here as Chapter 33. See the way in which the approach advocated by Turner is used to analyse particular cases, pp. 95–203.

Turner, V. W. (1974), *Dramas, Fields and Metaphors: Symbolic Action in Human Society* (Ithaca, NY, and London: Cornell University Press). A more advanced discussion of 'social drama' – see the preface and chapter 1.

For discussions of ethical problems including an analysis of the ethics of reporting social science data, see:

Barnes, J. A. (1979), *Who Should Know What?* (Harmondsworth: Penguin); provides a detailed survey of ethical issues and an extensive bibliography on the subject.

Becker, H. (1964), 'Problems in the publication of field studies', in A. J. Vidich, J. Bensman and M. R. Stein (eds), *Reflections on Community Studies* (New York: Harper & Row). A useful guide to ethical problems in reporting data.

Cassell, J. and Wax, M. L. (1980) (eds), 'Ethical problems of fieldwork', special issue of *Social Problems*, vol. 27, no. 3, pp. 259–378; contains a variety of papers on informed consent and associated field problems.

Douglas, J. D. (1970) (ed.), *The Relevance of Sociology* (New York: Appleton-Century-Crofts); contains the papers by Becker (1970c) and Gouldner (1970) in the 'taking sides' debate.

Polsky, N. (1969), *Hustlers, Beats and Others* (Harmondsworth: Penguin); provides a useful discussion on ethics in relation to the study of deviancy; although the remarks are relevant to other areas of study.

Sjoberg, G. (1967), (ed.), *Ethics, Politics and Social Research* (London: Routledge & Kegan Paul); consists of a collection of papers that raise many of the central issues.

EMPIRICAL STUDIES

All field research reports contain some form of analysis. However, some reports are more explicit about data analysis than others. The studies that are listed here have been chosen for their clarity regarding data analysis:

Anderson, N. (1923), *The Hobo* (Chicago: University of Chicago Press).

Becker, H. S., Geer, B., Hughes, E. C. and Strauss, A. L. (1961), *Boys in White: Student Culture in Medical School* (Chicago: University of Chicago Press).

Bell, C. (1968), *Middle Class Families* (London: Routledge & Kegan Paul) (see especially chapter 7).

Ditton, J. (1977), *Part-Time Crime: an Ethnography of Fiddling and Pilferage* (London: Macmillan).

Gluckman, M. (1942), *An Analysis of a Social Situation in Modern Zululand*, Rhodes-Livingstone Paper No. 28.

Loudon, J. (1961), 'Kinship and crisis in South Wales', *British Journal of Sociology*, vol, 12, no. 4, pp. 333–50; also reprinted in C. C. Harris (1970) (ed.), *Readings in Kinship in Urban Society* (Oxford: Pergamon), pp. 187–208.

Mitchell, J. C. (1956), *The Kalela Dance*, Rhodes-Livingstone Paper No. 27.

Nash, R. (1973), *Classrooms Observed* (London: Routledge & Kegan Paul).

Platt, J. (1976), *Realities of Social Research* (London: Chatto & Windus for University of Sussex Press).

Strauss, A., Schatzman, L., Bucher, R., Ehrlich, D. and Sabshin, M. (1964), *Psychiatric Ideologies and Institutions* (New York: The Free Press).

Whyte, W. F. (1955), *Street Corner Society* (2nd edn) (Chicago: University of Chicago Press).

A series of studies that raise ethical problems include:

Cohen, S. and Taylor, L. (1972), *Psychological Survival: the Experience of Long-Term Imprisonment* (Harmondsworth: Penguin).

Festinger, L., Riecken, H. W. and Schachter, S. (1956), *When Prophecy Fails* (New York: Harper & Row).

Humphreys, L. (1970), *Tearoom Trade* (London: Duckworth).

Parker, H. (1974), *View From the Boys* (Newton Abbot: David & Charles).

Patrick, J. (1973), *A Glasgow Gang Observed* (London: Eyre-Methuen).

Vidich, A. J. and Bensman, J. (1968), *Small Town in Mass Society* (2nd edn) (Princeton, NJ: Princeton University Press).

Wallis, R. (1976), *The Road to Total Freedom: a Sociological Analysis of Scientology* (London: Heinemann).

32

Participant Observation: The Analysis of Qualitative Field Data

HOWARD S. BECKER AND BLANCHE GEER

Introduction

Many people think of the work of science as the production of general propositions stating the relation between two or more variables under a specified set of conditions. Such propositions take, in the simplest case, this form: if A, then B – provided that conditions D, E, and F obtain. These kinds of propositions avoid taking account of the unique characteristics of any given case and attempt to abstract from the particular case only those variables contained in the proposition, while controlling all others. Students of small groups, for instance, work with propositions relating such variables as cohesion, communication and deviance in ways that are purposely independent of those qualities unique to the groups on which their studies are done.

Generating such propositions is an important part of scientific work, but sometimes the study of human organisation requires a different approach. For many practical and theoretical problems, we want to take account of as much of an organisation's complexity as our theory will allow. We may be interested in applying existing theory to a particular case in order to understand and possibly control it, or in developing theories about social systems and their relations with the environment, or in understanding the nature of a particular social problem. When our interests lie in these directions, we want to take account of those very characteristics which, when we seek general causal propositions, we want to control or otherwise render irrelevant to our problem.

Studies oriented to an understanding of an organisation and its local circumstances rather than to demonstrating relations between variables need not be untheoretical. But the person doing such research assumes that he does not know enough before beginning his study to identify relevant problems and hypotheses in the organisation chosen for study, nor to recognise valid indicators of the theoretical variables in which he is interested. He believes that a major part of his research must consist of finding out what problems he can best study in this organisation, what hypotheses will be fruitful and worth pursuing, what observations will best serve him as an indicator of the presence of such phenomena as, for example, cohesiveness or deviance.

Research aimed at discovering problems and hypotheses requires a data gathering technique that maximises the possibility of such discovery. Obviously, the more structured a technique, the less likely the researcher is to find facts whose existence he had not previously considered or to develop hypotheses he had not formulated when he began his study. A respondent in an unstructured interview is more likely to provoke a discovery by saying something unexpected than is the respondent who can only check one of six precoded replies to a questionnaire item. Techniques which maximise the possibility of coming upon unexpected data include the free or unstructured interview and participant observation.

Observation is not always a feasible alternative and is considerably more expensive and time-consuming than is interviewing. It provides, however, firsthand reports of events and actions and much fuller coverage of an organisation's activities, giving direct knowledge of matters that, from interviewing, we could know about only by hearsay. Whether or not one should use observation in any particular study, depends on the resources available and the character of the problem one is attempting to solve.

The term 'participant observation' covers several kinds of research activity.[1] The researcher may be a member of the group he studies; he may pose as a member of the group, though in fact he is not; or he may join the group in the role of one who is there to observe. Though the technical problems of managing one's research role and of gathering data differ greatly, the researcher in any of these three situations faces the same kinds of analytic problems. Consequently, as our interest here is in problems of analysis, we have made no distinction based on the character of the researcher's role, though this would obviously have great relevance in other contexts. In general, the participant observer gathers data by participating in the daily life of the group or organisation that he studies. He watches the people he is studying to see what situations they ordinarily meet and how they behave in them. He talks with the other participants and discovers their interpretations of the events he has observed.

In our own study of a state medical school we wanted, originally, to discover what a medical school did to students other than give them a technical education.

We assumed that students left medical school with a set of ideas about medicine and medical practice that differed from the ideas they entered with. Such changes presumably influenced the career choices students made once they became practising physicians: whether to go into general practise or a speciality, and if the latter, which speciality to enter; where to practise; and whether to practice alone, with a partner, or in some institutional setting. Our original focus, then, was on the medical school as an organisation in which the student, through his participation in it, acquired some basic perspectives on his later activity as a doctor.

We realised from the beginning that there was a great deal we did not know. We did not know what perspectives were characteristic of doctors in practice. We did not know what perspectives a student acquired while in school. We did not know the mechanisms by which the medical-school experience affected the student's views. We did not know the pattern of social relationships that students had in school. These gaps in our knowledge committed us to working with an open theoretical scheme, in which problems, hypotheses and variables were to be discovered rather than with a scheme in which predetermined problems would be investigated by isolating and measuring the effects of specified variables. We chose participant observation as our major mode of data gathering, because is allowed us to identify and follow up problems crucial to the medical students and to revise our thinking about the organisation as we learned more about it.

Before we turn to problems of analysis, we will briefly discuss our fieldwork procedures. These were dictated by the routine activities of the medical students. We went to lectures with students taking their first two years of basic science and frequented the laboratories in which they spent most of their time watching them and engaging in casual conversation as they dissected cadavers or examined pathology specimens. We followed students to their fraternity houses and sat around while they discussed their school experiences. We accompanied students in the clinical years on rounds with attending physicians, watched them examine patients on the wards and in the clinics, and sat in on discussion groups and oral exams. We ate with the students and took night call with them. We pursued interns and residents through their crowded schedules of teaching and medical work. We stayed with one small group of students in each of the many departments of the hospital for periods ranging from a week to two months, spending many full days with them. We found time for conversation and took advantage of this to interview students informally about things that had happened and were about to happen and about their own backgrounds and aspirations.

Such a programme of observation yields an immense amount of detailed description. Our files contain approximately 5,000 single-spaced pages of such description. The data are 'rich'; they contain material on a wide range of phenomena as seen from many points of view, but they also tend to be unsystematic. Though there are occasions when an observer follows up a particular problem in a systematic fashion for a while, the fact that the observation follows no 'design' means that the data reflect the shifting emphases dictated by new discoveries and are not pointed in any single-minded way towards the solution of a specific problem. In particular, there are no data specifically designed to test propositions of the 'if A, then B . . .' type.

What is the participant observer, with his file of 'rich' but unsystematic data, to do? He knows a good deal about the organisation he has studied, and he has a great deal of confidence in many of the conclusions he has drawn. But how does he present his conclusions and the evidence so as to evoke in other scientists the same confidence he himself feels? Participant observation has not done well with these problems, and the full weight of evidence for a given conclusion is usually not presented. The observer's conclusions often have a kind of *prima facie* validity, a 'ring of truth', but the reader of his research report has no way of knowing whether a solid basis of fact underlies this. The reader does not have the data available with which to convince himself and must rely on his faith in the researcher's honesty and intelligence. This is unfortunate, because we believe that most observational studies gather data of a kind that *would be* convincing, if it were assembled and presented in such a way that the reader could see why the researcher believes as he does in his conclusions. Towards this end, we utilised two modes of attack on these problems of analysis and research reporting, which we now consider.

First, the fact that the participant observer constantly redesigns his study as he uncovers new data deserves to be taken very seriously. It indicates that he engages in analytic activity most of the time that he is in the field. This analysis is often carried on unsystematically, without any consideration of its underlying logical structure or rationale. The observer's 'hunches' and 'insights' are, in fact, truncated and unformalised acts of analysis. We reasoned that, if we could make the nature of this analytic activity clear, participant observers could carry on a continuing or sequential analysis[2] in a more formal and self-conscious fashion. At the end of their fieldwork they would not have a mass of undigested field notes, but a set of tentative conclusions based on a running analysis of the field data.

Secondly, we decided that the model of the 'If A, then B . . .' conclusion, with its accompanying modes of proof based on probability statistics and analogy to the controlled experiment, had drawn our attention away from other modes of reasoning more suited to the kind of data and problems we worked with. Our reading of George Polya,[3] a mathematician, suggested that the statistical probability model is only one of the many which can be used to arrive at credible conclusions. Following his leads, we attempted to make explicit those elements in our data which led us to arrive at conclusions in which we had confidence and to explore the reasoning by which we decided that those conclusions were credible. This has led us to attempt to construct generalised models of the kinds of proof which might be offered for conclusions of various kinds based on fieldwork data. In the remainder of this chapter we shall consider these two problems at length.

Sequential Analysis in Fieldwork

What are the kinds of analytic operations carried on while the fieldwork is in progress? We can distinguish three stages:[4] (1) the selection and definition of problems, concepts and indices; (2) the check on the frequency and distribution of phenomena; and (3) the incorporation of individual findings into a model of the organisation under study. These three stages are differentiated, first, by their logical sequence: each succeeding stage depends on analysis in the preceding stage. They are further differentiated by the fact that varying kinds of conclusions are arrived at in each stage and that these conclusions are put to different uses in the continuing research. Finally, they are differentiated by the criteria used to assess evidence and to reach conclusions in each stage.

SELECTION AND DEFINITION OF PROBLEMS, CONCEPTS, AND INDICES

During the first stage of analysis in the field, the observer looks for problems and concepts that give promise of yielding the greatest understanding of the organisation he is studying, and he looks for items which may serve as useful indicators of facts which are harder to observe. The typical conclusion that his data yield is the simple one that a given phenomenon exists, that a certain event ocurred once, or that two phenomena were observed to be related in one instance. The conclusion says nothing about the frequency or distribution of the observed phenomenon.

By placing such an observation in the text of a sociological theory, the observer selects concepts and defines problems for further investigation. He constructs a theoretical model to account for that one case, intending to refine it in the light of subsequent findings. For instance, he might find the following: 'Medical student X referred to one of his patients as a "crock" today'.[5] He may then connect this finding with a sociological theory suggesting that occupants of one social category in an institution classify members of other categories by criteria derived from the kinds of problems these other persons raise in the relationship. This combination of observed fact and theory directs him to look for the problems in student–patient inter-

action indicated by the term 'crock'. By discovering specifically what students have in mind in using the term, through questioning and continued observation, he may develop specific hypotheses about the nature of these interactional problems.

Conclusions about a single event also lead the observer to decide on specific items which might be used as indicators[6] of less easily observed phenomena. Noting that in at least one instance a given item is closely related to something less easily observable, the researcher discovers possible shortcuts that will easily enable him to observe abstractly defined variables. For example, he may decide to investigate the hypothesis that medical freshmen feel that they have more work to do than can possibly be managed in the time allowed them. One student, in discussing this problem, says that he faces so much work that, in contrast to his under-graduate days, he is forced to study many hours over the weekend and finds that even this is insufficient. The observer decides, on the basis of this one instance, that he may be able to use complaints about weekend work as an indicator of student perspectives on the amount of work they have to do. The selection of indicators for more abstract variables occurs in two ways: the observer may become aware of some very specific phenomenon first, and later see that it may be used as an indicator of some larger class of phenomena, or he may have the larger problem in mind and search for specific indicators to use in studying it.

Whether he is defining problems or selecting concepts and indicators, the researcher at this stage is using his data only to speculate about possibilities. Later operations may force him to discard most of the provisional hypotheses. Nevertheless, problems of evidence arise even at this point, for the researcher must assess the individual items on which his speculations are based in order not to waste time tracking down false leads. We need a systematic statement of canons to be applied to individual items of evidence. Lacking such a statement, let us consider some commonly used tests. (The observer typically applies these tests as seems reasonable to him during this and the succeeding stage in the field. In the final stage, they are used more systematically in an overall assessment of the total evidence for a given conclusion.)

The credibility of informants. Many items of evidence consist of statements by members of the group under study about some event that has occurred or is in process. Thus, medical students make statements about faculty behaviour that form part of the basis for conclusions about faculty–student relations. These cannot be taken at face value, nor can they be dismissed as valueless. In the first place, the observer can use the statement as evidence *about the event*, if he takes care to evaluate it by the criteria a historian uses in examining a personal document.[7] Does the informant have reason to lie or conceal some of what he sees as the truth? Does vanity or expediency lead him to mis-state his own role in an event or his attitude towards it? Did he actually have an opportunity to witness the occurrence he describes, or is hearsay the source of his knowledge? Do his feelings about the issues or persons under discussion lead him to alter his story in some way? Secondly, even when a statement examined in this way proves to be seriously defective as an accurate report of an event, it may still provide useful evidence for a different kind of conclusion. Accepting the sociological proposition that an individual's statements and descriptions of events are made from a perspective that is a function of his position in the group, the observer can interpret such statements and descriptions as indications of the individual's perspective on the point involved.

Volunteered or directed statements. Many items of evidence consist of informants' remarks to the observer about themselves or others or about something which has happened to them; these statements range from those which are part of the running casual conversation of the group to those arising in a long, intimate *tête-à-tête* between observer and informant. The researcher assesses such statements quite differently, depending on whether they have been volunteered or have been directed by a question from the observer. A freshman medical student might remark to the observer or to another student that he has more material to study than he has time to master; or the observer might ask, 'Do you think you are being given more work than you can handle?', and receive an affirmative answer.

This raises an important question: to what degree is the informant's statement the same one he might give either spontaneously, or in answer to a question, in the absence of the observer? The volunteered statement seems less likely to reflect the observer's pre-occupations and biases than one which is made in response to some action of the observer, for the observer's very question may direct the informant into giving an answer which might never occur to him otherwise. Thus, in the example above, we are more sure that the students are concerned about the amount of work given them when they mention this of their own accord than we are when the idea may have been stimulated by the observer's asking the question.

The observer-informant-group equation. Let us take two extremes to set the problem. A person may say or do something when alone with the observer or when other members of the group are also present. The value of an observation of this behaviour as evidence depends on the observer's judgement as to whether the behaviour is equally likely to occur in both situations. On the one hand, an informant may say and do things when alone with the observer that accurately reflect his perspective but that would be inhibited by the presence of the group. On the other hand, the presence of others may call forth behaviour that reveals more accurately

the person's perspective but would not be enacted in the presence of the observer alone. Thus, students in their clinical years may express deeply 'idealistic' sentiments about medicine when alone with the observer but behave and talk in a very 'cynical' way when surrounded by fellow students. An alternative to judging one or the other of these situations as more reliable is to view each datum as valuable in itself but with respect to different conclusions. In the example given above, we might conclude that students have 'idealistic' sentiments but that group norms may not sanction their expression.[8]

In assessing the value of items of evidence, we must also take into account the observer's role in the group, for the way the subjects of his study define that role affects what they will tell him or let him see. If the observer carries on his research incognito, participating as a full-fledged member of the group, he will be privy to knowledge that would normally be shared by such a member and might be hidden from an outsider. He could properly interpret his own experience as that of a hypothetical 'typical' group member. On the other hand, if he is known to be a researcher, he must learn how group members define him and in particular whether or not they believe that certain kinds of information and events should be kept hidden from him. He can interpret evidence more accurately when the answers to these questions are known.

CHECKING THE FREQUENCY AND DISTRIBUTION OF PHENOMENA

In the second stage of analysis the observer, possessing many provisional problems, concepts and indicators, now wishes to know which of these are worth pursuing as major foci of his study. He does this, in part, by discovering whether the events that prompted their development are typical and widespread and by seeing how these events are distributed among categories of people and organisational subunits. He reaches conclusions that are essentially quantitative, using them to describe the organisation he is studying.

Participant observations have occasionally been gathered in standardised form capable of being transformed into legitimate statistical data.[9] But the exigencies of the field usually prevent the collection of data in such a form as to meet the assumptions of statistical tests, so that the observer deals in what have been called 'quasi-statistics'.[10] His conclusions, while implicitly numerical, do not require precise quantification. For instance, he may conclude that members of freshman medical fraternities typically sit together during lectures, while other students sit in less stable smaller groupings. His observations may indicate such a wide disparity between the two groups in this respect that the inference is warranted without a standardised counting operation. Occasionally, the field situation may permit him to make similar observations or ask similar questions of many people, systematically searching for quasi-statistical support for a conclusion about frequency or distribution.

In assessing the evidence for such a conclusion, the observer decides, if possible, how *likely* it is that his conclusion about the frequency or distribution of some phenomenon is an accurate quasi-statistic, just as the statistician decides, on the basis of the varying values of a correlation coefficient or a significance figure, that his conclusion is more or less likely to be accurate. The observer's confidence in the conclusion will vary with the characteristics of the evidence.

Suppose, for example, that the observer concludes that medical students share the perspective that their school should provide them with the clinical experience and the practice in techniques necessary for a general practitioner. His confidence in the conclusion would vary according to the nature of the evidence, which might take any of the following forms: (1) *Every* member of the group said, *in response to a direct question*, that this was the way he looked at the matter. (2) *Every* member of the group *volunteered* to an observer that this was how he viewed the matter. (3) *Some given proportion* of the group's members either *answered* a direct question, or *volunteered* the information that he shared this perspective, but none of the others was asked or volunteered information on the subject. (4) Every member of the group was asked or volunteered information, but *some given proportion said* they viewed the matter from the differing perspective of a prospective specialist. (5) No one was asked questions or volunteered information on the subject, but *all members were observed to engage in behaviour* or to make other statements from which the analyst *inferred* that the general practitioner perspective was being used by them as a basic, though unstated, premiss. For example, all students might have been observed to complain that the university hospital received too many cases of rare diseases that general practitioners rarely see. (6) *Some given proportion* of the group *was observed* using the general practitioner perspective as a basic premiss in their activities, but *the rest of the group* was not observed engaging in such activities. (7) *Some proportion* of the group *was observed* engaged in activities implying the general practitioner perspective, while *the remainder* of the group was observed engaged in activities implying the perspective of the prospective specialist.

The researcher also takes account of the possibility that his observations may give him evidence of different kinds on the point under consideration. Just as he is more convinced if he has many items of evidence than if he has few, so he is more convinced of a conclusion's validity if he has *many kinds* of evidence.[11] For instance, he may be especially persuaded that a particular norm is shared and affects group behaviour if the norm is not only described by group members, but also if he observes events in which the norm can be

'seen' to operate – if, for example, students tell him that they are thinking of becoming general practitioners and he also observes their complaints about the lack of cases of common diseases in the university hospital. It should be remembered that checks on frequency and distribution, when carried out in the field, may be so interrupted because of imperatives of the field situation that they are not carried on as systematically as they might be. Where this is the case, the overall assessment can be postponed until the final stage of post fieldwork analysis.

CONSTRUCTION OF SOCIAL SYSTEM MODELS

The final stage of analysis in the field consists of incorporating individual findings into a generalised model of the social system or organisation under study or some part of the organisation.[12] The concept of social system is a basic intellectual tool of modern sociology. The kind of participant observation discussed here is related directly to this concept, explaining particular social facts by explicit reference to their involvement in a complex of interconnected variables that the observer constructs as a theoretical model of the organisation. In this final stage, the observer designs a descriptive model which best explains the data he has assembled.

The typical conclusion states a set of complicated interrelations among many variables. Although progress is being made in formalising this operation through use of factor analysis and the relational analysis of survey data,[13] observers usually find current statistical techniques inadequate to express their conceptions and find it necessary to use words. The most common kinds of statements at this level include:

(1) Complex statements of the necessary and sufficient conditions for the existence of some phenomenon. The observer may conclude, for example, that medical students develop consensus about limiting the amount of work they will do, because (a) they are faced with a large amount of work; (b) they engage in activities which create communication channels between all members of the class; and (c) they face immediate dangers in the form of examinations set by the faculty.

(2) Statements that some phenomenon is an 'important' or 'basic' element in the organisation. Such conclusions usually indicate that this phenomenon exercises a persistent and continuing influence on diverse events. The observer might conclude that the ambition to become a general practitioner is 'important' in the medical school under study, meaning that many particular judgements and choices are made by students in terms of this ambition and many features of the school's organisation are arranged to take account of it.

(3) Statements identifying a situation as an instance of some process or phenomenon described more abstractly in sociological theory. These statements

imply that relationships posited in generalised form in some theory hold in this particular instance. The observer, for example, may state that a cultural norm of the medical students is to express a desire to become general practitioners; in so doing, he in effect asserts that the sociological theory about the functions of norms and the process by which they are maintained, which he holds to be true in general, is true in the case of the phenomenon he has labelled here as a norm.

In reaching such conclusions, the observer characteristically begins by constructing models of parts of the organisation as he comes in contact with them. After specifying the relationships among various elements of this part of the organisation, the observer seeks greater accuracy by successively refining the model to take account of evidence that does not fit his previous formulation,[14] by searching for negative cases (items of evidence which run counter to the relationships hypothesised in the model) that might force such revision, and by searching intensively for the interconnections *in vivo* of the various elements he has conceptualised from his data. While a provisional model may be shown to be defective by a negative instance which crops up unexpectedly in the course of the fieldwork, the observer may infer what kinds of evidence would be likely to support or to refute his model and may make an intensive search for such evidence.[15]

After the observer has accumulated several partial models of this kind, he seeks connections between them and, thus, begins to construct an overall model of the entire organisation. An example from our study shows how this operation is carried on during the period of fieldwork. (The reader will note, in this example, how use is made of findings typical of earlier stages of analysis.)

When we first heard medical students apply the term 'crock' to patients, we made an effort to learn precisely what they meant by it. We found through interviewing that the term referred in a derogatory way to patients with many subjective symptoms but no discernible physical pathology. Subsequent observations indicated that this usage was a regular feature of student behaviour and, thus, that we should attempt to incorporate this fact into our model of student–patient behaviour. The derogatory character of the term suggested that we investigate the reasons students disliked these patients. We found that this dislike was related to what we discovered to be the students' perspective on medical school: the view that they were in school to get experience in recognising and treating those common diseases most likely to be encountered in general practice. 'Crocks', presumably having no disease, could furnish no such experience. We were, thus, led to specify connections between the student–patient relationship and the student's view of the purpose of his professional education. Questions concerning the genesis of this perspective led to

discoveries about the organisation of the student body and communication among students, phenomena which we had been assigning to another partial model. Since 'crocks' were also disliked because they gave the student no opportunity to assume medical responsibility, we were able to connect this aspect of the student–patient relationship with still another tentative model of the value system and hierarchical organisation of the school, in which medical responsibility plays an important role.

Again, it should be noted that analysis of this kind is carried on in the field as time permits. Since the construction of a model is the analytic operation most closely related to the observer's techniques and interests, he usually spends a great deal of time thinking about these problems. But he is usually unable to be as systematic as he would like until he reaches the final stage of analysis.

An Example of Final Analysis: Reporting Conclusions about Group Perspectives

When the fieldwork ends, the observer will already have done a great deal of analysis. He must now put his material into such form that a reader will understand the basis on which he has arrived at his conclusions.[16] While statistical data can be summarised in tables and descriptive measures can often be reported in the space required to print a formula, qualitative data and their analytic procedures are often difficult to present. The former methods have been systematised so that they can be referred to in this shorthand fashion, and the data have been collected for a fixed, usually small, number of categories. The presentation need be nothing more than a report of the number of cases to be found in each category.

The data of participant observation do not easily lend themselves to such ready summary. They do not ordinarily meet the standards of comparability and of systematic collection necessary to satisfy the assumptions required for many statistical analyses. The observer may wish to bring together many different kinds of observations that seem to him to bear on the same point but that have been gathered in different ways and under different cicumstances. He may even wish to take account in his analysis of certain kinds of circumstances under which observations were made, in order to buttress a particular point. In the absence of any conventional procedures for achieving these purposes, the observer typically relies on anecdote and illustration to support his conclusions.

But anecdote and illustration do not furnish sufficient proof for the sceptical reader, who rightly wants to know what the entire body of data gathered show. Yet it is clearly out of the question to publish all the data one has collected. Nor is it any solution, as Kluckhohn has suggested for the similar problem of presenting life history materials,[17] to publish a short version and make the entire set of materials available on microfilm or in some other inexpensive way. Both these procedures beg the question of how one can indicate the ways that one's data constitute proof for a given proposition. No one method will solve such a general problem. It is our present view that classes of analytic problems can be distinguished for which models of the kind of proof possible can be constructed. We present one such model, designed to present evidence about certain characteristics of group perspectives. We do not mean to intimate, however, that these methods should not be kept flexible. When not suited to a problem they should be revised.

PERSPECTIVES

In analysing the material gathered in the medical school, we frequently made statements which took essentially this form: medical students customarily use perspective X on problem Y. Typically, our initial belief that such a statement was true came from a few striking incidents we observed or a few statements we heard students make. In our final analysis, however, we wanted to assess systematically the supporting data and present the results. In what follows we describe the method arrived at for presenting the content of a perspective and providing evidence about its frequency and distribution in tabular form. We explain both the steps taken in handling the data and the assumptions underlying them.

We use the term 'perspective' to describe a set of ideas and actions used by a group in solving collective problems. The content of a group's perspective includes a definition of the environment and the problems it presents as seen by group members, an expression of what members expect to derive from the environment and the ideas and actions group members employ in dealing with the problem situation. To demonstrate a perspective to our readers convincingly, we must present its content in some form briefer than the voluminous pages of our field notes, and we must present evidence about certain of its characteristics in such a way that readers may judge for themselves whether the perspective is in frequent, widespread and collective use and may, thus, be considered the customary way (for we define 'customary' in terms of these three characteristics) for students to define a situation and deal with the problems they see in it.

ASSEMBLING THE DATA

A systematic assessment of all data is necessary before we can present the content of a perspective in brief form or go on to assess how customary it is. We have found it useful, in preparing data for the kinds of analysis we describe below, to make a running summary of our field notes. We break the data down into separate incidents, summarising for each incident our observation of a

student's action or transcription of something he said. We have tentatively identified, through sequential analysis during the fieldwork, the major perspectives we want to present and the areas – for example, student–faculty relationships – to which these perspectives apply. We now go through the summarised incidents, marking each incident with a number or numbers that stand for the various areas to which it appears to be relevant. This is essentially a coding operation, though it differs from the usual coding operation in that its object is not to put items in mutually exclusive categories for counting, but rather to make sure that all relevant data can be brought to bear on a point. Several things should be kept in mind while doing this coding:

(1) The coding should be inclusive. That is, any incident should be coded under a category, if there is initially any reason to believe that it might be considered relevant. Many incidents will, therefore, be coded under several categories, for they may be relevant to all of them. An incident which on later analysis proves to be irrelevant can simply be discarded.

Take, for instance, the following summarised incident from our field notes:

> Mann says that now that he and the other students have found out what Dr Prince, the staff physician, is like, they learn the things they know he's going to try to catch them on and keep him stumped that way.

This incident contains some reference to student–faculty relations and would accordingly be coded under that category. It also refers indirectly to the phenomenon of student co-operation on school activities and would be coded under that category as well.

(2) The coding should be by incidents: either complete verbal expressions of an attitude, or complete acts by an individual or group. We see the necessity of this when the analyst has finished his general coding and moves on to the construction of a model of the students' perspective in one area. If, for example, we decide that we will consider as part of our tentative formulation of the perspective that students cheat on examinations or that they believe cheating is a good way to solve their problems, then we would code separately each observation of cheating and each complete statement by a student expressing the attitude that cheating is all right. Although it is not particularly important what criteria are used to decide what constitutes an incident, it is important that they be used consistently. Suppose one listens to a long conversation among three students about taking examinations. Each one takes a particular line about cheating and expresses it in essentially the same way several times during the conversation. One could count the whole conversation as an incident; one could count each statement about cheating as an incident; or one could count each person's participa-

tion in the conversation, as long as he continues to take the same line, as one incident. It seems to us reasonable, in this case, to use the latter definition of incident. Similarly, if one were to observe acts of cheating by students, counting as one incident an observation of several acts of cheating by the same student during an examination would seem more reasonable than counting each one separately.

(3) The coding should be full. That is, the incident being coded should be summarised in all its relevant detail: the ideas expressed, the actions taken, the people present, the date and the setting. Here are some samples of summarised incidents we coded as relevant to the students' perspective on student–faculty relations:

5/25/6 – p. 6 Jones talks about Smith not having done well on the OB oral – says Smith is really smart but of course they can get you in any oral, just by picking on something you don't know about.

10/22/6 – p. 6 Brown says he failed to get the lab work on a patient and got caught by Dr. Hackett. He copied the figures from the main lab, but drew some blood too in case Hackett checked up on him.

FORMULATING THE CONTENT OF THE PERSPECTIVE

The next step is to inspect the various incidents (statements and actions) described by the items coded under one area and formulate a more differentiated statement of the content of the perspective. In doing this we attempt to describe more specifically the kinds of statements and actions expressive of the perspective, trying to take into account all the items we have coded as being relevant to it. (In so doing, of course, we may be forced to revise our initial tentative statement of the perspective.)

For example, in looking over the material on the student's relations with the faculty in teaching situations, we derived a tentative statement of the students' perspective on this area. The coded incidents defined a problematic situation as the students saw it, stated what they wanted to get out of it and described the actions they took to this end. The content of the perspective could be briefly characterised by saying that students felt that they needed to exert all their efforts to get along with a faculty that was in many ways capricious and unpredictable and could vitally affect the students' professional futures.

In order to get a more differentiated picture of the content of this perspective, we went through all the incidents we had coded into the faculty–student category, noting each different kind of specific expression of the perspective as it appeared. Coming on the first of the items quoted above, we might jot down, 'Student says faculty can get you on an oral by picking on something you don't know'; and, coming on the second, might note, 'Student cheats in order to show faculty member he is doing his work'. Having accumulated a list of such notes, we then formulated a systematic and more general statement of the kinds of attitudes and actions which could be seen as expressing the basic perspective. Many incidents had in common the fact that students stated that you needed to please the faculty in order to get through school. Other incidents like the one about the faked lab work, showed students acting in ways calculated to make a pleasing impression on the faculty. Still other incidents, like the one about the OB oral, had as a common theme the students' expressed belief that it was impossible to tell what the faculty wanted of them. Each category we formed had some one underlying characteristic of this kind that could be interpreted as an expression of the perspective; taken together, the set of categories constituted the perspecive. Such an analysis serves two purposes. On the one hand, it adds richness and detail to our description of the perspective's content by spelling out the particular ways it is seen to operate in actual situations. On the other hand, it describes fully the kinds of items we will later use as evidence that the perspective is the customary way students handle the problem of their relations with faculty teaching situations. In the final written presentation of the perspective, each kind of item that expresses it is described in terms of the specific characteristics that do so. We find is useful to follow the tradition of presenting illustrative quotations from the actual field notes; we further specify exactly what it is about the quotation that is meaningful and assert that every item used in later analyses has at least the minimum characteristics of one of the kinds of items discussed.

The operations up to this point are directed towards arriving at a relatively brief presentation of the content of the perspective. We now turn to a discussion of the procedures by which we establish certain characteristics of the perspective – its frequency, range and collective character – in order to document the conclusion that it is the customary way students deal with the problem it refers to. Each of these procedures is designed to present evidence bearing on factual conclusions – such as a conclusion that use of the perspective is widespread – in such a way that the reader can make his own judgement of how much confidence to place in them.

CHECKING THE FREQUENCY OF THE PERSPECTIVE

In asking whether or not the perspective is frequently used by the students, we are first of all concerned with the number of positive items from the data (incidents in which students state or act out the perspective) as compared with the number of negative instances in which they use some alternative perspective in dealing with the same problem. Ordinarily, because the final perspective has been formulated after a great deal of observation and analysis in the field, there are relatively few negative cases. This fact lends some credence to the proposition that the perspective has a high relative frequency. If there should be a large number of negative cases, this would certainly require revision of any proposition that the perspective is in frequent use. In any event, a careful inspection of all negative instances is in order. We discuss later how we deal with them.[18]

Aside from the question of negative instances, the major consideration with regard to the absolute number of incidents is that this number should be sizeable. If it were very small, we would not be able to conclude that the perspective was frequently used. We might simply have seen a few odd cases in which it happened to be employed. But if the number of instances is as high, let us say, as 75 or 100, this could hardly be true. It would not be credible that so many instances should be observed, if the null hypothesis that the perspective was not frequent were true. That is, the absolute number does not indicate that the perspective is frequent so much as negate the null hypothesis that it is not.

Since the participant observer seldom observes the entire group at one time, it is legitimate to take into account the fact that the people he was not observing at any particular moment might well have been engaged in behaviour that he would have counted as an instance in favour of his hypothesis had he been there to observe it. For instance, we typically observed from five to eight (and never more than fifteen) students at a time while we were in the teaching hospital. Yet there were always approximately 200 students taking clinical work at the time. We consider it legitimate to estimate that probably ten times as many incidents as we observed to support our hypotheses probably occurred during the time we were making our observations and could, in principle, have been observed by us if there had been enough observers to go around.

Other points need to be taken into account in assessing the meaning of the absolute number of items from the data. For example, it is important to take into account the length of time during which observations were made. Obviously one can gather more material in a month than in a week, and in a year than in a month. Similarly, the number of items which consist of responses to direct queries by the observer must be considered. If the percentage of items so directed by the observer is very large, this means that less meaning can be attached to the absolute number, because it is now a function of the observer's activity rather than of the students'. In short, no strict rule of interpretation can yet be stated, though the absolute number obviously has some meaning.

CHECKING THE RANGE OF THE PERSPECTIVE

The next thing we check in establishing the characteristics of the perspective is how widely the items of data were distributed through the various observational situations. For example, we might observe student–faculty interaction in ten different places and find that the bulk of our items came from only one of these places. This might lead us to suspect that the perspective is a response to something unique in that particular situation. Similarly, the perspective might be used by students with regard to only one kind of activity or person.

Consequently, we make it a practice to list all the places in which observations of the problem we are considering were made and see in how many of them at least one instance of the perspective's use was observed. In the medical school, for example, students in the clinical years had some training in eighteen different departments of the hospital. It was a simple matter to check in how many of the eighteen some expression of the perspective was found. If no expression of it was found in observations made in some large proportion of these observational situations, we could not consider the perspective widespread. Similarly, where possible, we listed the kinds of activity the perspective might be relevant to and made a similar check to see that instances of it were observed in some sizeable proportion of these activities. Again, while this kind of check gives positive evidence that the perspective has a wide social range, it is also important in that it casts doubt upon the null hypothesis that the perspective was not widespread by showing that it occurred in many of the relevant situations. We check not only the situational range of the perspective, but also its temporal range. Since each example is dated, we can see how they are distributed over the period of observation. If most of the examples are confined to a short period of time, we should consider the perspective ephemeral; if there is a relatively even spread, we conclude that it persists. Our confidence in its persistence, however, depends upon the length of the observation period. We are more satisfied that the perspective persists, if we have had many opportunities to observe situations in which it is likely to occur (and then find that it does) than if we have not.

CHECKING THE COLLECTIVE CHARACTER OF THE PERSPECTIVE

Having established that the perspective is in frequent and widespread use by students, we now want to demonstrate that it is collective, that is, that it is shared by students and regarded by them as the legitimate way to think about and act in the area the perspective refers to. By 'shared', we mean that students not only use the perspective, but use it with the knowledge that their fellow students also use it. By 'legitimate', we mean that students see the ideas and actions which make up the perspective as the proper and necessary way to act in this area.

The first point to consider is whether or not expression of it is an artefact of the observer's techniques. If, for example, many instances consist in the observer's making a statement embodying the basic points of the perspective to students and asking them whether they agree or disagree, a high proportion of 'agree' answers will have some value but is open to the criticism that, while students may agree to this attitude, it is not one they themselves would ordinarily express. Therefore, each item should be classified according to whether it was directed by the observer's activities or arose 'spontaneously' from the students. One should not, however, assume that any statement by a student made in response to something the observer said is directed. The observer may make neutral remarks, or ask neutral questions that bring out important items, that should not be classified as directed. Only those items in which the observer himself injects the points characteristic of the perspective should be counted as directed. For example, we frequently made use of such neutral questions as 'What's happening?' and found these very productive of important information. But we would not classify these pieces of information as directed, because the questions themselves contained no reference to the terms of the perspective.

The second point to consider in asking whether or not the perspective is collective is the degree to which the statements or actions expressing it occurred in public. In the course of participant observation there will be many occasions when one of the persons observed will be alone with the observer and talk at some length about his problems and aspirations. Material of this kind can be considered evidence that the individual involved in the conversation held this view (and was willing to express it, at least in private) but does not give much clue as to whether the ideas expressed are held commonly or regarded as legitimate by all members of the group involved. It may, after all, be the case that many members of the group hold these opinions but hold them privately and neither express them, nor act on them in the presence of their fellows.

To check this point, all items should be classified according to whether they occurred in the presence of the observer alone or when other members of the group were also present. If, for instance, the observer sees a student doing something in the presence of several other students who take it as a matter of course, he is entitled to assume that this kind of activity is legitimate enough to excite no comment from other members of the group. He could not make this inference, if he saw the act performed when he was the only other person present. Similarly, if a member of the group makes a statement in conversation with other members of the group, we are entitled to regard this as a legitimate way to view things more than if the statement is made to the observer alone. We can argue that the appearance of terms of the perspective in the everyday conversation of group members indicates that they share the perspective, since they could not use these terms to communicate unless there was mutual understanding of them. Finally, we should also take note of the proportion of items which are made up of observations of activity rather than statements. If all the items consisted of observations of activity, or if all the items consisted of statements made by students, our conclusions would be affected by this disproportion. If all items were observations of activities and there were no statements on the subject, we know nothing of students' views. Similarly, in the opposite case, we might conclude that the perspective was 'all talk' and unrelated to the students' behaviour.

We have found it useful to present the findings of this kind of analysis in the accompanying tabular form (see Table 32.1), presenting in each cell both frequencies and the appropriate percentages. We have not developed any formulas for interpretation of a table of this kind, but we can state a few rules of thumb. In the first place, the number of directed statements should be small in comparison to the volunteered statements. Secondly, in the 'volunteered' column, the proportion of items consisting of statements made to the observer alone should not be overwhelming. This, of course, begs the question of just what proportion would be large enough to cause us to doubt our proposition that the perspective is collective. We are inclined now to think that any proportion over 50 per cent would necessitate another look at the proposition but cannot state any rationale for this inclination. Thirdly, there should be a reasonable proportion of activities as well as statements by

Table 32.1

		Volunteered	Directed by the Observer	Total
Statements	To observer alone			
	To others in everyday conversations			
Activities	Individual			
	Group			
Total				

students. Again, we cannot state any rigid formula but are inclined to think that somewhere in the neighbourhood of 20 or 25 per cent would be an appropriate figure. A table like this makes possible a quick summary presentation of a great deal of material and is, thus, very useful. It gives the reader much of the ground for concluding that the perspective is shared by students and regarded by them as legitimate and allows them to see the basis on which that conclusion was formed.

NEGATIVE CASES

The final step of the analysis is a consideration of those cases found in the field notes which run counter to the proposition that the students shared a particular perspective. Because the statement of the perspective is refashioned many times in the course of the fieldwork and later analysis with the idea of revising it to take into account as many of the negative cases as possible, this number will usually be quite small. Each one should be considered early, and whatever revisions it suggests should be incorporated in the analysis. Two generic types of negative instances should be noted, for we deal with them differently. In one type we find individuals not making use of the perspective, because they have not learned it yet. Negative cases of this kind typically consist of a student acting against the perspective and being corrected by his fellows. Such an instance obviously requires no change in the proposition, except to note that not everyone knows the perspective at first and that people acquire it in the course of their experience in the situation.

The second kind of negative instance consists of observations indicating that some people have a perspective other than that we postulate as the common one, or of cases in which students are observed to behave according to the perspective publicly but to deviate from it privately. In these cases, the most likely kind of revision we make is to say that apparently there exists confirmed deviance in the social body or that there may be marginal areas in which the perspective is not necessarily applied, even though our evidence indicates that in most kinds of situations it is the usual thing. This second kind of negative case permits further confirmation of the perspective as a collective phenomenon. If it can be shown that the person who acts on a different perspective is socially isolated from the group or that his deviant activities are regarded by others as improper, unnecessary, or foolish, then one can argue that these facts indicate use of the perspective by all but deviants, hence, its collective character. The analyst must exercise ingenuity in seeking possible alternatives to his hypothesis and in deducing the consequences of these in the students' behaviour. This gives him a set of indicators for identifying negative cases. This is an important part of the analysis and should not be slighted.

Conclusion

After completing the steps we have outlined, we can inspect the results of our analysis to see whether the perspective we have defined and described can be properly held to be customary for students to use in dealing with the relevant problem. We have already noted that we have no formal tests for making this judgement. We find it best to reason from the results in a manner suggested by the work of George Polya.[19] trying to establish whether our conclusion is plausible in the light of conceivable alternatives. Thus, if we should find that there are several hundred incidents in our field notes in which the perspective is expressed, the hypothesis that the perspective is infrequently used becomes highly implausible and the hypothesis that it is frequently used much more plausible. Similarly, if some sizeable proportion of the incidents consists of statements made by students to one another, the proposition that the perspective is held privately and not shared is highly implausible, while the opposite hypothesis is much more plausible. By presenting the results of our checks in the forms of counts and tables like those described, we make it possible for the reader to make his own judgement as to whether the degree of plausibility we assign to the conclusion is warranted. In this way, the acceptability of the conclusion comes to rest on more impersonal and objective grounds than is ordinarily the case in the analysis of qualitative observational data.

Notes: Chapter 32

Reprinted from Richard Adams and Jack Preiss (eds), *Human Organization Research: Field Relations and Techniques* (Homewood, Ill.: Dorsey Press, 1960), pp. 267–89.© Dorsey Press. This chapter was developed out of problems of analysis arising in the study of a state medical school. The study was sponsored by Community Studies, Inc., of Kansas City, Missouri, USA; the Carnegie Corporation of New York; and the National Institutes of Health. It was directed by Everett C. Hughes; Anselm Strauss was also a member of the research team. Some of the material presented here originally appeared in Becker (1958). Alvin Gouldner's comments on an earlier version of that paper were of great value. Another paper on participant observation is by Becker and Geer (1957).

1   There is little agreement on the specific referent of the term 'participant observation', See Gold (1958) for a useful classification of the various procedures that go by this name. Our own research, from which we have drawn our illustrations, falls under Gold's type, 'participant-as-observer'. The basic methods discussed here, however, would appear to be similar in other kinds of field situations.
2   In so far as they have this sequential character, the analytic methods we discuss here bear a family resemblance to the technique of *analytic induction*; cf. Lindesmith (1947), especially pp. 5–20, and the subsequent literature cited in Turner (1953).
3   See Polya (1954).

4 Our discussion of these stages is abstract and simplified and does not attempt to deal with practical and technical problems of participant observation study. The reader should keep in mind that, in practice, the research will involve all these operations simultaneously with reference to particular problems.

5 The examples of which our hypothetical observer makes use are drawn from our own current work with medical students.

6 The problem of indicators is discussed by Lazarsfeld and Barton (1951; 1955), whose important paper parallels the present discussion in many places; and Kendall and Lazarsfeld (1950).

7 Compare Gottschalk, Kluckhohn and Angell (1945), pp. 15–27, 38–47. See also papers by Back (1956), and Vidich and Bensman (1954).

8 See further, Becker (1956), pp. 199–201.

9 See Blau (1954).

10 See the discussion of quasi-statistics in Lazarsfeld and Barton (1955), pp. 346–8.

11 See Gouldner (1954), pp. 247–69.

12 The relation between theories based on the concept of social system and participant observation was pointed out to us by Gouldner (1956; 1957a).

13 See Gouldner (1957b; 1958), and Coleman (1958).

14 Note again the resemblance to analytic induction.

15 See Alfred Lindesmith's discussion of this principle (Lindesmith, 1952).

16 Becker (1958), p. 659, discusses some additional problems of final analyses.

17 Gottschalk, Kluckhohn, and Angell (1945), pp. 150–56.

18 Richard N. Adams and Jack J. Preiss have suggested to us that the number of negative and positive items may be strongly affected by the observer's unconscious biases in reporting. This is certainly true, and we have assumed here that the observer has already taken what steps are possible to avoid such bias. We cannot undertake any lengthy discussion of the problem here, but it obviously requires extended consideration in its own right.

19 Polya (1954), especially pp. 18–54, 109–41, suggests that it is useful to replace syllogistic reasoning and strict logical forms of proof with a 'calculus of plausibility' that systematises the kinds of considerations often made use of in everyday reasoning.

33

The Analysis of Social Drama

VICTOR TURNER

(EDITOR'S NOTE: This extract deals with the concept of social drama. For examples of the way in which this concept has been used to analyse five consecutive social dramas in Ndembu society see V. W. Turner, *Schism and Continuity in an African Society: A Study of Ndembu Village Life* (Manchester: Manchester University Press, 1957), pp. 95–168.)

Schism and Continuity in an African Society[1] is dominantly a study of social conflict and of the social mechanisms brought into play to reduce, exclude, or resolve that conflict. Beneath all other conflicts in Ndembu society is the concealed opposition between men and women over descent and in the economic system. Influenced by this basic opposition, but possessing their own autonomy, sets of struggles arise within the social structure: conflicts between persons and between groups who invoke different principles of residential affiliation to support and justify their own specific interests, political, jural and economic; struggles between persons and groups couched in terms of a common norm which each party claims the other has broken; and conflicts between persons, united by a single principle of descent and residence, for positions of authority determined by that principle. Struggles around succession to village headmanship are instances of the last type of conflict, and it is with these that I wish to commence the analysis of what I propose to call 'social dramas'. Formal analysis of a social system enables us to locate and isolate critical points and areas in its structure where one might expect, on *a priori* grounds, to find conflicts between the occupants of social positions carried in the structure. In the examination of the Ndembu system I have isolated the matrilineal descent group and shown how the office of village headman is vested in this group.[2] I have looked at different categories of matrilineal kin and shown how struggles for succession may be expected to take place between adjacent generations and between specific kinship positions, notably between mother's brother and sister's son. It remains to test out these hypotheses in a number of cases, regarded as typical, and to see whether struggles do in fact take place. But the task does not end at this point. If conflicts occur, we want to see in what way they are handled by the members of the society. In Ndembu society conduct has been regulated

over what we can assume to have been a very long period of time by norms, values, beliefs and sentiments associated with kinship. Conflicts of interests arising out of the social structure are perpetuated by the observance of these norms. Hence, the conflicts must also follow a regular course dictated partly by these norms, and take a shape grown familiar to the people through repetition. We can expect to find, in fact, a number of social mechanisms, of institutionalised ways of behaviour, which have arisen in response to an almost endless reduplication of such conflicts, and which have been designed by group experience to mitigate, diminish, or repair them. Conflict and the resolution of conflict have effects which are observable in statistical and genealogical data. But the hints and indications afforded by such data must be followed up by a close study of social dramas. There we observe the interlinked and successive events which follow breach, and make visible the sources of conflicts. This, in turn, leads to action which may restore the earlier set of relations, or reconstitute them in a different pattern, or even recognise an irreparable breaking of relationships between particular persons or groups. These last, nevertheless, fit into the wider pattern of the Ndembu system.

The Concept of the Social Drama

On a number of occasions during my fieldwork I became aware of marked disturbance in the social life of the particular group I happened to be studying at the time. The whole group might be radically cloven into two conflicting factions; the quarrelling parties might comprise some but not all of its members; or disputes might be merely interpersonal in character. Disturbance, in short, had a variable range of social inclusiveness. After a while I began to detect a pattern in these eruptions of conflict: I noticed phases in their development which seemed to follow one another in a more or less regular sequence. These eruptions, which I call 'social dramas', have 'processional form'. I have provisionally divided the social process which constitutes the social drama into four major phases:

(1) Breach of regular norm-governed social relations occurs between persons or groups within the same system of social relations. Such a breach is signalised by the public breach or non-fulfilment of some crucial norm regulating the intercourse of the parties.

(2) Following breach of regular social relations, a phase of mounting crisis supervenes, during which, unless the conflict can be sealed off quickly within a limited area of social interaction, there is a tendency for the breach to widen and extend until it becomes coextensive with some dominant cleavage in the widest set of relevant social relations to which the conflicting parties belong. The phase of crisis exposes the pattern of current factional struggle within the relevant social group, be it village, neighbourhood, or chiefdom; and beneath it there becomes visible the less plastic, more durable, but nevertheless gradually changing basic social structure, made up of relations which are constant and consistent.

(3) In order to limit the spread of breach, certain adjustive and redressive mechanisms, informal or formal, are speedily brought into operation by leading members of the relevant social grou. These mechanisms vary in character with such factors as the depth and social significance of the breach, the social inclusiveness of the crisis, the nature of the social group within which the breach took place and the degree of its autonomy with reference to wider systems of social relations. They may range from personal advice and informal arbitration, to formal juridicial and legal machinery and, to resolve certain kinds of crisis, to the performance of public ritual.

(4) The final phase I have distinguished consists either in the reintegration of the disturbed social group, or in the social recognition of irreparable breach between the contesting parties. In short, the *processional form* of the social drama may be formulated as (1) breach; (2) crisis; (3) redressive action; (4) reintegration or recognition of schism.

It must be recognised, of course, that in different kinds of group, in different societies, and under varying circumstances in the same kinds of group in the same society, the process may not run smoothly or inevitably from phase to phase. Failure, for example, in the operation of redressive machinery, may result in regression to crisis. In recently formed groups institutionalised legal or ritual means of handling social disturbance may be lacking, and breach may be succeeded immediately by the irreversible fission or fragmentation of the group.

In Ndembu society, although villages arise and perish, the ideal form of the village persists. Meanwhile, in order that any village life should be possible, it is necessary that members of a village should observe certain common values, and that the norms governing behaviour between village members, most of whom are interlinked by ties of kinship and affinity, should be upheld. Where customary norms and values are deeply entrenched, it is usual to find institutionalised machinery of redress. Each instance of breach in social relations is made the occasion of a restatement of their regulative norms. The nature of redressive machinery and the way in which it functions in specific situations is discussed later.

I have found the social drama a useful descriptive and analytical tool when taken in conjunction with more orthodox techniques of analysis, such as the genealogy, the census and the hut diagram. Analysis of numerical material obtained by the use of such techniques reveals regularities in social relations that we may call structural. Among Ndembu, for example, we find by these means that the core of villages tends to be the maternal descent group, that marriage is predominantly virilocal, that there is a high frequency of divorce, that alternate genealogical generations tend to build adjacently and adjacent genealogical generations in opposite sections of a village, and so on. We find that there is a tendency towards adelphic succession and that sisters' sons tend to be the most frequent founders of new villages. This leads us to suspect tension in the relationship of mother's brother and sister's son. The social drama shows vividly how these social tendencies operate in practice; how, in a given situation, some may support and others oppose one another; and how conflict between persons or groups in terms of a common norm or in terms of contradictory norms may be resolved in a particular set of circumstances. In the social drama latent conflicts of interest become manifest, and kinship ties, whose significance is not obvious in genealogies, emerge into key importance.

If we examine a sequence of social dramas arising within the same social unit, each one affords us a glimpse, as it were, of the contemporary stage of maturation or decay of the social structure of that unit. I hope to demonstrate this in presenting a set of five consecutive social dramas in a single long-established village.[3] The social drama is a limited area of transparency on the otherwise opaque surface of regular, uneventful social life. Through it we are enabled to observe the crucial principles of the social structure in their operation, and their relative dominance at successive points in time. Of the five social dramas based on material collected at Mukanza village, the last three came under my direct observation. The first two rest on data collected from a large number of interviews and conversations with living persons who actively participated in them.

Social Drama I[4] illustrates the conflict that may arise between mother's brother and sister's son, and between male parallel cousins, when only a few men remain in the senior, office-holding generation in a village, and there are several middle-aged men ripe for office in the junior generation. Other kinds of conflicts become overt within the framework of these crucial conflicts; but the former will not be analysed, since they involve other principles of village organisation than matriliny.

This social drama is one of a series,[5] each of which contains the same principal characters, and each of which reflects different aspects of the same structural conflicts. It may be objected that such factors as innate psychobiological constitution and personality variations determined by differential training in the early years of childhood take precedence over sociological factors in shaping the events to be described. But it is clear that the different personalities involved occupy social positions that must inevitably come into conflict, and each occupant of a position must present his case in terms of generally accepted norms. A person can avoid disputes over succession only by renouncing the claim to office vested in his position. In a society governed by rules of kinship, he cannot abrogate his position, into which he is born and by virtue of which he is a member of the village community. Personality may influence the form and intensity of the dispute, it cannot abolish the situation in which conflict must arise. A person who endeavours to avoid pressing his claim to office when the position of headman falls vacant is subject to intense pressure from his uterine kin and from his children to put it forward. If he fails to do so, there occurs a displacement of the locus of conflict, not a resolution or bypassing of conflict. Instead of leading a group of kin against the representatives of other pressure groups, he becomes the target of criticism from members of his own group. At some point in the social process arising from succession, he is compelled to turn and defend himself, whatever his temperament or character. The situation in an Ndembu village closely parallels that found in Greek drama, where one witnesses the helplessness of the human individual before the Fates: but in this case the Fates are the necessities of the social process.

Notes: Chapter 33

The material in this chapter originally appeared in V. W. Turner, *Schism and Continuity in an African Society: a Study of Ndembu Village Life*, pp. 89–94, first published in 1957 for the Rhodes-Livingstone Institute (Manchester University Press; reprinted by Manchester University Press for the Institute for Social Research, 1968, and for the Institute for African Studies, 1971). Reprinted by kind permission of the Institute for African Studies and the author.

1   See Turner (1957).
2   See Turner (1957), chapter 4.
3   See Turner (1957), pp. 95–168.
4   See Turner (1957), pp. 95–115.
5   See Turner (1957), pp. 95–168.

34

The British Association Scandal:
The Effect of Publicity on a Sociological Investigation

D. H. J. MORGAN

The fact that the findings of sociological investigations are often eventually published and that this publication brings with it a variety of personal, ethical and professional problems has already received some attention in the literature. Vidich and Bensman have provided a dramatic illustration of how a community study is received by the 'objects' of that research,[1] Fichter and Kolb have attempted to outline some of the ethical limitations on the reporting of sociological investigations[2] and, more recently, the British Sociological Association has been considering, among other matters of professional ethics, the various complex responsibilities of sociologists in the matters of publication and relationships with the press and the mass media.[3] Informal discussion with other sociologists has convinced me that this is a major source of concern within the discipline and many individuals appear to know of at least one story of unfortunate 'leaks' or misrepresentation.[4]

It is likely that this problem is particularly acute for studies based largely or wholly on the method of participant observation. On the one hand, the investigator feels required to present as much detail about his workshop or community as possible, so that his research can be subjected to the critical scrutiny of his colleagues; at the same time, the presentation of such detail can only make it more likely that the precise location of the community under investigation (and perhaps even some of the key actors) can be discovered and named by an enterprising journalist.[5]

The case presented here differs from some of the cases and arguments already mentioned in two respects. In the first place, the publicity came before the completion of the research project; it did not arise out of the publication of a final report. In the second place, the case is not presented primarily as a cautionary tale of a problem to be avoided or as an account of a research project which 'went wrong'. This is not to deny that the publicity caused me a fair degree of personal embarrassment and that it is likely that it did in fact damage – or at least alter – the whole project in certain respects. But the emphasis here is on what might be seen as being some of the more positive aspects of the case. At a fairly trivial level, the case may be seen as an example of the ways in which it is possible to turn something such as adverse press publicity to good advantage. At a more fundamental level, the case is seen as a particular example of the way in which observer and observed interact in the participant observation situation and of the necessity for incorporating the observer as an element in the situation under review. Thus, the stress is not so much on the problem *created* by the press publicity, but rather on the way in which the publicity brought home some of the issues involved in *any* piece of sociological investigation. An attempt is made to explore some of the implications arising out of the following statement by Sartre:

> Research is a living relation between men . . . Indeed, the sociologist and his 'object' form a couple, each one of which is to be interpreted by the other; the *relationship* between them must be itself integrated as a moment of history.[6]

In this chapter I shall first give a brief description of the field in which this particular case took place, namely, a workshop employing women workers. I shall then describe the particular set of events following a paper which I delivered at a meeting of the British Association for the Advancement of Science. This paper used some of my research findings as illustrative material. Against this background I shall introduce a brief discussion of the ways in which my role as a participant observer in the department was interpreted by various sets of workers. This will be followed by a discussion of the ways in which the responses within the workshop to the press publicity following my paper were patterned and hence revealed something about the nature of social relationships within that department. Finally, I shall attempt to look at both aspects – the role of the observer and the responses and social relationships of the observed – as together forming an interacting system. I need hardly add that this chapter cannot exhaust the possible range of themes which could be covered by a case of this kind.

The Project, the Factory and the Department

It is not necessary in this context to provide a detailed account of the research problems and the strategies adopted to tackle these problems. It is probably enough to say that the aim, expressed at its broadest level, was to continue and develop some of the lines of inquiry which had already been pursued by Lupton, Cunnison and Wilson.[7] In common with these other 'Manchester' studies we adopted the method of 'open participant observation'. The factory chosen in this study allowed the different members of the research team to study social relationships in different departments and at different levels. Emmett concentrated on the managerial and supervisory levels, while Walker and I studied two different departments at a shopfloor level.

The factory (which we call Citron Works) produced a variety of electrical components which were sold to other electrical goods firms. It was a branch of a much larger firm. The department where I worked produced small electrical components, although within this rather broad descriptive category there was a wide range of variation in terms of size and complexity. There were two sides to this department: the process, and the assembly. The process side (which was spread over several small rooms and workshops on the same floor) produced the cells which were the essential part of the electrical component, while the assembly side (spread over one larger room) used these cells, together with other parts, to assemble the final product. Although there was some rudimentary flow of work – from process to assembly to the paint shop and then to testing and packing – for the most part an assembler would make a complete item by herself. There were, as I have suggested, considerable variations in size, complexity and size of order facing any individual assembler. Thus, one assembler might produce the same item week after week, while another might produce a variety of short-run orders in the course of one week. Items were assembled by hand with the assistance of a few simple tools.

It can be seen that there were important functional differences between the two sides. On the process side there was a much more clearly structured flow of work, whereby the cells moved from room to room as various different operations were performed on them. This side was noisier, darker and more subject to fluctuations in temperature than the assembly side. There were also some differences between the workers on the two sides, although, with a few exceptions, they were all women. These differences are outlined in Table 34.1 and the importance of some of these differences will emerge later. The department (which enjoyed considerable autonomy in terms of the structure of the factory as a whole) was under the product manager, Mr Gollan. There were two foremen, Mr Sandhurst in charge of the process side and Dick Herman in charge of the assembly side. Herman was assisted by an assistant foreman, Joe Reynolds, and two female supervisors, Liz and Clare.

Table 34.1   *Characteristics of Women Workers on the Process and Assembly Sides**

	Assembly	Process
Number employed (100%)	124	56
Percentage married	59·7	67·9
Median length of service	11·6 months	10·5 months
Percentage with over ten years' service	6·4	10·7
Median age	28·0 years	41·1 years
Percentage living over five miles from work	13·7	25·0

*Data refer to the year 1963.

Just as there were differences between the assembly and the process sides in terms of the characteristics of the workers, so too were there differences within the assembly side between those workers under the supervision of Liz and those under Clare. The workers at Clare's end of the room for the most part assembled items described as 'miniatures': small electrical components enclosed in polythene cases. The work tended to be more standardised at this end of the room, while there was greater variety in the kinds and sizes of components assembled at Liz's end of the room. The workers under Liz tended to be older and with longer service than the workers under Clare.

The factory was located in an old working-class district of a northern city we call Dockford. Most of the workers in the department came from Dockford, 68·5 per cent on the assembly side and 71·4 per cent on the process side. An important minority of the workers came from a nearby city, which we call Chesstown. This reflects the history of this particular department, for it had originally been located in Chesstown and had moved some ten miles to Dockford five years prior to the research project. When the department moved, the workers were given the opportunity of continued employment and a special bus was laid on for them. At the time of the research 19·6 per cent of the workers on the process side came from Chesstown as opposed to 8·1 per cent on the assembly side. This factor also contributed to the distinction between the workers on the two sides of the assembly room as a greater proportion of the workers under Liz came from Chesstown. Inevitably, Chesstown workers tended to be older and to have longer service in the department.

The Paper and its Effects

In September 1964, some time after the completion of full-time participant observation, I read a paper to the British Association for the Advancement of Science entitled 'Women in industry – the factory and the home'.[8] In this paper I discussed in a general way the inter-relationships between a working woman's roles in the workplace and her domestic roles and, in presenting this argument, I used some of my field data as illustrative material. In particular I drew attention to the variety of ways in which the workplace was 'domesticated' and I described the responses on the part of some of the workers to the broadcast of the Royal Wedding between Princess Alexandria and Angus Ogilvie. I suggested that the rewards at work in terms of sociable relationships were at least as important as the rewards for the work in terms of the paypacket and probably more important than the rewards in the work itself. In this connection I raised the possibility of 'alienation in reverse'; that while men were alienated at work and sought partial alleviation from this in extra-work relationships, women were alienated at home and in some senses sought and obtained alleviation in the performance of work roles.[9]

On the following day several of the national newspapers carried a version of my paper. While most of my paper was concerned with the inter-relationships between home and work and this theme of 'alienation in reverse', most of the newspaper reporting of the British Association meeting concentrated on the illustrative material.[10] Thus, the *Daily Mirror* carried the headline 'A factory girl's dream of romance'; the *Daily Express* carried its story under the heading 'What a giggle! When a man tells the secrets of life among the girls'; and the *Daily Mail* referred to me in its headline as 'The eavesdropper'. More or less straightforward summaries of the paper appeared in the *Guardian* and the *Daily Telegraph*, neither of which, to my knowledge, appeared on the shopfloor. More distressing to me and the several people in the factory, from the managing director downwards, was the fact that two of the newspapers discovered and printed the name of the factory, information which had not been included in my paper and which I refused to give to newspaper reporters.

It may be useful at this point to give a fairly detailed account of the immediate responses as I saw them. On the advice of a senior colleague (R.F.), I went with him to the department on the day after the newspapers had come out. As we approached the department, I felt extremely apprehensive. While we walked through the department, crossing from the main door to the foreman's office, I was aware of a few whispers and comments from the workers. Dick Herman, the foreman, greeted me in a friendly and sympathetic manner and after a brief exchange of jokes and comments, he first called together the workers at Clare's end of the department. He argued that these workers (who were the ones I associated with most during my period of full-time participant observation) were the ones most affected by my report. I attempted to explain the purpose of my paper and how this had, in my terms,

been distorted by the press and I stressed that it had not been my intention to present the workers in an unfavourable light. The workers listened in silence until I asked if there were any questions. Then Judy (aged between 45 and 50, living in Dockford) argued that I had represented the workers as 'a lot of layabouts'. Edna (aged 45 to 50 from Chesstown) then muttered something to the effect that 'that's all there is to be said, then', and began to move away, taking some of the older women with her. At this point, however, a younger girl said in opposition to Edna that 'it didn't worry me, anyway' and some argument developed between the workers. The same procedure of calling the women together was adopted at the other end of the room. The responses here were broadly similar, although no arguments developed. June (aged 45 to 50, married and living in Dockford), an inspector on one of the lines and one of my best informants, became involved in a discussion with the senior colleague as to what I had meant by 'alienation in reverse'.

We then returned to the office and had some more discussion with Dick and Mr Gollan (the manager), and it was agreed that I should attempt to explain the situation to each of the girls individually. We left the department but, just as we were outside the door, a teenaged girl from the miniatures line stopped us and said: 'Some of the girls would like to thank you for coming in and explaining to us'. I did not know the girl by sight; she had not been working in the department during my period of full-time participant observation.

In my subsequent visits to the department I brought with me the cutting from the *Guardian*, both as an attempt to redress the picture presented by some of the other newspapers and also as an attempt to stimulate further discussion. I managed to speak to most of the workers on the assembly side as well as to one or two of the key workers on the process side. Some responses were cool, others were critical but open, and others were sympathetic. Nobody absolutely refused to listen to what I had to say. Later I was able to provide a full version of the paper and Dick had several copies made. I doubt whether many of the workers read the paper in full but Dick, who had initially been sympathetic, became more hostile. We had a fairly heated discussion about the objects of the research and of professional ethics. I completed this series of visits to the department after about two or three weeks.

The effects of this publicity and my subsequent return visits were twofold. In the first place I gained more information from and about some of the workers than I had gained during the period prior to the 'scandal'. In many cases this may have reflected a desire on the part of these informants to 'put the record straight'. More specifically, however, these responses may be seen as attempts on the part of the informants to define or redefine their positions in relation to me, the department and the other workers. Linked to this was a second consequence. The report underlined to me the importance of certain divisions within the department, divisions of which I had only been partially aware prior to the publicity. Responses to my paper and to the publicity differed in degree and in intensity, and these differences were not randomly distributed among the workers, but were patterned according to certain characteristics such as age, length of service, residence and type of work. It is the nature and significance of these divisions that I shall examine in this chapter.

The Role of the Observer

The role of the participant observer in the research situation has already received considerable attention and it is not my intention to provide a full account of the problem here.[11] It is enough to say that my role – in common with the reported experience of several other participant observers – was characterised by a high degree of ambiguity together with, and arising out of, an initial visible social distance. It was clear that I was not a worker in the sense of my directly relying upon employment at Citron Works for my livelihood, and I did not attempt to pretend that I was a worker. My sex, accent and mode of dress generally distinguished me from the workers. It was slightly less clear that I was not a manager or a foreman. One or two of the workers felt that I was there to 'learn the trade', presumably in some technical or potential managerial capacity. I deliberately attempted to separate myself from management and authority within the department as I felt that the main danger facing a participant observer in a workshop would be identification with authority. The foremen, supervisors and managers were seen to be telling me what to do in my day to day work. I observed normal working hours during the period of full-time participant observation and sat with one group of workers during the lunchbreaks. After my full-time period in the department, I continued to come in and made a point of not spending all the time with the foremen, managers, or technical staff. As the department was a small one, my movements and activities were always highly visible.

Given this ambiguity, attempts were made by the members of the department to categorise me in terms of some more meaningful identity. While I always attempted to explain the object of my research – although I now feel that I could have done more in this respect – it became clear to me that the role of a sociologist was not one with a high degree of social visibility in the Britain of the mid-1960s. Thus, where I was not categorised as some kind of management trainee, I was classified as a 'student' (to some, a theological student) or as someone who was 'writing a book'. In terms of this last identity, references were made by one or two of the workers to *Saturday Night and Sunday Morning*, *A Taste of Honey*, and to the television series *Coronation Street*.

My role, therefore, was characterised by both ambiguity and distance. But at the same time, there was the possibility of restructuring the situation in terms which were formally irrelevant to either the work, or to the research situation. I was (then) a young unmarried male in a department full of women; two obvious parameters according to which the situation might be restructured were, therefore, those of age and sex. Thus, to some of the younger unmarried girls I became the object of some mock flirtation and a certain amount of joking about girlfriends. The older married women tended to play more of a maternal role, expressing concern about the way in which I managed on my own in a bed-sitting room and even, in one case, offering to wash my shirts for me. Interestingly, several of the older women underestimated my age and were surprised when my real age was revealed in one of the newspaper accounts.

Thus, in a variety of ways, the initial ambiguity and distance inherent in my role as a participant observer was reduced by a reordering of the situation in terms which were more easy to handle on both sides. My presence became accepted in these diffuse, unspoken terms; my absences (in the case of sickness) and my lateness became the subject of comments. My departure from full-time participation in the work of the department was marked with the presentation of small gifts. It would not be true to say that I became indistinguishable from the workers, but at least I had a stable and relatively acceptable identity in the department. The effect of the publicity was to break this unwritten *modus vivendi*. The reports both made it 'clear' what I was really doing and, at the same time, also increased or reactivated a sense of ambiguity and dismay.

While there were obviously specific factors relating to my personality and to the particular social situation under observation which contributed to this ambiguity, it should be stressed that to varying degrees this ambiguity and potential instability is inherent in *any* social research situation. The investigator is pursuing what is both an individual (in the terms of career and personal interests), and a collective (in terms of the professional, scientific interests of the research team, the university or research department, and the discipline as a whole) project. Yet these individual and collective projects involve the sustained development of interpersonal relationships. As such, any research situation has, in part, an exploitative character involving the definition of the 'other' as an 'object' of research. This is true, even where – as was the case here – the research is *not* directly sponsored by some agency concerned with the ultimate manipulation of these 'others' in terms of governmental or managerial policy. When the aim of the research is known, some resentment and opposition on the part of the 'others' is likely.[12] While certain measures and techniques may be used to alleviate this problem – the deliberate setting up of an interview situation or the development of codes of professional ethics – they cannot fully resolve the dilemma.[13]

Yet, while the pursuit of sociological research has this exploitative element in it and involves the definition of the research 'others' as the 'objects' of research, this does not mean that these 'others' will necessarily respond in an undifferentiated way. An analysis of the relationship between the researcher and the persons under investigation cannot fully be analysed in terms of an ego–alter relationship unless it is realised that there are several alters and that their responses to the observer are mediated through particular aspects of the total social situation. For this reason I am interested in the variation between the responses to this 'crisis' (itself only an exaggerated and heightened dramatisation of the research situation) and the way in which these variations can be related to particular features of this workshop.

If, in the course of this discussion, I differentiate some of the responses in the department according to the labels 'old' and 'young' it should be stressed that I am using these terms as shorthand indicators for a cluster of characteristics which were to some extent linked and which had meaning in the life of the department. Thus, the term 'old' or 'older' implies not merely biological age, but also longer service in the department, greater commitment to the workplace, marriage and mother-hood, having lived through a certain period and set of historical circumstances, residence in Chesstown (in some cases), traditional working-class, and so on. The term 'young' or 'younger', on the other hand, carries with it connotations of an unmarried status, less identification with the workplace and traditional working-class values, greater identification with the prevailing 'youth culture', and so on. Furthermore, each was defined in terms of the other. Thus, a married woman in her early thirties might be defined as 'young' in this situation, although the same categorization might not apply elsewhere.

To the 'old' group it appeared that I had broken out of a role which had been assigned to me. The word 'betrayal' was apparently used by some of the workers in this category. During my everyday interaction, prior to the publicity, questions of difference in terms of age, education and social class had been suspended or at least muted. Now they were brought into the open. Some claimed that I had insulted the working class and, by concentrating on some of the 'play' aspects of work-shop behaviour, I had ignored the harsh realities of working-class life. Several workers in this category, after the publicity, described aspects of their personal circumstances which stressed the struggles and the set-backs – the sick children, the deserting husbands – that they had known at home and at work.

To the younger group it seemed that I appeared as something of a challenge to the older, more dominant, culture of the workshop. For the most part they were not offended by what it appeared I had written: indeed, they seemed to welcome it as a talking-point and a diversion. This was in spite of the fact that many of the activities I had described in the report appeared to be more about them than about the department as a whole. I was seen as a possible ally. Differences of sex and class were for the most part suspended in inter-action – as they had been during the whole research period – while the similarities in terms of age were implicitly stressed.

The way in which the ambiguous role of a participant observer is defined in a particular situation is not merely idiosyncratic or accidental. If the participant observer – or any 'stranger' – is defined in a particular way, it is largely because these latent identities have meaning in those particular circumstances. What is being described is not a dyadic or set of dyadic relation-ships between observer and observed, but rather a triad between observer, observed and others in the same situation. It is necessary, therefore, to examine the department more closely.

The Social Structure of the Department

The department in many respects presented a very fluid and unstructured social situation. On the one hand, it was difficult to discern any clearcut and permanently drawn lines of conflict and antagonism between different functional groups or categories of workers. Informal groups – of the kind often described in industrial sociology – could not be called the most central or the most important units in the department. On the other hand, there was no clear and coherent identification with the department itself. Thus, there was an absence of both an overall cohesion, and clear-cut internal divisions. Both cohesion and divisions were potentially present and which principle dominated depended upon particular situations. What we have here is a set of overlapping potential bases for identification. It is against this fluid background that this particular case must be understood.

It will already be clear that there was not a uniform response to the British Association paper. It was neither universally accepted, nor rejected. One of the problems here is that there was a high degree of ambiguity as to what the members of the department were responding. The various images of myself and of my British Association paper were mediated through two or three mass-circulation newspapers. Considerable selectivity and flexibility were adopted on the part of the members of the department in their responses to the total situa-tion. Thus, some people argued that the report was broadly true but that I should not have said it; others argued that the report was true – for other people in the department; others were more prone to blame the press than the actual paper, or me; and yet others were prepared to accept the situation in its entirety. Thus, when I came to attempt to classify the responses, I found that a simple favourable/unfavourable continuum did not accurately take account of these shades of variation.

An extreme response was presented by Reenie, who worked on the 'miniatures' line under the supervision of Clare. She was a married woman in her forties. She argued that the report had made a mockery of the working class. Women workers, she argued, *had* to work hard, especially if they were on bonus. They needed the money. She did not see much good coming out of the report although the 'upper classes' might like to read it. The rest of the people, the working people, knew all about it anyway. She said she had a tough life and was not sure how she had managed at times. Her friend, roughly in the same age group, supported this view. Thus, Reenie and her friend condemned the content of the report, doubted its usefulness, did not strongly differentiate between the paper and its presentation in the press and stressed the class issue.

At the other extreme were the views of a group of young girls, who also worked on this miniatures line (aged 17 to 21, approximately). In the context of a lively group discussion, they told me that they felt that the matter was a huge joke. Some of the older workers who had objected to the report were 'narrow-minded'. They described themselves to me – on another occasion – as 'revolution corner'. The girl who came and thanked me for coming into the department came from this group. They claimed that they had always had a laugh at their work and talked about everything apart from the job itself. This group, therefore, found some kind of affinity between certain themes in the report and their own situation in the department. Again, there was no attempt to differentiate between what I had actually said and what the newspapers reported me as saying.

These were extreme views but there were, as I have suggested, many possible stages between them and not all of them could be considered to be on the same continuum. Some argued that the report provided a 'good talking point' without committing themselves to a wholehearted approval or condemnation. Some used the report as an occasion to launch an attack on the younger workers in the room, thereby arguing that the report was true for some people but not for them. Others restricted their comments to statements about the press and the way in which the press 'distorted things'.

Recognising these difficulties in the classification of the responses in a simple unfavourable/favourable continuum, I have attempted a tentative classification according to the following criteria. Those who argued that my report was false or that it was accurate but unacceptable might be seen as taking a broadly unfavourable attitude. Similarly, those who argued that the report was accurate and acceptable – that it was acceptable for oneself and for one's own group and who made a positive appraisal of the behaviour reported in the paper – might be seen as adopting a broadly favourable attitude. These are logical categories in that, for example, to hold the former opinions and yet to hold a favourable attitude would represent a contradiction. There were, however, some responses that could not be so readily classified and which were often a mixture of favourable and unfavourable views. Thus, those who argued that the report was true for others but not for themselves might broadly be located in the unfavourable camp, although there were exceptions. Much depends upon such matters as tone of voice. I shall attempt in the next few paragraphs to classify the responses I received (and it should be noted that this was neither a total population, nor a random sample of views) and to assess what kind of association existed between responses and certain characteristics. It should be stressed that this cannot, under the circumstances, be a strictly statistical exercise and that I am necessarily simplifying a great deal.

A preliminary analysis suggests that, in the terms outlined above, the following groups could be broadly classified as being favourable or unfavourable:

Favourable	Unfavourable
assembly side of department X	process side of department X
within the assembly side, those workers under the supervision of Clare	within the assembly side, those workers under the supervision of Liz
younger workers	older workers
short-service workers	longer-service workers
workers living in Dockford	workers living in Chesstown

This list should, of course, be read as indicating that favourable responses were more likely to come from workers with the characteristics listed on the left-hand side than from those with characteristics on the right-hand side, the reverse being true for unfavourable responses. It will already be clear, however, that there were several exceptions and that, further, many of the categories used here overlap and include each other. We are dealing with broad clusters of characteristics, which are in various ways related and which interact with and reinforce each other.

To illustrate these clusters of related characteristics and the way in which they were related to the responses to the British Association paper, I took four characteristics which appeared to me to be particularly important. Looking through my field notes for this crisis period, I attempted to relate the favourable or unfavourable responses according to the presence or absence of one or more of these characteristics. The characteristics were as follows:

(1) age (over or under the age of 40);
(2) length of service (more or less than five years service);
(3) residence (Dockford or Chesstown);
(4) possession of authority (that is, supervisor).

A person with all four characteristics, therefore, would be over 40, have over five years' service, come from Chesstown and have some supervisory authority. We have seen how the first three characteristics are closely related, and it should be clear that the fourth characteristic is also closely related to the first three. I selected these four characteristics as together or singly indicating some measure of commitment to and identification with the workplace. Those responses which, according to my field notes, could be classified as being definitely favourable or unfavourable are grouped according to the possession or non-possession of one or more of these characteristics (Table 34.2). Again it should be stressed that the use of figures here should not mislead the reader into assigning an unwarranted degree of precision to these findings.[14] The suggestion is, therefore, that the kinds of response to the event depended to some degree – perhaps to a large degree –on a worker's degree of commitment to and identification with the workplace. On the one hand, there were those workers who had experienced many years of work and who had a fairly long experience with this particular plant. Some of them had come from Chesstown and had shared the experience of the move and of travelling together to and from work on the bus. Some – three – of them were supervisors.[15] To all or most of these workers, work was a 'central life interest', or at least it was more of a 'central life interest' than it was for the other workers.[16] When the workplace appeared to be attacked, they felt themselves to be under attack and reacted with various degress of hostility. On the other hand, there were those workers with relatively little experience of life and work, often single and who had spent little time with the firm. It was likely that several of them would leave the firm to get married, have children or find work elsewhere. Their identification with the work and the firm was marginal, their reference groups were largely external to the department. They were, therefore, not unduly offended by the publicity; indeed, they saw it as a diversion and as a chance to attack the numerically dominant older workers.

Table 34.2   *Characteristics Indicating Attachment to the Workplace and Response to the Paper*

	Unfavourable	Favourable
Possessing all four characteristics	3	–
Possessing any three characteristics	5	–
Possessing any two characteristics	2	2
Possessing any one characteristic	4	2
Possessing none	1	8
Total number of responses classified	15	12

One thing to be noted here is the way in which many of these responses and orientations were mediated through groups. Thus, there was a group of older, long-service women, who sat together working on coding and packing. Several of these women came from Chesstown. They had developed among themselves some schemes of rudimentary teamwork and mutual assistance should one worker happen to fall behind the others, or if work were scarce. Their opposition to the report was uniformly hostile, and this included the responses of a younger girl in her early twenties who happened to be working among this group of older women. On the favourable side there was the already mentioned 'Revolution Corner' and some members of the core of a more heterogeneous group that met in the lunchbreak to play cards. Again, this group included two older women, who shared the views of the younger workers they sat with. Thus, group relationships tended to reinforce the favourable or unfavourable views that the workers had of the report.

We can see, therefore, that the responses to the paper were not uniform and that the differences in response were related to a cluster of factors which, taken together, indicated some measure of commitment to the workplace. At the same time, it should not be felt that the publication of the report had created a major rift in the department, or even that the report had made manifest a major rift that was already present but latent. The following modifications must be recognised and incorporated into the analysis:

(1) The lines of difference which have been described in the previous paragraphs were differences largely in terms of latent characteristics which, while being reinforced by work experiences, did not have consequences for work relationships. As we have seen, there was a low degree of functional interdependence on the assembly side at least. Thus, patterned antagonisms did not arise out of work relationships of interdependence and neither were categorisations in terms of 'non-work' characteristics directly reinforced by work relationships.

(2) Although I have labelled some of the responses to the paper as being 'unfavourable', the actual degree of overt hostility was not great. Thus, even the most antagonistic responses were expressed calmly, at length and with a considerable degree of understanding. Only one or two of the workers to whom I spoke became noticeably cool or non-responsive after the crisis.

(3) Much of the mild antagonism was deflected towards the press and the way in which 'they' misrepresented things. Thus, Reenie, while she did not argue that the press distortion excused my report and was, as I have shown, one of the most vocal opponents of my report, expressed amusement at the way in which one of the newspaper 'follow-up' stories had attempted to reproduce the local dialect in print. (A kind of 'stage North Country'.)

(4) It should be emphasised that I have classified the extreme responses here – the unambiguously favourable or unfavourable. At least the same number of responses could be located between the two points or outside this continuum, although the broad pattern of

the responses according to the characteristics mentioned appears to be maintained.

In the context of these qualifications it should be noted that the 'scandal' was a relatively short-lived affair. One of the most favourable respondents and one of the most unfavourable respondents both used the same phrase to me to describe the affair: 'A nine days' wonder.' The report did not create division; it merely provided an issue in terms of which some of the already existing latent divisions could be expressed. Once these divisions had been expressed and positions had been defined or redefined, the department settled back to 'normal'.

Conclusion: The Observer, the Event and the Department

This particular event may be seen as a 'social drama', involving the observer, his paper and its reporting in the press, and the 'objects' of the research.[17] In the first place, we have the paper with its various themes based partly on some aspects of the life within the department. But this original paper was presented to the members of the department through the press, which highlighted some themes and played down or ignored others. In the second place, we have the observer, placed in an uncertain and ambiguous role situation and whose role was, as a result of this ambiguity, defined in terms of some extradepartmental identities. And finally we have the department, characterised by a high degree of fluidity in its social relationships, relatively unconstrained in terms of technological or administrative imperatives, possessing neither deep-rooted and persisting patterns of antagonism, nor a clear collective identity. Workers had differing degrees of commitment to and involvement in the workplace and assigned different meanings to different aspects of their work situation. These differences, although given meaning in terms of the workplace, were, partly at least, in terms of latent characteristics, that is, characteristics which were formally irrelevant to the requirements of the work.

The 'British Association Scandal' was a social drama which enabled the actors to define or redefine themselves in relation to the department as a whole and in relation to each other. Certain values relating to work, to class and to intergenerational conflict were given expression in terms of the particular content of the paper and its author. At the same time they were not responding to the paper as a whole, nor even to the newspaper reports as a whole, but to certain features with which each person individually felt that she had some kind of affinity. The members of the department, in other words, responded selectively to the paper and its author.[18] They responded selectively in terms of the particular meanings they assigned to work and to work relationships. Thus, one grouping was able to reaffirm their commitment to work, to working-class values and

to the ways in which these commitments were realised in the particular context of this workplace. Another grouping, similarly, was able to express its alienation from certain aspects of the workplace and to reaffirm other values, deriving largely from outside the workplace and expressed in terms of youth and a youth culture.

It is important to realise that here, as in many other situations, we are dealing with a set of overlapping potential identities, some of which were undoubtedly more central than others but none of which unambiguously structured the department. Thus, although the paper allowed people to redefine their positions in relation to others and to reaffirm their commitments, these redefinitions and reaffirmations were not pushed to the extent of provoking a major rift in the department. While there were references to the irresponsibilities of the young and to the conservatism of the old, it was also true that old worked alongside young, that they all worked together in the same room and shared common facilities, such as the stores or the canteen. It is possible to see some of the ambiguities of the crisis as enabling antagonisms to be expressed without their threatening to disrupt the day to day working consensus in social relationships. Hostility to some aspects of the paper – and through this hostility to those persons felt to be most associated with the activities described in the paper – could be modified to reference to the distortions made by the press or by jokes about its author. (Sometime after the 'scandal' the members of the department among others went on a boat trip, organised by the factory's social club. I was told that after a particularly risqué story had been told, one of the girls cried: 'Careful, look under the seat, David may be listening.')

This social drama, in common with all social dramas, can be seen in terms of a cycle. Prior to the scandal, I had a recognised if ambiguous position in the department, and the department itself had a relatively fluid structure made up of a set of overlapping identities. On the morning of the scandal, there was widespread consensus about the newspaper reports in that they were: (a) recognised as relating to the members of the department; (b) seen as a major talking-point; and probably (c) seen as a source of concern. My previously accepted position in the department was to some extent called into question. The initial shock gave way to more diverse and conflicting interpretations, expressing divisions and potential conflicts within the department. And finally, there was a return to the fluid, relatively harmonious state of accommodation that had existed prior to the scandal. Some divisions would undoubtedly remain and would be given further expression in future dramas, just as earlier dramas had laid the ground for some of the patterns revealed here. But the everyday pattern of accommodation and tolerance would also remain, largely because there was little in the structuring of the department to give these divisions permanent expression.

'In the social drama we see social structure in action', writes Turner.[19] This should not be interpreted, at least in this case, as meaning that the divisions and conflicting interpretations made manifest in the course of this drama represented the 'reality' beneath the apparent calm and consensus. Rather the drama revealed certain potential bases for identity. Certain identities in terms of class or age (in opposition to those of the investigator) were brought into play in the course of the particular drama, but these identities were not necessarily 'more real' than other identities brought into play on other, less dramatic occasions. If these identities were in terms of largely 'external' factors, this was because I had concentrated on these factors in the original paper and because these identities were particularly salient in terms of working women in this particular place and at this particular point of history. In analysing why certain identities were brought into play rather than others, we need to consider a whole set of factors: the relatively 'permissive' environment in terms of the absence of major technological or administrative constraints, the expectations brought to the workplace by the workers and the backgrounds and biographies of the workers themselves.

If the social drama reveals something about the nature of the department itself, it also highlights certain features of the research situation. In fact, it is probably difficult or impossible to distinguish between the research situation and the department, between the department as an object of research and the department as a place of work. One worker in the department wondered if I had not arranged the whole thing as an experiment. Put in these terms the statement is untrue, but in a sense all participant observation is a kind of uncontrolled experiment. The introduction of the participant observer creates a new situation. To understand this situation in full, it is necessary not only to analyse the particular features of social life in the community under observation, but also the interests, commitments and backgrounds of the observer himself. If some of the workers in the department responded to me at this time in terms of age and class, it was because of a perceived difference between us in these terms which became relevant in this situation. It should be clear from this account that all these elements – the observer, the observed and the social situation of the observed –should be seen interacting to form a new situation. It is not so surprising that *some* of the workers responded in terms of the following set of overlapping dichotomies: observer/observed, outsider/insider, male/female, young/old, middle class/working class, them/us and exploiter/exploited. It is likely that an increasing number of sociologists will be met with opposition expressed in these kinds of terms. What is interesting here is that some workers – probably the majority of the workers – did *not* overtly respond in these terms. To understand this, we must examine the particular social situation under investigation. The

events described in this chapter are in some senses unique and perhaps even particularly dramatic. But the situation and problems of the participant observer (or indeed any sociologist) are not necessarily unique. Similarly there are many social situations like department X where there are no clearcut lines of division or antagonism, but which appear humdrum, insignificant and everyday. Social dramas of the kind outlined here may tell us something not only about the community under investigation, but also about the process of research itself, with all its constraints, ambiguities and responsibilities.[20]

Notes: Chapter 34

Reprinted from *Sociological Review*, vol. 20, no. 2, 1972, pp. 185–206, by kind permission of the publisher and the author. This article arises out of research conducted during the period 1962–5, financed by what was then known as the Department for Scientific and Industrial Research (DSIR). The Senior Investigator was Professor Max Gluckman, and the project was under the immediate supervision of Professor Ronald Frankenberg and Dr Valdo Pons. My co-workers on the project were Isabel Emmett and Dr W. M. Walker. I have benefited greatly from discussion with these individuals and from other members of the Department of Sociology and Social Anthropology, University of Manchester, all of whom have contributed to my thinking on this and other topics. I am particularly grateful to Ian Craib for reading a draft of this article, and for stimulating my interest in the relationships between existentialism and sociology.

1   See the article by Vidich and Bensman (1964).
2   See Fichter and Kolb (1954).
3   For a brief statement, see the letter on 'professional ethics' by Stacey (1968).
4   The possible functional role of these stories as 'occupational myths', creating a professional identity and, perhaps, serving as a *rite de passage* cannot be discounted.
5   I should stress that this is not the only, or even the most important, ethical problem confronting the sociologist. The purpose of this article is not to list all the ethical dilemmas facing the sociologist, but to explore one particular dilemma in some detail.
6   See Sartre (1963), p. 72. The reader will be aware that this article does not live up to these somewhat exacting demands; in particular, the interpretation of the events as a 'moment of history' is given scant attention here.
7   See Lupton (1963); Cunnison (1966); and Wilson (1963).
8   It was the second of two related papers, the first being given by Dr Derek Allcorn.
9   This is clearly an oversimplification both of the actual situation of women at work, and my formulation of the problem.
10 The temptation, of course, is to cast the journalist in the role of villain. However, it is important to note that both the journalist and the sociologist can be seen as handling the same kinds of situation, faced with similar problems and operating under particular sets of constraints. The difference is in the nature of these constraints (the concept of a 'good story', the daily deadlines, and so on) and the

resulting differing frames of reference. The sharpest point where the two clash is, of course, over the question of confidentiality and identifiability.

11 For a useful collection of papers, see Filstead (1970).

12 Such opposition is likely to increase, especially among exploited or minority groups, such as workers on strike, immigrant communities, areas of poverty, and so on. It is also likely that this, more than any discussion of professional ethics, will cause a radical reassessment of the sociologist's role.

13 I am particularly grateful to Ian Craib for suggesting some of the points raised in this paragraph.

14 I do not hold the view that the use of figures and the use of participant observations are incompatible. Recent analyses of social networks show observation can be combined with measurement and quantification. See Mitchell (1969), especially the paper by Kapferer (1969).

15 Two were the supervisors already mentioned in this report; the third was a supervisor on the process side.

16 The term 'central life interest' comes from Dubin (1956).

17 For a discussion of social dramas, see Turner (1957), p. 93. (See the extract reprinted in this volume as Chapter 33).

18 This, of course, is not in itself unusual. The same could be said of perceptions of a television programme, a street accident or a football match.

19 See Turner (1957), p. 231.

20 Since writing this paper, I have read Gouldner's book; his discussion of 'reflexive sociology' clearly has some bearing on the themes raised here (see Gouldner, 1971, pp. 488–500).

References

Aberbach, J. D. and Walker, J. L. (1970), 'Political trust and racial ideology', *American Political Science Review*, vol. 64, no. 4, pp. 1199–1219.

Aberle, D. F. (1951), *The Psychosocial Analysis of a Hopi Life History*, Comparative Psychology Monographs 21 (1).

Ackoff, R. L. and Halbert, M. H. (1958), 'An operations research study of the scientific activity of chemists', Case Institute of Technology, Operations Research Group, Cleveland; mimeo.

Adams, R. N. and Preiss, J. J. (1960) (eds), *Human Organization Research: Field Relations and Techniques* (Homewood, Ill.: Dorsey Press).

Allan, W. (1949), *Studies of African Land Usage in Northern Rhodesia*, Rhodes-Livingstone Paper No. 15.

Allan, W. (1965), *The African Husbandman* (Edinburgh: Oliver & Boyd).

Allport, G. W. (1942), *The Use of Personal Documents in Psychological Science*, Social Science Research Council Bulletin 49.

Allport, G. W. (1961), *Pattern and Growth in Personality* (New York: Holt, Rinehart & Winston).

Alpert, H. (1952), 'Some observations on the sociology of sampling', *Social Forces*, vol. 31, no. 1, pp. 30–33.

American Anthropological Association (1971), 'Statements on ethics: principles of professional responsibility'; reprinted in T. Weaver (1973) (ed.), *To See Ourselves: Anthropology and Modern Social Issues* (Chicago: Scott, Foresman), pp. 46–8.

American Journal of Sociology (1956), 'Interviewing' (special issue), vol. 62, no. 2, pp. 137–217.

Anderson, M. (1971), *Family Structure in Nineteenth Century Lancashire* (Cambridge: CUP).

Anderson, M. (1972), 'The study of family structure', in E. A. Wrigley (ed.), *Nineteenth Century Society* (Cambridge: CUP), pp. 47–81.

Anderson, N. (1923), *The Hobo: the Sociology of the Homeless Man* (Chicago: University of Chicago Press).

Anderson, R. T. and Anderson, B. G. (1964), *The Vanishing Village: a Danish Maritime Community* (Seattle: University of Washington Press).

Angell, R. (1945), 'A critical review of the development of the personal document method in sociology, 1920–1940', in L. Gottschalk, C. Kluckhohn and R. Angell (eds), *The Use of Personal Documents in History, Anthropology and Sociology*, Social Science Research Council Bulletin 53, pp. 177–232.

Ardener, E. W. (1975), 'Language, ethnicity and population', in R. P. Moss and R. J. A. R. Rathbone (eds), *The Population Factor in African Studies* (London: University of London Press), pp. 48–56.

Arensberg, C. (1954), 'The community study method', *American Journal of Sociology*, vol. 60, no. 2, pp. 109–24.

Arensberg, C. M. and Kimball, S. T. (1965), *Culture and Community* (New York: Harcourt Brace Jovanovich).

Armstrong, A. (1974), *Stability and Change in an English County Town, a social study of York, 1801–1851* (Cambridge: CUP).

Arrington, R. E. (1943), 'Time sampling in studies of social behaviour: a critical review of techniques and results with research suggestions', *Psychological Bulletin*, vol. 40, no. 2, pp. 81–124.

Asad, T. (1973) (ed.), *Anthropology and the Colonial Encounter* (London: Ithaca Press).

Atkinson, P. (1977), 'Becoming a hypochondriac', in A. Davis and G. Horobin (eds), *Medical Encounters: the Experience of Illness and Treatment* (London: Croom Helm), pp. 17–31.

Back, K. W. (1956), 'The well-informed informant', *Human Organization*, vol. 14, no. 4, pp. 30–33.

Baeck, L. (1961), 'An expenditure study of the Congolese évolués of Leopoldville, Belgian Congo', in A. Southall (ed.), *Social Change in Modern Africa* (London: OUP for the International African Institute), pp. 159–81.

Bailey, K. D. (1978), *Methods of Social Research* (New York: The Free Press).

Baldamus, W. (1967), 'The category of pragmatic knowledge in sociological analysis', *Archives for Philosophy of Law and Social Philosophy*, vol. 53, no. 1, pp. 31–51.

Baldamus, W. (1972), 'The role of discoveries in social science', in T. Shanin (ed), *The Rules of the Game* (London: Tavistock), pp. 276–302.

Baldamus, W. (1976), *The Structure of Sociological Inference* (London: Martin Robertson).

Banks, J. A. (1957), 'The group discussion as an interview technique', *Sociological Review*, vol. 5, no. 1, pp. 75–84.

Banton, M. (1966) (ed.), *The Social Anthropology of Complex Societies* (London: Tavistock).

Barnes, J. A. (1963), 'Some ethical problems of modern field-work', *British Journal of Sociology*, vol. 14, no. 2, pp. 118–34; reprinted in W. J. Filstead (1970) (ed.), *Qualitative Methodology: Firsthand Involvement with the Social World* (Chicago: Markham), pp. 235–51.

Barnes, J. A. (1979), *Who Should Know What?* (Harmondsworth: Penguin).

Bartlett, F. C. (1937), 'Psychological methods and anthropological problems', *Africa*, vol. 10, no. 4, pp. 401–19.

Barton, A. H. and Lazarsfeld, P. F. (1955), 'Some functions of qualitative analysis in social research', *Frankfurter Beiträge Zur Soziologie*, pp. 321–61; reprinted in G. J. McCall and J. L. Simmons (1969) (eds), *Issues in Participant Observation: a Text and Reader* (Reading, Mass.: Addison-Wesley), pp. 163–96 and 239–44.

Bateson, G. and Mead, M. (1942), *Balinese Character: a Photographic Analysis* (New York: New York Academy of Sciences).

Beattie, J. (1965), *Understanding an African Kingdom: Bunyoro* (New York: Holt, Rinehart & Winston).

Bechhofer, F. (1974), 'Current approaches to empirical research: some central ideas', in J. Rex (ed.), *Approaches to Sociology: an Introduction to Major Trends in British Sociology* (London: Routledge & Kegan Paul), pp. 70–91.

Beck, B. (1970), 'Cooking welfare stew', in R. W. Habenstein (ed.), *Pathways to Data* (Chicago: Aldine), pp. 7–29.

Becker, H. (1956), 'Fieldwork among Scottish shepherds and German peasants', *Social Forces*, vol. 35, no. 1, pp. 10–15.

Becker, H. S. (1954), 'A note on interviewing tactics', *Human Organization*, vol. 12, no. 4, pp. 31–2.

Becker, H. S. (1956), 'Interviewing medical students', *American Journal of Sociology*, vol. 62, no. 2, pp. 199–201.

Becker, H. S. (1958), 'Problems of inference and proof in participant observation', *American Sociological Review*, vol. 23, no. 6, pp. 652–60.

Becker, H. S. (1963), *The Outsiders* (New York: The Free Press).

Becker, H. S. (1964) 'Problems in the publication of field studies', in A. J. Vidich, J. Bensman and M. R. Stein (eds), *Reflections on Community Studies* (New York: Harper & Row), pp. 267–84.

Becker, H. S. (1966), 'Introduction', in C. R. Shaw, *The Jack Roller: a Delinquent Boy's Own Story* (Chicago: University of Chicago Press, Phoenix edition), pp. v–xviii.

Becker, H. S. (1970a) (ed.), *Sociological Work* (New York: Transaction Books).

Becker, H. S. (1970b), 'Practitioners of vice and crime', in R. W. Habenstein (ed.), *Pathways to Data* (Chicago: Aldine), pp. 30–49.

Becker, H. S. (1970c), 'Whose side are we on?', in J. D. Douglas (ed.), *The Relevance of Sociology* (New York: Appleton-Century-Crofts), pp. 99–111.

Becker, H. S. (1980), 'Aesthetics and truth', *Transaction*, vol. 17, no. 5, pp. 26–8.

Becker, H. S. and Geer, B. (1957), 'Participant observation and interviewing: a comparison', *Human Organization*, vol. 16, no. 3, pp. 28–32.

Becker, H. S. and Geer, B. (1958), 'Participant observation and interviewing: a rejoinder', *Human Organization*, vol. 17, no. 2, pp. 39–40.

Becker, H. S. and Geer, B. (1960,' Participant observation: the analysis of qualitative field data', in R. N. Adams and J. J. Preiss (eds), *Human Organization Research: Field Relations and Techniques* (Homewood, Ill.: Dorsey Press), pp. 267–89.

Becker, H. S., Geer, B. and Hughes, E. C. (1968), *Making the Grade* (New York: Wiley).

Becker, H. S., Geer, B., Hughes, E. C. and Strauss, A. L. (1961), *Boys in White: Student Culture in Medical School* (Chicago: University of Chicago Press).

Becker, H. S., Geer, B., Riesman, D. and Weiss, R. S. (1968) (eds), *Institutions and the Person: Papers Presented to Everett C. Hughes* (Chicago: Aldine).

Bell, C. (1968), *Middle Class Families* (London: Routledge & Kegan Paul).

Bell, C. (1977), 'Reflections on the Banbury restudy', in C. Bell and H. Newby (eds), *Doing Sociological Research* (London: Allen & Unwin), pp. 47–62.

Bell, C. and Encel, S. (1978) (eds), *Inside the Whale* (Oxford: Pergamon).

Bell, C. and Newby, H. (1972), *Community Studies* (London: Allen & Unwin).

Bell, C. and Newby, H. (1977) (eds), *Doing Sociological Research* (London: Allen & Unwin).

Bellah, R. N. (1964), 'Research chronicle: *Tokugawa Religion*' in P. Hammond (ed.), *Sociologists at Work* (New York: Basic Books), pp. 142–60.

Benedict, R. (1934), *Patterns of Culture* (New York: Houghton Mifflin).

Bennett, J. W. (1948), 'The study of cultures: a survey of techniques and methodology in field work', *American Sociological Review*, vol. 13, no. 6, pp. 672–89.

Bennett, J. W. and Thaiss, G. (1967), 'Survey research and sociocultural anthropology', in C. Glock (ed.), *Survey Research in the Social Sciences* (New York: Russell Sage Foundation), pp. 271–313.

Benney, M. (1978), 'The legacy of mining', in M. Bulmer (ed.), *Mining and Social Change* (London: Croom Helm), pp. 49–58.

Bensman, J. and Vidich, A. J. (1960), 'Social theory in field research', *American Journal of Sociology*, vol. 65, no. 6, pp. 577–84; reprinted in M. Bulmer (1977) (ed.), *Sociological Research Methods* (London: Macmillan), pp. 259–71.

Berger, J. and Mohr, J. (1967), *A Fortunate Man: the Story of a Country Doctor* (London: Allen Lane).

Berger, J. and Mohr, J. (1975), *A Seventh Man: a Book of Images and Words about the Experiences of Migrant Workers in Europe* (Harmondsworth: Penguin).

Bernard, J. (1966), *Academic Women* (Cleveland, Ohio: World).

Bernheim, E. (1908), *Lehrbuch der historischen Methode* (Leipzig: Duncker & Humblot).

Bernstein, C. and Woodward, B. (1974), *All the President's Men* (London: Quartet).

Beynon, H. (1973), *Working for Ford* (Harmondsworth: Penguin).

Bick, M. (1967), 'An index of native terms', in B. Malinowski, *A Diary in the Strict Sense of the Term* (London: Routledge & Kegan Paul), pp. 299–315.

Bidney, D. (1953), *Theoretical Anthropology* (New York: Columbia University Press).

Billingsley, A. (1968), *Black Families in White America* (Englewood Cliffs, NJ: Prentice-Hall).

Bittner, E. (1968), 'Keeping the peace in skid row', in A. L. Strauss (ed.), *The American City: a Sourcebook of Urban Imagery* (London: Allen Lane), pp. 277–84.

Blau, P. M. (1954), 'Co-operation and competition in a bureaucracy', *American Journal of Sociology*, vol. 59, no. 6, pp. 530–35.

Blau, P. M. (1964), 'The research process in the study of *The Dynamics of Bureaucracy*', in P. Hammond (ed.), *Sociologists at Work* (New York: Basic Books), pp. 16–49.

Blau, P. M. and Scott, W. R. (1962), *Formal Organizations* (San Francisco: Chandler).

Blauner, R. (1964), *Alienation and Freedom* (Chicago: University of Chicago Press).

Blaxter, M. (1979) (ed.), 'The analysis of qualitative data: a symposium', special issue of *Sociological Review*, vol. 27, no. 4, pp. 649–827.

Bloch, M. (1976), *The Historian's Craft* (Manchester: University of Manchester Press).

Blumer, H. (1939), *Critiques of Research in the Social Sciences: an Appraisal of Thomas and Znaniecki's 'The Polish Peasant in Europe and America'*, Social Science Research Council Bulletin 44.

Blumer, H. (1954), 'What is wrong with social theory?', *American Sociological Review*, vol. 19, no. 1, pp. 3–10.

Blythe, R (1969), *Akenfield* (Harmondsworth: Penguin).

Boas, F. (1920), 'The methods of ethnology', *American Anthropologist*, vol. 22, no. 4, pp. 311–22.

Boas, F. (1932), 'The aims of anthropological research', *Science*, vol. 76, no. 1983, pp. 605–13.

Boas, F. (1940a), 'Some problems of methodology in the social sciences', in F. Boas (ed), *Race, Language and Culture* (New York: Collier-Macmillan), pp. 260–69.

Boas, F. (1940b), 'The aims of ethnology', in F. Boas (ed), *Race, Language and Culture* (New York: Collier-Macmillan), pp. 626–38.

Boas, F. (1943), 'Recent anthropology', *Science*, vol. 98, nos 2545 and 2546, pp. 311–14, 334–7.

Boase, F. (1956), *Modern English Biography* (Truro: Netherton & Worth).

Boehm, A. and Weinberg, R. A. (1977), *The Classroom Observer: a Guide for Developing Observational Skills* (New York: Teachers College Press).

Bogdan, R. (1972), *Participant Observation in Organizational Settings* (Syracuse, NY: Syracuse University Press).

Bogdan, R. (1974), *Being Different: the Autobiography of Jane Fry* (New York: Wiley).

Bogdan, R. and Taylor, S. J. (1975), *Introduction to Qualitative Research Methods* (New York: Wiley).

Boissevain, J. (1974), *Friends of Friends: Networks, Manipulations and Coalitions* (Oxford: Blackwell).

Boissevain, J. and Mitchell, J. C. (1973) (eds), *Network Analysis: Studies in Human Interaction* (The Hague: Mouton for the Afrika Studiecentrum).

Booth, C. (1889–1902) (ed.), *Life and Labour of the People of London*, 17 vols (London: Macmillan).

Bott, E. (1971), *Family and Social Network* (2nd edn) (London: Tavistock).

Bowen, E. S. (Laura Bohannan) (1964), *Return to Laughter* (Garden City, NY: Doubleday/Anchor Natural History Library.

British Sociological Association (1973), 'Statement of ethical principles and their application to sociological practice'; mimeo.

Brookover Bourque, L. and Back, K. W. (1966), 'Time sampling as a field technique', *Human Organization*, vol. 25, no. 1, pp. 64–70.

Brown, C., Guillet De Monthoux, P. and McCullough, A. (1976), *The Access Casebook* (Stockholm: THS).

Brown R. (1963), *Explanation in Social Science* (London: Routledge & Kegan Paul).

Brunskill, R. W. (1970), *Illustrated Handbook of Vernacular Architecture* (London: Universe).

Brunswik, E. (1944), 'Digital focussing of perception: size constancy in a representative sample of situations', *Psychological Monographs*, no. 254.

Brunswik, E. (1947), *Systematic and Representative Design of Psychological Experiments* (Berkeley, Calif.: University of California Press).

Bruyn, S. T. (1966), *The Human Perspective in Sociology: the Methodology of Participant Observation* (Englewood Cliffs, NJ: Prentice-Hall).

Buckley, W. (1957), 'Structural-functional analysis in modern sociology', in H. Becker and A. Boskoff (eds), *Modern Sociological Theory in Continuity and Change* (Hinsdale, Ill.: Dryden Press), pp. 236–59.

Bühler, C. (1933), *Der Menschliche Lebenslauf als Psychologisches Problem* (Leipzig: S. Hirzel) (Gottingen: Verlag für Psychologie, 1959, 2nd edn).

Bühler, C. (1962), *Values in Psychotherapy* (New York: The Free Press).

Bühler, C. (1967), 'Human life as a whole as a central subject of humanistic psychology', in J. F. T. Bugental (ed.), *Challenges of Humanistic Psychology* (New York: McGraw-Hill), pp. 83–91.

Bühler, C. (1968a) 'The course of human life as a psychological problem', *Human Development*, vol. 11, no. 3, pp. 184–200.

Bühler, C. (1968b), 'Introduction', in C. Bühler and F. Massarik (eds), *The Course of Human Life* (New York: Springer), pp. 1–10.

Bühler, C. and Massarik, F. (1968) (eds), *The Course of Human Life* (New York: Springer).

Bulmer, M. (1977) (ed.), *Sociological Research Methods* (London: Macmillan).

Bulmer, M. (1978) (ed.), *Mining and Social Change* (London: Croom Helm).

Bulmer, M. (1979), 'Concepts in the analysis of qualitative data', *Sociological Review*, vol. 27, no. 4, pp. 651–77.

Bulmer, M. (1980), 'Comment on the ethics of covert methods', *British Journal of Sociology*, vol. 31, no. 1, pp. 59–65.

Bulmer, M. (1982) (ed.), *Social Research Ethics* (London: Macmillan).

Bundy, C. and Healy, D. (1978), 'Aspects of urban poverty', *Oral History*, vol. 6, no. 1, pp. 79–97.

Burgess, R. G. (1978), 'Researchers come clean' (review of C. Bell and H. Newby (1977) (eds), *Doing Sociological Research*), *The Times Higher Education Supplement*, no. 325 (27 January).

Burgess, R. G. (1979a), 'Gaining access: some problems and implications for the participant observer', paper presented at SSRC Workshop on Participant Observation, University of Birmingham (September, 1979).

Burgess, R. G. (1979b) (ed.), *Teaching Research Methodology to Postgraduates: a Survey of Courses in the U.K.* (Coventry: University of Warwick).

Burgess, R. G. (1980), 'Some fieldwork problems in teacher-based research', *British Educational Research Journal*, vol. 6, no. 2, pp. 165–73.

Burnett, J. (1977) (ed.), *Useful Toil* (Hardmondsworth: Penguin).

Calhoun, C. J. (1978), 'History, anthropology and the study of communities: some problems in Macfarlane's proposal', *Social History*, vol. 3, no. 3, pp. 363–73.

Campbell D. (1955), 'The informant in quantitative research', *American Journal of Sociology*, vol. 60, no. 4, pp. 339–42.

Campbell, J. K. (1964), *Honour, Family and Patronage* (London: OUP).

Cannell, C. F. and Kahn, R. L. (1953), 'The collection of data by interviewing', in L. Festinger and D. Katz (eds), *Research Methods in the Behavioural Sciences* (New York: Holt, Rinehart & Winston), pp. 327–80.

Cannon, W. B. (1945), *The Way of an Investigator* (New York: Norton).

Carlin, J. E. (1966), *Lawyer's Ethics: a Survey of the New York City Bar* (New York: Russell Sage Foundation).

Carpenter, M. (1980), 'Asylum nursing before 1914: a chapter in the history of labour', in C. Davies (ed.), *Rewriting Nursing History* (London: Croom Helm), pp. 123–46.

Carr, E. H. (1964), *What is History?* (Hardmondsworth: Penguin).

Casagrande, J. (1960) (ed.), *In the Company of Man* (New York: Harper & Row).

Cassell, J. and Wax, M. L. (1980) (eds), 'Ethical problems of fieldwork', special issue of *Social Problems*, vol. 27, no. 3, pp. 259–378.

Caudill, W. and Roberts, B. H. (1951), 'Pitfalls in the organization of interdisciplinary research', *Human Organization*, vol. 10, no. 4, pp. 12–15.

Chafin, W. (1818), *Anecdotes Respecting Cranbourn Chase* (London: J. Nichols, Sons and Bentley).

Chamberlain, M. (1975), *Fenwomen* (London: Virago).

Chandler, M. (1954), 'An evaluation of the group interview', *Human Organization*, vol. 13, no. 2, pp. 26–8.

Chaplin, S. (1978), 'Durham mining villages', in M. Bulmer (ed.), *Mining and Social Change* (London: Croom Helm), pp. 59–82.

Chapple, E. D. (1949a), 'Field methods and techniques' (editorial), *Human Organziation*, vol. 8, no. 3, pp. 27–9.

Chapple, E. D. (1949b), 'Field methods and techniques' (editorial), *Human Organization*, vol. 8, no. 4, pp. 29–30.

Chapple, E. D. (1950), 'Field methods and techniques' (editorial), *Human Organization*, vol. 9, no. 1, pp. 29–30.

Chein, I. (1976), 'An introduction to sampling', in C. Selltiz, L. S. Wrightsman and S. W. Cook (eds), *Research Methods in Social Relations* (3rd edn) (New York: Holt, Rinehart & Winston), pp. 511–40.

Cicourel, A. V. (1964), *Method and Measurement in Sociology* (New York: The Free Press).

Clark, K. B. (1965), *Dark Ghetto – Dilemmas of Social Power* (New York: Harper & Row).

Clausen, J. A. (1968), 'A historical and comparative view of socialization theory and research', in J. A. Clausen (ed.), *Socialization and Society* (Boston, Mass.: Little, Brown), pp. 18–72.

Cleary, J. (1979), 'Demands and responses: the effects of the style of work allocation on the distribution of nursing attention', in D. Hall and M. Stacey (eds), *Beyond Separation: Further Studies of Children in Hospital* (London: Routledge & Kegan Paul), pp. 109–27.

Clément, P. (1956), 'Social patterns of urban life', in D. Forde (ed.), *Social Implications of Industrialization and Urbanization in Africa South of the Sahara* (prepared under the auspices of UNESCO by the International African Institute) (Paris: UNESCO), pp. 368–492.

Cochran, W. G., Mosteller, F. and Tukey, J. W. (1954), 'Statistical problems of the Kinsey report', *Journal of the American Statistical Association*, vol. 48, no. 264, pp. 673–716.

Codere, H. (1955), 'A genealogical study of kinship in the United States', *Psychiatry*, vol. 18, no. 1, pp. 65–79.

Cohen, P. S. (1968), *Modern Social Theory* (London, Heinemann).

Cohen, S. and Taylor, L. (1972), *Psychological Survival: The Experience of Long Term Imprisonment* (Harmondsworth: Penguin).

Cohen, S. and Taylor, L. (1977), 'Talking about prison blues', in C. Bell and H. Newby (eds), *Doing Sociological Research* (London: Allen & Unwin), pp. 67–86.

Coleman, J. S. (1958), 'Relational analysis: the study of social structure with survey methods', *Human Organization*, vol. 17, no. 4, pp. 28–36.

Coleman, J. S. (1964), 'Research chronicle: *The Adolescent Society*, in P. Hammond (ed.), *Sociologists at Work* (New York: Basic Books), pp. 184–211.

Coles, R. (1967), *Children of Crisis* (Boston, Mass.: Atlantic Little, Brown).

Coles, R. (1969), *Still Hungry in America* (New York: World).

Coles, R. (1971a), *Migrants, Sharecroppers, Mountaineers* (Boston, Mass.: Atlantic Little, Brown).

Coles, R. (1971b), *The South Goes North* (Boston, Mass.: Atlantic Little, Brown).

Coles, R. and Piers, M. (1969), *The Wages of Neglect* (Chicago: Quadrangle Books).

Collier, J. (1957), 'Photography in anthropology: a report on two experiments', *American Anthropologist*, vol. 59, no. 5, pp. 843–59.

Collier, J. (1967), *Visual Anthropology: Photography as a Research Tool* (New York: Holt, Rinehart & Winston).

Colson, E. (1954), 'The intensive study of small sample communities', in R. F. Spencer (ed), *Method and Perspective in Anthropology* (Minneapolis: University of Minnesota Press), pp. 43–59.

Coombs, T. (1974), '*Tis a Mad World at Hogsdon* (London: Hoxton Hall in association with the London Borough of Hackney).

Corbin, M. (1971), 'Problems and procedures of interviewing', in J. M. and R. E. Pahl, *Managers and Their Wives* (London: Allen Lane), pp. 286–306.

Corrigan, P. (1979), *Schooling the Smash Street Kids* (London: Macmillan).

Cottle, T. J. (1971), *Time's Children: Impressions of Youth* (Boston, Mass.: Little, Brown).

Cottle, T. J. (1972a), *The Abandoners: Portraits of Loss, Separation and Neglect* (Boston, Mass.: Little, Brown).

Cottle, T. J. (1972b), 'Matilda Rutherford: she's what you would call a whore', *Antioch Review*, vol. 31, no. 4, pp. 519–43.

Cottle, T. J. (1972c), 'No way to look but back', *Inequality in Education*, vol. 12, pp. 4–9.

Cottle, T. J. (1972d), 'A phalanz of children', *Appalachian Journal*, vol. 1, pp. 27–34.

Cottle, T. J. (1973a), 'A middle American marriage', *Harper's*. vol. 246, pp. 56–68.

Cottle, T. J. (1973b), *The Voices of School: Educational Images Through Pesonal Accounts* (Boston, Mass.: Little, Brown).

Cottle, T. J. (1973c), 'The life study: on mutual recognition and the subjective inquiry', *Urban Life and Culture*, vol. 2, no. 3, pp. 344–60.

Cottle, T. J. (1974), *Black Children, White Dreams: a Political Story about America* (New York: Dell).

Cottle, T. J. (1977), *Private Lives and Public Accounts* (New York: New Viewpoints).

Cottle, T. J. (1978), *Black Testimony: Voices of Britain's West Indians* (London: Wildwood House).

Cox, J. C. (1879), *How to Write the History of a Parish* (London: Bemrose).

Cressey, D. (1953), *Other People's Money* (Glencoe, Ill.: The Free Press).

Cressey, P. G. (1932), *The Taxi-Dance Hall: a Sociological Study in Commercial Recreation and City Life* (Chicago: University of Chicago Press).

Cunnison, S. (1966), *Wages and Work Allocation* (London: Tavistock).

Dalton, M. (1959), *Men Who Manage* (New York: Wiley).

Dalton, M. (1964), 'Preconceptions and methods in *Men Who Manage*', in P. Hammond (ed.) *Sociologists at Work* (New York: Basic Books), pp. 50–95.

Daniels, A. K. (1975), 'Feminist perspectives in sociological research', in M. Millman and R. M. Kanter (eds), *Another Voice: Feminist Perspectives on Social Life and Social Science* (Garden City, NY: Doubleday), pp. 340–80.

Davies, A. F. (1967), 'Criteria for the political life history', *Historical Studies*, vol. 13, no. 49, pp. 76–85.

Davies, A., Gardner, B. B. and Gardner, M. R. (1941), *Deep South* (Chicago: University of Chicago Press).

Davis, A. and Horobin, G. (1977) (eds), *Medical Encounters: the Experience of Illness and Treatment* (London: Croom Helm).

Davis, F. (1961), 'Deviance disavowal: the management of strained interaction by the visually handicapped', *Social Problems*, vol. 9, no. 2, pp. 120–32.

Davis, J. (1964), '*Great Books and Small Groups*: an informal history of a national survey', in P. Hammond (ed.), *Sociologists at Work* (New York: Basic Books), pp. 212–34.

Dean, J. P. (1954), 'Participant observation and interviewing', in J. T. Doby, E. A. Suchman, J. C. McKinney, R. G. Francis and J. P. Dean (eds), *An Introduction to Social Research* (Harrisburg, Pa: Stackpole), pp. 225–52.

Dean, J. P., Eichorn, R. L. and Dean, L. R. (1967), 'Observation and interviewing', in J. Doby, *An Introduction to Social Research* (2nd edn) (Des Mornes, Iowa: Meredith), pp. 274–304.

Dean, J. P. and Whyte, W. F. (1958), 'How do you know if the informant is telling the truth?', *Human Organization*, vol. 17, no. 2, pp. 34–8.

Dean, L. R. (1958), 'Interaction reported and observed: the case of one local union', *Human Organization*, vol. 17, no. 3, pp. 36–44.

Delamont, S. (1978), 'Sociology and the classroom', in L. Barton and R. Meighan (eds), *Sociological Interpretations of Schooling and Classrooms: a Reappraisal* (Driffield: Nafferton Books), pp. 59–72.

Deming, W. E. (1960), *Sample Design in Business Research* (New York: Wiley).

Dennis, N., Henriques, F. and Slaughter, C. (1956), *Coal is Our Life* (London: Methuen).

Denzin, N. K. (1970), *The Research Act* (Chicago: Aldine).

Deutsch, M. (1967), *The Disadvantaged Child* (New York: Basic Books).

Devons, E. and Gluckman, M. (1964a), 'Introduction' in M. Gluckman (ed.), *Closed Systems and Open Minds: the Limits of Naïvety in Social Anthropology* (Edinburgh: Oliver & Boyd), pp. 13–19.

Devons, E. and Gluckman, M. (1964b), 'Modes and consequences of limiting a field of study', in M. Gluckman (ed.), *Closed Systems and Open Minds: the Limits of Naïvety in Social Anthropology* (Edinburgh: Oliver & Boyd), pp. 158–261.

Diamond, S. (1964), 'Nigerian discovery: the politics of field work', in A. J. Vidich, J. Bensman and M. R. Stein (eds), *Reflections on Community Studies* (New York: Harper & Row), pp. 119–54.

Dickens, C. (1854), *Hard Times* (London: Bradbury & Evans).

Directory of Dealers in Secondhand and Antiquarian Books (1980), (London: Sheppard Press).

Ditton, J. (1977), *Part-Time Crime: an Ethnography of Fiddling and Pilferage* (London: Macmillan).

Dohrenwend, B. S. and Richardson, S. A. (1956), 'Analysis of the interviewer's behaviour', *Human Organization*, vol. 15, no. 2, pp. 29–32.

Dollard, J. (1935), *Criteria for the Life History* (New Haven, Conn.: Yale University Press).

Dotson, F. (1954), 'Intensive interviewing in community research', *Journal of Educational Sociology*, vol. 27, no. 5, pp. 225–30.

Douglas, J. D. (1970), *The Relevance of Sociology* (New York: Appleton-Century-Crofts).

Douglas, J. D. (1976), *Investigative Social Research* (Beverly Hills, Calif.: Sage).

Douglas, J. D., Rasmussen, P. K. and Flanagan, C. A. (1977), *The Nude Beach* (Beverly Hills, Calif.: Sage).

Driver, H. E. (1953), 'Statistics in anthropology', *American Anthropologist*, vol. 55, no. 1, pp. 42–59.

Dua, V. (1979), 'A woman's encounter with Arya Samaj and untouchables: a slum in Jullindur', in M. N. Srinivas, A. M. Shah and E. A. Ramaswamy (eds), *The Fieldworker and the Field: Problems and Challenges in Sociological Investigation* (Delhi: OUP), pp. 115–26.

Dubin, R. (1968), *Theory Building* (New York: The Free Press).

Dubin, R. J. (1956), 'Industrial workers' worlds: a study of the "central life interests" of industrial workers', *Social Problems*, vol. 3, no. 3, pp. 131–42.

DuBois, C. (1937), 'Some psychological objectives and techniques in ethnography', *Journal of Social Psychology*, vol. 8, no. 3, pp. 285–300.

Dyos, H. J. (1972) (ed.), *The Study of Urban History* (London: Arnold).

Earle, W. (1972), *The Autobiographical Consciousness: a Philosophical Inquiry into Existence* (Chicago: Quadrangle Books).

Easterday, L., Papademas, D., Schorr, L. and Valentine, C. (1977), 'The making of a female researcher: role problems in field work', *Urban Life*, vol. 6, no. 3, pp. 333–48.

Easthope, G. (1974), *History of Social Research Methods* (London: Longman).

Edinger, L. J. (1964), 'Political science and political biography: reflections on the study of leadership, I and II', *Journal of Politics*, vol. 26, nos 2 and 3, pp. 423–39, 648–76.

Edwards, P. J. and Marshall, J. (1977), 'Sources of conflict and community in the trawling industries of Hull and Grimsby between the wars', *Oral History*, vol. 5, no. 1, pp. 97–121.

Eggan, F. (1954), 'Social anthropology and the method of controlled comparison', *American Anthropologist*, vol. 56, no. 4, pp. 743–60.

Emmison, F. G. (1966), *Archives and Local History* (London: Methuen).

Emmison, F. G. and Gray, I. (1961), *County Records* (London: Historical Association).

Epstein, A. L. (1967a) (ed.), *The Craft of Social Anthropology* (London: Tavistock).

Epstein, A. L. (1967b), 'The case method in the field of law', in A. L. Epstein (ed.), *The Craft of Social Anthropology* (London: Tavistock).

Epstein, C. F. and Goode, W. J. (1971) (eds), *The Other Half: Roads to Women's Equality* (Englewood Cliffs, NJ: Prentice-Hall).

Erikson, E. H. (1958), *Young Man Luther* (New York: Norton).

Erikson, E. H. (1964), *Childhood and Society* (2nd edn) (New York: Norton).

Erikson, E. H. (1968a), *Identity, Youth and Crisis* (New York: Norton).

Erikson, E. H. (1968b), 'Life cycle', in D. L. Sills (ed.), *International Encyclopedia of the Social Sciences*, Vol. 9 (New York: Macmillan and The Free Press), pp. 286–92.

Erikson, K. (1967), 'A comment on disguised observation in sociology', *Social Problems*, vol. 14, no. 4, pp. 366–73.

Evans-Pritchard, E. E. (1937), *Witchcraft, Oracles and Magic among the Azande* (London: OUP).

Evans-Pritchard, E. E. (1973), 'Some reminiscences and reflections on fieldwork', *Journal of the Anthropological Society of Oxford*, vol. 4, no. 1, pp. 1–12.

Everitt, A. (1970), *New Avenues in English Local History* (Leicester: University of Leicester Press).

Ewart Evans, G. (1970), *Where Beards Wag All: the Relevance of the Oral Tradition* (London: Faber).

Ewart Evans, G. (1976), *From Mouths of Men* (London: Faber).

Fairbrother, P. (1977), 'Experience and trust in sociological work', *Sociology*, vol. 11, no. 2, pp. 359–68.

Faraday, A. and Plummer, K. (1979). 'Doing life histories', *Sociological Review*, vol. 27, no. 4, pp. 773–98.

Fenlason, A. F. (1952), *Essentials in Interviewing: For the Interviewer Offering Professional Services* (New York: Harper).

Festinger, L. and Katz, D. (1953) (eds), *Research Methods in the Behavioural Sciences* (New York: Holt, Rinehart & Winston).

Festinger, L., Riecken, H. W. and Schachter, S. (1956), *When Prophecy Fails* (New York: Harper & Row).

Fichter, J. H. and Kolb, W. L. (1954), 'Ethical limitations on sociological reporting', in J. H. Fichter, *Social Relations in the Urban Parish* (Chicago: University of Chicago Press), pp. 218–32.

Filstead, W. J. (1970) (ed.), *Qualitative Methodology: Firsthand Involvement with the Social World* (Chicago: Markham).

Finberg, H. P. R. (1953), *The Local Historian and his Theme* (Leicester: University College of Leicester).

Firth, R. (1951), *Elements of Social Organization* (London: Watts).

Firth, R. (1957) (ed.), *Man and Culture* (London: Routledge & Kegan Paul).

Flanders, N. A. (1970), *Analyzing Teacher Behavior* (Reading, Mass.: Addison-Wesley).

Fletcher, C. (1974), *Beneath the Surface* (London: Routledge & Kegan Paul).

Foley, A. (1973), *A Bolton Childhood* (Manchester: University of Manchester Extramural Department).

Foote, N. and Meyersohn, R. (1961), 'Allocations of time among family activities', in International Sociological Association, *Transactions of 4th World Congress of Sociology* (Louvain, Belgium: International Sociological Association), pp. 216–17.

Forge, A. (1967), 'The lonely anthropologist', *New Society*, vol. 10, no. 255, pp. 221–3.

Fortes, M., Steel, R. W. and Ady, P. (1947), 'Ashanti survey, 1945–46: an experiment in social research', *Geographical Journal*, vol. 110, nos. 4–6, pp. 149–79.

Foster, G. M., Scudder, T., Colson, E. and Kemper, R. V. (1979) (eds), *Long-Term Field Research in Social Anthropology* (London: Academic Press).

Foster, J. and Sheppard, J. (1980), 'Archives and the history of nursing', in C. Davies (ed.), *Rewriting Nursing History* (London: Croom Helm), pp. 200–14.

Frank, P. (1976), 'Women's work in the Yorkshire inshore fishing industry', *Oral History*, vol. 4, no. 1, pp. 57–72.

Frankenberg, R. (1957), *Village on the Border* (London: Cohen & West).

Frankenberg, R. (1963), 'Participant observers', *New Society*, vol. 1, no. 23, pp. 22–3.

Frankenberg, R. (1966), 'British community studies: problems of synthesis', in M. Banton (ed.), *The Social Anthropology of Complex Societies* (London: Tavistock), pp. 123–54.

Fraser, T. M. (1960), *Rusembilian: a Malay Fishing Village in Southern Thailand* (Ithaca, NY: Cornell University Press).

Freilich, M. (1977a) (ed.), *Marginal Natives at Work: Anthropologists in the Field* (New York: Wiley).

Freilich, M. (1977b), 'Fieldwork: an introduction', in M. Freilich (ed.), *Marginal Natives at Work: Anthropologists in the Field* (New York: Wiley), pp. 1–37.

Frenkel, E. (1936), 'Studies in biographic psychology', *Character and Personality*, vol. 5, no. 1, pp. 1–34.

Fujisaka, S. and Grayzel, J. (1978), 'Partnership research: a case of divergent ethnographic styles in prison research', *Human Organization*, vol. 37, no. 2, pp. 172–9.

Fürer-Haimendorf, C. V. (1964), *The Sherpas of Nepal: Buddhist Highlanders* (New York: Humanities Press).

Gallaher, A. (1961), *Plainville: Fifteen Years Later* (New York: Columbia University Press).

Gans, H. J. (1962), *The Urban Villagers* (New York: The Free Press).

Gans, H. J. (1967), *The Levittowners* (London: Allen Lane).

Gans, H. J. (1968), 'The participant-observer as a human being: observations on the personal aspects of field work', in H. S. Becker, B. Geer, D. Riesman and R. S. Weiss (eds), *Institutions and the Person: Papers Presented to Everett C. Hughes* (Chicago: Aldine), pp. 300–17.

Garraty, J. A. (1957), *The Nature of Biography* (New York: Knopf).

Garrett, A. (1942), *Interviewing: its Principles and Methods* (New York: Family Service Association of America).

Garrett, S. G. and Honigmann, J. J. (1965), 'Pakistani values revealed in the 1964 national election'; unpublished paper.

Gavin, H. (1971), *Sanitary Ramblings; Sketches and Illustrations of Bethnal Green* (London: Frank Cass).

Geer, B. (1964), 'First days in the field', in P. Hammond (ed.), *Sociologists at Work* (New York: Basic Books), pp. 322–44.

Geer, B. (1970), 'Studying a college', in R. W. Habenstein (ed.), *Pathways to Data* (Chicago: Aldine), pp. 81–98.

Geertz, C. (1963), *Peddlers and Princes* (Chicago: University of Chicago Press).

Gellner, E. A. (1963), 'Concepts and society', *Proceedings of 5th World Congress of Sociology, Washington, USA* (Louvain: Neualwaerts), pp. 161–89.

Gittins, D. (1979), 'Oral history, reliability and recollection', in L. Moss and H. Goldstein (eds), *The Recall Method in Social Surveys* (London: University of London Institute of Education), pp. 82–97.

Glaser, B. G. (1964a), 'Comparative failure of scientists', *Science*, vol. 143, no. 3610, pp. 1012–14.

Glaser, B. G. (1964b), *Organizational Scientists, their Professional Careers* (Indianapolis, Ind.: Bobbs-Merrill).

Glaser, B. G. (1968), *Organizational Careers: a Sourcebook for Theory* (Chicago: Aldine).

Glaser, B. G. (1978), *Theoretical Sensitivity* (Mill Valley, Calif.: Sociology Press).

Glaser, B. G. and Strauss, A. L. (1965), *Awareness of Dying* (Chicago: Aldine).

Glaser, B. G. and Strauss, A. L. (1967), *The Discovery of Grounded Theory: Strategies for Qualitative Research* (Chicago: Aldine).

Glaser, B. G. and Strauss, A. L. (1968), *Time for Dying* (Chicago: Aldine).

Glaser, B. G. and Strauss, A. L. (1971), *Status Passage, a Formal Theory* (Chicago: Aldine-Atherton).

Gluckman, M. (1942), *An Analysis of a Social Situation in Modern Zululand*, Rhodes-Livingstone Paper No. 28.

Gluckman, M. (1943), *Essays on Lozi Land and Royal Property*, Rhodes-Livingstone Paper No. 10.

Gluckman, M. (1960), 'Malinowski reassessed', *New Statesman*, vol. 59, no. 1514, (19 March), pp. 405–6.

Gluckman, M. (1961), 'Ethnographic data in British Social Anthropology', *Sociological Review*, vol. 9, no. 1, pp. 5–17.

Gluckman, M. (1963), *Order and Rebellion in Tribal Africa* (London: Cohen & West).

Gluckman, M. (1964) (ed.), *Closed Systems and Open Minds: the Limits of Naïvety in Social Anthropology* (Edinburgh: Oliver & Boyd).

Gluckman, M. (1967), 'Introduction', in A. L. Epstein (ed.), *The Craft of Social Anthropology* (London: Tavistock), pp. xi–xx.

Goffman, E. (1959), *The Presentation of Self in Everyday Life* (London: Allen Lane).

Goffman, E. (1963), *Stigma* (Englewood Cliffs, NJ: Prentice-Hall).

Goffman, E. (1968), *Asylums* (Harmondsworth: Penguin).

Gold, R. (1958), 'Roles in sociological field observation', *Social Forces*, vol. 36, no. 3, pp. 217–23.

Golde, P. (1970) (ed.), *Women in the Field: Anthropological Experiences* (Chicago: Aldine).

Goldfrank, E. S. (1948), 'The impact of situation and personality on four Hopi emergence myths', *Southwestern Journal of Anthropology*, vol. 4, no. 3, pp. 241–62.

Gorden, R. L. (1980), *Interviewing: Strategy, Techniques and Tactics* (3rd edn) (Homewood, Ill: Dorsey Press).

Gordon, C. W. (1957), *The Social System of the High School* (New York: The Free Press).

Gorer, G. (1955), *Exploring English Character* (London: Cresset Press).

Gornick, V. (1971), 'Woman as outsider', in V. Gornick and B. K. Moran (eds), *Women in Sexist Society: Studies in Power and Powerlessness* (New York: Basic Books), pp. 117–39.

Gottschalk, L. (1945), 'The historian and the historical document', in L. Gottschalk, C. Kluckhohn and R. Angell (eds), *The Use of Personal Documents in History, Anthropology and Sociology*, Bulletin No. 53 (New York: Social Science Research Council), pp. 79–175.

Gottschalk, L., Kluckhohn, C. and Angell, R. (1945) (eds), *The Use of Personal Documents in History, Anthropology and Sociology*, Bulletin No. 53 (New York: Social Science Research Council).

Gough, R. (1968), *Human Nature displayed in the history of Myddle* (London: Centaur Press).

Gouldner, A. W. (1954), *Patterns of Industrial Bureaucracy* (Glencoe, Ill.: The Free Press).

Gouldner, A. W. (1956), 'Some observations on systematic theory, 1945–1955', in H. Zetterberg (ed.), *Sociology in the United States of America* (Paris: UNESCO), pp. 34–42.

Gouldner, A. W. (1957a), 'Theoretical requirements of the applied social sciences', *American Sociological Review*, vol. 22, no. 1, pp. 92–102.

Gouldner, A. W. (1957b), 'Cosmopolitans and locals: toward an analysis of latent social roles I', *Administrative Science Quarterly*, vol. 2, no. 3, pp. 281–306.

Gouldner, A. W. (1958), 'Cosmopolitans and locals: toward an analysis of latent social roles II', *Administrative Science Quarterly*, vol. 2, no 4, pp. 444–80.

Gouldner, A. W. (1970), 'The sociologist as partisan: sociology and the welfare state', in J. D. Douglas (ed.), *The Relevance of Sociology* (New York: Appleton-Century-Crofts), pp. 112–48.

Gouldner, A. W. (1971), *The Coming Crisis of Western Sociology* (London: Heinemann).

Greenberg, E. S. (1970), 'Black children in the political system', *Public Opinion Quarterly*, vol. 34, no. 3, pp. 333–45.

Greenstein, F. I. (1969), *Personality and Politics* (Chicago: Markham).

Greenwood, J. (1876), *Low Life Deeps* (London: Chatto & Windus).

Gulick, J. (1977), 'Village and city field work in Lebanon', in M. Freilich (ed.), *Marginal Natives at Work: Anthropologists in the Field* (New York: Wiley), pp. 89–118.

Gupta, K. A. (1979), 'Travails of a woman fieldworker: a small town in Uttar Pradesh', in M. N. Srinivas, A. M. Shah and E. A. Ramaswamy (eds), *The Fieldworker and the Field: Problems and Challenges in Sociological Investigation* (Delhi: OUP), pp. 103–14.

Habenstein, R. W. (1970a) (ed.), *Pathways to Data* (Chicago: Aldine).

Habenstein, R. W. (1970b), 'Occupational uptake: professionalizing', in R. W. Habenstein (ed.), *Pathways to Data* (Chicago: Aldine), pp. 99–121.

Halbert, M. H. and Ackoff, R. L. (1958), 'An operations research study of the dissemination of scientific information', *Proceedings of the (1958) International Conference on Scientific Information*, pp. 87–120.

Hall, C. S. and Lindzey, G. (1957), *Theories of Personality* (London: Chapman & Hall).

Hall, D. and Stacey, M. (1979) (eds), *Beyond Separation: Further Studies of Children in Hospital* (London: Routledge & Kegan Paul).

Hallowell, A. I. (1956), 'Psychological leads for ethnological field workers', in D. G. Haring (ed.), *Personal Character and Cultural Milieu* (3rd edn) (Syracuse, NY: Syracuse University Press), pp. 341–88.

Hammond, P. (1964) (ed.), *Sociologists at Work* (New York: Basic Books).

Hannerz, U. (1969), *Soulside: Inquiries into Ghetto Culture and Community* (New York: Columbia University Press).

Hannerz, U. (1980), *Exploring the City: Inquiries Toward an Urban Anthropology* (New York: Columbia University Press).

Hansen, M. H., Hurwitz, W. N. and Madow, W. C. (1953), *Sample Survey Methods and Theory, Vol. I: Methods and Applications* (New York: Wiley).

Hanson, R. C. (1958), 'Evidence and procedure characteristics of "reliable" propositions in social science', *American Journal of Sociology*, vol. 63, no. 4, pp. 357–63.

Hanson, R. R. (1976), 'In quest of optimal health: the natural health movement in the United States', Department of Sociology, University of California, Davis; unpublished dissertation.

Hapgood, R. (1975), 'Courtship and marriage in Abingdon', paper given at History Workshop 9, Ruskin College, Oxford.

Hardy, T. (1886), *The Mayor of Casterbridge* (London: Smith, Elder).

Hargreaves, D. H. (1967), *Social Relations in a Secondary School* (London: Routledge & Kegan Paul).

Harkell, G. (1978), 'The migration of mining families to the Kent coalfield between the wars', *Oral History*, vol. 6, no. 1, pp. 98–113.

Harley, J. B. (1972), *Maps for the local historian, a guide to the British Sources* (London: National Council of Social Service).

Harrell-Bond, B. (1976), 'Studying elites: some special problems', in M. A. Rynkiewich and J. P. Spradley (eds), *Ethics and Anthropology: Dilemmas in Fieldwork* (New York: Wiley).

Harris, C. C. (1970) (ed.), *Readings in Kinship in Urban Society* (Oxford: Pergamon).

Hay, R. and McLauchlan, J. (1974), 'The oral history of Upper Clyde shipbuilders', *Oral History*, vol. 2, no. 1, pp. 45–58.

Heise, J. A. (1969), *The Brass Factories* (Washington: Public Affairs Press).

Herbert, G. (1948), *Shoemaker's Widow: Recollections of a Midland Town before the Railway Age* (Oxford: Blackwell).

Herskovits, M. J. (1948a), *Man and His Works* (New York: Knopf).

Herskovits, M. J. (1948b), 'The ethnographer's laboratory', in M. Herskovits (ed.), *Man and His Works* (New York: Knopf), pp. 79–93.

Herskovits, M. J. (1954), 'Some problems of method in ethnography', in R. F. Spencer (ed.), *Method and Perspective in Anthropology* (Minneapolis: University of Minnesota Press), pp. 3–24.

Heyerdahl, T. (1963), *The Kon-Tiki Expedition* (Harmondsworth: Penguin).

Hill, C. (1967), *Society and Puritanism in Pre-Revolutionary England* (New York: Schocken).

Hill, J. M. M. and Scharff, D. E. (1976), *Between Two Worlds: Aspects of the Transition from School to Work* (Richmond: Careers Consultants).

Hill, P. (1963), *The Migrant Cocoa-Farmers of Southern Ghana* (Cambridge: CUP).

Hilton, K. (1967) (ed.), *The Lower Swansea Valley Project* (London: Longman).

Himeloch, J. and Fara, S. F. (1955), *Sexual Behaviour in American Society* (New York: Norton).

Hine, R. (1946), *Relics of an Un-common Attorney* (London: Macmillan).

HMSO (1964), *Field Archaeology, some notes for beginners*, Ordnance Survey, Professional Papers, new series, no. 13 (4th edn) (London: HMSO).

Hobsbawm, E. (1974), 'From social history to the history of society', in M. W. Flinn and T. C. Smout (eds), *Essays in Social History* (Oxford: OUP), pp. 1–22.

Hobson, M. G. and Price, K. L. H. (1967), *Otmoor and its Seven Towns* (Oxford: Truex Press).

Hoffman, J. E. (1980), 'Problems of access in the study of social elites and boards of directors', in W. B. Shaffir, R. A. Stebbins and A. Turowetz (eds), *Fieldwork Experience: Qualitative Approaches to Social Research* (London: St Martin's Press), pp. 45–56.

Holmberg, A. R. (1955), 'Participant intervention in the field', *Human Organization*, vol. 14, no. 1, pp. 23–6.

Homan, R. (1978), 'Interpersonal communication in Pentecostal meetings', *Sociological Review*, vol. 26, no. 3, pp. 499–518.

Homan, R. (1980), 'The ethics of covert methods', *British Journal of Sociology*, vol. 31, no. 1, pp. 46–59.

Homans, G. (1950), *The Human Group* (New York: Harcourt Brace Jovanovich).

Honigmann, J. J. (1949), *Culture and Ethos of Kaska Society* Yale University Publications in Anthropology, no. 40.

Honigmann, J. J. (1953), *Information for Pakistan, Report of Research on Intercultural Communication through Films* (Chapel Hill: Institute for Research in Social Science, University of North Calfornia); mimeo.

Honigmann, J. J. (1964), 'Survival of a cultural focus', in W. H. Goodenough (ed.) *Explorations in Cultural Anthropology* (New York: McGraw-Hill), pp. 277–92.

Honigmann, J. J. (1973), 'Sampling in ethnographic field work', in R. Naroll and R. Cohen (eds), *A Handbook of Method in Cultural Anthropology* (New York: Columbia University Press), pp. 266–81.

Honigmann, J. J. and Carrera, R. (1957), 'Another experiment in sample reliability', *Southwestern Journal of Anthropology*, vol. 13, no. 1, pp. 99–102.

Honigmann, J. J. and Honigmann, I. (1955), 'Sampling reliability in ethnological fieldwork', *Southwestern Journal of Anthropology*, vol. 11, no. 3, pp. 282–7.

Honigmann, J. J. and Honigmann, I. (1965), *Eskimo Townsmen* (Ottawa; Canadian Research Centre for Anthropology, University of Ottawa).

Hoskins, W. G. (1968), *The Making of the English Landscape* (Harmondsworth: Penguin).

Hoskins, W. G. (1969), *Fieldwork in Local History* (London: Faber).

Hoskins, W. G. (1972), *Local History in England* (2nd edn) (London: Longman).

Howard, V. A. (1968), 'Do anthropologists become moral relativists by mistake?', *Inquiry*, vol. 11, no. 2, pp. 175–89.

Huber, J. (1973) (ed.), *Changing Women in a Changing Society* (Chicago: University of Chicago Press).

Hughes, E. C. (1958) *Men and Their Work* (New York: The Free Press).

Hughes, E. C. (1960), 'Introduction: the place of field work in social science', in B. Junker, *Field Work: An Introduction to the Social Sciences* (Chicago: University of Chicago Press), pp. v–xv.

Humphreys, L. (1970), *Tearoom Trade* (London: Duckworth).

Jacobs, J. (1974a), *Fun City: An Ethnographic Study of a Retirement Community* (New York: Holt, Rinehart & Winston).

Jacobs, J. (1974b) (ed.), *Deviance: Field Studies and Self-Disclosures* (Palo Alto, Calif.: National Press Books).

Jahoda, M., Deutsch, M. and Cook, S. W. (1951), 'Data collection: the questionnaire and interview approach', in M.

Jahoda, M. Deutsch and S. W. Cook (eds), *Research Methods in Social Relations, Part I: Basic Processes* (Hinsdale, Ill.: Dryden Press), pp. 151–208.

Jahoda, M., Lazarsfeld, P. F. and Zeisel, H. (1972), *Marienthal: the Sociography of an Unemployed Community* (London: Tavistock).

Jarvie, I. C. (1967), 'On theories of fieldwork and the scientific character of social anthropology', *Philosophy of Science*, vol. 24, no. 3, pp. 223–42.

Jarvie, I. C. (1969), 'The problem of ethical integrity in participant observation', *Current Anthropology*, vol. 10, no. 5, pp. 505–8.

Jenkins, D. (1971), *The Agricultural Community in South West Wales at the turn of the Twentieth Century* (Cardiff: University of Wales Press).

Johnson, J. M. (1975), *Doing Field Research* (New York: The Free Press).

Junker, B. H. (1960), *Field Work: an Introduction to the Social Sciences* (Chicago: University of Chicago Press).

Kahl, J. A. (1953), 'Educational and occupational aspirations of "common man" boys', *Harvard Educational Review*, vol. 23, no. 3, pp. 186–203.

Kahn, R. L. and Cannell, C. F. (1957), *The Dynamics of Interviewing: Theory Technique and Cases* (New York: Wiley).

Kanter, R. M. (1975), 'Women and the structure of organizations: explorations in theory and behaviour', in M. Millman and R. M. Kanter (eds), *Another Voice: Feminist Perspectives on Social Life and Social Science* (Garden City, NY: Doubleday), pp. 34–74.

Kapferer, B. (1969), 'Norms and the manipulation of relationships in a work context', in J. C. Mitchell (ed.), *Social Networks in Urban Situations: Analyses of Personal Relationships in Central African Towns* (Manchester: University of Manchester Press for the Institute of African Studies, University of Zambia), pp. 181–244.

Kapferer, B. (1972), *Strategy and Transaction in an African Factory* (Manchester: University of Manchester Press).

Kardiner, A. and Ovesey, L. (1951), *The Mask of Oppression* (New York: Norton).

Karp, D. A. (1980), 'Observing behaviour in public places: problems and strategies', in W. B. Shaffir, R. A. Stebbins and A. Turowetz (eds), *Fieldwork Experience: Qualitative Approaches to Social Research*, pp. 82–97 (New York: St Martin's Press).

Kassebaum, G. (1970), 'Strategies for the sociological study of criminal correctional systems', in R. W. Habenstein (ed.), *Pathways to Data* (Chicago: Aldine), pp. 122–38.

Katz, D. (1953), 'Field studies', in L. Festinger and D. Katz (eds), *Research Methods in the Behavioral Sciences* (New York: Holt, Rinehart & Winston), pp. 56–97.

Keating, P. (1976) (ed.), *Into Unknown England, 1866–1913: Selections from the Social Explorers* (London: Fontana).

Kendall, P. and Lazarsfeld, P. F. (1950), 'Problems of survey analysis', in R. K. Merton and P. F. Lazarsfeld (eds), *Continuities in Social Research* (Glencoe, Ill.: The Free Press), pp. 133–96.

Kendall, P. L. and Wolf, K. M. (1949), 'The analysis of deviant cases in communications research', in P. F. Lazarsfeld and F. W. Stanton (eds), *Communications Research, 1948–49* (New York: Harper), pp. 152–79.

Kerlinger, F. N. (1965), *Foundations of Behavioural Research* (New York: Holt, Rinehart & Winston).

Kerr, N. D. (1964), 'The school board as an agency of legitimation', *Sociology of Education*, vol. 38, no. 1, pp. 34–59.

Kimball, S. (1955), 'Problems of studying American culture', *American Anthropologist*, vol. 57, no. 6, pp. 1131–42.

King, R. (1978), *All Things Bright and Beautiful? A Sociological Study of Infants' Classrooms* (Chichester: Wiley).

Kish, L. (1953), 'Selection of the sample', in L. Festinger and D. Katz (eds), *Research Methods in the Behavioural Sciences* (New York: Holt, Rinehart & Winston), pp. 175–242.

Kish, L. (1965), *Survey Sampling* (New York: Wiley).

Klockars, C. B. (1974), *The Professional Fence* (London: Tavistock).

Klockars, C. B. (1977), 'Field ethics for the life history', in R. S. Weppner (ed.), *Street Ethnography* (Beverly Hills, Calif.: Sage), pp. 201–26.

Kloos, P. (1969), 'Role conflicts in social fieldwork', *Current Anthropology*, vol. 10, no. 5, pp. 509–12.

Kluckhohn, C. (1945a), 'The personal document in anthropological science', in L. Gottschalk, C. Kluckhohn and R. Angell (eds), *The Use of Personal Documents in History, Anthropology and Sociology*, Bulletin 53 (New York: Social Science Research Council), pp. 79–175.

Kluckhohn, C. (1945b), 'Field techniques and methods', in L. Gottschalk, C. Kluckhohn and R. Angell (eds), *The Use of Personal Documents in History, Anthropology and Sociology*, Bulletin No. 53 (New York: Social Science Research Council), pp. 109–32.

Kluckhohn, C. (1962), 'The limitations of adaptation and adjustment as concepts for understanding cultural behaviour', in R. Kluckhohn (ed.), *Culture and Behaviour* (New York: The Free Press), pp. 255–64.

Kluckhohn, F. R. (1940), 'The participant observer technique in small communities', *American Journal of Sociology*, vol. 46, no. 3, pp. 331–43.

Kohlberg, L. (1968), 'Moral developments', in D. L. Sills (ed.), *International Encyclopedia of the Social Sciences*, Vol. 10 (New York: Macmillan and The Free Press), pp. 483–93.

Komarovsky, M. (1962), *Blue Collar Marriage* (New York: Random House).

Kroeber, A. L. (1917), *Zuni Kin and Clan* (New York: Trustees of the American Museum of Natural History).

Kroeber, A. L. (1957), *Ethnographic Interpretations 1–6*, University of California Publications in American Archaeology and Ethnology 47, no. 2, pp. 191–234.

Kuhn, T. S. (1962), *The Structure of Scientific Revolutions* (Chicago and London: University of Chicago Press).

Kuper, A. (1973), *Anthropology and Anthropologists: the British School, 1922–1972* (London: Allen Lane).

Lacey, C. (1970), *Hightown Grammar: the School as a Social System* (Manchester: University of Manchester Press).

Lacey, C. (1976), 'Problems of sociological fieldwork: a review of the methodology of "Hightown Grammar"', in M. Shipman (ed.), *The Organization and Impact of Social Research* (London: Routledge & Kegan Paul), pp. 63–88.

La Farge, O. (1947), *Santa Eulalia: the Religion of a Cuchumatan Indian Town* (Chicago: University of Chicago Press).

Langenwalter, S. (1967), 'History of a questionnaire', (New York: Bureau of Applied Social Research, Columbia University); mimeo.

Langlois, C. V. and Seignobos, C. (1898), transl. by C. G. Berry, *Introduction to the Study of History* (London: Duckworth).

Langness, L. L. (1965), *The Life History in Anthropological Science* (New York: Holt, Rinehart & Winston).

Lansdown, M. J. (1968), *Trowbridge's Fight for Pure Water, 1864–1874* (Trowbridge: West Wiltshire Branch of the Historical Association).

LaPiere, R. (1938), *Collective Behavior* (New York: McGraw-Hill).

Larner, C. (1977), 'Dirty Linen' (review of C. Bell and H. Newby (1977) (eds), *Doing Sociological Research*), *New Society*, vol. 42, no. 785 (20 October).

Lazarsfeld, P. F. (1972), 'Foreword to the English edition: forty years later', in M. Jahoda, P. F. Lazarsfeld and H. Zeisel, *Marienthal: the Sociography of an Unemployed Community* (London: Tavistock), pp. vii–xvi.

Lazarsfeld, P. F. and Barton, A. (1951), 'Qualitative measurement in the social sciences: classification, typologies and indices' in D. Lerner and H. D. Lasswell (eds), *The Policy Sciences: Recent Developments in Scope and Method* (Stanford, Calif.: Stanford University Press), pp. 155–92.

Lazarsfeld, P. F. and Barton, A. (1955), 'Some functions of qualitative analysis in sociological research', *Sociologica*, vol. 1, pp. 324–61.

Lazarsfeld, P. F. and Rosenberg, M. (1955) (eds), *The Language of Social Research* (Glencoe, Ill.: The Free Press).

Lazarsfeld, P. F. and Thielens, W. (1958), *The Academic Mind* (New York: The Free Press).

Leach, E. R. (1958), 'An anthropologist's reflections on a social survey', *Ceylon Journal of Historical and Social Studies*, vol. 1, no. 1, pp. 9–20.

Leighton, A. H. (1949), *Human Relations in a Changing World* (New York: Dutton).

Leighton, A. H. (1959), *My Name is Legion* (New York: Basic Books).

Leighton, A. H. and Leighton, D. C. (1949), *Gregario, the Handtrembler: a Psycho-biological Personality Study of a Navaho Indian*, Papers of the Peabody Museum of American Archaeology and Ethnology, Harvard University, vol. 40, no. 1, pp. 3–177.

Leighton, D. C., Harding, J. S., Macklin, D. B., Macmillan, A. M. and Leighton, A. H. (1963), *The Character of Danger* (New York: Basic Books).

Leonard, D. (1980), *Sex and Generation: a Study of Courtship and Weddings* (London: Tavistock).

Leovinger, J. (1966), 'The meaning and measurement of ego development', *American Psychologist*, vol. 21, no. 2, pp. 195–206.

Lerner, D. (1958), *The Passing of Traditional Society* (New York: The Free Press).

Lewis, O. (1951), *Life in a Mexican Village* (Urbana, Ill.: Illinois University Press).

Lewis, O. (1953), 'Controls and experiments in fieldwork', in A. L. Kroeber (ed.), *Anthropology Today* (Chicago: University of Chicago Press), pp. 452–75.

Lewis, O. (1965), *La Vida: a Puerto Rican Family in the Culture of Poverty – San Juan and New York* (New York: Random House).

Liebow, E. (1967), *Tally's Corner: a Study of Negro Street Corner Men* (Boston, Mass.: Little, Brown).

Lindesmith, A. (1947), *Opiate Addiction* (Bloomington, Ind., Principia Press).

Lindesmith, A. (1952), 'Two comments on W. S. Robinson's "The logical structure of analytic induction"', *American Sociological Review*, vol. 17, no. 4, pp. 492–3.

Lipset, S. M. (1964), 'The biography of a research project: union democracy', in P. E. Hammond (ed.), *Sociologists at Work* (New York: Basic Books), pp. 96–120.

Lipset, S. M. and Hofstadter, R. (1968) (eds), *Sociology and History: Methods* (New York: Basic Books).

Lipset, S. M. and Lowenthal, L. (1961) (eds), *Culture and Social Character* (New York: The Free Press).

Littlejohn, J. (1963), *Westrigg* (London: Routledge & Kegan Paul).

Lofland, J. (1969), *Deviance and Identity* (Englewood Cliffs, NJ: Prentice-Hall).

Lofland, J. (1971), *Analyzing Social Settings* (New York: Wadsworth).

Lofland, J. (1974a), 'Styles of reporting qualitative field reports', *American Sociologist*, vol. 9, no. 3, pp. 101–11.

Lofland, J. (1974b), 'Analyzing qualitative data: first person accounts', *Urban Life and Culture*, vol. 3, no. 3, pp. 307–9.

Lohman, J. D. (1937), 'The participant observer in community studies', *American Sociological Review*, vol. 2, no. 6, pp. 890–7.

Loudon, J. (1961), 'Kinship and crisis in South Wales', *British Journal of Sociology*, vol. 12 no. 4, pp. 333–50; reprinted in C. C. Harris (ed.), *Readings in Kinship in Urban Society* (Oxford: Pergamon), pp. 187–208.

Lupton, T. (1963), *On the Shop Floor* (Oxford: Pergamon).

Lurie, N. O. (1966), *Mountain Wolf Woman, Sister of Crashing Thunder* (Ann Arbor, Mich: University of Michigan Press).

Luszki, M. B. (1957), 'Team research in social science: major consequences of a growing trend', *Human Organization*, vol. 16, no. 1, pp. 21–4.

Lynd, R. S. and Lynd, H. M. (1929), *Middletown: a Study in Contemporary American Culture* (New York: Harcourt Brace Jovanovich).

Lynd, R. S. and Lynd H. M. (1937), *Middletown in Transition* (New York: Harcourt Brace Jovanovich).

McCall, D. (1961), 'Trade and the role of wife in a modern West African town', in A. Southall (ed.), *Social Change in Modern Africa* (London: OUP for the International African Institute), pp. 286–99.

McCall, G. J. (1978), *Observing the Law* (New York: The Free Press).

McCall, G. J. and Simmons, J. L. (1969) (eds), *Issues in Participant Observation: a Text and Reader* (Reading, Mass.: Addison-Wesley).

McCall, M. (1980), 'Who and where are the artists?', in W. B. Shaffir, R. A. Stebbins and A. Turowetz (eds), *Fieldwork Experience: Qualitative Approaches to Social Research* (New York: St Martin's Press), pp. 145–58.

Maccoby, E. and Maccoby, N. (1954), 'The interview: a tool of social science', in G. Lindzey (ed.), *Handbook of Social Psychology* (Cambridge, Mass.: Addison-Wesley), pp. 449–87.

Macfarlane, A. (1970), *The Family Life of Ralph Josselin. A Seventeenth Century Clergyman* (Cambridge: CUP).

Macfarlane, A. (1977), 'History, anthropology and the study of communities', *Social History*, no. 5, pp. 631–52.

Macintyre, S. and Oldman, D. (1977), 'Coping with migraine', in A. Davis and G. Horobin (eds), *Medical Encounters: The Experience of Illness and Treatment* (London: Croom Helm), pp. 55–71.

Mackenzie, P. (1865–6), *Reminiscences of Glasgow and the West of Scotland*, 3 vols (Glasgow: J. Tweed).

McKinney, J. C. (1966), *Constructive Typology and Social Theory* (New York: Appleton-Century-Crofts).

Madge, J. (1953), *The Tools of Social Science* (London: Longman).

Malinowski, B. (1922), *Argonauts of the Western Pacific* (London: Routledge & Kegan Paul).

Malinowski, B. (1929), *The Sexual Life of Savages* (London: Routledge & Kegan Paul).

Malinowski, B. (1935a), *Coral Gardens and their Magic* (London: Allen & Unwin).

Malinowski, B. (1935b), 'The method of field work and the invisible facts of native law and economics', in B. Malinowski, *Coral Gardens and Their Magic*, vol. I (London: Allen & Unwin), pp. 317–40.

Malinowski, B. (1944), *A Scientific Theory of Culture* (Chapel Hill, NC; University of North Carolina Press).

Malinowski, B. (1948), *Magic, Science and Religion* (Glencoe, Ill.: The Free Press).

Malinowski, B. (1967), *A Diary in the Strict Sense of the Term* (London: Routledge & Kegan Paul).

Mandelbaum, D. G. (1953), 'On the study of national character', *American Anthropologist*, vol. 55, no. 2, pp. 174–87.

Mandelbaum, D. G. (1973), 'The study of life history: Gandhi', *Current Anthropology*, vol. 14, no. 3, pp. 177–96.

Marris, P. (1961), *Family and Social Change in an African City* (London: Routledge & Kegan Paul).

Marsden, D. and Duff, E. (1975), *Workless: Some Unemployed Men and their Families* (Harmondsworth: Penguin).

Martin, M. (1969), 'Understanding and participant observation in cultural and social anthropology', in R. S. Cohen and M. W. Wartofsky (eds), *Boston Studies in the Philosophy of Science*, Vol. IV (New York: Humanities Press), pp. 303–30.

Marx, G. T. (1967), *Protest and Prejudice* (New York: Harper & Row).

Mauksch, H. O. (1970), 'Studying the hospital', in R. W. Habenstein (ed.), *Pathways to Data* (Chicago: Aldine), pp. 185–203.

Mayer, P. and Mayer, I. (1974), *Townsmen and Tribesmen* (2nd edn) (London: OUP).

Mead, M. (1928), *Coming of Age in Samoa* (New York: Morrow).

Mead, M. (1932), *The Changing Culture of an Indian Tribe, Contributions to Anthropology*, no. 15 (New York: Columbia University Press).

Mead, M. (1933), 'More comprehensive field methods', *American Anthropologist*, vol. 35, no. 1, pp. 1–15.

Mead, M. (1935), *Sex and Temperament in Three Primitive Societies* (New York: Morrow).

Mead, M. (1939), 'Native languages as field work tools', *American Anthropologist*, vol. 41, no. 2, pp. 189–205.

Mead, M. (1940), 'The Mountain Arapesh', *Anthropological Papers of the American Museum of Natural History*, vol. 41, pp. 293–302.

Mead, M. (1951a), 'Research in contemporary cultures', in H. Guetzkow (ed.), *Groups, Leadership and Men* (Pittsburgh, Pa: Carnegie Press), pp. 106–18.

Mead, M. (1951b), 'The study of national character', in D. Lerner and H. D. Lasswell (eds), *The Policy Sciences* (Stanford, Cal.: Stanford University Press), pp. 70–85.

Mead, M. (1952), 'Some relationships between social anthropology and psychiatry', in F. Alexander and H. Ross (eds), *Dynamic Psychiatry* (Chicago: University of Chicago Press), pp. 401–48.

Mead, M. (1953), 'National character', in A. L. Kroeber (ed.), *Anthropology Today* (Chicago: University of Chicago Press), pp. 642–67.

Mead, M. (1954), 'The swaddling hypothesis: its reception', *American Anthropologist*, vol. 56, no. 3, pp. 395–409.

Mead, M. (1955), 'Effects of anthropological field work models on intercultural communication', *Journal of Social Issues*, vol. 11, no. 2, pp. 3–11.

Mead, M. (1961), 'National character and the science of anthropology', in S. M. Lipset and L. Lowenthal (eds), *Culture and Social Character* (New York: The Free Press), pp. 15–26.

Mead, M. (1964), 'The idea of national character', in R. L. Shinn (ed.), *The Search for Identity: Essays on the American Character* (New York: Harper & Row), pp. 15–27.

Mead, M. (1970a), *Culture and Commitment: a Study of the Generation Gap* (Garden City, NY: Doubleday).

Mead, M. (1970b), 'Fieldwork in the Pacific Islands', in P. Golde (ed.), *Women in the Field: Anthropological Experiences* (Chicago: Aldine), pp. 293–331.

Mead, M. (1973), 'The art and technology of fieldwork', in R. Naroll and R. Cohen (eds), *A Handbook of Method in Cultural Anthropology* (New York: Columbia University Press), pp. 246–65.

Mead, M. (1977), *Letters from the Field, 1925–1975* (New York: Harper & Row).

Mead, M. and Macgregor, F. C. (1951), *Growth and Culture: a Photographic Study of Balinese Character* (New York: Putnam).

Mead, M. and Métraux, R. (1953), *The Study of Culture at a Distance* (Chicago: University of Chicago Press).

Medawar, P. B. (1964), 'Is the scientific paper a fraud?', in D. Edge (ed.), *Experiment* (London: BBC), pp. 7–12.

Merton, R. K. (1947), 'Selected problems of field work in the planned community', *American Sociological Review*, vol. 12, no. 3, pp. 304–12.

Merton, R. K. (1949), *Social Theory and Social Structure* (Glencoe, Ill.: The Free Press).

Merton, R. K. (1957), *Social Theory and Social Structure* (2nd edn) (New York: The Free Press).

Merton, R. K. (1963), 'Resistance to the study of multiple discoveries', *Archives européenes de sociologie*, vol. 4, no. 2, pp. 237–82.

Merton, R. K. (1968), *Social Theory and Social Structure* (3rd edn) (New York: The Free Press).

Merton, R. and Kendall, P. (1946), 'The focused interview', *American Journal of Sociology*, vol. 51, no. 6, pp. 541–57.

Métraux, R. (1943), 'Qualitative attitude analysis – a technique for the study of verbal behavior', in M. Mead (ed.), *The Problem of Changing Food Habits*, National Research Council Bulletin 108, pp. 86–94.

Miller, S. M. (1952), 'The participant observer and "overrapport" ', *American Sociological Review*, vol. 17, no. 1, pp. 97–9; reprinted in G. J. McCall and J. L. Simmons (1969) (eds), *Issues in Participant Observation: a Text and Reader* (Reading, Mass.: Addison-Wesley), pp. 87–9).

Mills, C. W. (1956), *The Power Elite* (New York: OUP).

Mills, C. W. (1959), *The Sociological Imagination* (New York: OUP).

Mills, D. (1965), 'English villages in the eighteenth and nineteenth centuries: a sociological approach, part I: the concept of a sociological classification', *Amateur Historian*, vol. 6, no. 8, pp. 271–8.

Mintz, S. (1960), *Worker in the Cane: a Puerto Rican Life History* (New Haven, Conn.: Yale University Press).

Mitchell, J. C. (1956a), *The Kalela Dance*, Rhodes-Livingstone Paper No. 27.

Mitchell, J. C. (1956b), *The Yao Village: a Study in the Social Structure of a Nyasaland Tribe* (Manchester: University of Manchester Press).

Mitchell, J. C. (1966), 'Theoretical orientations in African urban studies', in M. Banton (ed.), *The Social Anthropology of Complex Societies* (London: Tavistock), pp. 37–68.

Mitchell, J. C. (1969) (ed.), *Social Networks in Urban Situations* (Manchester: University of Manchester Press).

Mitroff, I. I. (1974), *The Subjective Side of Science: a Philosophical Inquiry into the Psychology of the Apollo Moon Scientists* (Amsterdam: Elsevier).

Moore, R. (1974), *Pit-Men, Preachers and Politics* (Cambridge: CUP).

Moore, R. (1977), 'Becoming a sociologist in Sparkbrook', in C. Bell and H. Newby (eds), *Doing Sociological Research* (London: Allen & Unwin), pp. 87–107.

Morgan, D. H. J. (1972), 'The British Association scandal: the effect of publicity on a sociological investigation', *Sociological Review*, vol. 20. no. 2, pp. 185–206.

Morgan, D. H. J. (1981), 'Men, masculinity and the process of sociological enquiry', in H. Roberts (ed.), *Doing Feminist Research* (London: Routledge & Kegan Paul), pp. 83–113.

Moser, C. and Kalton, G. (1971), *Survey Methods in Social Investigation* (2nd edn) (London: Heinemann).

Nadel, S. F. (1939), 'The interview technique in social anthroplogy', in F. Bartlett, M. Ginsberg, E. J. Lindgren and R. H. Thouless (eds), *The Study of Society: Methods and Problems* (London: Routledge & Kegan Paul), pp. 317–27.

Nadel, S. F. (1951), *The Foundations of Social Anthropology* (London: Cohen & West).

Nadel, S. F. (1954), *Nupe Religion: Traditional Beliefs and the Influence of Islam in a West African Chiefdom* (London: Routledge & Kegan Paul).

Naroll, R. (1973), 'Cross-cultural sampling', in R. Naroll and R. Cohen (eds), *A Handbook of Method in Cultural Anthropology* (New York: Columbia University Press), pp. 889–926.

Naroll, R. and Cohen, R. (1973) (eds), *A Handbook of Method in Cultural Anthropology* (New York: Columbia University Press).

Nash, R. (1973), *Classrooms Observed* (London: Routledge & Kegan Paul).

Newby, H. (1977a), *The Deferential Worker* (London: Allen Lane).

Newby, H. (1977b), 'Editorial note (concerning Reflections on the Banbury restudy)', in C. Bell and H. Newby (eds), *Doing Sociological Research* (London: Allen & Unwin), pp. 63–6).

Nichols, T. and Beynon, H. (1977), *Living with Capitalism* (London: Routledge & Kegan Paul).

Oakley, A. (1981), 'Interviewing women: a contradiction in terms', in H. Roberts (ed.), *Doing Feminist Research* (London: Routledge & Kegan Paul), pp. 30–61.

Okely, J. (1975), 'The self and scientism', *Journal of the Anthropological Society of Oxford*, vol. VI, no. 3, pp. 171–88.

Okely, J. (1978), 'Privileged, schooled and finished: boarding education for girls', in S. Ardener (ed.), *Defining Females: the Nature of Women in Society* (London: Croom Helm in association with the Oxford University Women's Studies Committee), pp. 109–39.

Olesen, V. L. and Whittaker, E. W. (1967), 'Role-making in participant observation: processes in the researcher–actor relationship', *Human Organization*, vol. 26, no. 4, pp. 273–81; reprinted in N. K. Denzin (1970) (ed.), *Sociological Methods: a Sourcebook* (London: Butterworths), pp. 381–97.

Opler, M. and Singh, R. D. (1948), 'The division of labour in an Indian village', in C. S. Coon (ed.), *A Reader in General Anthropology* (New York: Henry Holt).

Osgood, C. (1940), *Ingalik Material Culture* (New Haven, Conn.: Yale University Publications in Anthropology), no. 22.

Osgood, C. (1955), 'Ethnological field techniques', in E. A. Hoebel, J. D. Jennings and E. R. Smith (eds), *Readings in Anthropology* (New York: McGraw-Hill), pp. 13–17.

Pahl, J. M. and Pahl, R. E. (1971), *Managers and their Wives* (London: Allen Lane).

Palmer, V. M. (1928), *Field Studies in Sociology: a Students Manual* (Chicago: University of Chicago Press).

Park, R. E. (1952), 'The city: suggestions for the investigation of human behaviour in the urban environment', in R. E. Park, *Human Communities* (Glencoe, Ill.: The Free Press), pp. 13–51.

Park, R. E. and Burgess, E. W. (1924), *Introduction to the Science of Society* (2nd edn) (Chicago: University of Chicago Press).

Parker, H. (1974), *View From the Boys* (Newton Abbot: David & Charles).

Parker, V. (1970), *The English House in the Nineteenth Century* (London: Historical Association).

Parsons, T. (1952), *The Social System* (London: Routledge & Kegan Paul).

Parsons, T. (1961), 'The point of view of the author', in M. Black (ed.), *The Social Theories of Talcott Parsons* (Englewood Cliffs, NJ: Prentice-Hall), pp. 268–88.

Parsons, T. and Clark, K. B. (1966) (eds), *The Negro American* (New York: Houghton Mifflin).

Parten, M. (1950), *Surveys, Polls and Samples* (New York: Harper & Row).

Patrick, J. (1973), *A Glasgow Gang Observed* (London: Eyre-Methuen).

Paul, B. D. (1953), 'Interview techniques and field relationships', in A. L. Kroeber (ed.) *Anthropology Today* (Chicago: University of Chicago Press), pp. 430–51.

Peel, F. (1888), *The Risings of the Luddites, Chartists and Plugdrawers* (2nd edn) (Heckmondwike: Senior).

Peel, F. (1893), *Spen Valley, Past and Present* (Heckmondwike: Senior).

Pelto, P. J. and Pelto, G. H. (1978), *Anthropological Research: the Structure of Inquiry* (Cambridge: CUP).

People's Autobiography of Hackney (1974a), *A Hackney Camera, 1883–1918* (London: Centerprise).

People's Autobiography of Hackney (1974b), *The Threepenny Doctor* (London: Centerprise).

People's Autobiography of Hackney (1976), *Working Lives, Vol. 1: 1905–1945* (London: Centerprise).

People's Autobiography of Hackney (1977), *Working Lives, Vol. 2: 1945–77* (London: Centerprise).

Perlman, M. L. (1973), 'The comparative method: the single investigator and the team approach', in R. Naroll and R. Cohen (eds), *A Handbook of Method in Cultural Anthropology* (New York: Columbia University Press), pp. 353–65.

Peters, D. U. (1960), *Land Usage in Barotseland*, Rhodes-Livingstone Communication No. 19.

Pettigrew, J. (1981), 'Reminiscences of fieldwork among the Sikhs', in H. Roberts (ed.), *Doing Feminist Research* (London: Routledge & Kegan Paul), pp. 62–82.

Pettigrew, T. (1964), *A Profile of the Negro American* (Princeton, NJ: Van Nostrand).

Piaget, J. (1968), 'Developmental psychology: a theory of development', in D. L. Sills (ed.), *International Encyclopedia of the Social Sciences*, Vol. 4 (New York: Macmillan and The Free Press), pp. 140–47.

Piddington, R. (1957), *An Introduction to Social Anthropology*, Vol. 2 (Edinburgh: Oliver & Boyd).

Pitt, D. C. (1972), *Using Historical Sources in Anthropology and Sociology* (New York: Holt, Rinehart & Winston).

Plant, M. (1975), *Drugtakers in an English Town* (London: Tavistock).

Platt, J. (1976), *Realities of Social Research* (London: Chatto & Windus for Sussex University Press).

Platt, J. (1981a), 'Evidence and proof in documentary research: some specific problems of documentary research', *Sociological Review*, vol. 29, no. 1, pp. 31–52.

Platt, J. (1981b), 'Evidence and proof in documentary research: some shared problems of documentary research', *Sociological Review*, vol. 29, no. 1, pp. 53–66.

Plotnicov, L. (1967), *Strangers to the City* (Pittsburgh, Pa.: University of Pittsburgh Press).

Polanyi, M. (1958), *Personal Knowledge* (London: Routledge & Kegan Paul).

Polsky, N. (1969), *Hustlers, Beats and Others* (Harmondsworth: Penguin).

Polya, G. (1954), *Mathematics and Plausible Reasoning, Vol. II: Patterns of Plausible Inference* (Princeton, NJ: Princeton University Press).

Pons, V. (1961), 'Two small groups in Avenue 21: some aspects of the system of social relations in a remote corner of Stanleyville, Belgium Congo', in A. Southall (ed.), *Social Change in Modern Africa* (London: OUP for the International African Institute), pp. 205–16.

Pons, V. (1969), *Stanleyville: an African Urban Community under Belgian Administration* (London: OUP for the International African Institute).

Pons, V. (1978), 'Contemporary interpretations of Manchester in the 1830s and 1840s', in *Stanford Journal of International Studies*, vol. 13, pp. 51–76.

Powdermaker, H. (1966a), *Stranger and Friend: The Way of an Anthropologist* (New York: Norton).

Powdermaker, H. (1966b), 'A woman alone in the field', in H. Powdermaker, *Stranger and Friend: The Way of an Anthropologist* (New York: Norton), pp. 108–14.

Pugh, R. B. (1954), *How to Write a Parish History* (London: Allen & Unwin).

Pym, B. (1952), *Excellent Women* (London: Cape).

Radin, P. (1913), 'Personal reminiscences of a Winnebago Indian', *Journal of American Folklore*, vol. 26, no. 102, pp. 293–318.

Radin, P. (1920), 'The autobiography of a Winnebago Indian', *University of California Publications in American Archaeology and Ethnology*, vol 16, pp. 381–483.

Radin, P. (1926), *Crashing Thunder: the Autobiography of an American Indian* (New York: Appleton).

Radin, P. (1933), *The Method and Theory of Ethnology* (New York: McGraw-Hill).

Rainwater, L. (1970), *Behind Ghetto Walls* (Chicago: Aldine).

Rapoport, A. (1959), 'Uses and limitations of mathematical models in social science', in L. Gross (ed.), *Symposium on Sociological Theory* (Evanston, Ill.: Row Peterson), pp. 348–72.

Rawlings, G. (1975), 'Bath in the 1930s', paper given at History Workshop 9, Ruskin College, Oxford.

Redfield, R. (1930), *Tepoztlán: a Mexican Village* (Chicago: University of Chicago Press).

Redfield, R. (1941), *The Folk Culture of Yucatan* (Chicago: University of Chicago Press).

Redfield, R. (1948), 'The art of social science', *American Journal of Sociology*, vol. 54, no. 3, pp. 181–90.

Redfield, R. (1950), *A Village that Chose Progress, Chan Kom Revisited* (Chicago: University of Chicago Press).

Redfield, R. (1955), *The Little Community* (Chicago: University of Chicago Press).

Rex, J. and Moore, R. (1967), *Race Community and Conflict* (Oxford: OUP).

Richards, A. I. (1939), *Land, Labour and Diet in Northern Rhodesia* (London: OUP for the International African Institute).

Richards, A. I. (1970), 'Socialisation and contemporary British anthropology', in P. Mayer (ed.), *Socialization: the Approach from Social Anthropology* (London: Tavistock), pp. 1–32.

Richardson, S. A., Dohrenwend, B. S. and Klein, D. (1965), *Interviewing: its Forms and Functions* (New York: Basic Books).

Richman, G. (1975), *Fly a Flag for Poplar* (London: Liberation Films).

Riesman, D. (1964), 'Foreword', in E. S. Bowen (Laura Bohannon), *Return to Laughter* (Garden City, NY: Doubleday Anchor Natural History Library), pp. ix–xviii.

Riesman, D. and Watson, J. (1964), 'The sociability project: a chronicle of frustration and achievement', in P. Hammond (ed.), *Sociologists at Work* (New York: Basic Books), pp. 235–321.

Riessman, F. (1962), *The Culturally Deprived Child* (New York: Harper & Row).

Riis, J. A. (1970), *How the Other Half Lives* (New York: Dover).

Riley, M. W. (1963), *Sociological Research, Vol. I: a Case Approach* (New York: Harcourt Brace Jovanovich).

Roberts, H. (1981a) (ed.), *Doing Feminist Research* (London: Routledge & Kegan Paul).

Roberts, H. (1981b), 'Women and their doctors: power and powerlessness in the research process', in H. Roberts (ed.), *Doing Feminist Research* (London: Routledge & Kegan Paul), pp. 7–29.

Robinson, W. S. (1951), 'The logical structure of analytic induction', *American Sociological Review*, vol. 16, no. 6, pp. 812–18; reprinted in G. J. McCall and J. L. Simmons (1969) (eds), *Issues in Participant Observation: a Text and Reader* (Reading, Mass.: Addison-Wesley), pp. 196–204.

Rogers, A. (1972), *This Was their World: Approaches to Local History* (London: BBC).

Rogers, C. R. (1945), 'The non-directive method as a technique for social research', *American Journal of Sociology*, vol. 50, no. 4, pp. 279–83.

Rosenberg, M. (1968), *The Logic of Survey Analysis* (New York: Basic Books).

Rossi, A. S. (1965), 'Women in science: why so few?', *Science*, vol. 148, no. 3774, pp. 1196–1202.

Roth, J. A. (1962a), 'Management bias in social science study of medical treatment', *Human Organization*, vol. 21, no. 1, pp. 47–50.

Roth, J. A. (1962b), 'Comments on "secret observation"', *Social Problems*, vol. 9, no. 3, pp. 283–4; reprinted in W. J. Filstead (1970) (ed.), *Qualitative Methodology: Firsthand Involvement with the Social World* (Chicago: Markham), pp. 278–80.

Roth, J. A. (1963), *Timetables* (New York: Bobbs-Merrill).

Roth, J. A. (1966), 'Hired-hand research', *American Sociologist*, vol. 1, no. 4, pp. 190–6.

Roth, J. A. (1974), 'Turning adversity to account', *Urban Life and Culture*, vol. 3, no. 3, pp. 347–59.

Roy, D. (1970), 'The study of Southern labor union organizing campaigns', in R. W. Habenstein (ed.), *Pathways to Data* (Chicago: Aldine), pp. 216–44.

Royal Anthropological Institute of Great Britain and Ireland (1951a), *Notes and Queries on Anthropology* (6th edn) (London: Routledge & Kegan Paul).

Royal Anthropological Institute of Great Britain and Ireland (1951b), 'Methods and techniques in social anthropology', in Royal Anthropological Institute of Great Britain and Ireland, *Notes and Queries on Anthropology* (6th edn) (London: Routledge & Kegan Paul), pp. 36–62.

Royal Commission on Historical Manuscripts (1973), *Record Repositories in Great Britain* (5th edn) (London: HMSO).

Rule, J. G. (1971), 'The labouring miner in Cornwall, c. 1740–1870: a study in social history'; University of Warwick unpublished thesis.

Rynkiewich, M. and Spradley, J. (1976) (eds), *Ethics and Anthropology: Dilemmas in Fieldwork* (New York: Wiley).

Samuel, R. (1975) (ed.), *Village Life and Labour* (London: Routledge & Kegan Paul).

Samuel, R. (1976), 'Local history and oral history', *History Workshop Journal*, no. 1, pp. 191–208.

Samuel, R. (1977) (ed.), *Miners, Quarrymen and Saltworkers* (London: Routledge & Kegan Paul).

Samuel, R. (1981) (ed.), *People's History and Socialist Theory* (London: Routledge & Kegan Paul).

Sapir, E. (1949), *Selected Writings of Edward Sapir*, ed. D. Mandelbaum (Berkeley, Calif.: University of California Press).

Sartre, J. P. (1963), transl. by H. E. Barnes, *The Problem of Method* (London: Methuen).

Sayles, L. (1954), 'Field use of projective methods: a case example', *Sociology and Social Research*, vol. 38, no. 3, pp. 168–73.

Scharff, D. E. (1976), 'Aspects of the transition from school to work', in J. M. M. Hill and D. E. Scharff, *Between Two Worlds: Aspects of the Transition from School to Work* (Richmond: Careers Consultants), pp. 66–332.

Schatzman, L. and Strauss, A. L. (1973), *Field Research: Strategies for a Natural Sociology* (Englewood Cliffs, NJ: Prentice-Hall).

Schenkel, W. and Sieber, S. D. (1969), *The Design of Survey Questionnaires: a Case History Approach* (New York: Bureau of Applied Social Research, Columbia University); mimeo.

Schofield, R. S. (1972), 'Sampling in historical research', in E. A. Wrigley (ed.), *Nineteenth Century Society* (Cambridge: CUP), pp. 146–90.

Schwartz, H. and Jacobs, J. (1979), *Qualitative Sociology: a Method to the Madness* (New York: The Free Press).

Schwartz, M. (1964), 'The mental hospital: the research person in the disturbed ward', in A. J. Vidich, J. Bensman and M. Stein (eds), *Reflection on Community Studies* (New York: Harper & Row), pp. 85–117.

Schwartz, M. S. and Schwartz, C. G. (1955), 'Problems in participant observation', *American Journal of Sociology*, vol. 60, no. 4, pp. 343–53.

Selltiz, C., Wrightsman, L. S. and Cook, S. W. (1976), *Research Methods in Social Relations* (3rd edn) (New York: Holt, Rinehart & Winston).

Sewell, W. H. (1949), 'Field techniques in social psychological study in a rural community', *American Sociological Review*, vol. 14, no. 6, pp. 718–26.

Shaffir, W. B., Stebbins, R. A. and Turowetz, A. (1980) (eds), *Fieldwork Experience: Qualitative Approaches to Social Research* (New York: St Martin's Press).

Sharp, C. J. (1972), *English Folk Song: Some Conclusions* (ed., M. Karpeles) (4th edn) (East Ardsley, Wakefield: EP Publishing).

Shaw, C. (1930), *The Jack Roller: a Delinquent Boy's Own Story* (Chicago: University of Chicago Press).

Shipman, M. (1976) (ed.), *The Organization and Impact of Social Research* (London: Routledge & Kegan Paul).

Shipman, M. (1981), *The Limitations of Social Research* (2nd edn) (London: Longman).

Sieber, S. D. (1973), 'The integration of fieldwork and survey methods', *American Journal of Sociology*, vol. 78, no. 6, pp. 1335–59.

Sieber, S. D. and Lazarsfeld, P. F. (1966), *The Organization of Educational Research*, Cooperative Research Project No. 1974 (USOE) (New York: Bureau of Applied Social Research, Columbia University).

Sieber, S. D. and Lazarsfeld, P. F. (1972), *Reforming the University: the Role of the Research Centre* (New York: Praegar).

Simmons, L. (1942), *Sun Chief: the Autobiography of a Hopi Indian* (New Haven, Conn.: Yale University Press).

Sims, G. R. (1883), *Horrible London* (London).

Singer, P. and Desole, D. (1967), 'The Australian sub-incision ceremony reconsidered: vaginal envy or Kangaroo Bifid penis envy', *American Anthropologist*, vol. 69, no. 3, pp. 355–8.

Sjoberg, G. (1967) (ed.), *Ethics, Politics and Social Research* (London: Routledge & Kegan Paul).

Smith. M. B. (1968), 'Competence and socialization', in J. A. Clausen (ed.), *Socialization and Society* (Boston, Mass.: Little, Brown), pp. 270–320.

Smith, R. T. (1963), 'Review of family structure in Jamaica: the social context of reproduction, by Judith Blake', *American Anthropologist*, vol. 65, no. 1, pp. 158–61.

Southall, A. (1961) (ed.), *Social Change in Modern Africa* (London: OUP for the International African Institute).

Southall, A. W. and Gutkind, P. C. W. (1956), *Townsmen in the Making*, East African Studies No. 9.

Spencer, G. (1971), 'Second careers of West Point officer retirees', unpublished paper presented at the annual meetings of the American Sociological Association, Denver, Colorado, USA.

Spencer, G. (1973), 'Methodological issues in the study of bureaucratic elites: a case study of West Point', *Social Problems*, vol. 21, no. 1, pp. 90–103.

Spicer, E. H. (1952) (ed.), *Human Problems in Technological Change* (New York: Russell Sage).

Spindler, G. D. (1955), *Sociocultural and Psychological Processes in Menomini Acculturation*, University of California Publications in Culture and Society, vol. 5.

Spindler, G. D. (1970) (ed.), *Being an Anthropologist: Field-work in Eleven Cultures* (New York: Holt, Rinehart & Winston).

Spindler, G. D. and Goldschmidt, W. (1952), 'Experimental design in the study of culture change', *Southwestern Journal of Anthropology*, vol. 8, no. 1, pp. 68–83.

Spradley, J. P. (1979), *Ethnographic Interview* (New York: Holt, Rinehart & Winston).

Spradley, J. P. (1980), *Participant Observation* (New York: Holt, Rinehart & Winston).

Spradley, J. P. and Mann, B. J. (1975), *The Cocktail Waitress* (New York: Wiley).

Spufford, M. (1974), *Contrasting Communities* (Cambridge: CUP).

Srinivas, M. N. (1979), 'Introduction', in M. N. Srinivas, A. M. Shah, and E. A. Ramaswamy (eds), *The Fieldworker and the Field: Problems and Challenges in Sociological Investigation* (Delhi: OUP), pp. 1–15.

Srinivas, M. N., Shah, A. M. and Ramaswamy, E. A. (1979) (eds), *The Fieldworker and the Field: Problems and Challenges in Sociological Investigation* (Delhi: OUP).

Srole, L., Langner, T. S., Michael, S. T., Opler, M. and Rennie, T. A. C. (1962), *Mental Health in the Metropolis* (New York: McGraw-Hill).

Stacey, M. (1960), *Tradition and Change: a Study of Banbury* (London: OUP).

Stacey, M. (1968), 'Professional ethics', *Sociology*, vol. 2, no. 3, p. 353.

Stacey, M. (1969a), *Methods of Social Research* (Oxford: Pergamon).

Stacey, M. (1969b), 'The myth of community studies', *British Journal of Sociology*, vol. 20, no. 2, pp. 134–47.

Stacey, M., Batstone, E., Bell, C. and Murcott, A. (1975), *Power, Persistence and Change: a Second Study of Banbury* (London: Routledge & Kegan Paul).

Stacey, M. and Burgess, R. (1979), 'The research process' (Oxford: Sussex Publications), taped discussion.

Stacey, M., Dearden, R., Pill, R. and Robinson, D. (1970), *Hospitals, Children and their Families* (London: Routledge & Kegan Paul).

Stavrianis, B. K. (1950), 'Research methods in cultural anthropology in relation to scientific criteria', *Psychological Review*, vol. 57, no. 6, pp. 334–44.

Steer, F. W. (1962), 'Probate inventories', *History*, vol. 47, no. 3, pp. 287–90.

Stein, M. (1954), 'Field work procedures: the social organization of a student research team', in A. W. Gouldner, *Patterns of Industrial Bureaucracy* (Glencoe, Ill.: The Free Press), pp. 247–69.

Stephens, W. B. (1973), *Sources for English Local History* (Manchester: University of Manchester Press).

Steward, J. H. (1950), *Area Research*, Bulletin No. 63 (New York: Social Science Research Council).

Stimpson, G. and Webb, B. (1975), *Going to See the Doctor: the Consultation Process in General Practice* (London: Routledge & Kegan Paul).

Stinchcombe, A. L. (1964), *Rebellion in a High School* (Chicago: Quadrangle Books).

Strauss, A. L. and Glaser, B. G. (1975), *Chronic Illness and the Quality of Life* (St Louis, Miss.: Mosby).

Strauss, A. L. and Glaser, B. G. (1977), *Anguish: a Case History of a Dying Trajectory* (London: Martin Robertson).

Strauss, A. L., Schatzman, L., Bucher, R., Ehrlich, D. and Sabshin, M. (1964), *Psychiatric Ideologies and Institutions* (New York: The Free Press).

Sudnow, D. (1967), *Passing On: the Social Organization of Dying* (Englewood Cliffs, NJ: Prentice-Hall).

Tate, W. E. (1946), *The Parish Chest, a Study of the Records of Parochial Administration in England* (Cambridge: CUP).

Thernstrom, S. (1965), 'Yankee City revisited: the perils of historical naïveté', *American Sociological Review*, vol. 30, no. 2, pp. 234–42.

Thernstrom, S. (1968), 'Quantitative methods in history: some notes', in S. M. Lipset and R. Hofstadter (eds), *Sociology and History: Methods* (New York: Basic Books), pp. 59–78.

Thomas, K. (1963), 'History and Anthropology', *Past and Present* no. 24, pp. 3–24.

Thomas, K. (1964), 'Work and leisure in pre-industrial society', *Past and Present* no. 29, pp. 50–66.

Thomas, K. (1966), 'The tools and the job', *Times Literary Supplement*, no. 3345 (7 April), pp. 275–6.

Thomas, K. (1971), *Religion and the Decline of Magic* (London: Weidenfeld & Nicolson).

Thomas, W. I. and Znaniecki, F. (1918–20), *The Polish Peasant in Europe and America* (Chicago: University of Chicago Press).

Thompson, D. (1975), 'Courtship and marriage in Preston', paper given at History Workshop 9, Ruskin College, Oxford.

Thompson, E. P. (1972), 'Anthropology and the discipline of historical context', *Midland History*, vol. 1, no. 3, pp. 41–55.

Thompson, E. P. (1976), 'On history, sociology and historical relevance' (review article), *British Journal of Sociology*, vol. 27, no. 3, pp. 387–402.

Thompson, F. M. L. (1974), *Hampstead: Building a Borough, 1650–1964* (London: Routledge & Kegan Paul).

Thompson, H. S. (1967), *Hell's Angels* (New York: Random House).

Thompson, P. (1978), *The Voice of the Past: Oral History* (Oxford: OUP).

Thorn, D. (1978), 'Women at the Woolwich Arsenal, 1915–1919', *Oral History*, vol. 6, no. 2, pp. 58–73.

Thrasher, F. (1927), *The Gang* (Chicago: University of Chicago Press).

Toulmin, S. (1961), *Foresight and Understanding* (Bloomington: Indiana University Press).

Travis, J. (1896), *Notes Historical and Biographical Mainly about Todmorden and District* (Rochdale: E. Wrigley).

Tremblay, M. A. (1955), 'Social disorganization in Stirling County according to a poverty–affluence indicator', Report 215, Stirling County Study; mimeo.

Tremblay, M. A. (1957), 'The key informant technique: a non-ethnographic application', *American Anthropologist*, vol. 59, no. 4, pp. 688–701.

Trice, H. M. (1956), 'The "outsider's" role in field study', *Sociology and Social Research*, vol. 41, no. 1, pp. 27–32; reprinted in W. J. Filstead (1970) (ed.), *Qualitative Methodology: Firsthand Involvement with the Social World* (Chicago: Markham), pp. 77–82.

Trow, M. (1957), 'Comment on "participant observation and interviewing: a comparison" ', *Human Organization*, vol. 16, no. 3, pp. 33–5.

Turner, R. H. (1953), 'The quest for universals in sociological research', *American Sociological Review* vol. 18, no. 6, pp. 604–11; reprinted in G. J. McCall and J. L. Simmons (1969) (eds), *Issues in Participant Observation: a Text and Reader* (Reading, Mass.: Addison-Wesley), pp. 205–16.

Turner, V. W. (1957), *Schism and Continuity in an African Society: a Study of Ndembu Village Life* (Manchester: University of Manchester Press on behalf of the Institute for African Studies University of Zambia).

Turner, V. W. (1964), 'Symbols in Ndembu ritual', in M. Gluckman (ed.), *Closed Systems and Open Minds: The Limits of Naïvety in Social Anthropology* (Edinburgh: Oliver & Boyd), pp. 20–51.

Turner, V. W. (1974), *Dramas, Fields and Metaphors: Symbolic Action in Human Society* (Ithaca, NY: Cornell University Press).

Udy, S. H. (1964), 'Cross-cultural analysis: a case study', in P. Hammond (ed.), *Sociologists at Work* (New York: Basic Books), pp. 161–83.

Urry, J. (1972), 'Notes and queries on anthropology and the development of field methods in British anthropology, 1870–1920', *Proceedings of the Royal Anthropological Institute of Great Britain and Ireland, 1972*, pp. 45–57.

Vaisey, D. (1976), 'Court records and the social history of seventeenth-century England', *History Workshop Journal*, no. 1, pp. 185–91.

Van Gennep, A. (1960), transl. by M. B. Vizedom and G. L. Caffte, *The Rites of Passage* (London: Routledge & Kegan Paul).

Vansina, J. (1973), *Oral Tradition* (Harmondsworth: Penguin).

Van Velsen, J. (1967), 'The extended-case method and situational analysis', in A. L. Epstein (ed.), *The Craft of Social Anthropology* (London: Tavistock), pp. 129–49.

Vidich, A. J. (1955), 'Participant observation and the collection and interpretation of data', *American Journal of Sociology*, vol. 60, no. 4, pp. 354–360.

Vidich, A. J. and Bensman, J. (1954), 'The validity of field data', *Human Organization*, vol. 13, pp. 20–27.

Vidich, A. J. and Bensman, J. (1964), 'The Springdale case: academic bureaucrats and sensitive townspeople', in A. J. Vidich, J. Bensman and M. R. Stein (eds), *Reflections on Community Studies* (New York: Harper & Row), pp. 313–49.

Vidich, A. J. and Bensman, J. (1968), *Small Town in Mass Society* (2nd edn) (Princeton, NJ: Princeton University Press).

Vidich, A. J., Bensman, J. and Stein, M. R. (1964) (eds), *Reflections on Community Studies* (New York: Harper & Row).

Vidich, A. J. and Shapiro, G. (1955), 'A comparison of participant observation and survey data', *American Sociological Review*, vol. 20, no. 1, pp. 28–33.

Voss, H. L. (1966), 'Pitfalls in social research: a case study', *American Sociologist*, vol. 1, no. 3, pp. 136–40.

Wake, J. (1925), *How to Compile a History of Present Day Village Life* (2nd rev. edn) (Kettering: T. B. Hart).

Wakeford, J. (1979) (ed.), *Research Methods Syllabuses in Sociology Departments in the U.K.* (Lancaster: University of Lancaster).

Walker, R. (1980), 'The conduct of educational case studies: ethics, theory and procedure', in W. B. Dockrell and D. Hamilton (eds), *Rethinking Educational Research* (London: Hodder & Stoughton), pp. 30–63.

Walker, R. and Adelman, C. (1975), *A Guide to Classroom Observation* (London: Methuen).

Wallace, A. F. C. (1952), *The Model Personality Structure of the Tuscarora Indians*, Bureau of American Ethnology, Bulletin 150.

Wallace, W. L. (1971) (ed.), *Sociological Theory: an Introduction* (Chicago: Aldine).

Wallis, R. (1976), *The Road to Total Freedom: a Sociological Analysis of Scientology* (London: Heinemann).

Wallis, R. (1977), 'The moral career of a research project', in C. Bell and H. Newby (eds), *Doing Sociological Research* (London: Allen & Unwin), pp. 149–67.

Wallis, W. A. and Roberts, H. W. (1956), *Statistics: a New Approach* (New York: The Free Press).

Warner, W. L. (1959), *The Living and the Dead: a Study of the Symbolic Life of Americans* (New Haven, Conn.: Yale University Press).

Warner, W. L. and Low, J. O. (1947), *The Social System of the Modern Factory, the Strike: a Social Analysis* (New Haven, Conn.: Yale University Press).

Warner, W. L. and Lunt, P. S. (1941), *The Social Life of a Modern Community* (New Haven, Conn.: Yale University Press).

Warner, W. L. and Lunt, P. S. (1942), *The Status System of a Modern Community* (New Haven, Conn.: Yale University Press).

Warner, W. L. and Srole, L. (1945), *The Social Systems of American Ethnic Groups* (New Haven, Conn.: Yale University Press).

Warren. C. A. B. and Rasmussen, P. K. (1977), 'Sex and gender in field research', *Urban Life*, vol. 6, no. 3, pp. 349–69.

Waters, M. (1977), 'Craft consciousness in a government enterprise: Medway dockyardmen, 1860–1906', *Oral History*, vol. 5, no. 1, pp. 51–62.

Watson, J. D. (1968), *The Double Helix* (Harmondsworth: Penguin).

Wax, M. (1972), 'Tenting with Malinowski', *American Sociological Review*, vol. 37, no. 1, pp. 1–13.

Wax, R. H. (1960), 'Reciprocity in field work', in R. N. Adams and J. J. Preiss (eds), *Human Organization Research* (Homewood, Ill.: Dorsey Press), pp. 90–98.

Wax, R. H. (1971), *Doing Fieldwork: Warnings and Advice* (Chicago: University of Chicago Press).

Wax, R. H. (1979), 'Gender and age in fieldwork and fieldwork education: no good thing is done by any man alone', *Social Problems*, vol. 26, no. 5, pp. 509–22.

Webb, B. (1926a), *My Apprenticeship* (London: Longmans, Green).

Webb, B. (1926b), 'The art of note-taking', in B. Webb, *My Apprenticeship* (London: Longmans, Green), pp. 364–72.

Webb, B. (1948), *Our Partnership* (London: Longmans, Green).

Webb, E. J., Campbell, D. T., Schwartz, R. D. and Sechrest, L. (1966), *Unobtrusive Measures: Nonreactive Research in the Social Sciences* (Chicago: Rand McNally).

Webb, S. and Webb, B. (1894), *History of Trade Unionism* (London: Longmans, Green).

Webb, S. and Webb, B. (1897), *Industrial Democracy* (London: Longmans, Green).

Webb, S. and Webb, B. (1898), *Problems of Modern Industry* (London: Longmans, Green).

Webb, S. and Webb, B. (1908), *The Manor and the Borough* (London: Longmans, Green).

Webb, S. and Webb, B. (1910), *English Poor Law Policy* (London: Longmans, Green).

Webb, S. and Webb, B. (1932), *Methods of Social Study* (London: Longmans, Green).

Werthman, C. (1968), 'The police as perceived by negro boys', in A. L. Strauss (ed.), *The American City: a Sourcebook of Urban Imagery* (London: Allen Lane), pp. 285–87.

West, J. (1945), *Plainville U.S.A.* (New York: Columbia University Press).

West, W. G. (1980), 'Access to adolescent deviants and deviance', in W. B. Shaffir, R. A. Stebbins and A. Turowetz (eds), *Fieldwork Experience: Qualitative Approaches to Social Research* (New York: St Martin's Press), pp. 31–44.

Westie, F. R. (1957), 'Toward closer relations between theory and research: a procedure and an example', *American Sociological Review*, vol. 22, no. 2, pp. 149–54.

Whiting, B. and Whiting, J. (1973), 'Methods for observing and recording behavior', in R. Naroll and R. Cohen (eds), *A Handbook of Method in Cultural Anthropology* (New York: Columbia University Press), pp. 282–315.

Whiting, J. *et al.* (1954), *Field Guide for a Study of Socialization in Five Societies*, SSRC Summer Conference at Laboratory of Human Relations, Harvard University, USA: mimeo.

Whiting, J. W. M., Child, I. L., Lambert, W. W. *et al.* (1966), *Field Guide for a Study of Socialization in Five Societies* (New York: Wiley).

Whyte, W. F. (1953), 'Interviewing for organizational research', *Human Organization*, vol. 12, no. 2, pp. 15–22.

Whyte, W. F. (1955), *Street Corner Society* (2nd edn), (Chicago: University of Chicago Press).

Whyte, W. F. (1956), 'Engineers and workers: a case study', *Human Organization*, vol. 14, no. 4, pp. 3–12.

Whyte, W. F. (1957), 'On asking indirect questions', *Human Organization*, vol. 15, no. 4, pp. 21–3.

Whyte, W. F. (1960), 'Interviewing in field research', in R. N. Adams and J. J. Preiss (eds), *Human Organization Research: Field Relations and Techniques* (Homewood, Ill.: Dorsey Press), pp. 352–74.

Wiener, N. (1954), *The Human Use of Human Beings, Cybernetics and Society* (2nd edn) (Garden City, NY: Doubleday).

Wilder, D. E. and Friedman, N. S. (1968), 'Selecting ideal-typical communities and gaining access to their schools for social research purposes', in D. E. Wilder, N. S. Friedman, R. B. Hill, E. E. Sandis and S. D. Sieber, *Actual and Perceived Consensus on Educational Goals Between School and Community* (New York: Bureau of Applied Social Research, Columbia University), appendix A, pp. 1–30.

Williams, G. (1966), 'The Merthyr of Dic Penderyn', in G. Williams (ed.), *Merthyr Politics: the Making of a Working Class Tradition* (Cardiff: University of Wales Press), pp. 9–27.

Williams, T. R. (1967), *Field Methods in the Study of Culture* (New York: Holt, Rinehart & Winston).

Williams, W. M. (1956), *The Sociology of an English Village: Gosforth* (London: Routledge & Kegan Paul).

Williamson, B. (1978), 'The leek', in M. Bulmer (ed.), *Mining and Social Change* (London: Croom Helm), pp. 83–9.

Willis, P. (1977), *Learning to Labour* (Farnborough: Saxon House).

Willmott, P. and Young, M. (1960), *Family and Class in a London Suburb* (London: Routledge & Kegan Paul).

Wilson, C. S. (1963), 'Social factors influencing industrial output: a sociological study of factories in N.W. Lancs.'; University of Manchester unpublished thesis.

Wilson, G. (1938), *The Land Rights of Individuals among the Nyakyusa*, Rhodes-Livingstone Paper No. 1.

Wirth, L. (1928), *The Ghetto* (Chicago: University of Chicago Press).

Wolff, K. (1960), 'The collection and organization of field materials: a research report', in R. N. Adams and J. J. Preiss (eds), *Human Organization Research: Field Relations and Techniques* (Homewood, Ill.: Dorsey Press), pp. 240–54.

Woods, P. (1979), *The Divided School* (London: Routledge & Kegan Paul).

Wormser, M. H. and Selltiz, C. (1951), 'Community self surveys: principles and procedures', in M. Jahoda, M. Deutsch and S. W. Cook (eds), *Research Methods in Social Relations* (Hinsdale, Ill.: Dryden Press), pp. 611–41.

Wrigley, E. A. (1972) (ed.), *Nineteenth Century Society* (Cambridge: CUP).

Yang, M. (1945), *Taitou: a Chinese Village* (New York: John Day).

Young, K. (1952), *Personality and Problems of Adjustment* (2nd edn) (New York: Appleton-Century-Crofts).

Young, P. V. (1966), *Scientific Social Surveys and Research* (4th edn) (Englewood Cliffs, NJ: Prentice-Hall).

Zelditch, M. (1962), 'Some methodological problems of field studies', *American Journal of Sociology*, vol. 67, no. 5, pp. 566–76.

Zetterberg, H. L. (1962), *Social Theory and Social Practice* (New Jersey: Bedminster Press).

Zimmerman, D. H. and Wieder, D. L. (1977), 'The diary: diary-interview method', *Urban Life*, vol. 5, no. 4, pp. 479–98.

Znaniecki, F. (1934), *The Method of Sociology* (New York: Farrar & Rinehart).

Znaniecki, F. (1936), *Social Actions* (New York: Farrar & Rinehart).

Zorbaugh, H. W. (1929), *The Gold Coast and the Slum* (Chicago: University of Chicago Press).

Name Index

Subject Index